Department of the Environment

# Assessing The Impact of Urban Policy

Brian Robson, Michael Bradford, Iain Deas,
Ed Hall, Eric Harrison
CENTRE FOR URBAN POLICY STUDIES,
UNIVERSITY OF MANCHESTER

Michael Parkinson, Richard Evans,
Peter Garside, Alan Harding
EUROPEAN INSTITUTE FOR URBAN AFFAIRS,
JOHN MOORES UNIVERSITY, LIVERPOOL

Fred Robinson
SOCIAL POLICY, UNIVERSITY OF DURHAM

London: HMSO

ISBN 0 11 752982 6

# Acknowledgements

The work discussed in this report has tackled an ambitious and novel project. Evaluating the overall impact of government's urban policy is a daunting undertaking, not least since urban policy covers so wide a range of interlocking programmes and since the content and emphasis of urban policy have changed progressively throughout the course of the last two decades. Without the help of innumerable individuals, we are conscious that we would have been unable to make many significant inroads into the task. We received great help from the various government departments from which we collected data on expenditure patterns. We would like to thank the many respondents to our 'expert' discussions for the time and effort which they took in discussing aspects of policy in Greater Manchester, Merseyside and Tyne and Wear: that they are not named is simply to preserve confidentiality. We would like to thank the residents and the employers who took part in the two local surveys in the three conurbations. We are much indebted to the help and guidance of the members of the inter-departmental Steering Group who were drawn from DoE, DTI, DE, HO, DTp, the Treasury, Scottish Office and Northern Ireland. In particular, the 'inner members' of the Steering Group - Mr Gerald Laufer, Mr Bernard Walsh and Mr Brian Wilson, all from DoE - provided sensitive and detailed advice which proved invaluable. To all of them we offer our thanks.

# Contents

ACKNOWLEDGEMENTS ........................................................................ iii

EXECUTIVE SUMMARY ...................................................................... vii

1. INTRODUCTION AND OUTLINE ................................................... 1

2. QUANTITATIVE ASSESSMENT:
   THE NATIONAL AND LOCAL PICTURES ............................... 19

3. THE VIEWS OF RECIPIENTS ...................................................... 33

4. THE VIEWS OF EXPERTS ........................................................... 37

5. CONCLUSIONS ............................................................................ 47

**APPENDICES**

    A. Input data and outcomes indicators ............................................ 57
    B. National-level analysis ............................................................... 157
    C. Local area portraits: the three conurbations .............................. 213
    D. Local analysis: the three conurbations ....................................... 325
    E. Residents' survey ........................................................................ 335
    F. Employers' survey ....................................................................... 367
    G. Discussions with key figures ...................................................... 404
    H. Summary of recommendations from the feasibility study ......... 431

# Executive summary

**1 METHODOLOGY**

(i)   The aim of the study is to evaluate the overall impact of central government urban policy in England over the period of the last decade.

(ii)   This is a difficult research task because of the numerous strategic and conceptual problems. First, changes to policy over the period make it difficult to characterise a single set of policy aims over the course of the whole period. However, since our terms of reference gave particular salience to the Action for Cities package (AfC), the core of the evaluation is based on its four aims and the 57 Urban Priority Areas (UPAs) which are the targets of AfC. Second, there are many conceptual difficulties. Not least among them is the 'counterfactual' problem, the difficulty of taking account of what might have happenened in the absence of public intervention. Where no policy impact is apparent there are also difficulties in knowing whether this arises from limitations of policy, theory or measurement.

(iii)   The research methodology has been designed to address such difficulties. It has three complementary facets or 'legs':

- quantitative or statistical analysis which examines the relationship between expenditure and socio-economic outcomes in a sample of 123 English authorities (comprised of the 57 UPAs, 40 similar 'marginal' authorities and 26 'comparator' authorities) to enable comparisons between places which have received more and less public assistance. These financial **inputs** are related to five measures of **outcomes** (unemployment, job change, small-firm creation, house price change and migration of 25-34 year-olds);

- qualitative information from surveys of the recipients of policy; both the residents of inner urban areas and of employers who operate within big cities; and

- qualitative information from discussions with experts at the sharp end of policy implementation.

(iv)   A national assessment of 123 local authority districts was used for the quantitative evaluation of inputs and outcomes. Local-scale case studies within the three conurbations of Greater Manchester, Merseyside and Tyne and Wear were used both for a more detailed quantitative study of financial inputs and for the qualitative approaches. The views which are developed are based on the triangulation of these three legs.

**2 QUANTITATIVE EVALUATION**

(v)   Formally, the quantitative evaluation is based on two null hypotheses: that the 57 UPA authorities will show no statistically significant difference from the 66 marginal and comparator areas in terms of the selected outcome indicators; and that greater urban policy expenditure in local authorities has no effect on the socio-economic indicators.

(vi)   The complex relationships between inputs and outcomes are disentangled through a variety of statistical techniques. Two principal approaches are used:

- various forms of regression analysis of inputs, outcomes and relationships between the expenditure and socio-economic change; and

- analysis of convergence or divergence in the conditions as measured by the outcome indicators between UPAs and other districts.

## 2.1 National scale: the 123 authorities

(vii)   **Inputs.**   A general point which emerges from the pattern of expenditure of the AfC resources over the course of the 1980s is the lack of fit between the classification of authorities as urban priority areas and the amounts of resource that they received per capita. While many elements of AfC expenditure were never intended to apply solely to the 57 UPAs, there nevertheless appears to be some ambiguity about the principle of targeting a limited set of authorities. This is compounded by the changes over time in funding; some places which experienced the largest percentage reductions in their overall per capita assistance were UPAs - and in many cases some of the 'worst' UPAs. Equally, looking at a wider definition of resources (the two mainstream programmes of Housing Investment Programme allocations and Revenue Support Grant, whose resources are much larger than AfC), it is clear that in the 1980s there were considerable reductions, especially in HIP allocations, to many UPA authorities.

(viii)   **Outcomes.**   A mixed picture emerges from the outcome measures. First, there are indications of deteriorating economic conditions in the UPAs over the period as a whole. Some of the indicators show a worsening position for the UPAs. The ratio of long-term unemployed to all unemployed (LT:U), for example, shows a widening gap as between the UPAs, marginals and comparators; thereby suggesting a deterioration of the areas with the worst conditions. Rates of new-firm formation also suggest that UPAs do somewhat worse than other authorities. On the other hand, there are also indications of areas of improvement; both the unemployment rate and the long-term unemployment rate taken separately, for example, show a narrowing gap. Taken together with the deterioration in the LT:U ratio, this implies that, while the UPAs were experiencing relative improvements as far as unemployment and long-term unemployment as a whole were concerned, amongst the unemployed in the UPA areas, higher proportions were long-term unemployed, thereby signifying an increasing degree of concentration of the most disadvantaged. There is nevertheless evidence in the improvements for the separate unemployment data that policy may have had a positive economic impact.

(ix)   Second, there is evidence of successful outcomes in terms of residential attractiveness. For the 25-34 year olds (which are used to signify the ability of areas to retain or attract a key and highly mobile cohort in the labour force), the gap between UPAs and other areas narrowed over the 1980s. Since long-term unemployment amongst this age group within UPAs does not suggest that the age group is trapped in inner areas, we conclude that some UPAs have been relatively more successful than the marginals or comparators in retaining this age group.

(x)   These positive indications of narrowing differentials on unemployment and migration provide evidence that urban policy may have had some success in slowing or reversing the erosion of the economic and residential base of cities.

(xi) **Relationships.** Many of the relationships between inputs of resources and socio-economic outcomes showed no statistical significance. However, there are some significant relationships. Most of these apply to measures of changes in unemployment levels which were examined for two periods, 1983-6 and 1986-90.

(xii) Inputs of regional assistance in the form of Regional Selective Assistance were positively related to relative improvements both in unemployment and long-term unemployment for both of the periods. Inputs from the Urban Programme were not significantly related to unemployment change in the first period, but for the second period were positively related to relative improvements both in unemployment and long-term unemployment. Furthermore, for this latter period, the significant positive associations with both Urban Programme and Regional Selective Assistance were independent of each other. In other words, at least for the second of the periods, there is evidence at the scale of districts that there were positive impacts associated with the expenditure of resources under urban policy.

(xiii) Expenditure is also related to the retention or attraction of the key 25-34 year old age cohort, and to house price change between 1986-9 (both within inner areas and for first-time buyers).

(xiv) These positive relationships between some of the financial inputs and some of the outcomes are clearly of considerable significance. They suggest that there are areas in which public expenditure has been associated with relative improvements in socio-economic conditions. This conclusion is further supported by the more detailed study of the socio-economic 'gaps' within selected conurbations. For example, in Greater London, there is a relationship between overall expenditure and improvements in long-term unemployment: whether or not boroughs were designated as UPAs, those places which received more overall resources showed greater rates of improvement than those places which were less well funded. These conclusions all imply that there are positive relationships between public expenditure and relative improvements in certain socio-economic outcomes.

## 2.2 Local scale: the three conurbations

(xv) Limitations of the data sources make it difficult to place great confidence in the patterns of spatial incidence at the finer scale of wards and the statistical analysis of ward data was unable to establish any significant relationships between expenditure inputs and socio-economic change. Nevertheless, the ward data show interesting spatial patterns from which one can draw inferences about policy impacts.

(xvi) First, in all three conurbations there appears to have been a consistent pattern of an increasing concentration of either unemployment or long-term unemployment (or of both) in the regional centres of each conurbation. Within each conurbation, economic problems have continued to grow in the worst of the areas, but there have been improvements outside the core. This suggests the apparent intractibility of the worst areas, but that policy may have made some inroads in places elswhere.

(xvii) Second, the patterns within each local authority consistently show that unemployment has become spatially more concentrated over time - there has been increasing polarisation. For example, unemployment change for the period 1983-90 shows that, in no fewer than 17 of the 20 districts which comprise the three conurbations, the inner areas increased their share of unemployment (the three exceptions being Manchester, Liverpool and Knowsley). This pattern is reinforced by a comparison of the share of unemployment and of long-term unemployment. In no fewer than 19 of the 20 districts the inner areas experienced a greater share of long-term unemployed than of unemployed. This strongly suggests a process of increasing polarisation at a within-district scale, in which the most deprived areas have seen their socio-economic problems grow increasingly severe.

(xviii)   The overall conclusion that might be drawn from the complex local patterns in the three conurbations is that, despite targeting on the defined worst areas, the benefits appear to have had as much or more effect on the broader surrounding areas as on the targeted areas themselves. If this interpretation is correct, it adds force to the need to develop effective linkages between policy targeted at areas and the disadvantaged residents living in those areas.

**2.3 Profiles of districts**

(xix)   A classification of authorities, based on the cross-tabulation of inputs and outcomes, suggests:

- that 18 of the 57 UPAs have mainly positive outcomes, 18 have mixed and 21 have poor outcomes. Given the severity of the social and economic problems in some of the authorities, this balance suggests a reasonable level of success. Only 9 UPAs had high inputs and poor outcomes.

- at a regional level, location in itself does not determine success or failure. There are areas with positive and with poor signs in all regions of the country.

- ten of the UPA districts had poor outcomes and, despite being designated as priority areas, received low overall inputs. This reinforces the arguments for better strategic planning and overall coordination of programmes.

- the very large cities are generally included within the category of 'poor' or 'relatively poor' outcomes. This reinforces the finding that it was precisely within these large core areas where expenditure inputs appeared to be less successful in influencing changes in socio-economic conditions.

**3 THE VIEWS OF RECIPIENTS**
**3.1 Residents' survey**

(xx)   The survey of residents involved a total of 1299 interviews in small areas within each conurbation. Most of the areas were selected to enable paired comparisons between areas broadly similar in socio-economic conditions but which had received different levels of financial resources.

(xxi)   The main points highlighted from the survey are:

- the paired comparisons show that in the areas which have received significantly more public resources the attitudes of residents towards the current and future desirability of their neighbourhood are more positive.

- there is an 'area loyalty' amongst most of the residents. Inner city residents perceive their own neighbourhood as being relatively more desirable than comparable areas as places in which to live, thereby suggesting scope for a more focused social dimension to urban policy to capitalise on the place-loyalty of local communities.

- the ranking of factors which residents saw as important for their quality of life suggests that policy has addressed issues of concern to most residents. The most important factors were crime, health care and the cost-of-living.

- there are marked differences between the views of Asian, Black and White respondents about employment prospects and crime.

**3.2 Employers' survey**

(xxii) The survey of employers' views was based on loosely-structured discussions with a small number of businesses in the three conurbations. Results suggest that:

- knowledge of government schemes was limited, even amongst those companies which had derived benefit from schemes. There was criticism both of the multiplicity of schemes and, more pointedly, of the bureacratic impediments seen as being associated with them.

- many capital-based schemes were generally welcomed; infrastructural programmes connected with DLG and UDCs in particular were widely praised.

- there was a widespread view that access to government departments was difficult.

- local authorities were generally seen as not being important players in the urban context.

- additional expenditure on security was seen as an important disincentive to urban location, thereby adding force to the emphasis given in recent policy to the crime dimension.

- there was little evidence of a corporate culture emphasising the involvement of business within the local community in which it happens to work.

**4 THE VIEWS OF EXPERTS**

(xxiii) Discussions with experts drew on interviews with some one hundred key figures in the policy communities in Greater Manchester, Merseyside and Tyne and Wear. In addition to providing portraits of the three areas, three recurring issues were raised.

(xxiv) **Partnerships.** Contextual differences between the areas have had effects on the viability of creating partnerships within each of the conurbations. At one extreme, powerful local consensus encouraged the growth of partnership and aided the achievement of government aspirations. At the other, conflicts between local interests restricted the evolution of partnership arrangements and constrained government ambitions.

(xxv) The common view of senior public, community and private sector figures in all the conurbations was that much of national policy throughout the 1980s had undermined the creation of partnerships at national and local levels, especially through financial restrictions which had reduced the capacity of local authorities to be successful partners.

(xxvi) There was widespread agreement, whatever limitations were expressed about the initiative, that City.Challenge represented a significant institutional innovation in the attempt to create local partnerships which even in the initial phase was showing some degree of success.

(xxvii) **Co-ordination.** In all three conurbations, it was widely believed that there is insufficient co-ordination between local authority departments, between central government departments and between central and local governments. In particular, there was little belief that the Action for Cities package constituted an integrated strategy since it did not link a clear vision of a region's future economic and social role to institutional mechanisms and resources. A common concern was the extent to which different government departments operated on different assumptions about the nature of the conurbations' problems. The compartmentalised nature of different departmental grant regimes and the different rules which accompany them clearly frustrate greater co-ordination and hamper the roles of local authority players. There was a clear feeling expressed by many policy experts in all three conurbations that government departments worked poorly together.

(xxviii)   A particular problem of co-ordination was seen as being the timing of policy introduction. Local authorities were particularly frustrated by the nature and scale of changes that polices which impact upon urban government and services have undergone during the decade. In the largest sense, the evolution of policy for the cities during the past decade was regarded less as an iterative process than as a series of policy oscillations. A narrower problem of timing is that of annuality of resources.

(xxix)   **Targeting.**   Two forms of targeting were raised in the discussions - that which differentiates the 57 designated UP authorities from the non-designated authorities and the targeting of areas or population groups within the 57 designated areas.

(xxx)   Opinion was divided on the merits of targeting **within** designated authorities. All of the policy experts were keenly aware of some of the dilemmas in targeting when resources were limited or declining. The consensus was that places had been the typical mode of targeting in the past. Many argued, however, that in future programmes would need to focus on population groups as well as areas. The view that targeting areas automatically benefited the people living within them was clearly challenged.

(xxxi)   Nevertheless, many of the initiatives which were regarded as most successful in the three conurbations were explicitly spatially-targeted programmes and projects. There was considerable support for focusing resources in future in narrowly defined areas.

## 5 IMPLICATIONS

(xxxii)   The pattern that emerges, both for employment opportunities and residential attractiveness, is very mixed. There has been beneficial change - some of it relative, some absolute. Across the whole set of targeted places and in the smaller areas within some of the conurbations, public resources appear to have made an impact on turning-around aspects both of the economic and residential distress in urban areas. But in the most deprived areas - and especially in the conurbation cores and in areas of high unemployment - policy has not been able to make significant inroads. The biggest and most deprived urban areas have generally experienced a continuing deterioration with 'inner city' conditions spreading more broadly out from the cores of the conurbations, despite the expenditure of public resources. On the other hand, some of the smaller and more peripheral authorities within the 57 UPAs have shown positive socio-economic change which can be related to urban expenditure. To this extent, both in terms of employment prospects and residential desirability, urban policy has achieved positive impacts. However, to set against this, within virtually all the authorities in the three selected conurbations, there is consistent evidence of increasing polarisation between the worst and the best areas. Despite the positive overall impacts, there are therefore strong suggestions of continuing decline in the worst areas. From this one might draw the conclusion that people-targeting, as against place-targeting, needs to be given greater weight than now.

(xxxiii) **Partnerships.** The attempt to encourage the formation of partnerships has been a valuable focus, but has been a goal only imperfectly achieved in practice. Many interviewees thought that policies to rein-back public expenditure and lever-in private investment have had the effect of reducing the ability of local authorities and communities to tackle their problems and to contribute to partnerships. Indeed, all the potential partners in future coalitions are faced with constraints. First, for local authorities, the expert discussions suggest that the transition to a new enabling role has proved more difficult in a context of overall pressures on their resource base and of a rapidly changing external environment created by government legislation. Second, local communities might have played a role in such coalitions, but it has generally not been a high priority of government policy to develop such community participation in the 1980s and this is seen by many as a missed opportunity. Third, there are questions about the long-term commitment of private investment to inner areas. Most of the respondents stressed that only if structures or mechanisms can be created which begin to develop long-term commitment to private-sector investment in cities will the benefits of creating partnerships be secured most effectively. A key to the successful creation of such growth coalitions is widely seen as being the consistent support of public resource and the creation of coherent frameworks through which to cement relationships. Policy changes do not create fertile ground for the development of such coalitions.

(xxxiv) **Coherence.** There is widespread evidence that policy has lacked the coherence that could have come through a more strategic approach to regeneration. This has two aspects. First is the financial dimension of targeting resources to assist urban areas. There is some contradictory evidence here. On one hand, most of the programmes have devoted a large (and usually stable or growing) proportion of resources to the 57 UPAs. This pattern of overall targeting to the UPAs, however, needs to be set alongside the substantial absolute decreases in many of the core resources of these local authorities and the ambiguities in the policy of targeting resources to individual authorities amongst the 57 UPAs.

(xxxv) The second and more fundamental aspect of the lack of coherence is the importance of co-ordinating programmes within and across various departments. There is an almost universal view that such co-ordination has not worked well either at central government or local government levels.

(xxxvi) Many of the best examples where more effective strategic coherence has been achieved through urban policy have involved area-based schemes. Two alternative approaches were suggested to capitalise on this: the development of regional or urban budgets which genuinely cut across departmental allocations; and an even greater emphasis on local area-based strategies through which local co-ordination might be developed more robustly on the ground.

(xxxvii) The experts suggested that the principles underlying City Challenge appear to have gone some long way to address many of the limitations argued above. Despite reservations about the competitive principle as a way of allocating resource, the operational principles applied to the successful authorities appear to embody much of value: an unambiguous role given both to local authorities and to local communities in the formation of coalitions with the private sector;

financial and institutional incentives which reinforce the creation of working partnerships and appear to place emphasis on quality as against expenditure; the spur to inter-departmental initiatives, through the area-based context of the schemes and through the explicit cross-sectoral emphases; encouragement to develop larger-scale more visionary proposals; the provision for monitoring and evaluation; the assurance of longer-term funding on which rolling programmes can be created. These principles are all ones which seem fundamental to good practice in urban regeneration.

(xxxviii) **Targeting people.** Over the course of the decade, the main thrusts of policy have increasingly been focused on economic and environmental goals and this has inevitably meant that social and community interests have had a lower profile. It was felt that the emphasis on infrastructure in the programmes of urban regeneration has ignored the needs of deprived inner-area residents and has missed the opportunity to utilise their skills and to mobilise their support.

(xxxix) Two findings reinforce the view that inner-city residents have not always benefited: conditions in the cores of the conurbations have deteriorated while there is some improvement across all of the 57 UPAs; and polarisation has increased between areas with worse and better socio-economic conditions. Social projects have suffered from the double disadvantage that Urban Programme resources have grown progressively less as a proportion of overall expenditure and that, within the Urban Programme, capital rather than revenue projects have been favoured.

(xl) Since most support for community-based schemes has come through the Urban Programme, the decision, following the 1992 Autumn Statement, to stop financial support for new schemes under the Urban Programme can only exacerbate the tension between infrastructural and social development. The evidence of increasing polarisation offers strong arguments for the community sector having access to some form of programme which addresses the need to strengthen the capacities of deprived communities.

(xli) **Conclusions.** Five policy conclusions are drawn from the impact assessment:

* There are clear indications of the importance of creating effective coalitions of 'actors' within localities and that these are most likely to result from the development of structures and mechanisms which encourage or require long-term collaborative partnerships.

* Local authorities - in their newly emergent roles as enablers and facilitators - need to be given greater opportunities to play a significant part in such coalitions.

* Local communities equally need to be given opportunities to play roles in such coalitions. The evidence of increasing polarisation suggests the need for specific resources to address the scope for community capacity-building within deprived areas.

* There remains a need to improve the coherence of programmes both across and within government departments. This requires a greater emphasis on the identification of strategic objectives which can guide departmental priorities. Area targeting has played an important part in those cases where separate programmes have been successfully linked so as to create additionality, thereby suggesting the value of giving yet greater emphasis to area-based approaches. Such creative linkage of

policy instruments would be helped by increasing the flexibility of expenditure through a more relaxed approach to virement.

* An important part of such coherence must derive from less ambiguity in the targeting of resources. There is a strong argument for the development of an urban budget which might be administered at regional level so as to reflect the varying constraints and opportunities across different regions and to improve co-ordination across programmes and departments.

# Section 1     Introduction and outline

1.1    There can be no doubt that British cities have experienced severe economic, social and environmental difficulties since the 1960s. Losses of population and jobs have reflected the massive withdrawal of investment from urban areas and this has left many of the big cities not only with extensive physical dereliction, but also with growing social problems associated with poverty, disillusionment and lawlessness. While there may be little argument over the facts of urban decay, the genesis of the problems remains a matter of dispute. The most widely canvassed view is that the economic restructuring of the last two decades has impacted differentially on cities because of the vintage of their stock of capital and because of the factor costs of urban locations: urban premises were old; land was expensive or difficult to recycle; labour was unionised or had skills only associated with 'traditional' industry; infrastructure was inadequate. Business restructuring therefore looked to concentrate or to redevelop in locations outside the cities and new investment sought green-field sites. There are many further arguments which have been brought into play: post-war redevelopment robbed cities of their stocks of cheap starter premises for small businesses; perceptions of cities - rightly or wrongly - emphasised their squalor and danger rather than the range of opportunities which comes with size and density; technological developments in transport and communications offered possibilities for activity to flourish in more remote areas. Some of the suggested causes are internal to cities; others are external. It is clear not only that the problems and causes are interwoven, but that how one interprets the genesis of the problems helps to determine whether the 'urban problem' is seen as a question of problems **of** the city or problems **in** the city.

1.2    Whatever the genesis, it has been especially within the inner areas of the big cities where the economic, social and environmental distress has been most concentrated. Government has responded to this with an evolving policy which has addressed inner-city problems. Its series of urban policy instruments has been elaborated over the last two decades, and the longevity of this policy span reflects the depth and complexity of the issues. The sets of policy instruments have continuously switched their focus, reflecting not only political priorities but also the changing interpretation of the nature of the problems. There has been a shifting target, a shifting set of priorities and a growing and fluctuating set of policies to tackle urban problems.

1.3    The impacts and effectiveness of many of the individual policy instruments have been evaluated in a series of studies conducted largely under the auspices of the Department of the Environment in the period since the middle 1980s. Recent DoE evaluations have included specific studies of the UrbanProgramme, Enterprise Zones, Industrial and Commercial Improvement Areas, the Urban Development Grant Programme, Derelict Land Grant schemes, Garden Festivals and other of the policy instruments of government. However, the functioning of cities cannot readily be partitioned into neatly discrete categories. The economies, environments and social structures of cities form a seamless interconnected web and the effectiveness of expenditure on any one of these distinctive elements of policy clearly intersects with the impact of expenditure on many of the other policy instruments. The obvious extension to such programme evaluations is to look at the effects of the broad swathe of policy as a whole over the span of time during which it has operated. That is the brief of this research project. Its aim is to evaluate the overall impact of government urban policy in England over the period of the last decade. We were specifically enjoined to look, not at any one of the elements of urban policy, but at the impacts of policy across the board. This is a difficult task. It faces both strategic and conceptual problems.

**Policy changes**

1.4    First, there is some difficulty both in determining unambiguously what government has aimed to achieve in developing its urban policy at any one time and in trying to characterise those aims over the course of the last two decades. During the 1980s, the government's aims have altered and the mix of policy instruments has changed. This can be seen in Table 1 which shows the pattern of public expenditure under the various departmental programmes for which we were able to collect data for a sample of local authorities during the 1980s. The streams of expenditure show new programmes coming into existence at various points throughout the decade, reflecting the changing balance of government aims. The multiplicity of programmes suggests the changing foci of policy. We can crudely recognise five policy phases.

* First was the so-called 'traditional' urban programme which began in 1968 and gave considerable weight to community-based projects and to addressing the needs of social deprivation.

* Second, with the development of the 'enhanced' urban programme in 1978, the focus was broadened to include economic and infrastructural needs. The delivery of policy was to be through the creation of partnerships between central and local government with the identification of 'partnership' and 'programme' areas.

* Third, from the early 1980s, the emphasis on economic and infrastructure was strongly reinforced with a switch of spending from revenue to capital expenditure. The stress on creating partnerships, which had originally been seen in terms of central and local government, was transformed to partnerships which involved the private sector and central government through the creation of new agencies such as Urban Development Corporations which were one of the key developments of the 1980s. It was this period that saw the appearance of many of the new policy instruments whose objective was to 'lever' private-sector investment into urban areas (for example, Enterprise Zones and the successive sequence of Urban Development Grants/ Urban Regeneration Grants/City Grants).

* Fourth, in the later 1980s, issues of co-ordination were added to government's concern, with bodies such as City Action Teams and Task Forces being added to the locally-based agencies. As part of this, in 1988 government formally determined a package of measures which comprised its *Action for Cities* (AfC) programme, rolling together a variety of programmes from across a range of government departments.

* Fifth (and outside the scope of this evaluation since it began after the period covered by our work), the most recent emphasis is on 'targeting' and 'simplification' within urban policy. An important part of the determination of expenditure allocations is now driven by a competitive process, reflected in City Challenge, in which places which appear more likely to succeed are more likely to receive resources for regeneration.

2

1.5 Within this changing mix of aims and of the associated policy instruments and objectives, the most explicit statement of the overarching aims of policy is that spelled out in AfC as:

- to encourage enterprise and new business, and help existing businesses to grow stronger;

- to improve people's job prospects, their motivation and skills;

- to make areas attractive to residents and to businesses by tackling dereliction, bringing buildings into use, preparing sites and encouraging development, and improving the quality of housing; and

- to make inner city areas safe and attractive places in which to live and work.

*Table 1*   **Expenditure in the sample of 123 districts: AfC and 'total' expenditure**

|  | 79/80 | 80/1 | 81/2 | 82/3 | 83/4 | 84/5 | 85/6 | 86/7 | 87/8 | 88/9 | 89/90 | 90/91 |
|---|---|---|---|---|---|---|---|---|---|---|---|---|
| **AfC** | 156 | 211 | 283 | 402 | 462 | 488 | 591 | 672 | 812 | 1115 | 1321 | 1099* |
| (of which) | | | | | | | | | | | | |
| UP | 120 | 163 | 170 | 221 | 222 | 232 | 226 | 224 | 242 | 227 | 230 | 233 |
| UDC | | | 30 | 67 | 94 | 91 | 93 | 109 | 168 | 316 | 445 | 588 |
| EZ | | | 30 | 32 | 26 | 63 | 115 | 111 | 96 | 171 | 207 | NA* |
| UDG/CG | | | | 1 | 31 | 18 | 36 | 33 | 48 | 60 | 64 | 52 |
| CATs | | | | | | | | 2 | 5 | 7 | 9 | 12 |
| DLG | 10 | 16 | 15 | 31 | 34 | 32 | 42 | 47 | 51 | 43 | 41 | 43 |
| EA | | | | | | | | 41 | 67 | 127 | 170 | NA* |
| SC | | | | | | | | | | | 2 | 5 |
| S11 | 26 | 34 | 42 | 52 | 60 | 55 | 59 | 67 | 68 | 77 | 80 | 83 |
| EMBI | | | | | | | 0.1 | 0.2 | 0.1 | 0.2 | 0.2 | 0.2 |
| EE | | | | | | | 26 | 26 | 37 | 42 | 36 | 41 |
| TF | | | | | | | | 12 | 30 | 45 | 35 | 41 |
| **HIP** | 1,628 | 1,449 | 1,153 | 1,451 | 1,414 | 1,221 | 1,056 | 1,034 | 996 | 988 | 827 | 1,309 |
| **RSA/RDGII** | 39 | 40 | 45 | 55 | 44 | 40 | 62 | 100 | 138 | 228 | 165 | 131 |
| **ERDF/ESF** | | | | | 265 | 178 | 157 | 131 | 137 | 109 | 33 | 35 |
| **RSG** | 4,225 | 4,963 | 5,297 | 5,336 | 5,383 | 5,416 | 5,639 | 5,578 | 5,884 | 6,199 | 6,304 | 6,438 |
| **TOTALS** | 6,047 | 6,662 | 6,779 | 7,244 | 7,569 | 7,343 | 7,505 | 7,514 | 7,967 | 8,639 | 8,650 | 9,011 |

Notes:
1. All figures are cash values and are shown in £ millions. Column totals may not add up up due to rounding.
2. *NA. When calculations were made, disaggregated data were not available for Enterprise Zones or Estate Action for 1990/91. The AfC total is therefore necessarily artificially depressed for that year.
3. The total European funding cannot be disaggregated for districts for the whole period: ERDF runs from 1983/4 to 1988/9; ESF runs from 1987/8 to 1990/1.
4. Abbreviations:

| | |
|---|---|
| AfC: | Action for Cities (of which) |
| UP: | Urban Programme |
| UDC: | Urban Development Corporation |
| EZ: | Enterprise Zone |
| UDG/CG: | Urban Development Grant, Urban Regeneration Grant, City Grant |
| CATs: | City Action Teams |
| EA: | Estate Action |
| SC: | Safer Cities |
| EMBI: | Ethnic Minorities Business Initiative |
| EE: | English Estates |
| TF: | Task Force |
| HIP: | Housing Investment Programme |
| RSA/RSGII: | Regional Selective Assistance/Regional Development Grant II |
| ERDF/ESF: | European Regional Development Fund/Social Fund |
| RSG: | Rate Support Grant |

1.6 There is clearly a good deal of overlap and inter-relationship amongst these four overall aims - the encouragement of enterprise will affect the job prospects of local residents; making local areas more attractive will enhance the likelihood of new enterprise-related investment in areas; increasing the safety of areas will increase their residential and business attractiveness. The stated aims also individually often refer to more than a single issue, for example job prospects and motivation and skills. Furthermore, there is a very large number of specific programme objectives amongst the policy instruments through which these four aims have been approached.

1.7 The policy changes make it difficult to suggest a single set of aims over the whole period of our evaluation. Not only did urban policy change, so too did a variety of other contextual circumstances over the course of the decade: economic and social policies more generally were affected by the government's encouragement of privatisation, of individual responsibility, of competition and deregulation; and they in turn reflected and responded to wider changes in the globalisation of economies. Any evaluation clearly needs to determine the policy domain which it will address. Since our terms of reference gave particular salience to the Action for Cities package, our focus is on the above aims and on the 57 Urban Priority Areas which were a central part of the targeting of the AfC package.

**Conceptual problems**

1.8 Second, the evaluation of a multi-stranded policy programme presents a host of conceptual conundrums which can be outlined under the heading of six 'Cs':

- the **counterfactual** problem of assessing what would have happened in the absence of government intervention;

- the **confound** problem arising from the fact that outcomes can be affected by many public policies (such as central government expenditure on mainstream programmes, EC intervention or the varying activity of local authorities) in addition to the specific government programmes under Action for Cities;

- the **contextual** problem that local authorities started the period from very different conditions and that this is likely to affect their capacity for improvement;

- the **contiguity** problem associated with the fact that intervention in one area can have positive 'spillover' or negative 'shadow' effects on adjacent areas which are not the subject of intervention;

- the **combinatorial** problem that public assistance has been delivered to places in differently constituted packages of programmes, some of which combinations may have worked better than others; and

- the changing **choice** problem which arises from the fact that the sets of places targeted to receive preferential assistance alters over time and across different programmes so that any decision to assign particular authorities to a 'policy-on' or a 'policy-off' set cannot apply unambiguously over the whole time span and for all elements of policy.

1.9 There are also conceptual problems in distinguishing and balancing between the variety of reasons which might account for any failures of policy. Failure could be the result of one or a combination of elements: theory failure (the incorrect identification of the genesis of problems and hence the development of an inappropriate set of policy instruments); implementation failure (the inadequate or ineffectual translation of policy into practices on the ground); or measurement failure (the absence or inadequacy of data or of techniques for measuring the impacts of policy).

1.10    Amongst these various difficulties, that of taking account of the counterfactual argument is by far the most problematic - and ultimately unsolvable. The traditional social science approach to addressing it is to make comparisons between 'experimental' and 'control' groups. This is clearly not an option in looking at the impacts of urban policy since there are no 'control' cities. All of the big cities in Britain have, to greater or lesser degree, been the recipients of urban policy; there are no equivalents of Liverpool or Birmingham which have not been the beneficiaries of government resources.

1.11    The nature of our research methodology has been designed to address such difficulties. The research design is elaborated below.

**Policy objectives**          1.12    The changes in the aim of urban policy over the decade clearly mean that an evaluation of impacts over the course of the whole decade must of necessity stand back from the detail of specific programmes and endeavour to pitch its conclusions at a meso-scale, looking at overall expenditure and overall changes. We do not attempt - and were not asked - to evaluate specific programmes.

1.13    In the initial feasibility study which preceded the research, we addressed the issues of determining what the objectives of policy could be considered to be and how best one could develop measures to evaluate the success of policy in meeting objectives (see Appendix H). We conducted national and local audits in order to clarify these issues.

1.14    The national audit involved primary data collection and ascertaining views about the evaluation of government policy through interviews with leading central departmental officers who are heavily involved in the implementation of programmes included in the Action for Cities package. The departments covered were DoE, HO, DE, DES, DTI and DTp (in London) and the TA and ES (Sheffield). In total, 30 of the 33 programmes listed in the original AfC document were discussed in face-to-face and telephone interviews (see Table 2). The purpose was to identify, for each programme, the formal objectives (or informal equivalents) used at departmental level, the relation of these objectives to impact assessments, the contribution made by the programme to the four stated objectives of AfC, current data collection arrangements relevant to impact assessment, the methods (if any) adopted by departments to assess impact on a programme-specific basis, and the limitations, shortcomings and lessons of all of the above for assessing the impact of the AfC package as a whole. The substantive conclusions from these discussions were reported in our Report to DoE on the feasibility phase of the evaluation.

1.15    The scrutiny of the published aims of urban policy showed that there are well over 100 such programme objectives. These, we would emphasise, are not our aims, but are the stated or imputed aims of government itself. There is inevitably a high degree of inter-relationship amongst these programme objectives, and this suggests the desirability of grouping together sets of objectives which are conceptually closely related - just as government itself has frequently reported its aims under the three heads of 'economic', 'social' and 'environmental'. Our consideration of the large number of objectives led us to the view that two levels of objective can be identified.

**Table 2    Programmes included in determining the objectives of policy**

| | |
|---|---|
| Urban Programme | (Inner City) Open Learning Centres |
| Urban Development Corporations | English Estates' Managed Workshop Programme |
| Enterprise Zones | Task Forces |
| City Grant | Enterprise Initiative |
| City Action Teams | Regional Selective Assistance |
| Derelict Land Grant | Transport Supplementary Grant |
| Housing Corporation | Jobclubs |
| Land Register | Loan Guarantee Scheme |
| Housing Action Trusts | Race Relations Employment Advisory Service |
| Estate Action | Small Firms Service |
| Garden Festivals | Employment Training |
| Safer Cities | Enterprise Allowance Scheme |
| Section 11 Grants | (School-Industry) Compacts |
| Ethnic Minority Business Initiative | Youth Training Scheme |
| City Technology Colleges | Headstart |

**First** is a *lower-level* set in which we can identify the following ten principal objectives:

1. *Enterprise development:* to improve the performance of existing enterprises and to encourage the formation of new enterprise;

2. *Sites for economic development:* to increase the rate of reclamation of sites and the improvement of existing buildings for private-sector development;

3. *Skills development:* to improve vocational and employment-related skills, adult numeracy and literacy;

4. *Motivation to work:* to enhance personal development and enterprise in job search;

5. *Inter-agency co-ordination:* to improve interdepartmental and intergovernmental co-ordination and public/private/voluntary sector joint working;

6. *Access to employment and services:* to remove barriers to recruitment and to access to publicly-provided services;

7. *Housing development:* to improve the quality of the housing stock and the quality of management of public housing and to increase the quantity of private housing;

8. *Built environment:* to improve infrastructural services and the provision and running of transport networks;

9. *Social fabric:* to strengthen communities and increase local self-help and community care; and

10. *Safety and security:* to reduce the incidence of crime and vandalism and of accidents.

**Second** is a higher-level set which identifies two principal objectives:

I. the creation of employment opportunities; and

II. the creation of cities which are more attractive places in which to live.

1.16    The ten objectives were derived from a classification of all the hundred and more objectives derived from the relevant programmes. The two higher-level objectives were in turn constructed from an examination of the ten lower-level objectives. This set of objectives can best be represented in a Venn diagram which suggests the degree of overlap between some of these elements across the two higher-level objectives (Figure 1). The ideal, for any form of monitoring and subsequent evaluation of performance, would be to assign specific measurable variables to each of such objectives. In practice such an ideal is unobtainable. There is no one-to-one relationship between such objectives and individual indicators which might be used to measure the impacts of policy on each of them. That reflects one of the innumerable difficulties associated with the whole field of evaluation. It means that, in using indicators of performance, one is inevitably forced to measure the performance of combinations of the lower-level objectives.

**Figure 1  Higher-level and lower-level policy objectives**

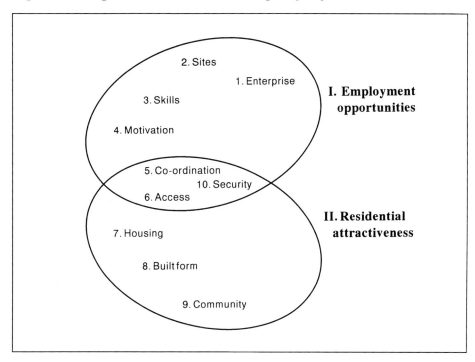

1.17   Despite the difficulties of attempting an evaluation of overall policy, what we would emphasise from our preliminary consideration of policy objectives is that:

(i)   in the great majority of the policy objectives, there is a focus on an essentially **spatial** view of the working of urban policy. Most of the policy instruments involve the definition of geographical areas (rather than groups of people) to which resources should be targeted. This suggests the appropriateness of using a geographical approach to our analysis (using aggregate spatial data rather than data for categories of individuals);

(ii)   the central requirement of the evaluation of impacts is to identify measures of **outcome** rather than of input or output. It is more important to know what substantive changes have occurred to employment or to the attractiveness of cities, than to know how much has been spent on environmental improvement or how many new houses have been built. This emphasis on outcomes reflects the fact that our work is concerned with impact assessment rather than with programme evaluation;

(iii)   any evaluation needs to focus on measures which are readily available at both the spatial scales and the temporal frequencies which might make evaluation practicable, even though this will force us to adopt imperfect and crude measures. There is therefore an inevitable compromise between what might be ideal and what is available; and

(iv) it is inevitable that one has to use **general** indicators rather than ones which claim to be highly specific to one or another objective. This is a result of the high degree of overlap between the aims of different policy instruments which means that any element of social and economic change will be affected by the inputs from a variety of policy instruments.

**Socio-economic indicators**

1.18 These points led us to consider a very large range of potential evaluative measures. The choice was restricted by our need to focus on outcomes rather than outputs and by the limited data sources available to study change at the scale of local authorities. Some of the less standard indicators which we considered included:

- property prices/valuations for both industrial and commercial property, as a measure of business confidence;

- investment and development trends, as a reflection of business confidence;

- housing applicants databases, as a measure of the popularity of local authority housing areas;

- DoE planning applications, as a measure of the ebullience of local housing and commercial markets;

- business confidence, as measured by Chambers of Commerce surveys;

- house condition surveys, as a reflection of public and private investment in property;

- evidence of crime from the British Crime Survey, as a measure of the real or perceived safety of areas;

- tourism statistics, as a measure of the ability of an area to attract external leisure-related custom; and

- poverty/quality-of-life surveys, as a measure of the perceived satisfaction of residents.

1.19 We eventually selected five socio-economic indicators. Many others which were considered were rejected principally for one of three reasons: they were measures of programme input or output rather than of outcomes; their relationship to the objectives of policy were too ambiguous; or data were not available at appropriate scales or with sufficient consistent geographical coverage or at the necessary sequential time intervals.

1.20 In selecting our five indicators we sought to choose socio-economic variables which were relatively simple and interpretable and ones for which data were relatively accessible. Such pragmatic considerations inevitably mean that the indicators are far from perfect; nor would we claim that they provide a comprehensive overview of the impacts of policy. We are not persuaded that there are such things as perfect indicators, given the conceptual difficulties surrounding policy evaluation. What we are convinced of is that the selected set of variables provide valuable, if coarse, indicators of the outcomes of different facets of the map of policy objectives which are outlined above. Taken in conjunction with the 'contextual' variables which we suggest as part of the quantitative interpretation of policy impact, they offer valuable indicators of the higher-level policy objectives (and of subsets of the ten stated policy objectives). The fact that these subsets overlap provides an effective way of developing a general interpretation of the impacts of policy 'in the round'.

Descriptive accounts of the patterns of each indicator are provided in Appendix A. A brief discussion of each indicator is provided below:

(i) **Unemployment and long-term unemployment, 1983-91** This addresses the higher-level objective of creating employment opportunities (and the lower-level combination of objectives 1, 2, 3, 4 and 6). Data were derived from the Department of Employment.

Unemployment has long been used as a key indicator of economic conditions. The principal limitations of the indicator are the frequent definitional changes of what constitutes unemployment and the difficulty of deriving an appropriate denominator to calculate rates from the raw figures of unemployment totals. To overcome the latter, we adopted two approaches. First was to use the ratio of long-term unemployment to unemployment - a measure which has increasingly been used to measure the economic health of areas and, computationally, has the advantage of drawing on data from a single source. Second, to calculate rates of unemployment we used as a denominator the estimated numbers of males aged 20-65 and females 20-60. This is a crude estimate because it includes economically inactive persons but, since most of the comparisons are based on changes over time rather than between areas, inaccuracies are likely to be minimised.

(ii) **Net job changes, 1981-89** This addresses the higher-level objective of creating employment opportunities (and the lower-level combination of objectives 1, 2, 3, 4 and 6). Data were drawn from the Census of Employment.

This indicator provides some overall indication of employment opportunities. It is more immediately interpretable and more readily linked with policy inputs than were we to have used Unemployment/ Vacancy ratios. It may be preferable to have had a more finely disaggregated indicator such as net change for particular types of job, but such data are not available at finer spatial scales. The indicator has the disadvantage of being work-place based which means that it fails to distinguish whether the beneficiaries of jobs are city-based or are commuters from outside urban boundaries. However, this difficulty was partly offset by examining job change alongside an analysis of relative changes in numbers of unemployed. As an outcome measure the indicator would seem to capture a high proportion of the higher-level objective of creating employment. It clearly needs to be distinguished from output measures of specific programmes such as cost-per-job.

(iii) **Percentage change in the number of small businesses, 1979-90** This addresses the higher-level objective of creating employment (and the lower-level objectives 1, 2, 4 and 5). Data are drawn from VAT registration records.

This indicator captures only part of what is meant by enterprise creation, but is a sector of the economy that has received considerable attention from government during the 1980s. If there has been change in the economic health of the 57 UPAs, it should be reflected in small business growth. It can be seen as a measure of the degree to which the assumed role of inner areas as 'seedbeds' has been restored. The data have limitations. Only businesses with a sufficient turnover to warrant VAT registration are captured. Amongst firm deaths, one cannot distinguish new firms of short life from those of longer duration. Nor is there any way in which one can isolate those deaths caused by displacement through competition from new firms. Nevertheless, this indicator is considered to be one of the most effective measures of the economic attractiveness and success of areas.

(iv) **House price changes, 1983-90** This addresses both of the higher-level objectives (and the lower-level objectives 2, 6, 7, 8, 9 and 10). Data have been drawn from building society information.

House prices are a good index of the perceived attractiveness of areas and they reflect both current and future confidence in the residential standing of an area. They also, indirectly, reflect business confidence through both the general demand for land and the readiness of the workforce to contemplate making future financial commitments within an area. As an indicator, house prices suffer from a number of limitations. They reflect the intersection of supply and demand and consequently some local knowledge of the types and numbers of available properties in local housing markets is required to make sense of the relative movements of prices. Second, they reflect only those houses which come onto the market and the price movements of this subset may not be typical of the stock as a whole. Third, they necessarily exclude housing outside the private market (although the substantial changes in the nature of the housing market during the 1980s included the growth of right-to-buy which considerably reduced the stock of non-private housing). Fourth, and most problematical, robust and interpretable data are notoriously difficult to collect. Nevertheless, since price changes are a good indicator of an area's general attractiveness, they remain a valuable outcome indicator and use was made of data on sales from the Nationwide and Halifax building societies held by the Centre for Urban and Regional Development Studies at Newcastle. In order to take account of the variation in types of housing, data were assembled for two categories of houses within each of the 123 local authorities in our sample: houses bought by first-time buyers; and all houses located within the 'inner areas' of each authority (the definition of 'inner areas' being based on 1981 Census data of unemployment and social composition).

(v) **Net change in the number/proportion of 25-34 year-olds, 1981-90** This primarily addresses the higher-level objective of making areas attractive for residence (and lower-level objectives 1, 7, 8, 9 and 10). Data were drawn from the OPCS mid-year population estimates.

Since one of the major problems of inner areas has been the scale of net outmigration which they have experienced, it is important to include a measure of the success of areas in retaining or attracting key age groups amongst their economically-active population. The 25-34 age group has relatively high residential mobility and it can therefore be argued that, if cities become more attractive, they should demonstrate this by capturing or retaining a significant proportion of this age cohort. There could be arguments for using younger age groups, but the age cohort between 15 and 25 is unduly affected both by fluctuating student populations and by the effect of educational policies which fall outside the remit of conscious urban policy and by the tendency in many large cities for such groups to include large proportions of unemployed or low-paid young people who drift into inner areas for negative rather than positive reasons. The choice of the 25-34 age group reflects the fact that this is a critical group both in terms of family life-cycles and of those most firmly established in the labour market.

1.21   We were tempted to use a sixth indicator; change in the amount of derelict land (using data from DoE surveys). However, even though it appears at first sight to be a good measure of environmental improvement, it is too close to being an output (or indeed an input) rather than an outcome measure. To be of value, given our focus on outcomes, we would need to be able to measure the additionality effect of derelict land having been converted through subsidies such as Derelict Land Grant (in other words to use a ratio of unassisted:assisted land conversion). Such data do not exist. We also explored, but decided against, other potential and sometimes innovative indicators.

**Research design**

1.22   The research design which we developed to address the evaluation of overall impacts is shown in Figure 2. It is based on the three facets or 'legs' which provide complementary evidence:

- first is a quantitative interpretation which examines the relationship between expenditure and socio-economic outcomes in a sample of English authorities, chosen so as to enable us to develop comparisons between places which have received more and less public assistance;

- second is a qualitative exploration of the views of the experts at the sharp end of policy implementation;

- third is a qualitative interpretation from surveys of the recipients of policy; both the residents of inner urban areas and of employers who operate within big cities.

**Figure 2    Design of the research**

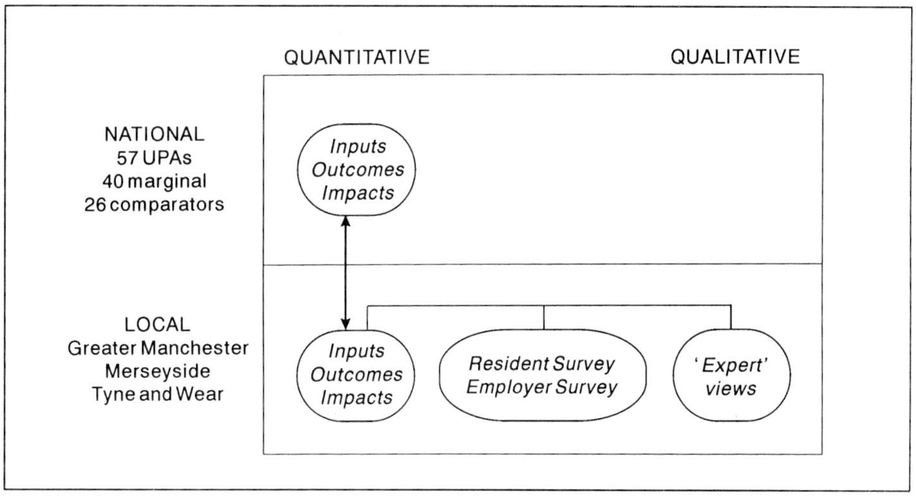

**The selection of case authorities**

1.23   The design embodies a division between the national scale of England as a whole and the local scale of the three selected conurbations of Greater Manchester, Merseyside and Tyne and Wear. The national scale was used for the quantitative evaluation of inputs and outcomes. The local scale was used both to develop a more detailed quantitative study of financial inputs and also for the qualitative studies using discussions and formal interviews. The design also allowed us to look both at the longer-term impacts over the course of the last decade (through the quantitative analyses) and the shorter-term impacts over the last three years (through both quantitative analysis and the perceptions of residents and others whose views are most reliable in relation to the immediate past). The views which we develop are based on the triangulation of these three legs; taken together the three facets can give a more rounded view of the achievements and limitations of overall government policy.

*Figure 3* **The sample 123 authorities**

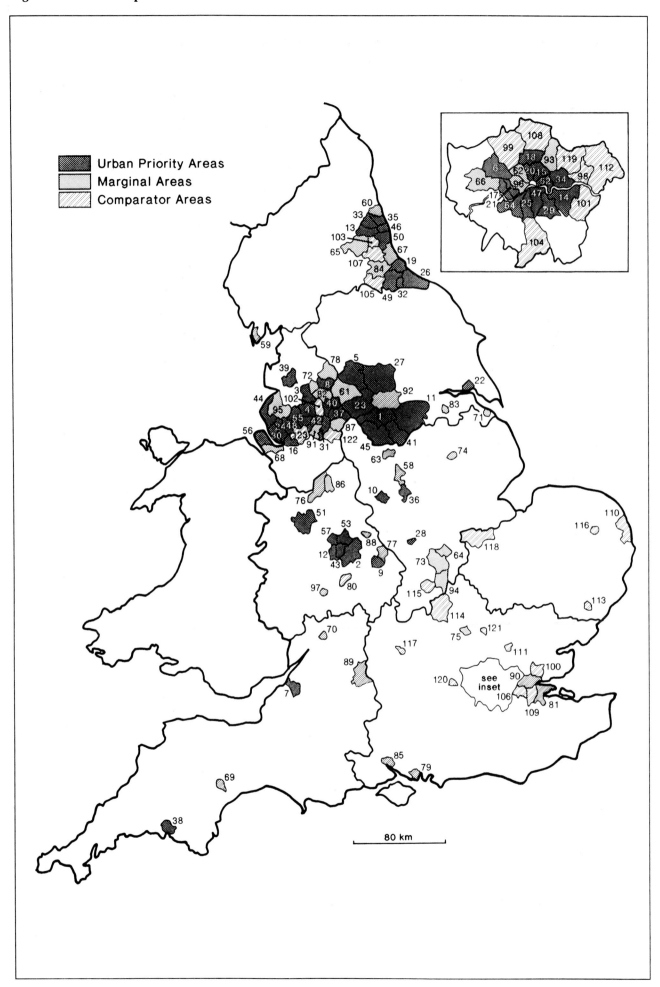

| Ref. No. | County | District | Category | Ref. No. | County | District | Category |
|---|---|---|---|---|---|---|---|
| 1 | S.Yorks | Barnsley | 1 | 63 | Derby | Chesterfield | 2 |
| 2 | W.Mids | Birmingham | 1 | 64 | Nhants | Corby | 2* |
| 3 | Lancs | Blackburn | 1 | 65 | Durham | Derwentside | 2* |
| 4 | Gr.Mcr | Bolton | 1 | 66 | OLond | Ealing | 2* |
| 5 | W.Yorks | Bradford | 1 | 67 | Durham | Easington | 2 |
| 6 | OLond | Brent | 1 | 68 | Chesh | Ellesmere Port/Neston | 2* |
| 7 | Avon | Bristol | 1 | 69 | Devon | Exeter | 2 |
| 8 | Lancs | Burnley | 1 | 70 | Glos | Gloucester | 2 |
| 9 | W.Mids | Coventry | 1 | 71 | Humber | Great Grimsby | 2* |
| 10 | Derby | Derby | 1 | 72 | Lancs | Hyndburn | 2* |
| 11 | S.Yorks | Doncaster | 1 | 73 | Nhants | Kettering | 2 |
| 12 | W.Mids | Dudley | 1 | 74 | Lincs | Lincoln | 2* |
| 13 | TyneWear | Gateshead | 1 | 75 | Beds | Luton | 2* |
| 14 | OLond | Greenwich | 1 | 76 | Staffs | Newcastle-u-Lyne | 2 |
| 15 | ILond | Hackney | 1 | 77 | Warw | Nuneaton | 2 |
| 16 | Chesh | Halton | 1 | 78 | Lancs | Pendle | 2* |
| 17 | ILond | Hammersmith/Fulham | 1 | 79 | Hants | Portsmouth | 2 |
| 18 | ILond | Haringey | 1 | 80 | HereWorc | Redditch | 2 |
| 19 | Cleve | Hartlepool | 1 | 81 | Kent | Rochester | 2 |
| 20 | ILond | Islington | 1 | 82 | Lancs | Rossendale | 2* |
| 21 | ILond | Kensington/Chelsea | 1 | 83 | Humber | Scunthorpe | 2* |
| 22 | Humber | Kingston-on-Hull | 1 | 84 | Durham | Sedgefield | 2* |
| 23 | W.Yorks | Kirklees | 1 | 85 | Hants | Southampton | 2 |
| 24 | Mersey | Knowsley | 1 | 86 | Staffs | Stoke-on-Trent | 2* |
| 25 | ILond | Lambeth | 1 | 87 | Gr.Mcr | Tameside | 2* |
| 26 | Cleve | Langbaurgh | 1 | 88 | Staffs | Tamworth | 2 |
| 27 | W.Yorks | Leeds | 1 | 89 | Wilts | Thamesdown | 2 |
| 28 | Leic | Leicester | 1 | 90 | Essex | Thurrock | 2 |
| 29 | ILond | Lewisham | 1 | 91 | Gr.Mcr | Trafford | 2* |
| 30 | Mersey | Liverpool | 1 | 92 | W.Yorks | Wakefield | 2 |
| 31 | Gr.Mcr | Manchester | 1 | 93 | OLond | Waltham Forest | 2* |
| 32 | Cleve | Middlesbrough | 1 | 94 | Nhants | Wellingborough | 2 |
| 33 | TyneWear | Newcastle-on-Tyne | 1 | 95 | Lancs | West Lancashire | 2* |
| 34 | ILond | Newham | 1 | 96 | ILond | Westminster | 2* |
| 35 | TyneWear | North Tyneside | 1 | 97 | HereWorc | Worcester | 2 |
| 36 | Notts | Nottingham | 1 | 98 | OLond | Barking/Dagenham | 3 |
| 37 | Gr.Mcr | Oldham | 1 | 99 | OLond | Barnet | 3 |
| 38 | Devon | Plymouth | 1 | 100 | Essex | Basildon | 3 |
| 39 | Lancs | Preston | 1 | 101 | OLond | Bexley | 3 |
| 40 | Gr.Mcr | Rochdale | 1 | 102 | Gr.Mcr | Bury | 3 |
| 41 | S.Yorks | Rotherham | 1 | 103 | Durham | Chester-le-Street | 3 |
| 42 | Gr.Mcr | Salford | 1 | 104 | OLond | Croydon | 3 |
| 43 | W.Mids | Sandwell | 1 | 105 | Durham | Darlington | 3 |
| 44 | Mersey | Sefton | 1 | 106 | Kent | Dartford | 3 |
| 45 | S.Yorks | Sheffield | 1 | 107 | Durham | Durham | 3 |
| 46 | TyneWear | South Tyneside | 1 | 108 | OLond | Enfield | 3 |
| 47 | ILond | Southwark | 1 | 109 | Kent | Gravesham | 3 |
| 48 | Mersey | St.Helens | 1 | 110 | Norfolk | Great Yarmouth | 3 |
| 49 | Cleve | Stockton-on-Tees | 1 | 111 | Essex | Harlow | 3 |
| 50 | TyneWear | Sunderland | 1 | 112 | OLond | Havering | 3 |
| 51 | Salop | The Wrekin | 1 | 113 | Suffolk | Ipswich | 3 |
| 52 | ILond | Tower Hamlets | 1 | 114 | Bucks | Milton Keynes | 3 |
| 53 | W.Mids | Walsall | 1 | 115 | Nhants | Northampton | 3 |
| 54 | ILond | Wandsworth | 1 | 116 | Norfolk | Norwich | 3 |
| 55 | Gr.Mcr | Wigan | 1 | 117 | Oxon | Oxford | 3 |
| 56 | Mersey | Wirral | 1 | 118 | Cam | Peterborough | 3 |
| 57 | W.Mids | Wolverhampton | 1 | 119 | OLond | Redbridge | 3 |
| 58 | Notts | Ashfield | 2 | 120 | Berks | Slough | 3 |
| 59 | Cumbria | Barrow-in-Furness | 2 | 121 | Herts | Stevenage | 3 |
| 60 | Northd | Blyth Valley | 2 | 122 | Gr.Mcr | Stockport | 3 |
| 61 | W.Yorks | Calderdale | 2* | 123 | Chesh | Warrington | 3 |
| 62 | ILond | Camden | 2* | | | | |

Notes

The categories are as follows:

1. Urban Priority Areas (as defined in Action for Cities)

2. Marginal districts (those which were targeted, largely as Other Designated Districts, in earlier phases of the Urban Programme are shown with asterisks)

3. Comparators

1.24 Our quantitative approach has necessarily taken account of the relative degrees of assistance given to different places, rather than to contrast the fortunes of a set of policy-on and a set of policy-off places. This is a way in which to tackle the difficulty of the couterfactual. We selected a sample of 123 authorities, all of which showed some degree of socio-economic distress, but some of which had received more and some had received less financial assistance. This sample of 123 authorities is divided into three categories:

- all of the 57 authorities which were defined as Urban Priority Areas in the Action for Cities programme. These are referred to as the 57 **UPAs**;

- 40 authorities which had either been included earlier in parts of the Urban Programme or whose socio-economic circumstances (measured in terms of high unemployment, low percentages of professional and managerial occupations, and the percentage of households in local authority housing) were little different from many of the UPAs. These are referred to as '**marginal**' authorities; and

- 26 authorities which have never been part of the targeted focus of urban expenditure, but which met two general conditions: first, that in the 1981 census they had above-average socio-economic vulnerability (again, as measured by their levels of unemployment, their low proportions of professional and managerial population and their housing tenure composition); and second that they included a regional coverage and provided complete coverage of a number of geographical areas - a swathe to the north and east of Greater London; all of the remaining districts within the four conurbations of Merseyside, Greater Manchester, South and West Yorkshire; and a continuous block of districts around Tyne and Wear and Cleveland. This set is referred to as '**comparator**' areas.

1.25 This sample provided the basis through which we have tackled two of the conceptual problems of the evaluation; the counterfactual and the contiguity issues. The geographical spread of the sample of 123 districts is shown in Figure 3. It provides a mechanism for taking account of some of the conceptual problems noted above: for example, it allows some control over the counterfactual problem since we can compare places which have all faced a degree of urban distress and have received varying amounts and kinds of support; it offers a way of examining the contiguity problem since the swathes of continuous areas allow us to look at spillover effects; and it takes account of the choice problem since it allows us to look at the relationship between amounts of expenditure and outcomes regardless of whether places are 'policy-on' or not. It also offers permutations of the sets of authorities: so, for example, we consider comparisons between the 57 UPAs, the 40 marginals and the 26 comparators; between the 57 UPAs and the 66 marginals and comparators; and between the 97 UPAs and marginals and the 26 comparators.

**Quantitative evaluation**

1.26 The sample provides the basis of our quantitative evaluation. This is divided into a **national** study of the 123 authorities and a more detailed **local** study of the three selected conurbations of Greater Manchester, Merseyside and Tyne and Wear. At each of these spatial scales we assembled data on public expenditure under a range of urban programmes and on the five socio-economic indicators. These data-sets enabled us to explore three elements:

(i) **inputs:** the amounts of public resource received by each authority. The aim was to see which authorities received more or fewer resources under the heading of urban policy. In order to take account of the 'confound' problem, we include not only the various elements of Action for Cities, but also some of the mainstream expenditure (such as Rate Support Grant, Housing Investment Programmes and various forms of regional assistance, which together form a critical element of local authority resources), plus expenditure from the European Community. The full range of data is shown in Table 1. For each of the programmes, expenditure data were disaggregated to the level of the 123 local authorities in our sample; where possible, these expenditure data were then further disaggregated to the scale of wards within each of the 20 authorities within the three conurbations of Greater Manchester, Merseyside and Tyne and Wear. It was in compiling these data that the most troublesome practical problems of our research became apparent. Especially for the earlier part of the period, data on expenditure have been very difficult to assemble and inevitably, throughout the period, the finer the spatial scale the greater those difficulties have been. Even though the data that we have assembled represent probably the best estimate that can be made of the incidence of expenditure, we are alive to their limitations. The outline of these data for each of the programme areas included in our analysis is provided in Appendix A.

(ii) **outcomes:** the changes in selected indicators of socio-economic conditions. The aim was to examine changes during the 1980s in five selected *outcome* indicators (based on unemployment, job creation, new-firm formation, house prices and migration). These indicators are taken as representing outcome changes related to the two broad policy objectives of improving employment opportunities and increasing the residential attractiveness of urban areas. Since our concern is with overall policy effectiveness rather than programme evaluation, we have not looked at *output* measures (such as numbers of houses built or hectares of land brought back into productive use) since these reflect simply the implementation of policy. Rather, as is argued above, we have been concerned with the broad outcomes related to the macro objectives of policy.

(iii) **relationships:** the goodness of fit between financial inputs and changing socio-economic outcomes. It is this relationship which gives us one of our principal indications of the effectiveness of policy. We used a variety of techniques based on correlation and regression to look at the relationship between expenditure and socio-economic change. Since we include measures of the socio-economic circumstances of places at the start of a particular period of change, we can thereby take some account of the 'contextual' problem. Even these input:outcome relationships, however, must be subject to qualification since the direction of any relationship can be interpreted in different ways: a negative relationship could suggest either that resource is 'properly' being targeted at places which are responding at a slower rate than other areas but would have responded even more slowly in the absence of inputs of public expenditure, or that policy inputs are ineffective; a positive relationship could be interpreted as suggesting either that resource is being inappropriately targeted to places which might have recovered even in the absence of assistance, or that public assistance is having beneficial effects.

1.27 Formally, our quantitative evaluation is based on two null hypotheses: that the 57 UPA authorities will show no statistically significant difference from the 66 marginal and comparator areas in terms of our selected outcome indicators; and that greater urban policy expenditure in local authorities has no effect on the socio-economic indicators. Any relative improvement in the UPAs can be attributed to the impacts of public expenditure; any relative deterioration can be interpreted either as a reflection of the failure of policy to create impacts or as a reflection of the counterfactual argument that, in the absence of public expenditure, conditions in the 57 would have grown relatively even worse. Likewise, any positive relationship across the whole set of 123 authorities between inputs and outcomes can be interpreted as the result of the expenditure of public resource.

1.28   We attempt to disentangle the complexity of such relationships in a variety of ways: by looking at time-lagged relationships (in other words, looking at the relationship between outcomes in one period and the inputs in earlier periods); by taking into account contextual indicators on the basis of which resources may have been allocated; and by making interpretations which are informed by the qualitative elements of our research design. The details of this quantitative evaluation are given in Appendix B (for the national scale) and Appendix D (for the local scale).

**Qualitative approaches**       1.29   This quantitative analysis is, in itself, far from being an adequate approach to an interpretation of the impacts of policy. There are many limitations to drawing inferences on the basis of quantitative relationships: the amounts of public resource cannot be a very sensitive measure of policy on the ground; the outcome indicators are a very imperfect and partial measure of socio-economic change; treating all of the component instruments of policy as equal parts of policy delivery does not recognise that different combinations in different circumstances can work better or worse; the input/outcome relationships act as black boxes which cannot tell us anything about the underlying processes or mechanisms of change.

1.30   It was for such reasons that we also developed the qualitative strands of our work. This involved two different attacks on the problem. First was an extensive series of discussions with experts in the three conurbations. These experts were senior policy makers, policy deliverers or policy 'influentials' in Greater Manchester, Merseyside and Tyne and Wear. In each conurbation, between 30 and 40 such discussions were held. Accounts of the experts' views are given in Appendix G. Their focus was on how well policy had worked and how the implementation and the implementors functioned. These discussions both sensitised us to many of the specific issues in each area and have fed into the accounts of expenditure in the three conurbations (Appendix C).

1.31   The second element of our qualitative approach was based on a formal questionnaire survey of some 1,299 residents in selected districts of the three conurbations and a survey of employers in the three areas. Details of the residents' survey are given in Appendix E. Its aim was to examine local attitudes to changes within local areas and to gauge residents' perceptions of future prospects. It also explored aspects such as safety and environmental issues which could not be examined through the quantitative work because of the absence of appropriate data; and it included a specific focus on ethnic groups. The employers' survey was based on more open-ended discussions with senior managers in a range of types of company and explores their views on business conditions, on the role of local circumstances and on how public policy has affected the operation of their businesses. Details of these discussions are given in Appendix F.

**Structure of the report**

1.32   It is therefore from the intersection - the triangulation - between these three legs of our work that our overall evaluation is based. The following four sections of the main report provide brief summary accounts of some of the conclusions of each of the elements of our work. Section 2 summarises the outcomes from the quantitative analyses both at the national and local levels; section 3 summarises the findings from the resident and employer surveys in the three conurbations; section 4 draws on the views of the experts in the same three conurbations. The final section draws these strands together and offers a view of the implications of the overall assessment of the impacts of policy.

1.33   These summaries need to be read in conjunction with the eight appendices which report in greater detail on the range of work which underlies our views. The appendices have been arranged to follow the sequence of work which was undertaken: Appendix A outlines the patterns of expenditure for the data which was collected on expenditure inputs at national level and for the indicator variables on outcomes; Appendix B provides detail on the quantitative analysis of the national sample of 123 authorities; Appendix C draws on the detailed expenditure data for wards in the 20 authorities within the conurbations of Greater Manchester, Merseyside and Tyne and Wear, to paint portraits of the three conurbation contexts; Appendix D discusses the results of the quantitative analysis for the local level of the 20 authorities in the three conurbations; Appendix E outlines the results of the residents' questionnaire survey; Appendix F summarises the views of employers in the conurbations; Appendix G outlines the views of experts in the three conurbations; and Appendix H provides a summary of the feasibility study which preceded the research itself.

# Section 2      Quantitative assessment: the national and local pictures

2.1   The quantitative assessment was based on study at both a national and local scale. The national scale involved the sample of 123 local authorities which comprised the 57 UPAs, 40 'marginals' and 26 comparators. As outlined in Section 1, these 123 authorities were spread throughout the regions of England. Our study focused on the incidence of inputs, changes over time in socio-economic outcomes and the relationships between these two. The local scale involved ward-level analysis within the districts of the three conurbations of Greater Manchester, Merseyside and Tyne and Wear.

**Techniques**

2.2   Our initial intention was to use multi-level modelling to explore the complex nature of the relationships between financial inputs and socio-economic outcomes. Multi-level modelling is a sophisticated form of regression analysis which enables one to examine the inter-relationship between 'levels' of analysis. Our aim was to explore the relationship between outcomes at different spatial scales (for example, to investigate whether the 'performance' of an inner urban area was statistically linked to the performance of its local authority; whether the authority's performance was related to its conurbation; whether the conurbation was related to the region in which it lies). For most of the analyses this proved impossible because of the spatial variability of the values of the outcome indicators. Had all of the targeted areas within a conurbation responded more slowly or more rapidly than non-targeted places, this would have been reflected in the outcomes and the model would have enabled us to interpret the interplay between changes in 'levels' or categories.

2.3   This situation, however, proved not to be the case. There was great variation within similar categories of areas, within conurbations, within regions and within city sizes and types. Regardless of what groupings we explored for authorities at the national scale or for wards at the local scale (for example, using the spatial definition of city, conurbation and region; or using various functional definition of groups of authorities), the variance of all of the outcome indicators was greater within the groupings than was the variance between. The outcomes therefore failed to show any discernible statistical pattern between 'levels'. This emphasises the complexity of the outcome indicators and hence of the relationships at which we looked: expenditure patterns prove highly complex spatially; outcome indicators are no less complex, even in the case of unemployment.

2.4   The exploration of the indicators through multi-level modelling, therefore, showed how great is the variation of outcomes across our sample areas. The differences between the targeted and non-targeted areas is often neither great nor consistent. This implies that there are some targeted areas which are responding better than others in socio-economic terms; and, indeed, are responding better than some non-targeted areas. Some of the more successful places may well adjoin other targeted areas which are not performing well. The multi-level model shows that there is no obvious classification of authorities or wards which can help to account for the varying fortunes of places. There is no simple categorisation of one type of place which has experienced uniformally bad socio-economic changes over the course of the 1980s and another set which has experienced uniformly good changes. The world proves more complex, and this may have something to do with policy interventions; the variation may reflect successful government intervention.

2.5   However, these patterns of variability meant that multi-level modelling proved impossible to use as the principal statistical vehicle for our detailed quantitative interpretations and, for this reason, our statistical analysis of the relationships between inputs and outcomes was largely based on two alternatives:

(i)   a large number of permutations of various forms of regression analysis of inputs, outcomes and relationships between the expenditure and socio-economic change; and

(ii)   analysis of trends in the 'gaps' or differences in the outcome indicators between UPAs and other districts (in other words, analysis of whether the UPA and non-UPA areas showed convergence or divergence over time).

2.6   Some of the details of the analysis are reported in Appendices B and D. Here, a number of relevant findings can be summarised both at the national scale for the 123 district authorities and for the ward scale within the three conurbations.

**National scale: the 123 Districts**
(i)   Inputs

2.7   The total public expenditure on Action for Cities was claimed to be over £3 billion in 1989/90 and over £4 billion in 1990/91. This expenditure needs to be set in the context of a total government expenditure of over £200 billion. Our evaluation is therefore concerned with changes which may have been achieved through targeting a mere 2% of total government expenditure. This merely reinforces the concern about the 'confounds' problem; that the impacts of AfC may have been swamped by the effects of other non-targeted public resources. While the absolute AfC expenditure may be considerable, its relative insignificance, may therefore make it reasonable to anticipate only modest impacts on the fortunes of the large cities in England.

2.8   Our compilation of AfC expenditure data for the 123 authorities is not (and cannot be) identical to the £4 billion benchmark figure used by government. Table 1 (in Section 1, above) shows the set of programmes for which we have been able to collect input data for our sample authorities over the period 1979/80 to 1990/91. Table 3 shows the difference between the government's calculation of overall AfC expenditure and our calculation of AfC expenditure in the 123 authorities. There are a number of reasons why the two calculations cannot be synonymous:

-   some expenditure is directed to people rather than places and cannot therefore be attributed spatially to areas. This applies in particular to training and enterprise assistance which accounts for some £1 billion.

-   some expenditure could not be disaggregated to the level of local authorities. This applies, for example, to expenditure under the Transport Supplementary Grant and, in particular, to Housing Corporation expenditure (which together account for almost £1 billion). While we were unable to derive place-specific expenditure from the Housing Corporation, we were able to assemble data on housing completions and housing refurbishment which are discussed in Appendix A.

- some expenditure falls outside England. The programmes in Scotland and Wales account for over one-third of a billion.

- some expenditure under main programmes, such as support for inner-city businesses through Regional Selective Assistance/Regional Development Grant or investment and innovation grants to small firms through DTI, is primarily directed at regional rather than urban objectives. While this expenditure was disaggregated to local authority areas and is used in our analysis of overall expenditure, it was decided not to include it in the urban-oriented AfC expenditure.

- some of the AfC expenditure necessarily falls outside our selected 123 authorities.

- some of the expenditure came on stream only after the end date of our evaluation (for example, Housing Action Trusts or the top-slicing of Housing Investment Programme resources as Inner City Special Allocations) .

*Table 3*  **Officially recognised overall expenditure on Action for Cities and expenditure included in the CUPS analysis**

(£millions)

|  | 1988/89 | 1989/90 | 1990/91 |
|---|---|---|---|
| * Urban Programme | 261 | 260 | 261 |
| * Urban Development Corporations | 234 | 439 | 542 |
| * City Grant | 25 | 35 | 49 |
| * City Action Teams | 7 | 6 | 8 |
| * Derelict Land Grant | 31 | 20 | 21 |
| * Estate Action | 140 | 190 | 190 |
| * Section 11 | 57 | 69 | 73 |
| * Task Forces | 16 | 19 | 23 |
| * Safer Cities | 0.2 | 2.5 | 6.5 |
| * Ethnic Minorities Business Initiative | - | - | - |
| * Enterprise Zones | - | - | - |
| * English Estates | | | |
| ** Regional Selective Assistance | 189 | 188 | 192 |
| ** Housing Investment Programme(ICSA) | - | - | 100 |
| ***Housing Corporation | 610 | 517 | 620 |
| Housing Action Trusts | - | - | 42 |
| Training/Enterprise | 1096 | 1035 | 1040 |
| Homelessness | - | - | 147 |
| Transport Supplementary Grant | 190 | 220 | 300 |
| Community Technical Colleges | 14 | 32 | 45 |
| Scotland and Wales | 300 | 350 | 400 |

**TOTALS**

| | 1988/89 | 1989/90 | 1990/91 |
|---|---|---|---|
| Total government expenditure | **3,170** | **3,382** | **4,060** |
| CUPS AfC evaluation expenditure (For details, see Table 1) | **1,115** | **1,321** | **1,099 #** |

**Notes:**
1988/89 data are out-turn; 1989/90 data are estimated out-turn; 1990/91 data are planned figures.
*    Programmes included in CUPS evaluation research definition of 'AfC expenditure' (Official figures do not include Enterprise Zones or EMBI expenditure in the AfC expenditure and do not show expenditure on English Estates separately.)
**    Programmes included in CUPS evaluation research definition of 'overall expenditure'
***    Programmes for which output rather than expenditure data are included in CUPS evaluation research (see Appendix A)
#    Spatially disaggregated data for Enterprise Zones and Estate Action for 1990/91 were not available at the time of calculating input/outcome relationships. This accounts for the lower figure for the CUPS totals for 1990/91.

2.9    As Table 3 shows for the three financial years 1988/9 to 1990/91, we were successful in compiling input data for the great majority of relevant programmes. In total, excluding expenditure on the Housing Corporation, training, Regional Selective Assistance and Scotland and Wales, virtually all of the total claimed under AfC has been incorporated into our quantitative analysis. The remaining expenditure for which we have been unable to assemble spatially-referenced data for authorities has to be thought of as 'background noise' which must be assumed to have been allocated to authorities in ways which do not discriminate systematically between the different urban areas in our 123 sample or in ways which discriminate no differently from other expenditure. While there is no way in which to test this assumption, the principal elements of the expenditure which is unaccounted for are related to training which can reasonably be assumed to reflect the patterns of unemployment which are already reflected in our categorisation of the sample of 123 districts and this makes the assumption not unreasonable.

2.10    This large financial data-set for authorities therefore gave us a variety of combinations of expenditure inputs at which to look. These comprised:

-    principally, total AfC expenditure;

-    within this, expenditure on the Urban Programme, since it applied to a large proportion of the authorities over the period studied;

-    Regional Selective Assistance, since again it applied to a large proportion of the sample authorities; and

-    total expenditure, by adding to AfC totals the expenditure on Regional Selective Assistance, Revenue Support Grant, Housing Investment Programme, European Social Fund and European Regional Development Grant.

2.11    Two general points can be made about the pattern of expenditure of the AfC resources over the course of the 1980s.

2.12    First, we found that there was a lack of fit between the classification of authorities as urban priority areas and the amounts of resource that they received per capita. It might have been expected that the 57 UPAs would have received the largest sums of financial inputs. In fact, ranking the top 57 authorities in terms of total per capita AfC resources over the period of the 1980s as a whole, no fewer than 12 were not UPAs. This may be a function of the changes in the designations of targeted areas over the course of the decade since the 57 UPAs were only formally used from the later part of the 1980s. However, if we restrict the period to 1988/9-1989/90 (during which the 57 UPAs **were** the officially designated target areas, and for which period we have full data for individual authorities), a similar pattern of expenditure targeting appears (Table 4). Of the 57 best-funded authorities, 10 were not UPAs (Scunthorpe, Corby, Trafford, Rochester, Rossendale, Hyndburn, Derwentside, Gravesham, Ellesmere Port and Wellingborough). Contrariwise, there were 10 UPAs which fell outside the best-funded 57 (Derby, Wigan, Leeds, Hammersmith, Wandsworth, Kirklees, Lewisham, Bristol, Sefton and Plymouth). While many elements of AfC expenditure were never intended to apply solely to the 57 UPAs, there nevertheless appears to be an ambiguity about the principle of targeting a limited set of authorities. (It also means that when we speak of 'assisted' and 'non-assisted' areas we use these terms to differentiate areas in terms of policy designations rather than the actual financial assistance received by districts.)

**Table 4**     **Targeting of AfC expenditure: ranking of the sample of 123 districts by per capita AfC expenditure, 1988/9 and 1989/90**

| Rank | District | Per capita | Designation (with main expenditure resource head for non-UPAs within the top 57) |
|------|----------|-----------|-------------------------------|
| 1. | Tower Hamlets | 1,717.11 | UPA |
| 2. | Newham | 799.51 | UPA |
| 3. | Scunthorpe | 269.27 | non-UPA (EZ) |
| 4. | Southwark | 225.56 | UPA |
| 5. | Gateshead | 206.07 | UPA |
| 6. | Corby | 189.35 | non-UPA (EZ and DLG) |
| 7. | Salford | 183.26 | UPA |
| 8. | Stockton-on-Tees | 177.02 | UPA |
| 9. | Hartlepool | 170.82 | UPA |
| 10. | Newcastle-on-Tyne | 148.63 | UPA |
| 11. | Trafford | 134.31 | non-UPA (EZ and UDC) |
| 12. | Sandwell | 132.40 | UPA |
| 13. | Rochester-on-Medway | 121.47 | non-UPA (EZ and EE) |
| 14. | Middlesbrough | 117.64 | UPA |
| 15. | Liverpool | 115.95 | UPA |
| 16. | The Wrekin | 105.86 | UPA |
| 17. | Manchester | 102.44 | UPA |
| 18. | Dudley | 98.58 | UPA |
| 19. | Kingston-on-Hull | 98.06 | UPA |
| 20. | Walsall | 96.87 | UPA |
| 21. | Islington | 89.53 | UPA |
| 22. | South Tyneside | 89.10 | UPA |
| 23. | Rochdale | 87.38 | UPA |
| 24. | Blackburn | 86.18 | UPA |
| 25. | Rossendale | 85.86 | non-UPA (EZ,DLG,EA and EE) |
| 26. | Wolverhampton | 79.88 | UPA |
| 27. | Burnley | 79.75 | UPA |
| 28. | Hyndburn | 77.67 | non-UPA (EZ,CG,DLG and EA) |
| 29. | Preston | 71.23 | UPA |
| 30. | Sunderland | 70.83 | UPA |
| 31. | Oldham | 68.96 | UPA |
| 32. | Coventry | 68.44 | UPA |
| 33. | Nottingham | 65.65 | UPA |
| 34. | Knowsley | 65.54 | UPA |
| 35. | Birmingham | 61.10 | UPA |
| 36. | St.Helens | 60.12 | UPA |
| 37. | Sheffield | 58.87 | UPA |
| 38. | Wirral | 57.66 | UPA |
| 39. | Hackney | 54.76 | UPA |
| 40. | Leicester | 52.82 | UPA |
| 41. | Bradford | 51.94 | UPA |
| 42. | Rotherham | 51.69 | UPA |
| 43. | Lambeth | 50.61 | UPA |
| 44. | Halton | 49.43 | UPA |
| 45. | Haringey | 49.06 | UPA |
| 46. | Kensington/Chelsea | 46.62 | UPA |
| 47. | Greenwich | 46.58 | UPA |
| 48. | Bolton | 43.58 | UPA |
| 49. | Brent | 43.58 | UPA |
| 50. | Derwentside | 43.40 | non-UPA (DLG and EE) |
| 51. | Barnsley | 42.80 | UPA |
| 52. | Gravesham | 42.69 | non-UPA (EZ) |
| 53. | North Tyneside | 41.85 | UPA |
| 54. | Ellesmere | 41.31 | non-UPA (DLG and EE) |
| 55. | Doncaster | 41.17 | UPA |
| 56. | Wellingborough | 39.64 | non-UPA (EZ) |
| 57. | Langbaurgh | 38.94 | UPA |
| 58. | Derby | 38.28 | UPA |
| 59. | Barrow | 34.60 | |
| 60. | Wigan | 33.89 | UPA |

| | | | |
|---|---|---|---|
| 61. | Pendle | 33.63 | |
| 62. | Leeds | 32.36 | UPA |
| 63. | Hammersmith/Fulham | 32.30 | UPA |
| 64. | Ealing | 27.89 | |
| 65. | West Lancashire | 26.39 | |
| 66. | Wandsworth | 25.23 | UPA |
| 67. | Kirklees | 24.53 | UPA |
| 68. | Lewisham | 23.33 | UPA |
| 69. | Bristol | 21.98 | UPA |
| 70. | Wakefield | 20.98 | |
| 71. | Waltham Forest | 20.92 | |
| 72. | Easington | 17.76 | |
| 73. | Chester-le-Street | 16.51 | |
| 74. | Calderdale | 15.45 | |
| 75. | Stoke-on-Trent | 12.05 | |
| 76. | Sefton | 11.00 | UPA |
| 77. | Enfield | 10.59 | |
| 78. | Bury | 10.40 | |
| 79. | Plymouth | 10.15 | UPA |

123.

---

**Note:**

Details are shown for the top 79 authorities so as to include all of the 57 UPAs.

2.13 The doubt is further compounded when we look at the changes over time in the levels of funding. Some of the places which suffered the largest percentage reductions in their overall per capita assistance were the UPAs - and indeed in many cases some of the 'worst' UPAs as measured by their socio-economic conditions. Within the North West, for example, Manchester and Salford both 'lost' significantly in terms of per capita resource.

2.14 Second, the lack of fit between UPAs and resource allocation is compounded when we look at the patterns for a wider definition of resources. As noted above, we were not able to incorporate disaggregated Housing Corporation resources in our calculations; details of housing completions and refurbishment under the Housing Corporation are given in Appendix A. Nevertheless, we were able to include the substantial expenditure on Housing Investment Programmes (HIP) and Revenue Support Grant (RSG). These two mainstream programmes greatly exceed the amounts of AfC resources. During the 1980s, considerable reductions in the levels of HIP and RSG allocations were experienced by many of the UPA authorities. In the case of HIPs, the reductions need to be put in the context of housing market changes such as the decreasing stock of local authority housing through the right-to-buy (with the associated capital receipts from sales, part of which were available to local authorities) and the growing role of housing associations in the non-owner-occupied market. Nevertheless, most local authorities experienced real or relative reductions in both HIP and RSG finances during the decade. Detailed examples for individual districts in Greater Manchester, Merseyside and Tyne and Wear are provided in Appendix C which shows for example that, allowing for inflation, RSG and HIP declined by over one-third between 1979/80 and 1989/90 in the five authorities of Tyne and Wear. These reductions meant that, even though AfC resources may have increased or been held steady (and thereby became an increasingly important part of total resources), such authorities experienced significant overall reductions in the public resource available to them. The recurring complaints of financial 'cuts' by many of the big cities are therefore difficult to refute.

2.15   For our purposes, the finding that UPAs did not receive consistently better financial treatment per capita than non-UPAs meant that the complications in tracing relationships between inputs and outcomes was inevitably likely to prove even more problematical than expected. The more substantive conclusion is that the 'bending' of mainstream spending seems not to have been a consistent feature of urban policy. Those authorities identified as deprived and worthy of public support have not been targeted for help in as co-ordinated or consistent fashion as might have been anticipated.

(ii)   Outcomes

2.16   The principal indicators of socio-economic change at which we looked were: unemployment and the ratio of long-term to total unemployed (LT:U); net job change; new-firm formation; migration of the young work force; and house prices. Because of the different availability of data, we have studied changes in these indicators over varying time periods during the 1980s.

2.17   Inevitably, the picture of change is complex. This is true in particular for the period 1983-86 when unemployment nationally was increasing; during this period, none of the indicators showed a consistent structure. Nevertheless, we can point to some valuable conclusions. First, there are indications of deteriorating economic conditions in the UPAs over the period as a whole. Some of the indicators show a worsening position for the UPAs. The LT:U ratio, for example, shows a widening gap as between the UPAs, marginals and comparators; thereby suggesting a deterioration of the areas with the worst conditions. Rates of new-firm formation also suggest that UPAs do somewhat worse than other authorities. On the other hand, there are also some indications of improvement. Both the unemployment rate and the long-term unemployment rate taken separately, for example, show a narrowing gap. Taken together with the deterioration in the LT:U ratio, this implies that the UPAs were experiencing relative improvements as far as unemployment and long-term unemployment as a whole were concerned, but that, amongst the unemployed in the UPA areas, higher proportions were long-term unemployed; signifying an increasing degree of concentration of the most disadvantaged. There is nevertheless evidence in the improvements for the separate unemployment data that policy may have had some positive economic impact.

2.18   There is also evidence of successful outcomes in terms of residential attractiveness. This is shown by the migration indicator - which was taken as signifying the ability of areas to retain or attract a key and highly mobile cohort in the labour force. For the 25-34 year olds, the gap between UPAs and other areas narrowed over the 1980s. While this could be interpreted as suggesting that this group is merely trapped in impoverished areas, there is no consistent evidence that the long-term unemployment of this age group within UPAs consistently increases relative to other unassisted areas over the period, even though there is great variation within the 57 UPAs. To this extent, the narrowing of the gap - the increasing retention of 25-34 year olds - can be interpreted in some cases in a positive fashion suggesting that UPAs have been relatively more successful than the marginals or comparators in retaining this age group. These positive indications of narrowing differentials on unemployment and migration provide evidence that urban policy may have had some success in slowing or reversing the erosion of the economic and residential base of cities.

(iii)   Relationships

2.19   In exploring the relationships between inputs and outcomes, we analysed a large number of permutations. As Table 5 shows, the combinations of the financial input data comprised: total AfC, Urban Programme and other separate components of AfC, Regional Selective Assistance, total expenditure, and various combinations of these elements. These were evaluated against each of the five outcome indicators, many of which were subdivided by time periods. Many of the sets of relationships between inputs and outcomes showed no statistical significance. For example, there are no significant relationships between net job change and any of the permutations of expenditure inputs nor between 25-34 year-old migration and inputs.

2.20   However, there are some significant relationships. Most of these occur with the measures of changes in unemployment levels. To explore this, we divided the 1980s into two periods: one between 1983 (when our unemployment data series starts) and 1986, a period when unemployment was generally rising; and the second between 1986 and 1990, when unemployment generally was falling. Inputs of regional assistance in the form of Regional Selective Assistance were positively related to relative improvements both in unemployment and long-term unemployment for both of these two periods. Inputs from the Urban Programme were not significantly related to unemployment change in the first period, but for the second period Urban Programme inputs were positively related to relative improvements both in unemployment and long-term unemployment. Furthermore, for this latter period, the significant positive associations with both Urban Programme and Regional Selective Assistance were independent of each other. In other words, at least for the second of the periods, there is confirmatory evidence at the scale of districts that there were positive impacts associated with the expenditure of resources under urban policy. Looking at the residuals from these regressions, none of the other expenditure programmes were able to 'explain' the pattern of residuals.

2.21   This pattern of relationships between unemployment and expenditure is also supported by the relationships between inputs and house price changes. For the first period, 1983-6, there are weak but significant **negative** relationships between AfC and HIP expenditure, on the one hand, and house price changes on the other. This suggests either that expenditure was having no impact or that it was targeted at places which had the greatest problems. For the second period, 1986-9, (and like the unemployment patterns) there are some positive relationships between Urban Programme and AfC expenditure, on one hand, and house price changes in inner cities and for first-time buyers, on the other. This provides some supportive evidence that government inputs were having positive impacts on house prices in the inner cities after 1986.

2.22   These positive relationships between some of the financial inputs and outcome indicators are clearly of considerable significance. They suggest that there are areas in which public expenditure has been associated with relative improvements in socio-economic conditions. This conclusion is further supported by our more detailed study of the socio-economic 'gaps' within selected conurbations. For example, in Greater London, there is a relationship between overall expenditure and improvements in long-term unemployment: whether or not boroughs were designated as UPAs, those places which received more overall resources showed greater rates of improvement than those places which were less well funded. These conclusions all imply that there are positive relationships between public expenditure and relative improvements in certain socio-economic outcomes.

**Local scale: the three conurbations**

2.23   The assembly of ward-level data on expenditure was a major undertaking. The limitations of the data sources make it difficult to place great confidence in the patterns of spatial incidence at this fine scale. Nevertheless, the data do provide a more accurate assessment of the detailed pattern of spending than anything that has yet been produced. A discussion of these patterns of spend in each of the three conurbations is provided in the portraits of each conurbation in Appendix C.

*Table 5*  **Input/outcome relationships**

| Socio-economic indicators | Financial inputs | | | | | | | | | | | | | | | | |
|---|---|---|---|---|---|---|---|---|---|---|---|---|---|---|---|---|---|
| | Total 79/80 81/2 | AfC 82/3 84/5 | UP 82/3 85/6 | UP 83/4 86/7 | UP 84/5 87/8 | UP 85/6 88/95 | UP 82/3 84/5 | UP 83/4 86/7 | RSA 84/5 87/8 | RSA 85/6 88/9 | RSA | RSA | HIP | EZ | DLG | UDC | EC |
| Unemployment '83-6 | ns | ns | *sig | *sig | *sig | ns | - | - | *sig | - | - | - | - | ns | ns | ns | ns |
| Unemployment '86-90 | ns | ns | - | - | - | ns | *sig | *sig | ns | ns | *sig | *sig | - | ns | ns | ns | ns |
| Long-term unemp '83-6 | ns | ns | ns | *sig | ns | ns | - | - | *sig | ns | - | - | - | ns | ns | ns | ns |
| Long-term unemp '86-90 | ns | ns | - | - | - | ns | *sig | *sig | ns | ns | *sig | *sig | - | ns | ns | ns | ns |
| LT:U ratio '83-7 | ns | ns | ns | ns | ns | ns | - | - | ns | ns | ns | ns | - | ns | ns | ns | ns |
| LT:U ratio '87-90 | ns | ns | ns | ns | ns | ns | ns | ns | ns | ns | ns | ns | - | ns | ns | ns | ns |
| Job change '81-4 | ns | ns | ns | ns | ns | ns | - | - | ns | ns | ns | ns | - | ns | ns | ns | ns |
| Job change '84-7 | *sig | ns | ns | ns | ns | ns | - | - | ns | ns | ns | ns | - | ns | ns | ns | ns |
| Job change '87-89 | ns | ns | ns | ns | ns | ns | ns | ns | ns | ns | ns | ns | - | ns | ns | ns | ns |
| Jobs pc'81-4,84-7,87-89 | ns | ns | ns | ns | ns | ns | ns | ns | ns | ns | ns | ns | - | ns | ns | ns | ns |
| VAT regs | ns | ns | ns | ns | ns | ns | ns | ns | ns | *sig | ns | ns | - | ns | ns | ns | *sig |
| House price IC '83-6 | - | *sig | ns | ns | ns | - | - | - | ns | - | - | - | *sig | - | - | - | - |
| House price FTB '83-6 | - | *sig | ns | ns | ns | - | - | - | ns | - | - | - | *sig | - | - | - | - |
| House price IC '86-9 | - | ns | - | - | - | ns | ns | *sig | ns | ns | ns | ns | ns | - | - | - | - |
| House price FTB '86-9 | - | *sig | - | - | - | ns | ns | ns | ns | ns | ns | ns | ns | - | - | - | - |
| 25-34 unemp | ns | ns | ns | ns | ns | ns | ns | ns | ns | ns | ns | *sig | - | ns | ns | ns | ns |
| 25-34 LT unemp | ns | ns | ns | ns | ns | ns | ns | ns | ns | ns | ns | *sig | - | ns | ns | ns | ns |
| 25-34 pop change | ns | ns | ns | ns | ns | ns | ns | ns | ns | ns | ns | ns | - | ns | ns | ns | ns |

**Notes:**

1. Entries show the statistical significance of correlations and partial correlations between financial inputs (columns) and socio-economic outcomes (rows). Time-lagged relationships were used to test relationships between earlier inputs and later outcomes. Only the results for UP and RSA are shown here by way of illustration. Entries in the table are as follows:

*sig : significant relationship at 0.05 level

ns : not significant at 0.05 level

- : inappropriate relationship (e.g. between a later input and an earlier outcome or between an economic indicator and non-economic outcome)

2. **Definitions:**

Inputs  All measures are per capita expenditure. **Total** - AfC, RSG, HIP, RSA, ERDF/ESF (See Table 1); **UP** - Urban Programme; **AfC** - Action for Cities (for composition, see Table 1); **RSA** - Regional Selective Assistance; **EZ** - Enterprise Zone; **DLG** - Derelict Land Grant; **UDC** - Urban Development Grant; **EC** - ERDF/ESF; **HIP** - Housing Investment Programme.

Outcomes  **Unemployment** - total unemployed divided by pop.aged 18-60/65; **Long-term unemp** - total unemployed > 1 year divided by pop.; **LT:U** - ratio of total long-term to total unemployed; **Job change** - total number of jobs; **Jobs pc** - number of jobs divided by pop.18-60/65; **VAT regs** - change in VAT registrations ratio with 1981 base year of 100; **House change** - absolute and percentage change in house prices for inner city areas (IC) and first-time buyers (FTB); **25-34 unemp** - total unemployed aged 25-34 divided by pop.25-34; **25-34 LT unemp** - total long-term unemployed aged 25-34 divided by pop.25-34; **25-34 migration** - change in population aged 25-34, 1981-90

2.24 Our statistical analysis of ward data was unable to establish any significant relationships between expenditure inputs and socio-economic change (as measured by the outcome indicators of changes in unemployment, long-term unemployment and job change) at this scale of wards. This may be a function of the partial nature of much of the expenditure data. Much of the expenditure in each conurbation could only be attributed to district-wide schemes and even that which could be attributed to specific wards will inevitably have had wider effects.

2.25   What our analysis has thrown some light on, however, are the patterns of change in the outcome indicators themselves. From this we can draw some tentative inferences about the impacts of policy at the between-district and within-district spatial scales.

2.26   First, in all three conurbations there appears to have been a consistent pattern of an increasing concentration of either unemployment or long-term unemployment (or of both) in the regional centres of each conurbation (the cities of Manchester, Liverpool and Newcastle). This tendency was most marked in Greater Manchester, where Manchester itself (along with Oldham) showed a marked increase in the overall share of both unemployment and long-term unemployment across the conurbation. By comparison, elsewhere within Greater Manchester, it was the more peripheral districts of Stockport, Bury and Trafford which showed the most markedly declining percentages of the share of unemployment. The same tendency for the piling-up of problems in the core of the conurbations is also suggested for the pattern of net job change where, for Greater Manchester, the district experiencing the heaviest and most consistent losses was Manchester itself. There appears to be a pattern which suggests that, within the conurbation, economic problems have continued to pile up in the worst of the areas, but that there have been improvements outside the core. The same tendency was apparent both for Liverpool's unemployment share within Merseyside and Newcastle's within Tyne and Wear. To this extent, the biggest cities of these three conurbations (those in which problems have been especially severe) have not shown measurable benefit from policy expenditure. Policy may, however, have had more beneficial effects in the areas outside the cores. This suggests the apparent intractibility of the problems in the worst areas, but that policy may have made some inroads in the places outside the most deprived areas.

2.27   Second, the patterns **within** each local authority district show considerable consistency. We explored the extent to which unemployment had become spatially more concentrated over time within each district - in other words, the degree to which the worst wards had become relatively worse through a process of increasing polarisation. Two conclusions emerge. First, within the regional centres of Manchester and Liverpool, unemployment does not become more spatially concentrated and the districts as a whole show a relative increase in their share of unemployment. This could be interpreted as a function of net outmigration from the districts, or of the initially very high levels of unemployment from which their inner areas began, or of the spreading of 'inner-city' problems across ever larger swathes of the cores of conurbations. Second, amongst the other districts there is a very complex pattern, but in the vast majority of districts there is an increasing polarisation of unemployment. To examine this we looked at the experience of 'inner areas' versus non-inner areas for each of the districts. The results are very clear for the 20 districts that comprise the three conurbations. For example, unemployment change for the period 1983-90 shows that in no fewer than 17 of the 20 districts the inner areas increased their share of unemployment (the three exceptions being Manchester, Liverpool and Knowsley). This pattern is reinforced by a comparison of the share of unemployment and of long-term unemployment. In no fewer than 19 of the 20 districts (the sole exception being Tameside in Greater Manchester) the inner areas experienced a greater share of long-term unemployed than of unemployed. This strongly suggests a process of increasing polarisation at a within-district scale, in which the most distressed areas have seen their socio-economic problems grow increasingly severe.

2.28    The overall conclusion that might be drawn from these complex local patterns in the three conurbations is that 'trickle down' (the assumption that any general improvement in local circumstances, whether or not it is of immediate benefit to the poor, will eventually work its way through to the disadvantaged) appears not to be working. The focus on the defined worst areas appears to have effect as much on the broader surrounding areas as on the targeted areas themselves. If this interpretation is correct, it adds force to the need to develop effective linkages between policy targeted at those areas and the disadvantaged residents living in the targeted areas.

**Profiles of districts**

2.29    Given the complex patterns of inputs and of socio-economic changes, an impression of the relationships can be gained by looking at 'profiles' of districts in terms of their inputs and outcomes. Some such profiles are outlined in Appendix B, first for Greater London, second for the North West, third for the North and finally for all of the remaining 57 UPAs outside these regions.

2.30    This set of profiles can be drawn upon to develop a crude categorisation of the relationships between inputs and outcomes. The classification is crude because it is difficult to classify districts into a simple two-by-two matrix showing high and low inputs and good and poor outcomes. Very few districts can be said to have received consistently high inputs since, for example, many of the districts which have high rankings on AfC inputs lost considerable amounts in overall inputs over the period. Many districts also show rather mixed socio-economic outcomes. A classification is attempted below (Table 6) based on levels of input and types of outcomes:

(i)    **Inputs** are divided into high, mixed, and low, based both on AfC and overall monies. A mixed class means that the district may be high on AfC, but lose significant overall resources, or low on AfC, but quite well resourced overall. In some cases, such as Manchester, the district is quite high on AfC, but has lost considerably in overall terms and is therefore categorised as being of low input.

(ii)    **Outcomes** are classified into poor, mixed and positive. A mixed outcome denotes that some of the indictors are positive and others are negative. The outcomes are measures of change and not the state at a particular time. The classification includes all of the 57 UPAs together with some of the 'marginal' districts which are shown as '(m)'.

2.31 We can make four observations from this set of relationships.

(i)    The classification suggests that 18 of the 57 UPAs have mainly positive outcomes, 18 have mixed and 21 have poor outcomes. Given the severity of the social and economic problems in some of the authorities, this balance suggests a reasonable level of success. Only 9 UPAs had high inputs and poor outcomes.

(ii)    The two districts with the greatest inputs, Tower Hamlets and Newham, appear at either end of the spectrum. One has been very successful; the other still has major problems. They are adjacent to one another. It could be argued that (even though Tower Hamlets is likely to have benefited more from the spillover benefits of its greater proximity to the City and the Isle of Dogs EZ) it is clear that regional location in itself is not critical in determining success in these cases. The only other district with a high input and positive outcomes is Corby which is not a UPA. Despite this, it has received the third highest amount of AfC resources. Four other marginal districts have mainly positive outcomes, two with high inputs and two with relatively low ones.

While Corby has no doubt benefited from the general growth of its region (recovering faster than Derwentside from similar problems), it should be noted that there are areas with positive and poor signs in all regions of the country. While having an effect, the regional context is not a determinant of success or failure. This reinforces our findings of the complexity of the pattern of outcomes derived from our work with multi-level modelling.

**Table 6    Inputs:outcomes - a categorisation of districts**

| Inputs | Outcomes | | | | |
|---|---|---|---|---|---|
| | Positive | Rel.high | Mixed | Rel. poor | Poor |
| **High** | Corby (m) Tower Hamlets | | | | Newham |
| **Rel. high** | | Dudley Gateshead Greenwich Hartlepool Sandwell Scunthorpe (m) Stockton Trafford (m) Wandsworth Wrekin | | | Coventry Hackney Hull Knowsley Lambeth Liverpool Newcastle Sunderland |
| **Mixed** | | Blackburn Bradford Derwentside (m) Hyndburn (m) | Brent Ellesmere (m) Hammersmith Preston Rochdale Rochester (m) Rossendale (m) Salford Southwark St Helens Wirral | Haringey Leeds | |
| **Rel. low** | | Bristol Burnley Middlesbrough North Tyneside Pendle (m) Sefton Walsall Wellingborough (m) Wolverhampton | Bolton Derby Doncaster Halton Kensington Kirklees Oldham Plymouth Rotherham Sedgefield (m) Tameside (m) Wigan | | |
| **Low** | | | | | Barnsley Birmingham Blyth (m) Camden (m) Islington Langbaurgh Leicester Lewisham Nottingham Manchester Sheffield South Tyneside |

Note: (m) refers to marginal authorities.

(iii) It is noticeable that ten of the UPA districts, despite being designated as priority areas, received low overall inputs, and had poor outcomes. This uncertain implementation of the targeting of designated areas recurs at the local scale. It reinforces the arguments for better strategic planning and overall coordination of programmes.

(iv) The final observation that can be made about the classification is to note that the very large cities are generally included within the 'poor' or 'relatively poor' outcomes categories. These are the districts with the most intractable problems. This reinforces our earlier findings on the concentration of unemployment which suggested that it was precisely within these large core areas where expenditure inputs appeared to be less successful in influencing changes in socio-economic conditions. The local analysis suggests that there is a growing number of areas within them that are disadvantaged and that the districts are home to an increasing share of the disadvantaged people within the conurbation of which they are the central area.

**Summary of quantitative analysis**

2.32   **First,** a variety of pieces of evidence suggest that greater expenditure is associated with relative improvements in socio-economic conditions:

* Urban Programme expenditure per capita and Regional Selective Assistance per capita have significant, and independent, associations with the rate of decline in unemployment and long-term unemployment between 1986 and 1990.

* Regional Selective Assistance has a significant beneficial relationship with long-term unemployment and overall unemployment during the period 1983 to 1986, when there is very little structure to the general increases that occur.

* Urban Programme expenditure per capita and changes in inner city house prices are positively related for the period 1986-9, as is AfC expenditure per capita and house price changes for first-time buyers.

* Comparisons between sets of UPAs and sets of comparators all show that there was a significant convergence in their amounts of long-term unemployment over the period 1983 to 1990. Higher levels of public expenditure are associated with more rapid falls in unemployment.

* The pattern of public expenditure is also associated with closing the regional gap between the north west and the south east. There is greater convergence between the north-west UPAs and the south-east comparators than between the north west comparators and the south east comparators

* There is evidence that some of the non-UPAs in the best-resourced 57 do better than expected in outcomes while some of the UPAs outside of the top 57 do worse.

* Three of the 12 non-UPAs in the best-resourced 57 experience falls in long-term unemployment and two have only very small increases during the period 1983-86, a period when all the other top 57 experience marked increases.

* The four London UPAs that lie outside the best-resourced 57 experience lower rates of improvement in long-term unemployment between 1983 and 1990 than all the other London UPAs except Hammersmith.

2.33   While these points suggest an association between better performance and government inputs, not all the gaps in indicators were closing, there were many combinations of indicators and time periods when there was no significant association between inputs and outcomes, and the variation within the experiences of UPAs as indicated by the profiles suggests that there are still many districts where problems have either not improved or indeed have worsened. Quantitative analysis is less effective than the subsequent case studies as a way of determining the extent to which this variation is a function of uncertain data, of the conceptual weakness of policy or of varying policy implementation on the ground.

2.34   **Second,** there are some interesting spatial findings from the quantitative analyses:

* Very large cities or the central areas of conurbations face the most difficult futures; nearly all have poor outcomes, which are confirmed in the local analysis, where the central areas of conurbations are shown to be the home of an increasing proportion of the disadvantaged.

* In contrast, many of the smaller places and many of the peripheral districts within the conurbations show relative improvement.

* Within most districts, there is evidence of an increasing polarisation between the most deprived wards and those with fewer problems.

* While the regional economic context of districts helps some districts to recover, it is no guarantee of success or indeed failure, there having been positive and poor outcomes in all areas.

* The link to the local analysis provides one further caveat. Analysis of the districts that appear to be improving, may at the local level show that their inner areas are getting worse relative to the outer ones. This is shown to be so for most of the case study conurbation districts. It may therefore be the improvement of the outer areas that accounts for the overall improvement of the districts. Whether or not the political boundaries of districts include wealthier suburbs may therefore help to explain their improvement.

# The views of recipients

3.1    The second leg of our research design explored the views of the recipients of urban policy. Within the three conurbations of Greater Manchester, Merseyside and Tyne and Wear, this involved forays into two different 'audiences': a major survey of local residents; and discussions with a range of employers. In both cases, the aims were similar: to investigate views about current socio-economic conditions in the conurbations; to see to what extent these conditions had altered over the recent past and were perceived as likely to alter in the immediate future; to identify whether government policy had impinged on its intended recipients and, if so, whether the experiences of those recipients supported or refuted the evidence culled both from our statistical analyses and from the views of experts. Details of the two surveys are provided in Appendices E and F.

**Resident survey**

3.2    The survey of residents involved a total of 1299 interviews, using a questionnaire design and schedule administered by MORI. We selected a variety of small areas within each conurbation (6 in Greater Manchester, including two area with high proportions of ethnic-minority households; 5 in Merseyside; and 4 in Tyne and Wear). Most of the areas were selected so as to enable us to develop paired comparisons between small areas which were broadly similar in respect of their socio-economic conditions but which had received different treatment under urban policy. In most areas, some 80 people were interviewed. We selected areas which included some of the most difficult conditions in each conurbation. Indeed, at the time of the survey, some of the areas were affected by the violent social disturbances which afflicted Salford in the summer of 1992. Clearly, the areas were not intended to be representative of the conurbations as a whole; because of this, the results of the survey cannot - and were not intended to - represent views across each conurbation. Rather, they attempt to tap the experiences and the perceptions of residents living in precisely the kinds of deprived circumstances to which policy is ostensibly addressed. Five main points can be highlighted from the survey.

3.3    First, by comparing the responses from paired areas in which one received significantly more public resources than the other, the survey shows that the expenditure of resource does have an impact on the attitudes of residents towards the current and future desirability of their neighbourhood. Examples are provided by the contrasts between Ordsall and Pendleton in Greater Manchester and between Cantril Farm and Clubmoor in Mersyside. In these and other cases, the former of the two sets of paired areas received significantly greater sums of public resource and have been more consistent targets of AfC expenditure. Residents agreed in perceiving the better-resourced areas (in this case, Ordsall and Cantril Farm) as being more generally desirable and better placed than those places which received less public assistance (Pendleton and Clubmoor). Such differences are repeated across all of the pairings of neighbourhoods; for example in Newcastle and Sunderland residents' responses reflected the awareness of recent financial inputs in neighbourhood schemes. To this extent there has clearly been a perceived benefit from the implementation of policy.

3.4   Second, there is ample evidence of a degree of 'area loyalty' amongst most of the residents. Asked for views on the residential desirability of their own neighbourhoods compared to other similarly deprived areas, there was a consistent pattern of people perceiving their own neighbourhood as being relatively more desirable as a place in which to live. This may have been a function of familiarity with the area; it nevertheless suggests that there are elements of community and local involvement on which regeneration can be based. Here is one of the planks on which policy can build. There is clearly scope for capacity-building within local communities. A more focused social dimension to expenditure could capitalise on the place-loyalty of local communities.

3.5   Yet, while people show this loyalty to their neighbourhood, it is equally clear that there is profound pessimism about conditions in inner-city areas. Most residents perceived conditions in their areas to be bad and to be growing worse. The prospects for the future were seen as being equally, or more, bleak than the present. The view of the future was less bleak for the overall desirability of their area than it was for crime and job opportunities which most people thought would worsen. Even in some of the areas of high unemployment, many respondents considered that the desirability and the physical appearance of their areas had improved. However even though many had an optimistic view of the future desirability of their area, larger proportions still thought that the gap with the outer suburbs would widen further in the future.

3.6   This latter aspect is one which must be a cause for concern; the perception of residents was that the gap between inner areas and outer suburbs was seen as likely to widen in the immediate future. Unfavourable spatial comparisons such as this provide the seed-bed for further out-migration of people and withdrawal of investment from inner urban areas.

3.7   Third, there are interesting variations across the conurbations especially in terms of perceptions about employment prospects and the current state of the labour market. The bleakest views were consistently found in Tyne and Wear, where the current situation was seen to be bad by more people than was the case in either Greater Manchester or Merseyside. Views in Merseyside and Greater Manchester differed little from each other, but were both more positive than those in Tyne and Wear. While such comparisons cannot be extended to the conurbations as a whole because the selected neighbourhoods are not representative, it is a noteworthy finding. Equally interesting, it was within Greater Manchester that employment conditions were seen as likely to worsen most markedly in the future. More people were pessimistic about the future in Greater Manchester than in the other conurbations, but fewer were optimistic in Merseyside than in the other two conurbations.

3.8   Fourth, the ranking of the dimensions which residents saw as important for their quality of life suggests that policy has addressed issues of concern to most residents. The most critically important dimensions affecting quality-of-life were seen as being related to crime, health care and the cost-of-living. Employment issues were ranked significantly lower; perhaps reflecting a degree of fatalism that nothing could significantly alter labour market issues. These local rankings are little different from national rankings covering similar quality-of-life dimensions. There is some reassurance in the fact that all of the major dimensions to which policy has given prominence were well represented in residents' own perceptions. The one area which was perceived as important to residents but is not formally incorporated into AfC is the health dimension.

3.9   Fifth, there were some marked ethnic divergences in the results. There were sharp - and expected - differences between some of the views of South Asian, Black and White respondents. Such differences were most marked in two fields. First, on crime, there were significantly higher levels of fear expressed by South Asians than by any other groups. Second, on employment, Black respondents showed greater concern about their employment prospects than did other groups. These two findings may cause little surprise, but they do reinforce the argument for the development of a specifically ethnic dimension to parts of urban policy.

**Employers' survey**

3.10   The survey of employers' views was based on loosely-structured discussions with a small number of businesses in the three conurbations. Details are provided in Appendix F. A number of points can be highlighted in a summary of the views of employers. In recounting them, it should be recalled that the survey was undertaken at a time of deep recession when most employers were preoccupied by macro-economic conditions and that such concerns tended to swamp the evaluation of the more subtle impacts of policy intervention.

3.11   First, knowledge of government schemes was shallow and patchy, even amongst those companies which had derived benefit from one or more scheme. There was criticism both of the multiplicity of schemes and, more pointedly, of the bureaucratic impediments seen as being associated with them. Such criticism focused on: the length of time taken to agree funding packages - delays which could mean that other private-sector funding might be lost; the inflexibility of grant regimes - that money came too much in tightly-constrained packages which could prevent a more flexible use of resources to achieve maximum benefit; the one-way nature of claw-back - that underspend was recouped by government but that unforseen and justified overspend did not result in an increase in allocations.

3.12   Second, many of the capital-based schemes were generally welcomed. Infrastructural programmes in particular were widely praised. This, for example, was the case with Derelict Land Grant and for the work of the Urban Development Corporations. Such views are unsurprising since they reflect the expected tension between the infrastructural emphasis in what employers look for from regeneration as against the greater social emphasis in the ostensible aims of regeneration policy.

3.13   Third, there was a widespread view that access to government departments was difficult. Praise for the work of the DTI, for example, was coupled with caveats suggesting the difficulty of dealing with its bureaucratic procedures.

3.14   Fourth, local authorities were generally seen as not being important players in the urban context. While the 'political climate' of a locality was seen as being important, local authorities did not feature as a central element of the environment in which business worked. This divorce between business and government generally extended to central government too. Most business saw the role of 'government', while important, as being to provide an infrastructure and to calm the external environment in which business operates; but, this apart, the view was that the less government intervened the better could business 'get on with doing its job'.

3.15   Fifth, on employment issues, there were some clear differences across the conurbations. Recruitment issues differed as between Merseyside and the other two areas. Merseyside employers had experienced few or no difficulties in recruitment, no doubt reflecting the state of its labour market; whereas somewhat more problems had been experienced elsewhere. Unsurprisingly, the levels of unemployment and restructuring meant that recruitment and labour costs were generally not seen as highly critical to most of the firms. The forecast demographic time-bomb has not materialised; and labour shedding and restructuring has meant that higher wages have been absorbed by higher productivity and smaller labour forces.

3.16   Sixth, a frequently recurring response on the question of changed operating costs was the additional expenditure on security. This adds force to the emphasis given in recent policy to the importance of the crime dimension.

3.17   Finally, on the image of the areas in which business operated, most respondents suggested that the image of the locality in which they worked was not of great importance, as against the national reputation of their product or their services. Where image was seen as important (as, for example, in some of the service sector), respondents argued that, regardless of outside perceptions, the image of their area was good or was improving. This no doubt reflects the fact that respondents were partly projecting a corporate image of their firms in the course of responding to the discussions.

3.18   Overall, a strong impression emerges: of businesses which recognised that benefits had accrued from those grants which they had been successful in winning, yet being largely unaware of many of the details of the measures taken by government to improve business performance; alive to the constraints surrounding policy instruments such as the confusing multiplicity of schemes, the inflexibility of grants and the bureaucratic procedures necessary to release resources. While many of the companies were active in local networking, there was little evidence that these were seen as important to business performance. Nor was there much evidence of a corporate culture that emphasised the involvement of business within the local community in which it happens to work. Few of the businesses had well-developed contacts with local bodies such as schools or with agencies in the non-statutory sector. There is clearly a long way to go before the arguments about the local responsibilities of business assume much flesh.

# The views of experts

4.1   The discussions with experts drew on interviews with some one hundred key figures in the policy communities in Greater Manchester, Merseyside and Tyne and Wear. Respondents included senior civil servants, local government officers, business people, local and national politicians and people from quangos and community organisations. A fuller account of the discussions is given in Appendix G. In broad terms, the aim of the discussions was to explore perceptions of the areas' problems, the ways in which policies have been implemented and the impacts of those policies on the conurbations over the last decade. The following summary draws directly on the views of the respondents themselves. It looks first at some of the different responses across each of the conurbations and then discusses the three most commonly recurring issues noted by discussants: those of partnership, co-ordination and targeting.

**Conurbation summaries**

(i) Greater Manchester

4.2   The Manchester conurbation is the largest and most complex of the three areas. It is characterised by fragmentation and this has affected its ability, at a regional level, to develop a single strategic view and, at a local level, has created jostling between authorities and considerable suspicion of Manchester as the 'lead' body.

4.3   Networking was continually stressed in the discussions. A strength of Manchester was that it was less introverted and 'provincial' than many conurbations. It has 'movers and shakers' who can get things done. A large number of people passed through the area, and those who were successful were not seen as outsiders. Networks, however, were seen as being diffuse and largely within rather than between the private and public sectors, each of which were seen as playing predominantly separate roles.

4.4   The private sector was seen as playing very different roles in different parts of the area. Many of the peripheral authorities emphasised the constraints that they faced because of the small number of large employers which meant that partnerships were more difficult to establish. Yet, even in Manchester with its much larger private sector, senior figures from both sectors believed that most companies had little commitment to the area since they were run from headquarters elsewhere and owed little allegiance to their local area.

4.5   Yet, business resilience was seen as a factor in the strengths of the conurbation: pharmaceuticals, foodstuffs and the continuing importance of banking and insurance in the area were seen as important nodes of economic potential. The area's weaknesses were familiar ones: a continuing dependence on a 'traditional' industrial structure; squalor, crime and unrest; a large 'dependent' population; a lack of vision and the fragmentation of the various districts.

4.6   Many elements of public policy were seen as having been successful. The resurgence of the Central Business District since the late 1970s was seen as a key success. Part of this was attributed to the successful working of the Central Manchester Development Corporation which was widely applauded. It was seen as having done things more quickly than the local authority could have managed and as having involved the right mix of key local actors. The experience of Trafford Park UDC was often used as a contrast to CMDC, although there was recognition of the problems that Trafford had faced through delays in CPOs and the problems of the impact of recession on lettings.

4.7   The co-operation between Salford and private developers was seen to represent the positive side of urban policy. Similar housing projects were widely praised elsewhere. Economic initiatives such as Bolton Business Ventures were seen as representing the new entrepreneurial face of local authorities. Various of the specific schemes had been used successfully to involve the private sector; Derelict Land Grant and City Grant being noted in particular. City Grant was seen in a generally favourable light, but was criticised for its slowness and its cumbersome bureaucracy.

4.8   Policy instruments which encouraged collaborative implementation across departments were generally welcomed. Housing Renewal Areas were widely praised as having offered incentives to co-ordinate action across a range of economic, social and environmental agendas. So too were Estate Action and Safer Cities; the latter being widely valued both for being closer to the grassroots and for the potential inter-agency co-ordination that it encouraged.

4.9   The policy failures which were stressed were of a more structural nature; poor inter-departmental co-ordination was widely noted, as was the lack of strategic direction. Local authorities argued that mainstream resources had all but dried up, as capital programmes had been pruned.

4.10   The issues of poverty, inequality and increasing social polarisation were a sub-text in many of the discussions. The voluntary sector was seen as having partly been sidelined over the period of the late 1980s. Housing associations, for example, were ill-equipped to take a wider role in tackling many of the problems since they had insufficient financial or manpower resources; in any case, housing was often less appropriate as a focus than were poverty, structural unemployment and general deprivation. The assumption that the voluntary sector in general could take on extra tasks was seen as doubtful in light of its financial difficulties. Ethnic communities were seen as a particular dimension of such limitations. The view of one respondent from the voluntary sector, for example, was that in practice ethnic groups had received little benefit from urban policy.

4.11   The sense in Manchester was of an area which had shown signs of a dramatic improvement in much of its physical infrastructure in the last three years and in which over that same period there had been a significant turning-around of business confidence vis-a-vis other parts of the country. The evidence of new building, the sense of a new vision associated with the Olympic bid, developments in the Central Business District and the Eastlands area and the promise that the longstanding problem of Hulme might be tackled through City Challenge; all these represented the bullish side of the evaluations of the changes of recent years. Against this, the continuing and deepening erosion of the position of the poor and of the areas outside the centre were seen to remain as problems which were only superficially scratched by urban policy.

(ii) Merseyside

4.12   There was considerable agreement on the region's strengths; the most commonly noted elements being its cultural and tourist potential, low-cost labour pool and accessibility to desirable areas. The offsetting weaknesses on which there was equal agreement were; location, communications and, particularly, the poor environment. To these were added a familiar array of economic weaknesses: poor skill levels in the labour force; a weak private sector; the decline in the manufacturing base; the dominance of multi-national corporations; the lack of an entrepreneurial small-firm tradition; the over-representation in the local economy of low-growth sectors.

4.13    Others made the related and familiar point that the expansion of AfC resources was drowned by cuts in main programmes. Particular criticism was directed at the resource cuts in the housing field. One senior official in the field emphasised the contrast between Estate Action, HATs and City Challenge resources, on one hand, and cuts in HIP which are creating a future crisis in the city, on the other.

4.14    A range of general and specific failures of policy were noted. The principal failure was seen as policy's reliance on a market-led strategy. The private sector is particularly weak on Merseyside - but it does not even punch the weight that it has got. There is a lack of civic commitment by the private sector. Regional policy was seen as having failed in the region and as having failed to support manufacturing. This was linked with a view of the failure of the DTI to commit resources to urban regeneration. The annuality rule was specifically mentioned by some in local government as preventing strategic approaches to housing. There was common agreement that weakly developed partnership is one of the problems of Merseyside.

4.15    The most frequently quoted specific failure was the Enterprise Zone, which was seen as not having been well marketed. Another area was training, which had not lead to jobs and was of low quality. TECs were seen as not adequate to their task and as having no connections with other regeneration policies.

4.16    Many of the successes on Merseyside were seen as having been in the housing arena rather than in economic development. Housing Renewal Areas had encouraged a multi-agency approach. The juxtaposition of housing association activity with the Safer Cities initiative had maintained and increased property values. While there were familiar criticisms of the Urban Development Corporation, it was seen as having achieved environmental improvement, flagship projects, a high profile and exploited the tourism and leisure potential of the area.

4.17    A number of specific projects were singled out for praise. Wavertree Technology Park, Freeport, Housing Action Areas, Housing Co-operatives, Ravenshead Renaissance (which one discussant claimed to be the model for City Challenge); all received praise, not least on the grounds that they were spatially confined and targeted. Equally, some institutions received plaudits. The Merseyside Task Force was regarded as important in giving access to central government and offseting the economic and institutional dominance of Manchester.

(iii) Tyne and Wear

4.18    Perhaps the most striking aspect of Tyne and Wear was that, despite the diversity of respondents' backgrounds, much common ground existed throughout the policy community. Indeed, consensus was one of the dominant features of the region. Many considered that this relied heavily on a series of intimate, well-developed networks revolving around personal contacts which derived from the geographical cohesiveness of the North East. There was a sense, too, in which the area settled on a form of political realism or pragmatism in the mid-1980s, which had led to co-operative working with government and the private sector.

4.19   There was a widespread feeling that the region's key problem was one of structural change in the economy. The implications of these economic changes were noted: unemployment, physical dereliction, poverty, crime and urban unrest were often viewed essentially as flowing from structural change. One widely shared concern was the problem of increasing social polarisation, leaving some marginalised groups trapped in unemployment and poverty. This issue seemed to be rising in importance on the local political agenda and has been given greater prominence since the Tyneside riots in September 1991.

4.20   While most interviewees argued that economic change is largely a result of market forces and that the private sector is central to wealth creation, there was a strong consensus on the relevance and value of public sector intervention. Local authorities, as well as central government, were identified as key 'players' in the policy community. Intervention - through regional policy, urban policy and local economic development initiatives - is a familiar feature of the local landscape, accepted by public and private sector alike.

4.21   Private sector involvement in public policy is confined mainly to a relatively small number of companies, often represented by a few active senior businessmen. Several large multi-national companies have little or no involvement in public policy, in terms either of policy formulation or delivery. A similar concern was expressed about voluntary sector participation. Whereas the general view appeared to be that private-public and central-local relationships had been fairly strong and steady, especially since the mid-1980s, links with the voluntary sector were perceived as working less smoothly. One interviewee commented that the high-level, tight-knit networks were good at delivering the 'big deals', but were less good at delivering projects and help at the local community level. One voluntary-sector respondent thought this problem was the best justification for the much criticised 'pepper-pot' spread of UP money which was a valuable - and highly flexible - source of 'seed corn' funding for a whole range of voluntary organisations which otherwise might not exist.

4.22   Many interviewees did, however, allude to the constraints on public sector activities. Local authorities complained about spending cuts undermining their ability to solve or ameliorate the area's economic and social problems. Some respondents pointed towards the need for more stability in public sector finance over the long-term. One senior official noted the limitations of a property-led approach to regeneration in times of recession in the property market.

4.23   The public sector was seen as constrained not only in terms of resources but also in relation to its abilities actually to solve economic problems since the economic development process itself is largely the province of the private sector. On the other hand, some interviewees noted the important economic role of the public sector as an employer and thus as an important source of incomes spent in the local economy. In addition, there was a general belief that the public sector has to be responsible for dealing with social problems and issues; the private sector was felt to be neither willing nor competent to address these concerns.

4.24   There was a degree of nervousness about over-reliance on inward investment because of past experience of branch plant closures in the early

1980s. However, inward investment was seen as crucial to the region. Hopes were expressed that more recent relocations to Tyne and Wear would be more permanent owing to the scale of their investment (notably Nissan) and lesser dependence on grants. Inward investment was also viewed as important in improving the region's 'image'.

4.25   Like inward investment and indigenous enterprise, a balance between both manufacturing and service industries also had to be encouraged. Several noted the downgrading of regional policy during the 1980s.

4.26   Various policy instruments were widely praised. Because of its greater visibility and its spatially concentrated aspect, the Enterprise Zone was regarded with some enthusiasm since it had been effective in generating or drawing in development. In general, the reaction to the UDC was favourable. It was seen as a valuable source of much needed funding denied to local authorities. Although there had been some initial friction with some local authorities, the UDC was generally regarded as a useful policy vehicle, having acted as a catalyst stimulating development, as an agency able to bring back into the market derelict land and, more strategically, as a way of re-focusing the conurbation on its rivers. Most saw the smooth relationship between UDC and existing institutions in Tyne and Wear as very different from the situation in other parts of the country.

4.27   Views on the Urban Programme were more mixed; local authorities saw it as important not least because such a significant proportion of capital spending came from this source, but several interviewees thought its 'pepper pot' approach gave it a lack of focus and impact. Several were critical of its emphasis on capital, rather than revenue, expenditure.

4.28   One senior civil servant identified the establishment of the City Action Team as one of the key landmarks in the last decade. The general feeling appeared to be that there was insufficient inter-agency co-ordination, even though the system managed to muddle through quite effectively via existing informal networks.

**Issues across the conurbations**

(i) Partnerships

4.29   The contextual differences between the areas have had effects on the viability of creating partnerships within each of the conurbations. National strategies and policies are implemented through local structures and institutions. These local forces, by encouraging or constraining national intentions, clearly shape their impact. And these local arrangements vary. This is particularly clear in the concept of partnership. The encouragement of partnerships at two different spatial levels - between actors in the public, private and community sectors at local level, and at intergovernmental level between central and local government - was seen as having been a clear ambition of the government's strategy for cities. But different patterns of relations between a range of local actors as well as between local and national governments have affected the experience of partnership, and hence the success of government policy, on the ground. At one extreme, powerful local consensus encouraged the growth of partnership and hence aided the achievement of government aspirations. At the other, conflicts between local interests restricted the evolution of partnership arrangements and constrained government ambitions. These local constraints upon national ambitions clearly need to be understood and accommodated. However, in addition the discussions revealed how, in the eyes of many decision-makers, national government strategies and priorities themselves restricted the capacity of local actors to form partnerships at local level as well as with national government itself.

4.30 The capacity of local institutions to form partnerships rests upon underlying institutional linkages and social relations. In Tyne and Wear, strong partnerships were able to emerge during the mid-1980s by exploiting a series of intimate, well-developed networks which were were frequently based upon close personal contacts. Partly this is explained by the relative geographical cohesiveness, almost isolation, of the north east, which guaranteed that a limited number of institutions and individuals dominated the social and professional networks. The limited scale of the region and the limited number of local authorities - for example in contrast to Manchester - also encouraged a greater capacity to network. One feature of these linkages is that they are frequently highly informal, resting on a range of frequent, ad hoc responses to particular initiatives.

4.31 A clear feature of partnership in the Tyne and Wear region was the lead role that the public sector, in particular the local authority, played. In many respects the private sector was willing to acknowledge that the local authority had the legitimacy as well as the capacity to take the lead in partnership arrangements and in creating a public-sector-led consensus. This contrasted sharply with the position in the other two conurbations.

4.32 In Manchester, local authorities were more numerous and regarded as less able to generate collective action. Equally they were commonly regarded as less in the lead in the policy-making process, important primarily when acting in association with the private sector or central government. This perception had altered over the period of the last three years, partly in response to the change in Manchester's political stance which increasingly reflected a pragmatic reaction to the opportunities presented by central government's policy initiatives and partly through externally-generated pressure to develop a co-ordinated regional response to strategic thinking to win European Community funding. These changes were reflected in the greater salience of public-private co-ordination seen in the Central Manchester Development Corporation and in the development of a Business Leadership Team.

4.33 In Merseyside, the prevailing view was that the absence of such a consensus had, until relatively recently, prevented the emergence of partnership and hence constrained the government's ambitions. In contrast with Newcastle, public and private institutions and individuals had not formed a consensus upon the strategic needs and priorities for the conurbation. The private sector was regarded as not contributing sufficiently to the local decision-making process, a factor acknowledged by senior private sector figures. In addition, the five local authorities in the region were frequently unable to achieve common approaches to regional problems and issues. It was commonly observed that the demise of the county council had eliminated one institution where local authorities could at least formulate common responses. In its absence, differences of economic and political views between the five local authorities in the area had prevailed.

4.34 In some respects, at least three of Merseyside's five local authorities were anxious to distance themselves from the problems that were associated with Liverpool. In part this was the result of the intense economic problems endured by the city during the 1980s. More generally, however, the economic strategies of the city council and its highly publicised conflicts with central government encouraged other authorities to distance themselves from Liverpool.

4.35 The strategies of the local council also constrained the development of partnerships with the private or community sector. Changes did occur in

Merseyside in the late 1980s. In Liverpool, the ruling administration changed its strategies committing itself to partnership with the private sector and national government. The private sector responded by creating an organisation, BOOM, to help market the area. These changes subsequently led in 1992 to the creation of the Mersey Partnership which involves the five local authorities, the Merseyside Development Corporation, the private sector, the voluntary and higher education sectors and the Merseyside Task Force whose aim is to promote and market the economic development of Merseyside. Central government made a substantial contribution to the emergence of these improved partnership relations through the Merseyside Task Force. This is seen locally as a clear example of the importance of the flexibility that key figures in the Task Force have to take initiatives. Indeed, senior figures in the region stressed that the government could achieve more than it does in the region by creatively using its influence in this way as much as by using financial resources.

4.36    However, in addition to local constraints which allowed only the belated development of partnerships in two of the conurbations, the common view of senior public, community and private sector figures in all the conurbations was that much of national policy throughout the 1980s had undermined the creation of partnerships at both levels. A variety of senior figures were highly critical of the impact of much policy in terms of institutions and resources which had made it more not less difficult for partnership to emerge at local level.

4.37    Senior figures frequently argued that much of government policy had reduced the capacity of local authorities to be successful local partners in a variety of ways. In the first case it was commonly argued that reductions in mainstream programme resources had restricted their capacity to deliver quality services and be efficient partners. There were two primary concerns. The first was that local authorities believed they had lost substantial resources through rate and charge capping and what they argue are arbitrary Standard Spending Assessments. The second major loss of autonomy was in the area of capital controls, in particular the restriction in the use of capital receipts from council house sales. Equally, institutional changes which had reduced local authority control over many areas had reduced the competence of local authorities. Senior figures argued that government reduction of local competence and capacity restricted local authorities' ability to play the part government was seeking to encourage them to play - to generate a clear vision for their area, to network with other local institutions, to create partnerships.

4.38    The impact of government strategy on encouraging partnerships in the three conurbation clearly varied. Partly, differences in local political arrangements and culture, in the capacity and commitment of the private sector as well as in the willingness of local authorities to provide a meaningful role for the community and voluntary sectors, created a variegated pattern of partnership. Local variation placed some constraint upon the capacity of government strategy to achieve its goal of increased partnership. In addition, however, the consensus in the three conurbations was that many of the institutional and resource priorities of central government throughout the 1980s had themselves constrained the ability of local authorities to create partnerships. The loss of local control and the alleged increase in central powers in many local eyes made central government a suspect partner. Finally, however, there was widespread agreement, whatever limitations there might be to the initiative, that City Challenge represented a significant institutional innovation in the attempt to create local partnerships which even in the initial phase was showing some degree of success.

(ii) Co-ordination

4.39　A second recurring issue to emerge from the discussions was the experts' views on the co-ordination of government programmes. This can be examined from three perspectives: the relationship between specifically spatial programmes and those sectoral policies which have a spatial impact; the relationship between policies which are not targeted at urban problems but which nevertheless have global impact upon urban governance and the relationship between policies which are specifically focused upon targeted urban areas and are, for example, in the Action for Cities programmes. Local experience and views of the degree of co-ordination of government programmes in many respects reflects those of partnership. In all three conurbations, it was widely believed that there is insufficient co-ordination between local authority departments, between central government departments and between central and local governments.

4.40　At the most general level substantial concern was expressed that the resources targeted at urban programmes are largely insignificant in relation to those invested in other policy sectors which have important spatial impacts. Central government policies, for example, in relation to research and development contracts in the defence industries, the allocation of national housing resources, the location of national airports or major infrastructure projects like the Channel tunnel were seen as collectively commanding greater resources than the Action for Cities programme and were considered to favour other regions.

4.41　A second widely-shared concern was the lack of co-ordination between government policies which operate within each conurbation. Senior local figures in all three conurbations consistently emphasised the fragmentation of government programmes and the lack of a coherent strategy at central level for local areas. In particular, there was little belief that the Action for Cities package constitutes an integrated strategy since it did not link a clear vision of the region's future economic and social role to institutional mechanisms and resources. In particular the Urban Programme was widely regarded as lacking a clear strategy. It did not specify what it was attempting to achieve. It was essentially resource-led. It had no clear exit strategy.

4.42　A common concern was the extent to which different government departments operated upon different assumptions about the nature of the conurbations' problems. Some departments were seen to have a spatial focus and priorities like the DoE whereas others like DTI, Transport, the DE or the Home Office have not. The failure of some government departments to commit sufficient political and financial resources to the conurbations was a constant source of criticism. The Department of Transport and to a lesser degree Trade and Industry were frequently cited as lacking commitment to urban problems and urban areas. As one senior government official put it; 'urban problems are multi-dimensional - government departments are not'. The compartmentalised nature of different departmental grant regimes and the different rules which accompany them clearly frustrate greater co-ordination and local authority players. It was widely believed that departmental strategies were driven by internal needs, frequently the political agendas of individual ministers. Indeed, government departments had little regard for their collective spatial impact upon the structure of governance at urban level.

4.43　The third problematic area of co-ordination was between departments, agencies and programmes which were specifically delivering urban programmes to inner urban areas. There was a clear feeling expressed by many policy experts in all three conurbations that government departments worked poorly together. City Action Teams, although achieving some successful projects, in general did not overcome the problem of inter-departmental differences and rivalries. Many regarded CATs' primary purpose as being to spend their own limited budgets, which were too small to encourage departments to collaborate. One senior government official observed that the CAT helped to avoid gross confusion between departmental actions, but it was not a mechanism to achieve a genuinely co-ordinated government approach to the conurbation. It did not even guarantee that the three departments with primary responsibility for urban economic programmes - DoE, DTI, DE - shared the same strategy, focused and targeted upon the same issues.

4.44    A particular problem of co-ordination was seen as being the timing of policy introduction. Local authorities were particularly frustrated by the nature and scale of changes undergone during the decade by polices which impact upon urban government and services. In the largest sense, the evolution of policy for the cities during the past decade was regarded as less an iterative process than a series of policy oscillations. A narrower problem of timing was that of the annuality of resources. Local authorities found Treasury rules and the inability to carry across funding between different years enormously frustrating.

(iii) Targeting

4.45    Two forms of targeting were also raised in the discussions - that which differentiates the 57 designated UP authorities from the non-designated authorities and the targeting of areas or population groups within the 57 designated areas. The impact of the targeting of the 57 in relation to other authorities has been discussed in a preceding section. The merits of targeting within designated authorities divides opinion.

4.46    On one hand, many of the initiatives which were regarded as most successful in the three conurbations were explicitly spatially-targeted programmes and projects. There was considerable support for focusing resources in future in narrowly defined areas. Estate Action initiatives for example were typically regarded as successful for concentrating resources in spatially limited ways as were some Safer Cities initiatives. Urban Development Corporations were equally regarded as having achieved progress as a consequence of having clearly defined boundaries as had a number of locally specific initiatives such as the Merseyside Freeport, the Wavertree Technology Park, Salford Quays and Ravenhead Renaissance. Task Forces equally were frequently mentioned as successful for their specific remit, areal basis and concentrated resources. In some cases the Enterprise Zones were regarded as achieving success.

4.47    Nevertheless, all of the policy experts were keenly aware of some of the dilemmas in targeting when resources were limited or declining. The same familiar concerns emerged in all three areas. One distinction emerges between the cores of the conurbations, where the inner urban areas can be relatively easily and clearly identified, and those local authorities on the periphery of the conurbations. In the latter case, many policy makers found it difficult to differentiate and target areas clearly. Spatially targeted strategies obviously excluded as well as included areas and groups. Those included in the boundaries clearly benefited. Those left out of boundaries clearly were discriminated against. This issue was most readily identified in the case of the UDCs. But the competition between areas to receive targeting within local authority boundaries as with the Urban Programme remains a major concern. It was particularly felt that City Challenge will find this a major problem in future. City centres may compete against peripheries. Ethnic minority groups may compete with non-ethnic minority areas.

4.48 This raised a second concern about targeting. The consensus was that places had been the typical mode of targeting in the past. However, many argued that, in future, programmes would need to focus as much upon target population groups as on deprived areas. The view that targeting areas automatically benefited the people living within them was clearly challenged.

# Section 5      Conclusions

5.1   In drawing together the strands of our evaluation, we can begin to reconcile the three legs of our work; the statistical analyses, the expert discussions and the surveys. We can do this first by returning to the two higher-level policy objectives from which our analysis began and looking at the conclusions that can be drawn from both the quantitative and qualitative assessments. The nature of our study means that while we have touched at various points on many of the 10 lower-level objectives, our main conclusions are related to the two broader and more generalised objectives of improving employment opportunities, on one hand, and enhancing residential attractiveness, on the other.

**Employment opportunities**

5.2   The most positive of our findings from the statistical analyses on the economic dimension is in terms of changes in unemployment where we have been able to demonstrate that the 'gaps' between UPAs and non-UPAs have narrowed over the latter part of the 1980s. This is not simply a reflection of the impacts of the service-sector recession of the late 1980s and early 1990s, which have had such marked effects on the erstwhile prosperity of the South East. Rather, in the period prior to the effects of the current recession, we have been able to show that, comparing the 57 UPAs targeted by urban policy with the other places in our sample, the UPAs have, at the margin, shown relative improvements by comparison with areas which have not received such assistance. This is reflected both in the positive relationship shown by the correlation and regression analyses between Urban Programme expenditure and unemployment outcomes, and in the closing of the 'gaps' between the 57 UPAs and the non-UPA areas. There is, of course, a dilemma in this since most of the evidence of relative improvement occurs for the period when the national economy was most healthy in the later part of the 1980s. Since the full set of AfC policy instruments were not in play (or their impacts were unlikely to have been felt) during the earlier recessionary period, it must remain an open question whether such relative successes are dependent on the state of the national economy.

5.3   Nevertheless, these positive relationships between expenditure and socio-economic outcomes are all the more encouraging a finding, first, because AfC expenditure is only a small proportion of total public expenditure and might therefore be expected to have had only a small impact on the socio-economic fortunes of urban areas and, second, because the economic experience of urban areas over the last two decades suggests that it would not be unreasonable to have expected that their employment fortunes would have grown progressively and markedly worse in the absence of public policy interventions. This being so, it could have been anticipated that, even with a policy of targeting assistance to selected urban areas, conditions would nevertheless have grown absolutely and relatively worse in the 57 UPAs, but that this would need to have been set against the counterfactual arguments suggesting that without the assistance of public resources the plight of such areas would have got even more severe. In fact, the general pattern which emerges is that, across the whole set of the 57 UPAs, there has been a relative improvement. Against this has to be set the fact that the cores of the large conurbations have experienced both absolute and relative deterioration - with 'inner city' conditions now extending more broadly across the hearts of the biggest cities. The categorisation of places in terms of inputs and outcomes suggests that the core districts of the conurbations have continued to deteriorate regardless of financial expenditure. It appears to be in many of the smaller places and many of the more peripheral districts within the conurbations where absolute or relative improvement has occurred. Likewise, the spatial patterns of unemployment change suggest that there has been an intensification of economic distress, with a greater concentration of economic problems in the cores and with a higher proportion of the unemployed in those cores being long-term unemployed. Similarly, within Greater Manchester, Merseyside and Tyne and Wear, there has been an almost universal pattern of increasing concentration of unemployment within the inner cores of the districts, within areas which already had high rates of unemployment. The general improvement across all of the 57 UPAs compared to the non-UPAs needs to be set against this evidence of increasing polarisation.

5.4    This positive conclusion about the improvements across the whole set of 57 UPAs is based upon the quantitative evaluation of one of our outcome indicators - unemployment and long-term unemployment. The second and third relevant indicators - job creation and new-firm formation - did not show the same relationship. Nevertheless, to have found for unemployment that there has been relative improvement is a testimony to the benefits of having targeted resources to the 57 UPAs. The weakest conclusion that one can draw is that the annual £4 billion spent on urban policy has not been misplaced. It has positively helped to underpin the economies of at least some of the areas.

5.5    This is a conclusion which applies to the longer-term impact of public expenditure (either over the period 1983-90 or 1986-90). It is a conclusion which at first sight appears to sit eccentrically with the views both of residents and of employers, whose attitudes both to employment and the local economy in the last three years and to economic prospects for the future were uniformly pessimistic. Despite this, we would reiterate the positive conclusions from the quantitative evaluation. The surveys have limitations which erode generalisations drawn from them. First, all of the resident surveys were conducted in some of the very worst of the inner-city areas which, as our statistical analysis has shown, have not been areas which have shared in the benefit of the closure of unemployment gaps. Somewhat different views might have emerged had our resident surveys been conducted in areas other than the hearts of the three big conurbations. Second, despite the area-based comparative focus of the survey design, many respondents were in a stronger position to discuss their experiences and expectations in an absolute sense rather than by making relative comparisons between themselves and others. Third, the employers' surveys were conducted in 1992 at a time of recession, when the difficulties of the macro-economic situation tended to swamp the subtler and more relative effects of policy intervention. Such caveats might temper the apparent discrepancies between the quantitative evaluation and the views of the recipients of policy.

**Residential attractiveness**

5.6    On residential attractiveness, our findings also provide evidence of the beneficial impacts of policy. The migration indicator in the quantitative analysis showed, on average, a closing of the 'gaps' between the 57 UPAs and the non-UPAs and this suggests the relative impact of the suite of programmes designed to attract or retain a key cohort of residents in targeted urban areas. Since it is not generally the case that unemployment has differentially increased amongst this group within the inner areas, we can take this as a positive finding rather than signifying that the 25-34 age cohort is merely trapped in inner areas. Likewise, on house price changes, the period 1986-9 provides some evidence of the positive impact of public expenditure on inner city housing markets (even though for the period 1983-6 the relationship was negative). Again, from these strands of evidence we can conclude that the expenditure of public resource has had an impact on the attractiveness of residential areas.

5.7   This positive conclusion is reinforced by many elements of the findings of the residents' survey. For example, the comparisons of 'assisted' and 'less assisted' neighbourhoods showed consistently that residents in areas which had benefited from more publicly-resourced projects took a generally more favourable view of the prospects and the current state of their neighbourhoods. Where more resources had been expended, views were consistently more favourable. If a critical element of the social problems of inner areas is the degree of hope of their residents, then this is an important indicator of the impact of expenditure. Much of the favourable reaction within such neighbourhoods was related to environmental and housing improvements, associated with expenditure under Derelict Land Grant, Estate Action and with environmental expenditure under the Urban Programme. Since crime is seen as the most important dimension of residents' perceived quality of life, it is not surprising that the relative optimism about local areas did not apply to crime. We might infer from this that the focus on programmes such as Safer Cities is a well-adjudged policy priority for the future. Given, on the other hand, the importance attributed by residents to health care, it is perhaps surprising that health has not featured as one of the elements of formal urban policy and therefore subject to the same degree of targeting.

5.8   It must be remembered, however, that these conclusions are based on relative evaluations between sets of areas. Our positive conclusions cannot gainsay the fact that the absolute levels of pessimism in inner areas are high and that most residents forsee a poor future for themselves and their areas. This conclusion, drawn from residents' own perceptions of their areas, is reinforced by the finding from our quantitative analysis that in most (but not all) of the authorities there was evidence of increasing polarisation between areas with better and areas with worse rates of unemployment.

5.9   The pattern that emerges, both for employment opportunities and residential attractiveness, is therefore a very mixed picture. There has been beneficial change - some of it relative, some absolute. Public expenditure has not been without effect. Across the whole set of targeted places and in the smaller areas within some of the conurbations, public resources appear to have made an impact on turning around aspects both of the economic and residential distress in urban areas. But in the most deprived areas - and especially in the conurbation cores and in areas of high unemployment - policy has not been able to make significant inroads into the socio-economic problems. The biggest (and most deprived) of the urban areas have generally experienced a continuing deterioration with 'inner city' conditions spreading more broadly out from the cores of the conurbations, regardless of the expenditure of public resources. On the other hand, some of the smaller and more peripheral authorities within the 57 UPAs have shown positive socio-economic change which can be related to urban expenditure. To this extent, both in terms of employment prospects and residential desirability, urban policy has achieved positive impacts. However, to set against this, within virtually all the authorities in our three selected conurbations, there is consistent evidence of increasing degrees of polarisation between the worst and the best areas. Despite the positive overall impacts, there are therefore strong suggestions of continuing decline in the worst areas. From this one might draw the conclusion that people-targeting, as against place-targeting, needs to be given greater weight than is currently the case.

**Conception and implementation**

5.10   Our overall views of the impacts of policy must, of course, distinguish between the thrust of what policy has aimed to achieve, on one hand, and how its chosen policy instruments have been implemented on the ground, on the other.

5.11   The statistical analyses are somewhat blunt instruments through which to address this distinction. We therefore draw the following conclusions predominantly on the qualitative views of experts, employers and residents. Three general conclusions emerge.

(i) Partnerships

5.12   There was a widespread consensus that the attempt to encourage the formation of partnerships has been a well-adjudged priority. Most of our discussions, however, suggested that it has been a goal which has been only imperfectly achieved in practice.

5.13   The goal of levering private-sector interest back into urban areas is widely seen as being critical to the plausibility of turning around the fortunes of big cities; the futures of cities can look more secure only if private-sector interest can be attracted and maintained. Public expenditure has been reined back through reductions for example in the Housing Investment Programme and in some areas in Revenue Support Grant, but the public expenditure targeted through urban policy has clearly levered-in private-sector investment to the urban areas. To this extent, the aim of policy has been achieved. Nevertheless, we have to conclude from the discussions with experts that while the project-led focus of most policy may have attracted private-sector interest on the basis of financial incentives, the widespread view amongst experts both from the public and private sectors was that it seems unlikely that such involvement outlasts the life-span of the projects concerned. This is reinforced by the limited sense of involvement or responsibility felt by most businesses towards the communities in which they operate. Most of our respondents stressed that only if structures or mechanisms can be created which begin to develop long-term commitment to private-sector investment in cities will the benefits of creating partnerships be secured most effectively. All of the evidence from this study suggests that coalitions between the private sector and local government are a key element in urban regeneration. The experience of Tyne and Wear shows how the intimate relationship of key private-sector players has produced a series of key agencies leading to the creation of the Northern Development Company and the Newcastle Initiative; the converse experience in Liverpool of fragmentation in the early 1980s goes some way to explain the difficulty of achieving similar developments in Merseyside. A key to the successful creation of such growth coalitions is widely seen as being the consistent support of public resource and the creation of coherent frameworks through which to cement relationships. Fluctuating policy does not create fertile ground for the development of such coalitions.

5.14   Furthermore, the overwhelming view from the expert discussions was that local authorities should now be given scope to play a more important role in such coalitions. The impatience which central government showed with the unwillingness or inability of some local authorities to 'deliver' urban regeneration in the early years of the 1980s may well have justified the policy response of by-passing local government. But local authorities are generally now seen as having an important role to play in the development and implementation of local strategies, especially now that an increasing number of such authorities have demonstrated their readiness to work in co-operation with a range of other partners. They have a key role to play as facilitators or enablers in establishing and maintaining the coalition structures through which longer-lasting and more securely-based regeneration can come about. Our discussions with local experts showed that the new roles expected of local authorities are ones to which they are attempting to come to terms, but that this transition has proved more difficult in a context of overall pressures on their resource base and of a rapidly changing external environment created by frequent changes in government legislation.

5.15    Local communities might also have played a role in such coalitions, but it has generally not been a high priority of government policy to develop such community participation in the 1980s. Our discussions - not merely those with experts from the voluntary sector and local authorities, but with some of the private-sector and quango representatives - suggested that the reduction in the availability of revenue resources for the voluntary sector had diminished the capacity of local communities to play active roles in regeneration and that this is seen by many as a missed opportunity.

(ii) Coherence

5.16    There is a widespread perception that policy has lacked the coherence that could have come through a more strategic approach to regeneration. There are two elements to this. First is the financial dimension of targeting resources to assist urban areas. There is some contradictory evidence here. On one hand, as Appendix A shows, most of the AfC and non-AfC programmes have devoted a large (and usually stable or growing) proportion of resources to the 57 UPAs. For example, the relative proportion of expenditure allocated to the UPAs during the 1980s increased for HIPs, RSG and Section 11 grants; it remained broadly constant for Youth Training, English Estates and Derelict Land Grant; it decreased for Housing Corporation expenditure and slightly decreased for Estate Action. This general pattern of sustained targeting to the UPAs, however, needs to be set alongside the substantial absolute decreases in many of the core resources of these local authorities. For example the local studies of the three conurbations show that the scale of the reductions in, for example, HIP allocations and RSG resources generally dwarfed the financial benefits of targeted Urban Programme expenditure. As Appendix C shows for Tyne and Wear for example, RSG and HIP budgets (which had accounted for over 90% of all expenditure in 1979/80) were over one-third lower in 1989/90 than they had been in 1979/80. Even though the roles of local authorities have altered during the course of the decade, this left them with the constant temptation to see urban policy resources as a mechanism for addressing the recurring pressures to underpin their statutory activities and thereby weakened their scope for developing longer-term and more imaginative schemes which could have formed the framework for coalitions with the private sector. If local authorities are to play a key enabling role, they need a secure resource base to give them political leverage within coalitions.

5.17    There are also curious ambiguities in the policy of targeting resources to the 57 UPAs. In practice, the 57 do cluster disproportionately within the set of places with highest per capita funding, but a significant number fall outside the list of best-funded places. If urban policy aims to identify places with socio-economic needs and to channel the resources necessary to them to help in tackling regeneration, the inter-relationship between many aspects of deprivation suggests the wisdom of a clearer targeting both of the whole range of AfC and of non-AfC resources to assist in this objective.

5.18   The second and more fundamental aspect of the lack of coherence is the importance of co-ordinating programmes within and across various departments. As many of our discussions suggested, there is an almost universal view that such co-ordination has not worked well. As one of our respondents commented; 'Urban problems are multifaceted: departments are not'. That verdict appears to apply as much to local authorities as to central government. While much of central government's urban policy has shown a move away from narrowly-defined projects, the views of experts suggest that insufficient attention appears to have been paid to the institutional mechanisms which might ensure better linkages between, for example, training, education and job creation, or between improvements to the environment, job creation and the strengthening of the capacity of local communities. This in turn has partly been a reflection of the failure to co-ordinate priorities and practices across and within the six main departments involved with urban policy. The two main departments involved - the Department of the Environment and the Department of Trade and Industry - have priorities which are overtly different, with the one being urban oriented and the other being regionally oriented. But the difficulty is the more general one of developing strategic objectives which might link cross-sectoral programmes either across or within all of the six departments involved in aspects of urban policy.

5.19   Some of our expert discussions suggested that European Community funds have encouraged a greater emphasis on strategic thinking, despite the cumbersome bureaucratic procedures which surround the release of EC resources. Once won, they appear to have been hedged around with somewhat fewer restrictions than are resources from central government. The accountability is more at arms length. Most significantly, the reforms of the structural funds have offered encouragement to integrate the various agencies and programmes - across the public and private bodies, across national and local agencies, and across sectors - in response to the different EC programmes. To this extent, the structural funds have helped to reinforce arguments about the need for more strategic thinking in the development of effective urban regeneration.

5.20   Many of the best examples where more effective strategic coherence **has** been achieved through urban policy have involved area-based schemes. For example, much of the work on crime prevention through Safer Cities initiatives has been concerned, within local areas, with creating inter-agency collaboration between, in this instance, the probation service, the police, local communities and local authorities. Similar cross-departmental strategies have been made possible through some of the Estate Action schemes. Equally, one of the growing strengths of Urban Development Corporations has been the fact that, operating within defined areas, there has been scope to develop more integrated programmes involving training, job creation, environmental and infrastructural improvements. It is understandable that departments argue, first, that they are faced with the constraints of Treasury rules which, for example, make it difficult to allow financial roll-over from one financial year to another, or are faced with the logic of departmentalism which gives priority to departmental budgets. But if the aim is to maximise the effectiveness of expenditure, it is clear that the issue of co-ordination needs to be squarely faced and that it appears most readily resolvable through area-based schemes and with a degree of financial flexibility that comes from grant-in-aid and with virement of expenditure across financial years. The general view is that the work of CATs seems not to have made major inroads into the difficulties, even though a more generous view might stress their more recent role in helping some local authorities to develop closer links with government departments in the context of City Challenge. Two alternative approaches were suggested in our discussions with experts; both depend on area-based approaches and were signalled in the manifesto of the present administration. First is the development of regional or urban budgets which genuinely cut across departmental allocations. In contradistinction to CATs, this would involve the direct determination of substantial resource allocation and be of a scale which might appear to make better co-ordination more plausible. Second is an even greater emphasis on local area-based strategies through which local co-ordination might be developed more robustly through implementation on the ground. Our discussions with policy experts and our local conurbation studies suggested a number of combinations of programmes which appeared to have worked effectively to create additionality within defined local areas; for example, the combination of Estate Action with Urban Programme expenditure and of Urban Development Corporation expenditure with City Grant. Likewise, we were also told of situations in which the barriers to combining resources across programe areas could work to the disadvantage of worthwhile area-based programmes; for example, in North Tyneside, the fact that Urban Programme expenditure has been disallowed within the boundaries of the Urban Development Corporation has prevented developments such as the introduction of security improvements at Point Pleasant - a scheme supported both by the local authority and the UDC - and has thereby prevented continuity of earlier valuable regeneration developments.

5.21    The experts suggested that the principles underlying City Challenge appear to have gone some long way to address many of the limitations argued above. Local authorities expressed great unhappiness at some of the elements of City Challenge - of competition for top-sliced resources and of a competition whose rules remain somewhat opaque. Nevertheless, the operational principles applied to the successful authorities appear to embody much of the 'wisdom' that derives from our earlier comments. There is an unambigous role given both to local authorities and to local communities in the formation of coalitions with the private sector. For both, this represents a helpful recognition of their potential contributions. There are financial and institutional incentives which both reinforce the creation of working partnerships and which appear to place a novel emphasis on quality as against expenditure. There is a spur to inter-departmental initiatives, not only through the area-based context of the schemes but also through the explicit cross-sectoral emphases. There is an encouragement to develop larger-scale more visionary proposals. There is provision made for monitoring and evaluation. There is the assurance of longer-term funding on which rolling programmes could be created. These principles are all ones which seem fundamental to good practice in urban regeneration.

(iii) Targeting people

5.22    Over the course of the 1980s, the main thrusts of policy were increasingly focused on economic and environmental goals and this inevitably meant that social and community interests have had a lower profile. Our discussions with experts suggested that it was not simply those from the voluntary sector or from local authorities who commented on the growing relative poverty of many inner-city residents and the narrowed scope to develop schemes to foster community development. Many of those from the private sector and from quangos shared such views. The emphasis on infrastructure in the programmes of urban regeneration has not addressed the needs of deprived inner-area residents and has missed the opportunity to utilise their skills and to mobilise their support. The view of policy-makers may well have been that targeting areas can simultaneously benefit the people in those areas. However (despite the existence of some policy instruments such as Task Forces which target people as well as places, and of such examples as Tyne and Wear Development

Corporation's schemes to target the unemployed of the Meadow Well estate linked to the flagship project at the Royal Quays), our work reinforces the view that 'trickle-down' has not generally been very effective. This is the most obvious interpretation of two of our findings: that conditions in the cores of the conurbations have deteriorated while there is some improvement across all of the 57 UPAs; and that polarisation has increased between areas with worse and better socio-economic conditions. The impact of public resource has been diffused and has been of little direct help to those living in the worst areas. Linkages between developmental programmes and distributional programmes appear not to have been very effective. The perceptions of most inner-city residents themselves confirm this; the widespread view is that infrastructural schemes may have had an impact on areas, especially those with commercial potential such as water-front areas or areas close to the central business district, but that the residents themselves see little direct or indirect economic benefit from most of them. The switch to capital as against revenue projects in the period since the early 1980s, has exacerbated the marginalising of local residents because the non-statutory sector has depended overwhelmingly on revenue programmes. Within this, it is also clear that ethnic groups (the very groups from which urban policy began in 1968) have begun to derive benefit from urban policy only late in the day and, ironically, at a time when the reduction in revenue-based projects has meant that they have been less able to capitalise on public resources. Community groups (and social projects generally) have suffered from the double disadvantage that Urban Programme resources have grown progressively less as a proportion of overall expenditure and that, within the Urban Programme, capital rather than revenue projects have been favoured.

5.23   The decision, following the 1992 Autumn Statement, to stop financial support for new schemes under the Urban Programme must severely limit the prospect of the non-statutory sector and local authorities continuing to make positive contributions to deprived inner areas, especially where City Challenge is not operating. There would be benefits were the balance to be redressed. Given the evidence of increasing polarisation between more and less deprived areas, there must be strong arguments for the community sector having access to some form of programme which addresses the need to strengthen the capacities of deprived communities. Such a conclusion can only be reinforced by the fact that the residents' survey showed evidence of a 'place-loyalty' effect amongst local residents; their attachment to their local communities can be inferred from the fact that they consistently assess the general desirability of their own neighbourhood more highly than that of other (similarly deprived) areas. This is a platform on which a stronger social dimension of urban policy could have been built.

**Policy conclusions**

5.24   The questions that we have addressed are inherently complex. It is therefore not surprising that most of our conclusions are hedged with caveats. We have been dealing with a wide range of policy instruments applied at different times over the course of the last decade and our aim has been to assess the overall impacts of the collection of those policies. The places which we have studied have tackled the issues of regeneration from different starting points, with different inherent strengths and weaknesses and with benefits derived from a wide mix of different public expenditures, only part of which are comprised of AfC resources. There is a host of permutations and combinations of the relationships even between the inputs and outcomes, and in reporting them we have selectively focused on those which can tell us something concrete about what is a confused and complicated set of patterns.

We have arrived at views on the overall impacts of urban policy through an exhaustive process of collecting and analysing data on financial inputs and socio-economic outcomes across a large sample of authorities, of discussing issues with experts who have influenced or determined policy and with those residents and employers affected by it.

5.25 We can draw five policy conclusions from our local assessments:

i) There are clear indications of the importance of creating effective coalitions of 'actors' within localities. Such coalitions are most likely to result from the development of structures and mechanisms which encourage or require long-term collaborative partnerships.

ii) Local authorities - in their newly emergent roles as enablers and facilitators - need to be given greater opportunities to play a significant part in such coalitions.

iii) Local communities equally need to be given opportunities to play roles in such coalitions. The evidence of increasing polarisation suggests the need for specific resources to address the scope for community capacity-building within deprived areas.

iv) There remains a need to improve the coherence of programmes both across and within government departments. This requires a greater emphasis on the identification of strategic objectives which can guide departmental priorities. Area targeting has played an important part in those cases where separate programmes have been successfully linked so as to create additionality, thereby suggesting the value of giving yet greater emphasis to area-based approaches. Such plaiting together of different policy instruments would be helped by increasing the flexibility of expenditure through a more relaxed approach to virement.

v) An important part of such coherence must derive from less ambiguity in the targeting of resources. There is a strong argument for the development of an urban budget which might be administered at regional level so as to reflect the varying constraints and opportunities across different regions and to achieve more effective co-ordination across programmes and departments.

5.26 Our quantitative evaluation clearly suggests a complex mixture of pluses and minuses. There have been positive impacts associated with the expenditure of AfC resources; there are, on the other hand, places where even large expenditures have had no demonstrable effect in reversing or slowing the urban decay reflected by increasing polarisation. The cores of the big conurbations present deep and multi-faceted problems which appear not to have been deflected by policy intervention; on the other hand some of the smaller and more peripheral UPA authorities have shown economic and residential improvements by comparison with non-UPA areas. Many of the criticisms levelled at the conception and implementation of urban policy - its lack of strategic coherence, the limited encouragement given to the full range of actors potentially involved in the creation of partnerships, its short-termism, its emphasis on property-led renewal at the expense of community development - seem likely to be addressed more effectively if many of the strategic principles which underlie City Challenge can be translated more consistently and broadly into the genesis and implementation of urban policy.

# *Appendix A*  Input data and outcomes indicators

The following accounts provide descriptive analyses of the expenditure data inputs assembled for the 123 English local authority districts (LAs) and for the outcome socio-economic indicators for those same districts. The initial 23 sections discuss the 'input' data and the final sections describe indicators for four of the five 'outcomes'.

## A1  THE URBAN PROGRAMME

**1  Programme background**

The Urban Programme has been at the core of the DoE's urban policy strategy over the last fifteen years or so. Targeted at its inception at a set of 'partnership' and 'programme' authorities, as well as to Other Designated Districts (ODDs), latterly it has been directed towards designated inner areas within the set of 57 UPAs. In recent years the focus of UP activity has largely been on economic and environmental projects, although ministerial guidelines continue to allow for around one third of expenditure on social and housing related projects.

The Urban Programme has been the longest-running of the government programmes tackling urban deprivation and as such has undergone various changes along the way, helping to support various 'special initiatives' responding to specific problems at particular times. This helps explain the plethora of different figures quoted in relation to the Urban Programme, and the confusion that sometimes results. Our requirements have been to amass a dataset which could be reasonably comprehensive for the full period under study, and also be comparable over time, by controlling for, or at least acknowledging, changes in the operation of the Programme and so on. In order to do this figures have been selected and applied in particular ways that we describe below.

Sources of finance

An early government publication commented; 'About 80% of the Government resources for the Urban Programme are provided by Department of Environment expenditure plans, the remainder coming from the Department of Health and Social Services [sic], the Department of Education and Science and the Department of Transport' (DoE, 1985:2). The figures quoted in that first report represented:

> '*the actual expenditure under the Urban Programme in each year. This expenditure is undertaken by local authorities, who are then reimbursed 75 per cent of the cost by the Government*' *(DoE, 1985:22).*

Since then, the contributions from other government departments have become less significant; it has effectively become a DoE programme, with a small input from the Department of Health. These allocations, spent by District Health Authorities have not always been shown separately in published figures; consequently it is not possible to break these down by area for the whole period under discussion, and so these have been excluded.

As policy instruments have grown in number, so there has been a tendency for commentators to conflate the Urban Programme with urban policy as a whole. Again some of the government's earlier publications have shown global UP figures which have included as components funds which are really separate programmes. The most obvious example of this is Urban Development Grant. Figures A1 and A2 are both taken from DoE reports and show the various components within a global total for a certain period (A1) or a single year (A2). Although the text of such documents at times seems contradictory, the Urban Programme is defined as:

> 'the collective term for the projects and activities supported under the Local Government Grants (Social Need) Act 1969' (DoE, 1985:2).

As mentioned above, for the purposes of this research it was necessary to compile a dataset consistent across time, and between authorities. In many years, elements of the overall Departmental budget have been put aside or 'top-sliced' for special purposes or projects. Examples of these are continuing commitments under the Traditional UP, the Low Attainers programme, the Merseyside Special Allocation and the Outward Bound Scheme. Such top-slices have been excluded from our figures as they were not readily available in disaggregated form.

Another problem with which we have had to deal has been the changing designations of authorities during the period 1979-87. These changes have been summarised as follows:

> 'By 1987, local authorities were requested to submit Inner Area Programmes which were to outline the objectives of Urban Programme funding, and to indicate how other funding programmes dovetailed into Urban Programme activities. Of these 57 authorities, 32 had been Partnership or Programme councils, and the remainder had a lower status either as Other Designated Districts or benefited from the traditional Urban Programme from which very many councils had gained some, often limited resources. The stratified approach to Urban Programme funding, with in essence a fourfold division of councils - was effectively to be abandoned. Instead a single Urban programme designation was to be introduced, and the traditional Urban Programme was to be phased out. This approach was adopted in order to concentrate resources on areas of greatest need. In the event in 1987-8 all 57 authorities submitted an Inner area programme and all were approved' (Lawless, 1989:53).

While there was in fact no formal system of stratification, the existence of a 'pecking order' was apparent, reflected in DoE publications, which did not provide as comprehensive information about ODDs, for instance. There are two main sources of historic Urban Programme data - the annual reports (DoE 1985, 1986, 1987) published by HMSO, and a series of Urban Programme Fact Sheets (for 81/82-89/90) produced by the Inner Cities Directorate within DoE. For 1979/80 - 1985/86, the source used is the former series produced prior to **Action for Cities**. These give only per authority figures for the Partnerships and the first group of Programme authorities, while a total figure is given for the group of ODDs and for the amount shared by the traditional UP authorities. As the Fact Sheets show, the traditional Urban Programme continued to fund committed projects throughout the 1980s, finishing finally in March 1992. This assistance was spread extremely thinly. For example, in 1984/5 approximately 190 local authorities shared £45m towards projects in urban areas with special social needs. Although each council would have received a very small allocation, the Traditional UP still accounted for 16% of total UP resources in that year. Unfortunately, the only existing records are the raw documents, the Final Audited Claims from the local authorities, and they are therefore absent from the figures. This may give the impression that certain councils 'came on stream' in 1987/8, whereas in fact most were merely upgraded from ODDs to full Programme authorities. In other words, there were no (or few) new resources supplied when the group of 57 UPAs was crystallised. On the contrary many councils which were excluded from the 57 experienced a reduction in funding, but this fails to show up in the statistics. It is possible to identify the authorities which were ODDs from 1981/2 onwards in the Fact Sheets, so for the missing years the ODD allocation has simply been divided equally between the number of authorities.

After 1986/7 the figures used are the 'base' figures (excluding topslices) from the DoE records at Marsham Street. In any year, the base figure would account for about 90% of all Urban Programme, and thus is a robust source of data. The database is compiled from the Inner Cities Reports, Regional Office returns and local authorities' claim forms.

A second problem with the 1979-84 period is the position of the Joint Partnerships in Manchester/Salford, Newcastle/Gateshead, Hackney/Islington and Docklands. Since Partnership funds are channelled through individual local authorities, it seemed probable that disaggregated data could have been available. This was not in fact the case, so each has been treated differently. Manchester/Salford figures come from the North West DoE. Prior to 1986/7 we have assumed that Manchester outspends Salford in the ratio 2:1. For Newcastle/Gateshead the overall figure is as per Marsham Street, and this is then apportioned between the partners in ratios corresponding to Northern Regional Office figures. Hackney and Islington formed a Joint Partnership until 1982/3, and for prior years the total has been apportioned on a ratio of 4:3 respectively.

The Docklands partnership is much more problematic. In the 1970s, central and local government co-operated to produce a London Docklands Strategic Plan agreed by the GLC and the five boroughs involved (Lawless, 1989:85). This became the basis of the Partnership area in 1979. However, the incoming Conservative administration decided to pursue an alternative policy by creating the LDDC. Until 1985/6, Docklands continued to receive funds to support committed projects (a total of £102.1m). Although we know that the Docklands partnership area covered the London boroughs of Tower Hamlets, Newham, Southwark, Lewisham and Greenwich, it has not been possible to uncover accurate records of how this money was split. This does not affect the analysis at the regional level. However, for the purpose of the statistical analysis of the 123 LAs, the money was equally apportioned among the five boroughs. In the attached tables the figures are in their gross form, since it shows the existence of the Docklands Partnership as a conduit through which funds travelled to these five local authority areas.

**2   Data analysis**

Since UP money is by definition limited to one (hierarchical) group of authorities, the only regional patterns of expenditure are those which reflect the distribution of the 57 within particular regions. The Partnership authorities received by far the largest shares. At the other end of the spectrum a number of small councils have consistently received small amounts of funding, first through their status as ODDs, and more recently within the main body of the Urban Programme. Figure A3 shows the overall growth of the UP over the 79-91 period, as well as how the regional share has fluctuated.

Naturally these patterns are affected by the number and size of authorities within a region. Two regions in particular, the North West and the West Midlands, took a larger percentage share of total expenditure than their 'share' of the 57 authorities would suggest. However, the regional location of an authority has less effect on the level of its allocation than its perceived needs - its rank in the notional pecking order, the major cleavage being between the Partnerships and the rest (Figure A4). Although the chart seems to indicate a drop in the Partnerships' share, this is accounted for by the rundown of the Docklands Partnership and the redesignation of its constituent boroughs as Programme authorities. In reality, Partnership areas have remained the focus of the largest parcels of Urban Programme funding.

**References**

DoE (1985), *The Urban Programme*, HMSO.
DoE (1986), *The Government's Inner City programmes 1985/6*, HMSO.
DoE (1987), *The Government's Inner City programmes 1986/7*, HMSO.
Lawless, P (1989), *Britain's Inner Cities*, 2nd edition, Chapman and Hall.

*Figure A1*　Urban programme allocations 1974/5 to 1983/4

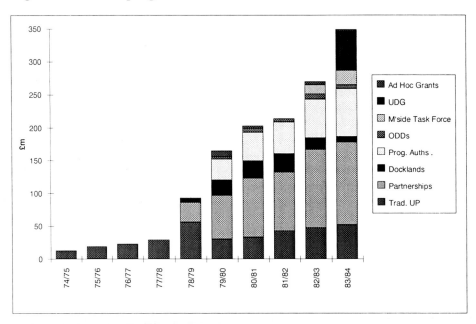

*Figure A2*　Composition of expenditure, 1986/87 final allocations

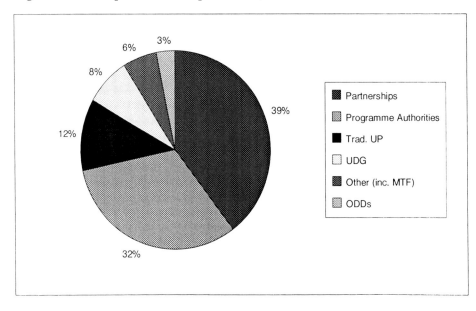

*Figure A3*  **UP expenditure by region 1979-91**

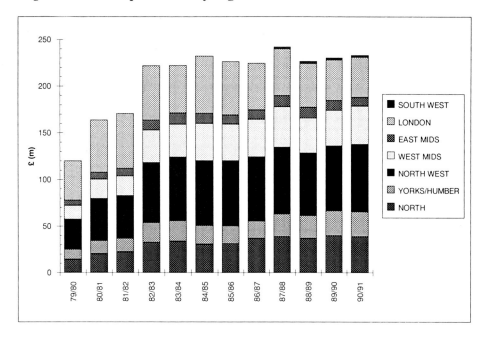

*Figure A4*  **Partnership and Programme Authorities: UP expenditure since 1979**

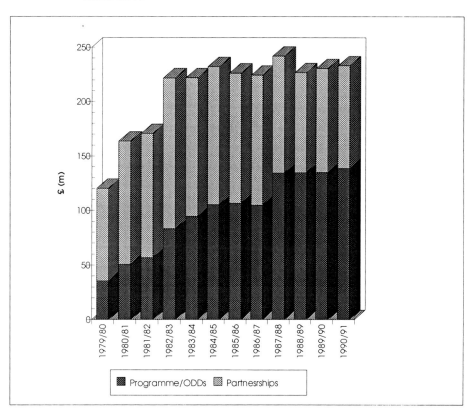

## 1 Programme background

Housing Investment Programme (HIP) is designed to create a comprehensive 'package' of measures for local authority council stock. Like the Urban Programme, the intention is to draw-up an annual plan for central government-funded expenditure on housing. Although HIP contains a 'special allocation for inner cities' which is included in Action for Cities, mainstream HIP expenditure is not counted as AfC money.

There are two sources of data which refer to local authority housing resources. We obtained expenditure data for the 123 areas, based on the HIP2 form returned by each authority. We collected separate figures for Sections B and C of the form. Section B includes all prescribed and non-prescribed capital expenditure, except for low-cost home ownership schemes which are shown within Section C. However, the workings of housing finance mean it is difficult to relate the figures to the level of resources made available to local government. The most important distinction is that between allocations and expenditure. Before 1981 HIP allocations were effectively a maximum borrowing approval which could not be exceeded, though many authorities did not use their full allocation. Any capital receipts had to be applied to reduce existing housing debt and therefore interest charges. As Malpass and Murie observe:

> 'After 1981-2, block allocation could be increased by a proportion (50%) of housing capital receipts in the year, and a proportion of accumulated unused receipts. The remaining percentage is distributed through the HIP allocations. Accrued receipts could carry forward to the subsequent year' (Malpass and Murie, 1990:106-110).

This led authorities to hoard capital receipts, and then spend them on repairs in subsequent years, and caused many to exceed the cash limit in 83/4 and 84/5. This, in turn, led the government to reduce the proportion of capital receipts eligible for re-use to 20%. The change in the allocation system therefore reduced its influence on local investment patterns. The shire districts and the South had the most stock to sell, and generated more receipts than the metropolitan districts and the Northern regions. To quote Malpass and Murie:

> 'By 1986/7, only 47% of borrowing permissions were allocated through HIP. The rest were determined in relation to capital receipts or held back for allocation in some other way' (ibid.).

If, prior to 1977, the pattern of investment reflected local political and professional predilections unaffected by relative national needs, then by 1987 investment bore no relation to either local or national estimates of need, merely to creative accounting, and where capital receipts fell. This trend has been continued by the introduction of supplementary routes for funding, most notably through the Estate Action programme. Some dispute exists over whether the latter represents a new initiative, or whether funds are merely topsliced from HIP allocations.

In the light of the above remarks, this discussion therefore draws on data both on allocations to, and reported expenditure by, the 123 authorities from 1978/79 to 1989/90, during which there was a basically consistent system of borrowing limits. Since allocations from DoE are not made for specific purposes, there is no corresponding 'Section B/Section C' split. In any case, the amount of expenditure on low-cost home ownership schemes is such a negligible proportion of the total that in all cases total figures have been used.

## 2 Data analysis

Before looking at patterns across time and space, it is worth establishing the national picture. Figure A5 compares HIP allocations with expenditure, and also shows (through the inflation index) how each has kept pace with inflation. Two main features are of interest here. The first is the divergence between allocations and expenditure, reflecting the use of sources of finance other than HIP borrowing limits (i.e. capital receipts). The second interesting trend is that both allocations and expenditure have fallen in real terms. Allocations were cut in every year of the 1980s except for 1982/3 and 1983/4, while actual expenditure rose and fell in roughly equal measure until 1986/87, after which it increased every year, rising particularly sharply since 1988/89. However, neither allocations nor expenditure kept pace with inflation. The inflation index shows the level of resources that would have been required to fund the housing investment programme at its 1978/79 level.

Figure A6 shows in another way the previous point, plotting cash allocations against their value at 1981/82 prices (the measure used in our statistical analyses). This shows more clearly that HIP allocations fell most in real terms between 1978/79 and 1981/82, and at a slower rate for the rest of the decade. In real terms, the only year HIP allocations rose was in 1982/3. If we compare allocations to different groups of authorities, we get the pattern in Figure A7. Although we obtained local authority data for just 123 places, we used the figures for 'All England' to work out what was happening to other places outside the '123'. The figure would seem to suggest that the 57 UPAs did not experience as large cuts as the rest of the country. The 66 non-UPA group suffered a reduction of about 60% over the period, while the 57 UPAs lost around 45% of their 1978/79 resources. Perhaps surprisingly, the 66 non-UPAs in our study actually fared worse than the UPAs, in percentage terms, falling by over 50 percent. If we look at relative shares of each year's HIP (Figure A8), the results are again interesting. There has been an increased targeting of the 57 at the expense of those outside the 123, with the non-UPA group retaining a static share.

**Reference**

Malpass, P. and Murie, A. (1990), *Housing Policy and Practice*, 3rd edition, Macmillan, Basingstoke.

*Figure A5* **HIP resources in England**

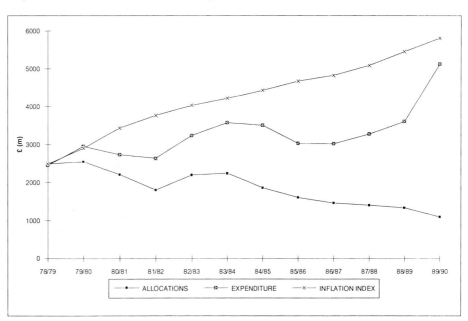

**Figure A6** **HIP allocations in England**

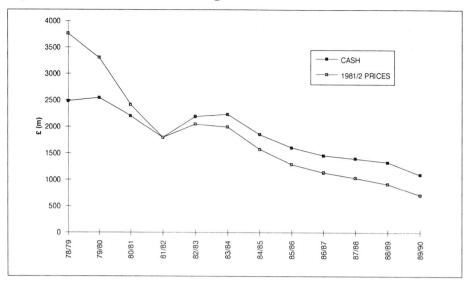

**Figure A7** **HIP allocations by type**

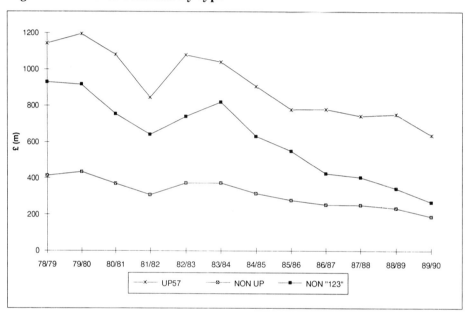

**Figure A8** **Share of HIP allocations by type**

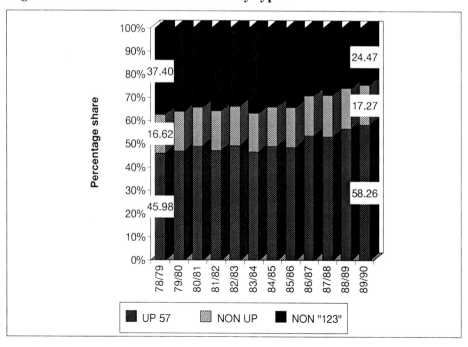

# A3  ESTATE ACTION

**1  Programme background**

Estate Action began life as the Urban Housing Renewal Unit, set up by Sir George Young in 1985 to offer 'a wide range of approaches for revitalising rundown estates and transforming unpopular properties into decent homes' (DoE, 1986). While Estate Action resources tend to be targeted towards estates in inner city areas, ministerial guidelines for the programme recognise that there are some estates outside the inner urban areas (and outside the 57 UPAs) which are suitable for Estate Action support. Estate Action, along with a number of other top-slices (e.g. Green House energy programme and the rural initiative) is an element of the Housing Investment Programme, but, unlike mainstream HIP, is included under the Action for Cities heading. The overall level of HIP is agreed in the light of policy priorities and perceived needs, and the top-slices are elements of HIP which are targeted on specific areas and needs, run-down housing estates in the case of Estate Action. Thus there is an important relationship between the level of basic HIP allocations and the amount of Estate Action resources received under **Action for Cities**.

There is also a close relationship with elements of the Urban Programme, through the Community Refurbishment Scheme. For instance in 1986/7, the Unit liaison with the Manpower Services Commission (MSC) to promote Community Refurbishment Schemes (CRS) on estates with high unemployment. In that year the MSC provided £454,000, with Estate Action contributing £456,000 of targeted Urban Programme support. It should also be noted that Estate Action funding is made available in the form of Supplementary Credit Approvals in the first year of a scheme, and mainly in the form of Basic Credit Approvals for subsequent years. Moreover, allocation works on the 'matching' concept:

> 'Local authorities will be expected to demonstrate their commitment to tackling the problems of their worst estates by maximising their contribution from their own resources, such as main HIP and/or capital receipts. Local authorities will also be expected to have taken all practicable steps to secure private sector investment. The general aim is for 50% of the total cost of the project to be resourced by the local authority' (DoE, 1991).

Naturally this results in an ever-increasing concentration of other urban resources (particularly HIP and UP).

**2  Data analysis**

Estate Action is a competitive national programme with no specified inner city objective, though experience shows that in practice around 75% of resources are allocated to the UPAs. Certainly the figures suggest Estate Action is less 'targeted' than when the programme was initiated in 1986/7 (in 1985/86 UHRU made many consultative visits to estates but had no specific budget). Figure A9 shows a slight decline in the percentage of resources made available to UPAs from just below 80% to a little under 75% in 1989/90. Within the 123 sample, UPAs get a much larger slice per authority than competitors in the 'near miss' group, or the remainder of the sample. If one examines the trajectories of the lines in Figure A10, the average for the sample is represented by the second line from the top. While it is fairly obvious that large UP authorities with many council estates will obtain funding above the sample average, over the life of EA the UP line has risen more steeply than the average, while both the 40 'marginals' and the 26 'comparators' have flattened out, effectively lagging behind. In other words, while the '123' has fractionally declined in its share of the national cake, the UPAs still dominate within our sample. This reflects the fact that there may be little to choose in terms of problem estates between places we have chosen for the '123' and those we have excluded.

There does seem to have been an emerging regional pattern over the period 1986/7 to 1989/90, with regional per authority averages having been pulled further apart, particularly since 1987/88. Even if one disregards the negligible contributions of the South East, East Anglia and the South West, there has been an increasingly broad spread between the top six regions. Since 1987/88, the North West has had the highest regional average, and, of the six regions which received some money at the programme's inception, the East Midlands has risen least steeply in the subsequent period. The most striking pattern has been the rise of the West Midlands's regional average from about £0.5m in 1987/88 to £1.6m in 1989/90.

It should be noted that at the time this report was written no figures were available for the period beyond 1989/90.

**References**

DoE (1986), *Urban Housing Renewal Unit Annual Report 1985-86*, HMSO, London.
DoE (1991), *New Life for Local Authority Estates: Estate Action Guidelines*, HMSO, London.

*Figure A9*  **Estate Action expenditure**

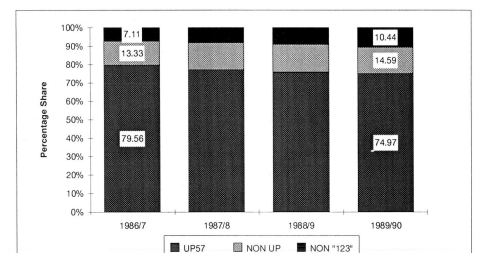

*Figure A10*  **Estate Action - mean expenditure per authority 1986-90**

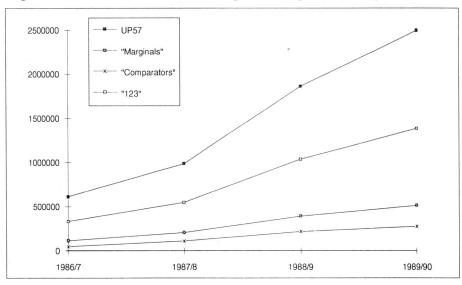

# A4 RATE/REVENUE SUPPORT GRANT

**1 Programme background**

Rate/Revenue Support Grant (RSG) is the main means by which central government underpins local authority mainstream expenditure and it constitutes the main source of local authority revenue. While RSG spending does not fall under the Action for Cities heading, the fact that RSG is calculated partly on the basis of local needs means that it may be skewed somewhat towards 'inner city' authorities.

**2 Data definitions**

The figures for Rate/Revenue Support Grant were obtained direct from DoE, and cover the period from 1977 to 1992. There are many problems involved with interpreting these statistics, some of which are outlined below. The two main changes during this period have been the alterations to the system of local government finance, and also the abolition of the Metropolitan counties in 1986.

There have been three systems of grant support during the period of study, and comparisons across the boundaries of these periods need to be treated with caution. These can be summarised thus:

- 1977-81 consisting of three elements: a Needs element; a Resources element; and a Domestic element.

- 1981-90 when there was a block grant, and a domestic element renamed Domestic Rate Relief Grant.

- 1990 onwards, since when a unitary payment called Revenue Support Grant has existed.

Initially, we collected figures for English districts. This turned out not to be satisfactory, due to the structure and functions of English local government since reorganisation. The two-tier system means that many districts are responsible for certain low-level services such as street cleaning, leisure facilities, and so on. The more strategic services are planned and provided by the upper tier, the County, which used to charge a precept to each district for Social Services, Education, Highways, Police and Fire, etc. Since sums in excess of 70% of the County budget are spent in providing services for the districts, it would be distorting reality to exclude grants to Counties from Central Government. In other words, some basis of apportionment was necessary in order to take account of upper- tier funding.

Various possibilities were available, but none is very satisfactory. Advice from the DoE suggested that the use of per- capita allocation was too crude, and that reapportioning on the basis of rateable value was a better alternative. This, however, seemed inappropriate to the Needs/Resources/Block elements, which are calculated on the basis of need. Since education expenditure forms such a large percentage of upper tier expenditure, the apportionment was eventually made on the following basis:

- 60% according to the number of 5-16 year olds in each district,

- 30% according to the total population of each district,

- 10% based on the proportion of overcrowded households and lone female parents in each district.

**3 Data analysis**

Figure A11 shows the relative shares of RSG taken by the different groups. In the late 1970s, the 57 UPAs accounted for a large and rising amount of overall RSG resources. This appears to have peaked in 1979/80, before dropping sharply in 1981/2. This can be explained by one of the changes there has been in the system of local government finance (see above section). The changes from needs/resources to a single block grant are widely considered to have worked in favour of shire counties and to the disadvantage of the metropolitan authorities, who are disproportionately represented in the UPAs (Travers 1986). Under the new system the UP authorities slowly regained this lost ground, apparently at the expense of those outside the 123 LAs, while the share of the marginals and comparators remained relatively stable. Figure A12 bears this out, showing that the UPAs doubled their RSG in cash terms between 1981 and 1990.

**Reference**

Travers, T. (1986), *The Politics of Local Government Finance*, Allen and Unwin, London.

*Figure A12* **Resources in the '123'**

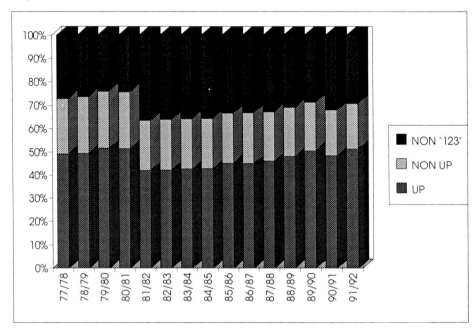

*Figure A11* **Share of RSG resources in England**

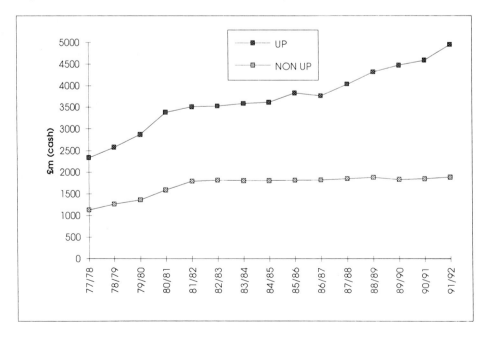

# A5  HOUSING CORPORATION

**1  Programme background**

The Housing Corporation provides funding for a range of housing providers, including housing associations and co-ops. Much of the Housing Corporation activity is focused geographically on areas of housing stress which, since 1990-91, has been defined as the 57 UPAs. Housing Corporation expenditure on supporting housing associations is covered by the Action for Cities heading.

**2  Data definitions**

We were unable to obtain figures from the Housing Corporation which were based on actual expenditure for completed projects. Given the wide variations in the take-up of money allocated to construction projects, and the slippage that often occurs during their completion, these data were too unreliable to be of much analytical use. However, we did feel that an output measure based on numbers of dwellings would be helpful as an index of activity in this sphere. Although an output measure is not really comparable to inputs measured as pounds of expenditure, it is consistent over time and free from the problems of price changes. The data for new builds were therefore obtained from the government publication Housebuilding in England by Local Authority Areas 1980 to 1989, with figures for renovations supplied separately from DoE. In the case of new build, we have used the figure for 'number of dwellings started'. Prior to 1981, the figures were not produced in a comparable format, therefore all our analysis concerns the period from 1981 to 1990.

**3  Data analysis**

Figure A13 shows that there are striking differences between the two main types of Housing Corporation project within the 123 authorities. The number of new builds rose by almost half between 1981 and 1982, and then fell back to their original level by 1985. The number of new builds rose again in 1986, decreased the following year and then remained stable, ending the decade at much the same level as it had started. The pattern for rehabilitations is more accentuated and more volatile. Between 1981 and 1982 the number of renovations funded by the Corporation nearly doubled, reaching more than 1200. Although this dropped slightly in the following year, there was another increase of around 40% in 1984, which proved to be the peak for this form of housing policy. After this, there was a sharp fall in the number of rehabs, which then flattened, before continuing a more gradual decline. In 1990, the number of HAG-assisted rehabs was less than half the level of 1981.

Figures A14 and A15 show the same information split by the sub-groups within the 123. Broadly speaking, these reflect the overall trends for the larger sample. In general, however, it is fair to say that the UPAs follow the pattern of the 123 particularly closely. The other two sub-groups are more static and at a lower level. In other words, most of the variation over time within the 123 is caused by changes within the 57 UPAs.

Obviously, the timing of construction projects means that yearly classification is somewhat arbitrary, and this means one needs to be cautious with any interpretations. It seems fairly clear that Housing Corporation renovations were extremely fashionable in the early 1980s, but then declined and gave way to new build as the principal form of Housing Corporation provision. This could be due either to the exhaustion of all available stock suitable for renovation, or to a change of policy direction in favour of new build, or both these factors could have been at work.

*Figure A13* Housing Corporation activity in the '123'

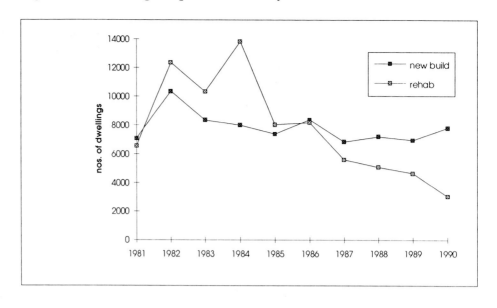

*Figure A14* Housing Corporation new builds in the '123'

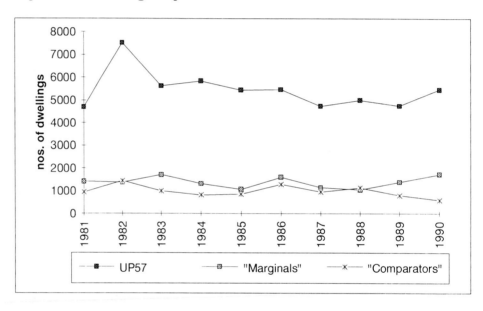

*Figure A15* Housing Corporation rehabs in the '123'

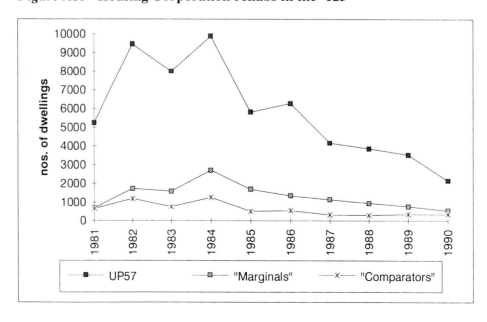

# A6 CITY ACTION TEAMS

**1 Programme background**

City Action Teams are designed to act as a co-ordinating mechanism for the range of urban policy initiatives provided under the auspices of the departments of trade and industry, environment, employment and the Training Agency. In addition to this co-ordinating role, CATs also have small budgets which may be used to fund specific initiatives, often in conjunction with other bodies such as government departments, local authorities and the voluntary and private sectors. At their inception in 1986/87, CAT activity was confined to the then partnership authorities, but subsequently they have been allowed to cross-cut formal boundaries where this was deemed appropriate. In practice, however, almost all CAT activity is confined to the inner areas of UPAs.

**2 Data definitions**

The data were drawn together from the various CATs and collated by Mr Brian Wilson at DoE. The dataset covers all years in which the various CATs had a budget of their own. It has not always been possible for the figures to be broken down between constituent boroughs and districts. This does not pose too serious a problem, given the relatively small sums of money involved.

**3 Data analysis**

Figure A16 shows that there is little discernible pattern, as different CATs have come on stream at different points in time. One footnote to the chart is to recognise that the 1988/89 figure for Tyne and Wear includes £2,525,000 for an additional package of expenditure in Sunderland only.

*Figure A16*  **Expenditure by City Action teams**

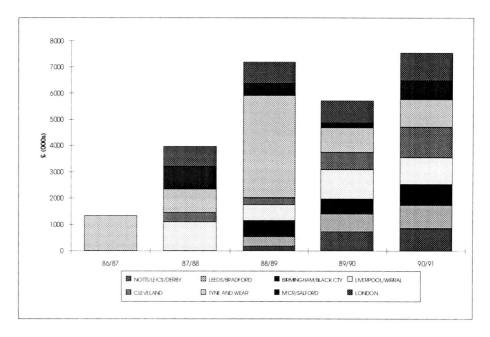

# A7  SECTION 11 GRANT

**1  Programme background**

Section 11 of the Local Government Act 1966 remains the only legislation specifically geared towards the provision of extra funding for local government services for ethnic minorities. More than four fifths of total S11 expenditure goes towards education staff costs, with the next largest recipient being social services. There has also been some funding for local authority staff secondment to voluntary organisations (Johnson *et al*, 1989:371).

Section 11 grant currently is paid by the Home Office at the rate of 75% of salary costs, with the rest funded by local authorities. Eligibility for grant is assessed on grounds of additionality, special need and community consultation. Despite the additionality requirement, however, many local authorities have used S11 funds to compensate for cuts to mainstream service programmes. This was especially true prior to the abolition of funding-by-formula in 1983/84 (Johnson *et al*, 1989:372).

S11 is also of interest in that until 1990 (following the Home Office review of 1988) it was one of the few government programmes not to be cash limited.

S11 has a clear spatial dimension in that it is concerned with 'ensuring that resources are directed towards the needs of ethnic minorities arising from racial disadvantage, particularly in the inner-cities' (Home Office, 1988, quoted in Johnson *et al*, 1989:372). S11 expenditure is included in Action for Cities expenditure.

**2  Data analysis**

Partly because it is related to differing local authority demands, Johnson *et al* (1989:378) point towards the strong variation across authorities in terms of the use of S11 funding, ranging from targeted racial equality strategies to straightforward substitution for cuts in mainstream programmes. This variability may be attributed to the lack of any clear guidance from the Home Office on the purpose of S11 grant prior to the review undertaken in 1988. Indeed, Johnson *et al* (p378) argue that Home Office advice itself evolved from existing local authority practice.

The inconsistency in terms of the use of S11 funding is apparently matched by variation in cash allocations to authorities. Lambeth and Newham, for example, spent £3.7m and £26.6m respectively during the period 1979/80-1989/90, despite having similar populations (246,000 and 209,000 at 1981 census) and similar ethnic compositions in 1981 (23.5% and 26.6%). However, this and other apparent anomalies can be explained by the fact that metropolitan LAs (e.g. Newham, Bradford) are Local Education Authorities (LEAs), while non-metropolitan and inner-London LAs (e.g. Leicester, Blackburn, Lambeth in the period before 1990) are not. The bulk of S11 expenditure is on education and is channelled through the LEA. This explains why, for example, Lambeth's S11 grant increased from £456,000 in 1989/90 to £1.47m in the following year when it became an LEA. Similarly, it explains the higher allocations for Bradford than for Blackburn and Leicester, and for Newcastle than for Stoke, despite their similarly-sized ethnic minority populations.

Even allowing for the fact that some LAs have acted as LEAs and some have not, there is still considerable variation in S11 spending levels between LAs (Johnson *et al*, 1989: 378). A number of factors help, in part, to explain this. These include; the political complexion of the local authority, the health of the local economy, the definition of need, the Asian/Afro-Caribbean mix (though the Leicester-Bradford contrast calls this into question), the degree of urbanisation of the authority, the spatial concentration of ethnic groups and the degree of racial unrest. Until 1983/84, when payments under formula were abandoned, the rate of increase of S11 expenditure amongst authorities in the 123 outstripped inflation. At 1981/2 prices, expenditure under the S11 heading increased from £33.6m in 1979/80 to £53.3m in 1983/4 (see Figure A17). As concern rose in the mid-'80s over the unfocused and capricious ways in which large sums of S11 money had been used by local authorities (Johnson et al, 1989:373), funding fell in real terms to £46.9m in 1984/5 and £47.7m in 1985/6. Thereafter, expenditure climbed and remained fairly steady in real terms from 1986/7 onwards, but still at a much higher level than at the beginning of the decade.

Figure A18 shows the variation in expenditure by region over the 1979/80 - 1989/90 period. (The numbers shown on the bars in Figure A18 show the number of LAs in each region of the sample of 123 which received S11 funding.) The predictable dominance of London is less pronounced in terms of the average expenditure per authority in each region. The average of the seven West Midlands authorities for the 1979/80 period is approaching £25m, whereas for London the average expenditure among 24 authorities is just over £10m. Again, however, this can largely be explained by the differing LEA structure of these regions, with large amounts of S11 expenditure in inner London having been channelled through ILEA and therefore missed by the dataset.

The time-series pattern for the regions shows how all have maintained an upward trend since 1979/80 (Figure A19). Amongst the big-spending regions (North West, Yorks/Humber, West Midlands and London), expenditure by the 24 London authorities is least steady. In particular, the decline of expenditure in London from 1983/4 -1984/5 is most pronounced. In fact, despite the abandonment of payments under formula at that time, expenditure in Yorks/ Humber and the Northwest actually rose. In total, 41 of the 57 UPAs received S11 funding from the Home Office between 1979 and 1990. The number of UPAs receiving funding increased from 34 in 1979/80 to 40 by 1985/6 and 41 thereafter. Both total and average funding for the UPAs has been higher than for the marginals which in turn has been higher than for the comparator authorities in the 123 sample. Indeed, that differential has increased over time. As Figure A20 shows, the increase in expenditure amongst UPAs has outstripped that of marginals or comparators. The dip in expenditure from 1983/4 - 1984/5 is most striking for the UPAs, which appear to have borne the brunt of the abandonment of payment under formula.

**References**

Home Office (1988), 'Brent S11 grant scheme to be monitored', press release, 20th May

Home Office (1990), 'S11 Grant administration proposals'

Johnson, M., Cox, B., and Cross. M., (1989), 'Paying for change?: Section 11 and local authority social services', *New Community*, 15, 371-90

*Figure A17*  **Section 11 Grant at constant 1981/82 prices for the '123'**

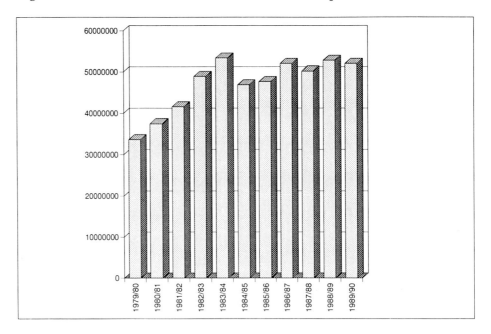

*Figure A18*  **Mean Section 11 Grant by region 1979-90**

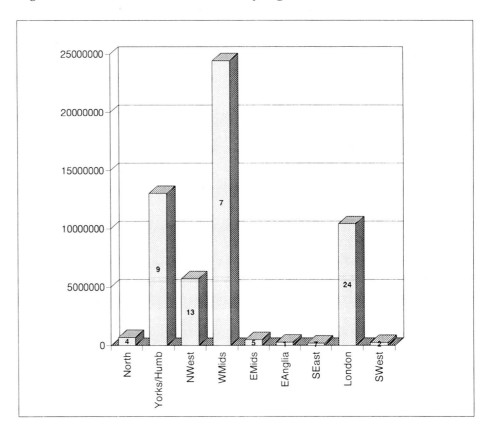

*Figure A19* **Section 11 funding by region**

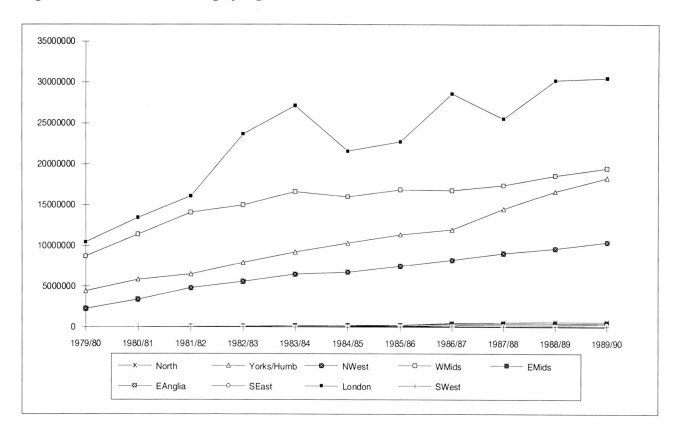

*Figure A20* **Section 11 Grant by LAD type**

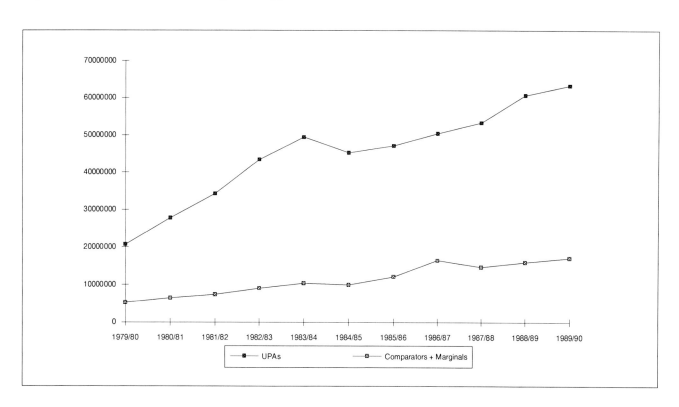

## A8  ETHNIC MINORITY BUSINESS INITIATIVE

**1  Programme background**

EMBI is a national programme, established in September 1985, with the twin objectives of encouraging ethnic minority entrepreneurship, and providing ethnic minority communities with business development services which offer a more accessible alternative to conventional agencies.

EMBI has three separate strands:

(i)   Five core enterprise agencies (EAs), funded jointly by the Home Office, local authorities and the private sector, and targeted at areas with sizeable ethnic minority populations. EMBI funding is earmarked for central administrative costs; none goes directly to ethnic minority businesses. Funding for the EAs comes from a variety of sources apart from EMBI funding, including Section 11 grants, finance from TECs (e.g. Ethnic Minority Grant), Task Forces and City Action Teams, and internal income generation (for example, fees from training seminars).

(ii)  Funding mainly outreach posts in a small number of mainstream enterprise agencies - after 1986/87 there was a shift in policy towards funding projects in existing mainstream enterprise agencies and other business advisory services. These are engaged in a wide range of activities, so it is difficult to disentangle their 'ethnic minority' efforts from their wider activities. This could have important conceptual and methodological implications for any output measures available (see below).

(iii) Between August 1989 and January 1992, funding and oversight of the Ethnic Minority Business Development Team (EMBDT), comprising secondees from Barclays and NatWest banks, Employment Department, DTI, Shell UK and others. Its functions were to help existing institutions such as TECs to address ethnic minority business issues; to improve the responsiveness of financial institutions to ethnic minority business needs; and to disperse good practice (for example, local purchasing schemes). Development Team activity was not always targeted spatially at inner-city areas. Funding amounted to £25,000 in 1989/90 and £75,000 in 1990/91, including some salary costs. The Development Team was time-limited and closed in January 1992.

While EMBI is not geographically targeted in any formal sense, the geography of ethnic minority communities means that, in practice, a large proportion of EMBI expenditure is directed towards inner areas. All five of the EMBI-supported enterprise agencies fall within the group of 57 UPAs, as do three of the five EMBI-funded outreach workers attached to other enterprise agencies (the exceptions being Ealing and Oxford).

**2  Data availability**

Input data

Expenditure data are available only for local enterprise agencies, several of which cover more than one local authority area. There were two potential ways of obviating this problem:

(i)   Divide the EA EMBI allocations by the number of LAs which they cover. Of course, the figures thus yielded would be purely nominal, with no way of identifying precisely what money went where. One solution would be to divide the EA sum according to a particular characteristic of the LAs. Ideally, the control variable would be the number of ethnic minority businessmen in each LA, though a viable option would be the proportion of ethnic minorities present in each LA.

(ii) Contact individually the four EAs which cover more than one LA to ascertain how their budgets were divided amongst the LAs. Initial indications from North London Business Development Agency suggested that this would be difficult. Indeed, in the case of the British Refugee Council, based in Lambeth, it would be impossible to disaggregate their spending totals.

An altogether more fundamental problem concerns the interpretation of expenditure by EAs. If EMBI funding is construed as input data, then expenditure by the EAs would constitute output data. If one accepts this argument (as seems reasonable), then it is not possible conceptually to disaggregate EMBI expenditure fully, other than in the purely nominal sense outlined in (i).

Output data

Output measures are collected for the five main Home Office funded EAs, each of which is asked to submit standardised forms on an annual basis. These include comprehensive information on:

- number of enquiries made

- number of clients (new/existing, male/female, ethnic origin, start-ups/existing businesses)

- number of counselling sessions held

- number of businesses assisted (start-ups/existing)

- survival rates

- number of jobs created/saved

- finance for clients (from financial institutions, central government, local authorities, EAs)

- agency support funds (grants/loans)

- private sector support (cash, donations, secondments)

- income generating activities

- training (number and type of courses, number of students, performance of students).

But while the data produced should be comprehensive, in practice there have been some problems with data collection, with resulting disruptions to time series.

For the EAs and other advisory services which fall outside the core funding programme, EMBI finance extends usually to the funding of an outreach post within the agency. In this case, HO monitoring is conducted from quarterly reports submitted by the agency. These reports are not standardised, reflecting the objectives and targets set for each individual post and the particular social circumstances, making cross-comparison difficult.

## 3 Data analysis

Total programme expenditure is shown in Figure A21. Figure A22 illustrates the variation across EAs in terms of average annual EMBI allocations. However, this does not take into account the fact that four of the EAs/advisory services cover a number of LAs.

One apparently interesting feature is the lack of funding for some of the five core EAs. Bristol Black Business Association, for example, receives less than South London Business Initiative, even though the latter's funding allocation is intended only to cover the cost of an outreach post. However, this can be explained by the fact that the five main black-led agencies (of which Bristol is one) receive substantial funds from other sources, utilising, for example, Section 11 Grant and the new Ethnic Minority Grant to meet salary costs. EMBI funding for mainstream business support services normally covers the costs of specific posts, sometimes using money from other sources.

**Reference**          Ward, R., R. Randall and P. Wilson (1989), *Evaluation of the Ethnic Minority Business Initiative: Final Report*, Nottingham: Trent Polytechnic

*Figure A21* **EMBI: total annual expenditure**

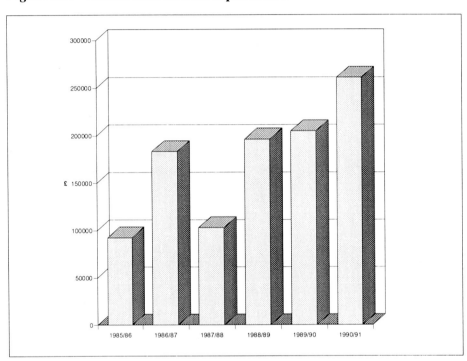

*Figure A22* **Enterprise Agencies - average annual EMBI allocations**

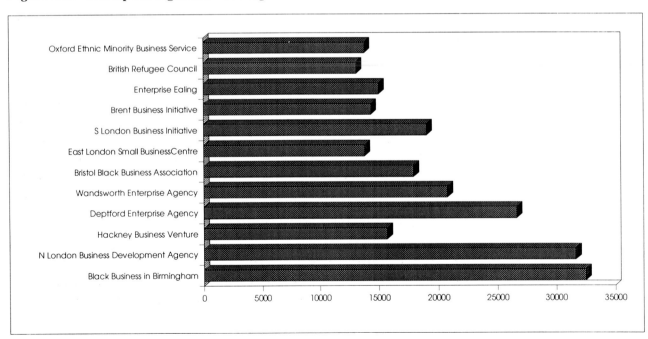

## A9    TASK FORCES

**1   Programme background**

Task Forces were launched in 1986 by the DTI under its Inner Cities Initiative, with the aim of boosting economic opportunities in inner city areas and assessing how best this might be achieved through existing government programmes. The areas targeted for Task Force support were chosen on the basis of high rates of long term unemployment, industrial development potential and the size and needs of constituent ethnic minority communities. All designated Task Forces fall within the group of 57 UPAs, and cover particular parts therein.

**2   Data availability**

Input data

Total expenditure figures are available, broken down into funding contributions by Task Force, by other public authorities, private sector and others (voluntary sector). The only significant caveats are, firstly, that in the period prior to the establishment of a computerised project monitoring system in 1989/90, there may be some under-counting of both input and output data. Fortunately, the only exception to this is expenditure falling under the Task Force heading. Secondly, the information contained on the computerised database is subject to constant revision as Task Forces update their records on a monthly basis. As a consequence, the data presented here constitute a 'snapshot' of Task Force expenditure and may be subject to minor revisions in future.

Output data

Under headings: jobs, training and business.

**3   Data analysis**

Inputs

The change in funding composition over time is shown by Figure A23. The main feature apparent is the virtual stability, in relative terms, of the proportions of public, private and Task Force funding sources.

Within the total of public expenditure in Task Force areas, it is not possible to say what proportion of this is new money. Although it may not be possible to generalise, evidence from DTI (1991) suggests that 50% (£12.8M) of public expenditure in Handsworth, Doncaster and Rochdale was new money. Of this new cash, £9.7M was directly attributable to the Task Forces, with only £3.1M in extra cash resulting from the bending of other government expenditure towards the Task Force areas.

Outputs

Figure A24 show that the number of Task Force funded projects increased year on year (with the exception of 1988/89 - 1989/90) over the programme's duration, reaching almost 900 by 1990/91. At the same time, the cost per project fell steadily from around £140,000 in 1986/87 to less than £60,000 in 1990/91 (see Figure A25). With total funding having been subject to a general upward trend (see Figure A23), this suggests that Task Forces have been funding a larger number of smaller projects. At the same time, the cost per job created by Task Force funding has increased over time (see Figure A26). While Figure A26 also shows that there was considerable variation in the cost per unit output (that is, the combined total of jobs, training and business outputs), it should be noted that there will have been a high degree of double counting and inter-correlation between output indicators. For example, money allocated for business support could also be beneficial in job terms.

Figure A27 shows the pattern of spending across Task Force areas. These totals include Task Force funding as well as other public expenditure diverted towards Task Force areas, and associated private and voluntary sector spending.

The graph shows the total expenditure over the whole duration of each of the Task Forces. Spending in Rochdale and Wolverhampton appears to rely heavily on Task Force funding. Doncaster and Middlesbrough rely heavily on private sector money, both in absolute and relative terms.

Figure A28 shows the leverage figures for each of the Task Forces. They vary from under 0.1 for Derby (which had only been running for one year) to around 0.9 in North Kensington and Doncaster. Overall, the leverage ratios increased from 1:0.26 in 1986/87 to around 1:0.45 from 1987/88 - 1988/89, before falling to 1:0.37 in 1990/91. This compares with DTI(1991) finding that every £1 of Task Force expenditure managed to lever £0.49 of private expenditure in Handsworth, Doncaster and Rochdale.

**References**

DTI (1990), *Task Forces in Action*, London: DTI
DTI (1990b), *Task Forces: an assessment - Leicester, Preston and Wolverhampton*, London: DTI
DTI (1991), *An evaluation of the government's inner cities Task Force initiative: Summary report*, London: DTI

*Figure A23* **Task Forces: change in funding composition**

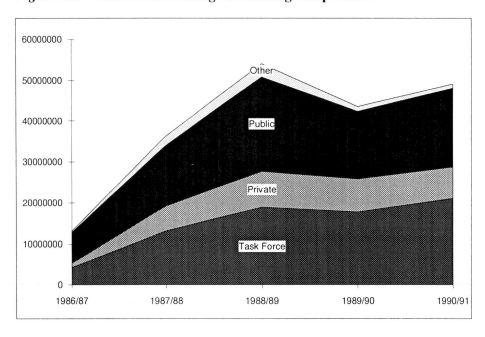

*Figure A24*   Number of projects - change over time

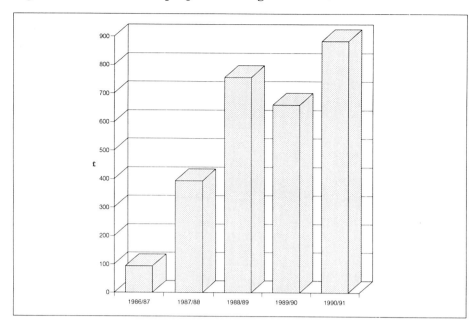

*Figure A25*   Task Forces: cost per project

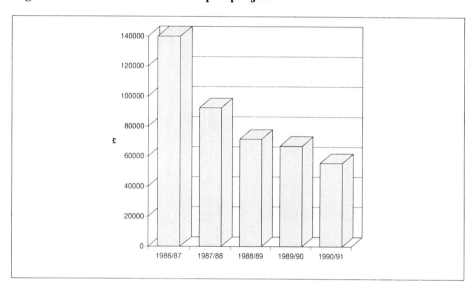

*Figure 26*   Task Forces: Cost per unit output

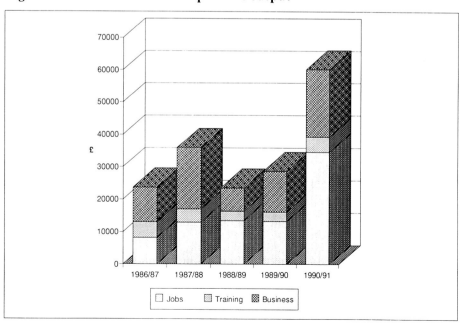

*Figure 27*   **Composition of funding for each Task Force**

*Figure 28*   **Leverage ratio (Task Force: Private)**

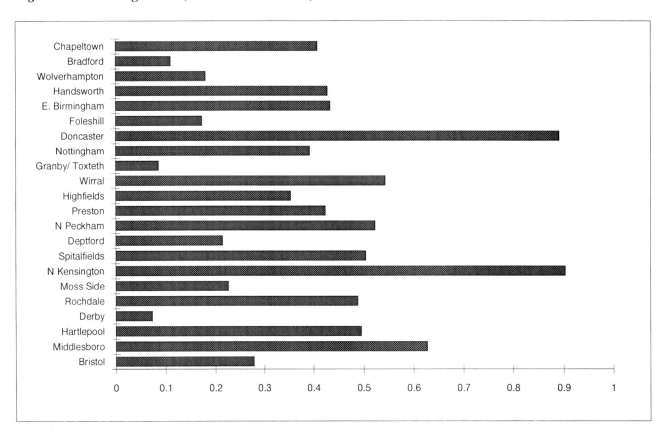

## A10   ET AND YTS

**1   Programme background**

Employment Training is intended to provide a broad range of training opportunities for longer-term unemployed people, as well as people with special training needs such as 'women returners', people with learning difficulties, ex-offenders and those requiring hi-tech skills lacking in the labour market. ET does have something of an inner city dimension in that a disproportionately large number of such groups are located in inner areas. According to departmental estimates, around half (48%) of all ET entrants in England were resident in the 57 UPAs.

Youth Training (formerly YTS) is designed to provide training to NVQ level II for 16-17 year olds, and, since the transfer of responsibility for the programme to Training and Enterprise Councils (TECs), to other age groups, at the discretion of YT mangers. While there is no specific commitment to spatial targeting, the higher levels of youth unemployment in inner areas means there will inevitably be some degree of geographical variation in YT expenditure.

**2   Data availability**

Expenditure data

ET - expenditure data are generally not available at LA level. Prior to the establishment of TECs in 1990/91, expenditure data were based around Training Agency Area Office boundaries, which followed county council or metropolitan district boundaries. In other words, data are available only for 46 of the 57 UPAs.

Expenditure at Area Office level is available for 1988/89 and 1989/90, and at TEC level for 1990/91. However, the 1988/89 data are of poor quality since this period covered the beginning of ET in September 1988, and the gradual wind-down of the Community Programme, Job Training Scheme and Voluntary Projects Programme. ET expenditure in 1988/89 is under-estimated since wages paid to CP participants who continued under ET were defined as CP expenditure, even though part of their funding was derived from the ET budget.

In 1990/91, expenditure ceased to be based around Area Offices as TECs gradually came on stream. Given that TECs were established in a series of batches over a number of months, the position for 1990/91 is also somewhat cloudy. In addition, there is a further problem with accessing TEC data in that there are many more TECs than Area Offices, with the effect that the new boundaries rarely coincide with LAs.

At LA scale, then, expenditure data are available only for 46 authorities and only for the single financial year 1989/90.

For YTS, again, expenditure data are available only at Area Office/TEC scale for the period 1988/89 to 1990/91.

Output data

Follow-up surveys are conducted for ET and YT leavers. Forms include a postal code reference for each respondent, which allows the Employment Department to aggregate totals to LA level.

For YTS, output data (number of starts and numbers in training) are available at LA level from 1982/3 to 1989/90. However, ET data are calculated only at TEC level, with all the attendant problems outlined earlier. While the follow-up survey is supposed to cover 100% of YTS leavers, in practice the response rate may be lower than 30% in some areas.

**3  Data analysis**

Although YTS data goes back to 1982/3, it was not until 1984/5 that any significant number of placements began (see Figure A29). For the sample of 123 authorities, the number of YTS starts climbed from 110,000 in 1984/5 to 196,000 in 1985/6, before falling steadily to 125,000 by 1989/90. This peak in YTS starts coincides with the peak for unemployment (all ages).

In 1984/5, there were 7 starts per 100 unemployed people. This figure rose to 11 the following year (when unemployment peaked), before falling to 10 per 100 as the level of unemployment fell. However, the figure rose to 11 in 1988/89 and 13 in 1989/90, even though unemployment continued to fall. This may be explained in part by the restriction of benefit entitlement for 16/17 year olds, introduced in September 1988 in line with the guaranteed offer of a YTS place (Lawlor, 1990:603).

**Regional pattern**

The number of YTS starts over the 1982/3 - 1989/90 period varies from 411 in Kensington and Chelsea to 48,551 in Birmingham. When the number of starts is expressed in relation to LA size, a clearer pattern begins to emerge. The most striking feature is the concentration of London authorities among those which have provided a low number of starts relative to numbers in the 15-19 age group. Sixteen of the eighteen worst performing LAs on this measure are London authorities. Indeed, all but one of the London authorities (Islington, which is 59th worst of 123) are contained in the 31 worst performing authorities. This pattern is confirmed by Figure A30, which shows the number of starts by region as a proportion of numbers unemployed in each region. On average, between 1984 and 1990 London authorities provided only 3 YTS places per 100 people unemployed (all ages). Seventeen of the 20 poorest performing authorities are in London. The best performing London authority is Redbridge, which provided, on average, 8 YTS places per 100 unemployed people.

Interpreting the relatively low level of YTS placements in London is problematic. It may well be that the London labour market(s) is more dynamic and able to soak up large numbers of 'young people' in the service sector. Historically, the turnover of, and demand for, labour (especially 'young' and short-term labour) has been high in London, with the effect that there has been a relatively low demand for YTS places. This is confirmed in a report by the Institute of Manpower Studies (IMS, 1990), which found that the contrasting 'north:south' pattern of local labour market conditions was matched by differences in the ways, and extent to which, YTS was used, both by employers and young people. IMS (1990: 15) found that employer participation rates in YTS during 1988 were lowest for London, where less than 10% of companies were involved with YTS. It seems, then, that lack of demand for YTS is the principal explanation for the low number of starts, rather than any problem on the policy-side such as a failure to deliver sufficient YTS places.

**LA-type pattern**

Figure A31 shows the distribution of YT starts amongst the three LA categories. In broad terms, the UPAs retained a similar share of YTS starts over the whole period.

**References**

Institute of Manpower Studies (1990), 'Regional variation in the development of Youth Training', *Manpower Commentary*, No. 45, IMS.
Lawlor, J. (1990), 'Monthly unemployment statistics: maintaining a consistent series', *Employment Gazette* 98, December 1990, 590-600.

*Figure A29* **Annual number of YT starts for the '123'**

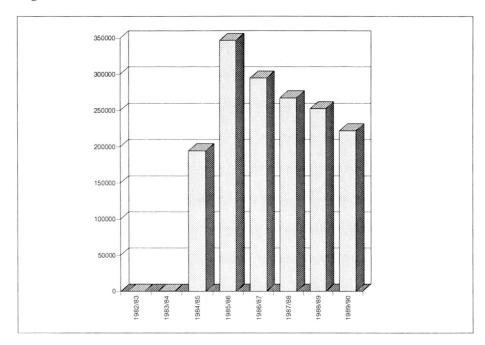

*Figure A30* **Starts as a % of unemployment (all ages) by region (average 1984-90)**

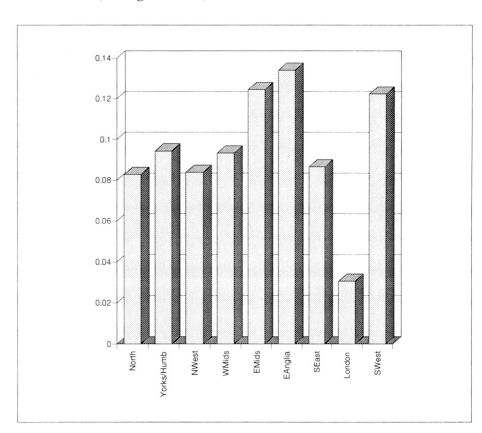

**Figure A31  Number of YT/YTS starts by LAD-type**

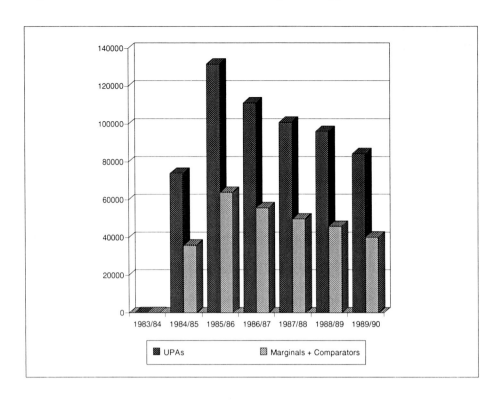

## A11  ENGLISH ESTATES

**1  Programme background**

English Estates is a DTI agency designed to manage an industrial and commercial land and property portfolio. It runs a number of programmes with substantial resources, but only one of these - the Managed Workspace Programme (MWP), launched in 1988 - is geared specifically towards inner areas. MWP is intended to provide managed industrial and commercial accommodation in inner city areas. However, the resources allocated to MWP are slim by comparison with overall English Estates expenditure, so all EE expenditure is included in this analysis.

**2  Data definitions**

Capital expenditure figures are available by LA from 1985/86 - 1990/91. This includes all expenditure by English Estates, although separate totals are available for the managed workspace programme (MWP). There is also a range of output measures available by LA and covering the same time period. These include number of units and floorspace, broken down into premises which are leased, not leased, reserved and available to let.

There are three significant caveats attached to the dataset. First, it should be noted that the expenditure and output data may be out of kilter. Output of statistics include information on development carried out before the start date of the financial data. Secondly, some expenditure does not have any physical results and therefore will not be echoed in the output data. Thirdly, expenditure on a particular development may be spread across several years, with the effect that it is impossible directly to compare expenditure with the physical appearance of units.

The managed workspace programme is English Estates' specific commitment to inner-city areas. It emerged following pressure in the mid-'80s for English Estates to devise a targeted inner-city programme. The result was MWP which, so far, has been limited to four authorities, Derby, Manchester, Lewisham and Kensington, with a total of five sets of sites.

Given the relatively small scale of the managed workspace programme, for the purposes of analysis, expenditure under this heading has been combined with the overall totals of English Estates expenditure.

The dataset includes figures for Rochester-upon-Medway, where English Estates embarked on a special programme to compensate for the rundown of Chatham dockyard. It should be noted that spending in Rochester accounts for a large proportion of EE expenditure, especially in the marginal and comparator authorities for 1989/90 and 1990/91.

**3  Data analysis**

Figure A32 shows English Estates expenditure for the 123 (including MWP money and expenditure in Chatham). It is clear that the share of English Estates money going to UPAs has remained relatively steady over time. The proportion going to UPAs is lowest in 1988/89 and 1990/91, but this is largely a result of the extra money going to Rochester (Chatham) which was additional to English Estates' other expenditure.

*Table A1*   **Managed workspace - capital expenditure**

|  |  | **1988/89** | **1989/90** | **1990/91** |
|---|---|---|---|---|
| Derby | Land | 0 | 40600 | 1353 |
|  | Works | 272633 | 109471 | 1804816 |
| Manchester | Land | 0 | 0 | 22849 |
|  | Works | 160138 | 130356 | 1098826 |
| Lewisham | Land | 0 | 0 | 2185188 |
|  | Works | 0 | 0 | 2000000 |
| Kensington | Land | 0 | 0 | 2800000 |
|  | Works | 0 | 0 | 0 |

*Table A2*   **English estates expenditure in Rochester-upon-Medway and Gillingham**

| **1985/86** | **1986/87** | **1987/88** | **1988/89** | **1989/90** | **1990/91** |
|---|---|---|---|---|---|
| 1,006,027 | 1,921,974 | 1,574,356 | 11,343,469 | 3,631,611 | 11,507,951 |

*Figure A32*   **English Estates - expenditure by LAD-type**

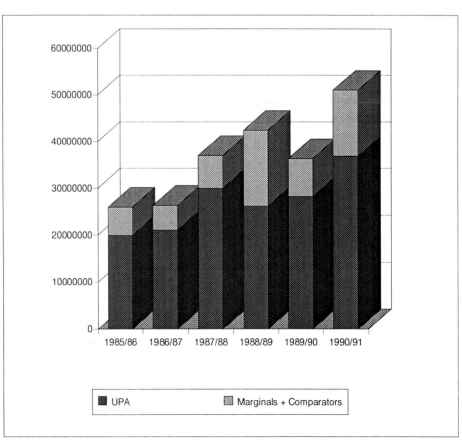

# A12   REGIONAL SELECTIVE ASSISTANCE

**1  Programme background**

Regional Selective Assistance (RSA) is provided to firms in the 'Assisted Areas' of Great Britain under Section 7 of the Industry Act 1982 (formerly the Industry Act 1972). Section 7 states that the objective of the scheme was 'to provide, maintain or safeguard employment in any part of the Assisted Areas'. A range of purposes for which assistance can be provided is listed as: promotion of development, modernisation, efficiency, expansion, reorganisation, and orderly contraction of an industry. In July 1979 two new criteria were added: firstly there was an 'additionality' or 'proof of need' criterion, i.e. the grant had to have a real effect on the firm's decision to undertake a project; secondly, the project had to be of benefit to the national economy as well as to the local area, the so-called 'Efficiency' criterion. The other criteria were; viability, employment link (i.e. the grant will lead to the creation of additional employment or safeguard existing employment), and the greater part of the cost of the project should be met by the firm or by sources outside the public sector.

The analysis conducted by the DTI in 1984 showed that 87% of projects in the 1980-84 period in Great Britain were either new projects or expansions which created employment, with the remainder for modernisation and/or rationalisation which safeguarded employment. However, the proportion of the value of offers made in support of the former type of project was only 72% as the aggregate size of offers in support of projects was less. Also, it is not always simple to distinguish between safeguarding existing jobs and creating new ones. Sectorally, it is no surprise that the vast majority of grants went to manufacturing industries, with only 2% going to the service sector.

There have been changes over the period in the Assisted Areas in England, towards which RSA is directed. Prior to 1979, the Assisted Areas - comprising Special Development Areas (SDAs), Development Areas (DAs), and Intermediate Areas (IAs) - covered the whole of the regions of the North, the North West, and Yorkshire and Humberside, parts of the South West, and the northern fringes of the East and West Midlands. In July 1979, some additional areas in the South West became IAs. In 1982 many areas were downgraded, but status was conferred on Corby. November 1984 saw a major overhaul of the Assisted Areas: SDAs were abolished, DAs were reduced, and IAs were expanded to include the West Midlands. The Assisted Areas were now constrained to the metropolitan areas of the North and North West, and parts of Cornwall, with Corby being an island in the South. These changes in areas are reflected in the patterns of the data.

**2  Data availability**

RSA expenditure is available for the period 1979/80 to 1990/91. Of the 123 LAs for which data were collected, 69 are situated in the Assisted Areas of England, and are therefore eligible for RSA.

**3  Data analysis**

For all areas, for the whole period, RSA expenditure (deflated at 1981/82 prices) begins at a level of £47 million (see Figure A33), and then falls steadily to £33 million in 1984/85, before climbing steeply to a peak of £61 million in 1988/89. The following year sees a small fall, while in 1990/91, spending drops down to a level approaching the early 1980s.

The totals for the whole period by region show that the North region, and to a slightly lesser extent the North West, have received the lion's share of RSA expenditure throughout the 1980s. Yorkshire and Humberside has less than half the North's total and the West Midlands is well below this. The East

Midlands, given that it is represented by the single area of Corby, does well. If one considers the whole time period, year by year, the pattern displayed in Figure A33 is largely repeated, but there are interesting internal variations (Figure A34). The North starts off well below the North West, but does not fall to so deep a trough, and rises steeply to a high peak in 1988/89, well above the North West. Both fall steeply in the final year. Yorkshire and Humberside, by comparison, remains fairly steady over the period, although it peaks steeply in 1988/89. The East Midlands (i.e. Corby) defies the trend and peaks in 1983/84, receiving much smaller grants in the 4 years following, and almost nothing in the first and last few years. The West Midlands began receiving grants in 1984/85. From this point it climbed steeply to levels comparable to the North and North West.

It should be noted that analysis of the data by Urban Type, a method used in other sections of the report, is potentially misleading in respect to RSA. The reason for this is that the major role of RSA is to attract significant inward investment projects which have a beneficial impact on the regional and the national economies, and not specifically to benefit individual urban authorities. This is reinforced when one considers the location of the major RSA funded sites: on 'greenfield' sites outside the inner areas.

*Figure A33* **Regional Selective Assistance: Totals 1979/80 to 1990/91, for the LADs situated in the Assisted Areas of England of the 123 selected**

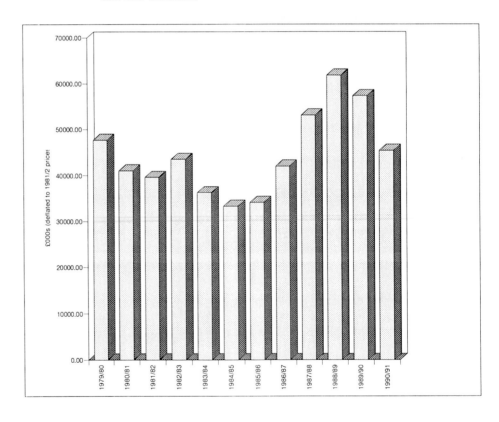

**Figure A34** **Regional Selective Assistance: Totals 1979/80 to 1990/91 by region, for the LADs situated in the Assisted Areas of England of the 123 selected**

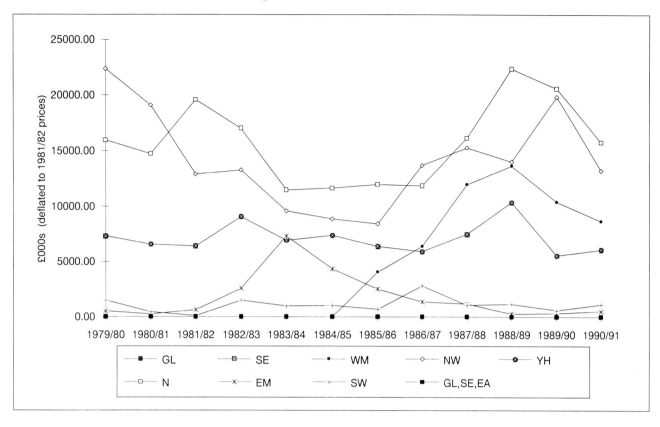

## A13   REGIONAL DEVELOPMENT GRANTS

**1   Programme background**

Regional Development Grant (RDG), like Regional Selective Assistance, operates in the Assisted Areas, although its geographical coverage has altered over time. In 1982 RDG was abolished for Intermediate Areas, and was reduced in Development Areas. The area covered by the Assisted Areas, and as a consequence the areas covered by RDG, have been reduced markedly over the 1980s; the area has been reduced to the old industrial heartlands of the North, the North West and parts of the South West.

RDG is in fact two schemes. RDG I, the original scheme, ran from 1977/78 to 1983/84, with last applications being accepted in November 1984. However, payments are not of a 'once and for all' nature, so money is still being paid out for RDG I. The aim of the second scheme, RDG II, introduced in 1984, was to be project- rather than asset-based, and applications had to include an explicit job creation element. While the original scheme consisted almost entirely of manufacturing industry projects (as with RSA), RDG II, included some service sector based projects. The revised scheme from 1984/85 to 1987/88, with applications closing on 31 March 1988. However, as with RDG I, payments continue to be made to the current year.

**2   Data availability**

The DTI were not able to provide full data for RDGI; only regional data are available from the annual reports compiled under the Industrial Development Act. The data for the period 1979/80 to 1990/91 for RDG I payments of £25,000 or more are published in the DTI journal 'British Business' 1988/89, and in 'Employment Gazette' thereafter. However, constructing a complete data set from these publications would be a hugely time-consuming, if not impossible, task: the RDG I grants are listed by firm using Employment Office Area, not a local authority locational reference. In addition, the number of payments of £25,000 or more for each quarter was until recently very large.

For RDG II, the situation is much more straightforward. Expenditure data are available for the full period, i.e. 1984/85 to 1990/91 for the selected 123 areas. Of these, 28 are situated in Development Areas of England, and were therefore eligible for RDG II.

**3   Data analysis**

Although RDG I expenditure data are not available at Local Authority District level it is important to note that RDG I is a significant source of funding. Over the period 1979/80 to 1990/91, the local authorities from within the 123 that were eligible for RDG I received a total of £1600 million (at 1981/82 prices).

RDG II rises steadily from a very low level in its initial year, 1984/85, to a level of £64m in 1987/88 (Figure A35). Then in 1988/89 there is a massive jump in grants to just under £140m. In the final two years grant levels return to 1987/88 levels.

On a regional basis, the pattern is similar to RSA. The North and the North West dominate, with Yorkshire and Humberside and the East Midlands (Corby) well below. Over time, all the regions begin at much the same level in 1984/85-1985/86 (Figure A36). After this there is a great divergence: the North and the North West climb steeply, while Yorkshire and Humberside and the East Midlands rise at much smaller rate. All regions peak in 1988/89, but the North and especially the North West make massive jumps in this year before falling to their 1987/88 levels by 1989/90.

As with RSA, an analysis by Urban Type for RDG II would not be appropriate, as the major RDG II projects are located outside inner urban areas on 'greenfield' sites.

**Figure A35  Regional Development Grant II: Totals 1984/85 to 1990/91, for the LADs situated in the Assisted Areas of England of the 123 selected**

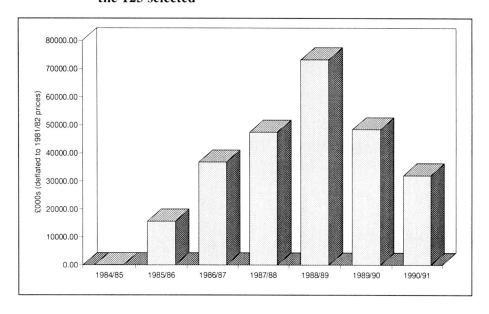

**Figure A36  Regional Development Grant II: Totals 1984/85 to 1990/91, for the LADs situated in the Assisted Areas of England of the 123 selected**

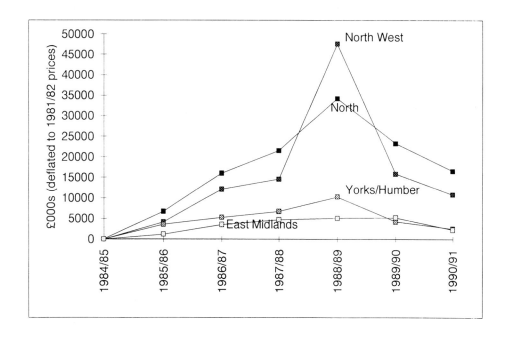

## A14   ENTERPRISE INITIATIVE

**1   Programme background**

The Enterprise Initiative was launched by the DTI in January 1988, and brought together into a 'comprehensive package' new and existing schemes. The services include:

- **Consultancy help:** free 'Business Review' of the individual firm, and financial assistance for hiring a consultant. Available to all firms. More support for Assisted Areas and UPA areas.

- **Managing into the '90s:** information and advice on management.

- **Exporting:** advice, information and contacts.

- **Regional Enterprise Grant:** available to firms with less than 25 employees in one of the Development Areas, or the Intermediate Areas of Derbyshire, South Yorkshire and Plymouth. REG provides grants of up to £15,000 for 15% of the costs of plant and equipment, and grants of up to £25,000 for 50% of the costs of improving products and processes.

- **Education and training:** the 'Teaching Company Scheme' creates partnerships between businesses, universities and polytechnics.

- **Innovation:** expert advice on introducing better technology; collaborative research projects involving businesses, universities and Government research institutes.

- **Single European Market:** information and a 'hotline' on the SEM.

- **Environment:** advice; assistance under three schemes

- **Environmental Technology Innovation Scheme** (ETIS) which offers financial support for research into environmentally clean technologies, EUREKA which encourages EC-linked research, and DTI Environmental Management Options Scheme (DEMOS) which supports good environmental practice.

**2   Data availability and analysis**

All the schemes are nationally oriented, and therefore individual local authority districts data are almost impossible to obtain.

- **Consultancy help:** data available are total expenditure by year for UPA areas. The figures are: 1987/88 £nil; 1988/89 £2.5m; 1989/90 £7.2m; 1990/91 £8.6m.

- **Managing into the 90s:** no local authority data are available; an estimated £3m a year is spent across all areas.

- **Exporting:** no local authority data are available; an estimated £154m per year is spent total, or £5.3m per region (some is spent overseas).

- **Regional Enterprise Grant:** data are available for the period 1988/89 to 1990/91 by local authorities for those areas in the 123 that received REG. The total expenditure is £12.6m. The regional breakdown is shown in Figure A37, which shows that the North has the majority of those local authorities which receive funding (14 of 29). The North also has the highest funding, at a figure of £4.6m. This compares with: £3.7m in the North West (9 authorities); £3.8m in Yorkshire and Humberside (5 authorities); and Corby, again the sole representative of the south, with £0.43m.

- **Education and training:** no data are available.

- **Innovation:** no data are available.

- **Single European Market:** no local authority data are available. Total expenditure is: 1987/88 £0.81; 1988/89 £11m; 1989/90 £4.3m; 1990/91 £3.3m. The overall total is £20.6m.

- **Environment:** no local authority data are available. The approximate total for the period from 1990 (when the project began) to 1993 is £21m.

*Figure A37*  **Regional Enterprise Grant: 1988/89 to 1990/91 by region, for the LADs situated in the Assisted Areas of England of the 123 selected**

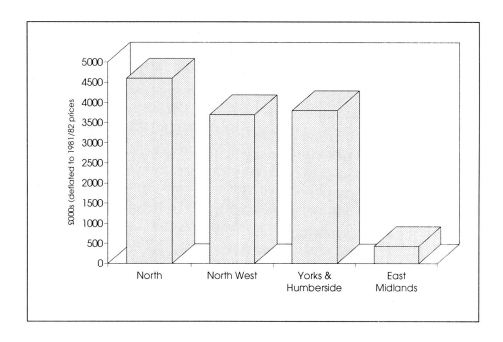

# A15    TRANSPORT SUPPLEMENTARY GRANT

**1    Programme background**

Transport Supplementary Grant (TSG) is intended as a source to allow local authorities to fund major road improvements ('roads of more than local importance'), but not trunk roads or motorways. A specific objective is to improve roads in urban areas, particularly the 57 UPAs benefiting from Action for Cities.

**2    Data availability**

Data are available for the metropolitan areas for the UPAs, marginals and comparators, but no local authority data are available for areas within the shire counties. The period for which data have been collected is 1986/87 to 1990/91.

**3    Data analysis**

The lack of a full data set means that detailed analysis is not possible. However, an impression of the data can be given by looking at the resources received by metropolitan areas.

Total spending rises steadily over the period, from a level of £105m in 1986/87 to £157m in 1990/91 (see Figure A38). The totals of TSG are made up of 'major schemes', of over £1m, and 'minor schemes', receiving spending of less than £1m. The major schemes are at the £90m level in 1986/87 and 1987/88, then climb steadily to £137m in 1990/91. For the minor schemes, except for the first year when expenditure was £14m, spending ran at a level close to £320m, with a peak of £29m in 1988/89.

Breaking down the data regionally, Greater London clearly received the lion's share of TSG expenditure in all years (see Figure A39). The West Midlands and the North West had similar levels of spending, while Yorkshire and Humberside, and particularly the North, had much lower expenditure. For Greater London, 1986/87 was the low starting point (£31m), 1989/90 the peak (£59m). For the other regions, the final year, 1990/91, was dominant in terms of levels of funding, with the other years being at lower but similar levels. The exception was the West Midlands where 1986/87 to 1987/88 were well below the high spending levels in 1988/89 and 1990/91, and the North, where 1989/90 was the peak year.

*Figure 38*    **Transport Supplementary Grant: Totals 1986/87 to 1990/91, for the 123 LADs selected**

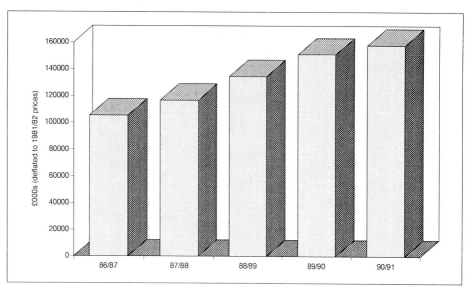

*Figure 39*    **Transport Supplementary Grant: Totals 1986/87 to 1990/91 by region and yer, for the 123 LADs selected**

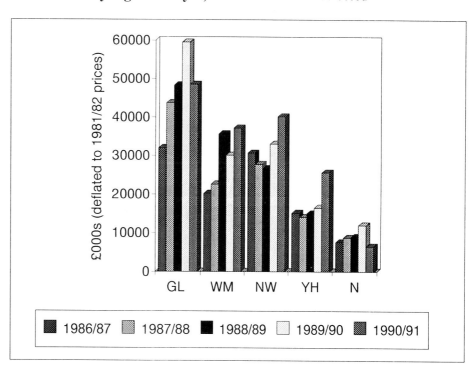

# A16. ENTERPRISE ZONES

**1 Programme background**

The Enterprise Zone (EZ) programme was designed as an 'experiment' to test the degree to which industrial and commercial regeneration might be promoted through the streamlining and simplification of planning procedures and administrative controls, and through the introduction of fiscal advantages (exemptions against rates and capital allowances) for companies in EZ sites. Although the EZ programme is included in Action for Cities, not all EZs lie within the set of 57 UPAs.

**2 Data availability**

The majority of work previously carried out to monitor the development and impact of EZs has been undertaken by PA Cambridge Economic Consultants (DoE, 1987) who are currently undertaking the second stage of the study. The reason for noting this, is to stress the problems that have already been incurred with regard to acquiring data on Enterprise Zones (EZs) which have also been acknowledged by PA Cambridge Economic Consultants (information supplied by Jonathan Lewis of PACEC who provided invaluable personal assistance with regard to data availability).

The main problem is the lack of detailed published information for which there are several reasons. First, because EZ policy minimised the involvement of local authorities and cut red tape to a minimum, detailed records of those zones which fall across authorities have not been disaggregated into the respective local authority areas. Second, there is no readily available data; the calculation of exact private investment and capital allowance figures by local authority for all EZs would be a daunting task.

The main source of information about the amount of private investment generated in EZs is given in the DoE annual reports on each zone. The first two reports, for 1981/2 and 1982/3, were prepared by Roger Tym and Partners. However, as noted above, this information is not divided into the local authorities in those cases where the zone constitutes more than one area and in some cases is entirely omitted from the reports to preserve confidentiality. The only way to analyse private investment data on a local authority basis was to utilise surrogate indexes (floor space development, number of establishments, numbers in employment) and to obtain the information not provided in the annual reports. For the majority of zones the missing information tended to be for only one or two years, however for Speke (Liverpool), during its ten years of operation, private investment was only published for two years.

Another problem with EZ records, on the input side (rate revenue foregone), is that they have never been committed to a computerised data base and require manual operation. However, the Land and General Statistics Division at the DoE manage a data base of EZ output measures (number of establishments and employment), which can be segregated into local authorities by the use of EZ sub-zones. It has therefore been possible to use these data, but their value is in question because there has been no continuous monitoring and some of the indicators are based on general estimates.

As an additional attempt to construct a robust data base on EZs, all of the zone authorities were contacted. This involved approaching both the economic and development departments and the finance departments of the authorities concerned, because of the uncertainty as to who would be involved in keeping records. This proved to be a thankless task because, of the fifteen authorities that did respond, only three admitted to having kept any form of data on the EZ within their area; and, of these, all were out of date by at least five years.

## 3  Data definitions

The main public inputs into the EZs are rate revenue forgone and capital allowances. In proportion to each other they have varied over time and between areas, depending on the number of establishments within each zone and the rate of inward private investment. For example, during the financial year 1983/84 the total cost of capital allowance to the exchequer was approximately £9 million, whilst rate revenue foregone totalled £14 million for all zones (DoE, 1984). However, in the financial year 1987/88 the cost of capital allowance was approximately £310 million and rate revenue foregone was £182 million for all zones.

The figures for the capital allowances listed in the annual EZ reports are approximate. They are estimates based on floor space figures relating to construction, and assume claim allowances in full. Because of this, it was possible - given a break-down of floor space development by local authority and an approximate estimate of inward private investment - to apportion capital allowance figures to each authority area.

The figures for rate revenue foregone were calculated for all the zone authorities, but as these only really provide half the picture of EZ expenditure, it is important to include some estimate of the capital allowances and private investment before a total analysis can be undertaken. To tackle this, the private investment figures were collated, as stated above, from the annual reports and Marsham Street. However they were not segregated for the five trans-boundary zones. Therefore, the following procedure was adopted. First, private investment was calculated for each zone authority utilising the following range of surrogate indexes:

- floor space development - taken from the first EZ annual reports;

- number of establishments and number in employment by sub-zone - taken from the Land and General Statistics data base, DoE;

- rate revenue foregone - provided by the UDC Division, Marsham Street.

- Then, utilising the annual rates of corporation tax (1981/82 - 52%, 1982/83 - 52%, 1983/84 - 50%, 1984/85 - 45%, 1985/86 - 40%, 1986/87 - 35%, 1987/88 - 35%, 1988/89 - 35%), the same percentage was extracted from the rates of private investment, thereby giving a rough guide to the capital allowance for each authority.

The overall calculation process was necessarily crude and based upon various different parameters, some of which were estimates. However, the assumptions at each stage do allow a direct comparison between zone authorities and the intention is to present a general picture of the levels of cost to the exchequer for all EZ expenditure.

## 4  Data analysis

(i) Rate revenue foregone

Figure A40 shows the full range of authorities receiving rate support through the EZ programme and plots the total cost to the exchequer over the period 1981/82 to 1988/89. Gateshead is the primary beneficiary, with Tower Hamlets and Dudley placed second and third. Caution is required in interpreting the rate relief data at local authorities rather than EZ area level. The relief received is primarily a function of the EZ area in an authority. Those receiving the lowest amounts - Burnley, Hyndburn, Pendle and Rossendale - together cover just 114 hectares.

The greatest concentration of the allocated funds falls to LAs in the North and the Midlands, fluctuating between the two areas over time. In 1981/82, due to such early designations as Dudley and Corby, the Midlands received the greatest mean input of revenue through rates foregone, £54,000, whilst the South only received an average of £2,250.

It is clear from Figure A40 that the main beneficiaries from rate relief through Enterprise Zones, have been UPA areas. The main exception to this overall pattern is Newham. Even though it is a designated UPA area, it consistently received low levels of support. This is largely a reflection of the small proportion of the borough which is occupied by the EZ by comparison with Tower Hamlets.

(ii)  Capital allowance and private investment

The other main investments going into Enterprise Zones are capital allowances and private capital, both inextricably linked. The data for capital allowance on private investment is not as straight-forward as rate revenue foregone, because of the confidentiality constraints. Briefly, the estimate involves deducting from the total investment eligible for capital allowances (construction investment), the investment that would have qualified even if it had taken place outside an EZ. The cost to the Exchequer is then based upon the main corporation tax during that year. Private investment for all zones is not publicised in the EZ annual reports and the figures assembled here have been provided at the discretion of the DoE. The figures, which have been broken down to local authority level, are not as robust as the information provided for rate relief and therefore the same level of description has not been attempted.

The total private investment in each zone authority over the period 1981/82 to 1988/89 is shown in Figure A41 which shows that Tower Hamlets has received by far the greatest amount of private investment. But, it is not just the southern authorities which have managed to attract private investment, since Gateshead and Salford encouraged more investment than any of the remaining authorities. However, it must be noted that the level of investment in these Northern areas is less than half of that in Tower Hamlets.

While generally similar to the patterns for rate revenue foregone, the pattern of private investment does show some marked differences; Dudley, Corby, Newcastle and Trafford show a relatively greater support from rate relief than from private investment in comparison to the other authorities. But, in Liverpool the relative difference between these inputs, in comparison to the other areas is dramatic and clearly shows that the leverage ability of public funds is severely hampered in this area.

Direct comparisons of rate revenue foregone and private investment are shown in figures A41 and A42, which display the total investments in EZs by authority and by year, respectively. Figure A41 highlights that in the majority of cases, private investment - and hence the capital allowances - are the main inputs into the EZ authorities. However, in certain cases (for example, Newcastle, Hartlepool, Middlesbrough, Wakefield, Trafford and Liverpool) the cost to the Exchequer (Capital Allowances and Rate Revenue Foregone) is virtually equal to the magnitude of private investment.

The overall pattern of investment in EZs on an annual basis (Figure A42) shows the general increase in funds, from their initial designation until 1988/89. The comparison of the inputs clearly shows the proportionally high contribution of private investment, but as previously noted this is in no way equal across all authorities. Apart from the overall rising trend of the inputs, there was a downward turn from 1985/86 to 1987/88, which indicates a short-term decline in investment, which changed to a dramatic upturn in 1988/89 to continue the general upward trend.

**References**

Department of the Environment (1987), *An Evaluation of the Enterprise Zone Experiment*, HMSO, London.
Department of the Environment (Annual Report 1983-1990). Department of the Environment, Enterprise Zone Information 1983- 1984, HMSO London.
Roger Tym (1982 and 1983) *Monitoring Enterprise Zones*, HMSO, London.

*Figure A40*  **Total rate revenue foregone in Enterprise Zone authorities 1981-89**

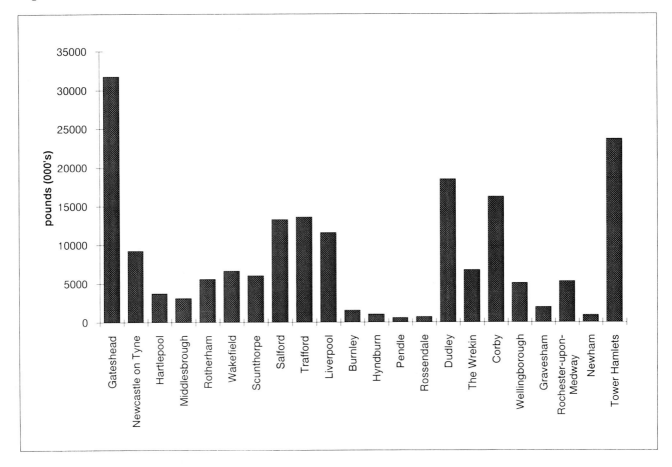

*Figure A41* **Total investment in individual Enterprise Zone authorities 1981-89**

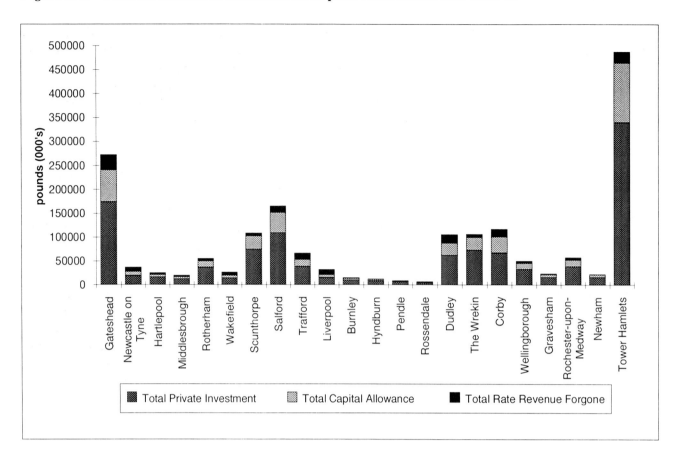

*Figure A42* **Total investment in Enterprise Zone authorities by year 1981-89**

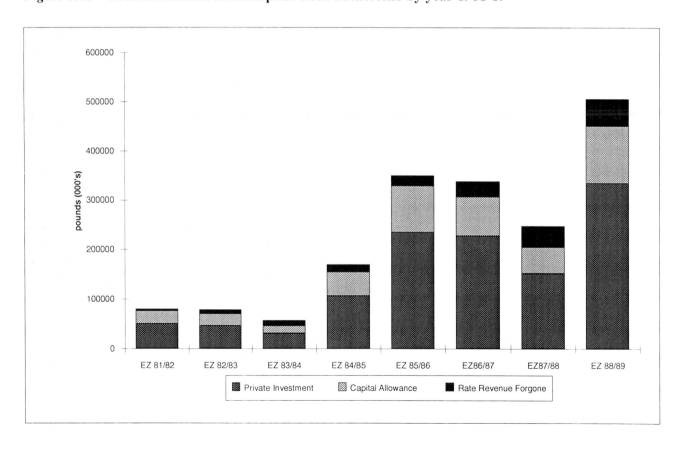

## A17  URBAN DEVELOPMENT CORPORATIONS

**1  Programme background**

Urban Development Corporations were created by the 1980 Local Government Planning and Land Act as part of a new wave of DoE initiatives, both to encourage the involvement of the private sector and to act as development agents directly accountable to central government. They were designated and are financed solely by central government and they displaced the local authorities as the planning authorities in the areas where they operate.

London Docklands and Merseyside were the first two designated development corporations, established in 1981, followed by a further eight UDCs throughout England in the course of the 1980s. A ninth UDC, Birmingham Heartlands, was created in 1992 and falls outside the scope of this study. The main role of the UDCs has been to concentrate on physical regeneration, allowing high profile operations and flagship developments to lead regeneration strategies.

**2  Data availability**

Initially the only data available concerning the expenditure of the UDCs came from the DoE, but because these data were extracted from the corporate plans of the corporations several problems arose. First, the expenditure figures were not broken down by local authority for the six areas with trans-boundary sites. Second, the data could only be presented in cumulative form for the first and second generation UDCs. Third, as the corporate plans were classified as commercially confidential, and request to examine them could only be relayed through a DoE representative, this meant both a protracted process and that a thorough examination of the plans could not be made.

These initial figures were deemed to be inadequate and the UDCs were contacted individually to assess their data bases. This provided the necessary expenditure figures by vote-head, but did not clearly define the levels of private investment attributable to the UDC. To ascertain the exact levels of private investment further discussions were necessary. All the UDCs were contacted and in certain cases the information provided was still based upon cumulative assessments. This arose as a result of the data monitoring exercises of the trans-boundary UDCs, which were not differentiated into local authority areas since the original essence of the UDCs was that they operated independently of local authorities. This involved further discussions with the respective corporations and only through personalised knowledge of the particular areas was an authority based segregation made possible.

The standard format that UDC expenditure data takes (annual reports and financial statements) is based upon a break-down of Administration/Estate Management and Projects costs. It is only possible to segregate the project expenditure by local authority area; other issues such as administration, promotion and publicity are area-wide operations unattributable to any one specific local authority. The only way to include these additional figures is to divide them proportional to the project investment totals for each local authority. By doing this the total expenditure for each UDC can be accounted for over the full range of local authority areas.

For each UDC the total grant expenditure has been accounted for and it is reasonable to assume that the calculations for the segregation of corporation-wide operations represent a reasonable estimate of the divisions of expenditure between local authorities. Even though the final figures may not be an exact reflection of the developments (expenditure) in each authority, their proportions indicate the magnitude of investment allocated to each authority.

103

The segregation of private investment and public project investment by local authority was primarily based upon advice given by key individuals. This was taken from an assessment of what parts of a project had occurred in particular areas and dividing the total expenditure (private and public) by these proportions. This sort of analysis is not necessarily replicable and may have differed depending on the person involved, but no alternative was available. This was especially relevant for transport projects, such as the Docklands Light Railway, which covers more than one authority. So, as before, the figures reflect the magnitude of investment in each authority, which otherwise would not have been visible on a project basis.

## 3  Data analysis

The spatial and temporal concentration of the investment in UDCs make it sensible to analyse the data by simple tabular and graphical representation.

Only the six authorities included within the Merseyside and the London Docklands Corporations received any form of investment throughout the whole of the 1980s. The majority of the other UDCs were not designated until 1987 and Bristol did not receive any funds until 1989/90. In the case of all the UDCs whose areas cover more than one local authority, public funds have been concentrated into one of the authorities. Liverpool and Tower Hamlets were primarily chosen for redevelopment within the first two designated UDCs. In the case of the second generation UDCs, the specifically targeted areas appear to be Newcastle upon Tyne, Stockton on Tees, Trafford and Sandwell. The third generation UDCs are all located within one local authority district. The three that started to receive funds in 1988/89 all received similar levels of public investment for the three financial years, but because Bristol only became operational in 1989/90 it is impossible to make any significant comment on its development.

In the majority of cases where a UDC crosses a local authority boundary the greatest portion of its designated area tends to be in the authority where expenditure is mostly concentrated (Figure A43). However, this is not the case for LDDC or Tyne and Wear. In the London case the greatest portion of its designated area is in Newham, with the rest being mainly in Tower Hamlets; and in Tyne and Wear, Newcastle had the overwhelming proportion of resources despite the fact that it has by far the smallest portion of the UDC within its boundary in comparison to the other three authorities.

The reason for excluding LDDC from Figure A43 is apparent from Figure A44. This shows the total investment in all UDC authorities and it is clear that the size of investment in the London area makes the other authorities' investment virtually impossible to register on the same scale. This clearly confirms the dominance of LDDC for attracting inward investment, but also the constant high input of public funds. Total public investment via LDDC into either Newham or Tower Hamlets, is greater than the total investment into any other single UDC.

The size of the public investment flowing into the LDDC, in comparison to the other UDCs, is even more disproportionate in the pattern of private investment (Figure A44). The figures show very clearly the magnified private investment into the Tower Hamlets area This is obviously a reflection of the massive developments in the area, such as the Limehouse Link Road and Canary Wharf, at the focus of the LDDC Corporate Plan. The private investment in LDDC is especially significant when contrasted with Merseyside Development Corporation since both have an equal life span. Throughout the 1980s the investment into London Docklands has dwarfed that attracted to Merseyside Docks. It would be expected that, considering MDC was operating at least six years prior to any other UDC (excluding LDDC), it would have the greatest total investment of the non-London UDCs, but as shown, Liverpool is surpassed by Stockton on Tees and Trafford.

The fact that Liverpool is the third highest investment area in total is because of the massive input of public funds, which far exceed those of any other UDC. By comparison to Liverpool, public investment in the other UDC authority areas has been minimal, even in the cases of those areas which have a similar total investment over a much shorter period of time (Salford, Sandwell, Newcastle and Manchester).

Figures A45 and A46 display the total investment over time going into the UDC authorities, including and excluding LDDC respectively. Figure A45 shows the peak in private investment in 1983/84 which occurred in London - a pattern not shown in the non-London areas in Figure A46. The second difference between London and non-London authorities is that, from 1988/89 onwards, the London data show that private investment begins to fall away and there is a considerable decrease from then on. This no doubt reflects the decline in the property markets and the economy in general. However, in the case of the other UDC authorities there is no sign of a decrease in private investment, even up to 1990/91, which is probably a result of the northern areas having been less affected by recession. The third difference is in the period before 1987, when the only designated UDCs were in London and Merseyside and when Merseyside's failure to attract private investment is noticeable.

**References**

Parkinson, M and Evans, R. 'Urban Regeneration and Development Corporations', **Local Economy**, 3, No. 2, 1988.
Department of the Environment (1986), **Urban Development Corporations - powers and functions, Background note**, London: DoE

*Figure A43*  **Total investment in UDC authorities excluding LDDC 1981-91**

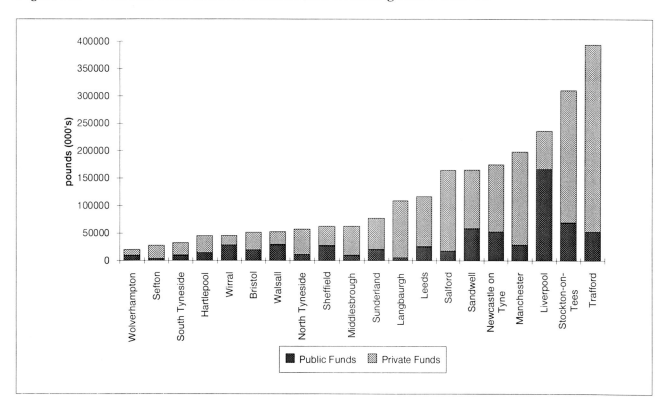

**Figure A44** Total investment in UDC authorities including LDDC 1981-91

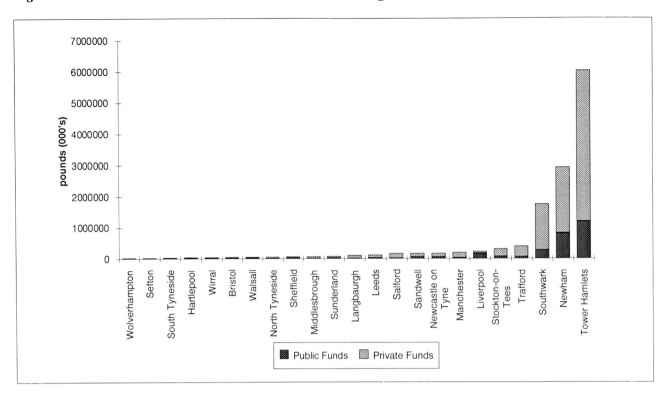

**Figure A45** Total investment in Urban Development Corporations

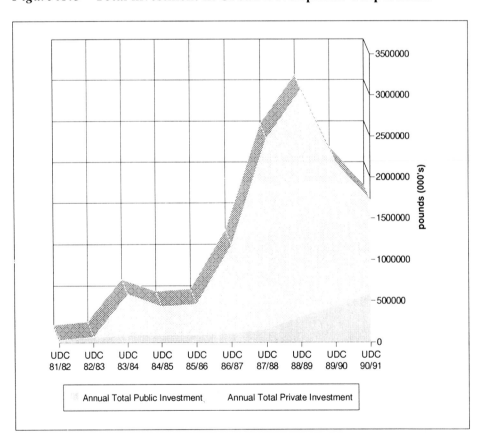

*Figure A46*  **Total investment in Urban Development Corporations (excluding LDDC)**

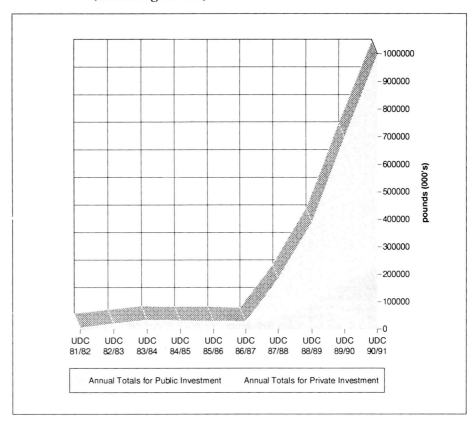

**1   Programme background**

In England, the European

Regional Development Fund is available within designated areas. It is not included under the Action for Cities heading. Until 1991 designated areas were based on the Department of Trade and Industry's Assisted Areas, but they have recently changed due to the various reforms of the structural funds (EC, 1989). It was decided at the Paris conference in December 1974 that the ERDF would be implemented as from 1 January 1975 and relied upon member states to outline their poorest areas, with the condition that governments would match any allocation with an equal contribution of their own. In 1985 the long standing quota system came under review, because its machinery allowed even the richest members to receive a certain allocation and as a result bidding was uncompetitive and inflexible. It was deemed the fund had moved away from its original ideology of a Community fund and had become a topping up scheme for national projects (Croxford, 1987).

The 1985 revisions introduced maximum and minimum percentage allocations which were fixed over a three year period. The minimum added up to 88% of the total fund with the further 12% to be allocated on the basis of need (Archer, 1990). The rules of the fund were also tightened during the 1989 reform and the Commission introduced a series of objectives which were to be used to concentrate funds into a smaller number of projects.

The five objectives of the EC structural funds are:

- Objective 1: The development and structural adjustment of regions which are currently underdeveloped. (N. Ireland is the UK's sole objective 1 region);

- Objective 2: The regeneration of areas seriously affected by industrial decline. Priorities for ESF support are principally small firms, tourism, R & D and training;

- Objective 3: Combating long term unemployment for those aged 25 and over;

- Objective 4: Facilitating the entry of young people aged under 25 into the labour market;

- Objective 5: (a) agricultural structural reform; (b) promoting the development of rural areas.

The 1989 reform also meant the introduction of National Programmes of Community Interest, Community Support Frameworks and Integrated Development Operations. These were designed to give a long-term perspective and enhance co-ordination of both funds and bodies involved, including the European Investment Bank.

In Britain, ERDF covers objectives 1, 2 and 5b, however in the context of this study only objective 2 applies, because Northern Ireland was the only objective 1 area in the UK and 5b applies specifically to rural areas. The structural fund is now channelled through Community Support Frameworks, which are drawn up between national governments and the Commission, which specify the amount of money to be allocated to each region. The general scheme is designed to facilitate a growth in business and tourism, with additional improvements in infrastructure.

Since 1989 there have been major developments for ERDF, which have tended to spatially concentrate the funds even more and induced more coherent management strategies. Prior to 1989 the funds were mainly used for projects and experimental programmes, run by local authorities through the DOE's regional offices. Post 1989, the funds have become based primarily upon programme schemes and focused upon objective 1 areas, which has meant a reduction in the money coming into England but a greater concentration of what is allocated. This has lead to a movement away from the general Assisted Area patterns to a more specific Urban Programme and Development Area status. For a detailed account of the reform of the Structural Funds see EC (1989) and EC (1991).

## 2  Data availability

The ERDF Division at the DoE was initially unable to access any figures for the fund on a local authority basis. Initial enquiry suggested that the DoE only kept manual records of programmes, which, especially after 1989, would take months to search through. Although a data base for ERDF is held by the Directorate of Planning Services at DoE, it is not possible to access certain authorities and, to retrieve the data required, all payments to all regions must be scrutinised.

This absence of readily-available information extended also to the Department of Trade and Industry. However, it transpired that the DTI journal 'British Business' recorded allocations of ERDF to local authorities in England. Unfortunately, the journal was terminated in 1988 and prior to 1983 the ERDF was only recorded by region. (Thanks are due to Mr Chris Kirby, accounts division of the DTI, for help in supplying photo copies of the journal.) Access was therefore gained to a list of the fund's allocation figures between 1983 and 1988 for local authorities in England.

## 3  Data analysis

Analysis of the allocation of ERDF data is based upon the data so far assembled from the DTI records. As stated, this is allocations only and may vary between 10% and 20% from the actual payments of ERDF to individual authorities, depending on the take-up rate. It is however a reasonable estimate of the payments made and on a comparative basis provides an accurate account of the differences between local authorities which received ERDF support.

An initial analysis of the ERDF involves all 123 local authorities, segregated into a three-area classification; 54 in the North, 13 in the Midlands and 56 in the South. The mean for the entire population decreases steadily over the six year period, 1983-1988. This decline is quite dramatic, with a fall from a 1983 figure of £2,158,317 to a 1988 figure of £638,057. It is a clear indication that during the period before the reform of the structural funds the input of ERDF into the selected authorities consistently declined. It is apparent that the majority of the funds were directed at the Midlands and the North. The mean value for the South is constantly less than one tenth of the means of the other two areas. At the same time, however, it is important to note that while ERDF resources for the sample of 123 LAs may have fallen, the overall sum for England has increased. At 1992 prices, ERDF funding for England increased from £174m in 1983 to £252m in 1992.

ERDF allocations have had a reasonably defined pattern throughout the 1980s and one of the more noticeable attributes has been its concentration into Urban Programme areas. In each region where allocations have been registered, the UPA areas have consistently received ERDF, whilst the non-UPA areas have fared significantly worse at attracting the structural fund. The mean allocation of funds has also been considerably higher in UPA areas irrespective of the region. The East Midlands until 1987 was the only region being allocated regional development funds that were not being directed at a UPA designated area The East Midlands has only three designated UPA areas, Leicester, Nottingham and Derby, of which Derby only became a designated authority in 1987. However, from 1987, after the consolidation of the fifty seven programme areas, two of the East Midlands programme areas received greater priority than any other authorities in the region.

The Urban Programme areas in the West Midlands and the South West have consistently been allocated the greater proportion of regional development funds. However, as Figure A47 shows, the higher regional averages as a whole have tended to be concentrated in the northern areas and the West Midlands. The South West and especially the East Midlands show a dramatically reduced regional average in comparison to the other regions, on both an annual basis and over the whole period. Figure A47 also clearly demonstrates two other points; first, that the authorities in East Anglia, the South West and London received no allocation of ERDF between 1983 and 1988, and second, that the annual average allocation over the period decreased in all regions.

Figure A48 displays a break-down of the average ERDF allocation on an annual basis by the '123' area classification. The consistent decrease in ERDF allocations is represented by the prominent slope of the graph, which denotes the dramatic reduction in these funds over the period. It also shows the continual priority of ERDF allocations given to UPA areas.

Figure A49 shows the allocation of ERDF to individual authorities over the six-year period. It highlights the individual authorities which have enjoyed high levels of ERDF allocation (Newcastle, Sheffield, Manchester, Birmingham) and graphically displays the magnitude of these allocations in comparison to the other authorities.

**References**

Archer, C. (1990) **Organising Western Europe**, Edward Arnold, London.
Commission of the European Communities (1989), 'Annual report on the implementation of the reform of the structural funds', EC Commission, Luxembourg.
Commission of the European Communities (1989), **Guide to the Reform of the Community's Structural Funds**, EC Commission, Luxembourg.
Commission of the European Communities (1991), **The regions in the 1990s**, Commission, Luxembourg.
Croxford, G. J. et al (1987), 'The reform of the European Regional Development Fund: a preliminary assessment', **Journal of Common Market Studies**, 26, 25-38.

*Figure A47*    Average ERDF allocation by region 1983-88

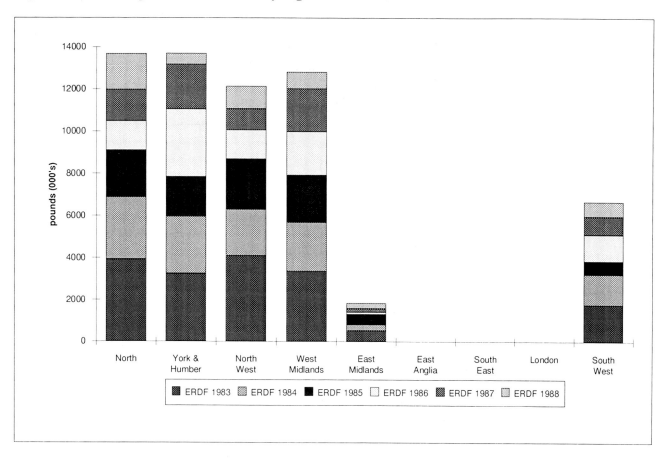

*Figure A48*    Average European Regional Development Fund, by local authority categorisation 1983-88

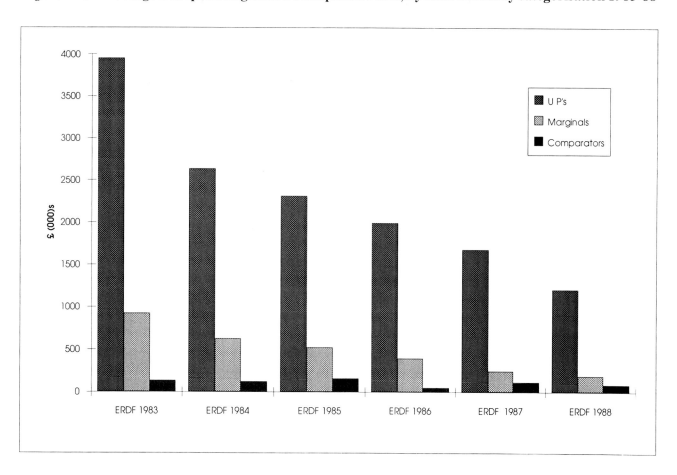

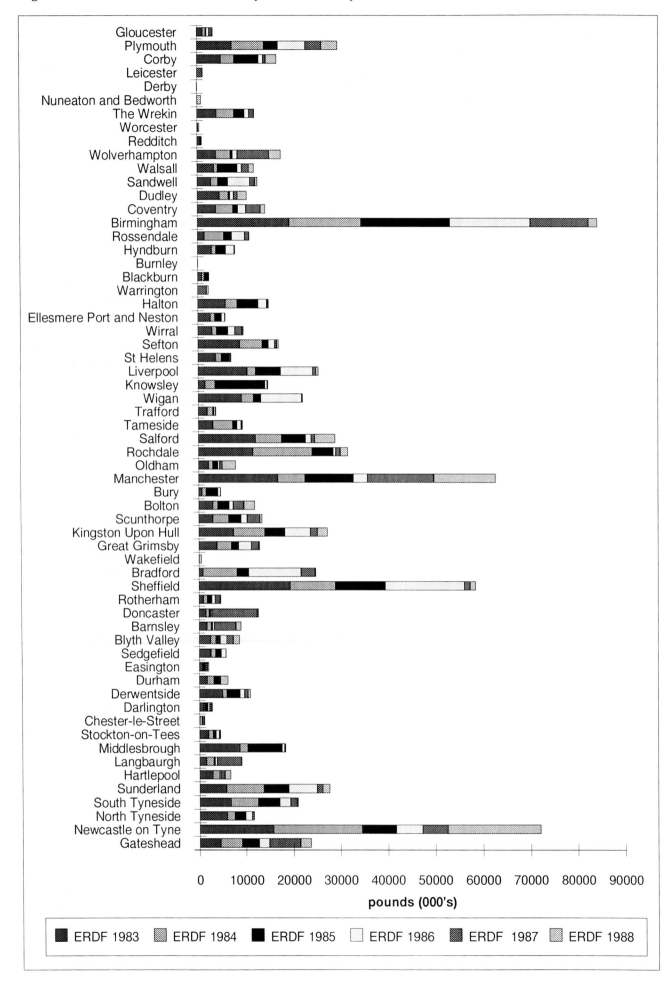

*Figure A49*   **Total ERDF allocation by local authority 1983-88**

pounds (000's)

■ ERDF 1983   ▨ ERDF 1984   ■ ERDF 1985   ☐ ERDF 1986   ▨ ERDF 1987   ▨ ERDF 1988

**1  Programme background**

The European Social Fund (ESF) was initiated by the Treaty of Rome, 1957, and since then has been primarily used to combat inequalities in the labour markets of member states. In the past it has also been used to assist both agricultural and industrial regions in need of regeneration (Bilsborough, 1991). ESF is not included within Action for Cities expenditure.

Two principles guide the main implementation of the fund: 'additionality', whereby the fund supplements member states' own expenditure on employment and training measures; 'matching funds', whereby all Social Fund support is matched pound for pound from an additional public body (Department of Employment, 1991). The Department of Employment works in conjunction with the European Commission, local authorities and other bodies, such as within the voluntary sector, to identify the most needy areas in which to direct the fund. Approximately half the fund goes to the Department of Employment programmes (Employment Training, Enterprise Allowance Scheme) and the rest is allocated to anyone who can satisfy the objectives set out in the 1989 reform criteria.

The fund aims to improve employment opportunities by providing financial support for the running costs of vocational training projects and employment measures. It works together with the other two structural funds (ERDF and European Agricultural Guarantee and Guidance Fund) under objectives 1, 2 and 5b. It is solely responsible for objectives 3 and 4 and it operates irrespective of location. All projects must fall within the broad spectrum of training, retraining or job creation, but there is considerable flexibility and any organisation (not individuals) involved in vocational training or employment development measures are eligible, conditional upon them being supported by a public body.

The priorities for the fund are set out by the Community and these are based upon training and employment objectives. The fund contributes towards the operational running costs of projects by matching amounts up to a level of 45% provided by public funds.

Since 1990 there has been a radical reform in the way the Social Fund is administered. Previously it was a highly centralised operation, involving the Commission at all stages of applications and was also very project oriented. Post 1990 the fund has become decentralised, so that it is the responsibility of each member state to select and approve bids in conjunction with all other organisations involved (local authorities, voluntary groups, etc.). In addition, operational programmes have become established in line with the developments of the ERDF, including the introduction of Integrated Development Operations (IDOs). These tend to cover all the priorities outlined for action within one package and give a more structured and coherent way of processing and implementing the fund. Because of these developments, all project applications have to relate to a particular operational programme.

**2  Data availability**

Information available for the assessment of ESF, is as limited as is information on ERDF. The central British organisation in charge of the fund - the European Social Fund Unit, within the Department of Employment - does not hold any figures pre-1987, because they are only at liberty to hold the records for a period of five years. The information they hold from 1987 onwards is only in list form for all applications by applicant. This means that any individual local authority can have multiple recordings on the list for all the objective headings including IDOs.

To collate the information was a time consuming exercise, which involved adding together all the entries for each local authority within a single year. Because some of the recordings are at a county level, all the funds going into specific local authority districts cannot be accounted for. Ultimately, this method will produce deficiencies in the accuracy of analysis, with perhaps 10% to 15% variation from actual payments, but it is the best approximation of the fund presently available.

## 3 Data analysis

The figures for the ESF funds demonstrate that throughout the later part of the 1980s the Midlands, northern and London regions dominated expenditure in England. However, it is also noticeable that over the four year period (1987-1990), the mean for the entire population continually increased, largely because the number of authorities receiving funds grew from 42 to 61.

Figure A50 shows the overall national pattern on an individual regional basis. All nine regions are recipients of ESF, but there is dramatic regional variation, with an expected lack of funds within regions in the south (East Anglia, South West, South East). However, on a regional basis, the London area obtained equal funds to most northern areas, apart from Yorkshire and Humberside, which utilised ESF more than any other region.

The average ESF expenditure for Urban Programme areas, in comparison to other areas is shown in Figure A51. It is clear that, over the four-year period, the Urban Programme areas were a focus for ESF expenditure. During this time (1987-1990), ESF went through various reforms, including the introduction of the Integrated Development Operations, but at no time were the funds specifically directed at pre-designated areas influenced by central government's Urban Policy. Therefore, the assumption must be that the objectives of the structural funds, pre- and post-reform largely coincided with Urban Programme priorities.

The detailed pattern of ESF support amongst the authorities receiving payments, segregated by the '123' area classification shows considerable variations in expenditure. In the case of non-UPA authorities, Wakefield received by far the most ESF support, far in excess of Bury and Stockport, which were the only other authorities to receive any noticeable support. There are dramatic differences between the marginal areas which acquired ESF support. Calderdale, Tameside and Trafford consistently show reasonable levels of ESF expenditure, whilst Sedgefield, Scunthorpe and Stoke-on-Trent register a minimal level of funds. The most dramatic level of ESF expenditure is attained by Birmingham, which is far in excess of any other Urban Programme authority. Some of the other UPA areas, such as Hartlepool, Preston, The Wrekin, Leicester, Greenwich, Hackney, Wandsworth and Plymouth, received virtually no support by comparison to Birmingham. Other authorities which attained a reasonable level of ESF support were Bradford and Leeds and the majority of this expenditure occurred in 1989 and 1990, after the reform of the fund. This was not the case with Birmingham which recorded the majority of its expenditure in 1987.

## References

Department of Employment, 1991), **European Social Fund - Guidance for 1992 Applications**, HMSO, London.
Bilsborough, M. (1991), 'The European Social Fund-partnership in action', **Employment Gazette**, April, pp. 237-40.

*Figure A50*   **Regional averages of the European Social Fund**

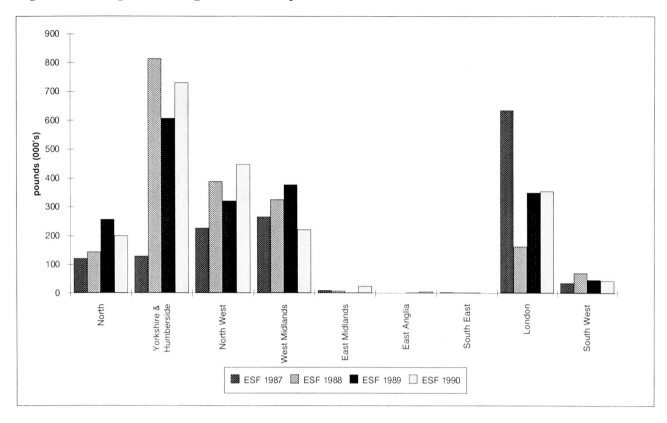

*Figure A51*   **Average European Social Fund, by local authority categorisation 1987-90**

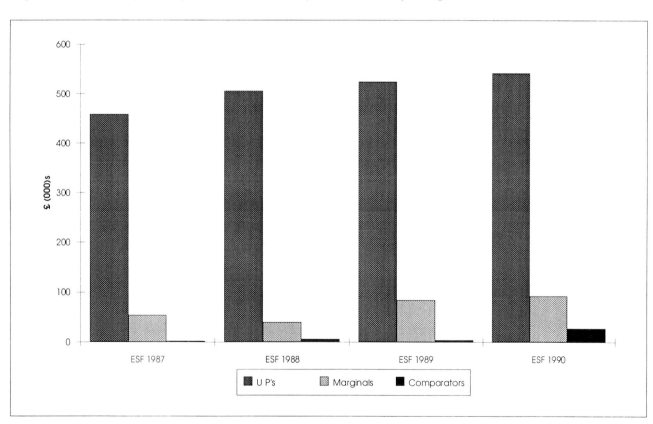

## A20. DERELICT LAND GRANT

**1  Programme background**

Derelict Land Grants have been available throughout the post-war period, but for the majority of this time they were used as an instrument to combat environmental and safety problems. It was not until the late 1970s that DLG became a facet of the government's wider urban regeneration scheme. But, as noted in previous research (DoE, 1987), government expenditure on DLG is still relatively small in comparison with other urban regeneration initiatives (Urban Development Corporations, City Grant).

DLG is available for the reclamation of derelict land to bring it into use or improve its appearance. Local authorities can claim grant of 100% of eligible costs in the Assisted Areas and Derelict Land Clearance Areas. Outside these areas, the rate of grant is 50% except for the National Parks and Areas of Outstanding Natural Beauty, where it is 75%. Non-local-authority grant is paid at 80% (100% for English Estates) in Assisted Areas and Derelict Land Clearance Areas and 50% elsewhere.

Priority is given to the treatment of land which in its present condition reduces the attractiveness of an area as a place in which to live, work or invest, or which because of contamination or other reasons is a threat to public health and the safety of the natural environment.

**2  Data availability**

Information identifying DLG allocations by local authority was made available by DoE. The figures given for the DLG are allocations, but before 1990/91 DLG allocations were issued retrospectively once the expenditure figures were known so that expenditure figures and allocation figures are the same.

The information has several drawbacks. First, the time period for the figures only runs from 1979/80 to 1990/91. The two previous years which should be included in the final analysis are not available because they were not included in the computerised data base and because manual archives such as these are only required to be kept for a period of ten years and have therefore been destroyed. This side-steps the problem of coping with the change-over from the old grant system to the new, which occurred in 1979/80, where the DLG was made available to private investors and public authorities other than local government (Derelict Land Act 1972). Second, the figures given for the local authority areas do not include the allocations to private investors or to other bodies which were or are publicly owned (Gas, Electricity, Water, etc.). This is because the records for these allocations are kept manually on a regional basis and cannot be segregated into local authority areas without sifting through thousands of allocation forms and checking developers addresses against local authority areas. The Minerals and Land Reclamation Division reliably indicated that the allocation directly given to local authorities makes up between 85% to 95% of all DLG allocations depending on the year in question, with the remainder going to other public or private bodies. Third, the figures given for 1990/91 represent grant paid (this is a change from previous years as a result of the new local authority finance system). In order for these figures to be totally comparable to previous years, supplementary credit approvals (part of the change in the local authority finance system) will need to be added in. These will not be available until a later date; however, they will only amount to approximately £2 million in total for the entire DLG payments in that year. Fourth, output figures for the local authority areas cannot be provided since these are not held centrally on an individual authority basis, the most detailed figures being at regional level. The DoE's own Review of Derelict Land Policy

(DoE, 1989) recognises one of the main problems in combating the problems of derelict land as being a lack of information and recommended that all local authorities should be encouraged to keep up to date information on all sites.

Apart from these caveats, the data provide a clear indication of the spatial distribution of DLG throughout the 1980s, which can be manipulated into any operational level.

## 3 Data analysis

The data for DLG show a broad increase in the level of DLG expenditure from 1979/80 until 1986/87, from when there is a general decline until 1990/91. In the early part of the decade priority was given to the northern regions and, proportionally, to the south. This pattern altered radically after 1981/82, when the average expenditure across all 123 authorities doubled from 118,453 to £252,773 and the means for the northern regions and the midlands accelerated far beyond that of the southern regions. The initial dominance of the northern regions in the first part of the decade, switched to the midlands from 1982/83 onwards.

Figure A52 illustrates the regional averages. These confirm the West Midlands and the North West as the two most prominent regions receiving DLG. The North and the East Midlands tended to follow the same pattern of DLG expenditure throughout the 1980s, but in general the North received greater DLG support. The peaks of DLG expenditure in the North consistently exceed those in the East Midlands, and in 1986/87 expenditure in the North, was also greater than in the North West. One of the most erratic patterns of DLG expenditure occurred in Yorkshire and Humberside. The level of DLG investment in this area remained relatively minor in the early part of the 1980s and even decreased from 1979/80 to 1984/85. From this year onwards the expenditure of DLG in Yorkshire and Humberside dramatically increased, surpassing that of the East Midlands, the North and the North West, only falling slightly short of the West Midlands in 1990/91.

Figure A53 represents DLG expenditure by the '123' area classification, illustrating the comparison between Urban Programme and other authorities. In the first two years the Urban Programme areas received the highest average input of DLG funds, but from 1981/82 to 1984/85 the 'gap' between UPA and marginal areas narrowed. In 1983/84, for example, average DLG expenditure in UPA and Marginal areas reached virtual parity. However, this trend altered after 1985/86 when the pattern reverted back to its pre 1981/82 days, with the UPAs once again receiving the highest average input of DLG funds. This final reverse in the trend was so pronounced that by 1990/91 the average expenditure of DLG in UPAs was more than double that of marginal authorities.

Individual local authority expenditure shows wide variations. For example, in the earlier part of the 1980s, areas such as Wigan and Stoke-on-Trent consistently had high levels of expenditure, whilst Peterborough and Nuneaton and Bedworth remained in the lower expenditure group. During the twelve year period, Preston moved from a position of low expenditure in 1980/81 to a position where, for two years, it received some of the highest levels of funding (1982/83 and 1983/84). But one of the most striking patterns from 1984/85 onwards is the dominance of the West Midland authorities (see Figure A52); Dudley, Sandwell and Walsall were regularly receiving some of the highest levels of DLG.

## References

Department of the Environment (1987), **Evaluation of Derelict Land Grant Schemes**, HMSO, London.

*Figure A52*  **Regional distribution of Derelict Land Grant 1979-91**

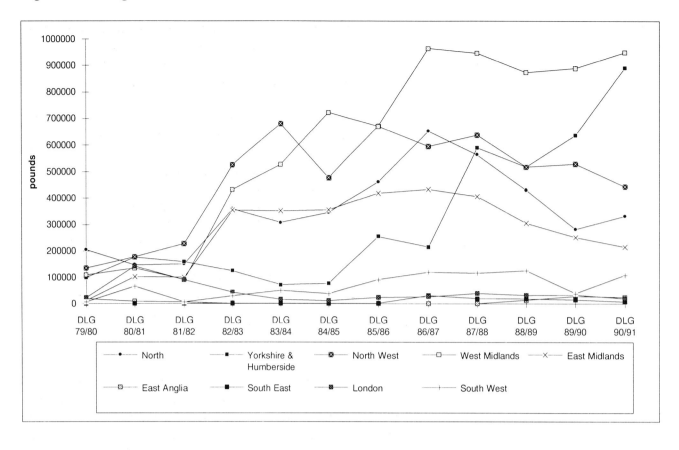

*Figure A53*  **Average Derelict Land Grant expenditure by local authority categorisation**

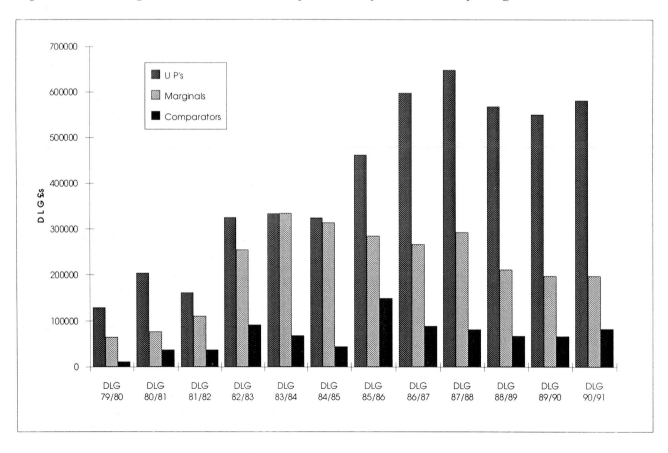

**1   Programme background**

In the wake of the 1981 riots, Michael Heseltine established the Financial Institutions Group to examine the issue of inner city regeneration. The main outcome of this exercise was the creation of the Urban Development Grant in 1982, modelled on the United States' 'Urban Development Action Grant' (Martin, 1990). The main purpose of this grant system was to attract private sector investment into the inner city areas by using public funds to bridge the 'funding gap'. In its initial stages - like the City Challenge scheme of 1991 - a number of local authorities (along with private investors) were invited to bid competitively for a portion of the £70 million budget available. The local authorities invited to bid were those who came under the designated districts for the Inner Urban Areas Act 1978 and those not designated but which had Enterprise Zones in their areas (DoE, 1988). Ultimately, with further designations, the list of local authorities grew to a total of 63. In the first round of the bidding stage 47 authorities were invited to submit proposals, but with the extension of the Inner Urban Areas Act (1978) and the increase in the number of Enterprise Zones in 1983, the number of areas eligible to bid increased by a further 16. In 1986, with the restructuring of the Urban Programme, the list of local authorities invited to bid for UDG became streamlined.

In 1987 a new grant regime was introduced, the Urban Regeneration Grant. This came under the Housing and Planning Act 1986 and was to target the type of development where UDG had failed to attract investment. As a result, its main priority, still primarily operating in the same areas, was to encourage the redevelopment of large sites (usually more than 20 acres) and the rejuvenation of building beyond the scope of the UDG. Under this new scheme the government tried to deal explicitly with the private sector, utilising the powers of the Housing and Planning Act to provide finance direct to anyone carrying out urban regeneration.

After the review of inner city policy (Cabinet Office, 1988) it was decided to simplify and streamline the urban grant system (DoE, 1988) by replacing the UDG and URG with a new system, City Grant. This followed the same policy initiative as URG, in terms of providing funds directly to the private sector, but there were changes in the payment criteria. City Grant was eligible for projects with end value of £200,000 or more and applications for less were to be passed on to the Urban Programme. Some changes were made to the type of projects and areas that were given priority, but for the most part the criteria remained the same.

The underlying aim of the grants throughout the 1980s also remained the same, to attract private investment into areas which it would have avoided without the stimulus of public funds. The directives under which the grants were provided were designed to involve a variety of aspects; reclamation, new build or refurbishment in inner city areas which provide new jobs or private housing, bring derelict land and empty buildings back into use, improve the local environment and help build confidence in inner city areas.

**2   Data availability**

The information provided by the Department of the Environment, covers the annual designation of these grant funds to all successful applicants, distinguished by local authority. This runs from the time of inception (1982) to the financial year 1990/91. Therefore, for each financial year a full list of grants allocated during that year has been made available. However, this does not take into account the annual incidence of expenditure for those which have been paid over a series of years, as the total grant figure is only related to the year of allocation.

The figures provided also included the amount of private investment designated to each project. These figures also only relate to the initial year the project received its allocation and do not reflect the staggered investment patterns which occur over more than one year.

The figures for both public and private investment do not take into account the claw-back of public funds on the sale of a particular project. This relates to the disposal of completed projects, partly funded by public investment, on which the private investor must repay part of the original grant received. Due to the complicated and confidential nature of this arrangement, it was impossible to include these figures and the data used in the analysis are purely based upon gross investment in each authority.

## 3  Data analysis

Figure A54 shows the national pattern of UDG expenditure, from both public and private sources, using the regional classification of Northern, Midlands and Southern areas. In all years, the level of private investment was of a much greater magnitude than public expenditure, reflecting the gearing mechanism of the grant programme. Levels, however, varied dramatically depending on the location.

The take-up of grant in the first year (1982/83) was minimal, but this greatly increased in 1983/84 with the highest expenditure occurring in the Midlands. On a more detailed regional basis, Figures A55 and A56 show the total public and private expenditure over the whole period of UDG. It is the West Midlands that attracted the highest rates of expenditure, closely followed by the North West. Of the southern areas it was only London that benefited from UDG expenditure.

Figure A57 clearly shows the spatial concentration of the UDG programme into Urban Programme areas throughout the whole of the 1980s. In every year, the majority or the whole of UDG expenditure was targeted at UPA areas, with the greatest private expenditure occurring in 1983/84 and the greatest public expenditure occurring in 1987/88. The overall pattern of expenditure in the UPAs tended to be an initial boom followed by a rapid decline in 1984/85, followed by growth to 1986/87, only to fall away towards 1988/89. The scheme was actually terminated in 1987, so that expenditure registered after this date tended to be outstanding claims, which explains the gradual fall away in expenditure. In only two years is expenditure recognisable in other than Urban Programme areas. In 1985/86 a small percentage of private funds, in comparison to public funds, was registered as being directed at marginal areas. In 1988/89 a considerable amount of private expenditure, in comparison to public expenditure, occurred in non designated areas, but in general the support directed at non-UPA areas was minute.

The expenditure pattern of the next most significant and final grant programme introduced in the 1980s, City Grant (CG), is shown in Figure A58. This programme was introduced in 1988 and it is clear that during the three-year period, the North West and the West Midlands were the major beneficiaries. The South East and East Anglia received no support from CG during this time (neither region, of course, containing priority areas) and the South West registered only a minimal level of expenditure in 1990/91.

The targeting of CG is quite marked. Of the forty four authorities in which CG expenditure occurred, only two were marginal areas - Calderdale and Trafford. Of those authorities which received CG support, the highest rates occurred in; Sheffield, Bradford, Bolton, Manchester, Oldham, St. Helens, Birmingham, Sandwell, Leicester, Nottingham and Southwark. Within London, only Southwark received grant.

The least significant and most short-lived grant programme to be introduced, the Urban Regeneration Grant (URG), was initiated in 1987 to deal with larger projects than UDG. This grant only lasted for one year. Each authority that received support through URG was a designated Urban Programme area and three out of the five were the central cities of large conurbations (Manchester, Liverpool and Birmingham).

**References**

Cabinet Office (1988), **Action for Cities**, London: HMSO.

Department of the Environment (1988), 'A Simplified Grant Scheme', **Consultation Paper**, Inner Cities Directorate, London: DoE.

Department of the Environment (1988), **City Grant Guidance Notes**', Inner Cities Directorate.

Department of the Environment (1988), **An Evaluation of the Urban Development Grant**, HMSO, London.

Martin, S. (1990) 'City Grants, Urban Development Grants and Urban Regeneration Grants.' in Campbell, M. 1990 (ed.) **Local Economic Policy**, Cassell, London, chapter 3.

*Figure A54*   **Urban Development Grant public and private expenditure: National pattern 1982-89**

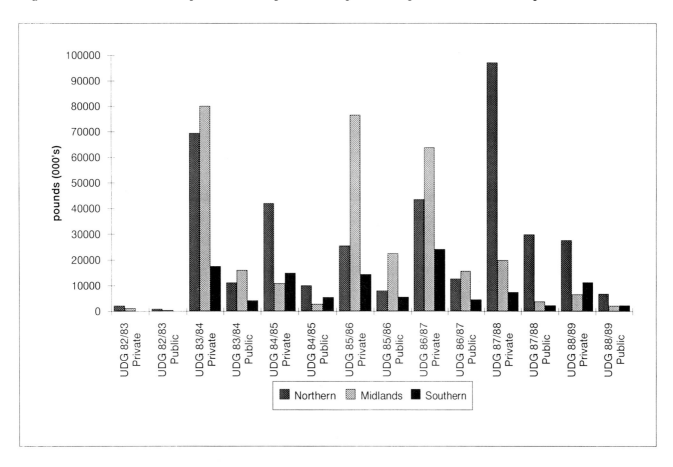

*Figure A55*  Urban Development expenditure: private investment by region 1982-89

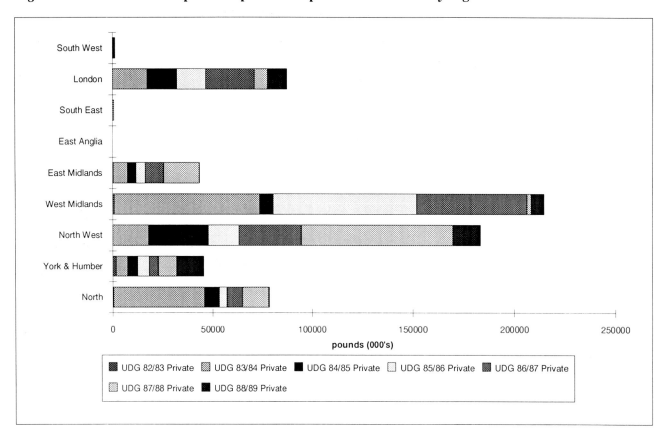

*Figure A56*  Urban Development Grant expenditure: public investment by region 1982-89

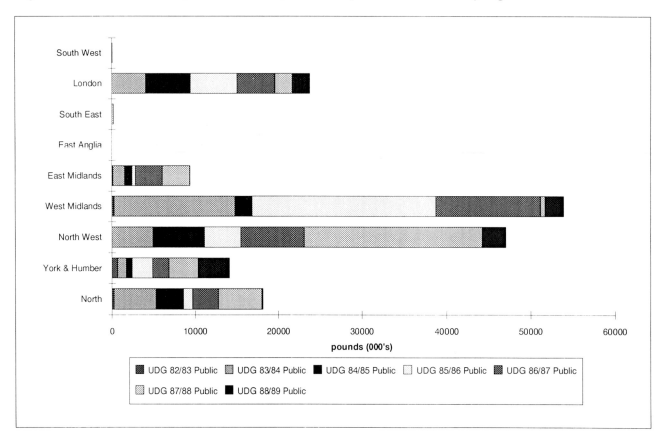

**Figure A57** **Total Urban Development Grant investment by local authority categorisation 1982-89**

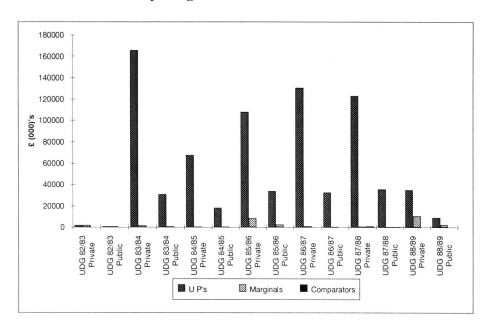

**Figure A58** **Total annual City Grant expenditure by region**

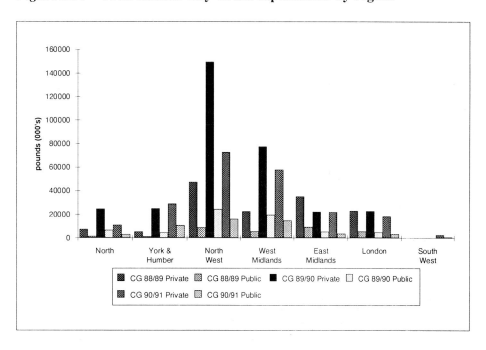

**1 Programme background**

Garden festivals were based upon a German concept. In Germany, however, such festivals were held every ten years. In the three English cases, Liverpool (1984), Stoke (1986) and Gateshead (1990) the longest planning period pre-festival was five years from designation to opening. In the case of other (European) festivals the management and planning time has been on average ten years (DoE 1990). The aim of the sites was to produce a series of environmental social and economic benefits from a focused point of investment. However, commentators have suggested that the long-term benefits seem slender, especially with respect to continued employment and regeneration after the closure of the festival (Warwicker, 1991).

**2 Data availability**

The information that has been provided for the assessment of the sites' expenditure has been drawn from a range of sources: central DoE; regional office of DoE in Newcastle; the Merseyside Task Force, the Merseyside Development Corporation and PA Cambridge Economic Consultants.

The expenditure cannot be broken down into public and private investment, due to the way the festival companies generated funds through the establishment of private operations and sponsorship deals. Figures have therefore been divided into operational and development costs. An additional problem with the available data, was the differences in the figures held by the different bodies for the same sites. In some cases the differences were merely a result of the net costs being taken as the final expenditure figure; the net cost of the sites were based upon the gross expenditure minus the revenue generated by the festival site operation (visitors, additional knock-on effects) and the sale of land for after use. However, in other cases, the differences appeared to be based upon what was included in or excluded from the overall cost of the festivals. For example, some institutions included separate running costs in addition to operational costs. The figures provided by the Merseyside Task Force included a separate section for running costs, which was not part of the totals provided by Marsham Street.

**3 Data analysis**

As these projects were predominantly isolated incidents, the range of data for a descriptive analysis of their development is limited. A comparative analysis of certain festival sites, including Stoke and Liverpool, has previously been carried out, providing detailed studies of the various experiments (DoE, 1990). This brief quantitative summary, simply provides an overview of the levels of expenditure that occurred in the English cases.

Table A3 provides a direct comparison of the three English sites showing the expenditure costs of the festivals in 1990 prices. Gateshead operation proves to have been the most expensive in overall costs, but the division between acquisition/reclamation and developments costs clearly shows the bias in expenditure towards gross development. In the case of the other two sites the split between these two costs is far more equitable, with only a slight bias towards gross development costs.

Table A4 displays some basic comparable achievements from the festival operations and as can be seen, the eventual outcomes differ significantly. In the Liverpool case, the effect of the festival development influenced a far wider area than was actually used for the specific festival site, as 93 hectares of land were reclaimed and only 49 hectares were used for the festival. In Stoke the land reclaimed and used for the festival was the same (73 hectares) and in Gateshead only a portion of the site area had to be reclaimed for use (46 out of 73 hectares), which explains the relatively reduced costs for gross acquisition and reclamation.

The Table also shows the cash price expenditures of the festival sites, showing the proportional division between the operating costs and the acquisition and development costs. It also incorporates data additional to that provided by the DoE at Marsham Street and indicates that there is no real agreement as to the final costs of the sites, which is highly dependent upon what is considered to be a 'cost'. In terms of proportional costs between the various functional categories, it appears that the operating cost of the Liverpool Festival was relatively minor, not only in comparison to its acquisition and development costs, but also in comparison to the other festivals. Further, even on a cash basis, the cost of developing the various different sites has risen, whilst the cost of their acquisition has decreased.

**References**

Department of the Environment (1989), **An Evaluation of Garden Festivals**, HMSO, London.
Warwicker , M. (1991), 'Festival's role defended', **Newcastle Journal**, June 1991.

*Table A3*  **Garden Festival statistics**

|  | Liverpool (1984) | Stoke (1986) | Gateshead (1990) |
|---|---|---|---|
| Gross acquisition and reclamation costs (£m, 1990 prices) | 14.1 | 14.3 | 7.1 |
| Gross development costs (£m, 1990 prices) | 18.9 | 16.8 | 34.2 |
| Visitors (millions) | 3.4 | 2.2 | 3.1 |
| Land reclaimed (hectares) | 93 | 73 | 46 |
| Area used for festival (ha) | 49 | 73 | 73 |

*Table A4*  **Outturn expenditure in real terms**

|  | Liverpool (1984) | Stoke (1986) | Gateshead (1990) |
|---|---|---|---|
| Acquisition costs | 13.2 | 9.9 | 6.9 |
| Development costs | 14.9 | 17.6 | 22.7 |
| Operating costs | 5.9 | 11.7 | 12.4 |

**Sources:**  *For Liverpool: Merseyside Task Force. For Stoke: DoE, 1990, table 2.2. For Gateshead: Northern Regional Office, DoE.*

# A23 SAFER CITIES

**1 Programme background**

The Safer Cities programme was established in 1989 with the aim of alleviating crime and fear of crime, and improving home and work place safety in designated cities. Policy is derived locally through steering committees comprising representatives of the likes of local authorities, the police, probation service, the voluntary sector, the business community, ethnic minority organisations, Task Forces and City Action Teams. Safer Cities operate within some of the 57 UPAs, with intra-LA targeting devised on the basis of high crime rates and social and economic problems.

Initial allocations to each of the first sixteen Safer City projects were based around a nominal figure for grant expenditure of £265,000 per Safer City in 1991/92. This is supplemented by funding under three separate budget headings: general administration, publicity and local surveys. In 1991/92, the nominal allocation figures under these headings are £10,000, £7,000 and £7,500 respectively to each Safer City. In practice, there is some scope for limited deviation from the initial grant funding allocations once reallocations are agreed later in the financial year, even though the principle is to allocate funding evenly across project areas. The same applies to general administration, publicity and local survey funding.

**2 Data availability**

For input data, annual funding allocations to each Safer City project are available for the financial years 1989/90 and 1990/91. Figures are broken down into actual grant expenditure categories: voluntary organisation, local authority, police, probation, business and other.

For output data, the indicators available have been limited to the number of grants paid per year for each Safer City project. However, this raises the conceptual quandary of whether or not grants paid out by Safer City project offices to voluntary organisation, the police and so on constitute an output or, conversely, whether they can be construed as inputs. More satisfactory output data could be yielded from the Home Office's scheme for categorising each scheme/grant. The four categories are: target hardening, work with young offenders, modifying public service management and educational and development opportunities. Of these, the target hardening category is most amenable to quantitative analysis. It may be possible to secure a range of quantifiable outputs under this heading, although these normally take the form of measures such as the number of spy holes and window locks fitted. Such outputs would exclude much of the work conducted under the Safer Cities heading.

**3 Data analysis**

Figure A59 illustrates the sectoral split in spending. The bulk of expenditure is directed via grants to voluntary organisations and local authorities. In proportional terms, grants to the voluntary sector accounted for a larger proportion of the budget in year two, increasing from 25% to 31%. By contrast, the proportion allocated to local authorities decreased from 52% to 36%.

Grant expenditure totals within local authority areas varied more in year one than in year two. During the first year there were no set rigid allocations, allowing projects some degree of flexibility in grant expenditure. In 1990/91, allocations were set at £265,000 per Safer City area, but total allocations ranged between £250,000 (Wandsworth) and £365,000 (Lewisham) because projects were allowed to exceed their allocations to offset the underspend elsewhere. The extent of this deviation from the initial allocation was relatively small, amounting to an extra £42,000 in Coventry. Underspending amounted to £45,000 in Wandsworth, £30,000 in Birmingham and £25,000 in Islington. Predictably, the number of grants during the second year of operation rose for all Safer City areas. More interesting however, is the contrast between cities, ranging from 48 over two years in Wandsworth to 147 in Rochdale (see Figure A61).

As Figure A62 demonstrates, cost per grant varies from £13,000 in Sunderland during 1989/90 and £8,500 in Coventry in 1990/91, to under £2,000 (1989/90) and £3,000 (1990/91) in Rochdale.

*Figure A59*   **Safer Cities - expenditure breakdown**

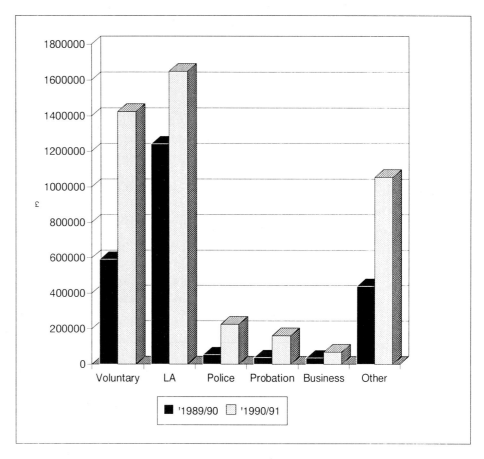

*Figure A60*   **Total expenditure by Safer Cities**

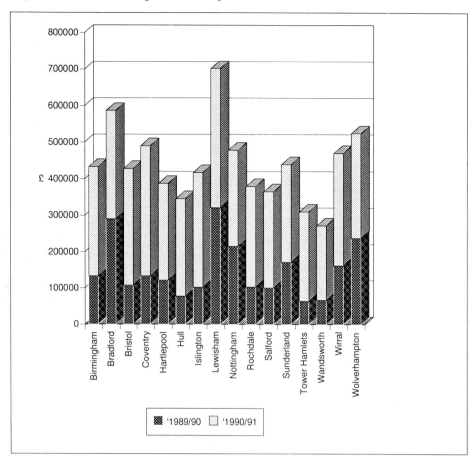

*Figure A61*   **Total number of grants for each Safer Cities**

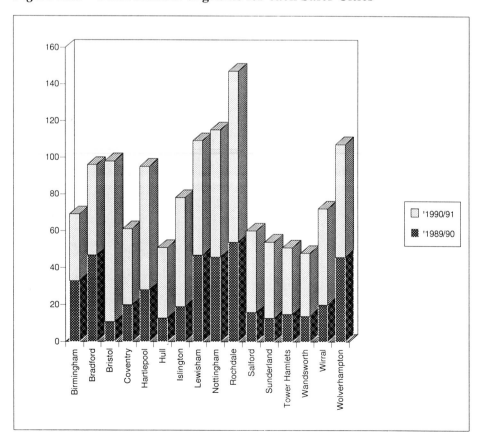

*Figure A62*   **Safer Cities expenditure breakdown**

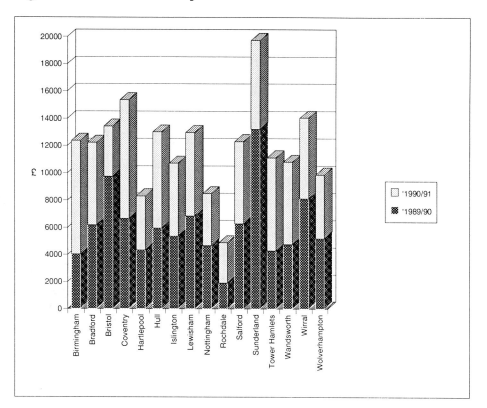

## A24  CHANGE IN UNEMPLOYMENT

**1  Data Availability**

The following data are available at LA scale, from 1983 onwards;

- unemployment totals (all ages)

- unemployment totals (25-34 age group)

- unemployment rate estimates (using 1981 census economic activity figures as the denominator)

**2  Data definitions**

The Employment Department (ED) currently maintains a consistent seasonally adjusted claimant count which takes account of some of the procedural changes in compiling unemployment statistics, thereby allowing relatively accurate cross-year comparisons to be made. At LA level, however, the monthly claimant count remains in unadjusted form, lacking any control for the various statistical discontinuities which apply to the data set. The implication of this, in effect, is that what is being measured changes from year to year, in contrast to the consistent coverage series available at regional and national levels. This presents something of a problem given that between 1983 and 1990 (the period of study) there were, according to Lawlor (1990) and Taylor (1989), at least seventeen changes to the coverage of the unemployment benefit count.

**3  Data analysis**

Unemployment

The analysis of change in unemployment across the set of 123 LAs suggests that, as expected, it is the large cities which fared best. Of the 24 London borough, 19 are amongst the lowest 23 places for percentage change. Conversely, 13 of the 15 worst performers are London boroughs, with only 4 northern authorities (Grimsby, Durham, Blyth Valley and Barrow) in the bottom quartile. While the larger cities performed well in terms of absolute change, in relative terms the fall in unemployment has been considerably less pronounced. Birmingham - which showed the largest absolute fall in unemployment - comes 41st in terms of percentage change, Liverpool falls from 2nd to 56th, Leeds from 3rd to 55th and Manchester 5th to 64th. At the same time, the concentration of northern and midland authorities as best performers on the absolute change variable is mirrored for percentage change. Corby, which came out top for the small business indicator, occupies a similar position for unemployment change. In fact, only one authority outside the north and midlands - Thurrock - is contained in the top quartile, while all but five of the bottom quartile fall in the south.

**Change over time.** As Figure A63 illustrates, the 1983-91 period can be divided into three broad parts running from 1983-86, during which the general trend was upward; from 1986-90, when the trend was downward; and 1990-91 when the trend once more is upward.

For each of these three periods, the ranking order of LAs alters significantly. The contrast between 1986-90 and 1990-91 is particularly striking. While authorities in the South occupy the top places for the 1986-90 period, in many cases it is the same authorities which perform least well from 1990-91. Milton Keynes, for example, goes from top rank (-72%) in 1986-90 to bottom (+162%) for 1990-91. Likewise, Redditch goes from 3rd top (-71%) in 1986-90 to 8th bottom (+99%), and Thamesdown from 5th top (-68%) to 4th bottom (+125%). Conversely, Liverpool goes from worst performer in 1986-90 (-39%) to second from top in 1990-91 (+10%) while Manchester moves from 6th worst (-42%) to 9th best (+17.6%).

**Regional trends.** Figure A64 shows the pattern for relative change by region for the whole 1983-91 period. There appears to be something of a north-south divide, with West Midlands and North West authorities performing best and London authorities showing the smallest decline. This overall regional pattern conceals significant variations within the eight year period. Figure A65 shows that while there are clear differences in unemployment levels between regions, the curve shapes are roughly similar. Most regions peak in 1986 and reach their trough in 1990, with the exception of the north and two midland regions which peak earlier. In general, the lag times (which exist for individual authorities, as outlined) lack any clear regional component. Interestingly, the only LAs to show increases in unemployment over the eight-year period are in London. Moreover, the degree of variation in change within each regional grouping appears to be strongest for London.

**LA-type pattern.** Figure A66 illustrates the time series patterns for the different LA types. These show that while unemployment levels are higher for UPAs, the gap appears to have narrowed over time (particularly during the 1986-90 period). The UPA unemployment is more capricious than for the other categories. This is borne out by the rate of increase over the last year, which is noticeably steeper for the UPAs.

Long-term
unemployment

**Change over time.** For all 123 authorities the pattern of change is not dissimilar to that exhibited for unemployment (all durations) - that is to say, an upward curve from 1983-86, downward from 1986-90 and upward thereafter. At the same time, however, the time series pattern for unemployment (all durations) appears significantly more volatile than for the long-term group (see Figure A63). In the last year, for example, the gradient for unemployment is considerably steeper than for long-term unemployment. It may be that some of the changes to the unemployment count (noted earlier) have contributed towards constraining the level of long-term unemployment to a greater extent than is the case for all unemployment.

**Regional trends.** There are some interesting inter-regional variations in the pattern of change over the whole 1983-91 period. As with the general pattern of unemployment, London fares worst of the nine regions, with a fall of some 40% over the 1983-91 period. But unlike the pattern for unemployment, the range of inter-regional variation for long-term unemployment is slightly narrower. Second, although there is something of a north:south divide in terms of absolute change in relative terms the performance of the southern authorities (with the exception of London) is no worse than that of their northern counterparts (Figure A67).

At regional level the time-series pattern (Figure A68) illustrates some interesting inter-regional disparities. While the curve shapes for each region are broadly similar (West Midlands being the most obvious exception), the gradients do vary across regions. In particular, London and the North West seem to be the most variable, while the curve shapes for the southern authorities (London excluded) and East Midlands are much smoother.

**LA-type pattern.** Predictably, the fall in long-term unemployment over the 1983-91 period amongst the 57 UPAs far outweighs the corresponding figures for the marginal and comparator categories. In relative terms, however, the differences between categories is less pronounced. The time series patterns (Figure A69) suggests that the variability amongst UPAs has been greater than for the other categories. For all three categories the peak falls in either 1985 or 1986, and the trough is 1990.

**References**  Lawlor, J. (1990), 'Monthly unemployment statistics: maintaining a consistent series', **Employment Gazette**, 98, December 1990, pp 590-600.
Taylor, D. (1989) **Creative Counting**, Unemployment Unit Briefing Note.

*Figure A63*  **Unemployment totals - long-term and all durations 1983-91**

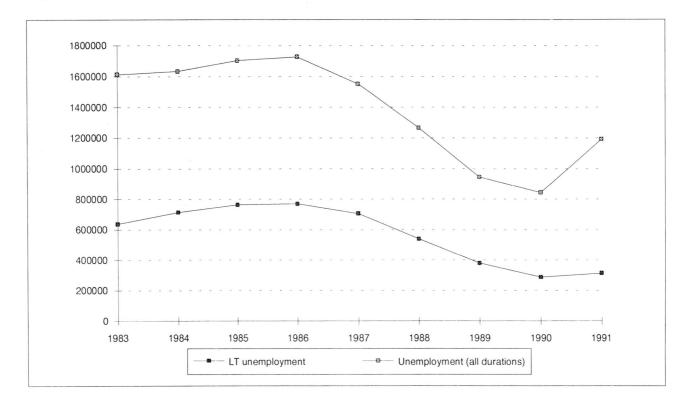

*Figure A64*  **% unemployment change by region 1983-91**

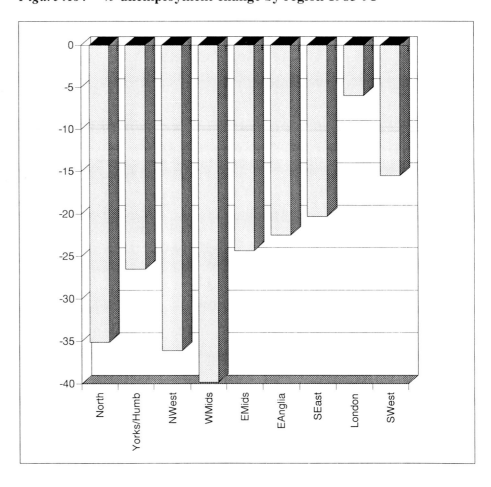

*Figure A65*   **Total unemployment by region 1983-91**

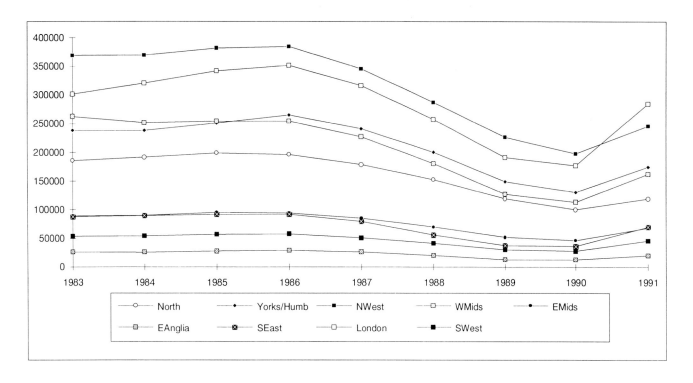

*Figure A66*   **Unemployment totals 1983-91 by LAD type**

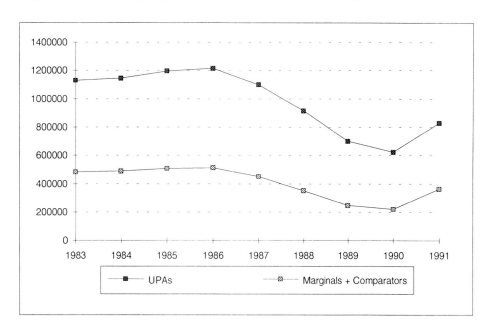

*Figure A67*  **% change in long-term and overall unemployment by region 1983-89**

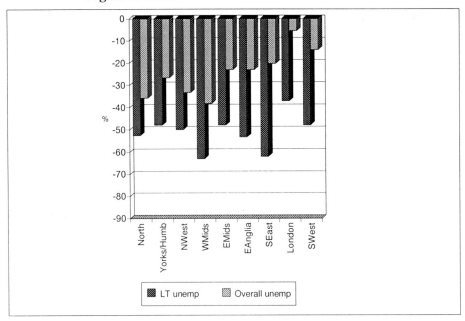

*Figure A68*  **Long-term unemployment totals by region 1983-91**

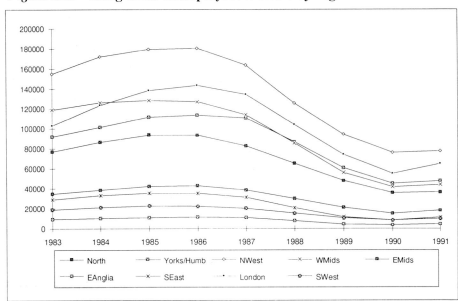

*Figure A69*  **Long-term unemployment totals by LAD type 1983-91**

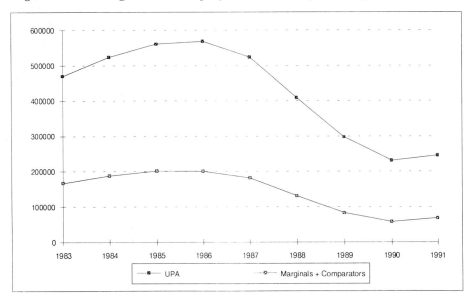

**1  Data definitions**

The Census of Employment is based on a postal survey of companies registered for PAYE with the Inland Revenue. Each PAYE point is required to give details of the number of employees at each of its worksites and in each distinct industrial activity. The area to which employees are apportioned is therefore the specific worksite location ('data unit') rather than the PAYE point address ('reporting unit'). The census covers employees in employment only. It takes no account of people in self-employment, the armed forces, private domestic service or homeworkers. Firms where all staff are earning less than the income tax threshold are also excluded from the census. This mainly affects the retail sector (Employment Gazette, 1991).

While the 1981 Census of Employment was a full survey of PAYE points, from 1984 onwards the census was carried out on a sample basis on line with the recommendations of the 'Rayner Scrutinies' of government statistics. The 1984, 1987 and 1989 censuses surveyed all units with 25 or more employees, together with a sample of those units employing fewer than 25. In total, some 90% of reporting units employ fewer than 25 people, accounting for around 15% of the total number of employees in employment. In 1984, around 150,000 of these small reporting units were polled in a sample stratified by location and type of industry (Employment Gazette, 1987: 408-409).

Given the introduction of sampling in 1984, care has to be taken when comparing 1984-89 figures with those for preceding years. This is especially true when the level of disaggregation is greater, in which case sampling error is likely to be higher because the number of employees being estimated may be very high in proportional terms (Employment Gazette, 1987:407).

There are three main problems with the 1984-89 census data (following Employment Gazette, 1987, 1991):

(i)   **Duplication**. The 1984 census attempted to match the list of PAYE points with updated information from the census in 1981. Problems arose, however, because employers often had multiple PAYE arrangements at any one (or group) of addresses, leading to duplication in survey results as employers were sent more than one census form to complete (Employment Gazette, 1991:225). Comparison with 1981 census returns was able only partially to offset such duplication. By scrutinising a sample of completed census forms, national and regional estimates were adjusted to take account of duplications and over-counting. However, according to Employment Gazette (1987:408), caution has to be exercised when looking at data below the regional level, where any remaining duplications could have a major effect. In the 1987 and 1989 censuses the problem of duplication is considerably less acute due to the use of employer VAT numbers to help identify firms (Employment Gazette, 1991:225).

(ii)  **Sampling error**. As noted above, work sites employing 25 or more people accounted for around 85% of all employment. For the remaining 15%, however, the reliance on sampling has created problems. In each of the censuses from 1984-89, the sample was stratified by size, location and industry, based on PAYE information and data from the previous census. However, the size indicators used to stratify the sample often differed from the actual employment levels, especially where the size was identified solely from PAYE information. The results were twofold. First, some large units were found in the strata supposed to cover small units. The effects of this can be serious because the results may be grossed up by a factor of 10 or more, which could inflate the estimate in a particular area or industry (Employment Gazette, 1991:225). Second, some large units employing more than 25 people were allocated to strata supposed to be for smaller units and therefore were not polled. In the 1987 and 1989 censuses, however, large units which had responded to previous censuses but which no longer registered on the PAYE list as a 'large' company were polled anyway. In addition, information on large companies collected for the 1989 census was scanned for errors in about 50% of local authorities.

The consequence of these points is that while national and regional employment totals are relatively accurate, sub-regional totals may be skewed by the erroneous inclusion of a large employer in a particular area or, alternatively, the exclusion of a large employer. Fortunately, most of the errors arising in this way apply to information at sub-regional scale below SIC division level. For job totals at LA level, the information should be reasonably accurate. As Employment Gazette (1987:225) puts it:

> 'the effect of sampling on the overall accuracy of the Census of Employment is extremely small. However, there are other types of error which are not large in relation to the main national and regional aggregates of employees but which could be significant for small employment aggregates'.

(iii) **Non-response.** This is a very limited problem due to the statutory obligation on employers to complete census forms. For the 1989 census, the response rate was almost 97%, accounting for around 99% of their employees. Moreover, estimates for non-responding units are calculated based on the employment characteristics of units with similar location, size and industrial type (Employment Gazette, 1991:225).

## 2 Data analysis

Figure A70 shows the pattern of employment change for all 123 LAs. Total change has been limited, with the number of jobs in the sample increasing by 51,400 between the censuses of 1981 and 1989.

**LA-type pattern.** Figure A71 shows the job change pattern across the three categories of local authority (UPA, marginal and comparator). While the time-series pattern for each category is broadly similar, with each dipping in the mid-year censuses before recovering in 1989. However, there is clearly some inter-group variation. In terms of percentage job change, the performance of UPAs is significantly poorer than the other categories.

**Regional pattern.** While between-region variations are not statistically significant, nonetheless there are important contrasts (Figure A72). The northern regions perform less well than those in the midlands or south. The exceptions to this broad pattern are the West Midlands, whose performance is more in line with the northern regions', and London, which bucks the positive trend apparent in the rest of the south.

**SIC breakdown.** Figure A73 illustrates the pattern of change by SIC division. In relative terms, UPAs perform worst for each of the SICs, with the notable exceptions of the service divisions 6, 8 and 9.

**LA league tables.** Tables A5 and A6 show how each of the LAs performed in relative terms for the periods 1981-84 and 1984-89, broken down into the three LA categories. Amongst UPAs, there is a group of authorities whose performance is similar over both time periods, such as Liverpool, Knowsley and South Tyneside, which do badly, and The Wrekin, which does well. Conversely, the performance of authorities like Rochdale and Dudley is more variable. Rochdale is the best performer amongst UPAs in the 1981-84 period (+6.41%) and 11th worst during the 1984-89 period (-3.0%). Likewise, Dudley's job total fell by 11.5% in 1981-84 (9th worst UPA), but grew by 16.28% in 1984-89 (7th best).

**References**

Employment Gazette (1987), '1984 Census of Employment', **Employment Gazette**, August 1987, pp 407-409

Employment Gazette (1991), ' 1989 Census of Employment: results for the UK', **Employment Gazette**, April 1991, pp 209-226

*Table A5* **Job change indicator - % change 1981-84**

| LA name | 1981-84 %change | Region |
|---|---|---|
| **UPAs** | | |
| Langbaurgh | -17.91 | North |
| Burnley | -16.52 | NWest |
| South Tyneside | -15.33 | North |
| Oldham | -14.62 | NWest |
| Knowsley | -14.37 | NWest |
| Liverpool | -13.41 | NWest |
| Hartlepool | -12.76 | North |
| Coventry | -12.45 | W Mids |
| Dudley | -11.05 | W Mids |
| Gateshead | -10.83 | North |
| Brent LB | -10.36 | London |
| Sheffield | -9.84 | Yorks/Humb |
| Stockton-on-Tees | -9.45 | North |
| Manchester | -8.98 | NWest |
| Newham LB | -8.92 | London |
| Halton | -8.80 | NWest |
| St Helens | -8.27 | NWest |
| Preston | -7.20 | NWest |
| Barnsley | -7.19 | Yorks/Humb |
| Doncaster | -6.73 | Yorks/Humb |
| Birmingham | -6.58 | W Mids |
| Wirral | -6.27 | NWest |
| Bolton | -6.01 | NWest |
| Middlesbrough | -5.90 | North |
| Wigan | -5.69 | NWest |
| Wolverhampton | -4.74 | W Mids |
| Salford | -4.67 | NWest |
| Haringey LB | -4.38 | London |
| Kirklees | -4.38 | Yorks/Humb |
| Greenwich LB | -4.13 | London |
| Sandwell | -4.05 | W Mids |
| North Tyneside | -4.01 | North |
| Tower Hamlets LB | -3.81 | London |
| Sunderland | -3.81 | North |
| Kingston-u-Hull | -3.77 | Yorks/Humb |
| Lewisham LB | -3.42 | London |
| Nottingham | -3.13 | E Mids |
| Hammersmith LB | -2.55 | London |
| Leeds | -2.34 | Yorks/Humb |
| Rotherham | -2.29 | Yorks/Humb |

*Table A5*   **Job change indicator - % change 1981-84** (continued)

| LA name | 1981-84 % change | Region |
|---------|------------------|--------|
| **UPAs** | | |
| Derby | -2.12 | E Mids |
| Walsall | -2.09 | W Mids |
| Bradford | -2.08 | Yorks/Humb |
| Lambeth LB | -1.84 | London |
| Hackney LB | -1.66 | London |
| Bristol | -1.10 | SWest |
| Leicester | -0.60 | E Mids |
| Newcastle on Tyne | 0.34 | North |
| Southwark LB | 0.49 | London |
| Kens/Chelsea LB | 0.68 | London |
| Islington LB | 0.91 | London |
| Blackburn | 1.26 | NWest |
| Plymouth | 1.90 | SWest |
| Wandsworth LB | 2.73 | London |
| Sefton | 2.84 | NWest |
| The Wrekin | 4.16 | W Mids |
| Rochdale | 6.41 | NWest |
| **Marginals** | | |
| Rochester-on-Medway | -24.61 | SEast |
| Ellesmere/Neston | -20.24 | NWest |
| Thurrock | -11.16 | SEast |
| Portsmouth | -11.01 | SEast |
| Easington | -10.67 | North |
| Great Grimsby | -9.08 | Yorks/Humb |
| Sedgefield | -8.16 | North |
| Waltham F. LB | -7.05 | London |
| Pendle | -6.95 | NWest |
| Barrow-in-F'ness | -6.80 | North |
| Trafford | -6.15 | NWest |
| Wakefield | -6.01 | Yorks/Humb |
| Hyndburn | -5.56 | NWest |
| Chesterfield | -5.47 | E Mids |
| Ealing LB | -3.66 | London |
| Calderdale | -3.52 | Yorks/Humb |
| Tameside | -3.22 | NWest |
| Ashfield | -2.87 | E Mids |
| Redditch | -2.68 | W Mids |
| Nuneaton | -2.42 | W Mids |
| Gloucester | -2.06 | SWest |
| Derwentside | -1.42 | North |
| Worcester | -1.02 | W Mids |
| Camden LB | -0.35 | London |
| Stoke-on-Trent | -0.15 | W Mids |
| Luton | 0.21 | SEast |
| Southampton | 0.41 | SEast |
| Exeter | 0.61 | SWest |
| Rossendale | 1.53 | NWest |
| Westminster LB | 1.79 | London |
| West Lancashire | 2.22 | NWest |
| Lincoln | 3.14 | E Mids |
| Newcastle u Lyme | 3.26 | W Mids |
| Scunthorpe | 4.25 | Yorks/Humb |
| Thamesdown | 5.03 | SWest |
| Wellingborough | 5.82 | E Mids |
| Blyth Valley | 7.21 | North |
| Corby | 11.96 | E Mids |
| Tamworth | 19.64 | W Mids |
| Kettering | 21.54 | E Mids |

*Table A5*   **Job change indicator - % change 1981-84** (continued)

| LA name | 1981-84 %change | Region |
|---|---|---|
| **Comparators** | | |
| Barking/Dag. LB | -16.20 | London |
| Dartford | -8.28 | SEast |
| Darlington | -7.61 | North |
| Bury | -6.99 | NWest |
| Basildon | -6.64 | SEast |
| Durham | -6.62 | North |
| Croydon LB | -6.44 | London |
| Slough | -6.38 | SEast |
| Barnet LB | -4.77 | London |
| Enfield LB | -4.00 | London |
| Norwich | -3.94 | E Anglia |
| Harlow | -3.57 | SEast |
| Stockport | -3.50 | NWest |
| Redbridge LB | -3.18 | London |
| Warrington | -2.27 | NWest |
| Chester-le-St | -1.66 | North |
| Oxford | -1.31 | SEast |
| Gravesham | -0.55 | SEast |
| Stevenage | 0.14 | SEast |
| Bexley LB | 0.53 | London |
| Havering LB | 0.69 | London |
| Ipswich | 2.55 | E Anglia |
| Northampton | 2.84 | E Mids |
| Peterborough | 5.61 | E Anglia |
| Great Yarmouth | 5.90 | E Anglia |
| Milton Keynes | 20.70 | SEast |
| **TOTAL** | **-4.07** | |

*Table A6*   **Job change indicator - % change 1984-89**

| LA name | 1984-89 %change | Region |
|---|---|---|
| **UPAs** | | |
| Newham LB | -11.36 | London |
| Barnsley | -9.62 | Yorks/Humb |
| Liverpool | -8.08 | NWest |
| St Helens | -7.70 | NWest |
| Knowsley | -6.86 | NWest |
| Lambeth LB | -6.40 | London |
| Lewisham LB | -5.17 | London |
| Hackney LB | -4.54 | London |
| South Tyneside | -3.45 | North |
| North Tyneside | -3.12 | North |
| Rochdale | -3.00 | NWest |
| Greenwich LB | -2.06 | London |
| Doncaster | -1.97 | Yorks/Humb |
| Sunderland | -1.74 | North |
| Sheffield | -1.38 | Yorks/Humb |
| Haringey LB | -1.13 | London |
| Birmingham | -0.87 | W Mids |
| Brent LB | 0.15 | London |
| Hartlepool | 0.27 | North |
| Leicester | 0.30 | E Mids |
| Manchester | 1.04 | NWest |
| Plymouth | 1.17 | SWest |
| Newcastle on Tyne | 1.27 | North |
| Hammersmith LB | 1.92 | London |
| Derby | 1.98 | E Mids |

## *Table A6*  **Job change indicator - % change 1984-89** (continued)

| LA name | 1984-89<br>% change | Region |
|---|---|---|
| **UPAs** | | |
| Blackburn | 2.39 | NWest |
| Sandwell | 3.45 | W Mids |
| Langbaurgh | 3.53 | North |
| Wolverhampton | 3.90 | W Mids |
| Southwark LB | 4.03 | London |
| Salford | 4.14 | NWest |
| Walsall | 4.33 | W Mids |
| Wirral | 4.37 | NWest |
| Rotherham | 4.48 | Yorks/Humb |
| Islington LB | 6.97 | London |
| Bristol | 8.17 | SWest |
| Sefton | 8.40 | NWest |
| Wigan | 8.42 | NWest |
| Nottingham | 8.96 | E Mids |
| Coventry | 9.39 | W Mids |
| Leeds | 9.63 | Yorks/Humb |
| Bradford | 10.15 | Yorks/Humb |
| Wandsworth LB | 10.26 | London |
| Kingston-u-Hull | 10.61 | Yorks/Humb |
| Gateshead | 10.76 | North |
| Preston | 11.91 | NWest |
| Bolton | 13.69 | NWest |
| Stockton-on-Tees | 14.35 | North |
| Kens/Chelsea LB | 15.66 | London |
| Middlesbrough | 15.73 | North |
| Dudley | 16.28 | W Mids |
| Oldham | 17.37 | NWest |
| Halton | 17.67 | NWest |
| Kirklees | 18.00 | Yorks/Humb |
| Burnley | 21.18 | NWest |
| Tower Hamlets LB | 28.17 | London |
| The Wrekin | 37.83 | W Mids |
| **Marginals** | | |
| Easington | -11.69 | North |
| Blyth Valley | -6.68 | North |
| Wakefield | -5.93 | Yorks/Humb |
| Kettering | -5.82 | E Mids |
| Westminster LB | -3.68 | London |
| Worcester | -3.23 | W Mids |
| Ashfield | -2.42 | E Mids |
| Sedgefield | -2.14 | North |
| Stoke-on-Trent | -0.64 | W Mids |
| Ealing LB | 0.02 | London |
| Lincoln | 1.19 | E Mids |
| Southampton | 1.21 | SEast |
| Waltham F. LB | 2.25 | London |
| Camden LB | 2.49 | London |
| Portsmouth | 3.30 | SEast |
| Newcastle u Lyme | 3.32 | W Mids |
| Thurrock | 3.40 | SEast |
| Tameside | 5.82 | NWest |
| Chesterfield | 6.64 | E Mids |
| West Lancashire | 8.74 | NWest |
| Great Grimsby | 9.35 | Yorks/Humb |
| Trafford | 9.41 | NWest |
| Ellesmere/Neston | 9.62 | NWest |
| Calderdale | 10.26 | Yorks/Humb |
| Derwentside | 11.16 | North |
| Hyndburn | 12.85 | NWest |
| Pendle | 13.34 | NWest |

*Table A6*  **Job change indicator - % change 1984-89** (continued)

| LA name | 1984-89<br>% change | Region |
|---|---|---|
| **Marginals** | | |
| Luton | 15.58 | SEast |
| Tamworth | 16.64 | W Mids |
| Thamesdown | 16.72 | SWest |
| Nuneaton | 17.00 | W Mids |
| Rossendale | 17.03 | NWest |
| Scunthorpe | 18.24 | Yorks/Humb |
| Rochester-on-Medway | 18.90 | SEast |
| Exeter | 18.94 | SWest |
| Gloucester | 19.65 | SWest |
| Redditch | 19.78 | W Mids |
| Barrow-in-F'ness | 22.00 | North |
| Wellingborough | 23.59 | E Mids |
| Corby | 55.89 | E Mids |
| | | |
| **Comparators** | | |
| Redbridge LB | -9.83 | London |
| Barking/Dag LB | -8.72 | London |
| Stevenage | -6.75 | SEast |
| Barnet LB | -3.53 | London |
| Harlow | -0.22 | SEast |
| Chester-le-St | 0.30 | North |
| Bexley LB | 1.30 | London |
| Croydon LB | 2.27 | London |
| Dartford | 2.64 | SEast |
| Oxford | 2.96 | SEast |
| Havering LB | 3.79 | London |
| Durham | 5.05 | North |
| Great Yarmouth | 5.76 | E Anglia |
| Gravesham | 5.93 | SEast |
| Bury | 7.62 | NWest |
| Peterborough | 8.46 | E Anglia |
| Ipswich | 9.68 | E Anglia |
| Stockport | 10.02 | NWest |
| Enfield LB | 10.19 | London |
| Slough | 10.65 | SEast |
| Darlington | 10.85 | North |
| Norwich | 13.56 | E Anglia |
| Basildon | 18.08 | SEast |
| Northampton | 19.87 | E Mids |
| Warrington | 19.91 | NWest |
| Milton Keynes | 30.18 | SEast |
| **TOTAL** | **4.74** | |

*Figure A70*  **Employment change 1981-89**

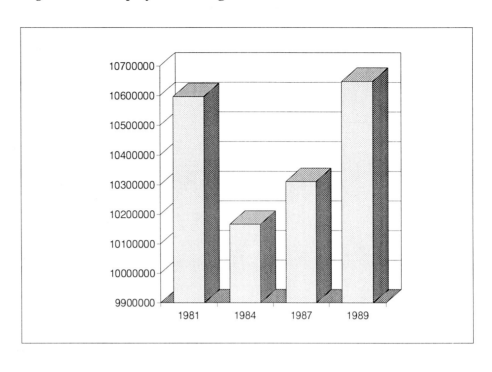

*Figure A71*  **% employment change by LAD type 1981-89**

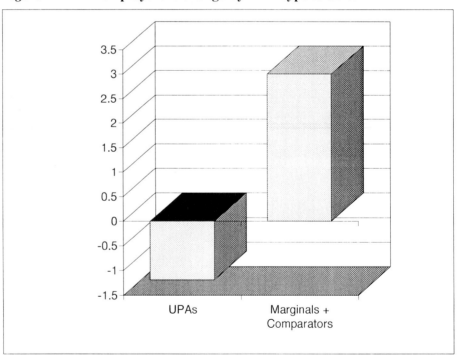

*Figure A72* **Employment change by region 1981-89**

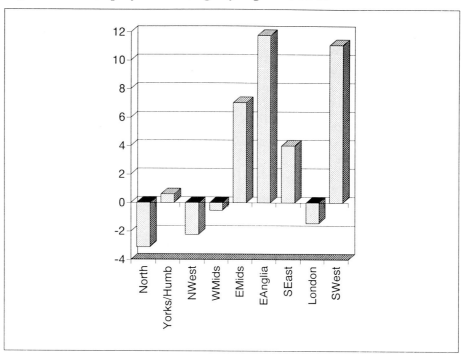

*Figure A73* **% job change by SIC and LAD type 1981-89**

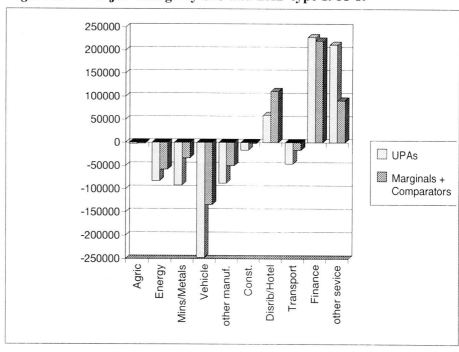

# A26    CHANGE IN NUMBER OF SMALL BUSINESSES

**1    Data availability**

The following data are available at LA, county and regional scales for the years between 1979 and 1990:

- total stock at end of each year (1979-90)

- overall percentage change each year (1980-90)

- registrations and deregistrations each year (1980-90)

**2    Data definitions**

Although VAT registration data cover more than just small businesses, it is nonetheless an accurate indicator of the health of the small business sector since the bulk of VAT registrations are accounted for by small businesses. In fact, estimates suggest that around 95% of all businesses on the register have an annual turnover below £1m (Figure A74). This, according to Daly (1990:563), equates with businesses employing fewer than 20-25 people. This is reinforced by the fact that the dataset records businesses, as opposed to individual branch sites, thereby skewing the distribution towards smaller firms.

**Thresholds**. Time-series analysis of the dataset could conceivably be undermined by substantive variations in the thresholds for registration. But while previous years have witnessed real changes in the thresholds - for example its increase from £5,000 to £10,000 between September 1977 and April 1978 - the period since 1980 has been marked by the index-linking of thresholds (see Table A7).

As noted earlier, registrations are skewed towards businesses with low turnovers. However, this could still exclude businesses whose turnover falls below the minimum qualifying threshold. Nevertheless, Daly (1990:564) identifies four reasons why such businesses frequently do appear on the register: firms register in the hope of reaching the threshold, but fail to do so; turnover may fall below the threshold, but firm remains registered; firms register for financial benefit; and firms register for kudos and credibility.

**VAT exemptions**. This too could impinge on registrations. Again, however, the situation has remained steady since 1980 (Daly, 1990).

**Industry codes**. The dataset is broken into industrial sectors which equate roughly with 1968 SICs, but not with the widely used 1980 SIC definition.

**Area codes**. Since the dataset registers businesses, rather than individual sites, the level of total activity could be underestimated. Larger firms, for example, will be registered only once, even though they may cover a number of sites in different LAs. But since the dataset is to be interpreted as a measure of the fortunes of small businesses, then this is relatively unimportant.

**Data interpretation**. A number of caveats apply. VAT registration and deregistration cannot necessarily be equated with firm birth and death. Registration may be of an existing business which has just reached the registration threshold. Actual firm births could therefore lag some way behind registration. Likewise, deregistration may be explained not by firm closure, but by other factors such as take-over (where the buyer is already registered) and contraction below the threshold for registration (Daly, 1990:563). In general, registration and deregistration figures will understate the real level of births and deaths. This could be important bearing in mind that some 27.9% of deregistrations are accounted for by take-overs - something which is not necessarily indicative of economic decline.

## 3   Data analysis

Figure A75 illustrates change in the number of VAT-registered firms, with the rate of increase steady throughout the period. Table A8 shows the upper and lower rankings for percentage change (1980-89) for each of the LAs. Only four authorities have suffered an overall decline in firms registered - Gloucester, Manchester, Bury and Newcastle. By contrast, Corby, Stevenage, Milton Keynes and Hammersmith fare best. The former extreme is unexpected: Gloucester's decline far outweighs any of its neighbours. Corby's success is a result of industrial contraction and closure, and the investment of redundancy payments in small businesses. LAs at both extremes cannot be interpreted as atypical outliers if one looks at their performance across industrial sectors (see Table A9). Gloucester is ranked between 1 and 10 for all sectors except property. Likewise, Corby's scores are remarkably consistent across all sectors. In fact, this consistency applies across the bulk of LAs, most of which perform relatively evenly across industrial sectors.

**Regional pattern**. The extent of regional variations in net change is illustrated by Figure A76, which suggests a rough North-South gradation in change values. There appears to have been some degree of polarisation over the ten years. The number of businesses registered for VAT in the South East and London, in particular, appears to have exceeded a more general growth trend.

**LA-type pattern**. Figures A77 and A78 show the overall change in VAT registrations for each of the 3 sub-groups within the 123 LAs. Analysis of variance indicated that there was no significant difference between the cores of each category. The performance of each category relative to one another has remained relatively steady over the ten years (Figure A79).

Analysis of variance suggested inter-group variations were not significant for any of the years from 1980-89. In other words, in statistical terms the position of each category relative to the others remained unchanged over the period. Figure A80 shows the change in the analysis of variance F-Value from 1980-89. While none of the F-values are significant, the graph does give a statistically crude indication of the relative positions of each category. If the aim of urban policy is to improve the position of urban authorities relative to the national position, then lower F-values would suggest some degree of success. However, the pattern has been uneven, although the F-Value for 1989 is lower than 1980.

## References

Anon (1989), 'VAT registrations and deregistrations of UK businesses: 1980-88', **British Business**, 34(8), 25 August 1989, pp. 10-12

Daly, M (1987), 'Number of businesses: data on VAT registrations', **Employment Gazette**, 95(4), pp. 176-183

Daly, M. (1990), 'The 1980s - a decade of growth in enterprise', **Employment Gazette**, 98(11), pp. 553-565

*Table A7*  **Change in VAT registration thresholds**

| From | To | Threshold (£) |
|---|---|---|
| Apr-73 | Sep-77 | 5000 |
| Oct-77 | Apr-78 | 7500 |
| Apr-78 | Mar-80 | 10000 |
| Mar-80 | Mar-81 | 13500 |
| Mar-81 | Mar-82 | 15000 |
| Mar-82 | Mar-83 | 17000 |
| Mar-83 | Mar-84 | 18000 |
| Mar-84 | Mar-85 | 18700 |
| Mar-85 | Mar-86 | 19500 |
| Mar-86 | Mar-87 | 20500 |
| Mar-87 | Mar-88 | 21300 |
| Mar-88 | Mar-89 | 22100 |
| Mar-89 | Mar-90 | 23600 |
| Mar-90 | | 25400 |

Source: *Daly (1990)*

*Table A8*  **Lower and upper quartile for change in number of businesses registered for VAT 1979-90**

| | 79-90 % | change actual | Region | LA-type |
|---|---|---|---|---|
| **Upper Quartile** | | | | |
| Oxford | 53.42 | 882 | SEast | comparator |
| Havering | 55.1 | 2361 | London | comparator |
| Haringey | 55.16 | 2245 | London | UPA |
| Ellesmere | 56.58 | 502 | NWest | marginal |
| Dartford | 58.23 | 753 | SEast | comparator |
| Bexley | 58.69 | 2216 | London | comparator |
| Warrington | 59.01 | 1553 | NWest | comparator |
| Brent | 59.12 | 3125 | London | UPA |
| Knowsley | 59.61 | 625 | NWest | UPA |
| Halton | 61.14 | 735 | NWest | UPA |
| Southwark | 61.58 | 2757 | London | UPA |
| The Wrekin | 62.09 | 1253 | WMids | UPA |
| Rochester upon Medway | 63.02 | 1396 | SEast | marginal |
| Wellingborough | 63.14 | 877 | EMids | marginal |
| Lewisham | 63.87 | 2160 | London | UPA |
| Lambeth | 66.11 | 2706 | London | UPA |
| Redditch | 66.4 | 832 | WMids | marginal |
| Thurrock | 67.77 | 1205 | SEast | marginal |
| Kensington and Chelsea | 68.15 | 3978 | London | UPA |
| Slough | 69.26 | 1204 | SEast | comparator |
| Luton | 72.16 | 2014 | SEast | marginal |
| Greenwich | 72.25 | 2090 | London | UPA |
| Basildon | 73.17 | 1789 | SEast | comparator |
| Harlow | 75.88 | 723 | SEast | comparator |
| Tamworth | 76.09 | 646 | WMids | marginal |
| Thamesdown | 80.62 | 1758 | SWest | marginal |
| Barking | 84.88 | 1425 | London | comparator |
| Wandsworth | 91 | 4319 | London | UPA |
| Ealing | 92.2 | 4564 | London | marginal |
| Hammersmith | 102.1 | 3710 | London | UPA |
| Milton Keynes | 105.45 | 2821 | SEast | comparator |
| Stevenage | 117.25 | 918 | SEast | comparator |
| Corby | 122.39 | 587 | EMids | marginal |

### *Table A8* **Lower and upper quartile for change in number of businesses registered for VAT 1979-90** (continued)

| | 79-90 % | change actual | Region | LA-type |
|---|---|---|---|---|
| **Lower Quartile** | | | | |
| Gloucester | -20.76 | -570 | SWest | marginal |
| Manchester | -11.93 | -1441 | NWest | UPA |
| Bury | -4.76 | -219 | NWest | comparator |
| Newcastle on Tyne | -0.05 | -3 | North | UPA |
| Salford | 2.09 | 90 | NWest | UPA |
| Liverpool | 3.83 | 330 | NWest | UPA |
| Westminster | 6.51 | 1731 | London | marginal |
| Bradford | 9.33 | 983 | Yorks/Humb | UPA |
| Birmingham | 9.42 | 1909 | WMids | UPA |
| Pendle | 10.15 | 215 | NWest | marginal |
| Great Grimsby | 12.25 | 245 | Yorks/Humb | marginal |
| Nottingham | 12.39 | 690 | EMids | UPA |
| Blackburn | 14.66 | 410 | NWest | UPA |
| Stoke-on-Trent | 14.85 | 705 | WMids | marginal |
| Sunderland | 15.02 | 495 | North | UPA |
| Sheffield | 15.69 | 1462 | Yorks/Humb | UPA |
| Hyndburn | 15.91 | 279 | NWest | marginal |
| Sefton | 16.07 | 813 | NWest | UPA |
| Burnley | 16.22 | 304 | NWest | UPA |
| Exeter | 17.42 | 394 | SWest | marginal |
| Norwich | 17.61 | 532 | EAnglia | comparator |
| Barnet | 18.03 | 1642 | London | comparator |
| Worcester | 18.62 | 320 | WMids | marginal |
| Ipswich | 18.9 | 420 | EAnglia | comparator |
| Southampton | 19.97 | 825 | SEast | marginal |
| Kingston upon Hull | 20.22 | 832 | Yorks/Humb | UPA |
| Walsall | 20.24 | 1097 | WMids | UPA |
| Barrow-in-Furness | 21.06 | 229 | North | marginal |
| Leeds | 21.15 | 3076 | Yorks/Humb | UPA |
| Leicester | 22.22 | 1467 | EMids | UPA |
| Preston | 23.17 | 633 | NWest | UPA |
| Durham | 23.19 | 279 | North | comparator |
| Bolton | 24.45 | 1192 | NWest | UPA |

*Table A9*  **Rankings (1-123) by industrial sector - upper and lower quartiles**

| | Agric | Constr | Wholesale | Property | Motor | Production | Transport | Retail | Catering | Other |
|---|---|---|---|---|---|---|---|---|---|---|
| Gloucester | 8 | 3 | 3 | 1 | 1 | 1 | 20 | 1 | 6 | 1 |
| Manchester | 25 | 2 | 1 | 9 | 2 | 39 | 5 | 41 | 2 | 3 |
| Bury | 18 | 13 | 7 | 8 | 32 | 2 | 27 | 5 | 7 | 7 |
| Newcastle | 13 | 10 | 6 | 4 | 4 | 21 | 7 | 20 | 3 | 5 |
| Liverpool | 11 | 9 | 4 | 7 | 5 | 29 | 2 | 47 | 5 | 4 |
| Salford | 27 | 16 | 8 | 10 | 10 | 4 | 74 | 2 | 18 | 6 |
| Westminster | 5 | 1 | 2 | 11 | 3 | 55 | 8 | 3 | 1 | 2 |
| Bradford | 26 | 15 | 16 | 30 | 18 | 37 | 28 | 12 | 44 | 13 |
| Birmingham | 3 | 8 | 10 | 16 | 8 | 54 | 11 | 14 | 26 | 10 |
| Grimsby | 35 | 18 | 23 | 36 | 11 | 84 | 6 | 28 | 10 | 24 |
| Pendle | 68 | 49 | 15 | 35 | 79 | 11 | 30 | 38 | 37 | 22 |
| Nottingham | 1 | 14 | 5 | 29 | 12 | 65 | 36 | 30 | 31 | 40 |
| Stoke | 32 | 35 | 20 | 12 | 31 | 45 | 4 | 8 | 33 | 39 |
| Worcester | 19 | 24 | 12 | 6 | 38 | 49 | 53 | 10 | 22 | 19 |
| Blackburn | 67 | 56 | 14 | 73 | 33 | 35 | 1 | 69 | 15 | 35 |
| Burnley | 76 | 78 | 51 | 28 | 23 | 16 | 15 | 18 | 34 | 18 |
| Sefton | 15 | 60 | 24 | 46 | 30 | 14 | 32 | 37 | 45 | 8 |
| Sheffield | 78 | 11 | 11 | 49 | 14 | 87 | 38 | 21 | 29 | 36 |
| Hyndburn | 98 | 53 | 40 | 63 | 27 | 9 | 77 | 15 | 81 | 38 |
| Exeter | 12 | 21 | 25 | 25 | 7 | 95 | 12 | 22 | 35 | 14 |
| Barnet | 115 | 4 | 37 | 57 | 16 | 5 | 21 | 23 | 19 | 16 |
| Sunderland | 22 | 47 | 18 | 50 | 22 | 19 | 69 | 85 | 12 | 34 |
| Ipswich | 17 | 17 | 53 | 22 | 40 | 7 | 22 | 17 | 27 | 17 |
| Hull | 20 | 30 | 38 | 20 | 13 | 99 | 13 | 34 | 17 | 11 |
| Barrow | 87 | 40 | 68 | 121 | 59 | 13 | 43 | 50 | 94 | 27 |
| Norwich | 9 | 7 | 13 | 18 | 17 | 104 | 35 | 68 | 68 | 12 |
| Southampton | 109 | 20 | 56 | 2 | 34 | 12 | 51 | 13 | 14 | 43 |
| Walsall | 33 | 29 | 30 | 13 | 41 | 69 | 20 | 79 | 43 | 15 |
| Leicester | 39 | 43 | 22 | 41 | 37 | 41 | 25 | 57 | 30 | 26 |
| Leeds | 41 | 23 | 28 | 45 | 25 | 66 | 45 | 31 | 49 | 44 |
| Bolton | 29 | 51 | 46 | 76 | 36 | 30 | 81 | 27 | 66 | 37 |
| | | | | | | | | | | |
| Haringey | 124 | 34 | 71 | 114 | 63 | 61 | 96 | 43 | 65 | 103 |
| Oxford | 107 | 48 | 86 | 115 | 99 | 90 | 41 | 93 | 32 | 86 |
| Ellesmere Pt | 51 | 120 | 88 | 6 | 89 | 101 | 75 | 100 | 114 | 98 |
| Dartford | 93 | 57 | 95 | 105 | 106 | 67 | 52 | 56 | 100 | 100 |
| Bexley | 4 | 76 | 106 | 56 | 68 | 34 | 37 | 104 | 42 | 93 |
| Brent | 123 | 31 | 103 | 116 | 60 | 47 | 88 | 121 | 89 | 81 |
| Wrekin | 103 | 97 | 113 | 38 | 88 | 109 | 84 | 65 | 117 | 102 |
| Warrington | 43 | 110 | 85 | 101 | 94 | 91 | 116 | 42 | 104 | 113 |
| Medway | 105 | 83 | 114 | 78 | 112 | 18 | 57 | 109 | 87 | 68 |
| Lewisham | 54 | 59 | 96 | 34 | 56 | 85 | 111 | 120 | 24 | 108 |
| Halton | 100 | 88 | 99 | 62 | 115 | 115 | 115 | 6 | 124 | 110 |
| Southwark | 121 | 27 | 82 | 44 | 48 | 114 | 100 | 112 | 52 | 104 |
| Wellingboro | 85 | 107 | 102 | 117 | 84 | 81 | 94 | 74 | 116 | 106 |
| Redditch | 108 | 62 | 98 | 124 | 102 | 78 | 99 | 111 | 120 | 101 |
| Kensington | 40 | 87 | 108 | 110 | 69 | 124 | 31 | 29 | 110 | 52 |
| Slough | 102 | 33 | 105 | 103 | 91 | 76 | 85 | 110 | 75 | 107 |
| Thurrock | 70 | 104 | 120 | 69 | 118 | 73 | 65 | 61 | 97 | 75 |
| Lambeth | 90 | 52 | 73 | 91 | 46 | 105 | 102 | 118 | 61 | 109 |
| Greenwich | 34 | 66 | 119 | 75 | 96 | 52 | 114 | 71 | 53 | 95 |
| Luton | 114 | 37 | 117 | 106 | 101 | 108 | 40 | 95 | 95 | 112 |
| Harlow | 28 | 32 | 116 | 82 | 110 | 122 | 39 | 55 | 115 | 97 |
| Basildon | 94 | 70 | 115 | 64 | 117 | 117 | 42 | 25 | 112 | 96 |
| Thamesdown | 71 | 119 | 110 | 118 | 113 | 86 | 120 | 88 | 109 | 119 |
| Tamworth | 101 | 112 | 111 | 42 | 123 | 106 | 103 | 96 | 122 | 122 |
| Barking | 113 | 80 | 122 | 70 | 75 | 111 | 95 | 124 | 111 | 114 |
| Ealing | 118 | 74 | 97 | 122 | 114 | 107 | 66 | 123 | 106 | 116 |
| Wandsworth | 31 | 89 | 90 | 111 | 92 | 112 | 117 | 113 | 72 | 117 |
| Hammersmith | 83 | 90 | 91 | 109 | 111 | 121 | 105 | 94 | 98 | 118 |
| Milton Keynes | 84 | 105 | 121 | 104 | 120 | 70 | 123 | 80 | 113 | 124 |
| Stevenage | 119 | 99 | 123 | 102 | 124 | 123 | 29 | 54 | 123 | 115 |
| Corby | 106 | 124 | 124 | 120 | 122 | 118 | 124 | 119 | 121 | 123 |

*Figure A74*   **Number of VAT registered businesses by turnover size**

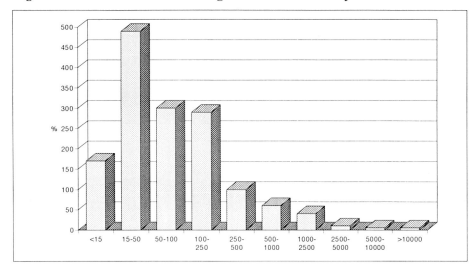

*Figure A75*   **Number of businesses registered for VAT**

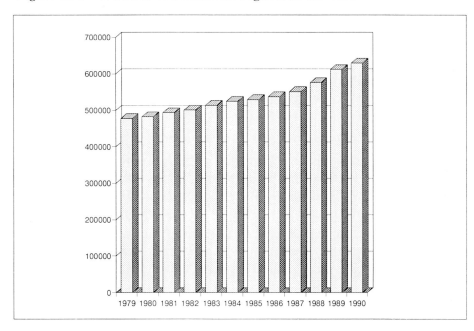

*Figure A76*   **% change in numbers of VAT registered businesses by region 1980-90**

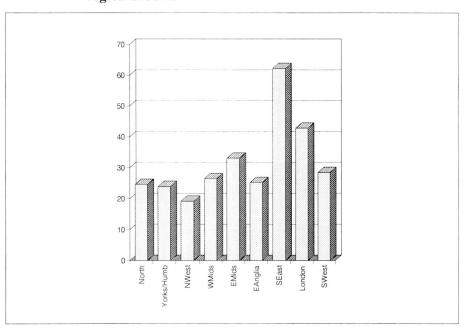

149

*Figure A77* **Absolute change in numbers of VAT registered businesses by LAD type 1979-90**

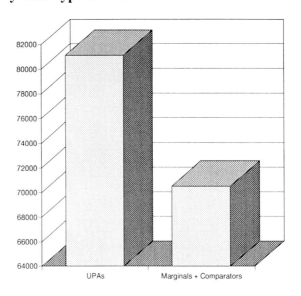

*Figure A78* **% change in numbers of VAT registered businesses in LAD type 1979-90**

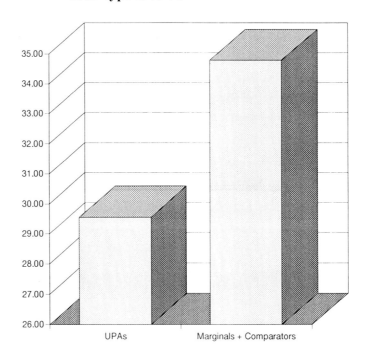

*Figure A79* **Number of VAT registered businesses by LAD type 1979-90**

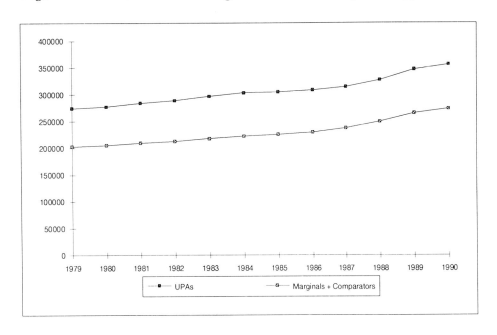

*Figure A80* **VAT registrations by LAD type - analysis of variance F-value**

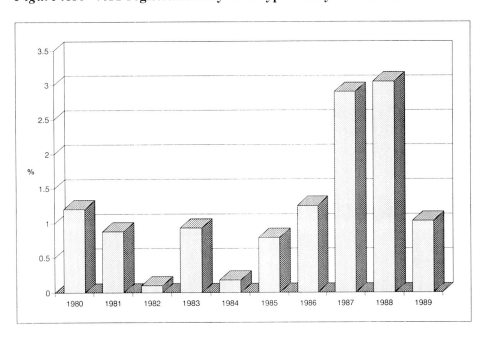

# A27   NET CHANGE IN NUMBER / PROPORTION 25-34 YEAR OLDS

**1   Data availability**

Population data are available at LA, county and regional scales for the years 1977-1990.

**2   Data definitions**

Population estimates are devised using results from the 1981 census as a base, and adding in natural change and migration estimates. While birth and death figures are highly accurate, the migration component is considerably more difficult to estimate since there is no migration register as such. Instead, estimates are based on two data sources: the International Passenger Survey (IPS) and the NHS Central Register.

IPS was designed specifically to measure migration at a national scale, resulting in problems when the scale of analysis is the LA. Although accurate at a national level, IPS is much less accurate at LA level because of the small sample size and because many immigrants are unsure of their final destination. Problems also apply to the NHS Central Register dataset, which was not designed as a source of migration information. The main problem is that data are available only for counties and metropolitan districts. Both IPS and NHSCR data are disaggregated to LA level by using electoral registration data - that is, changes in the electoral register at LA level are assumed to apply to IPS and NHSCR data.

There are two main qualifications which have to be attached to the dataset. First, while attraction of 25-34 year olds can be construed as an indicator of attractiveness, interpretation of the retention dimension is more problematic since it could imply the 'locking-in' of this group into a depressed local economy. Second, it is important to remember that all data are estimated and therefore have to be treated with caution. That the data are comprised of estimates will be obvious from some of the time-series patterns shown.

**3   Data analysis**

There are three different measures of population change, each with its own benefits:

- Absolute change - actual number gained/lost is important, even though the implications of a given level of change will vary according to the original size of the population.

- Relative change - change expressed as a proportion of the initial population

- Proportional change - change in the number of 25-34 year olds as a proportion of change for all age groups. Unlike relative change, this takes into account changes amongst other population groups, while still showing the proportional contribution of the 25-34 group. In other words, whereas relative change shows change in relation to that group itself, proportional change is affected by changes to other age groups.

This analysis is restricted to absolute and relative change. Table A10 shows the upper and lower quartiles of the ranking of LAs.

Figure A81 shows change in population over the 1977-1990 period. The totals increase to a peak in 1981, before falling until 1984 and rising steadily thereafter. There appears to be a clear breakpoint between years 1981 and 1982. This is because estimates for the years 1982-90 were based on the 1981 Census. In effect, the estimates from 1977-1980 and 1982-90 have to be considered as two separate sets.

**LA-type pattern.** If we look within this overall pattern at the contrast between LA types it appears that in relative terms the level of change is greater for the UPAs than for the comparators/marginals (Figure A82). Figure A83 shows the time-series pattern by LA-type. The shapes of the curves are broadly similar, although the increase in population over the 1986-90 period appears to be steepest for the UPAs. The 'bump' in the 1981 figures and the uniformity of the curve lines emphasise that the data are based on estimates and must be treated with caution.

**Regional breakdown.** Figures A84 and A85 show the pattern of regional change. The pattern of relative change is interesting because the East Midlands differs substantially from the similar change figures exhibited by the other regions, which fall within the range 6.06% (South West) to 9.06% (South East). Of the 16.7% growth in East Midlands, three quarters of this is accounted for by four of the region's ten authorities - Leicester, Nottingham, Derby and Northampton. The largest relative increases in the region are found in Lincoln (+31.8%) and Northampton (+39.9%). Interestingly, the population of Corby fell by 6.1% (-521) - a trend which sits oddly with Corby's performance on the other indicator variables.

Reference

OPCS (1992), 'Making a population estimate England and Wales', **Occasional Paper**, 37

*Table A10*  **Upper and Lower Quartile - ranking of LAs by percentage change in 25-34 year-old population, 1977-90**

| LA | change | %change | region | LA type |
|---|---|---|---|---|
| **Upper Quartile** | | | | |
| Kensington & Chelsea | -15646 | -41.95 | London | UPA |
| Westminster City | -9275 | -26.20 | London | marginal |
| Camden | -4747 | -13.30 | London | marginal |
| Norwich | -2135 | -12.49 | EAnglia | comparator |
| Hammersmith and Fulham | -3725 | -12.38 | London | UPA |
| Southampton | -3439 | -11.13 | SEast | marginal |
| Haringey | -3325 | -9.42 | London | UPA |
| Durham | -1206 | -8.93 | North | comparator |
| Scunthorpe | -747 | -8.30 | Yorks/H | marginal |
| Kingston upon Hull | -2939 | -7.90 | Yorks/H | UPA |
| Bristol | -4070 | -7.07 | SWest | UPA |
| Harlow | -787 | -6.90 | SEast | comparator |
| Thurrock | -1446 | -6.85 | SEast | marginal |
| Gravesham | -919 | -6.71 | SEast | comparator |
| Corby | -521 | -6.13 | EMids | marginal |
| Ipswich | -945 | -5.73 | EAnglia | comparator |
| Blyth Valley | -676 | -5.16 | North | marginal |
| Oxford | -821 | -4.72 | SEast | comparator |
| West Lancashire | -741 | -4.57 | NWest | marginal |
| Newcastle u Lyme | - 387 | -2.28 | WMids | marginal |
| Sedgefield | -131 | -0.96 | North | marginal |
| Barrow in Furness | -59 | -0.57 | North | marginal |
| Langbaurgh | -96 | -0.43 | North | UPA |
| Lambeth | -173 | -0.41 | London | UPA |
| Havering | -80 | -0.23 | London | comparator |
| Wigan | 108 | 0.22 | NWest | UPA |
| Liverpool | 158 | 0.24 | NWest | UPA |
| Coventry | 283 | 0.62 | WMids | UPA |
| Portsmouth | 555 | 1.98 | SEast | marginal |
| Salford | 750 | 2.25 | NWest | UPA |

*Table A10*  **Upper and Lower Quartile - ranking of LAs by percentage change in 25-34 year-old population, 1977-90** (continued)

| LA | change | %change | region | LA type |
|---|---|---|---|---|
| **Upper Quartile** | | | | |
| Ellesmere Pt and Neston | 288 | 2.34 | NWest | marginal |
| Bury | 701 | 2.60 | NWest | comparator |
| Derwentside | 356 | 2.89 | North | marginal |
| Rochester upon Medway | 776 | 3.25 | SEast | marginal |
| **Lower Quartile** | | | | |
| Great Grimsby | 1573 | 12.58 | Yorks/H | marginal |
| Exeter | 1642 | 12.63 | SWest | marginal |
| Sunderland | 5340 | 12.81 | North | UPA |
| Islington | 3683 | 13.49 | London | UPA |
| Nottingham | 5013 | 13.7 | EMids | UPA |
| Bolton | 5325 | 14.05 | NWest | UPA |
| Doncaster | 5666 | 14.09 | Yorks/H | UPA |
| South Tyneside | 2912 | 14.27 | North | UPA |
| Leicester | 5436 | 14.53 | EMids | UPA |
| Bradford | 9334 | 15.01 | Yorks/H | UPA |
| Stockton on Tees | 4018 | 15.76 | North | UPA |
| Manchester | 9631 | 15.87 | NWest | UPA |
| Chesterfield | 2200 | 16.18 | EMids | marginal |
| Chester Le Street | 1233 | 16.22 | North | comparator |
| Darlington | 2249 | 16.78 | North | comparator |
| The Wrekin | 3090 | 16.89 | WMids | UPA |
| Redditch | 2004 | 18.22 | WMids | marginal |
| Derby | 5529 | 19.54 | EMids | UPA |
| Great Yarmouth | 2146 | 20.06 | EAnglia | comparator |
| Calderdale | 5276 | 20.21 | Yorks/H | marginal |
| Sefton | 8013 | 21.37 | NWest | UPA |
| Luton | 5332 | 21.76 | SEast | marginal |
| Slough | 3542 | 25.48 | SEast | comparator |
| Worcester | 2764 | 26.32 | WMids | marginal |
| Peterborough | 6113 | 33.59 | EAnglia | comparator |
| Hackney | 8941 | 33.87 | London | UPA |
| Preston | 5272 | 34.68 | NWest | UPA |
| Warrington | 8350 | 35.08 | NWest | comparator |
| Lincoln | 3720 | 37.58 | EMids | marginal |
| Southwark | 10655 | 38.05 | London | UPA |

*Figure A81*  **Population in the 25-34 age band for sample of 123 Lads**

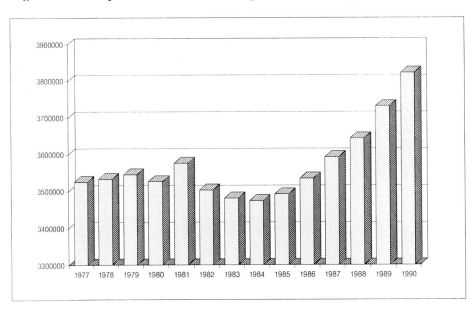

## Figure A82　%　change in 25-34 population by LAD type 1977-90

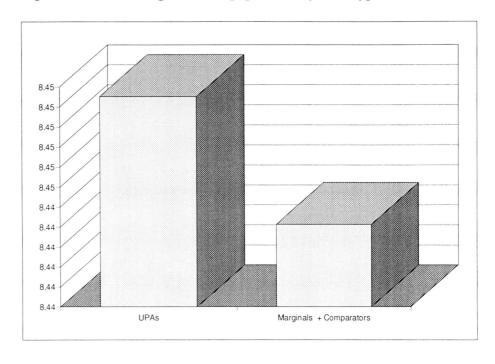

## Figure A83　25-34 population by LAD type 1977-90

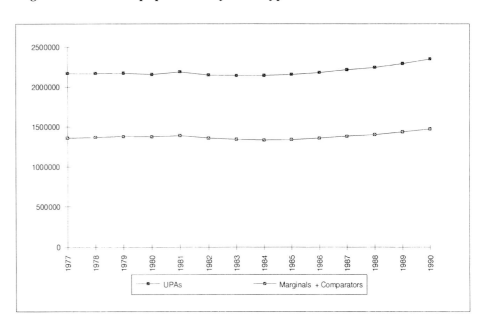

## Figure A84   % change in 25-34 population by region 1977-90

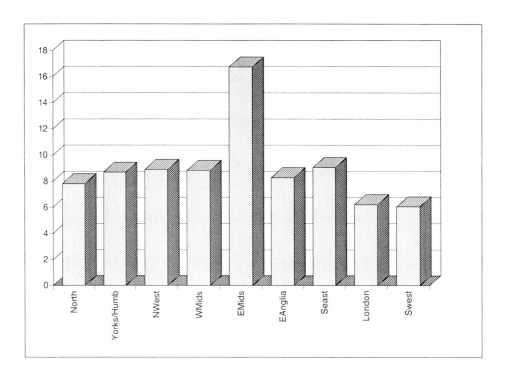

## Figure A85   Absolute change in 25-34 population by region 1977-90

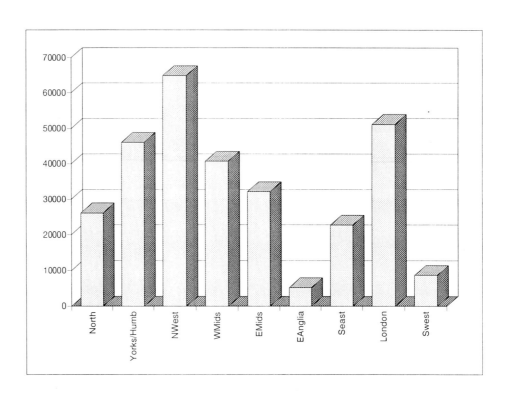

# *Appendix B* National-level analysis

## 1 INTRODUCTION

The overall aim of this analysis is to use a national sample of local authority districts to investigate:

- their national government financial inputs;

- their outcome experiences, measured on a set of socio-economic indicators; and

- the relationships between these inputs and outcomes, representing the overall impact of inner city policy.

### 1.1 Sample authorities

A sample of 123 district authorities was selected comprising:

- all of the 57 Urban Programme Authorities (UPA) as used in Action for Cities;

- 40 authorities which either, under earlier phases of urban policy had received Urban Programme resources (largely as Other Designated Districts) but were not subsequently included amongst the 57 UPAs, or whose unemployment levels and proportion of semi-skilled and unskilled populations in 1981 were little different from the UPAs. In socio-economic terms they are little different from many of the 57, and are here referred to as 'marginal' authorities; and

- a further 26 authorities that are used as comparators. These have not been targeted by government policy and the districts were selected: to include places with above-average unemployment and below-average proportions of professional and managerial households; to include places within each of the Standard Regions; and to provide contiguous swathes of coverage of certain parts of the country (north east of Greater London; the areas around and between the conurbations of the North West and West and South Yorkshire; and the two conurbations of the North East).

Comparisons are made between various combinations of these three subsets. The 123 sample is shown in Figure B1.

### 1.2 Outcomes: socio-economic indicators

In looking at the impacts of policy we were concerned to measure the outcomes of policy rather than the outputs. Outputs would include such measures as numbers of houses built, numbers of advance factories constructed, hectares of land reclaimed. They are in many ways indirect estimates of inputs and, to that extent, there would be circularity involved in looking at the relationship between inputs and outputs. To assess policy impacts it is therefore important to consider the more general changes which policy intervention may have effected - hence our concern with outcomes. In selecting appropriate measures, we first examined the written statements of intent behind all of the 40 policy instruments which have been used as part of urban policy. These suggested over one hundred 'first-order' objectives, many but not all of which overlapped. These were then aggregated into a set of 10 second-order objectives and they in turn into two third-order objectives. The second- and third-order objectives are suggested in the Venn diagram of Figure B2. The two third-level objectives are employment opportunities and residential attractiveness.

Five socio-economic indicators were selected to reflect these objectives. They are as follows:

- **unemployment and long-term unemployment** (addressing objectives 1,2,3,4 and 6).

  **Source:** NOMIS. Unemployment remains the single most potent measure of socio-economic conditions, with high levels reflecting poverty and having impacts on the stability and robustness of communities.

- **net job change 1981-87** (addressing objectives 1,2,3,4 and 6).

  **Source:** Census of Employment. This is included to give some overall measure of changing employment opportunities. However, at the ward level, only totals are available for all wards because of problems of confidentiality. Data may also be difficult to interpret at one point in time because of using the company rather than establishment as a base. However, by examining change over time this is less of a problem, even if still an important consideration. Perhaps the greatest problem with the indicator is the fact that it cannot distinguish who are the recipients of new jobs; commuters from out of cities absorb significant proportions of inner-city jobs.

- **house price change 1983-89** (addressing objectives 2,6,7,8,9 and 10).

  **Source:** building society records (both Nationwide-Anglia and Halifax building societies). Averages are calculated for two combinations of housing types and households: first-time buyers; and all houses in defined 'inner areas' (defined through 1981 Census data in terms of levels of unemployment and social composition). House prices reflect a combination of use value, exchange value and sign/symbolic values. The variation in house price change between areas within a city is obviously an indicator of the interaction of demand and supply, rather than simply of demand. There are a number of limitations with house prices. First they do not reflect the value of all houses. Some wards will be dominated by LA rented housing. There may be evidence of price changes in privately-bought council houses for the latter part of the period and in such low cost home ownership schemes as private refurbishment of council housing, and housing associations' improvement for sale and shared ownership. A second limitation is that any measure will be based on the property on the market at that time, which may not be representative of the property in the ward as a whole.

- **net change in the number/proportion of 25-34 year olds 1981-1991** (addressing objectives 1,7,8,9 and 10).

  **Source:** census. Since one of the major problems of inner cities has been net out-migration, it is important to include an indicator that measures the degree of retention and attraction of population. A particularly significant age group that has featured in out-migration is the 25-34 year olds. The changed number and proportion of this age group may reflect the confidence of both living and working in the inner city. It is a good indicator of any success in reversing the trend of population loss.

- **change in number of small businesses 1981-1990** (addressing objectives 1,2,4 and 5).

  **Source:** VAT registrations via Office of Customs and Excise. This is the best available indicator of variations in new firm creation over time. The index linking of the turnover threshold lends consistency to the data over time and the availability of data on a sectoral basis enables the effect of an area's industrial structure to be taken into account. The growth of new firms only captures part of what is meant by enterprise but it is a sector of the economy that has received much government interest during the 1980s. Nevertheless, if there has been any change in the economic health of the 57 UPAs, it could be argued that it should be revealed by this indicator. The data set does have a number of inherent limitations. The source gives details of all those firms with a turnover above an indexed-linked threshold that trade in mainly VAT-rated goods and services. It also identifies for each calendar year new registrations and also those firms deleted from the register. Not all new registrations are small firms and neither can it be assumed that all are new starts. Some small firms do not have to register for VAT either because they fall below the VAT threshold or because they trade only, or mainly, in exempt or zero-rated goods and services. Nevertheless, some companies which are exempt do opt for voluntary registration and the vast majority of registrations are small firms. Other limitations are that, among the number of deaths, new firms of short life cannot be distinguished from the death of older ones; nor is there any way of indicating if any deaths of older firms have been caused by the arrival of new ones in the same sector.

**1.3 Inputs**

Two forms of financial input are used. First is what are referred to as AfC resources (while Action for Cities was only launched in 1988, for the sake of simplicity we have used the term 'AfC resources' to cover identifiable targeted inner-city expenditure for the whole period of the analysis). This includes all of the measurable and attributable expenditure from the set of programmes which were rolled into the Action for Cities programme (details are given in Table 1 in the main text). Some expenditure is aspatial and, since it cannot be attributed to specific districts, has been excluded from the analysis; the best example of this being expenditure on training. Of the total AfC expenditure, our analysis has been able to incorporate some 60%. Second, is the 'overall' expenditure which comprises AfC expenditure together with expenditure on the Housing Investment Programme, Rate Support Grant, the regional programmes of Regional Selective Assistance and Regional Development Grants, and European resources under the Social Fund (ESF) and Regional Development Grant (ERDF). Expenditure data for all of these programmes were collected for all of the districts in the sample and this extensive data set provides the input statistics.

Inputs have been measured as amounts of money per capita. This common base allows the aggregate input of all programmes to be calculated. This approach has been taken because governments usually want to evaluate the impact of their expenditure. There are arguments against such an accounting approach but it has been adopted here as the main way of measuring the overall input into areas.

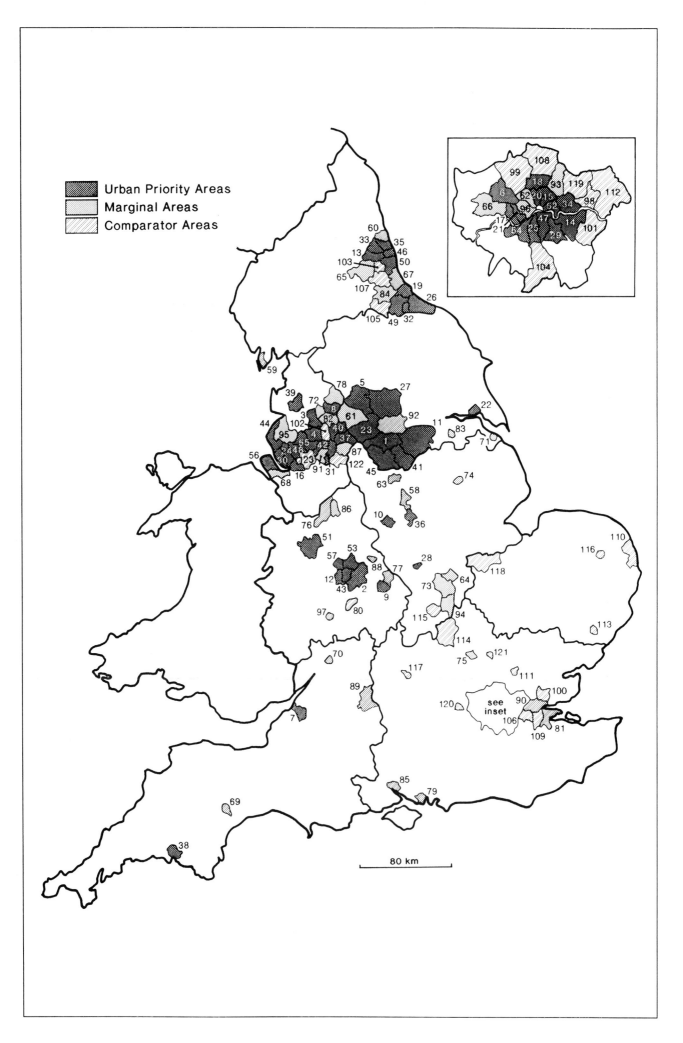

| Ref. No. | County | District | Category | Ref. No. | County | District | Category |
|---|---|---|---|---|---|---|---|
| 1 | S.Yorks | Barnsley | 1 | 63 | Derby | Chesterfield | 2 |
| 2 | W.Mids | Birmingham | 1 | 64 | Nhants | Corby | 2* |
| 3 | Lancs | Blackburn | 1 | 65 | Durham | Derwentside | 2* |
| 4 | Gr.Mcr | Bolton | 1 | 66 | OLond | Ealing | 2* |
| 5 | W.Yorks | Bradford | 1 | 67 | Durham | Easington | 2 |
| 6 | OLond | Brent | 1 | 68 | Chesh | Ellesmere Port/Neston | 2* |
| 7 | Avon | Bristol | 1 | 69 | Devon | Exeter | 2 |
| 8 | Lancs | Burnley | 1 | 70 | Glos | Gloucester | 2 |
| 9 | W.Mids | Coventry | 1 | 71 | Humber | Great Grimsby | 2* |
| 10 | Derby | Derby | 1 | 72 | Lancs | Hyndburn | 2* |
| 11 | S.Yorks | Doncaster | 1 | 73 | Nhants | Kettering | 2 |
| 12 | W.Mids | Dudley | 1 | 74 | Lincs | Lincoln | 2* |
| 13 | TyneWear | Gateshead | 1 | 75 | Beds | Luton | 2* |
| 14 | OLond | Greenwich | 1 | 76 | Staffs | Newcastle-u-Lyne | 2 |
| 15 | ILond | Hackney | 1 | 77 | Warw | Nuneaton | 2 |
| 16 | Chesh | Halton | 1 | 78 | Lancs | Pendle | 2* |
| 17 | ILond | Hammersmith/Fulham | 1 | 79 | Hants | Portsmouth | 2 |
| 18 | ILond | Haringey | 1 | 80 | HereWorc | Redditch | 2 |
| 19 | Cleve | Hartlepool | 1 | 81 | Kent | Rochester | 2 |
| 20 | ILond | Islington | 1 | 82 | Lancs | Rossendale | 2* |
| 21 | ILond | Kensington/Chelsea | 1 | 83 | Humber | Scunthorpe | 2* |
| 22 | Humber | Kingston-on-Hull | 1 | 84 | Durham | Sedgefield | 2* |
| 23 | W.Yorks | Kirklees | 1 | 85 | Hants | Southampton | 2 |
| 24 | Mersey | Knowsley | 1 | 86 | Staffs | Stoke-on-Trent | 2* |
| 25 | ILond | Lambeth | 1 | 87 | Gr.Mcr | Tameside | 2* |
| 26 | Cleve | Langbaurgh | 1 | 88 | Staffs | Tamworth | 2 |
| 27 | W.Yorks | Leeds | 1 | 89 | Wilts | Thamesdown | 2 |
| 28 | Leic | Leicester | 1 | 90 | Essex | Thurrock | 2 |
| 29 | ILond | Lewisham | 1 | 91 | Gr.Mcr | Trafford | 2* |
| 30 | Mersey | Liverpool | 1 | 92 | W.Yorks | Wakefield | 2 |
| 31 | Gr.Mcr | Manchester | 1 | 93 | OLond | Waltham Forest | 2* |
| 32 | Cleve | Middlesbrough | 1 | 94 | Nhants | Wellingborough | 2 |
| 33 | TyneWear | Newcastle-on-Tyne | 1 | 95 | Lancs | West Lancashire | 2* |
| 34 | ILond | Newham | 1 | 96 | ILond | Westminster | 2* |
| 35 | TyneWear | North Tyneside | 1 | 97 | HereWorc | Worcester | 2 |
| 36 | Notts | Nottingham | 1 | 98 | OLond | Barking/Dagenham | 3 |
| 37 | Gr.Mcr | Oldham | 1 | 99 | OLond | Barnet | 3 |
| 38 | Devon | Plymouth | 1 | 100 | Essex | Basildon | 3 |
| 39 | Lancs | Preston | 1 | 101 | OLond | Bexley | 3 |
| 40 | Gr.Mcr | Rochdale | 1 | 102 | Gr.Mcr | Bury | 3 |
| 41 | S.Yorks | Rotherham | 1 | 103 | Durham | Chester-le-Street | 3 |
| 42 | Gr.Mcr | Salford | 1 | 104 | OLond | Croydon | 3 |
| 43 | W.Mids | Sandwell | 1 | 105 | Durham | Darlington | 3 |
| 44 | Mersey | Sefton | 1 | 106 | Kent | Dartford | 3 |
| 45 | S.Yorks | Sheffield | 1 | 107 | Durham | Durham | 3 |
| 46 | TyneWear | South Tyneside | 1 | 108 | OLond | Enfield | 3 |
| 47 | ILond | Southwark | 1 | 109 | Kent | Gravesham | 3 |
| 48 | Mersey | St.Helens | 1 | 110 | Norfolk | Great Yarmouth | 3 |
| 49 | Cleve | Stockton-on-Tees | 1 | 111 | Essex | Harlow | 3 |
| 50 | TyneWear | Sunderland | 1 | 112 | OLond | Havering | 3 |
| 51 | Salop | The Wrekin | 1 | 113 | Suffolk | Ipswich | 3 |
| 52 | ILond | Tower Hamlets | 1 | 114 | Bucks | Milton Keynes | 3 |
| 53 | W.Mids | Walsall | 1 | 115 | Nhants | Northampton | 3 |
| 54 | ILond | Wandsworth | 1 | 116 | Norfolk | Norwich | 3 |
| 55 | Gr.Mcr | Wigan | 1 | 117 | Oxon | Oxford | 3 |
| 56 | Mersey | Wirral | 1 | 118 | Cam | Peterborough | 3 |
| 57 | W.Mids | Wolverhampton | 1 | 119 | OLond | Redbridge | 3 |
| 58 | Notts | Ashfield | 2 | 120 | Berks | Slough | 3 |
| 59 | Cumbria | Barrow-in-Furness | 2 | 121 | Herts | Stevenage | 3 |
| 60 | Northd | Blyth Valley | 2 | 122 | Gr.Mcr | Stockport | 3 |
| 61 | W.Yorks | Calderdale | 2* | 123 | Chesh | Warrington | 3 |
| 62 | ILond | Camden | 2* | | | | |

Notes

The categories are as follows:

1. Urban Priority Areas (as defined in Action for Cities)

2. Marginal districts (those which were targeted, largely as Other Designated Districts, in earlier phases of the Urban Programme are shown with asterisks)

3. Comparators

**1.4 Aims**

The specific aims of the analysis of the inputs are to:

- discover whether the 57 UPAs have in practice received more inputs from national government urban policy than the others in the sample;

- examine the variation of national government inputs for the 57 UPAs; and

- analyse the inputs of urban policy resources compared with other monies from national government and from the EC.

The specific aims of the analysis of outcomes are to:

- compare the indicators for the three groups, particularly to see whether the gaps between the UPAs and the comparators, and the UPAs and the marginals are closing;

- compare the indicators within the 57 UPAs to establish which of the 57 are exhibiting better outcomes; and

- compare indicators for UPAs and comparators across regions to see whether gaps between regions are closing.

The specific aims of the analysis of relationships between inputs and outcomes are to:

- see whether a multi-level model can be applied to the 123 so that a sophisticated analysis of associations and contextual variables can be carried out;

- examine lagged correlations, partial correlations and regressions between inputs and outcomes in order to establish whether there are any strong associations between inputs and outcomes for the 123, 97 or 57;

- analyse whether any closure of gaps between UPAs and comparators is associated with different overall inputs;

- analyse whether differential outcomes for the UPAs is associated with differential inputs of either AfC or overall monies;

- produce profiles for all UPAs and other areas receiving major amounts of inputs; and

- produce a classification of areas according to the relationship between their inputs and outcomes.

It is important to note that it is impossible to attribute causality from this analysis. Models can only show associations or directions of relationships and trends and need further in-depth analysis of a different kind in order to establish cause or causal mechanisms. Even then, most socio-economic outcomes are multi-causal; isolating the effect of one factor is difficult.

**1.5 Possible relationships and the methodologies**

Before outlining the results it is worth considering the possible relationships that might emerge and their meanings. For the inputs it would be expected that government monies would have been concentrated into the 57 UPAs, with fewer going to the marginals and still fewer to the comparators. Yet some AfC programmes, such as Enterprise Zones, are not restricted to the 57 UPAs. It is therefore possible that some non-UPAs will receive greater amounts of input and that targeting of overall monies has not corresponded to the priorities set. This would make the comparison of outcomes and impacts between the three groups of places more complex.

Positive impacts of the inputs on the outcome indicators could take a number of forms:

- an absolute improvement in the indicators for UPAs (i.e. less unemployment, more jobs etc);

- a relative improvement in the UPAs by comparison with the comparator areas; and

- in periods of overall economic downturn, a slower deterioration in the UPAs by comparison with the comparator districts.

Any such comparisons can only imperfectly take account of the counterfactual argument. There is no easy way of estimating this. Trends and projections from past periods may be used, but that depends on availability of data and being able to distinguish the effects of previous policies that may or may not continue and may or may not have lagged effects. The methodology used here has been one of comparison between places receiving policy inputs and ones that have not, or more precisely between those receiving more and fewer inputs; hence the choice of the 40 marginals and the comparators.

The difficulty with such comparisons is that the places do not start from the same position. Their initial conditions vary and one would expect given amounts of inputs to have different impacts partly because of this. So one planned method is to introduce contextual variables that would take account of the initial conditions.

**Figure B2  Higher-level and lower-level policy objectives**

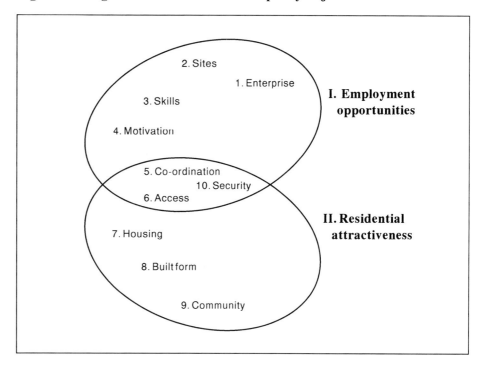

Places which are located in different regions may be responding to global economic restructuring in different ways, partly because of their regional economic structure. So places in different regions which receive the same amount of inputs, even though the initial conditions of the individual places may not differ appreciably, may still experience different impacts because of their regional context. The regional context has been taken into account in various ways, one being analysis of change within particular regions.

These considerations suggest comparisons of the UPAs, marginals and comparators at different geographical scales: national and regional. Within these analyses, the gaps between the three sets of places at particular points of time will be observed. The use of similar points on the economic cycle is important because places are differentially sensitive to the cycle, with some showing much greater rises and falls in unemployment for example. A narrowing of the gap between the three sets of places between comparable points on the economic cycle may be argued as an indication of the successful impact of policy inputs. A widening could be argued as failure but it could also be argued, again using the counterfactual point, that the gap would have been even wider without the government inputs. Clearly a narrowing gap could also be argued as a trajectory which would have happened anyway, without government inputs, but most evidence suggests that market forces lead to greater rather than smaller regional differences.

There are two other major points to make about the relationships between inputs and outcomes, as discussed in this section of the report. The aim of the research is to examine overall outcomes, not the outputs or outcomes of particular programmes. The links between inputs and outcomes are therefore examined at a wider, indirect level. There is no attempt in this part of the report to show the mechanisms by which any associations there might be between inputs and outcomes come about. That remains a black box here, but it is one which other parts of the report address, using different methodological approaches.

Finally it is necessary to try to untangle the relationships between inputs and outcomes. Lagged correlations are used to reflect earlier inputs and somewhat later outcomes, so that the outcomes as a possible response to inputs are modelled. However, the geographical distribution of inputs at one of point of time is often closely related to that at another point of time, especially the preceding and following years. Similarly the indicator outcomes may at times be closely related to those at other points of time. So it is possible to argue that any close relationship between inputs and outcomes may be a reflection of inputs being targeted on immediately past outcomes, rather than outcomes responding to inputs. By examining change in the outcome indicators, the autocorrelation with previous outcomes is removed. This helps us to distinguish interpretations that outcomes lead to inputs as against inputs leading to outcomes. It is less appropriate to examine change in the inputs (i.e. to remove the autocorrelation over time) because it is the spatially varying total amounts of the inputs that it is argued should be affecting the outcome changes.

Examining the strongest lagged correlations also partly offsets the interpretation that outcomes lead to inputs (i.e. if inputs made before outcomes show stronger correlations than inputs made just after outcomes, then the inputs to outcomes model is stronger than the outcomes to inputs one). Where there is a strong relationship between the outcomes of a particular year and change in following years, as there is with unemployment indicators in 1986 and change from 1986 to 1990, then a partial correlation between inputs and outcome changes has been carried out controlling for the effect of the outcome year eg inputs 1985/6 to 1989/90 with unemployment change 1986-1990 controlling for 1986 unemployment levels. We have therefore tried to disentangle the associations between inputs and outcomes by examining changes in the outcome indicators rather than levels, and using lagged correlations and partial correlations.

The remainder of this Appendix is divided into three major sections: inputs; outcomes; and impacts - the relationship between inputs and outcomes.

## 2 THE INPUTS

**2.1 AfC expenditure per capita: national level**

For the sake of simplicity inner city expenditure over the period 1979-90 is referred to as AfC expenditure, although it was not called that until 1988. This expenditure was deflated to 1981 prices and recorded per capita. It was aggregated for the overall period and for 1981-90. The resulting rankings below are indicated for the latter period, with the former in brackets where different. Twelve non-UPAs appear in the top 57, two of them in the top 10.

**Non-UPAs falling within the best-funded 57 LAs 1981-90**

| LA | rank | % of total | main expenditure heads |
|---|---|---|---|
| Corby | 3 | 6.97 | (EZ and DLG) |
| Scunthorpe | 7(8) | 2.28 | (EZ) |
| Durham | 24(28) | 1.12 | (EE) |
| Trafford | 27(25) | 1.01 | (EZ and UDC) |
| Derwentside | 34(39) | 0.87 | (DLG and EE) |
| Wellingborough | 36(42) | 0.86 | (EZ) |
| Rochester | 43(41) | 0.72 | (EZ and EE) |
| Sedgefield | 49(48) | 0.61 | (EE) |
| Rossendale | 51(54) | 0.59 | (EZ,DLG,EA and EE) |
| Ellesmere/Neston | 55 | 0.53 | (DLG and EE) |
| Blyth Valley | 56(52) | 0.53 | (EE and EA) |
| Hyndburn | 57 | 0.52 | (EZ,CG,DLG and EA) |

Contrariwise, the 12 UPAs which fall outside the 57 are:

**UPAs falling outside the best-funded 57 LAs 1981-90**

| LA | rank | % of total |
|---|---|---|
| Haringey | 60 | 0.43 |
| Wandsworth | 61 | 0.42 |
| St Helens | 63 | 0.41 |
| Wigan | 66 | 0.35 |
| Lewisham | 67 | 0.32 |
| Barnsley | 68 | 0.31 |
| Derby | 72 | 0.26 |
| Sefton | 74 | 0.23 |
| Plymouth | 76 | 0.23 |
| Kensington/Chelsea | 78 | 0.22 |
| Kirklees | 80 | 0.21 |
| Bristol | 87 | 0.11 |

Since the 57 UPAs have only formally been used as the targeted set of districts since the introduction of Action for Cities, it may appear more logical to look at such rankings for the period 1988/9 to 1989/90 (during which AfC was in operation and for which we have full expenditure data). This, however, makes little difference to the conclusion: for that period 10 of the UPAs fell outside the best-funded 57 districts (details are given in Table 4 in the main text).

Over the whole period, Greater London UPAs have attracted most government monies per capita (31.9%), with Tyne and Wear's six LAs being next best, attracting 10.19% of the total pc. The North East has done even better when Durham, Derwentside and Blyth Valley, all non-UPAs within the top 57, are taken into account.

Although the amount of AfC money going to the 57 increases over the period between 1979/80 and 1989/90 from £12.1pc to £61.6pc, the variation among the 57 increases dramatically, with standard deviations rising from 12 to 128. This variation among the UPAs is commented on further below.

## 2.2 Total inputs: national level

This takes into account 'AfC' monies together with other important inputs that could affect overall outcomes. These include Rate Support Grant (under varying names over the period), Housing Investment Programmes (HIPs), various types of Regional Assistance and European monies. These inputs are also calculated on deflated 1981 values and expressed per capita for ease of comparison. This allows some estimate of net monies entering LAs. It gives us some idea of the relative importance of AfC monies.

As well as being analysed for the whole 123, two major comparisons are made at the regional level: Greater London and the North West. In these two areas there is a mix of UPAs, marginals and comparators. The North East is also examined, but more briefly.

The major point to make about the change in overall inputs over the 1980s is that in most districts the declines in the amounts of RSG and HIPs have a greater overall effect than any change in AfC monies. It is therefore possible that any impact of increasing AfC inputs on overall outcomes may be more than offset by a much greater loss of other revenues.

The overall amount obtained by the 57 UPAs decreases from £367pc in 1979/80 to £298pc in 1989/90 (£244pc in 1990/91). There was a dip to 1985/6 (£287pc) and a rise in 1988/9 to £311pc, but over the decade there has been less overall input despite some new sets of monies coming on line, such as European monies.

The UPAs have lost less monies overall than the marginals and comparators (£69pc, £83pc and £98pc respectively), although this is not the case in 1990/91 when the comparators received more than they did in 1979, more than marginals in 1990/1 and nearly as much as UPAs.

The major point to make is that the experience of the UPAs becomes more varied over time, especially in the latter half of the 1980s. Whereas the standard deviation of overall inputs was 117 in 1979/80 (74 in 1985/6), it had grown to 172 in 1989/90 and to 198 in 1990/1. This variability among UPAs is demonstrated in more detail below for Greater London and the North West.

## 2.3 Inputs for Greater London

We include the 13 UPA authorities, four marginals (Camden, Ealing, Waltham Forest, and Westminster) and seven comparators (Barking, Barnet, Bexley, Croydon, Enfield, Havering and Redbridge). In many ways, Ealing and Waltham Forest are very like the comparators, while Camden and Westminster are more similar to the UPAs.

'AfC' monies. Over the period 1979/80 to 1990/91, two UPAs received considerably more money than any others. Tower Hamlets obtained 10.9% of all of the AfC monies going to our 123 districts, while Newham got 6.73%. The following received quite considerable percentages: Southwark 2.75, Hackney 1.69, Lambeth 1.63, Islington 1.51. Lesser amounts went to Hammersmith 0.91, Brent 0.84, Greenwich 0.72, Lewisham 0.59, Wandsworth 0.5, Haringey 0.48, and Kensington 0.16. Ealing (0.32) and Waltham Forest (0.18) had important slices, while Camden (0.06) and Westminster (0.02) had little.

166

Of the comparators, Bexley obtained most (0.4) and Havering the least (almost none). Most were between 0.09 and 0.05%.

**'Overall' inputs from national government and other sources.** In 1979/80, all the UPAs received more money per capita than the comparators. During the 1980s, however, despite their 'AfC' monies, many UPAs had a greater net loss than the comparators. By 1985/6 only Newham and Tower Hamlets were in a better situation than the comparators in terms of the loss of monies. Newham had a slight net gain since 1979/80 (£10.87 pc). The other 23 authorities had lost monies (Camden the most with £468.54 pc). If the authorities are ranked at this time according to their net gain/loss, Newham is ranked 1 and Camden ranked 24. The difference between the UPAs and the comparators is best shown by the ranks of the comparators, which were: 3,4,5,8,9,11 and 12. Ealing and Waltham Forest are ranked 6 and 7. Of the other UPAs, only Brent, ranked 10, comes above some of the comparators. The rest of the UPAs are well down the rankings list.

This pattern continues until 1989/90, when Tower Hamlets and Newham are clear net gainers (£1122.39 and £838.89). The rest are still net losers. The comparators still dominate the top ranks; of the UPAs only Greenwich (4th) and Haringey (10th) appear before them in the rankings. Brent has dropped back down to 15th.

In 1990/1 there is quite a change in expenditure patterns, through changes in RSG. Hackney had been well down the rankings as a net loser, but in 1990/1 it becomes a slight overall  net gainer over 1979/80. While still net losers over 1979/80, Lambeth, Wandsworth and Brent also improve their position considerably in 1990/1. The improvements in some UPAs means that the position of the comparators relative to the UPAs has changed. They now occupy middle to poorer rankings on the net gainers/losers scale (9th to 19th). Effectively this indicates that the individual UPAs were treated in very different ways in 1990/1. This change is a result of the changed allocation of RSG.

**A comparison between 1979/80 and 1989/90.** 1989/90 is more representative of the latter part of the period than 1990/1. Furthermore, fewer data are available for 1990/1. Consequently, a comparison has been made between the base year and 1989/90. By 1989/90 there was a considerable change in the net amounts coming into authorities. Whereas all the UPAs received more monies than the comparators in 1979/80, by 1989/90 Ealing and Waltham Forest were receiving more than Lewisham, Kensington and Wandsworth. There are other significant changes. There is a much greater difference in the range of amounts received by authorities. In 1979/80, inputs ranged from £782.09 (Islington) to £233.88 (Havering). By 1989/90, they ranged from £1582.34 (Tower Hamlets) to £104.66 (Camden). Dramatic changes have occurred to certain areas: Camden has dropped from 2nd to last; while Tower Hamlets has risen from 11th to 1st and Newham from 10th to 2nd. Other authorities which have lost four or more places in the ranking are: Islington (1 to 5), Kensington (5 to 14), Lewisham (8 to 13), and Westminster (16 to 21). Other climbers are: Ealing (17 to 12), Greenwich (13 to 8), Havering (24 to 20), Redbridge (21 to 17) and Waltham Forest (15 to 11).

**Greater London in summary.** Such rankings do not show amounts lost and can miss important changes. Taking two points in time can also be limiting (1989/90 has been used for comparison because the patterns are fairly consistent until then). It is therefore useful to summarise the whole period 1979/80 to 1990/1.

Southwark does not change rank in total monies coming in, but it has been a consistent loser over the period. Other consistent UPA major losers are Islington, Kensington, and Lewisham. Over the whole period other continuing losers are Hammersmith and Haringey. The dominant UPA gainers are obviously Tower Hamlets and Newham.

Of the non-UPAs, the most consistent loser of all is Camden. Westminster does poorly until 1990/1 when a major input of RSG makes it a net gainer over the period. Ealing and Waltham Forest have similar experiences to the comparators.

In conclusion, although AfC was being targeted at districts, few were net gainers of national government resources over the period, and most lost more money inputs overall than did comparator districts.

## 2.4 Inputs for the North West

In the North West there are 15 UPAs, 7 marginals and 3 comparators. Of the 15 UPAs, 6 are located in Greater Manchester, 5 in Merseyside, 3 in Lancashire and 1 in Cheshire. Of the 10 non-UPAs, 4 are in Greater Manchester (2 of them comparators), 3 in Lancashire and 2 in Cheshire (1 of which is a comparator).

**Allocation of 'AfC' monies per capita.** Over the period 1981-90, not surprisingly, the UPAs generally obtain more AfC monies than do the marginals or comparators. Unlike Greater London, there are, however, major exceptions. Trafford, a marginal, is 6th in the region (27th of the 123) with just over 1% of all monies. The UPAs of the region that obtain more than Trafford are: Liverpool (1st, 4th of 123, with 3.89%); Salford (2nd, 8th of 123, with 2.27%); Manchester (3rd, 11th of 123, with 1.76%); Rochdale (4th, 25th of 123, with 1.12%); and Knowsley (5th, 26th of 123, with 1.04%). Seven UPAs did worse than Trafford and were ranked between 28th and 50th of the 123 (Bolton, Wirral, Blackburn, Oldham, Burnley, Halton, and Preston). The remaining UPAs, however, obtain less AFC monies than some marginals. St. Helens (0.41%, 63rd) receives less than Rossendale (0.59%, 51st), Ellesmere (0.53%, 55th), and Hyndburn (0.52%, 57th); while Wigan (0.35%, 66th) also gets less than West Lancs ((0.38%) and Sefton (0.23%, 74th) receives less than Pendle (0.24%). Three of the North West's UPAs therefore fall outside the top 57 receivers of AfC monies, while 4 of its marginals fall within the top 57. The remaining marginal, Tameside (0.15%, 85th), obtains less than two of the comparators, Bury (79th) and Warrington (81st), but more than its neighbour, Stockport (90th).

In summary, there must be some question about the implementation of the aim of targeting 'AfC monies' over the 1980s. In particular, the existence of UDCs and EZs outside UP areas clearly has affected the targeting.

**'Overall' inputs from national government and other sources.** In 1979, Manchester received by far the most monies per capita (£518.23). Salford (£463.88) and Liverpool (£429.01) are next. Unlike Greater London, not all the UPAs received more monies than the comparators and marginals. The ranks of the marginals and comparators show this: respectively 6, 12, 13, 15, 19, 24, 25 and 16, 22, 23. The UPAs of Halton and Preston appear well down the list (20,21) while Wirral and Sefton rank lower than expected given their UPA status (17,18). Of the marginals, Tameside in 6th place, and of the comparators, Bury in 16th, obtain more monies than expected.

During the period 1979/80 to 1985/86, just as in Greater London, there are major differences among the experiences of the UPAs and some of the non-UPAs fare much better than the UPAs. Only Preston is a net gainer over the period. The rest of the 25 are all net losers. Preston's net gain (£11.59pc) contrasts with the greatest loss, in Manchester (-£232pc). Salford (-£123.09pc) and Warrington (-£106pc) are also substantial losers. The range of experiences within the UPAs is demonstrated by the contrasts of Preston, Manchester and Salford, but the ranks of the marginals (2,3,6,7,8,17,21) and the comparators (11,18,23) show how many UPAs lost more than their supposedly better-off neighbours.

A similar pattern occurs until 1989 with Manchester (25th), Salford (23rd) and Warrington (24th) being major losers and Blackburn, Hyndburn, Preston, and West Lancs actually being overall gainers. The ranks of the marginals (2,4,6,8,9,16,22) and the comparators (19,21,24) again demonstrates the great overlap in treatment as compared with the UPAs.

As in Greater London there is a major change in 1990, because of the RSG component. There are no net gainers, all are net losers compared to 1979. The rankings change considerably. Tameside, Salford and Burnley are now the greatest losers with Manchester moving up the rankings. Trafford is now almost a gainer, with Knowsley and Ellesmere not far behind. Of these only Knowsley is a UPA. However, 18 of the 25 are now net losers by more than £100pc over 1979 whereas in 1989 only 4 were. Although the individual ranking of UPAs have changed there is still a great variety of experience among the UPAs which the rankings of marginals (1,3,10,12,19,21,25) and comparators (11,14,17) demonstrates. The RSG settlement has promoted some of the UPAs relative to the marginals, but it has also promoted the comparators.

**The period 1979 to 1989**. As in the Greater London case, it is more representative to examine the change between 1979 and 1989 than 1990, since there has been a fairly consistent pattern over the period. Unlike Greater London the amounts of money coming into the North West declined and the range reduced. Manchester received most (£518pc) at the beginning of the period, but by the end Liverpool receives most, at only £360pc. The range has dropped from 142-518 to 84-360. Three districts have improved their absolute and relative positions: Blackburn(£24pc) and Preston(£11pc), both UPAs, and Hyndburn(£12pc), a marginal. Blackburn goes from 10th out of 25 in 1979/80 to 2nd in 1989/90 while Hyndburn moves from 15th to 7th and Preston from 21st to 14th. West Lancs, another marginal, receives about the same monies, while the rest lose. The major loser is Manchester (-£228pc). It falls from 1st to 8th over the period. Salford (2nd to 4th), Tameside (6th to 17th) and Warrington (23rd to 25th) all lose over £100pc. Salford is a UPA while Tameside is a marginal and Warrington, a comparator. Other significant losers (more than £80pc) include Oldham, Wigan, Sefton and Halton (all UPAs), Pendle (a marginal) and Bury and Stockport (comparators).

**The conurbations and the other areas**. Finally it is worth comparing the parts of the North West. Greater Manchester loses more monies overall per district than does Merseyside: £98pc compared to £46pc. Within Greater Manchester least is lost by the marginal, Trafford. The Lancashire districts lose least, £19pc, despite only 3 of its 7 districts being UPAs. This changed in 1990, but held for the 1980s. While it might be argued that Merseyside should receive more inputs than Greater Manchester, it is difficult to see that both should be cut more than the Lancashire districts.

**The North West in summary**. As with Greater London, it is helpful to summarise the position of UPAs, marginals and comparators. There are major UPA consistent losers over the period: Manchester, especially, and Salford. Other significant losers include Oldham, Wigan, Sefton and Halton. Other loser UPAs include Bolton, Liverpool, and Burnley, and to a lesser degree, Rochdale, Knowsley, St.Helens, and Wirral. Blackburn and Preston show minor gains over the period, but very little in comparison with the London boroughs of Tower Hamlets and Newham. Amongst the marginals, Hyndburn gains somewhat while West Lancs retains its position. Tameside is by far the greatest loser among the marginals. Pendle drops considerably too. Both warrant carefully monitoring. All three of the comparators lose considerably, but Warrington's loss is comparable with that of Salford.

## 2.5 Overall summary of inputs

While AfC monies have increased generally over the decade, other significant monies, namely RSG and HIPS have declined dramatically, offsetting this increase. There is a great and increasing variablity in both AfC and overall inputs among the 57 UPAs. Their experiences may be expected to be rather different. Despite the targeting of the 57 UPAs, a number of non-UPAs have received both more AfC monies and more overall inputs over the period. Two non-UPAs appear in the top ten places receiving AfC monies over the period 1981-90 (i.e. Corby and Scunthorpe). Twelve non-UPAs appear in the top 57, while six UPAs do not appear in the top 70. While some UPAs have been major net losers in overall inputs over the period, in contrast some non-UPAs have been relative and in some cases absolute gainers. The major loss of overall inputs by some UPAs and the relative gains of some non-UPAs suggest that differences in outcomes between the groups may be less than initially expected.

# 3 OUTCOMES: THE INDICATORS

Where data have been available, the main indicators (job change, unemployment, VAT registrations, migration and house prices) have been converted in various ways to aid analysis. Two general caveats should be noted:

- local authority districts have been used for data collection because they are the units for most government spending. Districts, however, do not correspond to labour market areas, units that are more appropriate for many of the outcome indicators; and

- varying proportions of the area and population of the local authority districts are classified as inner city, but the data are recorded for the district as a whole. This means, for example, that a decline in unemployment recorded for the district as a whole may not be occurring at the same rate for the inner city parts of the district.

The indicators are analysed in two basic ways: first by examining the differences between the sets of UPAs, marginals and comparators. This compares means for the sets of places, paying due attention to the variance within the sets, which is often quite large; and second by analysing the gaps between UPAs, marginals and comparators in Greater London and the North West, two regions where there are substantial numbers of observations. The analysis is repeated in brief for the North East, partly to provide a further region and partly to give the context for the local level analysis. Clearly in analysing the national sets, the regional differences within each set of places produces some of the variability within the sets. Using the three regional case studies offsets that problem to some extent.

## 3.1 Unemployment

There are many caveats linked with these data in addition to the two noted above. The raw data are collected as numbers unemployed and numbers unemployed long term (over a year). Two procedures have been tried to obtain some proxy of rates:

- first was to create an index of unemployment which measures the ratio of long-term unemployed and total unemployed (LT:U). This has been used in the literature to assess the economic health of an area. This has the advantage of using only the data collected from a single source and therefore has the additional merit of greater consistency.

- second was to produce a proxy rate for both unemployment and long-term unemployment by dividing the number unemployed by the number of males 20-65 and females 20-60 estimated for that year as living in the area. Obviously these are estimates and they include some economically non-active. Since the percentage of active females, for example, varies across the country, we should be careful about making comparisons across the country at one point of time. However most of our comparisons are over time and examine changes in estimated rates of unemployment or long term unemployment. Although there are changes in the numbers economically active over time, these variations are probably less than those among places. These are crude estimates but the best that can be achieved in the circumstances.

Data are available from 1983 to 1991. The index of long-term unemployment (LT:U) peaks in 1987. Our interpretation was therefore based on two distinct periods, 1983-87 and 1987-91. The lagged effect of long-term unemployment produced the 1987 peak in the index for our set of 123 places.

As may be expected the index is higher for the 57 UPAs than the marginals and comparators, at its peak in 1987 being 0.466 (i.e. 46.6% of all unemployment is long term). The variance within each set of places decreases from 1983 to 1987 and increases again to 1990, when it is higher than in 1983, i.e. there is greater variability of experience in 1990 for all three sets.

Comparing the means of the three sets of places over the period 1983-90 does have problems because of the different regional timing of unemployment in the early period and the greater variability around the means in 1990. Bearing these caveats in mind, it should be noted that the gap between the UPAs and both the marginals and comparators increases over the period.

|  | LT:U ratio | | |
|---|---|---|---|
|  | **1983** | **1987** | **1990** |
| difference in means | | | |
| 57 UPAs versus 40 marginals | 0.043 | 0.059 | 0.092 |
| 57 UPAs versus 26 comparators | 0.078 | 0.080 | 0.109 |

Therefore the UPAs have on average a relatively greater proportion of long-term unemployment at the end of the period than the beginning, despite any government assistance. This seems to indicate a relative decline in their economic health.

The rates of unemployment and long-term unemployment both peak in 1986. From 1990 unemployment rises again. 1990 is used as the end of the period. So two periods, 1983-86 and 1986-1990, have been analysed.

Unlike the LT:U index, the unemployment and long-term unemployment rates both show a closing gap between 1983 and 1990. It widens in the time of increasing unemployment (i.e. 1983-1986) and narrows when overall unemployment falls between 1986-1990. The gaps in 1990 are less than those in 1983.

|  | Unemployment rate | | |
|---|---|---|---|
|  | **1983** | **1986** | **1990** |
| gap between | | | |
| 57 UPAs and 40 marginals | 2.81 | 3.65 | 2.77 |
| 57 UPAs and 26 comparators | 5.10 | 5.77 | 3.69 |

|  | Long-term unemployment rate | | |
|---|---|---|---|
|  | **1983** | **1986** | **1990** |
| gap between | | | |
| 57 UPAs and 40 marginals | 1.65 | 2.32 | 1.43 |
| 57 UPAs and 26 comparators | 2.79 | 3.47 | 1.54 |

In 1990 the rates are lower than 1983, but it should be noted that the same parts of the economic cycle are not being compared. It could be argued that the difference between the mean rates for a particular year is not the best way of making comparisons and that the ratios of the rates should be compared, in other words the difference between 3% and 2% is not the same 'gap' as the difference between 7% and 6%, and that ratios of 3:2 and 7:6 are better comparisons. The same argument can be used for the LT:U index, but there the gap is widening, despite the reduction in the index. The difference in rates has been used here because it is thought that reducing unemployment from 14% to

7% is not the same as reducing it from 8% to 4%, even though in both cases, the rate has been halved. It is accepted, however, that as rates drop and approach zero or the minimum level of unemployment, the gaps are bound to narrow. Perhaps in 1990 that minimum level is being approached in the comparators. It would be interesting to compare 1986 with 1991 and 1992 figures to see whether the gap is narrowing when comparing higher periods of unemployment.

Overall, the message from the unemployment indicators is ambiguous. While the gap between the sets of places is closing for the rates, it is widening for the index. It is the index as a sign of economic health that presents some concern for the UPAs.

## 3.2 Job change

The total number of jobs was divided by the estimated working population (as with the calculation of unemployment rates, this is a crude estimate) in order to standardise for the size of the place. One indicator of change may then be expressed as the increase/decrease in jobs per capita. Both the absolute change in numbers of jobs and the percentage change in job totals have been analysed.

We cannot choose the periods of analysis, as we have with the unemployment indicators, because data are only available for 1981, 1984, 1987 and 1989. We analysed the indicators for the periods 1981-4, 1984-7, and 1987-9. The first period is one of declining numbers per capita. For the last two there is a rise.

Strangely, the means of the UPAs and the comparators are the same for the four points of time and so there is no change in the gap. There simply is no gap. It is worth noting that the variance for the larger set of UPAs is actually lower than that of the comparators. The extreme values and change of Westminster very much affect the means and variance of the marginals and make any analysis of that changing gap meaningless. For the record, it narrows.

## 3.3 VAT registrations

Available from 1979 and increasing throughout the period, these are indexed to 1981 in order to remove the size effect. Change is then related to the 1981 figures which are set at values of 100. By removing the effect of size, it must be remembered that a 1% increase in registrations in some of the UPAs is many more than a 1% rise in some of the comparators which are smaller.

There is very little difference between the growth in the three sets of places up to 1985 (109). After that, registrations increase more rapidly in the comparators (143 in 1990) than the UPAs (131), with the marginals' registrations (134) growing somewhat faster than those of the UPAs. In 1990 the standard deviations of the three sets are UPAs 20, marginals 22, comparators 25. There is therefore a greater variation within the comparators and overlap between the sets. However there is some evidence that the UPAs as a whole are doing less well over the latter half of the 1980s.

While there are great difficulties associated with VAT registrations, as an indicator of enterprise, these data suggest that the UPAs have not been developing as fast as the comparators, though not significantly differently from the marginals.

## 3.4 The net migration of 25-34 year olds

This age group is attributed key significance for the economic health of an area. Absolute or relative change of population in that age group implies the loss of a vital, dynamic element of the labour force. Retention or even

173

attraction of the age group, on the other hand, can be taken as good indicators of economic health, provided that they are not accompanied by an increase in the rate of long-term unemployment of the age group. Where the latter occurs it could be argued that retention or attraction is not a positive sign but simply an indication that the age group may be trapped in the area.

Both the absolute change and the change in the proportion of 25-34s in the district population have been analysed. Only 1981 is based on census data. The rest are based on Registrar-General estimates. An updated analysis will be carried out with 1991 census data.

In 1981, the UPAs on average had a similar proportion of 25-34 year olds to the comparators but less than the marginals. All three sets declined up to 1984 and rose again to 1990, when both the UPAs and the comparators exceed the marginals. There is no difference between the UPAs and the comparators over the period, although the UPAs decline slightly more and rise more rapidly during the two periods (i.e. they are more sensitve to cyclical change than the comparators). There is a significant change, however, between the UPAs and the marginals. In 1981 the UPAs are 0.24% behind, while in 1990 they are 0.28% ahead. Over the period the variability within both sets has decreased. While these changes are not statistically significant because of the variability within the sets, they are indicative. The UPAs are retaining or attracting more of their 25-34s over the period.

The question that therefore has to be posed is, are the 25-34s 'attracted' or are they 'trapped'? The latter interpretation could apply if the age group has become a disproportionately increasing element of the long-term unemployed. The 25-34s as a whole are becoming a higher percentage of the long-term unemployed, partly for demographic reasons, partly for reasons concerning economic restructuring. Between 1983 and 1991 they are a rising proportion for all three sets of places. For the period 1983-90 the rise is greatest for the UPAs. However there is increasing variance within all three groups over the decade and comparisons between them therefore become less meaningful. The variance in the 57 more than doubles between 1983 and 1990.

The rate of long-term unemployment of 25-34s increases slightly from 1983 to 1986, more for UPAs than the others, and then decreases sharply to 1990, with the fall being most dramatic for UPAs. This is another example of their greater sensitivity to economic fluctuations.

The rates for 25-34s are becoming closer to overall long-term unemployment rates, for example the rates for UPAs in 1983 were 5.13 and 5.65, while in 1990 they had closed to 2.53 and 2.69. The rates for the other two groups also became more similar. In short, long-term unemployment of 25-34s is becoming more similar to that for the economically active as a whole.

Not surprisingly, the rates are higher for the UPAs, but the gaps between the sets of places closes over the period.

| | Long-term unemployment amongst 25-34 year-olds | | |
| | 1983 | 1986 | 1990 |
| --- | --- | --- | --- |
| gap betwen | | | |
| 57 UPAs and 40 marginals | 1.60 | 1.39 | 1.49 |
| 57 UPAs and 26 comparators | 2.65 | 2.47 | 1.70 |

Unlike the changing gaps for overall long-term unemployment, they do not increase to 1986 and then decrease to 1990. The gap with the comparators shows a steady decline, despite the peak of unemployment in 1986.

So, even though the proportion of long-term unemployed that is made up of 25-34s is growing (and, up to 1990, at a faster rate in the UPAs than the other two sets), the gaps between the three sets in rates of long-term unemployment for the 25-34s is closing. There is therefore no evidence that 25-34s are being relatively increasingly trapped in UPAs as a group. The increased variation within groups, however, does suggest that further analysis within groups is needed.

## 3.5 House price changes

The data come from Halifax and Nationwide building societies' sources for the period 1983-1989. Two indicators have been used: sales occurring within inner-city wards of the district; and sales to first-time buyers within the whole district. Inner-city wards were defined according to data from the 1981 Census. The indicators are the average price of houses sold during the year. The reliability of the indicators depends to some extent on the total number of sales within the year. Three years were compared: 1983, 1986 and 1989. There were more sales in 1986 than in either 1989 or 1983 and fewest sales in 1983. The comparisons between 1986 and 1989 are therefore the more reliable of the two periods. Analyses were carried out using data for all 123, 97 and 57 districts for both periods. Because of the problem of small numbers of sales in some districts, further analyses were undertaken using only those districts with larger numbers of sales, districts with relatively few sales in 1986 (fewer than 100) being removed from the analysis. In all cases both the percentage change and the absolute change were analysed.

House prices may be used as an indicator of the overall impact of inner-city policies. Generally it can be suggested that increasing house prices indicate a degree of market confidence in an area. While prices may increase because of increased demand or a decrease on the supply side, over a three-year period the supply is unlikely to change substantially so that most change in prices over such a short period will probably be due to demand changes. Price rises can therefore be taken as evidence of increased demand which suggests confidence in the area. Increased prices mean a greater value of assets in the area and hence of residents' greater potential to borrow. Clearly, overinflated prices that cannot be sustained can have negative effects on the area. These eventually lead, among other things, to reduced prices, lower confidence and less value of assets on which to borrow. It should be remembered that at times during the period 1983-1989 such over-inflation occurred, especially in the south-east. It should also be noted that the timing and extent of the greatest increases in house prices varied by region during this period.

Between 1983 and 1986 the percentage changes of both inner-city and first-time buyer housing were closely related to the absolute change in prices (r=>0.9). Between 1986 and 1989, by contrast, the percentage changes were much more weakly related to absolute changes in prices (with values of r between 0.3 and 0.6, although still significant). The relationship was closer for inner-city housing than for first-time buyers'. 1986-89 is therefore a somewhat more complex period of change for house prices than 1983-6, the reverse of the case for the unemployment data.

There is a weak, but significant, positive relationship between the absolute and percentage changes in house prices for 1983-6, on one hand, and the changes in unemployment, long-term unemployment, and the LT:U index of long-term to all unemployment, on the other. These relationships are highest for the 97 UPAs and 57 marginal districts. The highest correlations have r-values lying in the high 0.4s. So to some extent in this period, in areas where house prices rose more rapidly, unemployment was also rising more rapidly. This is a weak association. Nevertheless, it is counter-intuitive as a causal relationship between unemployment and house prices. It should be remembered that there was little obvious structure to the unemployment changes in this period and this may explain the unexpected finding.

In the later period, 1986-89, there is only one significant correlation between house price increase and unemployment. This is for the case of the LT:U index. The relationship is weak, but negative. Where the ratio of long-term to all unemployment increased least, house prices increased most. An increasing proportion of long-term unemployed is weakly associated with low increases in house prices. This association seems to be more meaningfully interpretable.

## 3.6 Regional analysis of gaps: Greater London

Various comparisons were made between sets of areas to show the extent to which they had converged or diverged from one another over the period 1983 to 1990 in their experience of long-term unemployment, net migration, job change and VAT registrations. The average state on an indicator is compared at the beginning of a period and the difference (or gap) noted. This is then compared to the gap at the end of the period to establish whether the gap has closed (convergence) or has widened (divergence). The major caveat indicated throughout this analysis is the variation within each set of areas. For some indicators at certain times the variation is considerable, and differences between averages should therefore be taken only as indicative. Individual area profiles are needed because of the complexity of the data. The points of time used to make the comparisons between the sets of areas present some difficulties. For long-term unemployment, for example, 1983 is used as a base only because it is the start of our data. It is not the trough of a cycle, and it must remembered that different areas of the country can reach their peak and troughs at slightly different times.

**Long-term unemployment**. A comparison of the experience of long-term unemployment was made between the 13 UP London boroughs and the 7 that were included in our 123 as comparators. Whereas long-term unemployment in the comparators only rose by an average of 0.51% during 1983-86, it rose much faster in the UPAs, on average by 1.87% (the variations were, for comparators 0.3 - 0.64, for UPAs 1.15 - 2.85). The gap between the two sets of areas therefore grew over this period.

Between 1986-90, however, the gap narrowed. Long-term unemployment fell by 1.94% for the comparators and 3.86% in the UPAs (the variations were; for comparators -1.53 - -3.32, and for UPAs -2.79 - -5.32). As can be seen, the difference in the reduction of long-term unemployment is greater than the difference in its rise. Over the whole period 1983-90, therefore, the gap between the UPAs and comparators narrowed (by on average 0.56%).

**Greater London: net migration of 25-34 year olds.** Any analysis of net migration for the 25-34 age group has to be set within the context of rates of counterurbanisation to which this age group makes a marked contribution. It is known that counterurbanisation varies over time, being faster in times of economic and property booms than in recessions, when fewer people are moving. Comparisons between 1981 and 1990 mean that fairly similar points of time in economic and property cycles are being compared.

The process of counterurbanisation is complex, but it is worth noting that most moves are short-distance decentralising ones, for example from Inner London just into Outer London or Outer London outskirts to just across the boundary into the Home Counties. There is no evidence to suggest that movement into or out of any one concentric ring centred on the middle of London dominates the process, so that when the process slows down or quickens more or less of this particular age group will be concentrated in a particular ring. Comparison between the UPAs (mostly Inner London) and the comparators (outer London) therefore is not affected by varying rates of movement from outer London to ROSE because, when that movement is high, it would be accompanied by movement into the outer boroughs from Inner London, and when outward movement is low, movement from the Inner London to Outer London would be expected to be low. Comparing the gap between the UPAs and the comparators therefore captures the extent to which Inner London has been able to retain and attract this key age group over the 1980s.

In 1979 for the UPAs there was a considerable range in the proportion of 25-34 year olds (22.64% to 12.95%). By 1990 there was much less variation (19.24% to 15.94%). There was much variation in the changes in absolute numbers of 25-34s among the UPAs over the period (+69.88% to -34%). So the gains and losses among the UPAs have led to convergence rather than divergence among the UPAs which makes comparison with comparator areas more statistically meaningful.

The range of proportions of 25-34s among the comparators is much less than for the UPAs in 1979 (2%) and also narrows by 1990 (1.75%). There is an absolute growth of 9-11% for this cohort, except for Croydon (6.7%) and Havering (-0.9%).

The UPAs on average started out with a higher proportion of 25-34 year olds than the comparators (15.74% v 14.52%). The proportion increased for both groups but faster for the UPAs. The gap has widened significantly over the period. In 1990 it was 1.8% (17.43% v 15.63%) compared to 1.22% in 1979.

This suggests that as a whole the UPAs are improving relative to the comparators. However, as noted above, there is much variation among them in their growth paths on this indicator and it makes less sense to treat them as a set when considering this indicator than when considering others.

UPAs experiencing greater absolute growth than the comparators were Brent (12.5%), Hackney (30.9%), Southwark (33.29%) and Tower Hamlets (69.88%). UPAs with with similar growth to the comparators were Islington, Greenwich, Lewisham, Newham, and Wandsworth. Lambeth had somewhat lower growth (4.79%) and, more significantly, Hammersmith, Haringey and Kensington along with non-UPAs, Camden and Westminster, experienced declines of 10.9%, 9.42%, 34%, 12.81% and 24.5% respectively. Four boroughs experienced a proportional decline in 25-34s: Camden, Westminster, Hammersmith amd Kensington (in this last case a dramatic decline from 22.64% to 16.54%). All but Camden saw an overall loss in population. Clearly the loss of 25-34s was at a still greater rate. Haringey gained slightly proportionally, but also experienced an absolute loss of 25-34s, i.e. their loss was at a higher rate than for the population as a whole.

By contrast, there were large proportional increases in Tower Hamlets (12.95 to 19.24), Southwark (13.18 to 17.14) and Hackney (14.45 to 18.42). Brent, Greenwich and Islington also showed increases. The populations as a whole of this set of boroughs either increased or remained about the same. Newham, Lewisham, and Wandsworth showed substantial proportional increases and absolute growth of about 10% for 25-34s, but this was accompanied by an overall loss in population. For Lambeth too there was a significant proportional increase but a smaller absolute gain compared to an overall loss.

This indicator suggests that careful attention should be paid to Camden, Westminster, Hammersmith, Kensington and Haringey (the west central belt). The loss from these districts of this key element of the population does not bode well for the future of this area.

It is also necessary to examine the long-term unemployment of the gaining areas to ensure that some of the gain is not due to trapped 25-34 year olds. This is examined below in detail in the borough profiles, but generally this indicator showed a minor closing of the gap (from 2.19 to 2.08, these being the differences between the average rates for comparators and UPAs). As with all the other comparisons, a 'closing gap' has to be interpreted with some care. Our emphasis is on difference between rates and not percentage change in rates.

**Jobs per capita.** With easy travel over boundaries to work, this is a less important indicator, but it is suggestive of changes in local economic opportunities. Obviously it is affected by changing populations as well as changing jobs. Available data allow comparison between 1981 and 1989.

The major centres of jobs are Westminster and Camden. Both increase over time. The UPAs show considerable variation in 1981 (0.48 to 1.17). This increases slightly over time as it does for the comparators (for 1981, 0.46 to 0.88). When comparing the gap between the averages, these variations should be borne in mind. The gap increases over time (0.184 to 0.242). The average for the UPAs stays about the same whereas that for the comparators falls. On average then the circumstances have relatively improved. Those boroughs where there is an improvement are Islington, Kensington, Tower Hamlets and Wandsworth together with Camden and Westminster. There is little change in Hammersmith, Haringey and Southwark.

There is a decline in Hackney, Lambeth, Lewisham, Newham, Brent and Greenwich. In this respect they are similar to all the comparators except Havering and Enfield.

**VAT registrations.** On average the UPAs grow more rapidly than the comparators in VAT registrations (56.62% v 43.28% 1981-1990). However, there is very little difference between the gap in average number of VAT registrations at the two times. Although this measure has numerous caveats associated with it, there is another slight indication that on average the business/ employment outlook has improved. There is however considerable variation within the UPAs. Hammersmith, Wandsworth, Greenwich and Kensington experience above-average UPA growth, while Tower Hamlets, Hackney, Islington and to a lesser extent Brent and Newham show below-average growth. Both Camden and Westminster show below-average growth.

**3.7 Regional analysis of gaps: the North West**

**Long-term unemployment.** Similar comparisons were made for parts of the North West. First, for Greater Manchester, a comparison was made between its six UPAs, its two marginals (Tameside and Trafford) and three nearby comparator areas (Bury, Stockport and Warrington). Again the gap between

UPAs and comparators on long-term unemployment widened during the first period (0.49%) but closed during the second (1.0%). Overall therefore, there was a convergence of 0.51% on an original difference of 1.97%. So although the absolute closure was slightly less than in the case of Greater London, there was a greater relative convergence of about a quarter. The difference in the proportions of government monies was less dramatic than in the Greater London case, 7.35% for the UPAs compared to 0.51% for the comparators. A similar convergence has therefore been associated in the North West with less difference in input. There was also convergence between the UPAs and the two marginals over the period, the gap closing from 1.55% to 0.98%.

A similar comparison with the six UPAs in or adjacent to Merseyside showed a greater absolute overall closure of 1.27% on the three comparators. The initial difference was 4.33%, so the relative convergence is over a quarter. The six Merseyside UPAs received in total 7.2% of government monies over the period. Merseyside was also compared to the nearby areas of Ellesmere Port and West Lancashire. There was a slight closure of 0.14% on two areas that together received 0.91% of the AfC government money, not much less per area than was received by the UPAs.

Three other UPAs in the North West (Blackburn, Burnley and Preston) were compared to the three comparators for Greater Manchester and the marginals of Hyndburn, Pendle and Rossendale. The UPAs were converging on both sets of areas; to the comparators by 0.88%, and to the neighbouring places by 0.53%. Their position improved faster than that of the Greater Manchester UPAs, largely because they did not experience as great an increase in unemployment during the 1983-86 period. The decline in 1986-90 was very similar. They received in total 2.21% of AfC government monies, on average slightly less per place than those of Greater Manchester.

**Net migration of 25-34s.** The UPAs in Greater Manchester are not grouped in the same way as those in Greater London with its inner and outer comparison of UPAs and comparators, so similar differences to those in Greater London for this indicator may not be expected. While the percentage of 25-34s increases between 1981 and 1990 for the UPAs in Greater Manchester the gap between them and both the comparators and marginals does not close. This is due to the high increases in Warrington and Trafford rather than any difference between the UPAs and the others in general. Indeed Manchester, which had a smaller percentage of 25-34s than Bury, Stockport and Tameside in 1981, had caught up by 1990, increasing its proportion by over 2%. The gaps for long-term unemployment of 25-34s did close by about 0.4% in both cases between 1983 and 1990, so it would seem that as a whole there is not relatively more incidence of entrapment in the UPAs than in the other areas. Long-term unemployment of 25-34s, however, is becoming more similar to that of the economically active as a whole.

In Merseyside, the gap between the 5 UPAs and the two marginals (West Lancs and Ellesmere) for the percentage of 25-34s has narrowed from 0.87 to 0.08, but the gap for long-term unemployment of the group has widened by 0.43%. Here there does seem to be relatively greater entrapment. While Knowsley's rate of unemployment for the group is now below that of Liverpool, it is still very high (1981 11.83% to 1990 6.59% whereas Liverpool was 9.45% and by 1990 was 7.81%). In both places the rate for 25-34s is still higher than for that of the economically active as a whole. This is not the case for other parts of Merseyside except the Wirral, which moves into that position in the late 1980s.

For the 6 East Lancashire areas, not only does the gap narrow, it reverses. The UPAs start out with lower proportions of 25-34s and end up with more (-0.66 to +0.97). The gap in long-term unemployment also narrows but the rates are very low at the end of the period and the base level might be being approached.

**Job change and VAT registrations**. Again it should be remembered that the effect of commuting makes such comparisons less meaningful. Most districts have fewer jobs per capita in 1989 than in 1981. Only Bolton, Trafford and Stockport have recovered their 1981 position, with only the first two exceeding it. Manchester in particular is well down on its 1981 ratio (1.13 in 1989 compared to 1.28 in 1981). In addition its ratio fell from 1987 to 1989, whereas all others, except Bury, rose or stayed the same.

The gaps between the groups show little difference over the period. The marginals catch up with the UPAs because of the growth of Trafford, so that a 0.03 gap in 1981 becomes zero in 1989. The gap between the UPAs and the comparators closes from 0.1 to 0.09, so there is an almost neglible, catching up by the comparators.

The VAT data show greater changes. By 1990 the UPAs are at 112 compared to the marginals at 131, and the comparators at 126. There are however some major differences within groups. Manchester shows a major decline to 86 and Salford to 95, while Wigan increases to 130. Bury declines to 96 compared to the other comparators of Stockport (133) and Warrington (148). So the poor performances of Manchester, Salford and Bury need to be noted. Manchester is especially worrying because the drop in VAT registrations accompanies the decline in job change per capita.

In Merseyside, the jobs per capita are much lower. While Sefton, Wirral and Halton have recovered their 1981 position, Liverpool, Knowsley and St Helens are well down, with Liverpool having the same drop as Manchester but from a lower starting figure. The gap with the two marginals has slightly widened. VAT registrations are varied. Knowsley has a major rise to 161 and Halton and Ellesmere move to 149 and 144 respectively. In contrast Liverpool is at 104, better than the change in some parts of Greater Manchester but much lower than the rest of Merseyside, which averages 128.

By comparison, VATs expand less in the Lancs UPAs (115) and marginals (121), with only Rossendale above 120 at 128. In job change there has been greater success, with all but Preston regaining their 1981 position. Preston has dropped from 1.11 to 1.06. This has meant that the 3 marginals have caught up slightly on the UPAs, with Rossendale especially climbing from its low ratio in 1981.

**3.8 Regional analysis of gaps: the North East**

There are nine UPAs in the North East, five marginals and three comparators. A similar analysis of gaps was carried out for these districts, by examining the gaps between the means of the three groups for the beginning and end of a period. It is reported more briefly than the other two regions.

The gap in average long-term unemployment between the UPAs and marginals narrows from 1.63 in 1983 to 1.37 in 1990. The gap between the UPAs and comparators narrows from 3.13 to 1.5. The latter is a major change. This is associated with a very large difference in the amounts of AfC monies going into the areas. The 9 UPAs receive 13.04% of the 1981-1990 per capita monies, compared to the 3 comparators 1.68% (i.e. 1.45 versus 0.56 pc). The comparators' inputs are inflated by Durham's 24th place in AfC monies.

As in the other regions, 25-34 net migration results again in a form of narrowing of the gap. In this case the UPAs start with smaller percentage 25-34s and end up with exactly the same percentage as the comparators. A 0.8 gap reduces to zero. The UPAs start behind the marginals and finish ahead of them, with a gap of 0.9 becoming an excess of 0.41.

In some cases unemployment of the 25-34s has risen more than proportionately for the UPAs, for others it has even reduced. The variation is picked up in the district profiles at the end of this section of the report.

There is no difference between the growth of VAT registrations. There is so much within-group variation that it would be meaningless to compare the averages. Newcastle has a negative change (94), similar to Manchester, while North and South Tyneside have the greatest growth (116). This figure suggests the low rate of growth of companies in the North East. Similarly there is no real difference in the jobs per capita because there is a variety of experiences within the UPAs. Newcastle actually gains jobs per capita from 1981 to 1989 (+0.09) whereas Langbaurgh and South Tyneside lose (0.1).

In summary, although the gap is closing in unemployment and 25-34s, there is no evidence to suggest that it is closing for jobs or VATs.

## 3.9 Inter-regional comparisons

Further comparisons were made for long-term unemployment between Greater London/the South East and the North West to obtain some view of regional differences. The Greater London UPAs began somewhat better off than those of Greater Manchester (4.71% to 5.21% in long-term unemployment in 1983). They ended the period worse off by 0.3%. Although unemployment declined by about the same amount during 1986-90, it had risen much more in Greater London in 1983-86.

The two sets of control areas (the 7 in Greater London and the 3 in Greater Manchester) also converged, but not to quite such a degree. The gap narrowed by 0.67% to give a difference of only 0.43% in 1990. The three north-western areas received slightly more government monies per area (0.17% compared to 0.11%). The areas receiving major government support, the UPAs, were converging slightly faster than the two sets of comparator areas (0.8% compared to 0.67%).

Further comparisons with the 13 comparator areas in ROSE and East Anglia confirmed that the gap between the Greater Manchester UPAs and the South East was narrowing (by 0.7%). This is not just a regional effect because the gap between the Greater Manchester control areas and the South East 13 remained about the same.

Government AfC expenditure seems therefore to be associated with a convergence between regions as well as within regions.

## 3.10 Overall summary of outcomes

There are differences between the average outcomes for the three sets of places. The UPAs stay in the worst position over time for all indicators except 25-34 net migration and jobs per capita. There are considerable differences within groups, which for some indicators increase over time. The within-group differences suggest that there may be very varied stories about the impact of government policies. With the caveat about the within-group variation, there has been a narrowing of the gap between the sets of places for many of the indicators over the period, both at the national, inter-regional and regional levels.

# 4 ANALYSIS OF IMPACTS: THE RELATIONSHIPS BETWEEN THE INPUTS AND THE OUTCOME INDICATORS

This analysis has been carried out in a number of ways. First a whole set of ways was tried to apply multi-level analysis, which would have allowed the introduction of contextual variables at different scales, as well as government inputs at different scales (for example, training expenditure at a regional level). Second, a set of correlation and regression techniques were applied, finding and using the most appropriate lagged relationships between inputs and outcomes ('appropriateness' here applies to the strongest association). Third, the 'gap' analysis of outcomes was revisited, noting the relative inputs to the areas. Finally the places were examined individually to relate their individual stories, which, while useful in itself, also proved to be necessary because of the difficulty of establishing generalisations across the 123.

## 4.1 Classifications for multi-level modelling

In order for multi-level modelling to be used, the places and the indicators have to conform to a nested set of groups. Multi-level modelling was originally developed for individual data, such as pupils' attainment, where there is some inter-correlation within such groups as schools or forms within schools. The levels of the modelling refer to individuals (level 1) and to the various groupings that show inter-correlation (for example, level 2 may be forms and level 3 may be schools). The model can thereby investigate the attainment of a pupil within a form or within a school, taking account of the fact that attainment by one pupil is not independent of that of other pupils within the form or school.

Our intention was to apply this reasoning to the interpretation of the input:outcomes relationships in the sample set of districts. The model, if applicable, would allow us to introduce different 'explanatory variables' into the analysis at different levels, for example some at district level, and some at regional level. Contextual variables could also be introduced at the various levels.

It was unlikely that we would ever be able to obtain individual level data for this work. It was hoped that we could apply multi-level modelling to aggregate areal data, such as wards within conurbations, so long as we found inter-correlations within groups of wards and were careful not to commit ecological fallacies in the interpretation of results. Past analysis in geography has shown considerable inter-correlation within contiguous wards for some variables.

The application of such a model to the national scale of analysis uses many fewer observations and only works if there are very tight groupings with very little internal variation and considerable between-group differences. In such circumstances, the inter-correlation within groups of places could be interpreted as being due to similar processes impacting on them with similar consequences, for example regions of the country experiencing economic differential decline or growth with consequences for job creation and unemployment change.

In order to maximise the number of observations, a model design was used that had time at level 1 (i.e. unemployment each year), the district at level 2, and the region at level 3. No matter which unemployment indicator was used, the data did not fit the model. Using the unemployment change between 1983-6 at level 1 and regions at level 2 in a two-level model did not fit either. The reason for this is clearly shown in Figure B3. The means and standard deviations of various indicators are shown by region. The difference between the regional means compared to the variations within regions is not sufficient to give a good classification. The variations of change within regions is in many cases great. Regional classifications are, therefore, inappropriate in the cases so far analysed.

A second type of classification was tried, using the urban hierarchy. Analyses of job loss in the 1970s and 1980s suggested that there were greater differences by settlement size than by region. Such a hierarchy, modified by including one category for new or expanded towns again shows much greater variation within groups than between groups (Figure B4). Again this organisation of the data failed to fit the multi-level model.

A further classifaction was investigated following a meeting of the research Steering Committee. This classification drew on the cluster analyses of the 57 UPAs undertaken by a Bristol research group for the DoE. We used the employment grouping which was suggested by this research. Whilst this is the most appropriate classification, there is a danger of circular thinking. There is little point in grouping our data according to the indicators, if the resultant groupings do not have any wider meaning. As Figure B5 shows, even with this classification, there is still too much within-group variation relative to the differences in means. The cluster analyses were performed for a particular point of time and are useful descriptions of similarities and differences at that time. They do not apply very well, however, to change over time.

## Figure B3   Within and between variance: Regions

i) Unemployment 'rate' by region 1983 to 1990

|       | 1983  | 1984  | 1985  | 1986  | 1987 | 1988  | 1989 | 1990 |
|-------|-------|-------|-------|-------|------|-------|------|------|
| **GL** |       |       |       |       |      |       |      |      |
| Av.   | 10.73 | 11.33 | 12.02 | 12.29 | 7.27 | 9.04  | 6.66 | 6.12 |
| StDev | 3.73  | 3.90  | 4.24  | 4.35  | 2.69 | 3.58  | 2.93 | 2.73 |
| **SE** |       |       |       |       |      |       |      |      |
| Av.   | 9.26  | 9.33  | 9.44  | 9.42  | 5.25 | 5.59  | 3.77 | 3.68 |
| StDev | 1.33  | 1.35  | 1.46  | 1.52  | 1.14 | 1.35  | 1.02 | 0.89 |
| **WM** |       |       |       |       |      |       |      |      |
| Av.   | 13.53 | 12.84 | 12.89 | 12.74 | 7.40 | 8.68  | 5.85 | 5.14 |
| StDev | 2.47  | 2.45  | 2.52  | 2.74  | 1.59 | 2.28  | 1.90 | 1.81 |
| **NW** |       |       |       |       |      |       |      |      |
| Av.   | 12.72 | 12.58 | 12.91 | 12.91 | 7.48 | 9.39  | 7.19 | 6.21 |
| StDev | 3.12  | 3.31  | 3.43  | 3.50  | 2.28 | 3.23  | 2.94 | 2.68 |
| **YH** |       |       |       |       |      |       |      |      |
| Av.   | 12.16 | 12.14 | 12.73 | 13.38 | 7.99 | 10.21 | 7.53 | 6.54 |
| StDev | 2.31  | 2.18  | 2.32  | 2.41  | 1.66 | 2.31  | 1.82 | 1.62 |
| **N** |       |       |       |       |      |       |      |      |
| Av.   | 13.66 | 13.93 | 14.48 | 14.23 | 8.47 | 11.03 | 8.53 | 7.11 |
| StDev | 3.30  | 3.52  | 3.55  | 3.19  | 1.87 | 2.54  | 1.92 | 1.88 |
| **EM** |       |       |       |       |      |       |      |      |
| Av.   | 11.61 | 11.50 | 11.93 | 11.65 | 6.75 | 8.25  | 5.93 | 5.26 |
| StDev | 3.66  | 3.01  | 3.07  | 2.98  | 1.80 | 2.72  | 2.47 | 2.10 |
| **SW** |       |       |       |       |      |       |      |      |
| Av.   | 9.20  | 9.30  | 9.91  | 9.96  | 5.72 | 6.93  | 4.94 | 4.56 |
| StDev | 1.29  | 1.38  | 1.45  | 1.17  | 0.87 | 1.62  | 1.63 | 1.42 |
| **EA** |       |       |       |       |      |       |      |      |
| Av.   | 10.40 | 10.35 | 11.03 | 11.49 | 6.94 | 7.98  | 5.14 | 5.16 |
| StDev | 1.07  | 1.33  | 1.69  | 1.88  | 1.43 | 1.86  | 1.37 | 1.23 |

## ii) Unemployment 'rate' by region 1983-86 & 1986-90

|  | 1983-6 | 1986-90 |
|---|---|---|
| **GL** | | |
| Av. | 0.60 | -6.17 |
| StDev | 0.50 | 1.83 |
| **SE** | | |
| Av. | 0.16 | -5.73 |
| StDev | 0.99 | 1.00 |
| **WM** | | |
| Av. | -0.79 | -7.60 |
| StDev | 0.69 | 1.37 |
| **NW** | | |
| Av. | 0.19 | -6.70 |
| StDev | 0.70 | 1.12 |
| **YH** | | |
| Av. | 1.22 | -6.84 |
| StDev | 1.63 | 1.21 |
| **N** | | |
| Av. | 0.57 | -7.12 |
| StDev | 1.02 | 1.48 |
| **EM** | | |
| Av. | 0.04 | -6.39 |
| StDev | 1.93 | 1.74 |
| **SW** | | |
| Av. | 0.76 | -5.39 |
| StDev | 0.27 | 0.82 |
| **EA** | | |
| Av. | 1.09 | -6.33 |
| StDev | 1.37 | 0.84 |

## Figure B4  Within and between variance: Urban hierachy

i) Unemployment 'rate' by urban hierarchy 1983 to 1990

|  | 1983 | 1984 | 1985 | 1986 | 1987 | 1988 | 1989 | 1990 |
|---|---|---|---|---|---|---|---|---|
| **Dominant** | | | | | | | | |
| Av. | 15.35 | 15.29 | 16.04 | 16.40 | 9.87 | 12.92 | 10.24 | 9.03 |
| StDev | 3.35 | 3.46 | 3.45 | 3.61 | 2.35 | 3.46 | 3.24 | 2.92 |
| **Non-Dominant 'rich'** | | | | | | | | |
| Av. | 8.55 | 8.94 | 9.34 | 9.39 | 5.51 | 6.63 | 4.74 | 4.23 |
| StDev | 2.53 | 2.72 | 2.83 | 2.77 | 1.79 | 2.39 | 1.90 | 1.66 |
| **Non-Dominant 'poor'** | | | | | | | | |
| Av. | 13.32 | 13.58 | 14.12 | 14.35 | 8.44 | 10.67 | 8.04 | 7.12 |
| StDev | 3.10 | 3.19 | 3.33 | 3.17 | 1.97 | 2.74 | 2.28 | 2.09 |
| **Larger places** | | | | | | | | |
| Av. | 11.72 | 11.80 | 12.46 | 12.48 | 7.57 | 9.25 | 6.81 | 6.21 |
| StDev | 2.14 | 1.94 | 2.14 | 2.36 | 1.47 | 2.29 | 2.21 | 1.93 |
| **Smaller places** | | | | | | | | |
| Av. | 10.57 | 10.46 | 10.78 | 10.70 | 6.22 | 7.60 | 5.38 | 4.75 |
| StDev | 2.38 | 2.28 | 2.31 | 2.26 | 1.54 | 2.18 | 1.81 | 1.47 |
| **New/Expanding Towns** | | | | | | | | |
| Av. | 11.81 | 11.36 | 11.49 | 11.29 | 6.27 | 6.97 | 4.75 | 4.11 |
| StDev | 3.14 | 2.72 | 2.82 | 2.50 | 1.52 | 2.29 | 1.95 | 1.33 |

ii) Unemployment 'rate' by urban hierarchy 1983-86 & 1986-90

|  | 1983-86 | 1986-90 |
|---|---|---|
| **Dominant** | | |
| Av. | 1.05 | -7.37 |
| StDev | 0.84 | 1.01 |
| **Non-Dominant 'rich'** | | |
| Av. | 0.84 | -5.16 |
| StDev | 0.64 | 1.40 |
| **Non-Dominant 'poor'** | | |
| Av. | 1.03 | -7.23 |
| StDev | 1.33 | 1.30 |
| **Larger places** | | |
| Av. | 0.76 | -6.27 |
| StDev | 1.22 | 0.78 |
| **Smaller places** | | |
| Av. | 0.14 | -5.95 |
| StDev | 1.09 | 1.18 |
| **New/Expanding Towns** | | |
| Av. | -0.52 | -7.17 |
| StDev | 1.38 | 1.72 |

## Figure B5    Within and between variance: Bristol classification

i) Unemployment 'rate' by 'Bristol' classification 1983 to 1990

|  | 1983 | 1984 | 1985 | 1986 | 1987 | 1988 | 1989 | 1990 |
|---|---|---|---|---|---|---|---|---|
| **Bristol 1** | | | | | | | | |
| Av. | 14.84 | 14.94 | 15.41 | 15.60 | 9.24 | 11.85 | 8.94 | 7.80 |
| StDev | 2.57 | 2.52 | 2.53 | 2.17 | 1.32 | 1.96 | 1.83 | 1.63 |
| **Bristol 2** | | | | | | | | |
| Av. | 12.18 | 12.04 | 12.48 | 12.41 | 7.22 | 8.91 | 6.60 | 5.70 |
| StDev | 1.61 | 1.70 | 1.57 | 1.52 | 0.86 | 1.11 | 1.01 | 0.91 |
| **Bristol 3** | | | | | | | | |
| Av. | 15.56 | 16.09 | 17.00 | 17.36 | 10.39 | 13.43 | 10.59 | 9.57 |
| StDev | 2.67 | 2.54 | 2.59 | 2.35 | 1.53 | 2.09 | 1.83 | 1.62 |
| **Bristol 4** | | | | | | | | |
| Av. | 10.36 | 10.96 | 11.65 | 11.79 | 7.08 | 8.83 | 6.30 | 5.84 |
| StDev | 0.77 | 0.74 | 1.00 | 1.23 | 0.68 | 1.11 | 0.93 | 1.00 |

ii) Unemployment 'rate' by 'Bristol' classification 1983-86 & 1986-90

|  | 1983-6 | 1986-90 |
|---|---|---|
| **Bristol 1** | | |
| Av. | 0.76 | -7.80 |
| StDev | 1.32 | 0.83 |
| **Bristol 2** | | |
| Av. | 0.23 | -6.71 |
| StDev | 0.65 | 1.46 |
| **Bristol 3** | | |
| Av. | 1.80 | -7.79 |
| StDev | 1.12 | 1.15 |
| **Bristol 4** | | |
| Av. | 1.43 | -5.95 |
| StDev | 0.66 | 0.37 |

We have to conclude that for the selected indicators there are no groupings of places that make it appropriate to use multi level modelling in the analysis. In technical terms, whatever groupings are input into the model, there is no significant decomposition into levels for the indicator variables.

Although this finding has restricted the sophistication of our analysis and might seem a negative outcome, it does indicate that there is a strong message inherent in the indicator data. The values of the indicators vary greatly within regions and urban groupings. The overall outcomes that we are measuring therefore are highly varied. They do not show any simple patterns related to regions, urban hierarchy or any other classification with which we have experimented. Such patterns might have been more obvious if all the districts in the country were analysed, rather than a sample, since by definition most of this sample is at the worst end of the range of any indicator. Clearly within the smaller range there is considerable variability, which does not allow us to generalise across types of places.

## 4.2 Correlation and regression analyses of the impacts

Given the failure of the data to group into meaningful classes, lagged correlation, partial correlation and regression have been attempted, in order to examine the relationships between inputs and outcomes. We have used three sets of places in our analyses: all 123 places; the 57 UPAs; and an intermediate set of 97, which comprises the UPAs and marginals. Numerous combinations of correlations and regressions have been carried out, many of which yielded no significant results. Only the significant ones are reported here.

The data concern change and are complex. For example, the index of long-term unemployment (LT:U) shows complex changes between the period 1983 to 1991. It peaks in 1987 whereas both percentage unemployed and percentage long-term peak in 1986. Percentage unemployed and percentage long-term unemployed are not simply related. This means, for example, that places in the same region, level of the hierarchy or 'Bristol grouping' have very variable trajectories over the period.

The period of general unemployment increase between 1983-86 is particularly complex. The percentage unemployed in 1983 gives no prediction of the change in unemployment between 1983-86. There is therefore very little structure to the data. There are no prior states that help to predict the change.

The period of unemployment decline, however, is much more predictable, for instance being related to percentage unemployment in 1986.

Various analyses of the unemployment indicators and government expenditure examined the relationship over time between indicator and expenditure. Clearly there are two possible relationships which need to be distinguished: government expenditure as a contributory cause of the decline in unemployment; and government expenditure responding to and following past levels of unemployment. There is some evidence of both occurring. There are higher correlations of unemployment with the previous one or two years' government inputs and with the future one or two years' inputs. These are usually higher than the correlation with the input for that year. The correlations with the indicator of earlier input is usually higher than that with later input. The lagged effects for both the past and future are, however, not consistent. So we cannot say that the immediately preceding year's input has a greater correlation than the input of two years before.

We have therefore grouped the various forms of government input to reflect the possible effect of preceding years. To explain, for instance, change in unemployment 1983-6, we have used government expenditure over the period 1982/3-84/5. This also corresponds with a significant change in government expenditure between 1984/5 and 1985/6. For unemployment change 1986-90 we have used the equivalent period 1985/6-88/9. We have also examined other combinations and durations of years, such as 1984/5-86/7, which despite running across a change in expenditure patterns, for both unemployment and long-term unemployment change has the greatest correlation with total government expenditure per capita.

**Unemployment: the period 1983-6** As has already been said, unemployment change in this period is particularly complex. Urban programme money (1982/3-1984/5) is positively related to both the increases in percent unemployment and percent long-term unemployment in this period (i.e. where UP pc has been higher, unemployment has risen more). The correlations are greater for long-term unemployment than for unemployment. It could therefore be argued that government expenditure was not holding down the growth of unemployment, but the relationship is not strong, although statistically significant, and there is a greater correlation of unemployment change(1983-6) with Urban Programme pc in 1979/80-81/82 than with 1982/3-84/5 (for the 57, 0.41 to 0.29). Expenditure in the second period is closely related to the first. This could suggest that the UP money was relatively well targeted in the earlier period onto places where there was potential for unemployment growth, although it should be remembered that the variation of unemployment growth in this period was not easily predicted from earlier data. Unfortunately we do not have any comparable unemployment data before 1983 that might help us to unravel the relationships further.

On the other hand, Regional Selective Assistance shows a smaller but significant negative relationship with unemployment growth. In other words, for the 123 and 97, where RSA expenditure pc between 1982-5 is higher, unemployment growth is lower. This relationship, however, is not significant for the 57, where the absence of RSA inputs to the London boroughs may cloud the relationship more. European expenditure pc does not relate to the changes.

**Unemployment: the period 1986-90**. In this period unemployment is declining. There is greater structure to the data, as already mentioned. Expenditure is measured for the period 1985/6-88/9, unless otherwise stated. This is a period during which patterns of expenditure are fairly consistent, although for total expenditure as against per-capita expenditure there is a distinct change between 1987/8 and 1988/89. Between 1988/9 and 1989/90 there is a distinct change in both total and per-capita expenditure.

In this period both higher amounts of per-capita UP and per-capita RSA expenditure are associated with greater declines in unemployment to a significant degree. These are independent effects because UP and RSA expenditure are not related. European money is less significant for the 123 and not significant for the 97. Although significant, UP expenditure only accounts for between 16 and 25% of the variation in unemployment decline, with RSA accounting for a further 16%. An example of one of the results of multiple regression is shown below, demonstrating the significant improvement in levels of unemployment in the 1986-90 period associated with UP and RSA expenditure levels:

**Multiple regression for the period 1986-1990**

| | |
|---|---|
| Dependent variable: | % unemployed |
| Independent variables: | UP expenditure per capita; RSA expenditure per capita. |
| R-square value: | 0.384 |
| Beta coefficients: | UP= -0.483; RSA= -0.408 |

Partial correlations show the relationship between changes in unemployment and UP expenditure to be significant, even when allowing for the effect of the unemployment rates in 1986. This suggests that the association is much more likely to be inputs -> outcomes than outcomes -> inputs. If the former were the case, then allowing for the effect of the 1986 unemployment rates on which inputs may have been decided, would have resulted in no relationship at all between change in rates and inputs. The partial correlations are still significant for the 123, 97, and 57 for unemployment and for the 123, and 97 for long term unemployment, but of course the relationships are still not strong.

There is still much unaccounted variance in the changed rates. This is not due to other government programmes. However, given the lack of evidence in the first period of there being much effect of government expenditure, especially for inner-city oriented monies, this degree of association is worthy of note.

There is no relationship between total inputs per capita and changes in unemployment rates. While the mechanisms linking the total inputs to jobs are not obvious, the logic of such an accounting procedure suggested that it should be examined, especially since the changes in AfC inputs and the amounts of AfC inputs were offset by changes in other accounts, which would have direct effect on local government expenditure and an indirect effect on employment and the creation of an improved local context for employment opportunities.

Per-capita UP and RSA expenditure in previous periods are also related to unemployment decline, but not to such a high degree as expenditure in the period 1985-89. These associations may be due to the high correlations between periods of government expenditure, rather than to lagged effects of expenditure on unemployment decline.

The tentative conclusion for this period is that some elements of AfC expenditure are associated significantly with unemployment and long-term unemployment decline.

**Job change and VAT registrations**. Very little of the analysis carried out shows any relationship between government expenditure and job change. There is some significant positive association between total government expenditure per capita and percent change in the total number of jobs for the period of 1984-87 (i.e. more expenditure was associated with places with relatively more jobs). There is no association, however, with UP per capita expenditure. Here there is some possibility that government expenditure helped to increase the rate of job growth. There is, however, no relationship with job change per capita, so the first relationship may just be picking out a size effect.

There is a small degree of association between per capita European expenditure and the increase in VAT registrations for the late 1980s, but this is in a negative direction (i.e. more European money per capita is associated with smaller increases in VAT registrations). RSA per capita expenditure is also somewhat associated with VAT increases in the period 1984-7. In this case there is a positive association. Here again there is some evidence, along with percent job change, that government expenditure was associated with improving conditions in the places of greatest per-capita expenditure during the period 1984-87.

**Net Migration of 25-34 year olds**. There is no relationship at all between this indicator and AfC monies for any of the time periods. As has been shown above, there is great variation between places of a similar kind on this indicator. In a similar way to the change in the overall rates of unemployment, however, there is a significant relationship with RSA per capita for the 57, 97 and 123 for both unemployment and long-term unemployment of the 25-34s for change between 1986 and 1990. RSA accounts for between 13% and 25% of the variance depending on the sample size used. There is, however, no equivalent relationship between UP per capita and 25-34 year-old unemployment change.

These national-level analyses show few relationships between inputs and indicators. There are some for 25-34s unemployment changes for 1986-90 which suggest associations between inputs and outcomes that are not simply a reflection of inputs following outcomes. RSA monies have associations with both overall and 25-34 unemployment whereas UP per capita only relates to overall change. These are not strong associations, but they do suggest further types of analysis to discover whether there are causal mechanisms at work.

**House price changes, 1983-6**. No matter which sets of data are analysed for this period (absolute or percentage changes, or changes for the whole or the edited subset of districts, or for differing combinations of the 123), there are significant correlations between the two indicators and AFC investment per capita 1982/3 to 1985/6 and HIPS per capita 1982/3 to 1985/6. These are weak negative relationships, which still hold when partial correlations are carried out holding either the average 1983 price for inner-city or first-time buyers constant. These partial correlation analyses ensure that such a negative relationship is not simply a reflection of north-south differences in house prices. So, for the total 123 districts, the 97 UPAs and marginals and the 57 UPAs, and edited versions of these, AFC and HIPS inputs for this period were greatest where prices rose least.

This is the same negative relationship for this period as was found for the relationships between some inputs and the unemployment indicators (which suggested that unemployment was worsening most where inputs were greatest). It seems to be a period when government inputs were not having a direct, positive, effect on either unemployment or house prices. Public expenditure may have been preventing a worse situation from occurring, but that is not easy to prove.

One possible causal relationship has been examined between government inputs and house prices during this period. It is quite possible that the variation in house price changes was due to the variation in increases in long-term unemployment, although the previously observed weak positive relationship casts doubt on the more obvious direction of causality. Any relationship between government inputs and house price change may simply reflect the already observed relationship between some government inputs and increases in long-term unemployment. The use of partial correlation analyses again clarifies the relationships. If the effect of long-term unemployment change is allowed for, there is still a significant relationship between the above inputs and house price change. The relationships between government inputs and house price change are independent of the relationships between inputs and long-term unemployment change. This is also the case for the 1986-89 period.

Given that these various partial correlation analyses support the significance of straightforward correlations, it is useful to summarise the weak negative relationships for the different sets of places and the two indicators:

| | AFC pc '82/3-'85/6 | | | HIPS '82/3-'85/6 | | |
|---|---|---|---|---|---|---|
| | 123 | 97 | 57 | 123 | 97 | 57 |
| **absolute change** | | | | | | |
| - first-time buyers | -.21 | -.22 | -.32 | -.39 | -.47 | -.60 |
| - inner city | -.31 | -.32 | -.40 | -.43 | -.50 | -.58 |
| **percentage change** | | | | | | |
| - first-time buyers | -.21 | -.27 | -.40 | -.32 | -.43 | -.52 |
| - inner city | -.31 | -.35 | -.44 | -.33 | -.38 | -.49 |

An edited set of places (districts with more numerous incidence of sales) support the results of the larger sets:

| | AFCpc 82/3-85/6 | | | HIPS 82/3-85/6 | | |
|---|---|---|---|---|---|---|
| | 123ed | 97ed | 57ed | 123ed | 97ed | 57ed |
| **absolute change** | | | | | | |
| - first-time buyers | -.28 | -.29 | -.34 | -.51 | -.56 | -.58 |
| - inner city | -.38 | -.40 | -.44 | -.48 | -.50 | -.52 |
| **percentage change** | | | | | | |
| - first-time buyers | -.36 | -.38 | -.45 | -.47 | -.51 | -.52 |
| - inner city | -.44 | -.45 | -.49 | -.41 | -.43 | -.46 |

The regression analyses would be of more interest if the relationships between government inputs and house prices were positive. However, for the sake of completeness, one example is given to show that government inputs had a significant effect: 30% of the variation in the absolute change in inner-city prices for the 97 is accounted for by the inner-city prices of 1983. The inclusion of the AFCpc 82/3-85/6 adds a further 8% to the 'explanation'. This is significant, but as commented above, weak. The beta value for the AFC variable is -.28 (for inner-city prices 1983 it is 0.53). Many other such results could be shown to suggest the same weak but significant, negative relationship.

**House price changes, 1986-1989.** There are fewer consistent relationships between inputs and house prices over this period which, as already noted is a complex one for house price change. There are, however, some positive ones, but they are only for the absolute change in house prices and they are quite weak. Again the use of partial correlation analysis confirms that the relationships discussed are not just a reflection of north-south differences nor price differences in 1986. Some other weak negative relationships disappeared when partials were carried out.

For the absolute change in inner city prices there is a weak positive relationship with UP pc 1985/6-88/89 for all three sets of data, when holding constant 1986 prices. This narrowly fails to reach significant levels for percentage change. Similarly, there is a weak positive relationship between absolute change in first-time buyer prices and AFC pc 1985/6-88/9, again for all three sets of data.

The weakness of these relationships may be illustrated by the multiple regression for the 57 UPAs, where the dependent variable is absolute change for first-time buyers and the independent variables are the prices in 1986 and AFC pc 1985/ 6-88/89. 79% of the variation in absolute price increases is accounted for by the 1986 prices. While the government input is a significant addition, it only adds a further 2.7% to the 'explanation'. The beta values are 0.85 for the 1986 prices and 0.17 for the AFC variable. The residuals from this regression show that the Midlands and to a lesser extent some of Yorkshire are under-predicted. The over-predicted areas show less of a regional pattern.

While there is some evidence of positive relationships between government inputs and absolute house price change in this period, it is less consistent and weaker than the evidence of negative relationships in the earlier period. What evidence there is, does make some geographical sense. The Urban Programme resources across the country are more likely to have been allocated to inner city areas within local districts, whereas the wider set of AFC resources is probably less likely to have been so concentrated and may therefore have helped to improve the wider area and have contributed to the rise in first-time buyers' house prices.

This analysis simply shows an association. Given the weakness of the association, no causal explanation of the mechanisms that might link one to the other have been attempted.

## 4.3 Analysis by gaps

The national-level analysis of gaps between UPAs, marginals and comparators produces another way to examine impacts. For most of the indicators there was a closing gap and this is associated with more government inputs to the UPAs as a whole than to the others.

The variation of inputs and indicators within groups necessitates closer examination. Of the 12 non-UPAs in the best-funded 57, three experience falls in long-term unemployment during the period 1983-86 (Corby, Derwentside and Rossendale). Two others have very small increases (Wellingborough and Hyndburn). This was a time when the UPAs as a whole were experiencing large increases in long-term unemployment.

Of the 12 UPAs not within the best-funded 57, three experience rises in long-term unemployment of over 2.0% between 1983-86. Only 7 others of the 123 have such high increases. The four London boroughs within this 12 (Haringey, Kensington, Lewisham and Wandsworth) have lower rates of improvement in long-term unemployment over the period 1983 to 1990 than all but one other London UPA, Hammersmith. These five have gains of between 1.29% and 1.61% while the rest improve by 1.9% to 3.7%. In these terms there is an association between government inputs and outcomes.

Comparisons can also be made between districts with similar inputs but different policy status and hence, it may be assumed, different levels of socio-economic problems. Wigan, a UPA outside the top 57, has slightly less input per capita than nearby West Lancs, a marginal. In 1983 West Lancs exceeded Wigan's rate of long-term unemployment by 0.44 but by 1990 Wigan had a higher rate by 0.16, the gap reversing. Barnsley, a UPA outside the 57, shows a similar widening gap (0.12) with Wakefield, a marginal with similar inputs over the period. St. Helens obtains slightly more than West Lancs, but in this case the gap narrows by 0.1 between the UPA and marginal. So not all of the cases conform to the same pattern.

## 4.4 Regional level analyses

There are great variations of inputs and outcome indicators at the national level. Regional relationships between inputs and outcomes are examined through the above analyses of narrowing and widening gaps.

**Greater London**. Over the whole period 1981-90 the comparators obtained in total 0.77% of the total government expenditure per capita, while the UPAs had 31.9%. The proportions varied between 0 and 0.42% for the comparators and 0.22% and 13.63% for the UPAs. The averages were 0.11% and 2.45% rspectively. This difference in government support is associated with a narrowing of the gap in long-term unemployment between the two sets of areas from 2.57% in 1983 to 2.01% in 1990, so there was a convergence of about one fifth of the original difference. Expenditure is also associated with changing gaps in per capita jobs, VAT registrations and 25-34s. There is some support for an association between inputs and outcomes in Greater London, but the variation within UPAs suggests the need for individual analysis.

**The North West**. Merseyside receives a greater proportion of AfC monies than the other areas:

**Averages per district**

| | |
|---|---|
| Merseyside | 1.31 |
| with Halton | 1.20 |
| Gt Manchester | 1.23 |
| Lancs 3 UPAs | 0.73 |
| Gt Manchester marginals | 0.58 |
| E. Lancs marginals | 0.45 |
| W. Lancs and Ellesmere | 0.45 |
| Gt Manchester comparators | 0.17 |

The earlier gap analyses showed that Merseyside had closed the gap with comparators on long-term unemployment more rapidly than had the Greater Manchester UPAs, which receive less monies per district. The E. Lancs UPAs, however, had closed the gap even more. Although they received less monies, they also began from a less difficult situation. More comparably, the gap was also closed between them and the E. Lancs marginals, which received less monies. There is, therefore, considerable evidence of closure of gaps being associated with more inputs. However, not all the gaps for the indicators were closing. There were still problems, such as a widening gap in long-term unemployment of 25-34s and jobs per capita between Merseyside and its nearby marginals, and a difference between Greater Manchester's UPAs and the rest in VAT registrations.

In making these gap comparisons, however, considerable variation was noted within the North West and within Greater London at the individual district level, so individual profiles are presented below.

The inter-regional analysis of long-term employment changes showed that gaps were closing and that these were associated with different levels of government AfC inputs.

**4.5 District profiles**

The above analysis of gaps suggests evidence for there having been some improvement for the UPAs relative to the comparators. However, both the 'AfC' inputs and the 'overall' inputs show great variation within the UPAs and indeed within the whole set of districts. It is therefore useful to provide area profiles for districts within the three regions which have acted as case studies (see 4.2-4.3).

**Profiles for Greater London**. (Rankings within London are given before rankings within the set of 123).

Camden is not a UPA. Of the 24 sample London boroughs it was 19th in its receipt of AfC resources, in other words behind some of the comparators. It was 2nd in overall input in 1979/80, but had dropped to last by 1989/90. It has therefore experienced a rapid and continuing decrease in funds. The positive indicators are that its jobs per capita have been maintained and that it had the 3rd largest increase in numbers of VAT registrations (though the 22nd in rate of increase in VAT registrations). The negative indicators are that it has lost its 25-34s in absolute and relative terms. The proportion of long-term employment that was experienced by 25-34s had increased despite their relative decline in the population. The rate for 25-34s is now the same as that for the population as a whole.

Kensington has also had a big drop in inputs. It was 16th in receipt of AfC, again below some non-UPAs. Its overall input position has fallen from being 5th in 1979 to 14th in 1989. Its positive indicators are 4th in absolute growth of VAT registrations and 6th in rate of growth. Its jobs per capita are up, but it has lost population, so this partly explains the 'improvement'. It has a low level of 25-34 long-term unemployment. In negative terms, it experienced a great absolute and proportional loss in 25-34s. It was not surprising that the proportion that this group contributed to long-term unemployed fell. However the fall in 25-34 long-term unemployment was small.

Lewisham was 10th in receipt of AfC monies but on overall inputs it declined from 8th to 13th position. Positive indicators are that it gained 25-34s despite an overall loss in population and that it had the 7th largest increase in VAT registrations. Negative indicators are that its 25-34 long-term unemployment rate is now higher than the overall rate, with a very low drop in 25-34 long-term unemployed since 1986.

Islington has had quite a lot of AfC monies (6th highest) however it has dropped from 1st to 5th in overall inputs. The positive indicators are that it has gained 25-34s in both absolute and proportional terms. The negative indicators are that it has had a major change in 25-34 long-term unemployment - it had the 4th highest rise out of the 123 between 1986 and 1990 - and of the 24 boroughs, it has the 3rd highest level in 1990.

Westminster has received very little of the AfC monies (23rd of the 24). In overall inputs it has generally been low down the order. It dropped from 16th to 21st. However, it received more inputs in 1990. The positive indicators are low levels of long-term unemployment and jobs per capita are up (but not 1987-89). The negative indicators are that it has a lowish rise in VAT registrations and a big absolute and proportional loss in 25-34, yet a proportional rise in their long-term unemployment.

Tower Hamlets is clearly first in the country in receipt of AfC monies. From 11th position of the 24 in 1979 it has climbed to 1st in 1989 in overall inputs. The positive indicators are a massive increase in 25-34s and a proportional rise that is not echoed in long-term unemployment. It has the biggest drop in 25-34 long-term unemployment and a relatively low level. Its jobs per capita have risen. The only negative sign is that the VAT registrations increase is below average.

Newham obtained the next most AfC monies in the country and rose from 10th of 24 to 2nd in overall inputs. There are some positive signs: an increase in absolute and proportional terms of 25-34s. However, unlike Tower Hamlets, there are a number of negative signs: a relatively low decline in long-term unemployment, with the 25-34's rate now the same as that for all age groups; its jobs per capita are down (despite the drop in total population); and a relative low VAT registration rate and low absolute increase.

Southwark was 3rd of the 24 in receipt of AfC but its overall inputs were much lower than might be expected. A massive increase absolutely and proportionally of 25-34s is somewhat offset by their long-term unemployment being higher than long-term unemployment overall. Jobs and VAT registrations are average.

Hackney was 4th in AfC inputs. It shows high absolute and proportional gain in 25-34s but a worryingly high level of 25-34 long-term unemployment which is now higher than the overall rate. Jobs are down, despite little change in the population, while VAT registrations had a below-average increase.

Lambeth was 5th on AfC but its overall inputs were well down except in 1990/1. Its position dropped from 4th to 6th on overall inputs. Jobs were down despite a loss in population. 25-34s were slightly up but their long term unemployment exceeded the overall rate. However there was a large drop in this rate between 1986-90.

Hammersmith was 7th on AfC, but quite low on overall resources. It lost 25-34s absolutely and proportionally, yet showed very little decline in its long-term unemployment rate. On the other hand jobs and VAT registrations were more encouraging.

Brent is 8th on AfC. It did poorly on overall inputs in the late 1980s but did well in 1990/1. It had increasing 25-34s, but their long-term unemployment is now the same as the overall rate (however, comparatively low). It experienced job loss which, given a similar population, means an actual loss in jobs.

Greenwich was 9th on AfC and received overall inputs that increased it from 13th to 8th. VAT registrations show higher than average growth. It has an increase in 25-34s and a higher long-term unemployment rate than Brent and that for 25-34 now higher than overall rate. It seems to have derived benefits from relatively higher position on overall inputs, even if an overall loser since 1979.

Wandsworth was 11th on AfC. Its overall expenditure rank position remained nearly the same. It received a boost in 1990/1. VAT registrations and jobs per capita show good signs. Absolute and proportional increase in 25-34s without any great advance in long term unemployment rate. It has some healthy signs apart from overall population loss. It seems to have much lower priority for support than others.

Haringey was 12th on AfC and despite being a net loser in overall input, its position rose from 7th to 4th position in total inputs. It has lost 25-34s absolutely but at a slightly lower rate than the population as a whole. However the long-term unemployment rate for 25-34s is now considerably higher than the overall rate. It had the highest rise in 25-34 unemployment of the 123 from 1986-90. Its level is approaching that of Southwark. Jobs per capita are about the same, even though the population has fallen.

**Summary for London.** The overall picture is not simple. This is partly because the targeted monies are offset by variations in other monies. Although it can be argued that these are not contributing directly to many of the issues involved, they do contribute to the general attraction of the area as a place to live and to work. Since our outcome indicators reflect this, it seems appropriate to take these other inputs into consideration. The gaps analysis suggests some success of programmes but the rest of the analysis shows the variation within the UPAs and the positions of Westminster and particularly Camden as being close to some of the UPAs. At the extremes Tower Hamlets demonstrates what can happen with great inputs, while Camden shows the dangers of much reduced inputs. In between there are many stories, which are captured in the profiles.

**Profiles for the North West**

Bolton was a net loser in overall input by £142pc from 1979/80 to 1989/90. It dropped from 8th to 11th in NW. It was 28th ranked nationally as a receiver of AfC monies.  While its long-term unemployment fell considerably from 1983 to 1990, it was 3rd highest to Manchester and Salford in 1990 whereas it was 4th in 1983. Positively it has gained 25-34s without increasing their proportion of long-term unemployment. Its VAT and job change are about average for the conurbation. Jobs per capita rise. VAT is below average UPA level. It has relatively low inputs and mixed outcomes.

Manchester has been a major loser of overall inputs, dropping from 1st to 8th in the NW, by £223pc, the greatest loss in the NW. It was 11th in AfC inputs which clearly have been a positive gain in an overall extremely large loss through the period. On the positive side it has gained 25-34s, now being above rather than below average for the 6 UPAs and conurbation. Negatively, however, an increasing proportion of long-term unemployed are 25-34s, with long-term unemployment of that age group being higher than for overall long-term unemployment by 1990. This is associated with a large drop in jobs per capita and a decline in VAT registrations. Its input losses are associated with a decline in nearly all of the indicators.

Oldham has also been a loser dropping from 4th to 6th by £95pc. It was 37th in AfC input. VAT registrations are fairly buoyant for the region but below the UPA average but jobs per capita are down slightly (0.03). 25-34s have increased a little but have not increased as part of long-term unemployment by as much. It has had low inputs and mixed outcomes.

Rochdale has declined in overall inputs by £46, but risen in rank from 5th to 3rd. It was 25th in AfC spend. Its long-term unemployment rate dropped considerably, being now similar to that of Oldham and Wigan, which it exceeded by about 1% in 1983. It has a slightly higher proportion of 25-34s and this has been accompanied by a fall in their proportion of overall long-term unemployment. On the negative side its jobs per capita are still low and they have not quite recovered to 1981 levels and its VAT registrations, although growing, are less than Bolton, Olham and Wigan. So while there are some positive signs, there are still some problems.

Salford has declined from 2nd to 4th in overall inputs, by £140pc, a loss only exceeded by Manchester and Warrington. It was 8th nationally on AfC inputs, but this has been offset by the loss of other inputs. It has gained in 25-34s and they have not greatly increased as a proportion of long-term unemployed. It has nearly recovered its 1981 level of jobs per capita, but its VAT registrations have declined (95 in 1990 indexed on 1981). So, some good signs but some still to be concerned about.

Wigan has dropped from 11th to 15th with a loss of £84pc. Although an UPA it was outside the top 57 at 66th position on AfC. It has not done very well for inputs. It has a good VAT registration growth for a NW UPA (130). It has a slightly higher proportion of 25-34s without increasing the long-term proportion. However it has not recovered its jobs per capita ratio which, along with Bury's, is the lowest in the conurbation.

Knowsley is a net loser of £22pc but relatively moves up from 9th to 5th in the NW. It is 26th nationally on AFC monies. It has relatively boomed in VAT registrations (161). While its proportion of 25-34s have increased, so has their proportion of long-term unemployment. Even more negatively, the rate of unemployment of 25-34s exceeds the overall rate and exceeds it more by 1990 than it did in 1983. Overall unemployment is still very high in 1990 at 6.01%, even though it is much reduced from 11.74% in 1983. Its jobs per capita are 0.11 down on 1981 from 0.68 to 0.57. While there has been some improvement, there are still many problems and concerning signs.

Liverpool is a net loser by £69pc , the 13th largest loss in the NW. This still means it moves from 3rd to 1st in total inputs. It is 4th nationally on AfC receipt, well above Salford and Manchester. There is only slight positive news. It has a slight increase in VAT registrations, 104. There is a slight increase in 25-34s but it still has a small proportion. However by the end of the period, the long-term unemployment rate of 25-34s exceeds the overall rate by more than it trailed it in 1983. Both are still high, 7.81% and 6.96%, even though they have fallen from the 1983 levels. Jobs per capita are down 0.15 to 0.80, the largest in Merseyside, but considerably less than Manchester 1.13 and Preston 1.06, and the ratio expected of the centre of a conurbation. Any positive news is offset by continued problems, some that have been exacerbated.

St.Helens is a minor loser of £19pc and therefore moves from 14th to 5th in total inputs. This is even though it is 63rd for AfC, outside the top 57, despite its UPA status. It has gained in %25-34s without any increase in their proportion of long-term unemployment. Their rate has dropped more than that of the population overall. VATs are up 123 (below the UPA average), but jobs per capita are down by 0.13, the only negative sign.

Sefton has lost £81pc and gone from 18th to 20th. It has received relatively little AfC monies, being well out of the top 57 at 74th, with only 0.23% of total per capita input. It has slightly increased its jobs per capita and expanded VAT registrations, 123. Its proportion of 25-34s has increased considerably, by 2.66%, but the proportion of long-term unemployed has increased even more, so that the 25-34 rate is moving closer to the overall rate. But for this, there are mostly positive signs for a relatively low input.

Wirral is a loser by £43pc, but has a similar rank, from 17 to 16. It is 29th in AfC terms. VAT registrations are quite good at 131 and it gains %25-34s, but it does not quite regain its jobs per capita ratio and during the peak of unemployment the rate for 25-34s exceeded that for the overall population. The fall back below the overall rate by 1990, with a wider gap than in 1983, suggests that positive signs outweigh negative ones. It still has a high long-term unemployment level.

Halton is a large loser at £93pc, moving down from 20th to 22nd. In AfC terms it is 46th. It regains its jobs per capita ratio and VAT registrations are high at 143. It loses somewhat its %25-34s but from a high starting point but their long-term unemployment rate while beginning 1% below the overall rate, ends in 1990 at 0.8% above it. The 25-34s' proportion of long-term unemployment numbers has risen despite their drop as a proportion of the population. Again there are some positive signs but there are also some negative ones for 25-34s and their unemployment.

Blackburn is a small gainer of £23pc, rising from 10th to 2nd place in the NW. This rise is not due to its AfC monies, with its national ranking of 32nd. It improves its job per capita ratio over the period by 0.03, notably not declining in 1984 when nearly everywhere else does. Its %25-34s rises considerably and that is not accompanied by a proportional increase in their contribution of long-term unemployment, indeed it drops. However their long-term unemployment rate exceeded the overall rate in 1986, the peak year, but declined back nearly as far below it as it was in 1983. The only other negative sign is the VAT registrations which at 113 are relative low, being mainly due to slow growth from 1981 to 1987 (103). Recent signs then are relatively good.

Burnley is a net loser of £75pc, moving from 7th to 10th. It is 45th in AfC monies. It regains its 1981 jobs per capita ratio by 1987 having dropped in 1984, unlike Blackburn, but it does not exceed it. It gains in %25-34s without their proportion of long-term unemployment increasing, and their rates remain below the overall rate by about the same amount over the period. These positive signs are weakened by its VAT regs at 114, due to very little change from 1981 to 1986. More recent signs are good. For such a net loser it has not done badly.

Preston is a slight net gainer by £11pc, moving from 21st to 14th. It is 50th for AfC monies. It gains in %25-34s by over 3% without increasing their proportion of long-term unemployment by much and their rate of long-term unemployment remains well below the overall rate throughout the period. However jobs per capita fall 0.05, but from a high of 1.11, second to highest in the region and VAT growth is only to 117, with steady growth during the 1980s, not the recent growth of Blackburn and Burnley.

Trafford, as a marginal area, is a small net loser up to 1989/90 by £22pc, but it is almost in balance in 1990/1. It moves from 24th to 21st in 1989/90. In spite of not being a UPA it is 27th for AfC monies. Jobs per capita are slightly above 1981 levels and VAT registrations growth is at 137, the highest for Greater Manchester. The %25-34s has risen but with an increasing proportion of long-term unemployment. The 25-34s' rate has closed a little on the overall rate but it is still below it. It therefore shows mostly positive signs in an area that has received large sums of money, despite its status, and has not lost anywhere near as much in total inputs pc as others.

Tameside, as another marginal area, is a major net loser by £116pc, moving from 6th to 17th. It is 85th in AfC monies. Jobs per capita have not been regained, being 0.02 down. VAT registrations are at 125, average for the area. Its %25-34s has increased but their long-term unemployment rate and the overall one have closed and the proportional share risen. Despite the loss of monies its position does not seem to have worsened much.

**Profiles for the North**

Gateshead is a major receiver of AfC monies being 5th in the national ranking. In absolute terms it loses only £16.6pc between 1979/80 and 1989/90 in overall inputs and moves from 5th to 1st in inputs pc within the region. On the positive side its long-term unemployment has fallen greatly by 3.49% (83-90). Its %25-34s is up 1.6% and their proportion of unemployment has not risen any more than would be expected. Its VAT registrations are the highest for the region at 137. On the negative side its job per capita has not regained 1981 levels. While there are still problems on the jobs side it has a mostly positive picture. The high inputs are associated with mainly positive outcomes.

Hartlepool is 12th on the AfC ranking and is only a small net loser of -£10.8pc. It moves from 9th to 2nd on the amounts of overall inputs regionally. On the positive side long-term unemployment has dropped by 4.44%. Its %25-34s has risen by 1.96%. with a decrease in their % of the unemployment total. Its VAT registrations are 124, their growth having slowed in the later 1980s. The other negative sign is the failure to regain the 1981 job per capita level by 0.06. Considerable input has been met by many positive signs.

Langbaurgh only just gets into the best-funded 57 on AfC monies at 53. It has lost -£95.7pc and dropped from 13th to 15th in the northern region. On the positive side it drops 3.9% on long-term unemployment. It gains %25-34s. However their proportion rises more than expected in long-term unemployment and their rate is almost the same as the overall rate in 1990. Jobs per capita are down by 0.1 on 1981, a big drop, and VAT registrations are average for the region at 127. Here the negative signs outweigh the positive. The low AfC input and overall loss are associated with continuing problems.

Middlesbrough is 17th in AfC and loses £87.4pc. It drops from 3rd to 5th in overall inputs. The positive signs are an increase in jobs per capita by 0.09, a big increase. There is a 4.69% drop in long-term unemployment. %25-34s has risen a little and their long-term unemployment rate has dropped below the overall rate. VAT registrations are average for the region but lower than the national average. On the negative side its long-term unemployment rate is still very high. Although there are still problems, there are mostly positive signs from a very poor base and relatively low input.

Newcastle is 9th on AfC. It loses -£59.4pc but rises from 6th to 5th on overall inputs. It gains %25-34s but their long-term unemployment rate exceeds the overall rate by the end of the period. Its level of unemployment is still high. Its VAT registrations have dropped to 98. Jobs per capita have not quite regained 1981 levels. Despite the AfC input and quite a low drop in overall inputs there are mostly negative signs.

North Tyneside is quite low on AfC at 40th. It has lost a lot of overall inputs, the largest loss in the region at £129.8pc. It has dropped from 2nd to 8th on overall inputs. On the positive side it has gained 25-34s without their proportion of long-term unemployment rising more than expected. It has one of the highest regional rates of increase in VAT registrations at 135, above the national average. But it has not regained its 1981 jobs per capita level (-0.04). Its long-term unemployment only dropped by 2.55 % but it has the lowest rate of the UPAs in the region. There are some positive signs despite the relatively low inputs and net loss of overall monies.

South Tyneside is 16th on AfC. It too has dropped -£125.9 and dropped from 1st to 4th on overall inputs. There is a 2% rise in %25-34s but with some closing of their and the overall rate. VAT registrations growth at 133 is high for the region. However it is still 0.1 down on its 1981 jobs per capita. There are therefore both positive and negative signs. It can ill afford the large loss of overall inputs.

Stockton is 35th on AfC and with a gain, the only one in the region, of £42.51 it has risen from 7th to 3rd in overall inputs. The positive gain has only been in the later 1980s however. Long-term unemployment has dropped by 3.45%. The %25-34s has increased with some increase in their proportion of unemployment though. VATs are only at 125 and jobs per capita have not recovered to 1981 levels (0.02). There are still problems which the greater recent overall inputs may help to solve.

Sunderland is 23rd on AfC and only lost -£19.7 pc, rising from 7th to 3rd on overall inputs. Its long-term unemployment dropped by 3.84%. It has a greater %25-34s but with more than proportional rise in their long-term unemployment. Also on the negative side VAT registrations are low at 113 and jobs per capita are still down 0.05 on 1981. Despite the relative high inputs and low overall loss, there are still mostly negative signs. There seems to be much left to do here.

**Profiles for the remaining UPAs**

Barnsley is outside the top 57 at 68th on AfC. It has also had a loss of overall inputs of £104pc. On the positive side it has VAT registrations at 127. But it has not lowered its long-term unemployment rate very much, -1.62. It has only marginally increased its 25-34s, though on the positive side there has been no proportional increase in their long-term rates. Its major negative is a lowering of the job per capita level by 0.12.

Birmingham is 33rd on AfC and lost -£72.3pc. On the positive side it has seen a big drop in long-term unemployment (4.72). It gained in %25-34s but their rate of long-term unemployment is closing with the overall rate. It has low VAT at 104 and has lost jobs per capita by 0.09.

Bradford is 42nd on AfC and has lost £57.1 pc. Jobs per capita are slightly up 0.02 and %25-34s have increased without any effect on their proportion of long-term unemployment. However, VAT is only at 106. Mainly positive signs for a medium input.

Bristol is well down the AfC ranking at 87 with very little AfC monies for a UPA. It has also lost £71.8 pc. It has gained 0.1 on jobs per capita, a significant increase. It has a VAT growth of 128. But %25-34s are going down and their rate is nearing the overall rate of long-term unemployment. It has mostly positive signs with little inputs but there are some worrying changes.

Coventry is 22nd on AfC and has lost £58pc. Its VAT registrations are high at 138. Its long-term unemployment dropped substantially by 3.94% and its %25-34s have grown, but their rate of long-term unemployment has closed rapidly on the overall rate. Jobs per capita is down 0.03. There are some positive signs but some negative ones too, set against largish financial inputs.

Derby is a UPA but it is only 72nd on the AfC ranking. It has lost £54.4pc. On the positive side it has increased its %25-34 without changing their proportion of long-term unemployment. It has an about average VAT registration growth for a UPA of 130. On the negative side it has not regained its 1981 job per capita level (-0.04). It has low input and has mixed outcomes.

Doncaster is 54th on the AfC ranking. It has lost £126.8pc. It has slightly above average VAT registration growth at 133. It has increased its %25-34s without increasing their share of long-term unemployment. On the negative side, its drop in long-term unemployment was relatively low (2.52%) and it has lost jobs per capita (-0.09). Like Derby it has low inputs with mixed outcomes.

Dudley is 30th in AfC and has lost £30.85pc. Its long-term unemployment dropped considerably, by -3.56%. Its VAT is above average at 138. It has increased its %25-34s with only a slight increase in their proportional share of long-term unemployment. On the negative side it has not regained its 1981 job per capita level (-0.02). It has quite high inputs and mostly positive signs.

Hull is 18th on AfC and has lost £66.46pc. Its positive sign is its increase in jobs per capita (+0.12). It has a number of negative ones. Its VAT registrations are only 119. Its %25-34s has declined somewhat to a much lower level than most UPAs (13.97%) and at the same time their proportion of long-term unemployment has increased. It has reasonably high inputs and mostly negative signs.

Kirklees is the second-to-lowest UPA on the AfC ranking at 80th. It has the same input as Bury, a comparator. It has lost £42.5pc. It has gained jobs per capita (+0.04). It has a higher %25-34s but their rate and the overall rate of unemployment are closing. VAT registrations are slightly below average at 128. However it has a final long-term rate of 1.31%, lower than that of Tameside, a marginal authority. It has low inputs with some negative and some positive outcomes. It has not been generously treated as a UPA.

Leeds is ranked 15th on AfC. It has lost £97.6pc. It has just regained its 1981 job per capita level (+0.01). However while increasing its %25-34s their rate and the overall rate of long-term unemployment is closing. VAT registration is only at 117 and long-term unemployment only fell by 2.11%. It has mixed inputs and mixed outcomes.

Leicester is 52nd on AfC and lost £74.16pc. It has lost jobs per capita (0.03). It has a low VAT rate 119. It has increased its 25-34s but their rate and the overall long-term unemployment rate are closing. It has low inputs and still has quite a few problems.

Nottingham is 39th and lost £110.4pc. Its %25-34s grew a lot, 2.07% but their rate and the overall unemployment rate closed. Its long-term unemployment did not fall by much (2.7%) and is still high at 3.25%. Jobs per capita is slightly up (+0.01) but VAT registrations are low at 109. It has relatively low inputs and mainly negative signs.

Plymouth is 76th on AfC and has lost £80.4pc. It has increased its %25-34s without any change in their relative rates of long-term unemployment. VAT is somewhat below average at 125 and jobs per capita is down by (-0.04). It has low inputs and mixed outcomes.

Rotherham is 41st on AfC and has lost £119.3pc. There has been a rise in %25-34s but their rate and the overall rate of long-term unemployment are closing.

VAT is above average at 134 but jobs per capita is down (0.02). It has low inputs and mixed outcomes.

Sandwell is 19th on AfC and only lost £15.5pc. Its long-term unemployment fell by 4.94%. It has regained its jobs per capita level. It has increased its %25-34s by nearly 2% but their rate and the overall rate of long-term unemployment are closing. VAT is somewhat lower than average at 124. It has relatively high inputs and mainly positive outcomes.

Sheffield is 48th on AfC and has lost £81.2. Its %25-34s rose by 2.3% but their rate and the overall rate of long-term unemployment closed. VAT registrations are only at 113 and jobs per capita are down (0.08). Long-term unemployment only fell by 2.15% and remains at 2.8%. It has low inputs and has mainly negative outcomes.

The Wrekin is 14th on AfC and has lost £38.6pc. Its long-term unemployment fell by 5.49%. Its job per capita increased by (+0.15) and VAT registrations were high at 151. Its %25-34 only marginally increased but from a high level. There was though a closing of their and the overall rates of long-term unemployment. It has relatively high inputs and mostly positive outcomes.

Walsall is 38th on AfC and has lost £57pc. Long-term unemployment fell considerably by 4.56% and is now at 1.86%. It has a 2.05% rise in %25-34s and in contrast to many other areas their rate and the overall rate of long-term unemployment are getting further apart. VAT registrations are relatively low at 115 and job per capita has not quite risen to its 1981 level (-0.01). It has relatively low inputs and many positive signs.

Wolverhampton is 31st on AfC and has lost £88.7pc. Its long-term unemployment has fallen by 4.56% but it is still quite high at 2.99%. It has a 2.27% increase in %25-34s. Their rate of long-term unemployment begins higher than the overall rate and then drops below it, getting further from it over time. VAT registration is above average for a UPA at 135. Its job per capita has not recovered from 1981 yet (-0.02). It has relatively low input and mainly positive signs.

**4.6 A classification of districts**

It is difficult to classify the districts into a simple two-by-two matrix of high and low inputs and good and poor outcomes because the picture is complex. Very few districts can be said to have received high inputs when many of those which have high rankings on AfC inputs lose a considerable amount per capita expenditure in overall inputs over the period. Equally, many districts show rather mixed outcomes. Nevertheless, a classification is attempted below based on levels of input and types of outcomes.

Inputs are divided into high, medium/mixed, and low based both on AfC and overall monies. A mixed class means that the district may be high on AfC but loses resources overall, or low on AfC but does well overall. In some cases, such as Manchester, the district is quite high on AfC but has lost considerably in overall terms during the period and is therefore categorised as having low input. The outcomes are classified into poor, mixed and positive. A mixed outcome denotes that some of the indictors are positive and others negative. The outcomes are measures of change and not of the position at a particular time. The classification is as below:

**High inputs and positive outcomes**
Corby (marginal)
Tower Hamlets

**Relatively high inputs and mainly positive outcomes**
Dudley
Gateshead
Greenwich
Hartlepool
Sandwell
Scunthorpe (marginal)
Stockton
Trafford (marginal)
Wandsworth
Wrekin

**Relatively low inputs and mainly positive outcomes**
Bristol
Burnley
Middlesbrough
North Tyneside
Pendle (marginal)
Sefton
Walsall
Wellingborough (marginal)
Wolverhampton

**Relatively low inputs with mixed outcomes**
Bolton
Derby
Doncaster
Halton
Kensington
Kirklees
Oldham
Plymouth
Rotherham
Sedgefield (marginal)
Tameside (marginal)
Wigan

**Mixed/medium inputs and mainly positive outcomes**
Blackburn
Bradford
Derwentside (marginal)
Hyndburn (marginal)

**Mixed/medium inputs and mixed outcomes**
Brent
Durham (comparator)
Ellesmere (marginal)
Hammersmith
Preston
Rochdale
Rochester (marginal)
Rossendale (marginal)

Salford
Southwark
St. Helens
Wirral

**Mixed/medium inputs and mainly poor outcomes**
Haringey
Leeds

**Low inputs and poor outcomes**
Barnsley
Birmingham
Blyth (marginal)
Camden (marginal)
Islington
Langbaurgh
Leicester
Lewisham
Nottingham
Manchester
Sheffield
South Tyneside

**Relatively high inputs and poor outcomes**
Coventry
Hackney
Hull
Knowsley
Lambeth
Liverpool
Newcastle
Sunderland

**High inputs and poor outcomes**
Newham

**Summary**

16 of the 57 UPAs have mainly positive outcomes, 20 have mixed and 21 poor outcomes and continuing problems. Given the intractable nature of some problems in certain parts of the country, this balance suggest reasonable success. Only 9 UPAs had high inputs and poor outcomes, and some of these districts were better than others.

Some major observations may be made on the classification. The two districts with the greatest inputs, Tower Hamlets and Newham, appear at either end of the spectrum. One has been very successful. The other still has major problems. They are adjacent to one another. Clearly, regional location in itself is not critical in determining success in these cases.

The only other district with a high input and positive outcomes is Corby which is not even a UPA. Despite this, it has received the third highest amount of AFC monies. Four other marginal districts have mainly positive outcomes, two with high inputs and two with relatively low ones. While Corby has no doubt benefited from the general growth of its region, recovering faster than Derwentside from similar problems, it should be noted that there are areas with positive and poor signs in all regions. While having an effect, the regional context is not a strong determinant of success or failure. It is noticeable that ten districts had poor outcomes and, despite being UPAs, received low overall inputs, usually reflecting a major loss of overall inputs. This effectively poor implementation of the targeting of designated areas recurs at the local scale. It reinforces the arguments for better strategic planning and overall coordination of programmes. The absence of monitoring of the overall spend means that there may be little official awareness of such input patterns - running counter, as they do, to the idea of designated areas.

The final comment about the classification is to note that the very large cities generally occur within the category of poor outcomes with continuing problems. These are the hardest districts to change. The local analysis suggests that there are a growing number of areas within them that are disadvantaged and that the districts are the home of a growing share of disadvantaged people within the conurbation of which they are the central area.

# 5 UNEMPLOYMENT CHANGE 1990-1991

The initial analysis of the relationships between inputs and outcomes was undertaken before the results of the 1991 population census were available. Much of the analysis has therefore not been able to extend into the period of the early 1990s. Given the onset of recessionary trends in the 1990s, it is clearly important to look at the patterns for the unemployment indicators for the period following the period of healthy economic growth between 1986 and 1990. We were able to undertake a cursory examination of this once the census results became available in 1993. This section therefore extends the analysis of unemployment beyond the period 1983-1990 by looking at data for 1990 to 1991, incorporating data from the 1991 census. It examines changes in overall unemployment and long-term unemployment rates and those rates for the 25-34 year olds. It considers the data, the outcomes, the inputs and the relationship between inputs and outcomes.

The data used here draw on the 1991 census for the 1991 population base and on the Registrar General's estimates of population for 1990. For comparability, the numerator uses NOMIS unemployment and long-term unemployment data for both 1990 and 1991 rather than drawing on the census for 1991 unemployment. The major difference between the two sources is that NOMIS unemployment returns derive from benefit offices whereas the census is drawn from individual residents' views of their employment status. The denominators are the 20-65 male population and the 20-60 female population rather than the economically active because this is the base of the population estimates. The 1991 denominator from the census is obviously affected by the census undercount which varies by area and by age. The undercount particularly affects inner cities and younger age groups and this analysis must therefore be subject to cautions about the effects of undercount since it deals both with inner areas and with the 25-34 year old age group. The account of the analysis follows the pattern of the main study by looking at the pattern of outcomes and the relationship between inputs and outcomes.

## 5.1 Outcomes

For the total sample of 123 LAs, 1986 was the peak year for unemployment at 12.36%, while 1990 was the trough at 5.79%. All districts experienced increased rates in 1991 with an average rise of 2.64% to 8.43%. Long-term unemployment understandably shows a lag, with six districts still experiencing decline between 1990 and 1991. Overall, the long-term rate went up from 1.86% in 1990 to 2.08% in 1991. This compares with the peak year 1986 of 5.38%.

Unemployment for the 25-34s increased by 4.45% from 6.07% to 10.52%. This is a greater increase and to a higher level than for overall unemployment. This contrasts with the beginning of the period studied. In 1983 the rate for 25-34s was lower than the overall rate (10.26% compared to 11.82%). There is therefore a major change during the period in the ages of the unemployed. The same observation holds for long-term unemployment: for the 25-34s it increased from 1.69% in 1990 to 2.51% in 1991. Again, the increase is greater (0.82% compared to 0.22%) and the level is higher (2.51% compared to 2.08%).

This change in the ages of the unemployed was a trend observed and noted earlier in the Report. It is not a function of the census undercount, although this may have exaggerated the effect in 1991. Although it may partly be due to the changing methods of registering unemployment, in the main it probably reflects the changing nature of labour market. The decline in parts of the service sector during the late 1980s and early 1990s hit this key age group harder than previous declines in manufacturing. This is obviously a major change in the composition of unemployment. It makes it even more important to note that an increasing absolute and relative number of 25-34s in the inner cities may reflect their entrapment rather than attraction to inner areas.

## 5.2 Sub-sets of LAs

The rates for 25-34 year olds are higher than the overall rates across all three sub-sets of the data. The table below also shows that, as expected, the highest rates are for the 57 UPAs and the lowest for the comparators. The highest standard deviations for the 57 again shows a similar variability within the set to that observed in the earlier analysis.

**Unemployment rates in 1991**

|  | U% | LT% | U% 25-34 | LT% 25-34 |
|---|---|---|---|---|
| **57 UPAs** | | | | |
| average | 10.10 | 2.95 | 12.81 | 3.65 |
| (st.dev) | (2.36) | (1.14) | (3.26) | (1.66) |
| **marginals** | | | | |
| average | 7.27 | 1.44 | 8.84 | 1.62 |
| (st.dev) | (1.32) | (0.54) | (1.85) | (0.64) |
| **comparators** | | | | |
| average | 6.58 | 1.17 | 8.06 | 1.37 |
| (st.dev) | (0.99) | (0.39) | (1.59) | (0.47) |

The changes in the rates between 1990 and 1991 in the following table show little difference between the three sub-sets in overall unemployment. The increase in unemployment is greatest for the comparators. This is not the case for the 25-34s, but it is only within the long-term unemployment of 25-34s that there is any major difference between the sub-sets, with the 57 experiencing the highest rates.

**Unemployment change between 1990 and 1991**

|  | U% | LT% | U% 25-34 | LT% 25-34 |
|---|---|---|---|---|
| **57 UPAs** | | | | |
| average | 2.63 | 0.26 | 4.97 | 1.11 |
| (st.dev) | (0.93) | (0.19) | (1.28) | (0.55) |
| **marginals** | | | | |
| average | 2.56 | 0.18 | 3.99 | 0.58 |
| (st.dev) | (0.79) | (0.15) | (0.88) | (0.24) |
| **comparators** | | | | |
| average | 2.80 | 0.23 | 4.00 | 0.53 |
| (st.dev) | (0.74) | (0.12) | (1.01) | (0.18) |

## 5.3 Regional comparisons

Underlying these minimal differences among the sub-sets of authorities is a major regional difference in changes which is illustrated in the following table. It looks at three regions: the two regions with the largest sets of data (Greater London and the North West); and the South East. Greater London and the North West include examples from all three categories of district while the South East has no representative from amongst the 57 UPAs. Clearly the changes have generally been greater in the south-eastern part of the country.

Only Kensington and Dartford have lower increases than the North West average for overall unemployment; while only Manchester, with a 3.32% increase in overall unemployment, even approaches the averages of the two south eastern regions.

However, the story is different for the 25-34s. There is very little difference among the regions in the change in their unemployment, despite the differences in the overall rate; while for long-term unemployment for 25-34s the North West exceeds the other two areas. This emphasises the major underlying longer-term difficulties of certain districts in the North West. They are experiencing a larger increase in long-term unemployment for the key group of 25-34s, even though their overall long-term unemployment does not show such a change and unemployment for their 25-34s is little different in its rates of change from those experienced in other regions. Although there are regional differences in overall unemployment, these are reversed for long-term unemployment amongst the 25-34s.

## Changes in unemployment rates - Greater London, the South East and the North West

|  | U% | LT% | U% 25-34 | LT% 25-34 |
|---|---|---|---|---|
| **Greater London** |  |  |  |  |
| average | 3.52 | 0.32 | 4.30 | 0.65 |
| (st.dev) | (0.75) | (0.21) | (1.50) | (0.49) |
| **South East** |  |  |  |  |
| average | 3.42 | 0.27 | 4.36 | 0.55 |
| (st.dev) | (0.50) | (0.10) | (0.70) | (0.18) |
| **North West** |  |  |  |  |
| average | 2.02 | 0.17 | 4.38 | 1.00 |
| (st.dev) | (0.40) | (0.13) | (1.44) | (0.68) |

The other major point to note about the regions is that there is little difference in the south-eastern regions between the 57 UPAs and the rest. While Hackney, Islington, Newham, Tower Hamlets, Brent, and Southwark are all above-average in their increase in overall unemployment, so too are Barking, and Waltham Forest. The gap between the UPAs and the comparators within Greater London has closed, in the sense that there is very little difference in the rates of their increases. The same is the case for overall long-term unemployment and for 25-34s' unemployment and long-term unemployment. It should be noted, however, that there is great variation within the UPAs; with Tower Hamlets, Hackney and Newham standing out as having very high increases for the 25-34s on both measures. The closing gap is emphasised by the small difference between Greater London as a whole and the South East, which in the earlier period experienced much less unemployment of all kinds.

The rates for the other northern regions are very similar to those of the North West, as is shown in the following table. It is the two south-eastern regions which stand out in their increase in overall unemployment. They are followed by the Midlands and the South West. While the overall rates may show a lagged effect, with northern regions experiencing the recession later, this cannot be argued for the 25-34s where there is not a southern bias. This more general increase in rates for 25-34s across the country is a major finding.

**Average unemployment change 1990-91 for the 123 LAs by region**

|  | % U | % LT | %U 25-34 | %LT 25-34 |
|---|---|---|---|---|
| Greater London | 3.52 | 0.32 | 4.30 | 0.65 |
| South East | 3.42 | 0.27 | 4.36 | 0.55 |
| North West | 2.02 | 0.17 | 4.38 | 1.00 |
| North | 1.66 | 0.12 | 4.58 | 0.99 |
| Yorks and Humber | 2.32 | 0.15 | 4.85 | 0.87 |
| West Midlands | 3.42 | 0.27 | 4.36 | 0.55 |
| East Midlands | 2.82 | 0.37 | 4.54 | 0.92 |
| Sout West | 2.93 | 0.24 | 3.94 | 0.64 |
| East Anglia | 2.48 | 0.35 | 4.47 | 0.78 |

It is worth noting the districts where 25-34s' unemployment has increased sharply (i.e. above 7%). In addition to Tower Hamlets, Hackney and Newham in Greater London and Manchester, Knowsley and Liverpool in the North West, there are Wolverhampton, Doncaster, Great Grimsby, South Tyneside, and Great Yarmouth. For long-term unemployment the greatest rises (>1.5%) are found in Tower Hamlets, Hackney, Manchester, Knowsley, Liverpool, South Tyneside, Middlesbrough and Nottingham. The following lie just below this level, with rises above 1.45%: Birmingham, Wolverhampton, St Helens, Sefton, Wirral, Newcastle upon-Tyne, Sunderland, Langbaurgh, and Lincoln. Most, but not all, of these major rises therefore occur in UPAs. For these in particular the entrapment argument for 25-34s should be considered.

## 5.4 Relationships between the outcomes

We can also examine the relationship between the outcome measures and how they vary over time. The correlations between changes in unemployment and long-term unemployment for the 123, 97, and 57 are all around 0.6, not as high as in previous years. The relationship between these for the 25-34 year-olds is much higher, lying between 0.81 for the 123 and 0.87 for the 57. The regional effect influences the reduced strength of the overall unemployment/long-term relationship.

The correlation between unemployment change 1990-91 and the level in 1990 is not significant. It is almost zero for the 97, slightly positive for the 57 and slightly negative for the 123. In short, there is no structural effect of past levels on the change. This has been noted earlier when highlighting the greater increases in comparator areas.

There is a weak significant effect of the 1990 level of long-term unemployment on the 1990-91 change for the 123 and the 97, but this does not apply to the 57. Within the 57 there is a positive but insignificant relationship. The UPA districts with the highest levels are not all increasing at the highest rates.

This is much more the case for 25-34s, especially for long-term unemployment. The correlations are 0.44 and 0.62 for overall and long-term unemployment respectively. So districts in the 57 with higher levels of 25-34s' unemployment are much more likely to have larger increases between 1990 and 1991. The long-term relationship is even stronger for the 97 (0.72) and 123 (0.73) and also more for overall unemployment (0.55 and 0.52). The relationship for overall unemployment shows much more structure to the changes for the 25-34s than for all.

## 5.5 Input/outcome relationships

In looking at the input/outcome relationships, the period 1988/9 to 1989/90 has been used for financial inputs. This is the first part of the period of AfC policy. It coincides with the usual length of lagged response found for earlier periods and it uses input data which are relatively complete. Per capita input is used for UP, EZ, UDC monies, and AfC (project defined), RSA and Total (project defined) monies. The profiles of these inputs has already been discussed earlier in the Report.

The change in unemployment is positively related to AfC pc, Total pc, UDC pc and EZ pc for the 123 and 57. These are significant but weak correlations which still apply when partial correlations are carried out holding the 1990 level of unemployment constant. All but Total pc have similarly weak, significant correlations for the 97. The simple correlations are less than 0.27 for the 123, less than 0.31 for the 97 and less than 0.38 for the 57. This means that greater inputs have been going to some extent to districts where increases in overall unemployment have been greater.

The only significant negative relationship is recorded for RSA, which has a correlation of -0.52 for the 57 and -0.2 for the 123. Within the 57 UPAs, in particular, higher amounts of RSA are associated with lower increases in unemployment. This relationship holds in a partial correlation. The same negative relationship occurs for long-term unemployment change for the 123, 97 and 57. For the 97 and 123 it is stronger than for unemployment. For the 57 it is weaker at -0.28.

The general pattern of positive relationships occurs for long-term unemployment, but they are stronger than those for unemployment. So there is an even greater association between higher inputs and greater increases. The strongest relationship is for AfC pc for the 57 (at 0.57). Even here, therefore, there is still less than 36% of the variability in long-term unemployment change accounted for.

The 25-34s' overall and long-term unemployment have similar positive relationships to AfC pc, Total pc, EZ pc and UDC pc. The relationship with Total pc disappears for the 123 and 97 long-term and the 57 overall unemployment when partial correlation is carried out. Neither Total pc nor UDC pc are significant for the 57 for long-term unemployment. UP pc shows as significantly positive for many of the relationships, but again becomes insignificant once the 1990 level of 25-34s' unemployment is taken into consideration. There is no relationship with RSA pc inputs for this age group.

For the most part it can only be argued that government inputs, if they have had any effect on patterns of relative unemployment in the recessionary period 1990-91, have held down the increase in unemployment levels, which otherwise would have been higher. Only for RSA pc is there any evidence to suggest that inputs have been associated with lower rises in overall unemployment. Whether this is a causal relationship and what the mechanisms are by which causation operates are questions posed for a further, different form of analysis.

## 5.6 Conclusions

The analysis of change over a one-year period is obviously fraught with dangers, but there are some interesting and important changes in the outcomes. These concern the relative growth in overall and particularly long-term unemployment in the 25-34 age group, the national nature rather than south eastern bias to the unemployment increase and the northern bias to long-term unemployment growth. There is only one input that has a negative correlation with unemployment growth - both overall and long-term - and that is RSA pc, where higher inputs are associated with smaller increases. This does not influence the unemployment change for 25-34 age group however. There are a number of positive relationships which can be variously interpreted. If there is any causal effect which can be argued, it can only be that financial inputs have reduced rises that would have otherwise been greater.

# 6 OVERALL CONCLUSIONS

* There is evidence that some of the non-UPAs in the top 57 do better than expected in outcomes while some of the UPAs outside of the top 57 do worse. Three of the 12 non-UPAs in the top 57 experience falls in long-term unemployment and two only very small increases during the period 1983-86, a period when all the other top 57 experience marked increases. The four London UPAs that lie outside the top 57 experience lower rates of improvement in long-term unemployment between 1983 and 1990 than all the other London UPAs except Hammersmith.

* Urban Programme monies per capita and Regional Selective Assistance per capita have significant, independent associations with the rate of decline in unemployment and long-term unemployment between 1986 and 1990.

* Only Regional Selective Assistance has any significant effect on long-term unemployment and unemployment during the period 1983 to 1986, when there is very little structure to the general unemployment increases that occur.

* Regional Selective Assistance has also been shown to be the only programme associated with change in long-term unemployment rates for the 25-34s.

* Comparisons between sets of UPAs and sets of comparators all show that there was a significant convergence in their amounts of long-term unemployment over the period 1983 to 1990. More government money is associated with more rapid falls in unemployment.

* Government money is also associated with closing the regional gap between the north west and the south east. There is greater convergence between the north west UPAs and the south east comparators than between the north west comparators and the south east comparators

* House price changes for 1983-6 suggest a negative association with government expenditure under AfC. This could be interpreted to suggest either that resources were being channelled to those areas in greatest need or that expenditure in this period was of little effect in changing the attractiveness of residential areas.

* House price changes for 1986-9 suggest a weak positive association between Urban Programme expenditure and inner-city house price changes and between AfC expenditure and first-time buyer house prices. This provides some evidence that policy had positive effects on the inner areas after 1986.

* While the above points suggest an association between better performance and government inputs, not all the gaps in indicators were closing, there were many combinations of indicators and time periods when there was no significant association between inputs and outcomes, and the variation within the experiences of UPAs as indicated by the profiles suggest that there are still many districts where problems have either not improved or indeed worsened.

* While the regional context helps some districts to recover, it is no guarantee of success or indeed failure, there having been positive and poor outcomes in all regions.

211

*   Very large cities or the central areas of conurbations face the most difficult futures, nearly all have poor outcomes, which are confirmed in the local analysis, where the central areas of conurbations are shown to be the home of an increasing proportion of the disadvantaged.

*   The link to the local analysis provides one further caveat. Analysis of the districts that appear to be improving, may at the local level show that their inner areas are getting worse relative to the outer ones. This is shown to be so for most of the case study conurbation districts. It may therefore be the improvement of the outer areas that accounts for the overall improvement of the districts. The degree to which their delimitation includes wealthier suburbs may therefore be an element in explaining their improvement.

*   The absence of monitoring of the overall spend on districts leads to a poor implementation of targeting on designated areas. Such monitoring would assist strategic and coordinated policy making and delivery, the need for which are argued for elsewhere in the report.

Local area portraits: the three conurbations

To investigate impacts at a local level, we gathered data on expenditure in the three conurbations of Greater Manchester, Merseyside and Tyne and Wear at the scale of individual wards; thereby building up a spatial picture of how money had been spent in a number of key areas. These so-called 'ward data' have largely been obtained from local authorities themselves, usually second-hand. Given that Merseyside and Tyne and Wear include fewer authorities than Greater Manchester, we have been able to assemble more robust data for the former areas than for the latter.

In the case of the Urban Programme data, the figures were taken directly from DoE's former information system, known as UPCS. It is well-known that UPCS has its weaknesses, one of the most severe being the absence of a ward identifier in particular records. We have tried to minimise this difficulty by using the site address to make educated guesses about the ward in which a project is located. The quality of the UPCS data is clearly very variable. For example, in Greater Manchester, UPCS figures consistently underestimate expenditure by about 50%, due to omissions. The figures for the last year, 1990/91, are particularly poor in this regard. There are other discrepancies; for example, the 'ward data' figures for URG/UDG/City Grant projects in both Greater Manchester and Tyne and Wear do not total up to the figures collected at district level. This may simply be the difference between interim estimates supplied in statistical returns to DoE, and final figures later refined by local authorities.

The data for each conurbation are therefore of variable quality, with the most reliable being those for Merseyside and the least those for Greater Manchester. Despite all of the reservations, the data that we have collected, however, do cover a large number of programmes over a long period of time, and in many cases are the only (and therefore best) figures available. They at least enable us to make some sensible observations about the thickness or thinness of the policy spread at local scales, and point to geographical areas which seem to have attracted expenditure consistently over a long period.

Because of the variable quality of the data, each of the following three 'essays' on the conurbations adopts a somewhat different approach: the most exhaustive is for Tyne and Wear which discusses background issues on the local economy; that for Merseyside draws on the very full data set for wards that we were able to assemble; that for Greater Manchester reflects the weaker statistical basis of the data for the conurbation and the larger number of authorities within it. All three, however, provide descriptions of the geographical spread of resource allocation and thereby provide a descriptive account of the resource inputs at a local level.

*Figure C1*  **Greater Manchester wards**

BOLTON
1. Astley Bridge
2. Blackrod
3. Bradshaw
4. Breightmet
5. Bromley Cross
6. Burnden
7. Central
8. Daubhill
9. Deane-cum-Heaton
10. Derby
11. Farnworth
12. Halliwell
13. Harper Green
14. Horwich
15. Hulton Park
16. Kearsley
17. Little Lever
18. Smithills
19. Tonge
20. Westhoughton

BURY
21. Besses
22. Church
23. East
24. Elton
25. Holyrood
26. Moorside
27. Pilkington
28. Radcliffe Central
29. Radcliffe North
30. Radcliffe South
31. Ramsbottom
32. Redvales
33. St.Marys
34. Sedgley
35. Tottington
36. Unsworth

MANCHESTER
37. Ardwick
38. Baguley
39. Barlow Moor
40. Benchhill
41. Beswick and Clayton

42. Blackley
43. Bradford
44. Burnage
45. Central
46. Charlestown
47. Cheetham
48. Chorlton
49. Crumpsall
50. Didsbury
51. Fallowfield
52. Gorton North
53. Gorton South
54. Harpurhey
55. Hulme
56. Levenshulme
57. Lightbowne
58. Longsight
59. Moss Side
60. Moston
61. Newton Heath
62. Northenden
63. Old Moat
64. Rusholme
65. Sharston
66. Whalley Range
67. Withington
68. Woodhouse Park

OLDHAM
69. Alexandra
70. Chadderton Central
71. Chadderton North
72. Chadderton South
73. Coldhurst
74. Crompton
75. Failsworth East
76. Failsworth West
77. Hollinwood
78. Lees
79. Royton North
80. Royton South
81. Saddleworth East
82. Saddleworth West
83. Shaw
84. St.James
85. St.Marys

86. St.Pauls
87. Waterhead
88. Werneth

ROCHDALE
89. Balderstone
90. Brimrod and Deeplish
91. Castleton
92. Central and Falinge
93. Healey
94. Heywood North
95. Heywood South
96. Heywood West
97. Littleborough
98. Middleton Central
99. Middleton East
100. Middleton North
101. Middleton South
102. Middleton West
103. Milnrow
104. Newbold
105. Norden and Bamford
106. Smallbridge and Wardleworth
107. Spotland
108. Wardle

SALFORD
109. Barton
110. Blackfriars
111. Broughton
112. Cadishead
113. Claremont
114. Eccles
115. Irlam
116. Kersal
117. Little Hulton
118. Ordsall
119. Pendlebury
120. Pendleton
121. Swinton North
122. Swinton South
123. Walkden North
124. Walden South
125. Weaste and Seedley
126. Winton
127. Worsley and Boothstown

STOCKPORT
128. Bredbury
129. Brinnington
130. Cale Green
131. Cheadle
132. Cheadle Hulme North
133. Cheadle Hulme South
134. Davenport
135. East Bramhall
136. Edgeley
137. Great Moor
138. Hazel Grove
139. Heald Green
140. Heaton Mersey
141. Heaton Moor
142. Manor
143. North Marple
144. North Reddish
145. Romiley
146. South Marple
147. South Reddish
148. West Bramhall

TAMESIDE
149. Ashton Hurst
150. Ashton St.Michaels
151. Ashton St.Peters
152. Ashton Waterloo
153. Audenshaw
154. Denton North East
155. Denton South
156. Denton West
157. Droylesden East
158. Droylesden West
159. Dukinfield
160. Dukinfield Stalybridge
161. Hyde Godley
162. Hyde Newton
163. Hyde Werneth
164. Longdendale
165. Mossley
166. Stalybridge North
167. Stalybridge South

TRAFFORD
168. Altrincham

169. Bowdon
170. Broadheath
171. Brooklands
172. Bucklow
173. Clifford
174. Davyhume East
175. Davyhume West
176. Flixton
177. Hale
178. Longford
179. Mersey St.Marys
180. Park
181. Priory
182. St.Martins
183. Sale Moor
184. Stretford
185. Talbot
186. Timperley
187. Urmston
188. Village

WIGAN
189. Abram
190. Ashton-Goldborne
191. Aspull-Standish
192. Atherton
193. Bedford-Astley
194. Beech Hill
195. Bryn
196. Hindley
197. Hindley Green
198. Hindsford
199. Hope Carr
200. Ince
201. Langtree
202. Leigh Central
203. Leigh East
204. Lightshaw
205. Newtown
206. Norley
207. Orrell
208. Swinley
209. Tyldesley East
210. Whelley
211. Winstanley
212. Worsley Mesnes

# 1 GREATER MANCHESTER

Greater Manchester is a large metropolitan area encircling the twin cities of Manchester and Salford. The whole area contains around two and a half million people, of whom some 18-19% live in Manchester itself. There are ten district councils, all with powers as unitary authorities. Apart from Manchester and Salford, the county comprises the adjacent areas of Trafford, Tameside, Stockport, as well as five satellite towns inherited from pre-1974 Lancashire; Bolton, Wigan, Bury, Oldham and Rochdale.

Although the national focus is frequently on Manchester and (more recently) Salford, the metropolitan area as a whole has been the recipient of significant amount of urban policy activity. Since 1979, over a billion pounds has been spent in Greater Manchester through urban renewal, although some of this has been aid from the European Community. The area has also been the locus of a bewildering array of agencies and policy instruments; there have been six urban programme authorities, a two-district Enterprise Zone, two Task Forces, two Urban Development Corporations, two Safer Cities projects, and a City Action Team. In addition to these designations, there have been other forms of grant aid which some or all of the ten districts have made use of; City Grants, help in clearing derelict land, the Estate Action initiative, English Estates, and Section 11 grants. All but Stockport have at some time gained support from the European Community.

In the light of our previous work on resources made available to 123 local authority districts, it might be useful to clarify our definition of 'local data', in order to justify the approach taken below. The analysis of Greater Manchester will be tackled in two stages. First, we will examine the overall 'shape' of funding in the conurbation over the period involved, showing the pattern over a number of years, and also which authorities and which programmes have taken particular shares of the policy cake. Although not strictly 'ward-level' data, this is an exercise which has not previously been undertaken, and is essential for setting the context within which to assess urban policy spending. In the second part we present 'pen pictures' of the ten authorities, showing how the make-up of their funding relates to the conurbation as a whole, and how this has altered over time. In addition, for a number of particular programmes, we describe the way in which resources have been located in certain areas (i.e. wards) within that local authority's boundaries, and discuss the reasons for this dispersion across time and space.

## 1.1 Urban policy in the conurbation

Over the period as a whole, Greater Manchester attracted more than a billion pounds in grants of various types. This was broken down as follows:

|  | £ |
|---|---|
| Total Urban aid resources | 1,031,252,000 |
| (of which) | |
| Urban Programme | 370,280,000 |
| Urban Development Corporations | 97,562,000 |
| Enterprise Zones | 84,424,000 |
| UDG/URG/City Grant | 44,854,000 |
| City Action Teams | 3,246,000 |
| Derelict Land Grant | 60,732,000 |
| Estate Action | 73,021,000 |
| Safer Cities | 877,000 |
| Section 11 Grant | 72,332,000 |
| English Estates | 10,451,000 |
| Task Forces | 15,022,000 |
| European Community (ERDF/ESF) | 198,501,000 |
| Ethnic Minorities Business Initiative | 0 |

There are a number of points of interest in this table. First, despite the proliferation of policy tools during the decade, the Urban Programme has proved to be the mainstay over the whole of the decade, accounting for at least a third of the total. Second, it is clear that there has been a significant amount of support obtained from the European structural funds, proving to be the second highest contributor. Other features of the table are the large amounts of money spent by the Development Corporations and by the Estate Action programme, despite their relatively short history. The former were restricted to just three local authorities, representing a remarkable concentration of resources; the latter, while available to all councils, represents just four financial years (commencing 1986/7 - there are no figures available for 1990/91 yet, so this figure is a large underestimate). It is interesting, for instance, that these two policy initiatives have each chanelled more funds to the conurbation than the longer-running Derelict Land Grant. The table is illustrated graphically in Figure C2.

*Figure C2*    **Urban policy instruments in Greater Manchester 1979-91**

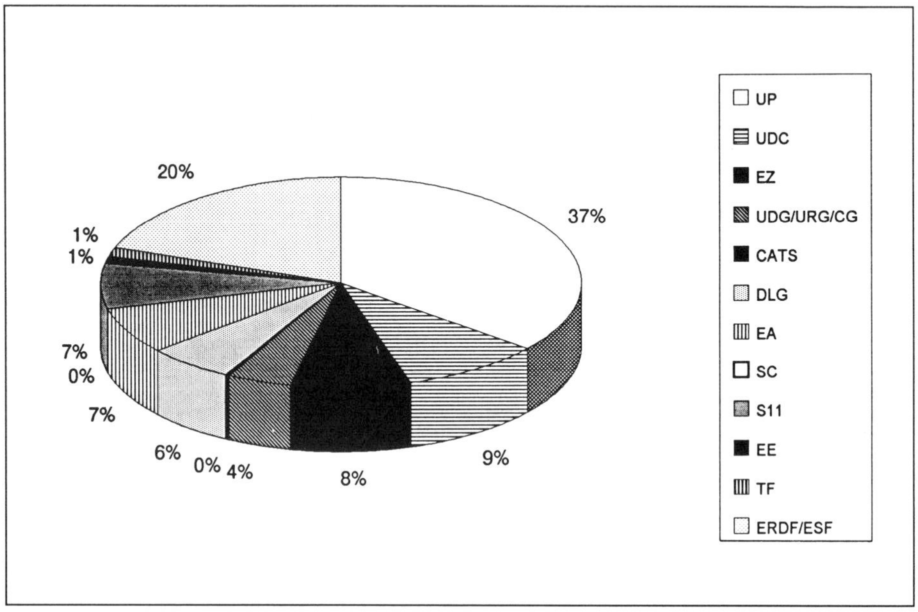

Although urban policy expenditure has amounted to increasingly large sums as the decade has progressed, this has to be set in context, by comparing these with other mainstream sources of funding. For instance, the £1,031,252,000 spent on the various urban policy instruments during the period was only 60% of the amount provided by one mainstream source, the Housing Investment Programme. Moreover, in 1991/92 the Revenue Support Grant settlement for the Greater Manchester authorities was more than £700 million - for a single year. Clearly then, mainstream funding will have made a major impact upon the conurbation.

What has been the pattern of expenditure over the period we are studying? Figure C3 shows both the growth of total spending and also the constituent elements within it. The key feature would seem to be the endurance of the Urban Programme as the bedrock of policy. Although this has remained broadly flat since 1983/4 it has survived remarkably well. So too have Section 11 grants and DLG, without ever being of large proportions. The chart makes clear the emergence of the Enterprise Zone and the UDCs, as well as the heavy use of Estate Action. The re-vamping of City Grant appears to have led to increased take-up too. The apparent falling away of expenditure after 1988/89 should be discounted. This is due to incomplete data. EZ figures were unavailable after 1988/89 and Estate Action figures for 1990/91 are also still in preparation.

*Figure C3*   **Urban policy instruments in Greater Manchester 1979-91**

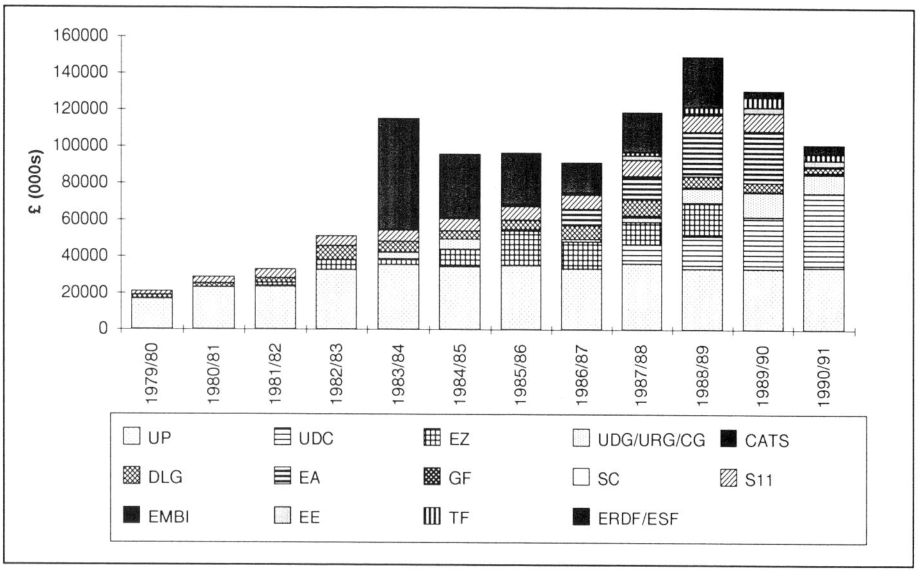

160000
140000
120000
100000
£ (000s)
80000
60000
40000
20000
0

1979/80 1980/81 1981/82 1982/83 1983/84 1984/85 1985/86 1986/87 1987/88 1988/89 1989/90 1990/91

☐ UP      ☰ UDC     ⊞ EZ      ☐ UDG/URG/CG   ■ CATS
▨ DLG     ☰ EA      ▨ GF      ☐ SC           ▨ S11
■ EMBI    ☐ EE      ▥ TF      ■ ERDF/ESF

Another interesting aspect is the distribution of resources between the ten authorities of Greater Manchester. The overall input of £1.03 billon can be broken down as shown in the table below:

| Authority | Policy Input, 1979-91 (£) |
|---|---|
| Manchester* | 329,335,000 |
| Salford * | 242,902,000 |
| Rochdale * | 100,696,000 |
| Trafford | 92,089,000 |
| Oldham * | 84,594,000 |
| Bolton * | 79,866,000 |
| Wigan * | 60,071,000 |
| Tameside | 23,328,000 |
| Bury | 11,414,000 |
| Stockport | 6,952,000 |

Notes:
*Figures for EZ not available for 89/90 onwards, Estate Action unavailable for 90/91.*
*\* denotes Urban Programme status.*

It is clear that Manchester remains the top priority for funding within the conurbation, followed closely by Salford. It is of interest that, although not designated as a UP authority, Trafford has secured substantial support from other sources which has given it a total of public assistance above many of the UPAs. However, apart from Trafford, inputs tend to reflect a kind of 'needs hierarchy', topped by the Partnership authorities, progressing though established UPAs (Bolton and Rochdale), down through the more recently recognised (Wigan) and on to 'near misses' like Tameside which, although non-UPA, has made extensive use of DLG and Estate Action. At the base of this inverted pyramid come the more well-to-do areas of Bury and Stockport.

Funding from mainstream sources is shown in Figures C4 and C5. The first of these shows the large cuts in HIP allocations to the Greater Manchester authorities, although as we shall see some have been hit worse than others. Between 1979/80 and 1989/90, HIP allocations were cut by more than half; a loss of around £110 million on the 1979/80 figure. Curiously, specific urban aid programmes increased from about £20m to £130m during the same period. In effect, therefore, the conurbation is financially back to square one (note however, the rise in HIP subsequently under the new Capital guidelines which are difficult to compare).

217

**Figure C4**  Housing Investment Programme in Greater Manchester (cash)

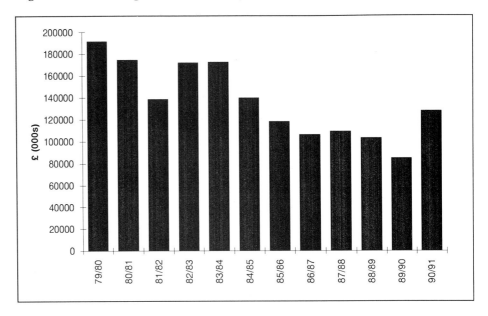

On RSG expenditure, Figure C5 demonstrates how there has been a less drastic reduction than in the case of HIP. In cash terms, the grant has remained relatively static. Broadly, the conurbation did well until 1981/2, when Needs and Resources elements were combined in Block Grant, a process which is acknowledged to have disadvantaged the Metropolitan authorities. The grant actually fell in 1982/83 and 1986/87, but otherwise maintained shallow upward progress until a steep drop in 1990/91; although again this was another new system, accompanying the introduction of the ill-fated Community Charge. Once again, it must be stressed that these are aggregate figures for Greater Manchester, and individual places have fared differently, as we shall see. Moreover, all these figures are in cash terms; they would look very different if adjusted for inflation. The relative funding through urban policy, HIP and RSG can be seen on the same scale in Figure C6.

**Figure C5**  Rate/Revenue Support Grant in Greater Manchester (cash)

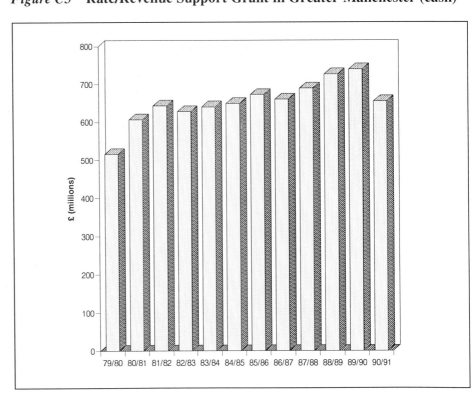

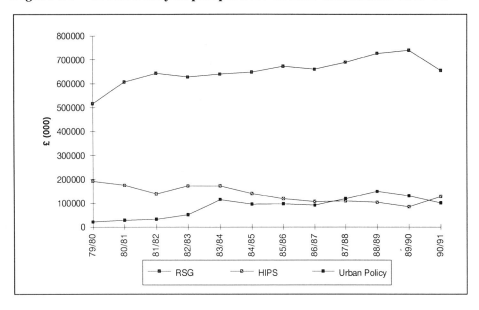

*Figure C6*   Urban Policy in perspective: Greater Manchester 1979-91

**1.2 Urban policy in the metropolitan boroughs**

The above account allows us some idea of how the metropolitan region has fared with regard to the various funding regimes, but Greater Manchester is a peculiarly diffuse assortment of ten councils, some with very different profiles and interests from Manchester itself. This makes it essential to understand the more detailed spatial picture as far as resource allocation is concerned. To that end, we shall examine the experience of each of the ten metropolitan boroughs in turn.

Manchester

With the largest population (450,000), Manchester is established as the capital of both the conurbation and, increasingly, the region too. It is also the most endemically deprived authority in the conurbation. In April 1991, it had the highest rate of unemployment in the conurbation. This was true for the 16-19, 20-24, and 25-54 age bands, as well as for long-term unemployment (whether defined as one or two years). At this date, only two of Manchester's 33 wards (Didsbury and Moston) had unemployment rates below the average for the conurbation. Of the worst 50 wards for unemployment within the whole conurbation, no fewer than 22 were within the Manchester itself.

This strong concentration of deprivation makes it unsurprising that Manchester should have taken such a large share of the urban policy resources available. For the period covered by the study, Manchester attracted £329,335,000 (more than 30% of the total urban policy expenditure). It has taken over 40% of the Urban Programme expenditure, a third of City Grant and Section 11 grants, and its Task Force alone spent £12 million. It has also received £65 million from Europe, around a third of Greater Manchester's share.

As for mainstream funding, there is a less positive story to tell. Manchester has suffered disproportionate cuts in its HIP allocations, losing almost 70% between 1979/80 and 1989/90, although a large increase under the new Capital system has recently cut this to just a quarter. In terms of RSG, although there were falls in 1982/3 and 1986/7, Manchester actually fared better than some of its neighbours, although the level of grant was broadly flat until the recent large increase in 1990/91. Obviously, these figures are based on levels of cash; the patterns look very different if one takes account of inflation.

Between 1983/4 and 1990/1 Urban Programme monies were highly concentrated. Taking the period as a whole, around 85% of expenditure has either been boroughwide or located in just six wards: Central (42%), Beswick & Clayton, Bradford, Hulme, Moss Side and Gorton North. This pattern has not changed radically over the period, and there is no apparent shift toward greater concentration more recently. Boroughwide expenditure rose from under 10% in 1983/4 to almost a quarter in 1990/1. There has also been a high degree of consistency in the locations chosen for UP funding. Taking the six best-funded wards for each of the eight years since 1983/4 (excluding boroughwide expenditure), a number of places recur:

**Number of times within the top six places over eight years**

| | |
|---|---|
| Central: | 8 times - first every year |
| Beswick: | 7 times - four second places |
| Hulme: | 6 times - third since 1986/7 |
| Bradford: | 6 times - second in 1989/90 |
| Moss Side: | 6 times - second in 1988/89 |
| Gorton North: | 4 times - second in 1985/6 & 1987/8 |

This 'hit parade' approach to the ward data helps to ameliorate the weaknesses of the data in certain years, first because we use percentages, and second because the focus is on relative positions within the districts.

Another factor to consider is the share of UP allotted to Capital and to Revenue. Figures are not available for the individual authority, but for the Manchester/Salford partnership as a whole, there was a steady trend toward Capital projects. In 1981/2, 68% of the Partnership's proposed expenditure was on Capital, by 1989/90 this had risen to 76%. Another change was the breakdown between the various 'end-use' classifications of projects. In 1981/2, 56% of Manchester/Salford's spending was on Social schemes, 23% Economic and 21% Environmental. By mid-decade, in 1985/6, these proportions had altered to become 39%, 32%, 29% respectively; a rise in the latter two at the expense of the former. By 1989/90, Social spending was down to just 17%, while Economic accounted for just over half. To complicate the picture, a new category of project, 'Housing' had been created and in that year accounted for as much as 20%.

But what did Manchester City Council use its UP money for? Many of the larger projects have been concerned with restoring roads, bridges or buildings in the City Centre. Some of the major uses of UP money have been the restoration of Philips Park in Bradford, and a million pounds spent in 1983/4 and 1984/5 refurbishing the Upper Campfield and Smithfield Markets. In the City Centre in 1983, £250,000 was spent in restoring Manchester Opera House, while on the social side, £327,000 was spent on the Broom Avenue Day Nursery in Levenshulme, and £238,000 for the Moss Side Play Centre at Alexandra Park. In 1984/5, Longsight received a Pakistani Community Centre worth £319,000, and under the aegis of the County Council a grant was paid to Greater Manchester Council for Voluntary Service for £29,000. In more recent times, the largest sums have been reserved for preparatory work supporting the introduction of Metrolink, the LRT system into the City.

Manchester has seen the take-up of eighteen City Grants and their predecessors. The most notable of these have been Phase 2 of Manchester Science Park in Hulme ward (half a million pounds), Granby House Mark II in Central (£600,000) and over £2 million over four years in the mid-1980s granted to the Royal Brewery. Again in Central ward, the City Council has had some success with a Council estate in Miles Platting which has had more than £7 million since 1986/87, with Waterloo Road in Cheetham receiving up £2m in 1988/9 and 1989/90.

The most striking degree of policy concentration, inevitably, is the Urban Development Corporation, which has spent in excess of £28 million since 1988 on a number of sites in an area of 470 acres within the City Centre, once more in Central ward. Projects undertaken have involved compulsory purchase of land, environmental improvements, housing projects, leisure developments and retail opportunities. By the UDC's own admission, several of these initiatives were inherited 'off the shelf' from previous Council-led schemes. This fact, supported by the ward data as a whole, clearly reinforces the widely-held opinion that the City Council has viewed making Manchester a regional centre as a priority since the late 1970s.

## Salford

The City of Salford is a curious hybrid; part (Blackfriars) adjoins the Centre of Manchester, nominally separated by the River Irwell, then there is the heart of traditional Salford's residential areas, such as Pendleton, Ordsall and Langworthy. The borough is completed with a variety of suburbs and outlying areas which belonged to South Lancashire prior to reorganisation. This pattern has an effect on the urban policy spend of Salford as against an authority like Manchester.

Salford has received £242,902,000 since 1979, the equivalent of £1000 for every resident of the borough. The composition of this amount is different from that of Manchester. Whereas half of Manchester's money came from Urban Programme, in Salford UP accounts for just a third of the total. Indeed, Salford appears to have been more successful in gaining and using funds from a variety of sources. Salford has of course been fortunate in the designations it has attracted. While not only enjoying joint Partnership status, the City has also shared an Enterprise Zone and a UDC which have netted £71 million between them. However, Salford has made more use of Estate Action and Derelict Land Grant than its neighbours, all contributing to a more diverse collection of grant aid.

Over time, Salford has had a meteoric rise as a destination for urban funding. Even if one leaves aside its success with European money, the underlying trend is still steadily upward during the 1980s, with the influence of the EZ, Estate Action and the UDC always underpinned by a consistently high level of UP (Figure C7). Its overall success in attracting resources is most graphically illustrated if one maps Salford's profile against its neighbour Manchester and sees the latter actually dip below Salford in 1986/7 (Figure C8). Even more remarkable is the effect of removing European money from the equation. On this measure (which 'smoooths' the trend lines), Manchester's drive for funds seems to have stalled, while Salford rises from half of Manchester's total in 1979 to overtake in 1985/6 and remain ahead thereafter (after 1988/9 the figures are distorted by the missing data). When one remembers that Manchester's population is some 80% larger and that its problem areas are both extensive and concentrated, this pattern of resourcing must be a cause for some surprise.

For the Urban Programme, there is a heavier concentration than in Manchester. For the period as a whole, 90% is boroughwide or in just the following seven wards: Blackfriars (City centre); Broughton; Eccles; Langworthy; Ordsall; Pendleton; and Weaste & Seedley. The pattern over the decade is different from that of Manchester, however. Over time, the proportion of boroughwide spend has declined, and Ordsall has become the focus of UP expenditure, increasing from 14% in 1983 to 47% by 1989, having represented almost 60% mid-decade. Blackfriars and Broughton are adjoining wards which border on Bury New Road, making it difficult to apportion some expenditure, but their collective share seems to have remained at around 25% throughout the period. The above wards contain the sites of most recent UP expenditure, namely the Trinity Estate and the Salford Quays flagship development. The influence of Salford Quays on Urban Programme expenditure is reflected in the level of expenditure (since 1985/6 a little under £9m has been spent there). Clearly this has reduced the level of resources available for other work being carried out in the authority's road, rail and water corridors, as well as on its Industrial and Commercial Improvement Areas.

*Figure C7*   **Salford - composition of urban funding 1979-91**

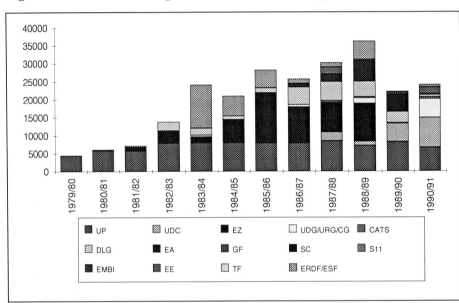

*Figure C8*   **Manchester and Salford urban funding (inc Europe)**

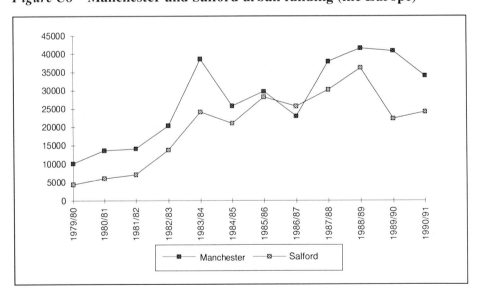

Derelict Land Grant has been used in the key area of Salford Quays, where £14m was spent in a three year rolling programme to 1990. DLG has been used to support tourism and leisure uses by acquiring and reclaiming disused sites such as the River Irwell walkway, but also to promote nature conservation in some outer areas. The emphasis on the Quays is partly a function of the DLG rules concerning hard-end use.

In terms of Estate Action, the main winners have been: Blackfriars which got £3.3m for the Trinity Estate; Weaste & Seedley which attracted £2.3m for the Ladywell estate; and Ordsall which took the lion's share again, with £4m for the Barracks and another £900,000 for the briefly notorious Ordsall estate itself. There has been relatively little City Grant activity, although Kersal benefited from £1m for a private housing project, and Blackfriars was the site of almost £2m worth of UDG projects, involving the Adelphi Riverside project, and money to complement the Estate Action funds for the Trinity project.

In addition to these grant regimes, Salford has also benefited from its position adjacent to Trafford Park. The areas of Weaste Quay and Ordsall Lane are within the boundaries of the Trafford Park Development Corporation (TPDC see below), which has been operating since 1988 and has already spent £16m in the Salford segment of its area. Still more successful, however, has been the other, older, policy designation which it shares with Trafford - the Enterprise Zone. Again based around former dock development, the zone ran from 1981 to 1991 and offered exemption from payment of rates, 100% capital allowances and short-cuts to planning permission. This has been worth an estimated £55m to those on the site.

Yet another shared, and lucrative, designation is the Manchester/Salford/ Trafford Integrated Development Project (MST-IDOP). Salford's share of the IDOP area covers the main Inner Area wards adjacent to the City, and allows it access to ERDF/ESF funding for business development, environmental works, improved physical communications and support for vocational training. Salford's inner wards have benefited from around £30m of this resource during the 1980s.

To summarise, Salford is an anomolous authority, in that it draws both upon the Urban Programme, City Grant and also money from the Countryside Commission. As much of a third of the 'City' is actually official 'countryside'. It has attracted a great deal of Urban Policy expenditure. At the same time, it lost around 60% of its HIP allocation between 1979 and 1989. Unemployment levels are high, but only the central wards are afflicted to the same extent as Manchester. Salford had seven wards in the top fifty wards with high unemployment rates in April 1991. The authority has a serious but partial urban problem. While 44% of Manchester's total land area is within the Partnership area, only 16% of Salford's lies there. However, Salford has a much higher percentage of publicly-owned stock, and hence its involvement with housing initiatives. In 1981, although the two cities owned 45% of the stock, within the defined Partnership area more than 60% of Salford's housing was in the public sector, almost half as high again as the proportion in Manchester.

Rochdale

Located to the north east of the City of Manchester, Rochdale has been a recipient of a variety of government resources. It suffers from unemployment - in April 1991 its rate of 9.5% was higher than the Greater Manchester average, and half of its twenty wards had rates in excess of that figure. The borough is distinctive in two ways; first it has a high proportion of Asians in its population, and second it has three large council estates, two of which are 'overspill' sites owned by Manchester City Council. Unlike the larger cities of Manchester and Salford, the borough is based on a number of non-contiguous inner areas; in central Rochdale, Middleton and Heywood. This can be problematic. Taken together, all these features mean that targeting is by no means an easy exercise.

In terms of the policy mix, there are a number of interesting features too. Urban Programme resources have formed some 30% of the inputs into the borough since 1979. What is striking, however, is the enormous amount of Estate Action resources (£18m), accounting for more than a quarter of all the EA monies granted in the conurbation. Also remarkable is the £34m of Euromoney, making up Rochdale's largest single element of urban aid. Of less size, but of equal interest, are the special initiatives which Rochdale has attracted, being one of only two areas in the conurbation to have its own Task Force (Hulme/Moss Side being the other). It has also recently been part of the national Safer Cities project.

The Urban Programme has developed piecemeal in Rochdale. Defined under the 1978 Act as an 'Other Designated District', the borough was awarded Programme status in 1983/4. Instead of being one of 14 authorities sharing some £8m, Rochdale was able to prepare a formal IAP for its own budget of £3.5m by 1984/5. For most of the decade the Council's strategy was based on its interim proposals of 1985 which were updated on an annual basis. By 1990/ 91, this was starting to appear dated, and a new strategy was adopted for that year. In other words, although there are areas of consistency, the targeting of resources does not show the same concentration as in the Partnership authorities.

In terms of breakdown by types of project, the figures are only available from 1984/5 onwards. Despite some fluctuation in both directions, the ratio between Capital and Revenue remained virtually static at about 2 to 1. This contrasts with the Manchester/Salford Partnership's increasing emphasis on Capital. As far as categories of project are concerned, again the relative stability contrasts with Manchester/Salford. Over the period Social schemes were down slightly from 35 to 31%, but Economic expenditure stayed static at 42%. There was a halving in the Environmental category which made way for spending on the fourth category of Housing.

In 1983/4 more than 90% of funds were either boroughwide (42%) or in one of five wards: Central & Falinge; Heywood North; Middleton Central; Middleton North; and Castleton. This expenditure was primarily concerned with small grants to industry and commerce, environmental works and highway improvements. Both Heywood and Middleton town centres received 'facelifts' to improve their attractiveness, and in the latter case, pedestrianisation. In 1986/7, well into full IAP status, the picture had changed somewhat. The focus had moved firmly towards town centre Rochdale, although the number of wards taking some share of UP funding was increasing too. In 1986/7, only 16% of projects were boroughwide, with 43.5% targeted on three wards which form the core of Rochdale's town centre: Central & Falinge; Smallbridge and Wardleworth (NE of the centre); and Brimrod & Deeplish (SW of the centre). Although Central & Falinge had been well funded in 1983, the wards flanking it had received negligible amounts. As well as spending on general physical improvements, a considerable sum was spent in 1986 on training for the ethnic minorities, who represent a fifth of the population of the town centre wards.

Away from the centre, funding continued to flow to sites in Middleton and Heywood. Middleton North consisted mainly of small businesses, while Middleton Central's money reflected the growing priority of the Langley estate. Similarly, Heywood North contains industrial and commercial activity based on the town centre, while Heywood West is the location of the Darn Hill estate. While the lion's share of funding continued to be swallowed by two or three key wards, UP expenditure was clearly spreading throughout the borough, with increasing numbers of wards picking up meaningful shares of the overall resources.

By 1990/1, the first year of the Council's new strategy, the basic pattern remained the same, with a few minor changes. Borough-wide projects accounted for more than a quarter of the spend, and the core wards were still highly represented. The alternative centres at Heywood and Middleton continued to receive support, and wards with rundown housing estates also loomed large in the IAP. The position of the ethnic minorities is a key priority within the IAP, with community support being provided both at Darn Hill (Mother Tongue teaching) and on Langley (improved shops, well-women clinic, and funding a project worker).

The authority's other success story is the use of Estate Action funding, befitting a borough with so much large-scale public housing. Of the nearly £19m spent under this scheme between 1986 and 1990, more than half was spent in the ward of Balderstone on the Kirkholt estate, which has been the subject of many innovative policy drives. The greater part of this spending related to the 'warm and dry' project, which consisted of insulation, heating and garden improvements. Some £2.2m was spent in Brimrod and Deeplish, primarily on Freehold, where a three phase programme of cladding and central heating was undertaken. Two Heywood wards netted over £3m; Angel Meadow was refurbished with the help of UP funds, while on the Back o'th Moss estate, 52 difficult-to-let properties were converted to a mix of bungalows and large family houses for rent. Smallbridge & Wardleworth received in excess of £2.5m, the greater part for the provision of fences and porches on the Cloverhall estate.

As a footnote on housing, it should be noted that Rochdale fared rather well in terms of HIP allocations, which in cash terms ended the decade 15% up on their 1979 level. This is well above the trend for Greater Manchester as a whole, for the North West region, and indeed for England as a whole.

Little use has been made either of DLG or City Grants, but Rochdale did boast a Task Force for four years during the mid to late 1980s. The Task Force Initiative was launched in 1986, with the aim of supplementing other inner city policies, and ensuring disadvantaged groups benefited from mainstream programmes. Although criticised to some extent for its rather slight impact, the same critics have acknowledged that it did enjoy excellent relations with the ethnic community, and went some way to close the gap between ethnic groups and mainstream programmes. During its life the Task Force spent more than £3m in an area more or less coterminous with the central core wards identified earlier.

## Oldham

Also bordering Manchester to the north east, Oldham has a population of 220,000; larger than Rochdale, but with many of the same problems. In April 1991, Oldham's unemployment rate was 8.5%, exactly the same as that for Greater Manchester. However, this authority-wide figure disguises sharp polarisation between wards. Eight of Oldham's twenty wards have unemployment above the Greater Manchester average, and well above - none of these wards' rates is within 2.5 percentage points of the mean. Thus wards in Oldham are either areas of high or of low unemployment, with little clustering around the mean. This said, there are no areas with the 'blackspot' reputation of a Hulme or an Ordsall. Oldham's four entries in the unemployment top 50 all figure in the bottom half of the table, a similar representation to Rochdale's five.

This profile may be slightly misleading, as with all aggregate figures. Oldham Council's own research does reveal stark concentrations of deprivation. For example, the 1990 Inner Area Housing Appraisal indicated concentrations of unemployment at the neighbourhood level; those of Glodwick (37.1%), Coppice (19.8%) and Coldhurst/Westwood (18.4%) had the highest rates. These three communities are also home to most of the borough's Bangladeshi, Indian and Pakistani families. This survey also pointed to the economic disadvantage suffered by these groups; in April 1990 the Council's own measure of unemployment showed levels that were three-and-a-half times higher among the Asian population of the 'inner area' than among non-Asians. 84% of the borough's Asians are believed to live within the 'inner area'.

As one of the original Programme Authorities, Oldham has received a steady flow of Urban Programme money throughout the 1980s. However, its policy profile is a curious one, dependent as it is on this one policy instrument for support. UP constitutes almost one half of all funding received since 1979. Another notable feature is that it is second only to Manchester in its level of Section 11 grant, despite having a smaller ethnic population than neighbouring Rochdale.

With regard to the distribution of the Urban programme, Oldham tends to focus on a small number of key wards. In 1984/5, over 80% of the spend was either boroughwide or in one of half a dozen wards. In this case, however, the concentration of spend may be even greater than it first appears. The way in which ward boundaries are drawn means that Oldham's town centre does not principally lie within any one ward, it is actually a point of convergence for the boundaries of several. It could be argued that the town centre is formed by the junction of St. Mary's, St. James and St. Pauls. Once this is accounted for, it can be seen that the great majority of expenditure is targeted on the town centre or is boroughwide. The proportion of the latter varied between 15 and 25% for most of the period, leaping to over half in 1990/1, apparently due to a high number of industrial and community grants, but possibly due to the eccentricities of the data.

Having argued for concentration of policy on the 'town centre', it could be argued that Oldham's centre sprawls unusually widely, and hence policy inputs are not really highly concentrated. This is supported by the defined 'inner area', which extends from the Borough's south-western boundary with Manchester through the Town Centre to the Watersheddings area. In addition, five of its outer housing estates have official approval to receive UP resources. Although the borough has other centres at Chadderton and Failsworth, these do not attract resources in the manner of Heywood and Middleton; the focus is much more on one place in this case.

Looking at spending by category, Oldham's approved programmes demonstrated a remarkable consistency with their strong emphasis on Capital projects. In 1981/2, 83% was allocated for capital spending, a proportion that fluctuated and perhaps declined slightly, touching 77% in 1989/90. As for the types of end-use, despite 1981/2 when 74% of expenditure was earmarked for social schemes, the pattern has remained fairly. Although environmental projects were squeezed by the other two categories in mid-decade, the broad ratio was 3:4:2 between Social, Economic and Environmental respectively, with the housing category picking up the residual spend.

In terms of City Grant and its precursors, fifteen grants have been awarded, mostly in relatively small parcels, reflecting the absence of large-scale flagship projects. The great majority of the schemes took place in the town centre wards, at least five being within St. Pauls' ward. Very recently, Oldham's town centre was redeveloped with the aid of City Grant, in a scheme which in total amounted to £4.8m.

Housing initiatives have also been few in number, and of limited overall cash value. The great bulk of the Estate Action money was spent on Shaw Road in St. Mary's ward, totalling almost £1.9m. It is also worth mentioning that Oldham has had one of the most severe cuts in its Housing Investment Programme. Like Manchester, the authority experienced reductions of nearly 70% in its allocations between 1979/80 and 1989/90, against a cut of around half for the conurbation and for the North West region.

Bolton

Bordering Salford to the north west, this authority takes its name from an ex-Lancashire mill town which (reluctantly) became part of Greater Manchester in 1974. It contains a population of nearly 260,000 spread over a mixture of rural settlements and urban centres. Much of the borough is actually countryside, but the core urban areas of Bolton, Farnworth and Breightmet show many of the worst features of economic and physical decline. Although the 'inner area' technically contains three discrete areas, these are not rival 'centres' in the same way as is the case in Oldham and Rochdale. Bolton's 'inner area' is in fact more or less contiguous, forming a kind of 'C' shape with a small break in each arc.

Bolton's unemployment rate is one tenth of a percentage point above that of Oldham's, which as we saw, was identical with that for the conurbation (April 1991 figures). Eight of Bolton's twenty wards have higher unemployment than the Greater Manchester average. All of these wards are explicitly targeted by the local authority. The worst-hit of them, Central, came out worst on five unemployment measures: males (25.4%), females (10.4%), totals (20.1%), long-term (33.3%) and the 16-19 age group (17.8%). It is clear from the Council's own documents that the borough has a significant ethnic population which is disproportionately located in four wards; Derby (42% of households), Central (31%), Burnden (27%), and Halliwell (19%). However, the most recent IAP strategy, unlike Rochdale and Oldham, signals no specific intent to target them. Even the word 'ethnic' does not appear in the opening section.

Bolton has a very standard policy profile, entirely in keeping with its status as one of the 15 'original' Programme Authorities designated in 1978. Over half its funding has come from the UP, and it has also made use of other conventional and long-standing instruments such as UDG/City Grant, Section 11 and DLG. What is lacking in Bolton's case is the attraction of any extra designations until its recent success with its City Challenge bid. UDCs, Enterprise Zones, Task Forces and City Action Teams have passed Bolton by. It is simply another large metropolitan town making use of a consistently high level of UP support.

Bolton's Urban Programme expenditure displays elements of both evolution and continuity. In 1983/4, as well as a sizeable spend on borough-wide projects (37%), a great deal of attention was paid to the north east of the borough. Although the data for this year had no ward identifiers, the wards in this sector would have been Breightmet, Halliwell and Tonge. In 1984/5 the pattern started to change. From then on, 70% of the expenditure was consistently either borough-wide or in the four wards of Central, Derby, Burnden and Farnworth. The exact proportions have fluctuated a good deal, reflecting both variations in policy and the limitations of the data. In the earlier years, between 20 and 30% of the spend was borough-wide. The last two years of the series appear to show a rise above 40%. Of the individual wards, Central has invariably taken the next largest slice of projects, though in 1988/89 it was just pipped by Derby ward.

By 1990/1, the UP expenditure was clearly focused on a number of specified areas, in anticipation of DoE's recent guidance on this matter. Half of the wards in the borough were receiving no assistance from the Urban Programme. Again, there is a thread of continuity here, for a number of these - Westhoughton, Bromley Cross and Blackrod, for instance - have never loomed large in the authority's resource allocations, but nevertheless the decision to concentrate on target areas to the exclusion of all others is in marked contrast to other districts in the conurbation which have attempted to maintain dispersed support albeit at a residual level.

In terms of expenditure categories, although there has beeen fluctuation in recent years, the longer-term trend has been one of stability. In 1982/3 capital amounted to 79% of the UP as opposed to only two thirds in the previous year. Since that time it has risen as high as 83%, but ended the decade at 78%, similar to its starting point. More change is apparent in the type of projects undertaken. In 1981/2 the Council planned to spend more than half of its UP on social projects, with economic and environmental sharing the rest equally. The following year saw a transfer of 20% of the budget from social to economic schemes. By 1984/5 social spending amounted for less than a quarter of the total allocation. Since then it has recovered its share. By 1989/90, the position was roughly that economic and social/housing projects were each taking about 40%, with the balance devoted to environmental improvements.

Bolton has benefited from more than £9m of City Grant and its forerunners. More than a third of this has been spent in Central ward on a scheme to upgrade shopping facilities in the town. This reflects a long-running theme in the Council's strategy. Earlier in the decade a great deal of UP was devoted to the refurbishment of an old market hall as the site for a covered shopping centre. Other schemes have included the building of the Moat House hotel behind a restored facade, the conversion of a handful of the 160 under/unused mills identified by the 1985 Mill Strategy. Housing schemes have also benefited, and industrial units were funded at Raikes Clough in Burnden.

Estate Action has been spread widely across the authority's stock; DoE data records 13 separate EA claims between 1986/7 and 1989/90. The biggest parcels of funding have gone to the Oldhams estate in Astley Bridge (£1.2m) and to the restoration of Breightmet Hall, again another million pound scheme. Also worthy of mention is the continuing work supported by EA on the Willows estate in Derby ward (£44,000 from 1988-90), which achieved fame as one of the earliest Priority Estates tackled by PEP in 1979.

Wigan

With its population of 309,000, Wigan is the second largest borough in Greater Manchester. Also covering a large physical area, the borough functions as a satellite town both for Manchester and for Liverpool, both being roughly equidistant. Another Lancashire town colonised by the reorganisation of 1974, Wigan suffers from many of the same types of economic difficulties as Rochdale, Oldham and Bolton, but without the ethnic subtext. In April 1991, its rate of unemployment was actually higher than that of Bolton and Oldham. Interestingly, long-term joblessness is also a feature of the borough; the ward of Norley has a fractionally lower rate than the Langworthy area of Salford, and a rate higher than many deprived wards in East Manchester.

In addition to these statistics, the authority also has the problem of very extensive areas of derelict land which tends to create a negative image. In terms of housing, the authority has twin problems. First, there are 120,000 residential properties in the borough, a quarter of which date from before 1919, and a third from before 1945. The older stock is concentrated in the inner areas of Wigan and Leigh; 70% are owner-occupied by low-income households, with the attendant problems of maintenance. Second, since 1985 the authority has identified six public housing estates in need of major input, and has sought to address their needs through urban policy.

Wigan's policy mix reflects its relatively recent incorporation as one of the 57 Urban Priority Areas. The borough received small packages of funding through its status as an Other Designated District for most of the 1980s. Its uprating to full Programme status as one of the 57 took place in 1987/88, and increased its level of resources to over a million pounds. By 1990/1 this had risen to £2.5m. This historical development explains the fact that UP has formed only about a sixth of total urban aid. Indeed, the total amount is only greater than the funds attracted by DLG and Estate Action. The truly striking feature of this profile, however, is Wigan's success in getting and spending European monies, £23m since 1983, the greater part of which was concentrated in the earlier years. This reflects the extent of derelict land within the area. As a proportion of total urban aid, this is extremely important to Wigan; it is an amount equivalent to the total funding received through UP, City Grant and Estate Action.

As far as the Urban Programme is concerned, there are no figures on categorical expenditure during the period as an ODD. However, since Programme status, spending on Capital projects declined from 82% in 87/8, to 75% in 88/9, reaching 70% by 1989/90. Economic priorities have always been important, accounting for more than half the expenditure from 1987 to 1990. Social expenditure declined from 36% to 21% during the same period, and was replaced by an increased concern with environmental and housing improvements.

The spatial distribution of UP resources since 1983 has followed a parabola. During the years 1983 to 1985, the limited funds available meant that targeting was essential in order for projects to be meaningful. Most of this spend concentrated on the town centre, on Noley and Newtown wards, or benefited the whole borough. As funding increased, the Council seems to have cast the net more widely, turning its attention to Abram ward, and to the centres of the borough's other towns, Leigh and Atherton. Towards the end of the decade, however, funding had begun to be re-concentrated, if measured by the number of wards receiving little or no support. In the mid to late 1980s the figures show an element of 'pepper-potting', indeed in 1988/89, more than a quarter of the UP was spent outside the defined 'inner areas', primarily due to one large commitment in Hindsford. However, in the following year, this was cut back to just 4%, with 35% spent on borough-wide projects and the balance spent in the inner areas, the main focus of which continued to be on Newtown and Norley.

Some £9m was spent in the period under the DLG scheme. Once known as the authority containing the most derelict land of any in England, there has been an enormous drive to remove the worst of these areas. A review in 1989 showed that the major concentration of this land was in the Makerfield Basin, which stretches between Wigan and Leigh, and covers a number of wards. It is estimated that about 50% of the borough's total disused land lies in three wards; Leigh Central, Ince and Abram.

Estate Action has been used on seven different sites, and much of it in large parcels. The Millers Lane estate in Abram received some £2.5m between 1986 and 1989, with just under a million pounds each going to Scholes in Ince, and Norley Hall in Norley. Some £1.5m has been spent since 1988 on two sites in Atherton, and during the same period £2m went to Higher Fold in the ward of Bedford/Astley. The largest individual beneficiary, however, in terms of Estate Action money, was the ward of Worsley Mesnes, which attracted almost £3m between 1987 and 1990, to benefit the estate of the same name.

## Trafford

The six Greater Manchester authorities so far discussed have all had Urban Programme status of one kind or another during the period 1979-91 and they have been discussed in the order of their descending resources. In the case of Trafford, we move to the expenditure hierarchy at a higher level. Although not enjoying UP designation, Trafford has the fourth highest expenditure total for the period under study, at around £92m. Another 1974 creation, the borough of Trafford lies to the south west of the conurbation, bordering both Manchester and Salford. Encompassing a number of Manchester's western suburbs, the authority has two major urban centres; one in Stretford in its inner area, and the other in the residentially-desirable outer area of Altrincham. It also contains a large stretch of land on the south bank of the Manchester Ship Canal, facing the new Salford Quays development. The three wards which comprise this area - Talbot, Clifford and Bucklow - each has unemployment rates well in excess of the rest of the borough, and of the Greater Manchester mean.

It was this strip of land which became the fiefdom of the Trafford Park Development Corporation which was formed in 1987 as a 'second-wave' UDC, prior to its more glamourous neighbour in City Centre Manchester. In addition to a good deal of vacant land on the waterside, the UDC inherited a once-thriving industrial estate which had been in steady decline since the 1970s, the 3,000-acre business park currently employs around 27,000 people, and is estimated to have a labour catchment of 1.5 million people. Development Corporation surveys show that between its designation and the summer of 1992, 460 new companies located their businesses in Trafford Park, making the total number of firms 1,188. The highest level of employment in Trafford is in the engineering sector, and 48% of all employees are in manufacturing.

A notable feather in the cap of the UDC was the recent confirmation of Trafford Park as the site for one of Railfreight Distribution's nine Channel Tunnel terminals within the UK. This terminal will cover around 20 acres and cost £11m. Together with the existence of deep-sea traffic facilities and the proximity of Manchester's International Freight Terminal, this will set out Trafford Park's stall as the UK's largest road/rail interchange complex outside London.

As well as the recent massive injection of funds in the form of TPDC, the Canal area has also benefited from having a portion of land within the Salford/Trafford Enterprise Zone. This has attracted £28 million since 1981/2, and was due to be wound up after its ten-year life span. Together, the funding from the UDC and EZ, both model policy instruments of the 1980s, totalled more than 85% of Trafford's total input. Certainly, it is a striking case of spatial targeting, with the UDC and EZ cheek-by-jowl in the three-ward area. It is in contrast to an authority such as Bolton, with a much greater proportion of its population deprived, and with recognised UP assistance, yet lacking funding with a critical mass to kick off a regeneration of the size attempted in Trafford. It can be argued that the concentration of schemes around the waterfront reflects the importance attached by government to large-scale strategic 'flagship' developments, and the massive employing capacity of Trafford Park makes it of more than merely totemic importance.

Tameside

This authority is adjacent to the City of Manchester on its east flank, and is a post-1974 cocktail of Ashton under Lyne, Hyde and Stalybridge. For many years the 'Cinderella' of Greater Manchester, Tameside has consistently missed out on urban resources. Unlike Trafford B.C. which distances itself rather from the idea of inner-city deprivation, Tameside proclaims its case from the rooftops, and recently made an unsolicited bid in Round Two of City Challenge. In its bid, the authority made a compelling case for the West End of Ashton, which has a 20% ethnic component, male unemployment of 23%, and a combined Z-score of 4.6, compared with a figure for Greater Manchester of 1.7.

Looking at more conventional geographical definitions of deprivation, there is some support for the borough's argument. Unemployment for the borough (April 1991) was identical to the Greater Manchester average of 8.5% (the same level as in Oldham), and 8 of the borough's 19 wards had higher-than-average unemployment rates. In fact, Hyde Godley had worse unemployment than Ashton St. Michaels, and youth unemployent was half as high again.

In terms of policy input, Tameside has attracted just £23m in the whole period, more than half gathered from European sources. Derelict land reclamation in the Tame Valley and Section 11 grants relating to the ethnic population provided a further £8m. The residual contact with formal urban policy resources has come through some £2m from the Estate Action programme, an amount which divided more or less equally between West Pennine in Stalybridge North, and a brace of sites within Ashton St. Peter's.

Bury

Covering a semi-rural belt to the north of Manchester and Salford, Bury is increasingly becoming a pleasantly-located dormitory town for commuters who work in the Regional Centre. Bury is rightly considered by DoE to be a low priority for urban resources; it achieved the distinction of having unemployment below not just Greater Manchester's average, but below that for Great Britain too. Nevertheless, in Redvales, Radcliffe South and Sedgley there are small concentrations of more persistent unemployment. Moreover, in common with a number of ex-mill towns, there is a problem with the condition of pre-war private sector terraced housing.

Of the £11m received by Bury since 1979, a little under half came from the EC. The remainder came primarily from two sources: Derelict Land Grant, much of which was used for the reconstruction of the East Lancashire Railway as a tourist attraction; and Estate Action, comprising a four-year programme on the Springs estate in Redvales and sums used in 1989/90 on Littlewood in Moorside and Chesham Fold in East ward.

Stockport

Generally considered to be the conurbation's most affluent borough, Stockport has low unemployment (5.7%). It offers all of the locational advantages a local authority economic development officer could wish for; the centre of Stockport lies ten minutes from Manchester on the InterCity rail link to London, and is itself extremely convenient for the Airport, as well as being excellently connected to the extensive motorway network. Despite this, the wards of Brinnington and South Reddish both have an unemployment problem; the former having a rate twice that of the conurbation average.

The authority has derived money from just two sources: DLG, which has mostly involved expenditure on disused railway tunnels and tracks; and the Estate Action programme. Between 1985 and 1987 the rundown Walnut tree estate in Cheadle Heath underwent comprehensive renewal, a process which involved the provision of a local housing office, diversification of tenure, and environmental improvements in the whole area. The massive Adswood estate had suffered from the highest level of voids and transfer requests in the borough. Partnership with a private builder brought renewal in Burwood Drive, and more than £2m in EA contributed to improvements throughout the estate. The high-rise blocks of the Brinnington estate also attracted a little under £2m, and improvements there have included another local housing office and a 24-hour concierge system.

## 1.3 Conclusions

The problem of assembling ward-level data proved to be more intractable for Greater Manchester than for the other two conurbations. Much of the data on Urban Programme expenditure was derived from the DoE's UPCS database which, in Manchester's case, appeared to exclude significant elements of expenditure. Greater Manchester also differs from the other conurbations in that some of its consituent boroughs are not included amongst the set of 57 UPAs and have received only small sums of public resource and, for them, there is thereby less on which comment can be made. Nevertheless, the analysis of the patterns of resource allocation does suggest a number of valuable conclusions. First, it is clear that most of the districts in practice target their resources to a limited number of wards, whether or not this is part of their stated policy. Regardless of whether there are or are not designated 'inner areas' within districts, there is a high degree of discrimination between those areas which receive assistance and those which do not. Second, as was evident from the national figures, the 'fit' between programme designation and the receipt of resources is only relatively close. Part of this is a function of specific attributes of the districts; for example, Wigan's extensive use of DLG in light of its severe difficulties with derelict land; Rochdale's success in attracting Estate Action resources, given its legacy of large council estates; most strikingly, Trafford's attraction of resources through the fact of its sharing in both an Enterprise Zone and a UDC. Part of the disparity seems also to be a function of the enterprise and political style of local authorities; perhaps most dramatically evident in Salford's case where (at least until its recent repeated lack of success with City Challenge bids) the authority has succeeded in attracting considerable resources on the basis of successful co-operation with the private sector, as in the Salford Quays development or in a variety of public-sector housing refurbishment schemes. Third, especially for the two most deprived areas of Manchester and Salford, the loss of 'mainstream' resources has cancelled out much of the financial benefit of targeted UP resources. Fourth, non-UPA authorities such as Tameside can be seen to have areas little if any better than those of some of its neighbouring UPA districts such as Oldham or Bolton. Being part of a single conurbation and yet without access to some of the UP resources enjoyed by its neighbours appears to leave it at a competitive disadvantage. Fifth, most of the districts have shown a progressive switch of resources away from 'social' spending and towards 'environmental' and, especially, 'economic' expenditure during the course of the decade. This has had inevitable consequences for the ability of the non-statutory sector to address the needs of local communities within most of the districts of the conurbation.

The patterns of expenditure described in the following sections illustrate the spatial targeting of thirteen programmes operating on Merseyside during the 1980s. These were:

|       |                                  |        |                      |
|-------|----------------------------------|--------|----------------------|
| i)    | English Estates                  | viii)  | Derelict Land Grant  |
| ii)   | Estate Action                    | ix)    | ERDF                 |
| iii)  | Urban Development Corporations   | x)     | HIP Allocation       |
| iv)   | Section 11 Grants                | xi)    | Housing Corporation  |
| v)    | Enterprise Zone                  | xii)   | Urban Programme      |
| vi)   | Safer Cities                     | xiii)  | City Grants          |
| vii)  | Loan Guarantee Scheme            |        |                      |

Some of the expenditure data relating to these programmes only cover certain periods of the 1980s and these durations do not necessarily coincide for each programme. There two basic reasons for this; first, the short life history of certain programmes (Estate Action, Safer Cities, Urban Development Grants) and second, the lack of historical monitoring records, which primarily applies to the longer-running programmes (Urban Programme, Housing Corporation). In certain cases the programmes were only operative in restricted areas, which for some was a direct result of spatial targeting (Safer Cities). However, other programmes were targeted as a contingent result of their operational priorities: for example, Section 11 Grant, which, because it was directed at a particular section of the community, became spatially confined.

Of the five districts in Merseyside, only Knowsley had changes to its ward boundaries after the 1981 census. Even though the changes made very little difference, it was not until 1983 that the present boundaries came into being. The data set however, has not been altered to accommodate this minor discrepancy, because it only applies to three programmes over a two-year period (HIP, DLG and ERDF over the period 1981/82 to 1982/83). Any expenditure that occurred in Knowsley prior to redesignation has been located and assigned to the present ward areas. This not only provides continuity throughout the analysis, but also allows area comparisons to be made over the whole study period.

In addition to the targeting of funds by specific programmes (Merseyside Development Corporation), a concentration of resources is also to be expected in the 'inner areas' of districts because the policies are directed at alleviating chronic social and economic problems. Such areas might be expected to have attracted disproportionately more of the resources available. The designated 'inner areas' are as follows:

**Liverpool**
Abercromby/Everton
Granby/Toxteth (Dingle)
Speke/Garston (St. Mary's)
Netherley/Valley
Croxteth/Gillmoss (Outer Estates)

**Wirral**
Birkenhead/Seacombe
Rock Ferry (Tranmere)
Beechwood (Bidston)
New Brighton

## *Figure C9*   **Merseyside wards**

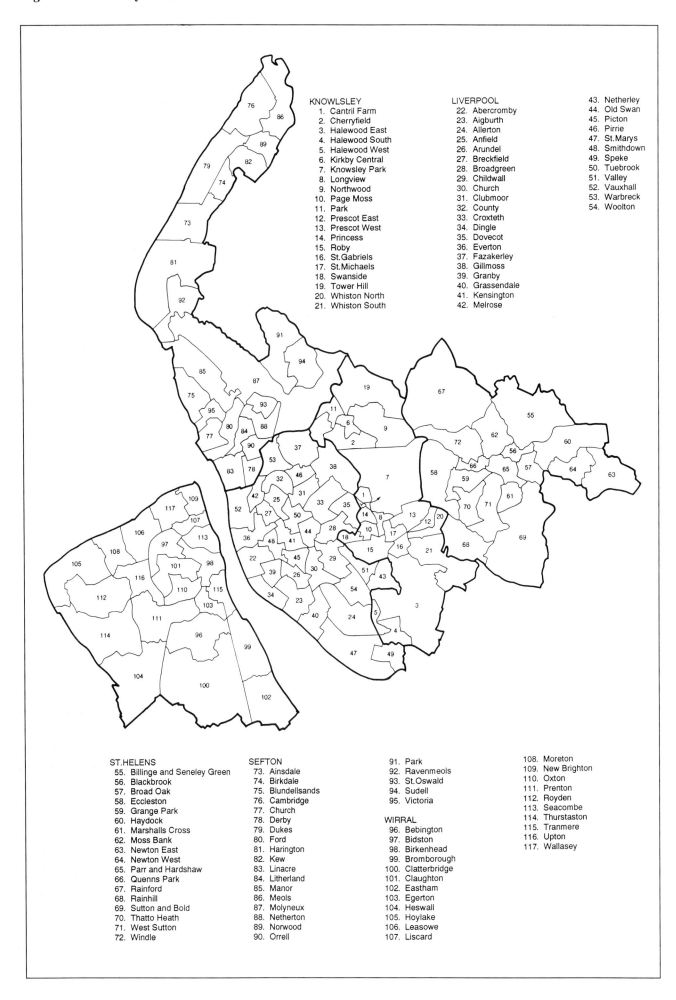

KNOWLSLEY
1. Cantril Farm
2. Cherryfield
3. Halewood East
4. Halewood South
5. Halewood West
6. Kirkby Central
7. Knowsley Park
8. Longview
9. Northwood
10. Page Moss
11. Park
12. Prescot East
13. Prescot West
14. Princess
15. Roby
16. St.Gabriels
17. St.Michaels
18. Swanside
19. Tower Hill
20. Whiston North
21. Whiston South

LIVERPOOL
22. Abercromby
23. Aigburth
24. Allerton
25. Anfield
26. Arundel
27. Breckfield
28. Broadgreen
29. Childwall
30. Church
31. Clubmoor
32. County
33. Croxteth
34. Dingle
35. Dovecot
36. Everton
37. Fazakerley
38. Gillmoss
39. Granby
40. Grassendale
41. Kensington
42. Melrose

43. Netherley
44. Old Swan
45. Picton
46. Pirrie
47. St.Marys
48. Smithdown
49. Speke
50. Tuebrook
51. Valley
52. Vauxhall
53. Warbreck
54. Woolton

ST.HELENS
55. Billinge and Seneley Green
56. Blackbrook
57. Broad Oak
58. Eccleston
59. Grange Park
60. Haydock
61. Marshalls Cross
62. Moss Bank
63. Newton East
64. Newton West
65. Parr and Hardshaw
66. Quenns Park
67. Rainford
68. Rainhill
69. Sutton and Bold
70. Thatto Heath
71. West Sutton
72. Windle

SEFTON
73. Ainsdale
74. Birkdale
75. Blundellsands
76. Cambridge
77. Church
78. Derby
79. Dukes
80. Ford
81. Harington
82. Kew
83. Linacre
84. Litherland
85. Manor
86. Meols
87. Molyneux
88. Netherton
89. Norwood
90. Orrell

91. Park
92. Ravenmeols
93. St.Oswald
94. Sudell
95. Victoria

WIRRAL
96. Bebington
97. Bidston
98. Birkenhead
99. Bromborough
100. Clatterbridge
101. Claughton
102. Eastham
103. Egerton
104. Heswall
105. Hoylake
106. Leasowe
107. Liscard

108. Moreton
109. New Brighton
110. Oxton
111. Prenton
112. Royden
113. Seacombe
114. Thurstaston
115. Tranmere
116. Upton
117. Wallasey

| **Sefton** | **Knowsley** |
|---|---|
| Linacre | Kirkby Central |
| Netherton | Northwood |
| | Southdene (Cherryfield) |
| **St. Helens** | Westvale (Whitefield) |
| Parr and Hardshaw | Longview/Page Moss |
| Grange Park | Halewood West/South |
| Thatto Heath | |
| Sutton and Bold | |
| West Sutton | |

These 'inner areas' give a clear indication of the areas in Merseyside which should have received priority attention. This will not necessarily apply to the full range of programmes listed above, but should provide a template for assessing the effective spatial distribution of Urban Programme resources.

Finally, the chosen format for the interpretive analysis requires a brief explanation, as it could have been approached in several ways. Essentially, the expenditure data is a two-way matrix, consisting of programme expenditure and ward areas, and it would have been feasible to present the analysis on a district basis using the ward categories as the primary classification for each programme. However, as the principal aim of the study is to present a conurbation-wide analysis, it is more beneficial to examine each programme throughout the entire area and then finally to compare the ward areas on the basis of total expenditure. Therefore, the following sections critically examine each programme in turn, comparing their expenditure distributions on both a district and ward basis.

## 2.1 Programme-based data

### Urban Programme

The figures representing Urban Programme (UP) expenditure clearly show that the distribution of 'inner areas' and high levels of spend corresponded closely during the study period (Figures C10 to C14). In Liverpool the wards receiving the majority of resources during the period 1984/85 to 1990/91 were: Everton, Speke and Abercromby; whilst Gillmoss, Granby and Dingle, while not as prominent, also attracted noticeable levels of investment. However some anomalies occurred in Liverpool's UP expenditure, as the priority wards of Valley and Netherley received minimal levels of UP support, whilst non-priority areas Breckfield, Vauxhall and Tuebrook enjoyed expenditure levels close to those of Dingle.

In Sefton, Linacre received over three times more UP expenditure than any other ward during the seven-year period. Even though the other 'inner area' in the district, Netherton, recorded the second highest level of expenditure, it received virtually the same level of support as did Litherland, Ford and Church. Comparing Netherton with Linacre, there was a higher level of investment in Litherland from 1986/87 to 1990/91. Netherton's designation as an 'inner area' was not reflected in its UP expenditure.

UP expenditure in St. Helens differs from elsewhere since there is no borough-wide category. The economic development unit of the local authority assigned all expenditure to individual wards and therefore expenditure can be calculated for each ward. The five wards that received the greatest levels of UP expenditure are the designated 'inner areas'; Parr and Hardshaw, West Sutton, Sutton and Bold, Grange Park and Thatto Heath. They are all adjacent to the town centre and reflect very closely the key areas of redevelopment, including the 'Ravenhead Renaissance' project and the Technology Campus. The other areas of St. Helens which received the next highest level of UP investment were Broad Oak and Marshalls Cross which are also deindustrialised areas near the town centre, but not severe enough to warrant 'inner area' designation.

The UP expenditure pattern in Wirral, as with the other districts, predominantly occurred in the 'inner areas'. Birkenhead and Seacombe - the key priority areas - received the greatest levels of support, far in excess of any other ward. The other targeted areas were Rock Ferry in Tranmere, Beechwood in Bidston and New Brighton. Tranmere and Bidston received virtually identical totals of UP investment over the period, yet the majority of Tranmere's expenditure occurred in 1989/90 and 1990/91, whilst Bidston recorded the bulk of its expenditure in 1987/88 and 1988/89. New Brighton received less total UP investment than Upton and virtually the same as Bromborough, Claughton and Prenton. However, in both Upton and Prenton there was a disproportionate level of expenditure in 1984/85, mainly directed at the Woodchurch estate. It is only because of this major project that the figures are distorted and on an annual basis New Brighton received consistently more UP funding than both Upton and Prenton.

The pattern of UP expenditure in Knowsley showed the poorest fit with 'inner areas'. This was not merely a result of Cantril Farm having received a disproportionate amount of the area's UP resources, but also because of the minimal expenditure rates within the designated 'inner areas'. Only Northwood recorded a reasonably high level of expenditure, whilst the remainder received relatively low levels of UP investment. This is especially true in the case of Cherryfield, which contains the 'inner area' of Southdene and yet had the third lowest level of expenditure of all the Knowsley wards. Apart from the dramatic expenditure that occurred in Cantril Farm, due predominantly to the presence of Stockbridge Village, other non-'inner areas' such as Tower Hill, St. Gabriel's and Princess also received high levels of investment, reflecting the presence of large residential areas in desperate need of financial assistance.

This brief account has outlined the spatial distribution of UP expenditure. However, the magnitude and type of UP investment are equally as important, since they may determine the resultant effects of the programme. Figures for the magnitude of investment show that during the seven-year period the rank order for the greatest expenditure by district was; Liverpool, Knowsley, Wirral, Sefton and St. Helens. The expenditure in Liverpool far outweighed that in any other district. Everton received the greatest support in any one ward, approximately seven million pounds more than the next highest ward expenditure, Cantril Farm. Even some of the more average examples of ward expenditure in Liverpool were far beyond those of other districts, with nine wards receiving around or more than four million pounds during the whole period. This is despite the fact that in Liverpool over thirty million pounds of UP expenditure was allocated on a borough-wide basis, which was more than six times the annual allocation to any other district.

The five top ranking wards on Merseyside (in order) which received the greatest total UP investment from 1984/85 to 1990/91 were; Everton, Cantril Farm, Speke, Abercromby and Birkenhead. Apart from the two wards outside Liverpool, the remaining top-ranking wards from the other districts - Tower Hill, Northwood, Seacombe, Linacre and Parr and Hardshaw - only compare with the mid-ranking ward expenditure in Liverpool - Vauxhall, Tuebrook, Smithdown, St. Mary's, Kensington, Dovecot, Dingle and Breckfield. The ward areas which received minimal support in Liverpool compare favourably with those wards in other districts which recorded above-average expenditure levels within their districts. For example, Warbreck, Valley, Melrose, Fazakerley, Croxteth, Allerton, Anfield and Aigburth all indicate a total expenditure of approximately one million pounds, whilst only two wards in St. Helens, West Sutton and Parr and Hardshaw, display expenditures in excess of this total.

Of all the districts, Sefton had by far the most stringent targeting policy, since over half of its wards did not receive any UP support. However, this must be set against the two million pounds which has been categorised as borough-wide, which may have filtered through to these areas, but for logistical reasons it cannot be allocated to them. The main division in UP expenditure is between revenue and capital, and the expenditure figures (apart from St. Helens) reveal the break-down of these types of expenditure. In the case of Liverpool, the revenue expenditure across the district decreased consistently from over eight million in 1984/85 to just over one million in 1990/91. By comparison the capital expenditure increased from just under eight million in 1984/85 to around ten million in 1990/91, after reaching a peak in 1989/90 of over twelve million.

To illustrate the types of projects that fall into either revenue or capital programmes, it is possible to draw representative samples from some of the more detailed UP records. Under Liverpool's capital programme, some of the high expenditure wards, Everton, Abercromby and Speke, show a reasonable level of consistency in the type of projects that were undertaken. They reflect the mixture of different projects, but in general, resource priority was given to the economically related operations. These included; the refurbishment of shopping areas (St. James Street), business centres (Black Business Centre), retail centres (St. John's Precinct), area regeneration (London Road Regeneration) and improvement of industrial areas (Speke). To appreciate whether a project is economically, environmentally or socially related is impossible under certain circumstances, for example, the effects of environmental works (regenerating Speke Boulevard) are multifaceted. And these were the types of project that were becoming more common towards the end of the 1980s, based upon the improvement of an area's infrastructure and environmental fabric. On the other hand, the small, specific, leisure and community activities (Central Youth Club Improvements, Young Women's Media Project) became less of a feature of ward expenditure. These changes occurred in Liverpool's capital programme and, as indicated by the types of project included in the other districts' capital programmes, it appears that similar changes also took place in their expenditure, but not to the same extent. In Wirral, Sefton and Knowsley, the small community-based leisure schemes were still part of UP expenditure into the late 1980s. However, these projects tended to be more prevalent in the wards with lower levels of expenditure and those with large residential improvement operations.

St. Helens is not included in the above list because a detailed breakdown of its UP projects was not available. However, local authority analysis indicates that there was a similar shift in bias towards economic projects, as with Liverpool. But, the relatively low level of expenditure indicates a constraint upon UP playing anything other than a supportive role in major regeneration projects. The revenue programme in the other four districts sustained a much better level of expenditure than it did in Liverpool. On an annual basis the revenue/ capital ratio maintained a reasonably consistent level, but overall there was still a gradual decrease in revenue expenditure. To a certain extent the UP maintained its support for socially related projects throughout Merseyside, but in general, the ward areas which received the greatest levels of support, did so through an increase in economic expenditure and a switch away from small-scale traditional UP projects. The reasons for this were as much a reflection of the change in UP policy as the need for local authorities to integrate UP expenditure into their large-scale redevelopment plans.

Derelict Land Grant

The figures of Derelict Land Grant (DLG) for each district demonstrate that, during the period 1981/82 to 1990/91, the majority of expenditure occurred in the 'inner areas' (Figures C15 to C19). Yet, as with the UP expenditure, there were several anomalies to this general pattern.

In Liverpool the most striking expenditure rate occurred in Kensington, a non-'inner area'. The DLG investment in this ward, over the ten-year period, was double that of any other Liverpool ward and in excess of all other wards on Merseyside. Its total DLG expenditure was £1,721,299, whilst the next highest occurred in Tower Hill, Knowsley. Kensington is obviously a special case and the reason for this unusually high level of DLG expenditure is the development of Wavertree Technology Park. Prior to 1983/84 this ward had used very little DLG, but the reclamation of railway sidings for the site development utilised over £200,000 of DLG during the mid 1980s. But, even this was made to look insignificant by the expenditure rate in the early 1990s, when over £1,000,000 of DLG was used for the second-stage development of the Technology Park.

The second-highest ward expenditure occurred in Tower Hill, Knowsley. The total DLG for Tower Hill over the ten-year period was £1,271,584. This was because, in the mid to late 'eighties the area was subject to a massive demolition exercise, followed by vast tracts of wasteland being restored. The majority of this demolition involved the removal of derelict flats, which occurred in several major stages over a four-year period. These included Ravenscroft Co-op and Radshaw Court, along with other operations named Tower Hill 'A', 'B' and 'C'.

Apart from the two special cases described above, the remaining DLG expenditure was fairly consistent with the distribution of 'inner areas'. In Liverpool, apart from Kensington the only other non-'inner area' ward that recorded a significant level of DLG expenditure was Vauxhall, the majority of whose money was spent on redevelopment projects such as Great Homer Street, Vauxhall Road and Limekiln Lane. Other Liverpool wards which accounted for the majority of the districts DLG support and experienced an expenditure total in excess of £300,000 were the 'inner areas' of Everton, Abercromby, Granby, Netherley.

The Liverpool wards which experienced more moderate DLG expenditure were; Smithdown, St. Mary's, Valley, Tuebrook and Dingle. Smithdown however, recorded a reasonably high total over the ten years (even though it is not an 'inner area') because a section of Wavertree Technology Park falls within its ward boundary. In contrast, Speke, a designated 'inner area', apparently used very little DLG, because the majority of DLG work undertaken in Speke fell outside the ward boundary, since a large section of Speke's urban area is located in St. Mary's ward.

In Sefton there were four wards in addition to Linacre which received substantial DLG support; Litherland, Molyneux, Netherton and Orrell. These all recorded DLG expenditure in excess of £200,000 for the ten-year period. Expenditure in Linacre was mainly concentrated in Bootle, with projects such as the Hawthorne Road Trading Estate and Langton Branch (derelict railway land). The reason why Litherland and Molyneux feature strongly in the DLG programme, is because of the clearance work undertaken at the Charles I King Factory and the Aintree Triangle Site, respectively.

Even though no single ward in St. Helens matched the significant expenditure levels of Kensington or Tower Hill, the district recorded the most consistently high expenditure across several wards in the whole of Merseyside. West Sutton, Thatto Heath, Sutton and Bold, Grange Park and Haydock all received DLG support in excess of £500,000 during the ten-year period. These projects mainly consisted of rejuvenating mineral works (Bold Colliery, Elephant Lane Clay Pit), the regeneration of deindustrialised wasteland (Ravenhead) and extensive redevelopment of the disused Leeds/Liverpool Canal.

In Wirral, the greatest DLG expenditure occurred in Tranmere and this mainly consisted of projects based around Rock Ferry, New Chester Road and Old Chester Road. From the brief project descriptions it appears that the majority of these operations were planned for industrial after-use. Housing was the second priority in this ward and education and office after-use received minimal support. One of the key distinguishing features about DLG expenditure in Wirral, is the large number of small projects it has supported. A considerable number of schemes were under 0.5 hectares and several were only 0.02 hectares, with the bulk of these being housing projects. However, this pattern of small schemes diminished in the late 1980s with the introduction of the rolling programme, which allowed the local authority to tackle larger projects over a number of years (Bromborough Power Station, 26 hectares). In the majority of cases, DLG expenditure in Wirral was focused in the 'inner areas' (Tranmere, Seacombe, New Brighton and Birkenhead), and these projects were mainly connected with the redevelopment of derelict dock land and the associated residential and industrial areas. In the early 1980s these projects were generally intended for industrial after-use, however towards the end of the decade the pattern became dominated by housing and commercial after-use.

The expenditure in Tower Hill dominated the ward pattern of DLG support in Knowsley, with Northwood and Whiston South clearly defined as second and third priority areas. Of these, only Northwood is a designated 'inner area' and the majority of its expenditure funded the redevelopment of the Gores Road site for industrial units. Tower Hill has already been noted for its massive residential redevelopments and the most notable project in Whiston South was the establishment of Whiston Enterprise Park, which involved derelict land reclamation and mine capping for industrial after-use. Apart from the three wards mentioned, the individual ward expenditure in Knowsley was relatively low over the ten-year period. But its overall pattern of DLG support is comparable to Sefton, in that the majority of expenditure was directed at a distinct set of wards split into three tiers, with the remaining wards recording expenditure rates of approximately £200,000 or below.

Across all districts, it appears that DLG expenditure at ward level became more spatially focused in the late 1980s and early 1990s. The levels of expenditure increased greatly in the key wards, whilst the expenditure in the less funded wards consisted of investment generated in the earlier part of the decade. Additionally, the size of project tended to increase over the period, predominantly as a result of the introduction of the rolling programme. This contributed to the focusing of DLG, since the larger projects were located in the key wards because of the extensive problems that already existed in these locations.

Housing Corporation

The pattern of ward expenditure for the Housing Corporation indicates that Sefton had the most focused programme of support (Figures C20 to C24). Linacre and Litherland received a disproportionate level of investment from the Housing Corporation compared to the other wards in the district. This concentrated pattern was not repeated in the other districts, as the level of investment in the other wards on Merseyside was much more evenly dispersed.

From 1983 to 1991 Liverpool had the greatest level of support from the Housing Corporation, with fifteen of its wards recording total project costs in excess of £4,000,000. One of these, Abercromby, with total project costs of £15,979,710, received the highest concentration of funds of any Merseyside ward. Of the three wards that show their total project costs to be only slightly less than this, two are in Liverpool, Dingle and Granby, and the other is in Sefton, Linacre. All of these wards are designated 'inner areas' and to a certain extent, this targeted funding of priority areas represents the general pattern of project expenditure, but within each district there were anomalies.

In St. Helens the ward which recorded the highest total project costs was Queen's Park, a non-'inner area'. However, of the five designated 'inner area' wards, four were amongst the top five wards in terms of project expenditure; Parr and Hardshaw, Grange Park, West Sutton and Thatto Heath. Even though Sutton and Bold, the fifth 'inner area' in St. Helens, witnessed one of the greatest investment levels in 1986, it still only recorded seventh position in terms of total project costs, behind Broad Oak.

In the other districts there were notable differences between the pattern of key investment wards and designated priority areas. In Liverpool, Vauxhall and Tuebrook accounted for a large proportion of the project costs in the district and their totals were in excess of the majority of other wards on Merseyside. In Sefton, Netherton (an 'inner area') received only an average level of investment, whilst Litherland (non-'inner area') had much migher expenditure than any other Sefton ward, apart from Linacre.

The wards in Wirral which received the greatest levels of Housing Corporation expenditure tended to follow the pattern of designated areas, with Birkenhead, Tranmere and Seacombe acquiring the most significant levels of investment. However, the non-designated areas of Wallasey and Claughton also display substantial project cost totals, whilst New Brighton and especially Bidston (non-'inner areas') received notably less support.

Of all the districts, the ward pattern of project investment in Knowsley differs the most from its designated priority areas. The ward showing the greatest level of investment, Cantril Farm, is a non designated area and it received virtually all its support between 1983 and 1985. In the case of the other key investment wards (Tower Hill, St. Michael's, Princess and Kirkby Central, of which only the latter is designated), the greatest proportion of expenditure occurred in the late 1980s and 1990. In the case of Cantril Farm, the majority of the expenditure was centred upon Stockbridge Village which makes up a large proportion of the ward area. In 1983 the project area was primarily Waterpark Drive, where virtually all the support was taken-up through shared ownership sale. In 1984 the same pattern occurred, but with the addition of major new-build projects in Stockbridge Village at Little Moss Hey, Birtle Croft and The Spinney. In 1985 the same pattern of expenditure continued in Stockbridge, but with a shift in the shared ownership sales to The Woodlands Plot and the major new-build took place in Roughsedge Hey.

From 1986 onwards, the type and location of expenditure in Knowsley moved away from shared ownership sales and Stockbridge. The main thrust of investment became concentrated into Kirkby and Huyton, and the projects diversified into a variety of categories, including, 'Major Repair' and 'Leasehold Schemes for the Elderly', with the major expense shifting to 'Rehab'.

In the other districts, the level of support to individual wards was more consistent on an annual basis. This was especially true of the wards with the highest levels of expenditure, which acquired reasonable levels of investment each year throughout the nine-year period. If any funding bias can be inferred from the figures, it is only that in Sefton and St. Helens the bulk of expenditure occurred in the mid 1980s, whilst in Liverpool and Wirral it was in the late 1980s and early 1990s.

The types of schemes that were realised in Liverpool, St. Helens, Sefton and Wirral were reasonably diverse at ward level. However, from this general pattern, it is possible to discern certain trends amongst groups of wards. For example, in Liverpool the northern wards (Tuebrook, Anfield, Everton) were more prone to 'Shared Ownership Sale' in the early 1980s than were the southern areas. Whilst the expenditure that occurred in wards such as Dingle and Granby was mainly confined to 'Major Repair' and 'Rehab'.

In the case of Sefton there was more of a defined pattern of scheme types throughout the 1980s. In and around Bootle (Linacre) the schemes were consistently based upon 'Major Repair' and 'Rehab'. However, in the majority of other Sefton wards there was a tendency for the schemes to be dominated by 'Shared Ownership Sale' and 'Improved for Sale'. This pattern was also replicated in Wirral and St. Helens, where the key wards receiving the greatest levels of support, did so through schemes dominated by 'Repair' and 'Rehab', whilst the wards not specifically targeted tended to incur developments for sale.

The patterns described above dominated the early and mid 1980s, but there was a distinct change in the operations of the Housing Corporation following the 1988 Housing Act. The principal change was the introduction of support for the rented sector, which applied to all wards throughout Merseyside. This radically changed the pattern of schemes, so that from 1988 onwards there were virtually no improvements for sale and the schemes became more consistent across all wards.

European Regional Development Fund

One of the more striking features about the European Regional Development Fund (ERDF), in comparison to the other programmes, was its spatial targeting (Figures C25 to C29). The figures representing the ward distribution of ERDF across Merseyside clearly show that during the 1980s the fund was only operational in specific areas and, outside of these, support was minimal. Therefore, the pattern of distribution is much starker than with the other programmes and this is primarily a result of the explicit project nature of ERDF.

The figures reveal that from 1981 to 1991 each district had a range of key wards outside of which the support was minimal or nothing. In St. Helens, Wirral and Liverpool, the main bulk of the funds went into the designated 'inner areas', even though certain non-designated areas received substantial levels of support; for example Wallasey in Wirral. In Knowsley ERDF investment was slightly biased in favour of the non-designated areas,

St. Gabriel's, Whiston North and Knowsley Park, but the designated areas of Northwood, Kirkby Central and Halewood South recorded reasonable levels of support. In Sefton the pattern of aid to 'inner areas' was totally reversed, as the main resources went to the non-designated areas of Duke's and Kew, whilst, of the 'inner areas', only Linacre received notable support.

Overall, Liverpool received the highest level of ERDF investment, with high expenditure rates in 1983 and 1984, but with the majority of support occurring in the late 1980s. This was also true of Wirral and Knowsley, with significant investment in 1983 and the main expenditure occurring in the late 1980s and early 1990s. If the 1985 investment in Duke's (Sefton) was not included, virtually the whole of Sefton's ERDF expenditure would have occurred at the end of the decade and in the early 1990s. The ERDF support in St. Helens during the 1980s was extremely low, but from 1989 onwards the level of support increased dramatically and the vast majority occurred in 1990 and 1991.

The pattern indicating a massive increase in ERDF expenditure at the end of the 1980s was a result of a change in the fund's operational policy. From 1988 onwards, the ERDF became assimilated into the new Integrated Development Operations (IDOs) and because of this, long-term project strategies were developed which vastly increased the funding for successful applicants. This was the case in St. Helens, which received 29% of the total ERDF programme for the Merseyside Integrated Development Operation, by far the largest share of all the Merseyside Authorities.

The reason for the decline in the ERDF during the mid-1980s was primarily a result of the abolition of the county council. Before this the Merseyside County Council was the main administrator dealing with submissions for the ERDF. However with its demise the district councils were not fully prepared to take on this role and it was not until the introduction of the IDOs that the district councils could fully access the ERDF.

In Liverpool the most prominent expenditure of the ERDF occurred in Abercromby and Everton. The projects in Abercromby were a mixture of transport and tourism, and they included the development of the Maritime Museum, highway improvements around Lime Street Railway Station and improvements to Church Street and St. George's Hall. In Everton the types of project were very similar, primarily aimed at tourism and transport, including developments around the railway station and improvements to William Brown Street and Hunter Street.

In the rest of Liverpool four other wards received significant levels of ERDF investment. Kensington mainly benefited because of ERDF contributions to Wavertree Technology Park, St. Mary's investment was due to improvements around the Enterprise Zone and the airport, Woolton utilised the support for part of its retail development and transport system around Gateacre, and the investment in Vauxhall was part of a sewerage and transport development.

During the 1980s ERDF investment in Sefton primarily occurred in Southport (Duke's), which included a wide range of projects from sewage works to a space theatre. At this time the rest of the ward areas received very little support and it was not until the introduction of MIDO that wards such as Linacre and Kew fully benefited from the fund. These projects included a tourist information centre, an adult education training unit, a business centre and various schemes of landscaping.

In Knowsley the bulk of ERDF investment was split between St. Gabriel's and Northwood, with the main programme of expenditure being taken up by financial assistance to industry. However, other schemes in these two wards included, Depot Road Improvements, the construction of Huyton Industrial Service Road, Kirkby Industrial Improvement Area and Woodward Road Security Works. The expenditure incurred in Knowsley in the late 1980s and 1990s was primarily a result of investment in the various industrial estates in Knowsley Park and Northwood and the business park in Whiston.

In Wirral, Wallasey was the main recipient of ERDF and the main projects were embankment sea defences, the Wallasey Technology Centre and Gorsey Lane Business Centre. The projects in New Brighton mainly consisted of beach stabilisations and sea defences, whilst in Birkenhead the projects were predominantly based upon road and environmental improvements (Hamilton Square, Four Bridges, Corporation Road). The general theme of the projects in Seacombe centred upon the Docklands Industrial Improvement Area, but also included general road developments and improvements to the ferry operations. Some of the smaller expenditure totals in Wirral occurred in Upton, due to the development of a by-pass, and Hoylake, which devoted its investment to the West Kirby Marina and Sailing School.

Finally, of all the authorities the most impressive track record for obtaining ERDF is held by St. Helens. This refers solely to their operations within MIDO, but far outweighs the majority of pre-1988 funding in the other districts. The projects are clearly reflected by the wards which have received the greatest support. Parr and Hardshaw recorded the highest expenditure due to the development of St. Helens Technology Campus. West Sutton is close to this expenditure because of the development of a link road from the centre of the town to the M62 Motorway and Grange Park has had a reasonable level of support because of the redevelopment works in the deindustrialised area of Ravenhead.

| Housing Investment Programme | The Housing Investment Programme (HIP), along with Estate Action, local authority assets and capital receipts, are all an integral part of a local authority's housing capital programme. The actual proportions that each contributes to the capital programme will vary from authority to authority, but in the main, the HIP allocation tends to be between seventy and ninety percent of an authority's total capital expenditure on housing. Given this, it is impossible to relate directly the HIP allocation to direct expenditure, as it merely makes up a pool of funds upon which an authority draws. The only way of relating the HIP allocation to a spatial distribution of expenditure, is to use the total capital programme as an index against which to allocate HIP expenditure. However, this is not a faithful representation of allocation since there is still a degree of uncertainty as to how HIPs resources are actually used. |
|---|---|

The location of the GIAs and HAAs was obtained from the various local authority housing departments, along with a project breakdown of the capital programme. This allowed an accurate picture of the capital expenditure to be constructed for the ward areas, which was then used proportionally to allocate the annual total HIP allocation for each district.

On a district basis, the figures reveal that Liverpool received by far the largest allocation and, of the other districts, only Wirral can be distinguished as having received an above-average allocation. This pattern of expenditure is a reasonably accurate reflection of the housing situation in Merseyside during the 1980s, with Liverpool having the greatest problems and the largest expenditure, notwithstanding the political climate of the time.

The ward distribution of HIP expenditure in Liverpool closely followed the pattern of designated 'inner areas', but because housing problems are more widely spread, each ward shows a reasonable level of expenditure. The expenditure levels were guided by two influences; first, the council's Urban Regeneration Strategy, which initially selected seventeen renewal areas and eventually concluded with twenty four, and second, the location of 119 HAAs (GIAs) that existed at various stages throughout the 1980s. The combination of these eventually led to the concentration of funds in the wards indicated, with priority being given to Vauxhall, Gillmoss, Everton, Dingle, Croxteth, Clubmoor and Abercromby; these areas in particular reflecting the ward concentration of urban renewal areas, HAAs and GIAs.

On an annual basis the amount of private sector expenditure in Liverpool was generally between twenty and thirty percent of the public total, but this does not apply to the other districts which had far fewer HAAs and GIAs. However, the peak expenditure which occurred in Liverpool between 1983 and 1985 is comparable to the other districts, as this was the height of the new construction policy, which has now been taken out of the hands of the local authorities. The Liverpool wards which received a total allocation of approximately £10,000,000, such as Valley, Speke and Smithdown are the areas which contained just one priority renewal area and some of the smaller HAAs. Whilst those areas which received minimal support, Woolton and Childwall, contained no places in receipt of mandatory awards, but due to changes in the housing legislation at the end of the decade, certain grants were available in any location.

The pattern of HIP expenditure in Wirral closely follows the five designated areas; Tranmere, Seacombe, New Brighton, Birkenhead and Bidston. This is primarily because of the twenty one HAAs/GIAs, of which the larger operations containing over a thousand dwellings were in Tranmere and Birkenhead, and also because the five wards contain large areas of public sector housing. These areas, such as the former Ford Estate (now the Beechwood Estate) in Bidston received high levels of public expenditure throughout the decade. The other less supported wards in Wirral, which still received a noticeable level of investment were; Moreton, Eastham, Claughton and Bromborough. The main bulk of expenditure in these wards occurred between 1983 and 1985, which was a result of large public sector spending on estates such as Noctorum in Claughton, but in the case of Bromborough it was also due to the presence of a large GIA at New Ferry which attracted additional resources.

In the case of Knowsley, Tower Hill, Princess, Longview and Cantril Farm were the four key wards which received preferential HIP allocations. The Tower Hill Estate received a substantial amount of allocation throughout the whole period, which was mainly spent on demolition and general improvements, and a wide range of specific operations, such as lift modernisations, re-wiring, heating and fencing. In Princess the main expenditure occurred in and around Fincham and the Woolfall Area, supporting a whole range of projects as with Tower Hill. Knowsley Heights and the Blue Bell Estate were the focus of attention in Longview, whilst in Cantril Farm it was not only Stockbridge Village, but the areas adjacent to Knowsley Park, Princess and Longview which received particular attention.

Unfortunately, even though the figures for Knowsley are generally representative, the exact detail of the records used is in question. This primarily refs to the areas of Southdene (Cherryfield Ward) and Westvale (Whitefield Ward), which are some of the most dependent residential areas in the district. Cherryfield also contains specific areas such as Cherryfield Heights, which have been subject to key renovation works. But, both these wards are not represented in the figures as having received any form of special attention. Therefore, it must be assumed that in the case of Knowsley, the picture presented has been biased by a lack of information.

During the 1980s the Sefton wards containing either HAAs or GIAs were; Linacre, Derby, Litherland, Orrell, Ford, Church and Kew. Of the eighteen designated private sector areas receiving support, virtually all were situated in or around Bootle, at the intersection of Linacre, Derby, Orrell and Litherland. This has influenced the pattern of expenditure, but was not the major contributory factor in the distribution of HIP allocation shown for Sefton. Of all the Sefton wards Linacre received the largest portion of HIP allocation during the ten-year period. This was not merely because of the presence of GIAs (Marsh Lane and Peel Road), but because of major public-sector expenditure in areas such as Stanley Road, Balliol Road and Strand Road. In Orrell, which received the second largest total HIP allocation, the greatest expenditure occurred around Johnston Avenue, which was the site of a major 'new build' programme in the early 1980s. In Litherland the majority of the expenditure occurred in the south of the ward, around Hawthorne Road. This involved a mixture of projects from slum clearance to the construction of new dwellings, but there was a decline in the 'new build' programme towards the end of the 1980s and an increase in renovation and slum clearance. This pattern was replicated in the other wards receiving a similar or moderate allocation; Victoria, Netherton, Manor, Ford, Derby and Church.

In general, the majority of the HIP allocation was concentrated into south Sefton, whilst the northern wards, especially Ainsdale received virtually nothing. In Southport, Kew and Dukes recorded minimal expenditure and this was primarily a result of the development of prefabricated accommodation for elderly and disabled residents, and the presence of one GIA and one HAA in Kew.

The adjacent wards of Grange Park and Thatto Heath were the two wards in St. Helens which received the largest portions of HIP allocation. Within these areas the expenditure was mainly concentrated into three locations; Grange Park, West Park and Portico, which in the early 1980s contributed to the development of new dwellings, but towards the end of the period 'remedial works' took over the majority of the expenditure. Vulcan Village and Earlstown were the main focus of expenditure around Newton-Le-Willows, which is located in the wards Newton West and Newton East. Whilst the other wards which received above average-levels of support, Rainhill and Marshalls Cross, had their expenditure distributed throughout the entire ward. The distribution of HIP allocation in St. Helens was primarily concentrated in the wards surrounding the town centre and in most cases each ward received in excess of £1,000,000 throughout the ten-year period. However, Rainford, a semi-rural, self-contained centre to the north of St. Helens received virtually no allocation, a situation similar to the distributive patterns of the other programmes previously discussed.

Safer Cities

The Safer Cities Programme is a Home Office crime prevention initiative which aims to tackle crime and the fear of crime in the inner city, through local multi-agency projects. In Merseyside, the Safer Cities Programme was only operative in Wirral (Figure C35). It also reveals that it is one of the newer Action for Cities programmes, as funding only began in 1989.

During the first year of operation, Claughton was the key ward receiving support and the majority of the funds entering this area were directed at the Noctorum Estate. These grants were specifically designed to tackle the problems of burglary and vandalism, by increasing security and awareness in the area. The other ward in 1989/90 which received a reasonable level of support was Tranmere. Its total expenditure in this year was spread across a number of different locations, all within close proximity to Rock Ferry and all the grants except one were used for the provision of security for the elderly. The other wards receiving grants in 1989/90 - Wallasey, Seacombe, Moreton, Eastham, Hoylake, Bromborough, Birkenhead, Bidston and Bebington - all operated a range of different schemes including; 'Lack of awareness', 'Lack of facilities for children', 'Children's personal safety-abduction' and 'Fear of re-victimisation'.

In 1990/91 only Tranmere continued to receive significant levels of support, whilst attention shifted from the other existing priority areas to new wards. In addition, far more of the overall grant entering Wirral was allocated on a borough-wide basis for general education of crime prevention. Birkenhead received far greater attention in the second year of operation, as its grant award increased from £488 to £54,950. The majority of finance to this area was used to avert vandalism and burglary and to combat juvenile crime. The highest grant awards in 1990/91 went to Bidston and specifically the newly named Beechwood Estate. The main aim of these grants was to prevent crime and vandalism, especially against the property of elderly people. The massive increase in borough-wide grant spending tended to cover two main issues; firstly, to educate people and prevent crime against women, and secondly, to reduce juvenile crime by means of education and providing recreational opportunities.

Enterprise Zone

The figures showing the breakdown of expenditure in Liverpool's Enterprise Zone (Speke), are segregated into two wards on the basis of the proportion of the zone in each area (Figures C36 and C37). This is because it is impossible to assess accurately the exact finance in each ward, due to the lack of monitoring records. Consequently a pro-rata division of funds was adopted based on the size of the zone in individual wards.

Even though the Enterprise Zone was entitled 'Speke', none of its operations occurred within Speke ward. The figures clearly demonstrate the zone was only operative in St. Mary's and Allerton and that twice the amount of investment occurred in the former. This has resulted because of the methodology adopted, as approximately two thirds of the zone is located in St. Mary's. All the figures relating to the investment in Enterprise Zones are confidential and it is not possible to relate the pattern shown to the commitments of any one firm. However, the breakdown does allow an insight into the divisions between public and private expenditure. During the early years of designation the levels of private investment, even though they were relatively small, were consistent up to 1984/85. From this year onwards private investment was discontinued until the final two years of the decade. In 1987/88 and 1989/90 there were two large injections of private capital and correspondingly the Capital Allowance increased proportionally.

Over the nine-year period the amount of Rate Revenue Foregone paid to the local authority steadily increased for both wards. This could be a result of two factors; first, the number of firms operative in the wards increased, but with virtually no investment in new construction until 1987/88, and second, the increase in the general rate level accelerated the rate differential from within to outside the zone, raising the payments to the local authority.

Loan Guarantee Scheme

The Loan Guarantee Scheme (LGS), initially under the auspices of the Department of Employment, was set up to guarantee loans issued by approved lenders to small firms, against default by the borrower. The general level of guarantee was 70% of the outstanding loan, but this was increased to 85% in Inner City Task Force Areas. Expenditure, as recorded in the figures, only occurred when the businesses failed and the lender called upon the Department to honour the guarantee.

The figures for Merseyside (Figures C38 to C42) do not appear to be particularly reliable as the LGS became operative in June 1981 and if the figures are taken as correct, there were no business failures in the entire area until 1988. It must be assumed that the earlier records and even those for 1988, which only show failures in four wards (Everton, Kensington, Bromborough and Hoylake), cannot reflect the true pattern of LGS expenditure on Merseyside. However, another contributory factor to the recorded increase in firm failures and scheme expenditure after 1988, was the increase in firms reliant upon the scheme. This occurred because in January 1988 a simplified arrangement for loans of £15,000 or under was introduced. This had a significant impact on the numbers of applications and on the level of expenditure, with far more smaller firms becoming reliant upon the programme.

Of the five districts, Liverpool received the highest levels of expenditure during the four-year period, not only because of the large amounts recorded in individual wards, but also because it had nearly twice as many wards involved in the scheme than any other district. The main wards in the district which received the largest amounts of expenditure were; Abercromby, Everton, Dingle St. Mary's and Kensington. The first three are key 'inner areas' where premiums for loans were at their lowest and the rate of guarantee was at its highest. The final two are special cases because of the influence of Speke Enterprise Zone in St. Mary's and Wavertree Technology Park in Kensington, which will have encouraged the establishment, but not the survival, of small firms.

The pattern of expenditure in Liverpool and in the other districts is a reflection of the number of loans guaranteed. The proportion of expenditure in Liverpool was far greater than in the other areas and as a result the failure rate and expenditure level was much higher. This ratio of loans guaranteed to actual firm failure has guided the expenditure levels in each district, as in Wirral which received the second highest level of expenditure and also had the second highest rate of loans guaranteed.

The proportional ratio of loans agreed to expenditure levels also applies on a ward basis. In Wirral, for example, the ward which had the greatest amount of loans agreed over the entire period was Birkenhead. Logically, this meant there was a greater potential for firm failure in the ward and it therefore incurred the highest LGS expenditure rate in the district. Unfortunately, unlike the other programmes these expenditure rates are not indicative of additional support for an area, as they signify business failure rates.

Apart from Wirral and Liverpool, the other districts recorded minimal expenditure rates, which are a reflection of the smaller numbers of loans guaranteed. Sefton and St. Helens recorded expenditure in five wards, whilst Knowsley received funds in only four wards. In St. Helens virtually all the expenditure occurred in 1990 and in almost all cases across the county, the majority of expenditure occurred in 1990 and 1991, possibly a reflection of the downturn in the wider economy.

In Liverpool, Wirral and Sefton the high expenditure wards tended to be in 'inner areas', where business was encouraged, but failed in the inner areas. In Knowsley, only one 'inner area', Northwood, received LGS expenditure, but this was greatly exceeded by the expenditure in St. Gabriel's and Knowsley Park. The reason for this is the presence of Knowsley Industrial Estate in Knowsley Park, and Huyton Industrial Estate in St. Gabriel's.

The most striking anomaly of all LGS expenditure on Merseyside occurred in St. Helens. Here, three key 'inner areas', West Sutton, Grange Park and Parr and Hardshaw recorded average levels of expenditure for Merseyside, but the ward which received the greatest level of support was Rainford. This is noted for being a reasonably affluent, semi-rural area and there is no definite reason for the large failure of firms in this ward. It can only be assumed, that due to the collapse in the wider economy, certain businesses in this area were more fragile than in other wards which received additional support measures.

## Estate Action

Estate Action (EA) was introduced in 1986, but as the figures reveal (Figures C43 to C46), it did not have any influence on the Merseyside districts, apart from Knowsley, until 1987/88. During 1986/87 only three wards in Merseyside, all within Knowsley, received support from the Estate Action programme: Halewood South, Knowsley Park and Tower Hill. Over the whole period Tower Hill received the largest ward-based sums due to investment into three estates within the area: Tower Hill, Ravenscroft and Fallowfield. However, Bidston (Wirral) which received the second greatest EA support, had all its investment concentrated into the Ford Estate. This estate, eventually renamed Beechwood, received the greatest amount of investment of all the housing estates on Merseyside through the Estate Action programme.

Of the districts, Liverpool recorded the highest level of expenditure over the four-year period, as three of its ward areas received a total investment of over £4,000,000; Breckfield, Granby and Netherley.

The pattern of ward expenditure for the EA programme does not exactly follow the distribution of designated 'inner areas', as there are certain key wards which are conspicuous by their absence from the scheme; Abercromby, Everton, Seacombe, Parr and Hardshaw, Northwood. This could be explained by the number of residential areas in these wards which received reasonable levels of support via other programmes. The pattern of investment has obviously been directed at some of the larger housing estates in need of desperate attention, which could not simply rely upon other programme measures to remedy housing problems. In Liverpool the estates selected were; Netherley/Belle Vale, Phythian, Princes Park, Queens Road and Netherley Central. In Wirral the areas were; Ford Estate, Noctorum, Leasowe, Rock Ferry, Moreton (Town Meadow and Curlew Way), and Central Birkenhead. In Knowsley the areas were; New Hutte, Hillside, Knowsley Heights and Tower Hill. In St. Helens the areas selected were; Deanway, Portico, Queensland Place, Cherry Tree Drive, St. Thomas Square and Gillar's Green.

The most noticeable pattern of district investment occurred in Sefton. Its total EA expenditure was concentrated into a single ward, Orrell. There was no definite area specified for this support, only that the investment was spread over three phases. It may appear puzzling that no other ward in Sefton received EA expenditure, considering the vast tracts of housing in Linacre, Derby, Netherton and Litherland, but such estates will undoubtedly have received resources via other government programmes.

Merseyside Development Corporation

It was only possible to gain access to figures for the Merseyside Development Corporation's (MDC) largest projects and the level of expenditure in each district. As a result of this, disaggregation of the earlier expenditure was relatively simple, especially for Sefton.

Expenditure in Sefton had already been calculated on an annual basis and with a detailed map of the MDC area it was possible to ascertain that all its activities occurred in Linacre, which resulted in the provision of 4,000 square metres of small industrial units at Millers Bridge, Bootle. In the case of Wirral, the main work in the earlier years was carried out in Birkenhead, with the reclamation of the Wallasey and Morpeth Dock for the development of the Four Bridges Route and the Woodside Business Park. In the earlier years operations in Seacombe were minimal compared to Birkenhead, with small areas of land being reclaimed and re-allocated around Scott's Field. Therefore, of the two wards in Wirral receiving investment from 1981/82 onwards, Birkenhead recorded nearly four times the level of expenditure.

Prior to the extension of the MDC's area in 1988, the developments in Liverpool were predominantly concentrated into Abercromby (Albert Dock) and Dingle (Brunswick Business Park and International Garden Festival). These projects dominated the operations of the MDC up until 1987/88 and consequently the majority of the MDC's expenditure occurred in these wards, with the Albert Dock being the flagship of the organisation.

Everton and Aigburth also received a certain amount of investment prior to 1988. In the case of Everton the work of the MDC centred upon the development around Pier Head and the dock area which extended north from Abercromby. Investment in Aigburth was a result of the redevelopment of Otterspool, including the promenade, as part of the International Garden Festival project.

After the redesignation of the MDC's area, investment in Liverpool switched from Dingle and Abercromby to Everton and Vauxhall. In Vauxhall the main projects initiated were redevelopments of Stanley Dock, Hartley Quays, Clarence Dock and the regeneration of the areas around the Leeds/Liverpool Canal, Sandhills and Derby Road. Also, as part of the MDC's operations in Vauxhall, they were also involved in the development of the Eldonian's Housing Project. In Everton the new projects were concentrated into the redevelopment of the Waterloo Docks, Princes Dock and Pier Head. During this time developments were still taking place in the South Docks, with the construction of a marina, continuing works on the Brunswick Business Park and the provision of housing estates in Dingle, Fullwood and Riverside.

In Wirral, the MDC's redesignated area extended far more into Birkenhead, allowing work to take place on Hamilton Square and the development of highway improvements around Queensway tunnel exit and in Woodside, with the aim of improving traffic flows. However, the main difference in the new area is the MDC's involvement in Tranmere and New Brighton. In the former, the main part of the development is planned for the Cammell Laird shipyard which is underutilised and supposedly has potential for industrial redevelopment opportunities. In New Brighton the expenditure recorded was related to the development of the commercial core and coastal protection. But studies have also been undertaken into the potential of the Floral Pavilion, possibilities for improving road access and increased help with the Wirral's housing improvement programme.

Apart from the public expenditure of the MDC, the figures also display the level of private investment. However, these are not as reliable as the public figures, because of the confidentiality involved and the lack of records charting their expenditure. Therefore, to give an indication of the (possible) magnitude of private investment in each ward, the annual totals for each district have been divided on a proportional basis to the public expenditure. Fortunately, in the majority of years this inaccurate process is insignificant, as the level of private investment was minimal up to 1988/89.

## English Estates

Of the districts, Liverpool received the greatest amount of support from English Estates (EE) from 1985/86 to 1990/91 (Figures C49 to C51). Much of this represents expenditure in Kensington and Everton and this can be explained by the development of two major projects. In the earlier part of the six-year period, funds were concentrated into Everton because of the Mercury Court Development. This modernised office accommodation in the centre of Liverpool is where the operations for EE on Merseyside are now based. The other large investment of funds, during the later part of the period, was for the development of Wavertree Technology Park. Apart from these two major developments, other smaller projects were also undertaken in Liverpool. The majority of these were factory, advanced factory or workshop developments at Speke, Speke Hall (St. Mary's), King Edward Street, Commercial Road, Binns Road and Holt Lane. In addition to these factory developments there was also another office development at Love Lane, which accounts for the majority of expenditure which occurred in Vauxhall.

In the other districts all the projects were factory-based developments and occurred in only a limited number of ward areas. In St. Helens, the main target for investment was Parr and Hardshaw and this was because of the development of the new technology campus. EE had been involved in the provision of workshop units on the new site, which had been developed in the late 1980s. The other EE projects in St. Helens were at Sherdley Road, Baxters Lane and Beech Park, Haydock.

In Sefton the main expenditure occurred in Ford, because of a factory-based development at Bridge Lane. However, in 1985/86 the bulk of EE investment went into Netherton Industrial Estate, which accounted for all the districts expenditure during the year. The other ward expenditures were only small workshop developments in Southport and Bootle.

In Knowsley the main developments were in Huyton, which is covered by the wards of Roby and St. Gabriel's and includes Huyton Industrial Estate. The other major expenditure occurred in Knowsley Park, which encompasses the majority of Knowsley Industrial Estate. In this case all the developments were factory-related ventures.

Finally, in the case of Wirral, the most significant investment was in Bromborough, whilst Tranmere, Seacombe and Birkenhead recorded negligible levels of expenditure. The reason for the concentration of funds into Bromborough was because of the Croft Business Park development, which is a mixture of business and factory units situated on the New Chester Road. The other moderate developments in Wirral were the Argyle St. Industrial Estate in Birkenhead, where the vast majority of expenditure occurred in 1985/86, and the West Float Industrial Estate in Seacombe, which recorded its highest expenditure in 1990

## Section 11 Grants

These grants were specifically designed to help ethnic minority communities, especially where there were certain constraints on their ability to benefit from educational, social and economic opportunities. Consequently, because of this targeting, Section 11 Grants have only been operational in Liverpool, which is the only Merseyside district to contain a distinctive ethnic minority community.

From 1983/84 to 1990/91 the grant increased from £23,253 to around £170,000, which constitutes 75% of the cost of all the projects support by the grant. As the ethnic minority community is only present in three wards in Liverpool: Abercromby, Dingle and Granby, and is especially concentrated in the latter the distribution of grant expenditure closely reflects this pattern. However, because of the nature of the grant, the schemes it supported were not specifically tied to one area, as the funds tended to be used to employ people who were operative throughout the three wards. For example the grant helped to finance community relations officers, multi-cultural education advisors, language teachers, bi-lingual nursery teachers, race complaints officers and various social workers.

It was therefore impossible to assign the expenditure accurately to any particular ward, but it was possible to ascertain that the majority of the labour resource was utilised in Granby. Because of this, the total grant figures for Liverpool were separated on a ward basis to reflect the magnitude of operation, rather than exact expenditure patterns.

## City Grants

Of the three urban grants that were in operation during the 1980s, City Grant (CG), Urban Regeneration Grant (URG) and Urban Development Grant (UDG), the latter was the longest running and contributed most to the redevelopment of Merseyside.

Only three out of the five districts in Merseyside received UDG and Knowsley benefited most from the scheme, with six successful projects. The majority of these were concentrated into Kirkby and Halewood and covered a wide range of operations from developments at Kirkby Football Club to a housing development at Kempsell Walk. Liverpool had only one successful application and this was used for the development of Plessey's operations on Wavertree Technology Park, Kensington. Sefton had two grant awards, one in Manor for a housing development and one in Church for improvements to Seaforth Freeport.

The other two schemes that followed UDG; Urban Regeneration Grant and City Grant had very little general effect on Merseyside. Abercromby was the only ward to receive any support from URG, which was used to build the Anglican Cathedral precinct. City Grant, which was introduced in 1988, was only used in St. Gabriel's (Knowsley) prior to 1991/92, for the redevelopment of an old Huntley and Palmer Factory Building into new office units. From 1991/92 onwards, several wards in Liverpool and St. Helens were also awarded grants, but these fall outside the time scale of the study.

The purpose of the grants was to provide funds for specific large-scale operations and not to offer a blanket approach to regeneration. The general effect of the various regeneration projects has been fairly limited and the approved schemes have been specifically concentrated into single large-scale developments, the largest of these being the development of the cathedral precinct, which now provides student accommodation and a site for the new cathedral college.

## 2.2 Global expenditure totals

This final section examines total expenditure levels for all thirteen programmes on a ward basis (Figures C52 to C56). Over the ten-year period, Liverpool received by far the highest levels of support. It has a total expenditure in approximately four times greater than any other district; the closest being Wirral, then Knowsley, Sefton and St. Helens. Even though the total expenditure in these other four districts was reasonably similar, the annual patterns of expenditure in each district were distinctly different. In Liverpool the level of expenditure quickly reached its peak in the early 1980s, which then progressed with small increments until 1988/89, after which there was a dramatic drop, followed by a slight recovery in the final two years of the study period.

Wirral and Knowsley recorded similar patterns of annual expenditure, represented by a bimodal cycle. Their expenditure peaked in the early part of the decade and than again in the late 1980s. The dip in expenditure that occurred in these two districts during the mid 1980s was more prominent in Knowsley than Wirral and overall Wirral sustained a higher level of expenditure.

The levels of support received by St. Helens and Sefton display opposing trends over the decade. In St. Helens total expenditure increased throughout the period, reaching its peak in 1990/91. In Sefton, the trend shows that the higher levels of expenditure occurred in the earlier part of the decade, but towards the end of the period expenditure tailed off.

On an individual ward basis, the total expenditure charts show that each district had a reasonably unique set of expenditure profiles. The most distinctive of these occurred in Sefton, where a single ward, Linacre, received twice as much funding as any other Sefton ward. Apart from Linacre, there were six other wards in Sefton which received notable levels of support: Litherland, Orrell, Ford, Church, Netherton and Derby. However, these were dwarfed by the expenditure in Linacre, which as an 'inner area' is understandable. But this is not the case for Netherton, which received a relatively low level of support even though it had been given 'inner area' status.

The ward pattern of total expenditure in Liverpool shows that there were five tiers of investment levels during the period. The first was restricted to one ward, Abercromby, which recorded a substantially higher level of investment than any other Liverpool and Merseyside ward. Its expenditure rate for the whole period was in excess of £140,000,000, with the majority occurring in the early and mid 1980s. The wards of Everton and Dingle made up the second tier of investment, with expenditure levels for the whole period in excess of £80,000,000. Everton received a slightly greater level of investment than Dingle and as with Abercromby, the majority of this occurred in the early and mid 1980s. The next discernable tier of investment occurred in St. Mary's and Vauxhall which received funds in excess of £40,000,000, but the timing of this investment was different to the wards already discussed. St. Mary's received a large proportion of its funds in one year, 1987/88, and because of this, nearly half its expenditure occurred in the late 1980s and early 1990s. In Vauxhall, the same pattern was even more exaggerated, with over half its expenditure occurring between 1987/88 and 1990/91. The fourth tier of investment covers those wards which received funds in excess of £10,000,000, which accounts for the majority of Liverpool wards. Those at the upper limit of this group are Granby, Speke, Kensington, Gillmoss and Clubmoor, and those close to the bottom threshold are Dovecot, County and Broadgreen. The fifth and final range of investment comprises those wards below £10,000,000, which defines the areas which were not given any form of priority aid. These wards mainly include the outer suburbs such as Woolton, Childwall and Grassendale, which would have been expected to receive low levels of investment.

The ward expenditure pattern for Knowsley clearly shows how funds were concentrated into two key wards; Tower Hill and Cantril Farm. However, these expenditure levels did not occur at the same time. In Cantril Farm the majority of funds were spent during the mid 1980s, and in Tower Hill the greatest levels of expenditure occurred in the late 1980s and early 1990s. These two wards were consistently targeted by all programmes and the primary reason they dominated the expenditure in Knowsley is because of their severe housing difficulties. The remaining wards in the district received considerably less investment than these two primary areas, but of this general group, six can be distinguished as having received marginally more funds than the majority; Princess, Kirkby Central, Longview, Northwood, Halewood South and Knowsley Park. Of these, only Princess and Northwood recorded large-scale investment during the earlier part of the decade, whilst the rest received their support towards the end of the study period. The Knowsley wards which recorded the lowest levels of expenditure - Swanside, Park, Halewood West and Halewood East - still received a noticeable level of investment in comparison to the other wards. This means, that no one ward received negligible funding and that all areas were able to attract a discernible amount of support.

Wirral's investment profile shows a much more polarised distribution of funds across its wards. The greatest concentration of funds occurred in Birkenhead, which received a total in excess of £35,000,000, whilst Heswall received the lowest level of support £160,122. During the 1980s there were seven ward areas in Wirral which received highly visible levels of investment, in excess of £10,000,000; Birkenhead, Tranmere, Bidston, Seacombe, New Brighton, Bromborough and Claughton. Of this group, Bidston was the only ward which received the majority of its investment during the later part of the decade, all the rest attracted the main bulk of their funds during the early and mid 1980s. A large proportion of Wirral's wards received a total investment of around £5,000,000, such as Oxton, Prenton, Leasowe and Liscard. However, there are six wards which do not fit into this secondary category: first, Wallasey stands alone because it received a total investment of £8,552,132, which distinguishes it from the high and middle range investment bands; and second, there is a group of five wards which received a minimal rate of investment below £2,000,000 - Thurstaston, Roydon, Hoylake, Heswall and Clatterbridge.

One of the most noticeable features about the investment pattern in St. Helens, is that a large number of wards received the majority of their funds in the late 1980s and early 1990s, which could possibly be linked to the district's success in attracting European Funds. This would indicate that the level of support from central government has for the most part taken a back seat in several wards. The four wards in St. Helens which received the highest levels of investment (Parr and Hardshaw, Grange Park, Thatto Heath and West Sutton) all show that a large proportion of their expenditure was concentrated into the final four years of the study period. This is especially true of West Sutton, which spent over 75% of its total programme support between 1987/88 and

1990/91. The majority of the remaining wards in St. Helens recorded expenditure levels between £2,000,000 and £10,000,000, apart from Windle and Rainford, which received investment of £1,017,894 and £352,115, respectively.

## 2.3 Conclusion

The main conclusion that can be drawn from the descriptive analyses, is that the targeting of funds increased during the study period. The ward investment during the earlier part of the decade tended not to be as concentrated as it was at the end of the period. The result of this increased focus, was to accentuate the different levels of investment across wards and to highlight those areas which were prioritised. In general, the 'inner areas' tended to be the most targeted areas, but in certain cases this did not apply. In Sefton, for example, only Linacre could be discerned as a targeted area and this appeared disproportionate to the other wards in the district.

In the later part of the study period the effect of European Funds was quite dramatic in increasing the levels of investment in key areas. This is predominantly due to the restructuring of the funds, which initiated the introduction of the Merseyside Integrated Development Operation.

There appear to have been two contrasting forces which generated the investment profiles of the ward areas. Initially, the targeted operations such as the Merseyside Development Corporation and other large capital developments (DLG, URG) tended to bring about a clear distinction between the wards. Then second, superimposed on this, the social programmes, especially housing operations, tended to reduce these differences in investment. But where there tended to be a lack of large single capital developments, as with Knowsley, the housing investment was utilised under more of a targeted regime.

In the majority of cases, the ward areas which were targeted at the start of the period tended to be those selected throughout the period. It therefore appears that, in terms of targeting, there was no radical change in policy during the past decade. And it was only under certain conditions, where single large-scale developments took place, such as the Upton By-Pass on Wirral, that this general targeting became distorted.

Even though the actual policy changes in the programmes are not revealed by the analysis of total investment, the distribution of the individual schemes gives a certain insight into the way they adapted during the 1980s. Priorities are clearly subject to the wider influences of market forces and changes in legislation. This applies to economic forces, such as rents and house prices, and to legislative and fiscal mechanisms, such as the 1988 Housing Act and interest rates. Such external influences doubtless help to explain the predominant shifts towards capital expenditure and towards 'economic' as opposed to 'social' priorities.

*Figure C10*   **Knowsley Urban Programme expenditure**

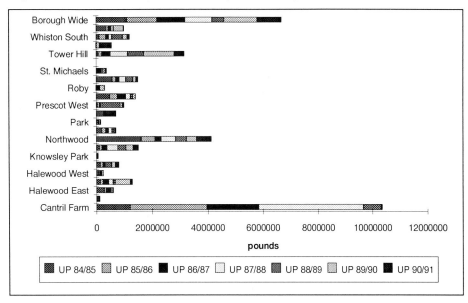

*Figure C11*   **Liverpool Urban Programme expenditure**

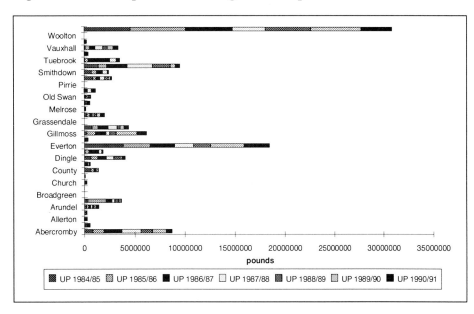

*Figure C12*   **Sefton Urban Programme expenditure**

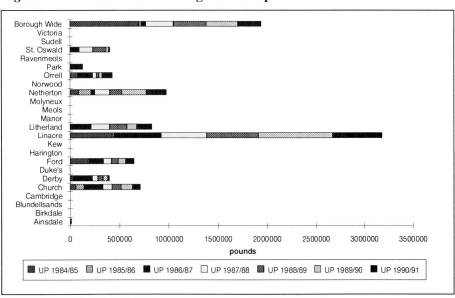

*Figure C13*   **St Helens Urban Programme expenditure**

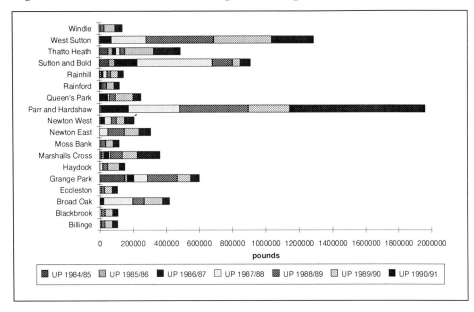

*Figure C14*   **Wirral Urban Programme expenditure**

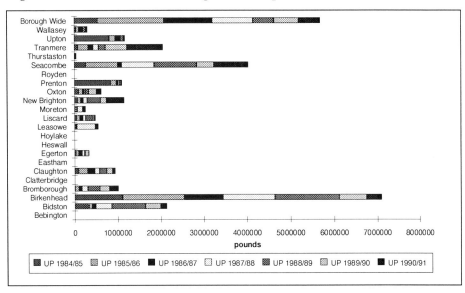

*Figure C15*   **Knowsley DLG**

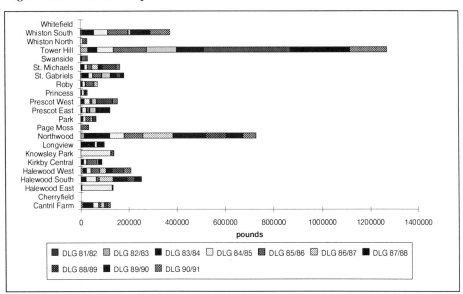

## Figure C16  Liverpool DLG

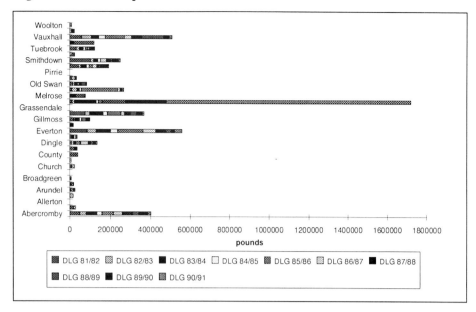

## Figure C17  Sefton DLG

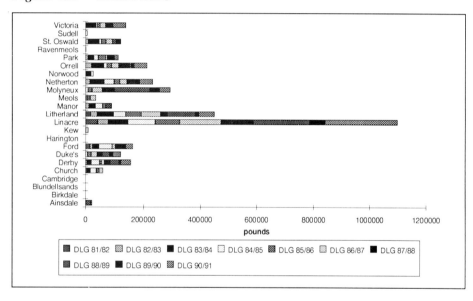

## Figure C18  St Helens DLG

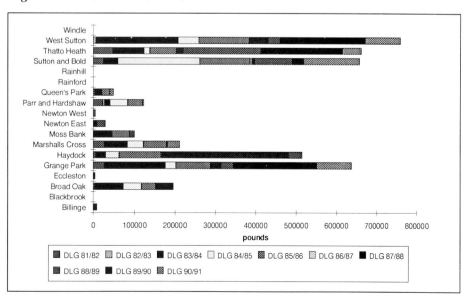

*Figure C19* **Wirral DLG**

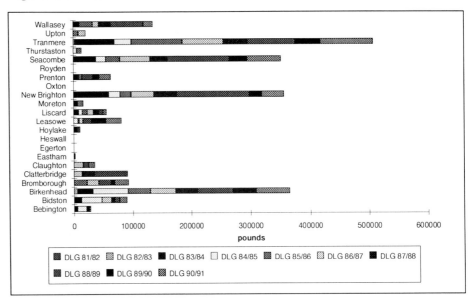

*Figure C20* **Knowsley Housing Corporation expenditure**

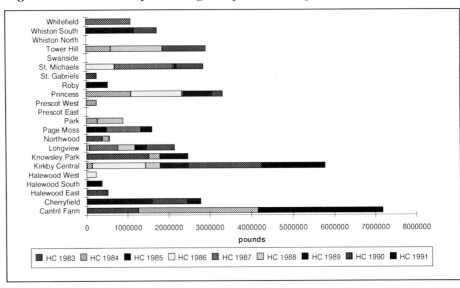

*Figure C21* **Liverpool Housing Corporation expenditure**

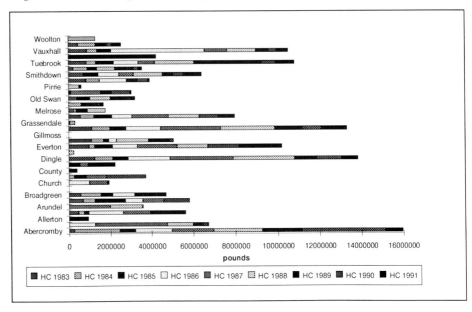

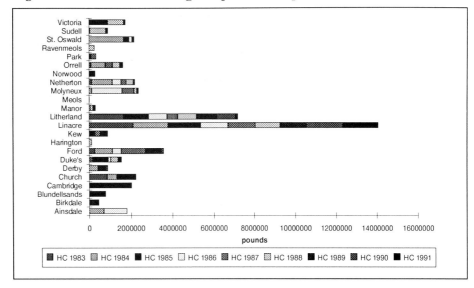

*Figure C22*   **Sefton Housing Corporation expenditure**

*Figure C23*   **St Helens Housing Corporation expenditure**

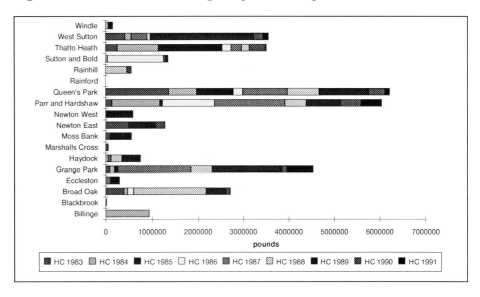

*Figure C24*   **Wirral Housing Corporation expenditure**

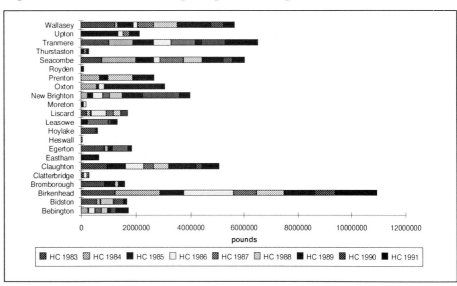

## Figure C25  Knowsley ERDF

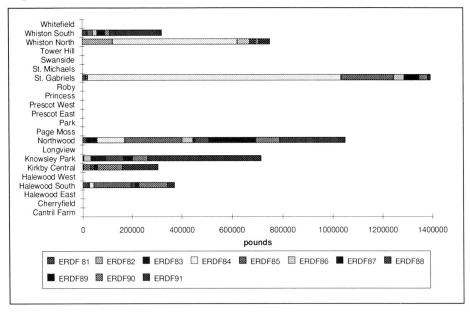

## Figure C26  Liverpool ERDF

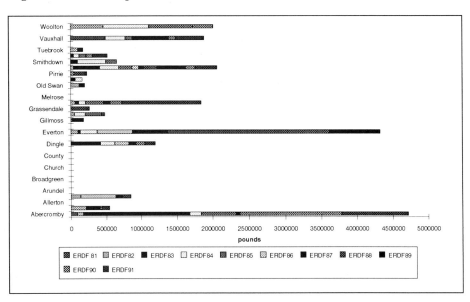

## Figure C27  Sefton ERDF

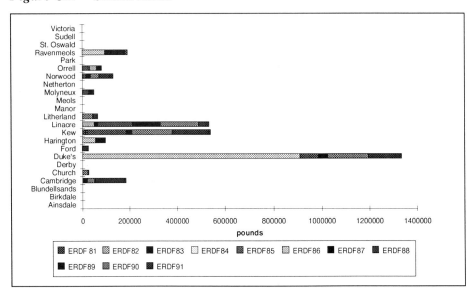

## Figure C28  St Helens ERDF

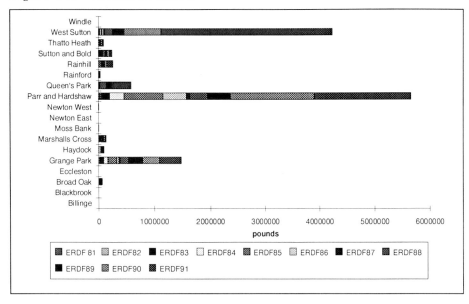

## Figure C29  Wirral ERDF

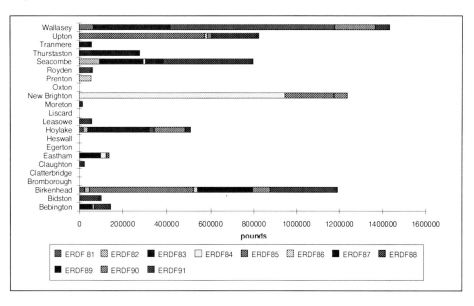

## Figure C30  Knowsley HIP allocation

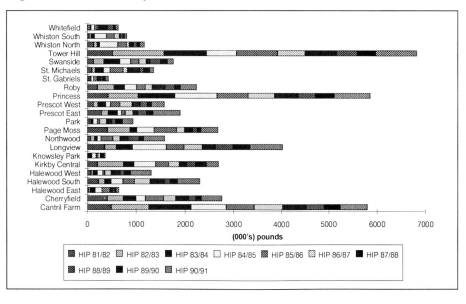

261

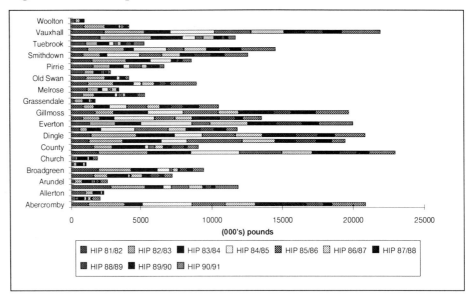

*Figure C31*  **Liverpool HIP allocation**

*Figure C32*  **Sefton HIP allocation**

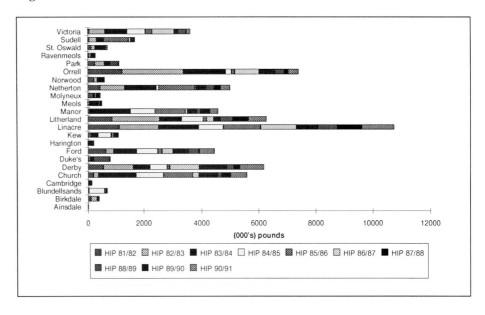

*Figure C33*  **St Helens HIP allocation**

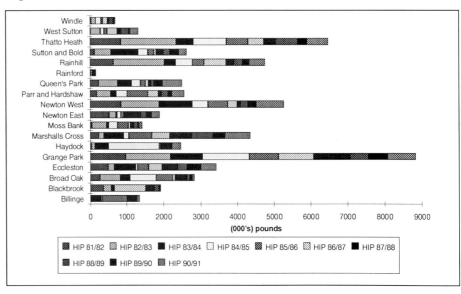

## Figure C34   Wirral HIP allocation

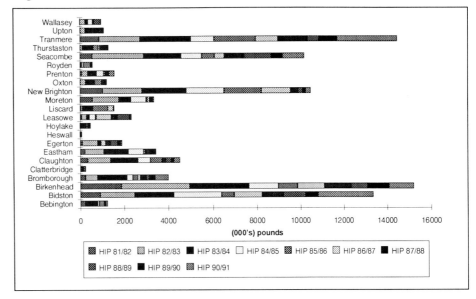

## Figure C35   Wirral Safer Cities expenditure

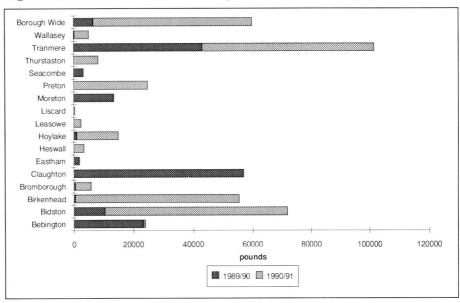

## Figure C36   Allerton EZ expenditure

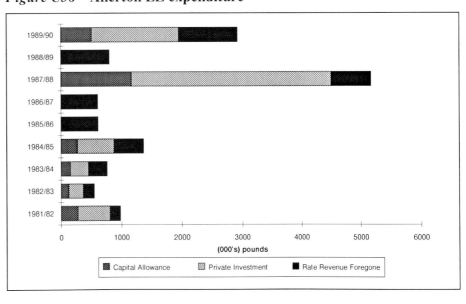

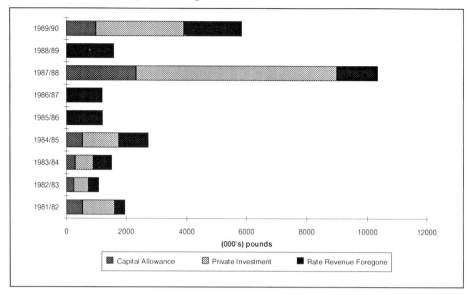

*Figure C37*  St Mary's EZ expenditure

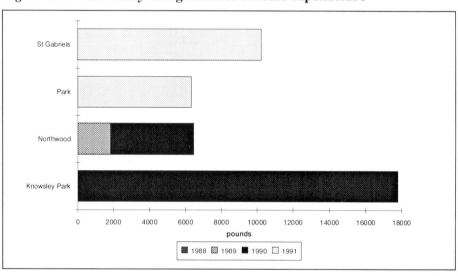

*Figure C38*  Knowsley loal guarantee scheme expenditure

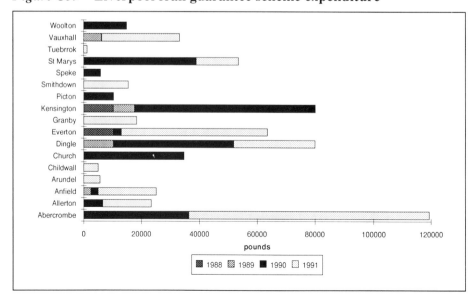

*Figure C39*  Liverpool loan guarantee scheme expenditure

264

**Figure C40**    Sefton loan guarantee scheme expenditure

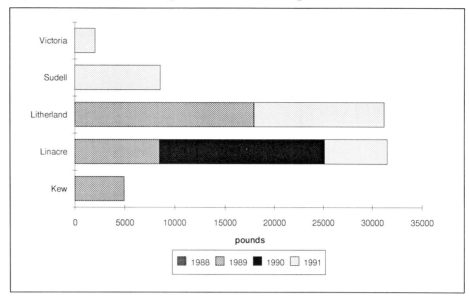

**Figure C41**    St Helens loan guarantee scheme expenditure

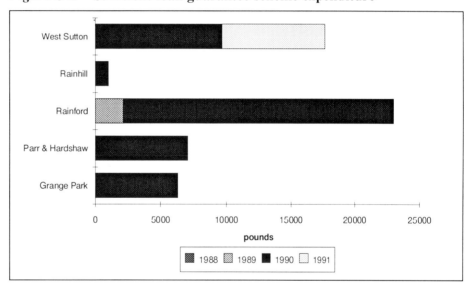

**Figure C42**    Wirral loan guarantee scheme expenditure

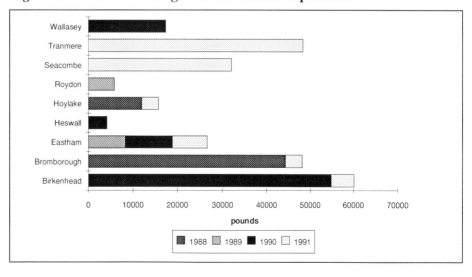

*Figure C43*   **Knowsley estate action expenditure**

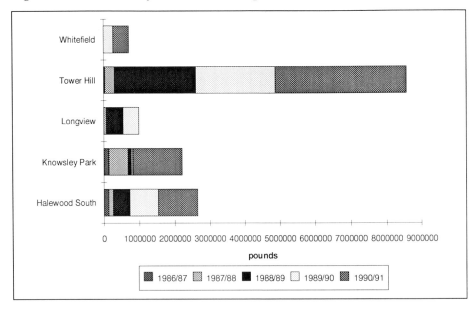

*Figure C44*   **Liverpool estate action expenditure**

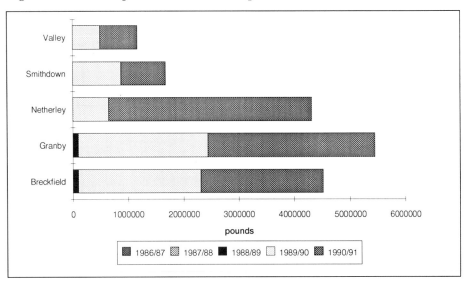

*Figure C45*   **St Helens estate action expenditure**

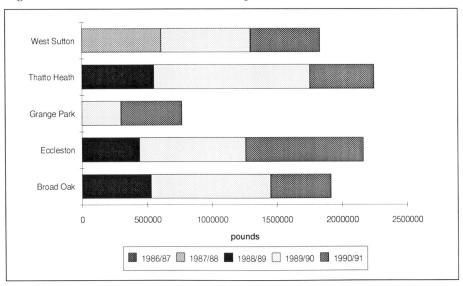

266

*Figure C46* **Wirral estate action expenditure**

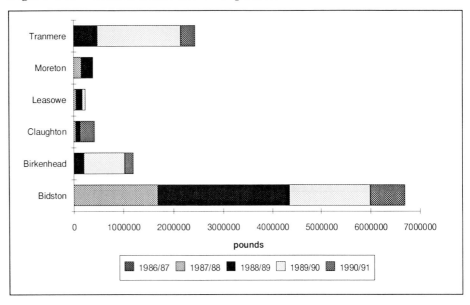

*Figure C47* **Knowsley English Estates expenditure**

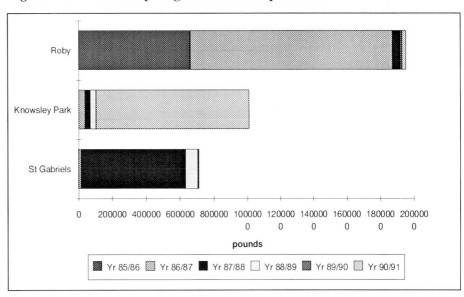

*Figure C48* **Liverpool English Estates expenditure**

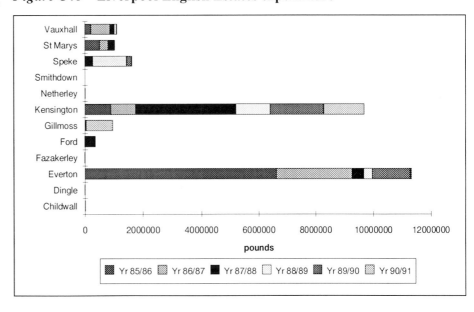

**Figure C49**   Sefton English Estates expenditure

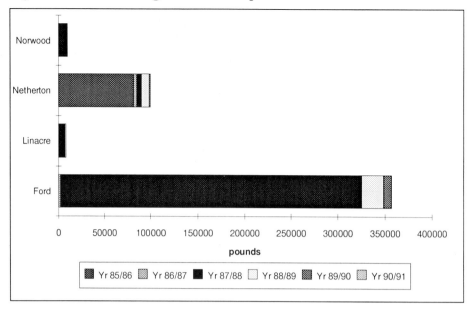

**Figure C50**   St Helens English Estates expenditure

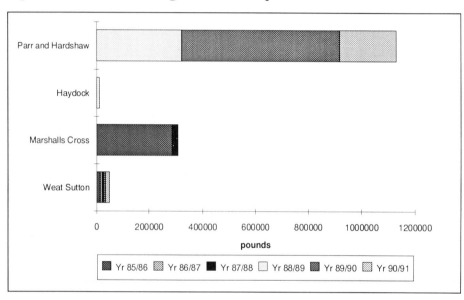

**Figure C51**   Wirral English Estates expenditure

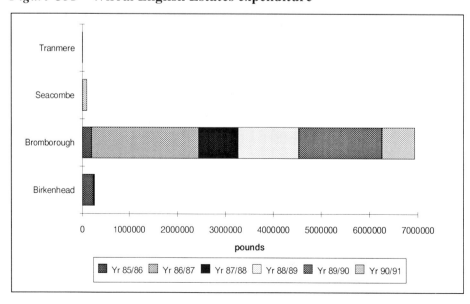

## *Figure C52*  Knowsley total ward investment

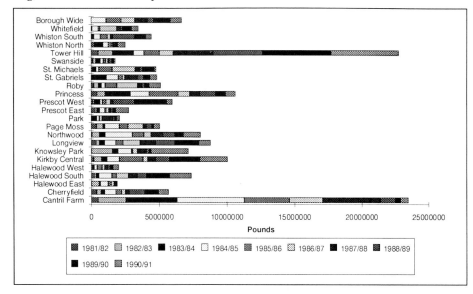

## *Figure C53*  Liverpool total ward investment

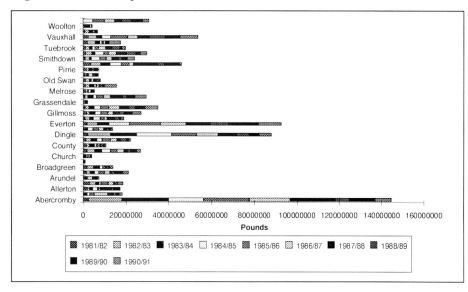

## *Figure C54*  Sefton total ward investment

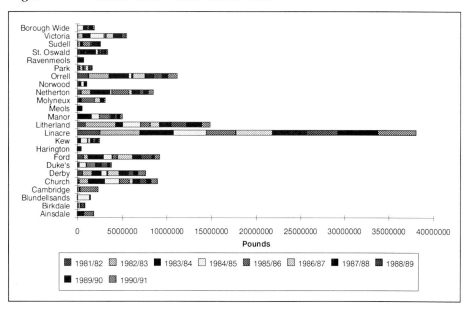

## *Figure C55*   St Helens total ward investment

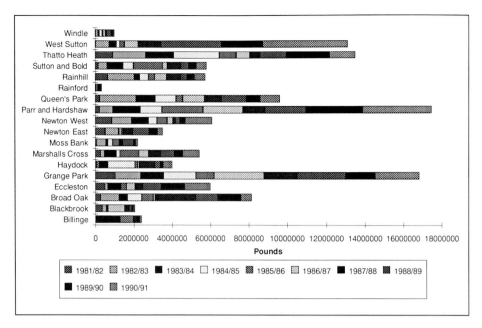

## *Figure C56*   Wirral total ward investment

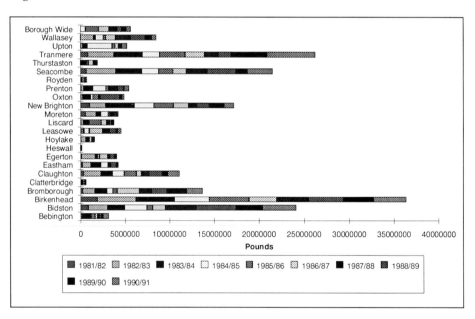

# 3 TYNE AND WEAR

The North East has long been the subject of government attention aimed at countering the effects of economic downturn and poverty, with industrial, employment and, in particular, regional policies directed at the area since the 1930s and 1940s. Together with Merseyside and Clydeside, Tyneside has traditionally been perceived as one of Britain's most deprived areas and has, as a consequence, been something of a testing ground for government policy. From the early regional policy initiatives of the 1930s, through the comprehensive redevelopment programmes following the war, the social and community initiatives of the late 1960s and early 1970s, and the property-led regeneration of the 1980s, Tyneside has been in receipt of a vast range of diverse policy instruments. In the last decade alone, the area has seen a whole raft of initiatives, ranging from grand 'flagship' developments promoted by Tyne and Wear Development Corporation, to small-scale community projects funded by the Urban Programme. But throughout all of these measures, and over all of these years, the feeling has remained, amongst government and public alike, that economic, social and environmental conditions in the conurbation continue to present a problem. This account seeks to review how this range of policy measures has evolved in the conurbation over the last decade by looking at the ways in which policies have impinged upon economic change, and, in turn, how social and economic conditions have helped mould and shape the ways in which policy has been implemented locally. This entails an evaluation of the development and change of the vast array of measures which have impacted upon the area in the last decade, including targeted Action for Cities programmes, funds from the European Community, continued regional funding, and central government cash allocations to local authorities for housing and other mainstream service provision.

Based on interviews with a range of senior policy makers in the North East and the refraction of an extensive database of programme expenditure compiled for the last decade, the first section attempts to trace the development of different strands of urban regeneration by looking, in a broad way, at some of the dominant themes to have emerged with the introduction of a succession of new policy programmes, as well as the shifts in direction and emphasis in existing ones. Many such themes have a distinctively local flavour, in terms both of their conception and implementation, and these are placed within the context of the development of urban policy nationally. This involves an account of the change and development of the local economy and how this has related to the development of policy. In turn, this necessitates an examination of the differing approaches to urban policy and the ways in which these have been implemented through different projects and policy initiatives. In particular, it is useful to look at the contrasting approaches offered, on one hand, by policies geared towards attracting inward investment and, on the other, those which rely on support for small firms; and secondly, by strategies which revolve around the targeting of particular places of need and (in recent years) opportunity, and those people-based strategies which attempt to link local economic development with community needs.

The second section goes on also to look at the evolution of policy in the North East, but this time in a more quantitative way by examining changes in the shape and structure of the policy 'inputs' flowing into the conurbation. Using data compiled for policy programme expenditure in Tyne and Wear, it examines the degree to which local areas have benefited from Action for Cities resources in the light of changes in other sources of funding, such as Rate Support Grant, Housing Investment Programme, regional funding and the European Structural

*Figure C54* **Tyne and Wear wards**

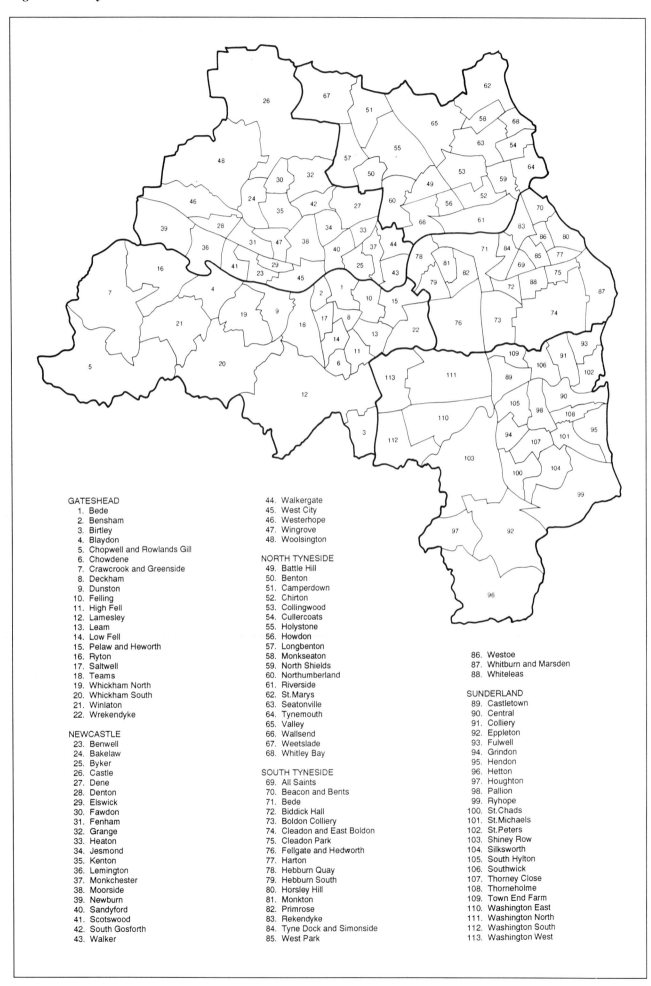

GATESHEAD
1. Bede
2. Bensham
3. Birtley
4. Blaydon
5. Chopwell and Rowlands Gill
6. Chowdene
7. Crawcrook and Greenside
8. Deckham
9. Dunston
10. Felling
11. High Fell
12. Lamesley
13. Leam
14. Low Fell
15. Pelaw and Heworth
16. Ryton
17. Saltwell
18. Teams
19. Whickham North
20. Whickham South
21. Winlaton
22. Wrekendyke

NEWCASTLE
23. Benwell
24. Bakelaw
25. Byker
26. Castle
27. Dene
28. Denton
29. Elswick
30. Fawdon
31. Fenham
32. Grange
33. Heaton
34. Jesmond
35. Kenton
36. Lemington
37. Monkchester
38. Moorside
39. Newburn
40. Sandyford
41. Scotswood
42. South Gosforth
43. Walker

44. Walkergate
45. West City
46. Westerhope
47. Wingrove
48. Woolsington

NORTH TYNESIDE
49. Battle Hill
50. Benton
51. Camperdown
52. Chirton
53. Collingwood
54. Cullercoats
55. Holystone
56. Howdon
57. Longbenton
58. Monkseaton
59. North Shields
60. Northumberland
61. Riverside
62. St.Marys
63. Seatonville
64. Tynemouth
65. Valley
66. Wallsend
67. Weetslade
68. Whitley Bay

SOUTH TYNESIDE
69. All Saints
70. Beacon and Bents
71. Bede
72. Biddick Hall
73. Boldon Colliery
74. Cleadon and East Boldon
75. Cleadon Park
76. Fellgate and Hedworth
77. Harton
78. Hebburn Quay
79. Hebburn South
80. Horsley Hill
81. Monkton
82. Primrose
83. Rekendyke
84. Tyne Dock and Simonside
85. West Park

86. Westoe
87. Whitburn and Marsden
88. Whiteleas

SUNDERLAND
89. Castletown
90. Central
91. Colliery
92. Eppleton
93. Fulwell
94. Grindon
95. Hendon
96. Hetton
97. Houghton
98. Pallion
99. Ryhope
100. St.Chads
101. St.Michaels
102. St.Peters
103. Shiney Row
104. Silksworth
105. South Hylton
106. Southwick
107. Thorney Close
108. Thorneholme
109. Town End Farm
110. Washington East
111. Washington North
112. Washington South
113. Washington West

Funds. Expenditure 'profiles', showing the changing relative and absolute contributions of programmes under each of these headings to the total local 'budgets', are drawn for each of Tyne and Wear's five authorities. This approach is taken further in the third section, which attempts to dissect Action for Cities expenditure by looking in more detail at the ways in which the policy focus has shone on different places and projects at different times. This section concentrates specifically on the Urban Programme, the longest established of the current Action for Cities policy instruments, in order to assess the ways in which it targets particular places, how it focuses on particular types of project and how it relates to spending under other urban policy programmes.

## 3.1 Approaches to urban regeneration in Tyne and Wear: continuity and change in policy

In many respects, Tyne and Wear typifies the development, decline and change of the economies of the older industrial urban regions of Britain and, indeed, of Europe. It is a text-book case of an area which witnessed rapid industrialisation in the nineteenth century, followed by the long-term decline of its staple industries during the twentieth century. It has also served as something of a seedbed for a highly diverse range of public policies aimed at ameliorating the impacts of this industrial decline and the particular problems posed by urban deprivation.

Since the early 1920s, the area's interrelated traditional industries - coal mining, shipbuilding and heavy engineering - have diminished in significance. There have been periods of economic prosperity, notably during the 'long boom' of the 1950s, but the overall trend has been one of gradual decline of this traditional base. For most of the past seventy years or so, Tyne and Wear has been trying to cope with this change, and to establish new kinds of economic activity and attendant opportunities for employment. Public policy has played an important role in this process and Tyne and Wear - and the North East as a whole - has been characterised as a 'policy laboratory' where regional, urban, industrial and labour market policies have been implemented by successive governments. Policy initiatives have had some notable successes, in particular the attraction of new industries under the aegis of regional policy, especially during the 1960s. In spite of such successes, however, high levels of unemployment have remained a prominent and intractable feature of the local economy for many years.

This experience of economic difficulty over a long period of time has helped create and mould an often distinctive set of local institutional policy responses. Concerns about economic development and unemployment have been dominant issues for the area's civil servants, local authorities and many other local agencies in Tyne and Wear. There is a strong sense of some overarching 'regional interest', often distinctive from other parts of the country, which has helped, in many cases, to foster policy initiatives geared towards local and regional needs. And because public policy has been so important in Tyneside and Wearside for so long, a set of well-established institutional structures has coagulated around this regional interest. Complex networks have been created within the local policy community enabling often diverse institutions to work together to deliver policy in a more coherent way, based on considerable consensus amongst a small group of 'key players'.

Over the past decade, this consensus has, if anything, grown stronger and the 'policy community' has become increasingly extensive, complex and pragmatic in response to a stream of new initiatives and institutional mechanisms. Virtually all the policy innovations of the last ten years have been introduced in Tyne and Wear: Enterprise Zones (1981 in Tyneside, 1991 in Sunderland); a City Action Team (1986) an Urban Development Corporation (1987); a Garden

Festival (Gateshead in 1990); a Task Force (South Tyneside in 1991) and City Challenge (1992 in Newcastle, 1993 in North Tyneside and Sunderland). The area has also continued to benefit from regional policy measures and the Urban Programme, while European Funding has become important with the setting up of a Integrated Development Operations Programme (IDOP) and the establishment of the RENEVAL scheme for declining shipbuilding areas. Among many institutional changes, Tyne and Wear County Council was abolished (in 1986) and a new region-wide promotional agency, the Northern Development Company was established.

The past decade has seen considerable policy development which, to a large extent, the area has welcomed, worked with, and used creatively. But how has the direction of policy altered over time, and what have been the dominant themes to have emerged for the region's policy makers? In addressing this question, it is necessary first of all to outline in more detail the changing economic context within which local and regional policies have developed.

## 3.1.1 The policy context: economic development and change

A review of the fortunes of Tyne and Wear over the last ten years necessarily highlights the continuing economic difficulties which the area has had to face, but also reveals significant examples of development and adaptation to economic change. Changes in the economic structure - principally the emergence of a more diverse industrial base - have rendered the local economy less vulnerable in the current economic recession than was the case in the early 1980s. There are also important new developments which symbolise changes wrought in the 1980s, most notably the Metro Centre shopping complex at Gateshead and the Nissan plant at Washington. At the same time, however, it has been a decade in which high unemployment has been a constant feature in Tyne and Wear, relieved only partially during the short-lived boom of the late 1980s, but now, once again, increasing.

The economic recession and restructuring of the early 1980s was expressed in an especially intense and traumatic way in Tyne and Wear. The long-term and steady decline of the traditional industries - which had seen employment in manufacturing industry decline by one third over the course of the 1970s - accelerated rapidly with extensive closure and contraction yielding massive job losses, especially in shipbuilding and heavy engineering. Substantial losses also took place in the branch-plant sector, removing much of the employment in the lighter industries attracted to the area in the 1960s and 1970s. Between 1981 and 1989, over one quarter of employment in manufacturing industry in Tyne and Wear was lost - a fall of almost 38,000 jobs in the space of just eight years. Modest growth in the service sector, mainly in the form of private sector services and especially in part-time employment, was insufficient to compensate for these losses. Although employment in the service sector increased by around one tenth over the course of the 1980s - adding an extra 28,300 jobs - this was insufficient to offset the much larger losses in the primary, manufacturing and construction sectors which, between them, lost almost 46,000 jobs over an eight year period. With an expanding labour force as participation in the labour market increased throughout the decade, the result was that unemployment rates increased markedly.

This major economic upheaval had long-lasting effects and the area had still not fully recovered from the impacts of this process of deindustrialisation when the current recession began. Throughout most of the 1980s, unemployment in Tyne and Wear remained obstinately high, peaking at 18.1% in 1985 and falling until 1990, after which the rate once more began to increase as the current recession took hold. But even at its lowest point in 1990, almost one in ten of the area's economically active population were out of work. Moreover, unemployment rates in Tyne and Wear have consistently been higher than in the country as a whole or, indeed, in the rest of the Northern region. That Tyne and Wear's economy is weak relative to other parts of the country is clearly borne out by a comparison with the South East region, whose unemployment rates during the early and mid 1980s were less than half - and in 1989 less than one third - of those in Tyne and Wear. Only during the current recession has there been some convergence in unemployment rates across parts of the country, although even this is a product of the current recession whose impacts have been particularly severe in the south, rather than any absolute improvement in the Tyne and Wear's economy.

This contrast between north and south is also evident in terms of the nature of unemployment in Tyne and Wear. The unemployment suffered by the area during the 1980s was notable both for its intensity and duration. In contrast to the South East, the unemployment total was composed of a disproportionately large number of long-term unemployed people. Between 1984 and 1986, over 8% of the economically active population of Tyne and Wear had been unemployed for more than one year; in the South East the figure was around 3%.

A further characteristic of unemployment in the North East - and one which has had definite implications for the development of policy - is that the economic recession and restructuring of the 1980s had a clear geographical dimension. Much of the impact of unemployment has been concentrated geographically in a relatively small number of inner-city wards and peripheral estates, where unemployment rates have often exceeded 25% during the 1980s. In 1986, for example, more than two of every five economically active people in Newcastle's West City ward were estimated as out of work and claiming benefit. And although unemployment had fallen by the end of the decade, inner-city areas like Scotswood in Newcastle continued to suffer unemployment rates in excess of one fifth of their economically active populations.

The removal of so much industrial capacity in the early 1980s and the consequent acceleration of unemployment meant that it would take years to rebuild the employment base by attracting new inward investment in manufacturing and by stimulating service sector growth. This process, still far from complete, was brought (temporarily?) to a halt by the present recession. Unemployment once more has begun to rise, again with greatest impact on inner-city areas. After a short-lived period of falling unemployment in the late 1980s, in 1991 and 1992 numbers unemployed again exceeded one in ten. In fact, whereas the unemployment rate in Tyne and Wear, with the exception of one year, has exceeded 10% since 1983, in the South East there has consistently been fewer than one in ten people out of work.

The shake-out of industrial capacity in the early 1980s certainly changed the area's economic structure. In particular, the result was less manufacturing industry and very much less 'traditional' industry, though manufacturing employment subsequently stabilised in the latter half of the 1980s. Much of what was left of the traditional sector after the recession at the start of the decade was removed in subsequent years, now leaving, for example, only one shipyard and (possibly) two collieries in Tyne and Wear. This is one of the main reasons why the recent economic downturn has not hit the area so hard: quite simply, there was much less older industry left which could be vulnerable to falling demand, intensified competition and consequent job loss. By 1989, towards the later part of the 1980s boom, fewer than 100,000 people were employed in manufacturing industry - less than half the number employed at the start of the 1970s and less than three quarters of the number employed just eight years earlier.

But another reason for Tyne and Wear being less hard hit by the current recession (at least, so far) than in the early 1980s, is that it began principally as a reaction to increased indebtedness and falling consumer demand in the south, and the resultant impact on that area's over-expanded service sector. Lower house prices and more manageable mortgages, coupled with an economy less reliant on employment in the hard-hit service sector during the latter part of the 1980s has left Tyne and Wear in a relatively strong position. Moreover, the Northern region's traditional reliance on public sector employment, allied with the substantial proportion of the population dependent on state benefits for their income, meant that a consumer-led boom of the type seen in the South East in the late 1980s was unlikely ever to take full hold of the regional economy. Tyne and Wear missed out on much of the expansion of 1987-89, but has not had to suffer the effects of subsequent retrenchment.

Alongside de-industrialisation there has been a partial re-industrialisation. Nissan's car plant near Sunderland is the best-known example of recent inward manufacturing investment, but equally important has been the build up of offshore fabrication yards on the Tyne, although signs are beginning to emerge that this sector is unlikely to grow much more in future years. There has also, to some extent, been a move towards 'post-industrial' forms of economic development, exemplified by the massive Metro Centre retail complex at Gateshead, waterfront schemes such as the East Quayside development on the Tyne planned by Tyne and Wear Development Corporation (TWDC), and the growth of business parks (rather than 'industrial' estates) like TWDC's 'flagship' Newcastle Business Park, (which houses, among others, offices for British Airways and the AA) and the Boldon Colliery Hi-Tech Village in South Tyneside. De-industrialisation in traditional sectors, coupled with these kinds of new development, has created an economic structure which is now more diverse, dominated less by a small number of interdependent large employers, and therefore less prone to collapse.

This uncertain and partial regeneration notwithstanding, the recession and restructuring of the early 1980s appears to have produced a local labour market which, arguably, is now characterised by a virtually permanent base-load unemployment rate of around one in ten, and much more than this in inner-city areas and deprived peripheral estates. Employment has only just returned to its 1981 level, but remains substantially lower than in the 1970s; there has been a relative decline in regional GDP; and household incomes have fallen. While there is widespread recognition of the gains made in regenerating the area in the last decade - some of them, like the growth of the Team Valley Trading Estate and the Nissan plant, created with direct policy support - there is also a pragmatic acceptance amongst the region's policy makers that the fundamental structural weaknesses of the local economy remain - as exemplified by high unemployment, lack of jobs, a low regional GDP, and low household incomes. Clearly, there are significant problems for policy to address.

3.1.2 Problems and policies

The continuing weaknesses of the local economy present real dilemmas for public policy. Given the local economy's development over the last decade and its likely direction in future, should policies be concerned primarily with economic development, property-led regeneration, or social development?

276

Should policy aim to secure inward investment or indigenous growth, manufacturing or service employment? Is it best to focus policy on places or people, localities or whole regions? These are not, of course, 'either/or' issues but matters of emphasis and degree. In Tyne and Wear, the balance has varied over the past decade with the wax and wane of the numerous policy initiatives applied. But something of a pragmatic consensus appears to have emerged: that all approaches are worthwhile and, perhaps above all, that all resources - whatever the conditions attached to them may be - are worth pursuing to help deal with the area's problems.

There is widespread agreement amongst the area's policy makers that the key issue to be addressed is the structurally-rooted decline of the regional economy and its staple industries. Within the economic context sketched earlier - that is, one of deindustrialisation, high unemployment, limited recovery and, now, a less severe recession than in the south - the problem for policy makers is thus to find and promote new economic activities to replace those which have declined. This has proved difficult, especially in times of recession. But the alternatives - policies aimed at lessening the impacts of unemployment, poverty and physical dereliction - while having more immediate impacts, are often seen by policy makers merely as addressing symptoms, not causes. In Tyne and Wear experience has perhaps shown that both kinds of policy are relevant - and that their effects are likely to be limited. Amongst the conurbation's policy community the general feeling is that many of the area's underlying structural problems remain as stubbornly intractable as ever; realistically, policy initiatives are regarded only as having a marginal, but nonetheless important, impact in the face of wider market forces.

*Attracting inward investment*

The attraction of inward investment in manufacturing industry - 'branch plants' - has traditionally been at the centre of economic development policy in Tyne and Wear. Starting with the Team Valley Trading Estate in Gateshead in the 1930s, successive governments have supported the provision of sites and premises for incoming industry, principally undertaken by English Estates. On a lesser scale, local authorities - particularly the former Tyne and Wear County Council - and more recently, Tyne and Wear Development Corporation, have done the same, and the public sector has long dominated an industrial property market in which the private sector is reluctant to invest.

As well as the provision of sites, premises and infrastructure, incoming industry has also benefited from policy programmes which offer financial subsidies. In previous years this has almost wholly taken the form of regional policy assistance, but now more complex arrangements prevail. Regional aid has become less generous and more selective, but during the last ten years alternative sources of assistance have emerged, notably through Enterprise Zone tax concessions, grants from the UDC, advice and support from the Northern Development Company and, nowadays on a small scale, from the local authorities. Indeed, the availability of assistance from such a wide range of bodies itself is viewed by some as constituting a problem. The result is that agencies often come together under the collective banner of organisations like the Northern Development Company or The Wearside Opportunity (TWO) to present a single case to potential investors. In the case of TWO, for example, an industrial-sites strategy was established in the late 1980s, under the guidance of Nissan's Managing Director, to co-ordinate the promotional and development activities of the local authority, the UDC, English Estates and the Commission for New Towns.

Alongside initiatives geared towards the provision of sites and premises and financial subsidies to investors, the network of agencies - and, in particular, the Northern Development Company - has also striven to cultivate links with foreign companies through intensive promotional work marketing the region's attractions. The attraction of foreign investment in this way has become an even greater priority with the apparent success of Nissan and the fact that Far Eastern plants accounted for 40% of all new jobs provided by new inward investment in the 1980s. This explains the focus on Japan and the Far East, as with The Newcastle Initiative's promotional programme - 'Japan Links: Where East Meets West' - designed to build upon existing Japanese investment in the region by encouraging new links with companies in the Far East.

These strategies for attracting inward investment differ substantially from those of the 1960s, when economic expansion, coupled with considerable regional policy intervention, helped stimulate industrial mobility, with the result that Tyne and Wear was able to attract many branch plants. Subsequently, however, in the late 1970s and early 1980s, many of these branches closed as companies, under pressure, sought to cut capacity, reduce costs and restructure, prompting a reassessment of the worth of inward investment amongst policy makers. The branch-plant syndrome came to be seen as damaging, and the wisdom of heavy subsidies called into question. A major criticism among today's policy community is that the 'untargeted' system of grants distorted the relocations process so that many branch plants were set up as short-term operations which moved away once the cash-flow benefits of those grants had worked their way out of the system.

In the past ten years, the attraction of industry to the area through the mechanisms outlined has proved much more difficult than it was in the 1960s, for a variety of reasons. For a start, there have been fewer mobile plants, and much more competition for them, often from other regions in the UK and Europe, many of them possessing formal development agencies with greater resources, such as the Welsh Development Agency and Scottish Enterprise's overseas promotional arm, Locate in Scotland. Moreover, in the last two years or so recession has reduced even further the supply of potential inward investors. Nevertheless, Tyne and Wear has been successful in attracting some significant inward investors during the decade. The largest and most celebrated example is Nissan's car factory, but the 1980s also witnessed the arrival of Findus, Komatsu, Mitsumi and Goldstar - all of them foreign-owned. Inward investment has undoubtedly helped in the regeneration of the local economy and has provided large numbers of jobs. Team Valley, for example, has continued to attract new industry and now provides over 16,000 jobs, making it the most important industrial centre in Tyne and Wear. In recent years, much of this expansion has taken the form of office-based 'B1' employment (as in the case of much of the Fifth Avenue Business Park within Team Valley) which differs markedly in character from 'traditional' industrial uses.

But the greatest success remains Nissan, which is almost universally held up by the policy community as perhaps the single most encouraging and important event in the regeneration of the North East in the 1980s. Since setting up in Washington in the mid-1980s, the plant has developed and grown, and now employs over 4000 people. There has also been a significant number of component suppliers and sub-contractors which have been established on the back of the car plant, adding to its impact. Furthermore, policy makers point towards the importance of Nissan in terms of the area's image and self confidence, which in turn has knock-on benefits in helping to foster further economic development. Nissan is regarded as providing an exemplar - in its concern with quality and customer care, for example - which existing firms can learn from and follow.

Nevertheless, worries still remain about the strategy of promoting inward investment. It is hoped that more recent arrivals, like Nissan and Komatsu, are more committed to the area, because of their levels of investment and supply networks, than were the 1960s' branch plants. This commitment to the area would certainly seem to be borne out by Nissan's recent decision to centralise its import-export facility at a deep water port at South Tyneside owned and managed by the Port of Tyne Authority, and by the company's decision to increase the number of cars produced at the plant by 100,000 to 270,000 in 1993. It is also argued by policy makers that newer relocations are 'more genuine' now that 'bribes' (that is, grants for relocation) are fewer in number and lower in value. There is nervousness, though, about the powerless that comes with the external control of much of the area's industry, although this is tempered by an understanding that the local economy must inevitably be an open one. Indeed, it is this openness which, in many cases, has attracted companies like Nissan which want to produce within the Single European Market.

In any case, the policy community has a strong imperative to compete for mobile investment since the potential pay-off can be large, bringing significant investment and many jobs. The local and regional institutions (particularly the Northern Development Company) are geared up to 'selling' the area, marketing a package of incentives and an environment which is pro-business and good on 'quality of life'. In attempting to do this, the region has significant advantages over the promotional agencies of similar regions competing for inward investment. While its counterparts in the North West and Yorkshire and Humberside are restricted mainly to smaller-scale promotional activities, the NDC itself is able to offer a much broader package of incentives to inward investors. Compared to other agencies, the NDC is better resourced (with a budget in 1990/91 greater than the combined total for its counterparts in Yorkshire and Humberside and the North West), has more staff, has more overseas offices and operates in something more akin to a 'natural' region. Moreover, the NDC - following from its predecessor, the Northern Economic Development Council, which was supported by the former Tyne and Wear County Council - has stronger support from its constituent local authorities, both in terms of funding and co-operation.

Interestingly, it has proved easier to sell the area to overseas investors than to British industrialists, apparently not least because there is less need to overcome prejudices. The competitiveness is, however, intense, and while these efforts do yield results from time to time the strategy is unlikely significantly to reduce the area's unemployment problems. While new inward investment during the 1980s provided almost 15,000 new jobs in the Northern region, this represents only one twentieth of total manufacturing employment in the region. The general feeling in the policy community in Tyne and Wear appears to be that while inward investment has an important role to play, this should form only one of a number of linked strategies for regeneration.

*Small business development*

Inward investment appears often to be viewed by the region's policy makers as essentially a short-term strategy; necessary, but limited. In the longer-term, the establishment of indigenous enterprise is generally felt to be crucial in fostering a sustainable economy and creating a wider provincial regeneration. Throughout the 1980s, there was an increasing emphasis on assisting the growth of indigenous enterprise, promoting self-employment and developing small firms. In Tyne and Wear, a substantial support infrastructure for such enterprise was created; a complicated network of increasingly specialised agencies was built up and the local authorities' economic development units also developed expertise in this field. This support infrastructure is now highly complex - to the point, almost, of engendering confusion - but seems to be reaching some maturity through specialisation, 'signposting' between agencies and a degree of rationalisation towards 'one stop' agencies such as Tyne and Wear Enterprise Trust (Entrust), the Northern Development Company (NDC) and The Wearside Opportunity (TWO). Many of these organisations work together in partnership, as in the case of Northern Enterprise, a body set up by the NDC, Project North East and Entrust to provide loans for expansion to small and medium sized companies; or the Tyne and Wear Enterprise Loan Fund, established by Entrust, the City Action Team and Barclays Bank to offer a lower rate loan scheme to small businesses. There have also been some attempts to tap into sources of European funding for small businesses. Wearside TEC, for example, has established an office in Brussels to represent the area's business community in Europe, to increase awareness amongst companies of the benefits on offer and to promote Wearside in Europe.

Tyne and Wear, with its 'employee culture' and tradition of large employers, has had relatively few small businesses so that this sector has had to be built up from a low base. The relative lack of personal capital and the lack of buoyancy in the local economy as a whole also sets limits on the growth of small businesses. Nonetheless, there has been some success in stimulating small business development, though growth - from a low base - has been well below levels achieved in many other parts of the country. While the number of small businesses in Tyne and Wear grew by almost one fifth between 1979 and 1990, this was considerably lower than the near one third increase in small firms in the UK as a whole. Perhaps more encouragingly, a relatively large proportion of this growth in Tyne and Wear was of manufacturing companies, which grew in number by over one third. Conversely, the most rapid rate of growth in the South East region was of construction and service based small firms, very much reflecting the particular characteristics of the economic boom, and subsequent recession, in that region.

After several years of initiatives and considerable policy commitment and effort, it is increasingly becoming clear that while stimulating the small business sector is a useful approach it is unlikely to make much of an impact on the local economy except, possibly, in the very long term. The majority - around three quarters - of small businesses are service-based, a figure which has remained constant throughout the last decade. Moreover, this figure is, if anything, slightly greater than in the South East region, which is viewed as an area whose economy is over dependent on service industries. The feeling amongst many of the region's policy makers is that the small business sector is too service-oriented; that new small businesses often simply displace other local businesses; that many fail after a short period; and that few grow to become substantial employers. This view has led to the beginnings of a reorientation of support services for small businesses in the region, with the scaling down of efforts to encourage small-firm start-ups and a growing emphasis on concentrating support on the small number of established small businesses which are growing, or show the potential to grow, at a rapid rate and which could employ large numbers in future years. But while there is widespread recognition of the worth of bodies like Entrust in supporting small-firm expansion in this way, as with inward investment strategies there is a strong feeling in the policy community that small business strategies are of value, but only when coupled with other strategies for economic development.

While regional policy covers the whole of Tyne and Wear (and much of the North East), most other policies are more spatially focused. Urban policy concentrates resources specifically on the inner areas but, within this, different measures operate within different boundaries. The spatial scale ranges from the relatively small areas covered by Enterprise Zones to the extensive coverage of the Urban Programme. The resulting policy map is one of a series of overlapping policy areas of differing levels of priority and assistance.

In general, these spatially targeted policy instruments have had the effect of distorting markets and structuring spatial opportunities for investment. At the regional policy level, Tyne and Wear's Assisted Area status has enabled it to compete with other regions for inward investment, while within Tyneside and Wearside urban policy has made some inner-city locations more attractive than they would otherwise have been. The aim, and the result, in essence has been to influence the location of economic development.

The Tyneside Enterprise Zone, in operation between 1981 and 1991, was especially effective in attracting - or, arguably, in diverting - economic development. Two of the key property development projects of the last ten years, the Metro Centre and Newcastle Business Park, were developed within the EZ area adjacent to the Tyne. Likewise, the southern part of Team Valley, also with Enterprise Zone status, took a large share of new peripheral office development in the 1980s. The tax concessions and rates holiday undoubtedly helped make these locations more attractive to developers. But the particularly strong backing for the Tyneside EZ 'experiment' amongst the region's policy makers seems to be as much to do with the supportive policies of other public sector institutions, such as English Estates (in the case of Team Valley), Gateshead Council (for the Metro Centre) and Tyne and Wear Development Corporation (in relation to the Business Park). Many policy makers argue that the apparent success of the Tyneside Enterprise Zone can be explained not just by the tax concessions on offer, important though these were, but by the whole 'package' offered by this network of support agencies.

It remains a moot point whether much of the new development would have taken place without the support of Enterprise Zone incentives. In the absence of the EZ, much of the development may have taken place elsewhere in Tyne and Wear, though the EZ may have resulted in these developments being larger and more coherent than they would otherwise have been. What is less debatable - and more disappointing - is that there may have been little net increase in economic activity and employment. The Metro Centre inevitably displaces retail employment from other parts of Tyne and Wear and the region, while many of the newcomers to the Team Valley area and Newcastle Business Park have merely relocated from other parts of the conurbation. Over two-thirds of the jobs at Newcastle Business Park, for example, have simply been moved from other locations in Tyne and Wear. Equally, it may be the case that many of the relocated jobs would have moved outside the region altogether were it not for the incentives offered by siting in an EZ area, exacerbating the area's already severe economic problems.

Tyne and Wear Development Corporation (TWDC) has had a similar impact in the inner areas along the banks of both the Tyne and the Wear. Site acquisition, reclamation, servicing and subsidies have encouraged development in these areas and supported existing activities. But - as in the case of Newcastle Business Park, which is in the TWDC's area as well as having been in the Enterprise Zone - much of the incoming activity has comprised short-distance moves and, arguably, some of the new companies would otherwise have gone to locations elsewhere in Tyne and Wear. But, also like the Enterprise Zone, proponents of TWDC point out that developments such as the Business Park serve to 'lock in' to the regional economy companies which might otherwise have relocated outside the North East.

Perhaps the main achievement of spatially targeted policies like the Enterprise Zone, the UDC, City Grant, Urban Programme economic development initiatives, and even the Garden Festival, has thus been to promote and retain development, bringing inner-city sites into use and, indeed, making them usable and marketable. These policies do connect, up to a point, with efforts to attract inward investment in economic activity, but the main impact may be to divert development which might 'naturally' have gone to the periphery. Furthermore, it is apparent that neither the attraction of inward investment nor the diversion of development is facilitated by recession - as shown by Sunderland's new Enterprise Zone which, so far, has attracted very little development either from within the conurbation or from incoming investors.

This emphasis on the inner areas in terms of specific policy instruments does not, however, go unchallenged. One of the lessons from the success of Washington New Town in the 1970s and the attraction of Nissan in the 1980s, has been that large-scale incoming industry generally has a preference for greenfield peripheral sites with good road links. Consequently, Newcastle is proposing in its Unitary Development Plan the opening up of peripheral green belt sites for industrial and business park development, thereby overcoming what the council views as a chronic shortage of developable land - a shortage which, according to some commentators, applies particularly to large industrial sites. Similarly, North Tyneside, through its successful City Challenge bid, is attempting to promote large-scale industrial development in the A19 corridor, while South Tyneside has used Urban Programme funding to market Boldon Business Park (which, again, is linked into the A1 and A19 trunk routes south) for sizeable incoming companies, arguably in competition with TWDC's attempts to regenerate the inner riverside area of the borough. This spatial competition, between inner and outer areas and 'brownfield' and 'greenfield' sites, is also accompanied by competition between Tyne and Wear's districts. Gateshead's Metro Centre thus acts as a competitor to Newcastle's Eldon Square, while Sunderland's efforts to attract industry to what the local Business Leadership Team (BLT) - The Wearside Opportunity - term the 'Advanced Manufacturing Centre of the North' mean that it competes with the other districts, all no less anxious to secure investment and jobs.

*Targeting people*

In past years policy in Tyne and Wear has predominantly targeted particular places, but recently there has been a discernible shift from place-based to people-based targeting - or at least a coupling of the two. Increasing concern about marginalised groups, the perceived failure of 'trickle down' and disappointment with property-led regeneration has brought new interest in the idea of targeting particular groups of people, often in particular places. This has been reflected in changes within government policies - notably the development of City Challenge - and is particularly pertinent in the Tyne and Wear context in the wake of the 1991 riots on the Meadow Well estate and in the West End of Newcastle. These events came as a real shock to the local policy community and prompted something of a re-assessment of existing policy approaches.

To a large extent, the urban policies pioneered in the 1980s were in the inner city, but not of it. They helped stimulate development in Tyne and Wear's inner areas, but this was not linked to local communities, with, in many cases, the benefits to local people living in the inner areas at best hidden and at worst absent. Without relevant experience or skills many of these people, often long-term unemployed, have been unable to compete for those new jobs which have been created. Conventional 'head-counting' training initiatives like Youth Training and Employment Training have been perceived largely as failing to reach the most disadvantaged groups and increasingly are regarded with scepticism by policy makers and deliverers. Moreover, the need is often not for specific training but, rather, confidence building and basic numeracy and literacy skills.

A number of innovative projects aimed at addressing this fissure between economic development and community benefit have been developed in Tyne and Wear in recent years. The best known is the Cruddas Park initiative in the West End of Newcastle, which provides counselling for unemployed people, a local job centre service, access to training and support for community businesses, all of it co-ordinated from the Community Employment and Enterprise Centre based in the local shopping centre. This project was established with help from The Newcastle Initiative, one of the first Business Leadership Teams, and has successfully drawn in resources from a wide range of private and public institutions such as Bunzl plc, Barclays Bank, Ernst and Young, Newcastle City Council, the Departments of Environment and Employment, the Employment Service, TWDC and Tyneside TEC.

The Cruddas Park estate, which has some of the highest levels of unemployment, deprivation and poverty in the whole city, has gained some improvements through this targeted approach. Some residents have benefited through finding work or training places, and there is a range of services on offer to residents to help them secure work. Under the Job Interview Guarantee heading, for example, residents and businesses in the Cruddas Park and Loadman Street areas are offered a service matching employer vacancies with local residents' skills; funding for work-place trials for unemployed people; job preparation courses which seek to boost confidence amongst unemployed people through counselling; and customised training packages for both job seekers and employers. In addition, much of the area is benefiting from Estate Action support, most notably for security improvements, following liaison with community groups under the Community Trust umbrella.

Similar, though less intensive (and less expensive) projects have been developed throughout Tyne and Wear. In many of these projects the employment impact has often been limited in strict numerical terms - not surprisingly given the dearth of jobs region-wide - but, for some people at least, they have provided an opportunity to escape unemployment and benefit from economic development projects which might otherwise go to people already in employment, people from outside the immediate area, or people already possessing skills. Small-scale and locally tailored and delivered projects, involving counselling, training and some community-based employment have been set up, with funding from various sources including the Urban Programme, the TECs, the Employment Service and local authorities. The communities of Town End Farm, Hylton Castle, Downhill and other deprived areas in the north western part of Sunderland, for example, have benefited from the North Sunderland Community Business Centre, offering pioneering training projects geared to the needs of long-term unemployed people. This involved direct input from large employers to the creation of training packages, following on from the early involvement of Nissan in the project. The Town End Farm estate benefited from the establishment of a Community Enterprise Forum which, with the support of public sector bodies, employers and the Community Business Centre, offers a

Community Job Shop and pre-employment training courses. The latter, which cater for small groups of 10-12 people over a six-week period, have an 80% success rate of getting people into jobs.

Initiatives of this sort have also increasingly been pursued by TWDC, anxious to try to ensure that some of the benefits from property-led regeneration reach local people living in areas adjacent to its 'flagship' projects. In particular, on the Meadow Well estate, which adjoins the Corporation's Royal Quays development - a mixed use scheme at the former Albert Edward Dock containing housing, retailing and industry but which focuses upon a proposed waterpark, marina and leisure facilities - TWDC have supported pre-employment counselling courses, training schemes, and community self help initiatives. Many of these initiatives are co-ordinated from a Community Employment Office established by the Corporation at its Royal Quays site. TWDC has also sought to encourage local recruitment, through a Code of Conduct for contractors and developers which encourages them first to advertise jobs locally and to provide regular information on the recruitment they have undertaken. The Corporation, with backing from Wimpey and Tyneside TEC, has also established a construction crafts training centre at nearby West Chirton which also aims to ensure that local people benefit from the development. Many of these initiatives have been overseen by a local 'monitoring panel', established by the Corporation to liaise with the local community.

The focus on people, and on residential areas, often involving a multi-agency partnership approach, was becoming well established in Tyne and Wear even before the introduction of City Challenge. Indeed, it is claimed by some in the policy community that the experience of a multi-agency approach in targeting Cruddas Park helped to mould the City Council's successful bid for City Challenge funding for 1992-97. City Challenge itself has been taken up with enthusiasm in Tyne and Wear. The West End of Newcastle is the area chosen by the city during the first 'pacemaker' round of City Challenge, while North Tyneside and Sunderland were successful bidders in round two and are currently preparing their Action Plans. The dominant view amongst policy makers appears to be that City Challenge offers the opportunity to put into practice a more 'corporate' approach, which expands upon and formalises the successful pioneering efforts of partnership initiatives targeted on people in defined places, such as the Cruddas Park initiative. Local political criticisms about the competitive nature of the exercise have been relatively muted, though concerns about the wider lack of resources - cuts in mainstream spending alongside the extra money provided by City Challenge - have been prominent. In general, however, the policy community in Tyne and Wear has responded to City Challenge in the same pragmatic way it has responded to almost all of the diverse range of new initiatives which have been directed at the area over the last decade: keen to win resources and implement policy as effectively as possible by taking account of local circumstances and adding a distinctively local flavour to policy initiatives.

## 3.2 The changing structure of urban policy in Tyne and Wear

The five authorities of Tyne and Wear have been subject to a wide range of programmes over the course of the 1980s. These differ considerably in size and extent, varying not just from year to year, but also between authorities. They range from the key set of core programmes, like Rate Support Grant and Housing Investment Programme, through large-scale spatially-targeted programmes like Enterprise Zones and Urban Development Corporations, to project-oriented programmes like Derelict Land Grant and the Urban Programme.

In total, expenditure data have been collected for sixteen central government programmes in England; fourteen of which were in operation in Tyne and Wear during the period 1979/80-1990/91. Figure C59 shows these programmes, ranked in order of their total contribution to expenditure between 1979/80 and 1990/91. Together, they have provided over £5 billion of expenditure since 1979/80.

*Figure C59*   **Tyne and Wear - total programme expenditure 1979/80-1990/91**

| | Undeflated totals | | | | Deflated totals (constant 1981/82 prices) | | |
|---|---|---|---|---|---|---|---|
| | Total | PC | % Total | | Total | PC | % Total |
| RSG | 3717880.13 | 3252.46 | 70.68 | RSG | 3148887.01 | 2754.70 | 71.17 |
| HIPS | 497336.00 | 435.08 | 9.45 | HIPS | 466386.10 | 408.00 | 10.54 |
| UP | 301010.00 | 263.33 | 5.72 | UP | 247030.52 | 216.11 | 5.58 |
| REG | 211662.79 | 185.17 | 4.02 | REG | 164323.60 | 143.75 | 3.71 |
| EURO | 167718.00 | 146.72 | 3.19 | EURO | 134225.60 | 117.42 | 3.03 |
| EZ | 136057.45 | 119.03 | 2.59 | EZ | 105571.67 | 92.36 | 2.39 |
| UDC | 92811.00 | 81.19 | 1.76 | UDC | 59129.92 | 51.73 | 1.34 |
| DLG | 39316.44 | 34.39 | 0.75 | DLG | 30816.16 | 26.96 | 0.70 |
| EE | 39081.58 | 34.19 | 0.74 | EE | 27232.29 | 23.82 | 0.62 |
| UDG/URG/CG | 22590.00 | 19.76 | 0.43 | UDG/URG/CG | 16733.49 | 14.64 | 0.38 |
| EA | 23067.50 | 20.18 | 0.44 | EA | 16220.80 | 14.19 | 0.37 |
| CAT | 8126.69 | 7.11 | 0.15 | CAT | 5597.00 | 4.90 | 0.13 |
| S11 | 3127.30 | 2.74 | 0.60 | S11 | 2193.74 | 1.92 | 0.50 |
| SC | 439.17 | 0.38 | 0.10 | SC | 270.95 | 0.24 | 0.10 |
| EMBI | 0.00 | 0.00 | 0.00 | EMBI | 0.00 | 0.00 | 0.00 |
| TF | 0.00 | 0.00 | 0.00 | TF | 0.00 | 0.00 | 0.00 |
| | 5260224.05 | 4601.73 | 100.00 | | 4424618.85 | 3870.74 | 100.00 |

Rate Support Grant (RSG) is by far the most important source of central government funds to local areas. Over the twelve financial years for which data have been compiled, RSG for the five districts amounted to £3,148.89m at constant 1981/82 prices. This represents 71.17% of the combined total of programme expenditure in the conurbation. When combined with expenditure under the Housing Investment Programme (HIP), which accounts for 10.54% of all expenditure, the five local areas received 81.71% of spending from just two programmes.

Although the remaining twelve programmes account for less than one fifth (18.29%) of total expenditure, nonetheless their spatially and/or project-oriented focus means, in many cases, that they have strong and tangible effects for tightly defined areas. The Urban Programme (UP), for example, contributed some 5.58% towards total expenditure in Tyne and Wear (£247.03m), but concentrated largely within targeted 'inner area' boundaries. Likewise, Enterprise Zone (EZ) expenditure amounted to £134.22m (3.03% of total spend), but unlike HIP and RSG, concentrated on a tightly defined area in only two of the five authorities (Gateshead and Newcastle). Moreover, it should be borne in mind that many of the fourteen programmes have been in operation for only a few of the twelve years for which data have been collected. Tyne and Wear Development Corporation's £59.13m of spending has been compressed into four financial years, again in specific, well-defined parts of four of the five authorities (Gateshead being the exception).

**3.2.1 Squeezing 'core' resources?**

In absolute terms, expenditure in the five authorities rose from £339.28m in 1979/80 to £547.82m in 1989/90, an increase of 61.46%. At constant 1981/82 prices, however, this represents a reduction in expenditure of almost one fifth

(19.39%), falling from £440.23m to £354.90m. Figure C60 illustrates how total expenditure in Tyne and Wear has declined steadily through the 1980s. In real terms, the conurbation was receiving £85.33m less in 1989/90 than in 1979/80. This overall loss is explained principally by large reductions in local authority RSG and HIP budgets. Together, the reductions in expenditure on these programmes more than outweigh the smaller expenditure gains accruing through the introduction of new programmes over the decade. Figure C61 shows how expenditure in Tyne and Wear has changed since 1979/80, and the changing contributions made to the annual expenditure totals by different government programmes. RSG and, to an even greater extent, HIP expenditure have been heavily squeezed, but not fully compensated for by the expansion of other programmes, under the Action for Cities, 'European' or 'regional' headings.

*Figure C61*   **Tyne and Wear - composition of funding (constant 1981/82 prices)**

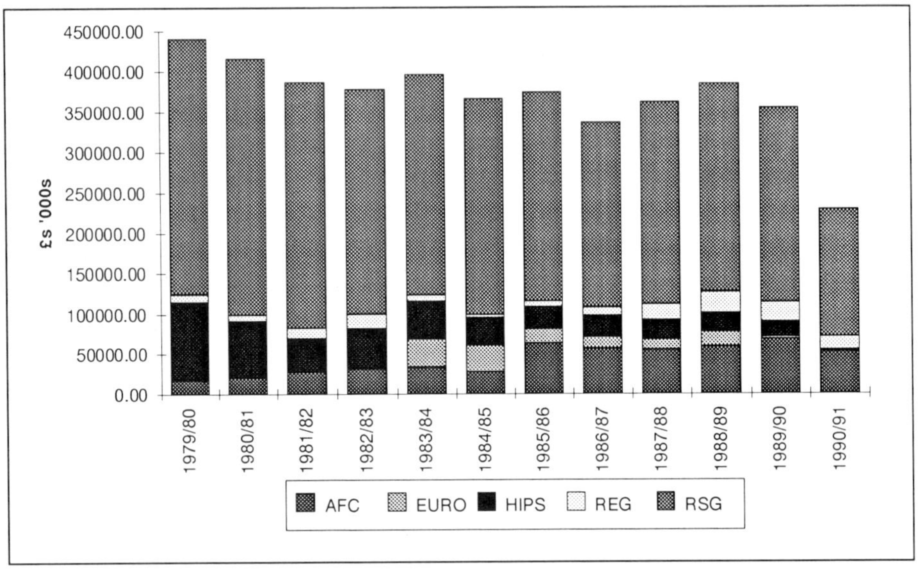

*Rate Support Grant (RSG)*

While RSG remains by far the largest package of funding to local areas, it now runs at a substantially lower level than in the late 1970s and early 1980s. In absolute terms, the five Tyne and Wear authorities jointly received £21.95m more in RSG funding in 1990/91 than in 1979/90. In real terms, however, this represents a decline of £157.25m (or £137.57 per person) - a fall of around half (49.83%) in the period from 1979/80 to 1990/91. This decline is all the more severe given the five authorities' heavy reliance on RSG as a source of funding. Over the period 1979/80 - 1990/91, the RSG budget accounted for 71.17% of total expenditure in Tyne and Wear. But while the conurbation's RSG budget fell by half in real terms over the 1980s, local authority budgets remain dominated by RSG. In 1979/80, 71.69% of expenditure in Tyne and Wear was accounted for by RSG monies; by 1990/91, this proportion had fallen only marginally to 69.14% of total expenditure, despite the considerable decline in the size of the RSG budget. In relative terms, Tyne and Wear authorities remain almost as reliant in 1990/91 on RSG as a source of funding as they were in 1979/80 (Figure C62).

*Housing Investment Programme (HIP)*

The reduction in HIP expenditure in Tyne and Wear has, if anything, been even more severe than that experienced by RSG. HIP expenditure fell in real terms by £79.13m between 1979/80 and 1989/90, a decline of 80.58% (or £69.23 per head of population). Unlike RSG, moreover, the HIP budget actually fell in absolute terms by £46.24m (61.10%) from £75.86m in 1979/80 to £29.44m in

1989/90. Even allowing for top-slicing of the HIP budget - Estate Action, for example, contributed £6.54m to the conurbation in 1989/90, over one-fifth of the size of the HIP budget for that year - this represents a sizeable loss of resource for the five local authorities. While RSG, despite considerable cuts in funding, remains vitally important to local authority budgets in relative terms (as outlined), HIP has progressively accounted for a smaller share of total programme expenditure in Tyne and Wear. In 1979/80, HIP expenditure amounted to over one fifth (22.31%) of all expenditure, but by 1989/90 made up only one twentieth (5.37%) of the conurbation total for that year.

*Figure C62*  **Tyne and Wear - composition of funding (constant 1981/82 prices)**

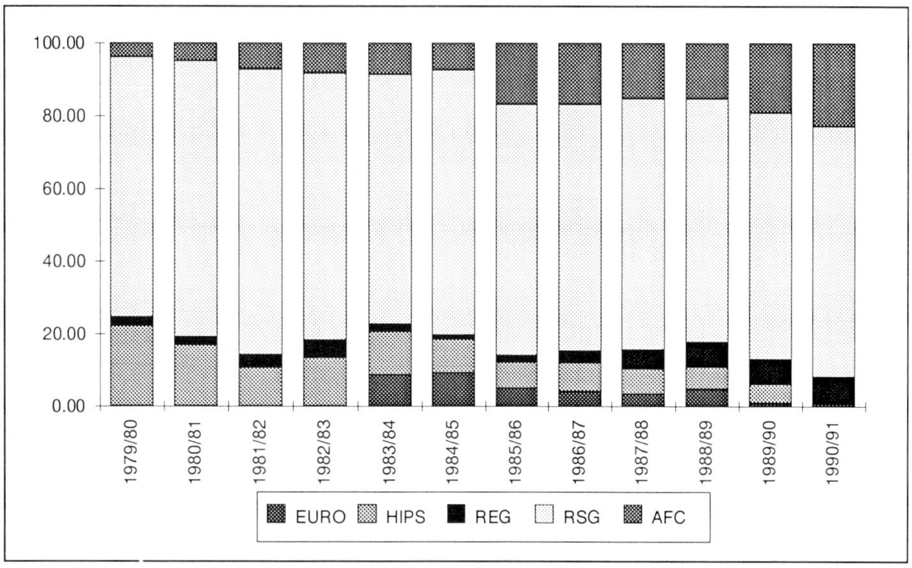

Taken together, the RSG and HIP budgets in Tyne and Wear were over one third (37.11%) lower in real terms in 1989/90 than in 1979/80. Whereas total expenditure declined in real terms by £85.33m, RSG and HIP declined by a total of £153.59m. Moreover, while the two programmes jointly accounted for 94% of all expenditure in 1979/80, this had fallen to 73.32% in 1989/90.

3.2.2 Filling the gap? The growth of 'new' programme expenditure

As outlined, the decline in RSG and HIP expenditure outweighs the growth in spending under new programme headings such as UDCs, Enterprise Zones and Estate Action, existing urban initiatives such as the Urban Programme and Derelict Land Grant, and monies spent under the European structural funds and DTI 'regional' programmes. At the same time, however, the growth of these programmes has gone some way towards offsetting the larger decline in RSG and HIPs. Whereas the latter in combination declined by more than one third in real terms by 1989/90, total expenditure in the conurbation fell by one fifth (19.38%).

Expenditure under the European (ESF, ERDF), regional (RSA, RDGII) and Action for Cities headings have increased over most of the 1980s. In 1983/84, for example, they accounted for 19.21% of total expenditure in Tyne and Wear. By 1989/90, however, their share of total expenditure had increased to 26.68%, with the Action for Cities programmes alone comprising 19.09% of total expenditure (Figure C62, which shows the different fund headings and their relative contributions to total expenditure).

*Action for Cities (AfC)*

Action for Cities expenditure has increased markedly in the conurbation in relation to the other headings since 1979/80, running counter to the pronounced decline in the level of HIP expenditure over the same period. While programmes under the AfC heading accounted for 3.81% of all expenditure in 1979/80 and 19.09% in 1989/90, HIP contributed 22.31% and 5.37% respectively. In each of the years from 1985/86 onwards AfC expenditure has been responsible for more than 15% of all expenditure, running in excess of £55m in each of the years from 1985/86-1989/90 (constant 1981/82 prices). The bulk of the increase in Action for Cities expenditure is explained by the establishment of new programmes. The Newcastle/Gateshead Enterprise Zone and Tyne and Wear Development Corporation, for example, contributed £136.06m and £92.81m respectively (absolute values) to the AfC total. With the exception of English Estates, City Action Team and UDG/URG/City Grant expenditure, all Action for Cities programmes increased their expenditure in real terms between the start and end dates for which data were collected.

Expenditure data run continuously for only two of the twelve Action for Cities programmes studied: Derelict Land Grant and the Urban Programme. The value of both programmes has increased substantially in real terms. Derelict Land Grant expenditure has more than doubled (+109.15%) over the period 1979/80-1989/90, rising from £1.01m to £2.11m and peaking at £4.92m in 1986/87. Similarly, Urban Programme expenditure has increased in real terms by over one fifth (22.99%) in the five authorities, rising from £15.76m to £19.39m.

*Regional funding*

Regional monies have also made an increasing contribution towards total expenditure in the five local authorities, accounting for a greater share of spending in each year from 1984/85 onwards. Regional expenditure increased by 150.24% from £9.64m in 1979/80 to £24.14m in 1989/90. They accounted for 2.19% of all spending in 1979/80, rising to 6.8% in 1989/90.

*European funding*

The EC structural funds (European Social Fund and European Regional Development Fund) made up a significant proportion of total expenditure during the mid 1980s. From 8.67% of total expenditure in Tyne and Wear in 1983/84, European funding increased its contribution to a peak of 9.04% in 1984/85. In financial years 1989/90 and 1990/91, however, European funding accounted for only 0.79% and 0.87% respectively of total expenditure.

Clearly, the increases in Action for Cities, regional and, to a lesser extent, European monies have made only a limited dent in the more severe decline in RSG and HIP expenditure. Overall, the conurbation has lost out in real terms, to the tune of £153.54m in lost HIP and RSG expenditure between 1979/80 and 1989/90. Substantial proportional increases in expenditure on programmes like DLG, the Urban Programme and Estate Action, as well as the injection of extra funds through the establishment of new policy vehicles such as the Urban Development Corporation and Enterprise Zone, are of limited value when placed beside the altogether more sizeable withdrawal of RSG and HIP funds.

3.2.3 'Winners' and 'Losers': the distribution of programme resources among localities

Although programme expenditure overall has declined in Tyne and Wear, this masks significant shifts in the importance of different programmes in different places at different times. Moreover, county-wide expenditure figures fail to reveal important changes in the extent of policy targeting both within and between local authorities.

Figure C63 shows total programme expenditure (undeflated figures) in each of the Tyne and Wear districts over the period 1979/80 - 1990/91. Sunderland received the largest share of expenditure, (£1327.97m), while North Tyneside received the smallest share (£812.23m). The largest sums per head of population went to South Tyneside (£5215.36) and Gateshead (£5200.72).

*Figure C63*  **Total programme expenditure by local authority 1979/80-1990/91 (undeflated totals) (£s '000s)**

|  | Total | pc total |
|---|---|---|
| Gateshead | 1090095.61 | 5200.72 |
| Newcastle | 1195637.27 | 4236.32 |
| N Tyneside | 818234.26 | 4197.75 |
| S Tyneside | 828285.99 | 5215.36 |
| Sunderland | 1327970.92 | 4463.47 |
| Tyne & Wear | 5260224.06 | 4601.73 |

As outlined earlier, the five authorities jointly lost £85.34m between 1979/80 and 1989/90 (constant prices). North and South Tyneside account for the largest shares of this reduction, their expenditure totals falling by around one third in real terms (35.75% and 31.59% respectively). Controlling for inflation, the expenditure totals in both North and South Tyneside have declined at a steady rate, in contrast to the rather more capricious expenditure patterns of Newcastle and Gateshead (Figure C64). This pattern also applies to the proportions of total spending in the conurbation claimed by North and South Tyneside, which have declined steadily from 17.56% and 16.90% respectively of all expenditure during 1979/80 to 15.81% and 15.90% in 1990/91. Conversely, the share of the 'county budget' taken by Gateshead and Newcastle has varied more widely. Gateshead's share of total spending leapt from 19.11% in 1984/85 to 26.60% in 1985/86 - which equates with an increase of £29.61m in real terms - mainly due to the injection of a substantial sum of Enterprise Zone cash (£41.04m or £33.04m at constant prices). There was also a considerable fall in the share of expenditure going to Newcastle between 1985/86 and 1986/87, dropping from 19.78% to 15.16%. This was mainly a result of the low RSG allocation for 1986/87, which, at £27.16m represented a drop of 44.94% on the previous year's total of £49.33m. Programme expenditure in Newcastle fell by £21.04m (19.98%) in real terms.

*Figure C64*  **Total programme expenditure (constant 1981/82 prices)**

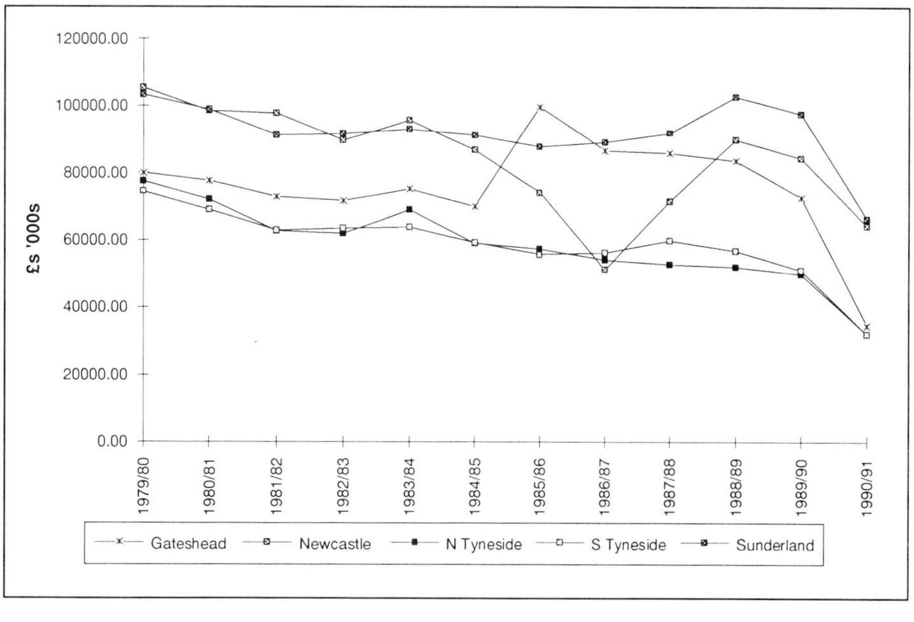

Sunderland, in contrast to Newcastle, North Tyneside and South Tyneside, has seen its expenditure levels maintained at a level closer to that in 1979/80, 'losing' 5.59% in real terms (£9.75m). This is explained principally by sizeable DTI regional expenditure in the district, amounting to £11.93m in 1989/90 out of a total regional expenditure figure for the five authorities of 24.14m (1981/82 prices). Likewise, the reduction in total expenditure in Gateshead - a decline of around one tenth (9.19%) - is moderated by the large public subsidies associated with the Enterprise Zone, which on average contributed one tenth (11.42%) annually to the district's total expenditure during the period 1979/80-1989/90. The significance of this EZ expenditure is apparent in the fact that it exceeds the authority's HIP allocation in each of the years from 1985/86 - 1989/90. Whereas HIP expenditure was responsible for around one twentieth (5.34%) of total expenditure over that period, EZ expenditure contributed 18.51% towards the total.

While spending under programme headings such as DTI regional monies in Sunderland and the Enterprise Zone in Gateshead have been significant in their own right, they have had only marginal effect in offsetting reductions in RSG and HIP funding. The most severely affected authority has been Newcastle, whose RSG allocation fell by £20.33m (29.82%) in real terms over the period 1979/80-1989/90. Of the five authorities, only Sunderland experienced a fall in its RSG budget below 20% (-18.02%) in real terms. Indeed, of all the districts, Sunderland is most 'dependent' on RSG for the maintenance of its total expenditure, 80.22% of the city's expenditure between 1979/80 and 1990/91 coming from the RSG budget. Newcastle, by contrast, is least heavily dependent on RSG money, which accounts for 61.70% of all spending over the twelve-year period. Similarly, Gateshead has a low 'dependence' on RSG, particularly in the period following the growth in importance of Enterprise Zone expenditure after 1985/86.

Tyne and Wear authorities have also been reliant on HIP cash for a substantial proportion of their budgets. But unlike RSG, this reliance on HIP monies has declined since 1979/80, when it accounted for 22.31% of all expenditure in the conurbation, to 5.37% by 1989/90 - a reduction in real terms of 80.58%. Of the five authorities, Newcastle, North Tyneside and South Tyneside are most 'dependent' on HIP cash, with 12-14% of their total expenditure deriving from the HIP budget. HIP expenditure accounts for 8.63 and 6.25% of all expenditure in Gateshead and Sunderland respectively.

All five authorities experienced declines in HIP levels in excess of 75% in real terms. Reduced HIP allocations ranged from 76.95% in Newcastle to 87.16% in South Tyneside. The severity of these losses is suggested by the fact that for three of the five authorities - Gateshead, Newcastle and Sunderland - the decline in HIP allocations is greater in real terms than is the case for total expenditure figures. HIP losses range from £102.27 per person in South Tyneside to 37.89 per person in Sunderland. However, the share of the total Tyne and Wear HIP budget going to each of the five districts has remained fairly steady through the decade. Indeed, the particularly severe fall in HIP experienced by South Tyneside can be explained largely by the district's peculiarly low share of the Tyne and Wear total during 1989/90, while the less pronounced decline in Newcastle's HIP expenditure is a result of its increased share of the budget during that same year. In total, the combined reductions in RSG and HIP budgets have been substantial for each of Tyne and Wear's district authorities, whose losses ranged from £25.28m in Gateshead to £41.58m in Newcastle. Only two of the five authorities - Sunderland and Gateshead - experienced losses in real terms below 40% (26.69 and 34.66% respectively).

Notwithstanding their limited contribution towards offsetting the cuts in RSG and HIP budgets, it is clear that AfC programmes have increased in significance in their own right. In each of the five Tyne and Wear authorities, AfC expenditure more than doubled in real terms over the period 1979/80-1989/90. However, this masks considerable variation in the extent to which each authority has benefited from additional AfC money. While North Tyneside received an extra £2.13m (101.68%) over the eleven-year period, Newcastle received an extra £19.84m (421.95%) in real terms. Indeed, as with HIP, it is North and South Tyneside which gain least from extra AfC expenditure in both percentage and absolute terms.

Unlike RSG or HIPs, Action for Cities funding is often project-oriented and therefore is more episodic. Figure C65 bears this out, showing, for example, how Gateshead's AfC total is related to particularly heavy spending in the Enterprise Zone during 1985/86. Likewise, Newcastle's total rises heavily from 1988/89 to 1989/90 largely as a result of the expansion of UDC expenditure, increasing from £11.75m to £22.04m (undeflated prices).

*Figure C65* **AfC as a proportion of total expenditure (constant 1981/82 prices)**

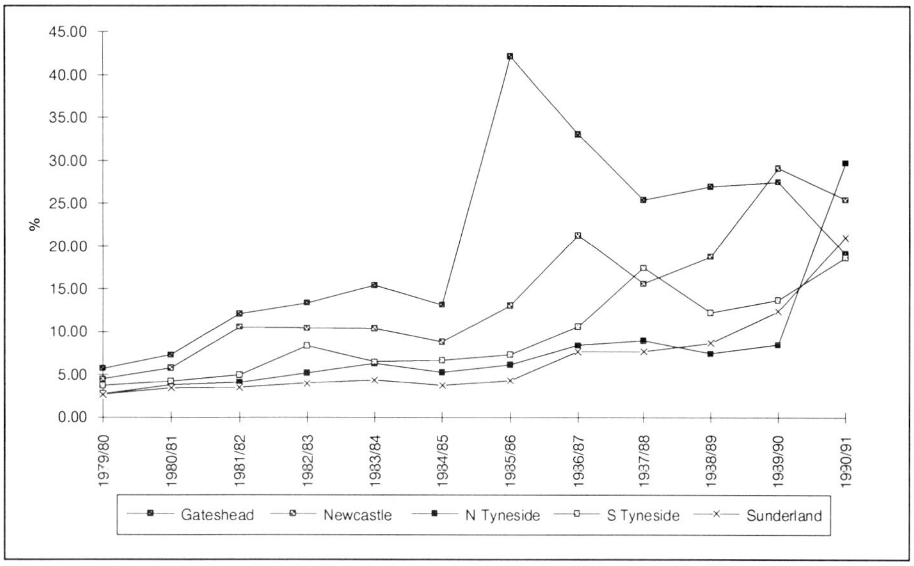

Over the period 1979/80-1989/90, Gateshead and Newcastle received the largest share of AfC expenditure in the conurbation, accounting for 37.34% and 26.79% of all AfC monies. However, AfC expenditure in Gateshead is more variable, accounting for 27.17% of all AfC cash during 1979/80, but peaking at 66.65% in 1985/86. The share of AfC expenditure taken by Sunderland remains relatively constant, ranging from 11.25% of total AfC funding in 1981/2 to 17.82% in 1989/90. North Tyneside receives the lowest share of AfC expenditure, gaining 9.44% of total AfC cash from 1979/80-1989/90. In each of the years 1985/86-1989/90, North Tyneside received less than one tenth of all Action for Cities expenditure.

Both Gateshead and Newcastle rely on AfC programmes for a significant proportion of programme expenditure within their areas. In total, one fifth (20.97%) of Gateshead's expenditure, and 13.57% of Newcastle's, came from Action for Cities programmes. North and South Tyneside and Sunderland were, by contrast, considerably less reliant on AfC monies, which, in each case, accounted for less than one tenth of all expenditure (6.90%, 8.86% and 6.58% respectively).

Just as AfC funding, though significant in its own right, has failed to compensate for reduced RSG and HIP budgets in each of the five authorities, so too European and regional monies have been insufficient to balance these losses. Although regional funding increased in Tyne and Wear by 150.24% (+£14.49m) in real terms between 1979/80 and 1989/90, this must be set against losses of £79.13m for HIPs and £74.45m for RSG. In 1989/90, for example, regional and European funds accounted for only 7.59% of all expenditure in Tyne and Wear, whereas RSG, in spite of considerable cut backs, continued to account for 67.95% of all expenditure. Moreover, the distribution of regional monies has been uneven, with Sunderland gaining £11.12m in real terms over the period to 1989/90, but Newcastle losing £0.11m.

Figure C66 illustrates the more episodic nature of a large proportion of regional monies - in contrast to the more incremental pattern of change shown by the HIP and RSG budgets. In Newcastle, for example, regional monies rose from accounting for 4.12% of all expenditure in the city during 1980/81, to 10.16% and 15.50% in subsequent years, before falling back to 5.37% by 1983/84. Moreover, at constant prices, the level of regional funding in Newcastle varied from £0.59m in 1986/87 to £13.88m in 1982/83. Newcastle has been particularly reliant on EC cash, which during financial years 1982/83, 1983/84 and 1988/89 accounted for more than 10% of all expenditure in the city. Of the five Tyne and Wear authorities, Newcastle has benefited most from European money. As Figure C67 shows, the city gained over two fifths (44.75%) in real terms of all European funding flowing into Tyne and Wear. North Tyneside, by contrast, received less than one tenth of all European monies over the period 1979/80-1989/90 - a situation which is mirrored for the district's share of Action for Cities and regional resources.

*Figure C66* **Regional funding as a proportion of all expenditure (constant 1981/82 prices)**

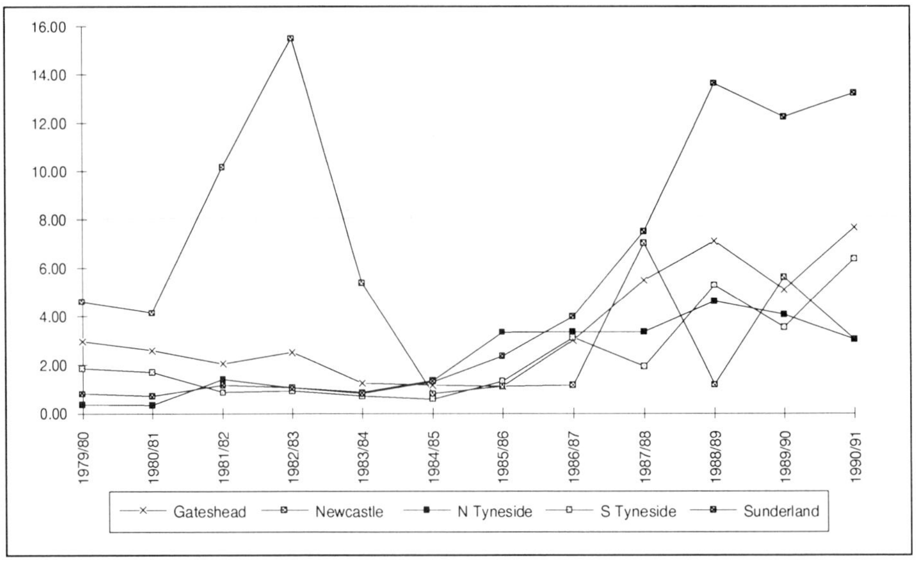

3.2.4 Summary

- Total programme expenditure in Tyne and Wear has declined in real terms by 19.38% between 1979/80 and 1989/90. Reduced RSG and HIP allocations account for the bulk of this decline. Increased Action for Cities, regional and European expenditure has not compensated fully for these cutbacks.

- Action for Cities expenditure accounts for an increasing proportion of funding to local areas. Over one-fifth of total expenditure in Tyne and Wear is now spent under the Action for Cities heading.

- Regional monies have made an increasing contribution towards expenditure in the five local authorities, accounting for a greater share of total spending in each year from 1985/86 onwards. European funding made up a significant proportion of total expenditure during the mid-1980s (1983/84-1988/89), but declined substantially in importance thereafter.

- The extent of programme targeting towards authorities has varied through the 1980s. North and South Tyneside have, with the exception of 1986/87, consistently received the lowest share of total expenditure. Sunderland, by contrast, has consistently received a substantial proportion of monies in the conurbation, while the share of spend going to Newcastle and Gateshead is more variable.

- The pattern of spending amongst the five authorities varies between different programme headings (Figure C67). In general, however, the largest share of expenditure under the five programme headings goes to Sunderland, Newcastle and Gateshead. Conversely, South and North Tyneside receive the lowest share of expenditure for Action for Cities, European and regional programmes, and for RSG. This pattern is not matched under the HIPs budget, where North and South Tyneside receive a larger share of expenditure than either Gateshead or Sunderland.

*Figure C67*     **% share of budgets taken by each local authority (constant 1981/82 prices)**

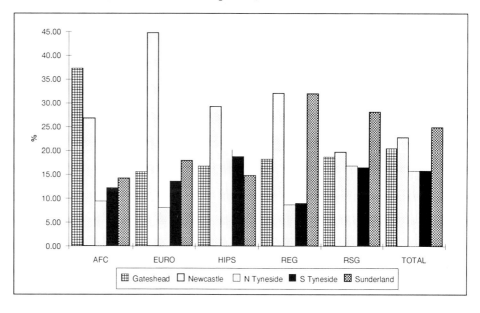

**3.3 Targeting urban policy initiatives: Action for Cities and the Urban Programme**

Each of Tyne and Wear's five local authority districts are designated UPAs and receive urban programme funding. Prior to the redesignation of Urban Programme funded authorities in 1987/88, Gateshead and Newcastle had enjoyed partnership authority status and had jointly submitted annual Inner Area Programmes (IAPs), outlining planned projects in subsequent years, for approval by the DoE. North Tyneside, South Tyneside and Sunderland had been given programme authority status in the period before 1987/88. Although the terms 'partnership' and 'programme' authority continue to be used, and Newcastle and Gateshead still submit their IAPs jointly, in theory there is a single UP designation which replaces the distinction between partnership and programme authorities.

*Figure C68*    **Urban Programme funding for Tyne and Wear (constant 1981/82 prices)**

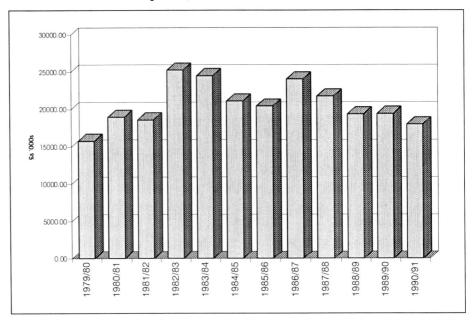

For the five Tyne and Wear authorities jointly, Urban Programme funding has increased significantly over the period 1979/80-1990/91, rising from £12.15m to £30.15m. In real terms, the amount of Urban Programme cash going to the five authorities has risen by 14.20% (constant 1981/82 prices) (Figure C70). Urban Programme funding peaked at £25.25m in real terms during 1982/83, before falling back to £18.00m in 1990/91 (Figure C68). While all five authorities increased their UP expenditure by more than 100% over the period 1979/80-1990/91, at constant prices the picture changes somewhat. In real terms, UP funding in Newcastle fell by 5.38%, while the increase in expenditure in North Tyneside was restricted to 4.06% (Figure C70). Conversely, South Tyneside, Gateshead and Sunderland received increases in excess of the county-wide rise of 14.20%. UP expenditure in Sunderland rose by 36.24% in real terms over the twelve-year period. Although the increase in Sunderland's UP budget outweighed that in any of the other Tyne and Wear authorities, by 1990/91 UP expenditure in Sunderland per head of population remained well below the figure for Tyne and Wear as a whole (Figure C69). Over the twelve-year period, UP expenditure in Sunderland in real terms represented £118.29 per person, compared to per capita figures of £216.11 for Tyne and Wear and £352.74 for Gateshead.

Figure C70 shows the pattern of change in expenditure over time for each of the five authorities. Funding levels for Gateshead and Newcastle are more variable from year to year than is the case for the three programme authorities. There is some divergence in funding levels, with the degree of increase in Gateshead, Sunderland and South Tyneside outweighing those in Newcastle or North Tyneside.

While there have been important changes in the levels of Urban Programme funding in each of the five authorities, there remains a marked difference between UP expenditure in Newcastle and Gateshead, on one hand, and North Tyneside, South Tyneside and Sunderland on the other. Although the distinction between partnership and programme authorities was formally ended with the designation of the 57 UPAs in 1987/88, in practice it appears that the distinction between authorities has remained. Over the whole twelve-year period, Gateshead and Newcastle jointly received well over half (57.41%) of total Urban Programme funding for the conurbation, with Gateshead alone receiving close

294

*Figure C69*     **Urban Programme funding per head of population (constant 1981/82 prices) (£s)**

|  | 1979/80 | 1980/81 | 1981/82 | 1982/83 | 1983/84 | 1984/85 | 1985/86 | 1986/87 | 1987/88 | 1988/89 | 1989/90 | 1990/91 | Total | change |
|---|---|---|---|---|---|---|---|---|---|---|---|---|---|---|
| Gateshead | 20.03 | 24.90 | 25.23 | 34.72 | 34.72 | 35.40 | 31.13 | 31.03 | 34.79 | 28.66 | 30.74 | 30.35 | 352.74 | 5.08 |
| Newcastle | 15.97 | 19.20 | 18.23 | 27.70 | 27.70 | 25.06 | 20.13 | 18.74 | 24.38 | 22.60 | 15.47 | 17.29 | 240.50 | -0.90 |
| N Tyneside | 10.21 | 12.39 | 11.78 | 14.55 | 14.55 | 15.56 | 13.57 | 13.46 | 15.41 | 13.38 | 12.12 | 11.06 | 154.48 | 0.43 |
| S Tyneside | 15.00 | 16.90 | 18.46 | 28.02 | 28.02 | 24.06 | 22.54 | 21.46 | 23.06 | 23.42 | 19.89 | 19.54 | 251.30 | 3.41 |
| Sunderland | 7.76 | 9.61 | 9.01 | 9.20 | 9.20 | 10.43 | 9.08 | 8.98 | 11.39 | 10.73 | 10.86 | 10.70 | 118.29 | 2.81 |
| Tyne&Wear | 13.52 | 16.31 | 16.08 | 21.96 | 21.96 | 21.37 | 18.47 | 17.91 | 21.17 | 19.15 | 17.09 | 17.19 | 216.11 | 1.99 |

*Figure C70*     **Urban Programme funding (constant 1981/82 prices)**

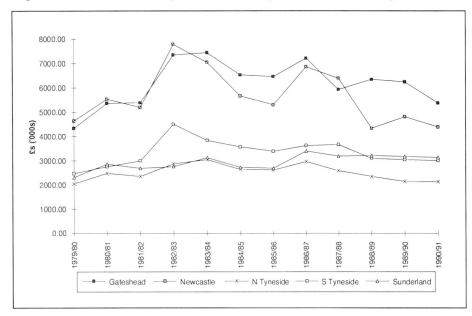

on one third (29.93%) in real terms. The share of Urban Programme expenditure taken by each authority has remained relatively steady over time (Figure C71). Over the twelve-year period, Newcastle and Gateshead jointly received more than 55% of all UP expenditure in each year except 1990/91. Conversely, North Tyneside, with the exception of 1982/3, has consistently received the lowest share of UP money, ranging from 10.99% in 1989/90 to 13.02% in 1980/81. This steady pattern of Urban Programme expenditure is interrupted only by the increasing share of expenditure taken by Sunderland, which rose in each successive year from 1982/83 onwards. Whereas UP expenditure in Sunderland in 1982/83 accounted for 10.91% of the county-wide UP budget, by 1990/91 this had risen to 17.38%.

Over the course of the decade, the Urban Programme has played an increasingly important role in relative terms as part of the conurbation's urban policy budget. In 1979/80, UP expenditure accounted for 3.58% of all expenditure in Tyne and Wear. By 1989/90, the conurbation was reliant on UP money for 5.46% of all expenditure. This increasing reliance on UP money is especially significant given that the decade witnessed such a profusion of urban policy instruments in the conurbation. Despite the introduction of new programmes such as Estate Action and City Grant, and the funding provided by new policy vehicles such as Enterprise Zones, UDCs and City Action Teams, the Urban Programme has actually become more important, both in relative and absolute terms, as a source of funding for local areas.

Of the five Tyne and Wear authorities, Gateshead has been most reliant on Urban Programme monies for its expenditure, 8.13% of which came from the UP during the period from 1979/80-1990/91. In fact, the two partnership authorities are most 'dependent' on UP cash, with 6.73% of Newcastle's total expenditure coming from the UP. This contrasts with North Tyneside and Sunderland, both of which rely on UP money for less than one twentieth of their total expenditure (4.30% and 3.19% respectively).

*Figure C71*    **% share of Tyne and Wear Urban Programme budget going to each authority (constant 1981/82 prices)**

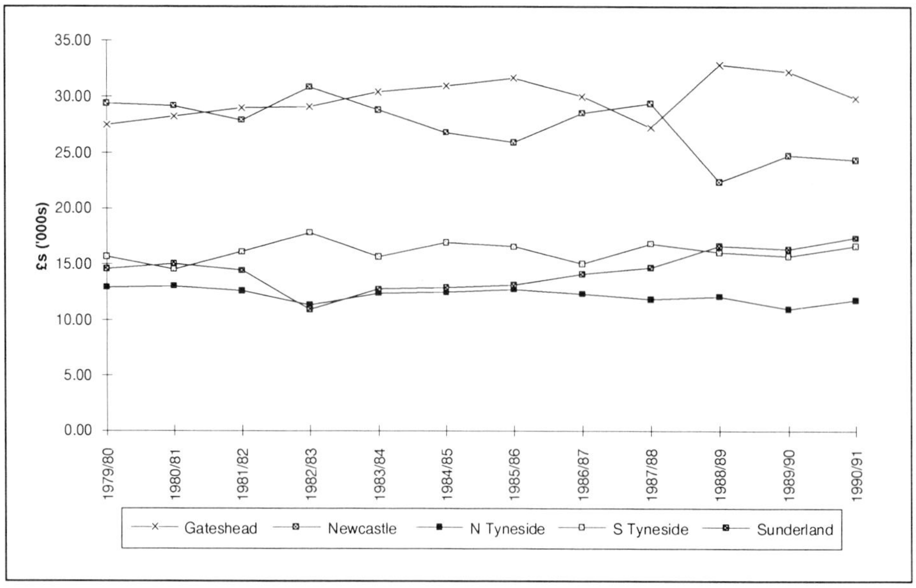

**3.3.1 Targeting Urban Programme resources**

The above discussion reveals in a broad way how Tyne and Wear's local authorities have fared in terms of UP expenditure levels. This section aims to complement this by taking account both of the diverse range of places within each of the five authorities and the array of policy measures implemented, looking in greater detail at the differing ways in which urban policy programmes have impinged upon different places at different times. This, in turn, necessitates a closer examination of the spatial and temporal pattern of urban policy resource allocation in the conurbation. To these ends it is necessary first, to look at the distribution of Urban Programme resource across and within wards in the conurbation; and second, to look at the qualitative and quantitative picture of Urban Programme funding in these wards. In addition, this section also looks at how Urban Programme expenditure relates to the policy input provided by the range of AfC programmes in the conurbation, including Tyne and Wear Development Corporation and Tyneside Enterprise Zone. Moreover, use is made of an extensive ward expenditure database compiled for urban policy projects funded through Estate Action, City Grant, Urban Development Grant, Derelict Land Grant and English Estates, as well, of course, as the Urban Programme.

Over the period 1983/84-1990/91, a total of 98 of the 113 wards in the five authorities of Tyne and Wear received some Urban Programme funding. These include the seventy-one wards which currently fall within the Inner Urban Areas ('inner areas'), as defined in the annual Inner Area Programmes (IAPs) submitted by local authorities for approval by the DoE (Figure C72). Of the remaining forty-three wards in the county, twenty-eight have received Urban Programme funding at some time during the period from 1983/84-1990/91.

The range of Urban Programme money received by the county's wards is considerable. While Sunderland's Central ward received £12.58m of UP cash over the eight financial years studied (representing 30.13% of all UP expenditure in Sunderland), Whickham South in Gateshead received just £200. There are also some interesting contrasts between the amounts received by some of the 'targeted' wards and those which fall outside the defined 'inner areas'. Fellgate in South Tyneside, for example, received a total of only £6,646 over the whole eight-year period, despite its designation as an 'inner area'. Conversely, Sunderland's Houghton ward received a total of £590,502 even though it is not defined as an 'inner area' ward. Seven non-'inner area' wards fall within the seventy best-funded wards in the conurbation. These are (in order of funding received): Houghton, Fulwell and Eppleton in Sunderland, Cleadon and East Boldon ward in South Tyneside, and Lemington, Wolsington and Heaton in Newcastle. The seven 'inner areas' which fall outside the seventy best-funded wards are Chowdene in Gateshead, St Chad's and Thorney Close in Sunderland, Westoe and Whitburn in South Tyneside, St Michael's in Sunderland and Fellgate in South Tyneside.

*Figure C72*   **'Inner areas' in the Districts**

| | | |
|---|---|---|
| **GATESHEAD** | SANDYFORD | ALL SAINTS |
| BENSHAM | BLAKELAW | PRIMROSE |
| DUNSTON | FENHAM | WEST PARK |
| FELLING | | HARTON |
| SALTWELL | | CLEADON PARK |
| BLAYDON | **N TYNESIDE** | HORSLEY HILL |
| BEDE | WALLSEND | WESTOE |
| TEAMS | TYNEMOUTH | WHITBURN |
| WHICKHAM N | NORTH SHIELDS | FELLGATE |
| PELAW | HOWDON | BIDDICK HALL |
| HIGH FELL | RIVERSIDE | |
| LEAM | LONGBENTON | |
| DECKHAM | CHIRTON | **SUNDERLAND** |
| CHOWDENE | BENTON | CENTRAL |
| | NORTHUMBERLAND | THORNEHOLME |
| | COLLINGWOOD | SOUTHWICK |
| **NEWCASTLE** | | COLLIERY |
| WALKER | | ST PETERS |
| WEST CITY | **S TYNESIDE** | HENDON |
| SCOTSWOOD | REKENDYKE | SOUTH HYLTON |
| ELSWICK | BOLDON COLLIERY | TOWN END FARM |
| BYKER | BEACON AND BENTS | CASTLETOWN |
| KENTON | BEDE | SILKSWORTH |
| MONKCHESTER | HEBBURN QUAY | PALLION |
| BENWELL | WHITELEAS | GRINDON |
| WALKERGATE | MONKTON | ST.CHADS |
| MOORSIDE | HEBBURN SOUTH | THORNEY CLOSE |
| FAWDON | TYNE DOCK | ST MICHAEL'S |

While there are some anomalies of this kind in the geographical distribution of Urban Programme funding, it should be borne in mind that the bulk of expenditure falls within the defined inner urban area. In fact, 97.37% of 'targeted' (i.e. non-borough-wide) expenditure was directed toward 'inner area' wards over the period 1983/84-1990/91. In other words, over half (54.82%) of all Urban Programme money (including borough-wide projects) in Tyne and Wear benefited 'inner area' wards directly. This concentration of resources is still stronger if one looks more closely at the share of Urban Programme funds directed to 'inner area' wards. Over one-third (35.76%) of all 'targeted' UP funding was directed towards the ten best-funded wards in the conurbation, all of which received over £4m in UP cash during the period 1983/84-1990/91. Moreover, the twenty best-funded wards received over half of all targeted UP money (58.54%); and the thirty best-funded wards received over three quarters of all money (75.78%).

Clearly, the majority of Urban Programme funding (56.30%) has been taken by projects targeted at specific areas; and the bulk of that money (97.37%) has gone towards 'inner area' wards. This still leaves a significant proportion of money (43.70% of total expenditure) which has gone towards projects which benefit most or all of the local authority area rather than any identifiable geographical part of the authority.

The general trend for Urban Programme expenditure in Tyne and Wear has been for an increase in borough-wide expenditure (Figure C73). At the same time, however, borough-wide spending has remained at a level below half of all UP expenditure in each year from 1983/84-1990/91. Borough-wide expenditure levels have been particularly high in the partnership authorities, Gateshead and Newcastle. Indeed, more than half of all expenditure in Gateshead over the eight years (57.33%) has been on borough-wide projects. By contrast, borough-wide expenditure in the three programme authorities over the same period amounts in each case to around one third of total UP expenditure.

*Figure C73* **Expenditure on borough-wide projects as a % of all Urban Programme expenditure**

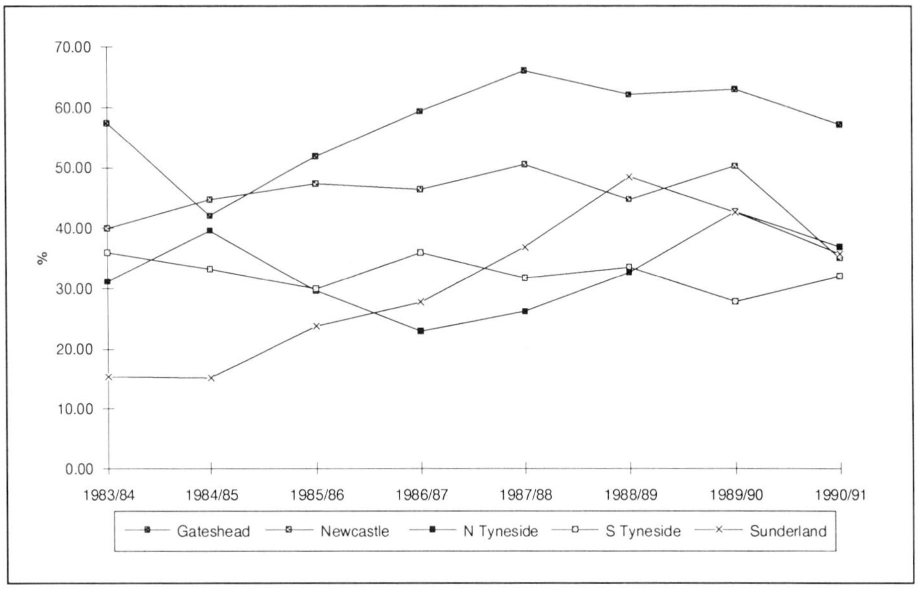

The relatively high proportion of borough-wide expenditure in Newcastle is unsurprising given its status as regional capital, with many UP-funded projects geared not just to local needs but to wider regional needs. Projects such as the refurbishment of Grey Street in the city centre or the funding of Newcastle Tourist Forum quite clearly are pitched at a market beyond the city's boundaries. What seems more surprising, however, is the higher proportion of borough-wide expenditure in Gateshead. This is mainly a result of considerable UP expenditure on the National Garden Festival - which explains in part the increase in borough-wide expenditure during the period 1985/86-1990/91 - and in the Enterprise Zone, most of which is located in Gateshead.

Clearly, then, the bulk of Urban Programme resource in the conurbation has been focused upon a limited number of wards, although some wards not included in the defined 'inner areas' have also benefited from smaller sums of UP cash. Against this context, we can consider in more detail the geographical spread of these Urban Programme resource for each of the conurbation's five authorities, and the shifting urban policy themes which have informed the changing ways in which the UP has been implemented.

*Gateshead*

Gateshead received a total of £84.60m over the period 1983/84-1990/91, shared between all twenty two of the borough's wards. Over the whole period, funding ranged from £9.22m in Bensham and £5.32m in Dunston to less than

298

£1000 in Ryton, Winlaton and Whickham South. Amongst the thirteen 'inner area' wards in the borough, the lowest funding totals were received by Deckham and Chowdene, both of which received less than £1m and 1% of total UP expenditure. Chowdene received only £0.14m, but this can be explained by the fact that only a small part of the ward falls within the defined 'inner area'.

The thirteen best-funded wards in the borough are the thirteen 'inner areas'. Unlike the situation in the metropolitan county as a whole, there are no aberrant cases of non-'inner area' wards receiving a greater share of Urban Programme resource than any of the 'inner areas'. In fact, 99.43% of all 'targeted' (i.e. non-borough-wide) expenditure went to inner area wards. In total, non-'inner area' wards received only £0.21m of Urban Programme resource over the period 1983/84-1990/91.

While the bulk of 'targeted' Urban Programme resources clearly have gone to the thirteen wards within the defined 'inner area', it should be borne in mind that of the five Tyne and Wear authorities, Gateshead devotes by far the lowest share of expenditure to targeted projects. Whereas a total of 57.33% of all UP monies in Gateshead was devoted to borough-wide expenditure, in Tyne and Wear as a whole borough-wide expenditure amounted to only 44% of all expenditure. 'Targeted' (i.e. non-borough-wide) expenditure comprised less than half (42.69%) of all Urban Programme money over the period 1983/84-1990/91. Of the total UP expenditure of £84.99m in Gateshead, £36.28m went to 'inner area' wards, while only £0.21m (0.24%) was directed to projects outside the defined inner area. However, the general trend over the eight years has been one of contraction of the share of resource devoted to 'inner area' wards. From a peak of over half (57.84%) of all expenditure in 1984/85, the proportion of spending taken by inner area wards declined to 33.75% by 1987/88. Between 1987/88 and 1990/91, however, expenditure targeted at the inner area increased again, comprising 42.68% in 1990/91. But with the exception of 1984/85, less than half of all Urban Programme cash has gone to inner area wards in each financial year. In contrast, for Tyne and Wear as a whole, 'inner area' wards have taken more than half of all expenditure in each year over the same period.

Amongst targeted wards themselves, there is a wide range of Urban Programme expenditure levels. The central ward of Bensham, Dunston in the western part of the riverside and Felling in east Gateshead have all received in excess of 5% of all Urban Programme monies (and more than 10% in the case of Bensham). In fact, these three wards together account for over half (51.65%) of all targeted UP money. Moreover, over three quarters (77.28%) of all targeted UP money was concentrated in six of the thirteen UPPA wards: the three mentioned above together with Blaydon and Teams wards in the western riverside area either side of Dunston, and Bede in central Gateshead adjoining Bensham.

Targeted Urban Programme resources have been spread amongst four broad geographical areas: the riverside area to the west of the town centre, containing most of the Gateshead portion of the Tyneside Enterprise Zone as well as the Garden Festival site at Dunston/Teams, and including the wards of Blaydon, Dunston, Teams and Whickham North; the central wards of Bede, Bensham, Deckham and Saltwell; the wards of Pelaw & Heworth and Felling to the east of the town centre; and the 'outer' wards of Chowdene, High Fell and Leam. The bulk (over three quarters) of targeted UP expenditure has gone to the eight wards in the central and western riverside areas. Between them, Dunston, Blaydon, Teams and Whickham North took 38.6% of all targeted UP expenditure, while spending in Bensham, Saltwell, Bede and Deckham accounted for 37.07% of the 'targeted' total of £36.49m. Of the remaining quarter of targeted funding, the majority (16.87%) was taken by Felling and Pelaw in east-central Gateshead, the former alone accounting for 11.81% of targeted money (Figure C74).

*Figure C74*    **Gateshead - % share of 'targeted' expenditure taken by each ward**

|  | TOTAL | % |
|---|---|---|
| BENSHAM* | 9,223,810 | 25.27 |
| DUNSTON* | 5,318,342 | 14.57 |
| FELLING* | 4,310,445 | 11.81 |
| BLAYDON* | 3,247,968 | 8.90 |
| BEDE* | 3,110,243 | 8.52 |
| TEAMS* | 2,994,468 | 8.21 |
| WHICKHAM N* | 2,524,338 | 6.92 |
| PELAW* | 1,845,891 | 5.06 |
| HIGH FELL* | 1,225,861 | 3.36 |
| LEAM* | 1,149,416 | 3.15 |
| DECKHAM* | 693,163 | 1.90 |
| SALTWELL* | 502,172 | 1.38 |
| CHOWDENE* | 140,996 | 0.39 |
| CHOPWELL | 74,671 | 0.20 |
| WREKENDYKE | 50,461 | 0.14 |
| CRAWCROOK | 42,243 | 0.12 |
| BIRTLEY | 18,465 | 0.50 |
| LAMESLEY | 10,500 | 0.30 |
| LOW FELL | 10,000 | 0.30 |
| RYTON | 865 | 0.00 |
| WINLATON | 400 | 0.00 |
| WHICKHAM S | 200 | 0.00 |
| **TOTAL** | **36,494,919** | **100.00** |

* 'inner area' ward

This concentration of Urban Programme resources on two broad geographical areas - western riverside and central wards - can be explained to a large extent by a number of sizeable projects associated with the National Garden Festival and Enterprise Zone in the case of the western wards, and the regeneration of the commercial area and older housing areas in the case of the central wards. The Enterprise Zone wards, for example, have been in receipt of substantial Urban Programme and Derelict Land Grant funds channelled through the Blaydon and Dunston Industrial Improvement Areas. Likewise, Team Valley Trading Estate received a significant input of UP funds through the former Tyne and Wear County Council's landscaping, infrastructure and promotion efforts. Between 1982/83 and 1985/86 (the last year for which large amounts of UP resource were committed for infrastructural work within the EZ area, the Enterprise Zone wards of Blaydon, Dunston, Teams and Whickham North received a total of £3.10m in UP allocations from Gateshead MBC (£1.73m) and Tyne and Wear County Council (£1.37m) for infrastructural works associated with the Zone. Over the period 1983/84-1985/86, Urban Programme projects under the 'Enterprise Zone' heading in the annual Inner Area Programme submissions accounted for one third (33.14%) of all UP expenditure in the four EZ wards. The importance of EZ-associated Urban Programme expenditure can be seen by the fact that the four EZ wards jointly received between 18.79% and 26.62% of UP funding in the borough during the period 1983/84-1985/86. In 1986/87 and 1987/88, however, the same wards received only 16.95% and 9.26% of all expenditure. As UP expenditure on major infrastructural projects within the Enterprise Zone was wound down, EZ associated Urban Programme expenditure amounted to £0.92m in 1985/86, but only £0.21m the following year.

Part of the reason for the apparent success of the Tyneside Enterprise Zone - especially in relation to EZs elsewhere in the country - was that the local authorities and English Estates were able jointly to offer a complete 'package' of help for companies, rather than relying solely on the statutory financial incentives to encourage the area's development. This appears particularly to be true in the case of Team Valley, where the local authorities and English Estates were able to build upon the area's attractive reputation, which had developed over a long period. Indeed, the support from English Estates has exceeded by some way that provided by the Urban Programme. Between 1985/86 and 1990/91, for example, English Estates support for Team Valley ran to some £14.86m, amounting to £4.68m in 1987/88 alone.

In total, over three quarters of all targeted Urban Programme resources have been directed towards two areas: the western riverside area (as outlined) and the four central wards of Bede, Bensham, Deckham and Saltwell. Just as the western riverside area has received a significant proportion of its UP cash for infrastructural and environmental projects associated with the Enterprise Zone, Industrial Improvement Areas and the National Garden Festival, so too the central wards have received much of their UP funding in the form of commercial regeneration projects (Gateshead town centre, for example) and housing improvements (the Avenues Agency in Bensham, for instance).

The majority of UP expenditure in this central group of wards has gone to Bensham, which received £9.22m between 1983/84 - 1990/91. This represents over a quarter (25.27%) of all targeted Urban Programme monies in Gateshead, or 10.85% of all UP expenditure. Much of this expenditure has been related to the rehabilitation of a core area of high density older housing which straddles the Bensham and, to a lesser extent, Saltwell areas. The most notable example is the Avenues Agency, established as a 'community refurbishment' scheme in 1986/87, involving Gateshead MBC, North Housing Association, the Northern Rock Building Society and the former Manpower Services Commission. Between 1986/87 and 1989/90, a total of £3.10m was directed towards Bensham under the Avenues heading in the form of funding a block repairs package, a community refurbishment programme using Community Programme-funded staff to carry out minor repairs, a housing advice officer and associated environmental improvements. Funding for the rehabilitation of the Avenues accounted for over half (52.39%) of all Urban Programme expenditure in Bensham during the period 1986/87-1989/90.

Substantial funds have also flowed into the area for the rehabilitation of the St Cuthbert's Village estate, which has been the subject of a highly diverse range of initiatives tackling housing, environmental and community service problems. In 1983/84 alone, initiatives targeted at the estate encompassed a housing management project, redevelopment of the central area, a diverse set of community development projects and numerous small scale environmental improvements. This policy focus on St Cuthbert's Village has remained through the duration of the study period. In both quantitative and qualitative terms the depth of focus on the estate was similar at the start and end dates of the study. In 1983/84, Urban Programme resources funded a community park, an anti-graffiti programme, fencing and planting schemes, external building feature work, and landscaping projects. Funds directed towards the estate during that year totalled approximately £235,000. Between 1986/87 and 1988/89, the area received a total of £2,998,000 from a package of Estate Action measures, while in 1990/91 the Urban Programme provided around £190,200 for a range of projects including a youth club, shrub planting, fencing, a community play project and a family centre. That tackling the problems of St Cuthbert's

Village has remained a priority throughout the 1980s is evidenced by the fact that Gateshead's unsuccessful 1993/4 City Challenge bid planned large-scale demolition of the estate's corridor access maisonettes. According to the bid, the estate remains 'unpopular and unattractive...despite numerous initiatives'.

Like Bensham, Felling to the east of the central area - which also received in excess of one tenth (11.81%) of all targeted UP resource - was the subject of targeted policy expenditure in the form of both commercial improvements and the rehabilitation of an area of older housing. Felling town centre, for example, received some £735,000 for shopping environmental improvements between 1983/4 and 1989/90. Urban Development Grant also provided £574,999 to private commercial interests as part of the second phase of improvements to Felling town centre in 1986/87 and 1987/88. Expenditure on a package of improvements for the Old Fold estate (including tenant management, environmental improvement and home security initiatives) contributed around £343,000 of UP money during the five years between 1984/5 and 1988/9, as well as £481,511 from Estate Action. In addition, the ward also saw an injection of UP cash in the form of estate security programmes, including the Community Protection Scheme aimed at improving defensible space in around three hundred homes (£121,000 during 1988/89).

While economic development, housing and environmental schemes account for the bulk of Urban Programme expenditure in Gateshead, there have also been a wide range of social and community-oriented projects which benefit particular areas. For the Newcastle/Gateshead partnership as whole, expenditure under the community services heading has ranged from 22.4% of all UP expenditure in 1988/89 to 30.8% in 1985/86, and averaging out at 28.3% over the period 1983/4-1990/91 (Figure C75). This equates, on average, to £6.129m per annum on community services, ranging from £4.533m in 1988/89 to £7.20m in 1985/86. Unlike spending under the economic development heading - which, increasingly, comprises high profile 'flagship' schemes - community services expenditure tends to be shared amongst a much larger number of projects, a large proportion of which have direct benefits for local areas and particular client groups. Some of this expenditure is in the form of revenue support for the likes of nursery provision, community centres, advice and community support, elderly services and, increasingly, ethnic minority community projects and crime prevention and security schemes. But while a great deal of community services expenditure takes the form of small scale revenue support, there have been some social projects which have contributed major sums towards the total amount of cash targeted at a particular ward in any one year. The Dunston Centre, for example, which houses a range of local authority and voluntary sector services, was established at a cost in 1983/84 of £70,000, representing almost one tenth (9.21%) of all targeted project expenditure in Dunston during that financial year. Similarly, Bensham received £250,000 during 1987/88 in the form of funding for the Bensham Day Hospital for the elderly - a sum which represents 16.61% of the ward's expenditure total in that year.

*Figure C75*    **% Share of total Urban Programme budget for Newcastle/Gateshead Partnership**

|  | 1983/84 | 1984/85 | 1985/86 | 1986/87 | 1987/88 | 1988/89 | 1989/90 | 1990/91 |
|---|---|---|---|---|---|---|---|---|
| Economic development | 42.20 | 45.20 | 45.00 | 46.00 | 48.90 | 56.30 | 54.50 | 49.20 |
| Housing/environment | 28.10 | 24.80 | 24.20 | 24.00 | 25.30 | 21.40 | 15.30 | 22.50 |
| Community/social services | 29.70 | 30.00 | 30.80 | 30.00 | 25.00 | 22.40 | 30.20 | 28.30 |

Source: *Newcastle/Gateshead Inner Area Programme submissions*

Urban Programme expenditure in Newcastle amounted to £90.58m over the period 1983/84 to 1990/91. Funding was spread amongst twenty-three of the city's twenty six wards, ranging from Walker, which received over one tenth (10.25%) of all UP expenditure, to Westerhope, which received only one hundredth of the total. Castle, Grange and South Gosforth wards received no Urban Programme money. Over half (55.16%) of all Urban Programme resource over the eight financial years examined was devoted to projects which benefited particular wards or groups of wards. A minority of expenditure (44.84%) went on projects whose aim was to benefit the entire city. While this is a lower proportion of borough-wide expenditure than is the case for Gateshead - which devotes over half its Urban Programme budget to such projects - it remains significantly higher than in the three programme authorities (North and South Tyneside and Sunderland), all of which devoted around two thirds of total expenditure to targeted projects.

A large proportion of this borough-wide expenditure has been on highly visible 'flagship' project based in the city centre. Frequently, the aim of such projects has been to improve the city centre - in real and image terms - as a centre for commerce and new office based service and retail uses, and for leisure, entertainment and tourist uses. In such projects, there has often been an explicit focus upon boosting the city's image, both for potential investors and customers. In recent years the Urban Programme in Newcastle has devoted substantial sums to block projects of this type, including the Regional Capital Initiative, the Tourism Development Fund and the Theatre Village/Chinatown rehabilitation project. In many cases, this has taken the form of funding for promotion and marketing, and for environmental improvements. The refurbishment of the Grey Street and Dean Street areas in the city centre, which contain much of the city's financial services and prestige offices, benefited from the refurbishment of building exteriors and a series of paving and lighting improvements (using UP grants). In addition, the areas received support for refurbishment costs from the City Grant budget, amounting to a total of £443,793 (Grey Street) and £351,000 (Dean Street) in 1990/91 and 1991/92. Likewise, the Clayton Street regeneration scheme - which was linked in to the Regional Capital Initiative - involved the refurbishment of a declining shopping area through general environmental and infrastructural improvements, grants for the refurbishment and re-use of properties and the promotion of the area as part of the city's historic Blackfriars area. The Stowell Street and Blackfriars area also received around £300,000 in the form of Urban Development Grants in 1989/90 and 1990/91.

Alongside these city centre projects, the Urban Programme has also funded a series of environmental projects whose aim is to refurbish and promote the riverside area, again in the hope of attracting prestige office employers and tourists. The Quayside initiative and the Elswick River Strategy, for example, have received substantial UP funding. The Quayside initiative, in particular, is one of the Urban Programme's key flagship programmes, involving environmental improvements at Hanover Street and All Saints Churchyard, and the refurbishment of the Princes Buildings to provide housing, office and retail space. As with the city centre flagships outlined above, these projects are often linked in to initiatives under other headings, such as TWDC's East Quayside project, and even the National Garden Festival in Gateshead.

Expenditure on targeted projects accounted for more than half (55.16%) of all Urban Programme expenditure in the city - again, a significantly larger proportion than is the case in the neighbouring partnership authority of Gateshead. Moreover, the bulk (99.59%) of this total of targeted money has been directed towards wards within the defined inner urban area. Expenditure targeted at the inner area has ranged from almost two thirds (63.43%) of all spending during 1990/91 to less than half (47.80%) during the preceding year. Of the eight financial years examined, expenditure in the inner urban area fell below half of all spending in only two years, 1987/88 and 1989/90.

Like Gateshead, the fourteen 'inner area' wards in the city occupy the fourteen top positions in terms of share of total Urban Programme funding. However, there is a huge range within the 'inner area' wards themselves, from Walker, West City and Scotswood - each of which received more than one tenth of total targeted expenditure - to Fenham, which received only 1.41% of the total or less than a tenth of the cash total directed towards Walker (Figure C76). While spending within the fourteen 'inner area' wards accounts for almost the entire total of targeted UP expenditure, a small number of 'inner area' wards themselves have been the focus for the bulk of policy attention. In fact, two wards, Walker and West City, account for almost one third of (32.07%) of targeted expenditure, while over half (52.71%) falls within these two wards plus Scotswood and Elswick. More than two thirds of the total of targeted expenditure falls within just six of the city's twenty-six wards: the four wards mentioned together with Byker and Kenton.

*Figure C76* **% share of 'targeted' expenditure taken by each ward in Newcastle (1983/84-1990/91)**

|  | TOTAL | % |
|---|---|---|
| WALKER* | 9,280,836 | 18.58 |
| WEST CITY* | 6,741,242 | 13.49 |
| SCOTSWOOD* | 5,979,389 | 11.97 |
| ELSWICK* | 4,331,917 | 8.67 |
| BYKER* | 3,689,154 | 7.38 |
| KENTON* | 3,491,599 | 6.99 |
| MONKCHESTER* | 3,170,015 | 6.35 |
| BENWELL* | 3,047,817 | 6.10 |
| WALKERGATE* | 1,961,811 | 3.93 |
| MOORSIDE* | 1,807,620 | 3.62 |
| FAWDON* | 1,574,596 | 3.15 |
| SANDYFORD* | 1,554,596 | 3.11 |
| BLAKELAW* | 1,421,514 | 2.85 |
| FENHAM* | 703,595 | 1.41 |
| LEMINGTON | 509,964 | 1.02 |
| WOLSINGTON | 263,695 | 0.53 |
| HEATON | 252,296 | 0.50 |
| JESMOND | 53,000 | 0.11 |
| NEWBURN | 43,634 | 0.90 |
| DENTON | 36,300 | 0.70 |
| DENE | 25,000 | 0.50 |
| WINGROVE | 15,800 | 0.30 |
| WESTERHOPE | 5,000 | 0.10 |
| **TOTAL** | **49,960,391** | **100.00** |

* 'inner area' ward

In terms of Urban Programme expenditure, the geographical focus of policy attention has very much been on the 'West End' wards of West City, Scotswood, Elswick and Benwell, together with the East Newcastle wards of Walker, Byker, Monkchester and Walkergate. This group of eight wards occupy eight of the nine 'top' positions for UP funding, accounting, between them, for almost three quarters (72.54%) of all geographically targeted expenditure in the city. All four wards in the western area and three of the four in the eastern area (the exception being Walkergate) received more than £3m (UPCS figures) over the whole period from 1983/84-1990/91. This constitutes considerable expenditure not just within the context of the city itself, but also in relation to Urban Programme spending over the entire county. Indeed, Walker and West City wards received a greater total of UP cash than any other ward in the county, with the exception of Sunderland's Central ward. All eight of the wards in the eastern and western areas fall within the thirty best funded wards in Tyne and Wear.

That the western riverside areas should be the subject of substantial Urban Programme attention is unsurprising given the geographical focus of other policy initiatives on the area. The western wards at present are targeted under the city's successful City Challenge bid for 1992/3-1996/7, together with existing Estate Action and HIP schemes at Buddle Road, Cruddas Park, the Bentinck Estate, Loadman Street and Scotswood. Moreover, the targeting of this area has become an explicit aim of policy with the inclusion of the Riverside West area - covering West City, Elswick, Scotswood and Benwell wards - as a 'target area' within the existing inner urban area.

Although the level of spatial targeting of resource towards the western riverside area has been consistently high, this conceals some significant shifts over time in terms of the geographical and sectoral distribution of funding within the area. The most notable trend is the increasing level of funding for projects in West City. Whereas Scotswood received a greater 'allocation' in the period from 1983/4 to 1987/8, in subsequent years the position was reversed. Indeed, in the final three years examined, West City received between two and three times as much cash as was targeted at Scotswood.

This change in the balance of funding between two of the western riverside wards is significant for two reasons, both of which are instructive in terms of the overall direction of the Urban Programme. First, the increase in resource directed towards West City is symptomatic of the Urban Programme's increasing focus on city-centre-based economic regeneration, often through a combination of property-led commercial regeneration and 'place marketing' initiatives to boost the city's image as a location for investment. West City ward, or at least the portion of it which falls within the city centre, has increasingly benefited from projects of these sorts, frequently including environmental improvements and refurbishment of buildings with the aim of aiding city centre commerce, tourism and leisure.

Second, and equally importantly, the growing policy focus on West City is symptomatic of a general trend in public policy, namely the intensive targeting of relatively small, well-defined areas. West City has benefited from a range of local economic and social projects, many of them linked to other urban policy programmes, particularly Estate Action. Under the Estate Action heading, West City ward has received £199,441 at Loadman Street, £1,182,801 at Cruddas Park flats and £2,550,877 on the Rye Hill estate. In recent years, Urban Programme money in West City has helped support Estate Action projects in areas like Cruddas Park and Loadman Street, which have also benefited from the efforts of the private sector-led Newcastle Initiative and Cruddas Park Community Trust. Urban Programme projects have included, for example, home security improvements associated with Estate Action, improvements to the run down Cruddas Park local shopping centre, and community development work in Cruddas Park and Loadman Street areas in association with the Community Trust. Indeed, the combined input provided by spending under the Urban Programme, Estate Action, The Newcastle Initiative, the Employment Service, Cruddas Park Community Trust and 'mainstream' local authority funding for community workers together constitute something akin to the 'corporate' approach to targeting which is now being formalised and extended in the area through City Challenge.

The western riverside wards have also been the subject of substantial Urban Programme funding aimed at boosting local economic development. In some cases, this has taken the form of site preparation, infrastructure and access works for industrial and business park accommodation, often linked with other policy vehicles such as the Enterprise Zone, or, in the case of Newcastle Business Park, Tyne and Wear Development Corporation. In other cases, UP support has involved funding for small business workspace accommodation. Urban Programme money was used to provide around 35 workshop units for small businesses at the Lynwood Terrace Workshops in Elswick, while the Whitehouse Enterprise Centre in Scotswood secured money for the conversion of redundant buildings to provide ten low-cost workshop units for expanding small firms.

Like the western riverside area, the four East Newcastle wards - Byker, Monkchester, Walker and Walkergate - have also been the focus of considerable Urban Programme attention, and have been the subject of Newcastle's unsuccessful City Challenge bid for 1993/94-1997/98. In total, the four East Newcastle wards drew in over one third (36.24%) of all targeted UP resources over the period 1983/84-1990/91, with Walker alone taking almost one fifth (18.58%) of targeted expenditure (Figure C76). This represents some £18.1m of expenditure in the four wards over an eight year period, over £9m of which went to Walker.

As in the West End, East Newcastle has seen a wide range of Urban Programme funded projects. These have ranged from environmental improvements in the local shopping areas at Shields Road and Welbeck Road, to the numerous small scale social and community projects which rely on the Urban Programme for start-up costs, one-off capital projects and revenue support. But the bulk of expenditure has been on projects whose aim has been to improve the area's housing and to promote industrial development.

Considerable sums of Urban Programme cash have been devoted to housing rehabilitation programmes in East Newcastle such as those in the Pottery Bank, Daisy Hill and St Anthony's areas. The Rochester Estate Renewal Project in Walker epitomises the approach to housing improvement which has been developing over the course of the decade. The Rochester Project was based on the emerging idea of 'area regeneration', the targeting of significant proportions of available resource in a limited number of strategic locations in which it is hoped that a greater impact will be made than if resources were more uniformly distributed. And in addition to this strengthening idea of spatial targeting, the Rochester Project also emphasised another of the emerging concerns amongst urban policy makers, namely the creation of partnership agreements. In addition to DoE involvement through Urban Programme funding, the project also involved Newcastle City Council and North British Housing Association, their combined efforts going towards the redevelopment and rehabilitation of housing for sale and rent, environmental improvements and the development of community facilities.

East Newcastle has also witnessed attempts at regenerating the area's industrial base, most of them focusing specifically on the riverside area. Industrial Improvement Areas at Walker and Riverside East received Urban Programme support after 1983/4, while money also went on riverside reclamation works, funded both through the UP and Derelict Land Grant. However, much of the environmental work along the riverside has been very different in character to some of the developments on the central Tyneside riverside area, where the concern over recent years, as outlined earlier, has primarily been to attract office employment, support entertainment and leisure facilities and boost the city's image. By contrast, riverside developments in East Newcastle have been of an altogether more prosaic nature, stressing the need to rebuild the area's industrial base. These have included attempts to support emerging types of river-based manufacturing activity, through, for example, sizeable UP and DLG funding, and smaller amounts of English Estates funding, for Newcastle Offshore Technology Park.

*North Tyneside*

Over the course of the period from 1983-91, Urban Programme spending in North Tyneside amounted to some £35.14m, according to the DoE's UPCS database. This was shared between twelve of the city's twenty wards, ranging for Wallsend, which received almost one fifth of all expenditure, to Holystone, which received only one quarter of one per cent of the total. Less than one third (32.60%) of this total of Urban Programme expenditure was devoted to projects which benefited the entire borough. Little of the borough-wide total has gone on the grander city centre developments found in Newcastle. Instead, North Tyneside's borough-wide spending has included large block projects to improve the environment of industrial areas or to improve the riverside area. Other projects have included the North Tyneside Young Persons Job Subsidy Scheme, Operation Corridor (environmental improvements along prominent transport routes) and the financial assistance to businesses block fund. There have also been attempts to stimulate tourism and recreation in the more affluent coastal areas such as Whitley Bay by funding projects such as the Tyne Tunnel Tourist Information Centre, and, in recent years, by funding environmental improvements in the coastal area itself.

The degree of spatial targeting in North Tyneside appears, initially in any case, to be more precise than in either of the partnership authorities. Spending on geographically-grounded projects has been shared amongst twelve of North Tyneside's twenty wards. Gateshead, by contrast, allocated UP funding to all twenty-two of its wards, while only three of Newcastle's twenty-six wards received no UP cash. Moreover, nine wards in Gateshead and twelve in Newcastle which fall outside the 'inner area' received some amount of UP funding, whereas only two wards outside North Tyneside's 'inner area' - Battlehill and Holystone - have received funding. In part, the nature of the distribution of North Tyneside's Urban Programme resource is governed by the geography of its social and economic problems. It is unsurprising that the borough's UP expenditure should be concentrated on a relatively small number of wards given that the incidence of social and economic problems is also concentrated in a limited geographical area. In 1991, for example, unemployment exceeded one in ten of the economically active population in Longbenton, Camperdown, Wallsend, Howdon, Riverside and Chirton wards, whereas in the northern coastal wards of Monkseaton and St Mary's fewer than one in twenty were out of work. In general, the social and economic geography of North Tyneside is more varied than in the other Tyne and Wear authorities and this has been reflected in the way in which UP money in the borough has been distributed.

In addition to the concentration of UP resource on a relatively small number of wards, North Tyneside is also notable in that it has devoted a high proportion of its UP budget directly towards the inner urban area. In total, over two thirds (66.83%) of expenditure over the period 1983/4-1990/1 was in the borough's ten 'inner area' wards. By contrast, expenditure targeted towards the 'inner area' comprised just 42.69% of all expenditure in Gateshead and 53.83% in Newcastle. In other words, in North Tyneside a greater proportion of the Urban Programme budget has been shared amongst a smaller number of wards. Expenditure targeted towards the ten 'inner area' wards has ranged from just over half (54.90%) of the borough's budget in 1989/90, to over three quarters (76.99%) in 1986/7. Moreover, projects within the 'inner area' have accounted for the vast majority of all targeted expenditure. In fact, projects outside the defined 'inner area' accounted for under 1% of all such targeted monies.

As with Gateshead and Newcastle, it is the borough's ten 'inner area' wards which have received the biggest share of the Urban Programme budget. Within this, however, there has been considerable variation, with Wallsend receiving over a quarter of targeted UP monies, while Northumberland and Collingwood have received less then one fiftieth of the total. Over half of the total of targeted project expenditure fell within the three best funded wards: Wallsend, Tynemouth and North Shields. Over three-quarters of expenditure fell within the five best funded wards: the three mentioned together with Howdon and Riverside (Figure C77).

*Figure C77*   **% share of 'targeted' expenditure taken by wards in North Tyneside (1983/84-1990/91)**

|                   | TOTAL      | %      |
|-------------------|-----------|--------|
| WALLSEND*         | 6,590,495  | 27.80  |
| TYNEMOUTH*        | 3,268,493  | 13.79  |
| NORTH SHIELDS*    | 3,179,828  | 13.41  |
| HOWDON*           | 2,593,518  | 10.94  |
| RIVERSIDE*        | 2,399,319  | 10.12  |
| LONGBENTON*       | 1,859,792  | 7.84   |
| CHIRTON*          | 1,671,363  | 7.05   |
| BENTON*           | 1,104,081  | 4.66   |
| NORTHUMBERLAND*   | 448,646    | 1.89   |
| COLLINGWOOD*      | 392,493    | 1.66   |
| BATTLEHILL        | 111,835    | 0.47   |
| HOLYSTONE         | 87,434     | 0.37   |
| **TOTAL**         | **23,707,297** | **100.00** |

\* 'inner area' ward

This high degree of spatial targeting is a result not only of the borough's particular economic and social geography, but also of deliberate policy decisions made by the local authority itself. In the 1984/85 Inner Area Programme submission, for example, the council noted a shift in Urban Programme projects in the borough away from 'supporting a relatively broad range of projects towards the concentration of resources in a limited number of 'activity areas''. Likewise, the 1986/87 submission talked of 'concentrating [UP] expenditure in particular localities', based either on need ('acute problems') or opportunity ('scope for strengthening the local economic base ... and where a high visual impact can be made'). In some respects, this approach, with the designation of 'activity areas', can be seen as the precursor of the current system of Target Areas within the defined inner areas of each of the 57 UPAs.

Much of the targeted UP money spent in North Tyneside has itself been concentrated on particular types of projects, most notably environmental and infrastructural projects aimed at reinvigorating the area's declining industrial base. This has largely been directed at the borough's riverside industrial areas, which have increasingly been falling out of everyday use with the pronounced contraction of shipbuilding and marine engineering on the Tyne. The Point Pleasant Industrial Estate, for example, was developed with substantial UP support which helped fund advance managed workshop units, nursery units, low cost office and workshop accommodation, advance factories, offices for the North Tyneside Community Programmes Agency, workshops for community businesses and 'sheltered' workshop accommodation for people with physical or learning disabilities. In addition, this funding from the Urban Programme was supplemented by around £60,000 in 1986/87 and 1987/88 in the form of Derelict Land Grant support for land reclamation and preparation works. The area also benefited from the expansion of offshore marine engineering, with sub-contracting to firms on the estate, and through the reclamation (using UP money) of the Wallsend Slipway site for North Sea oil and gas platform fabrication.

Another significant 'activity area' has been the Fish Quay area in North Shields, catering for the fish processing and catching industries on the Tyne. The Urban Programme has funded major environmental improvements including landscaping and repairs to the external fabric of buildings, and, through the Riverside Industrial Improvement Area, financial assistance to firms for investment in plants and machinery. The Urban Programme has supported the conversion of fish processing plants to new workshop accommodation in an attempt to diversify the area's economic base, as well as funding the relocation of processing facilities to new premises closeby. These changes have involved several different agencies and policy programmes, including support from Urban Development Grant and City Grant, English Estates, English Heritage, housing associations and, in recent years, Tyne and Wear Development Corporation. The Borough's own view is that the Fish Quay has 'probably [been] the main focus of the Inner Area Programme', explaining, in part, why North Shields ward received almost one tenth of available Urban Programme resources.

In recent years, the spatial focus of Urban Programme support for industrial regeneration in North Tyneside has shifted somewhat. With the arrival of TWDC in 1988, and the consequent loss of much of the riverside portion of the inner urban area, areas such as Point Pleasant Industrial Estate and Fish Quay have ceased to benefit from new Urban Programme money. As a result, the wards covered by TWDC - Wallsend, North Shields and Riverside - have been denied some of their earlier UP 'allocations'. North Shields, for example, has seen its UP budget shrink substantially, from a peak of 16.09% of all expenditure in 1985/86 to 8.37% by 1990/91. Wallsend's budget has declined over a longer period, from a peak of 40.30% in 1983/4 - more than was allocated for borough wide projects during that year - to 20.71% in 1986/7 and 11.70% in 1990/91.

The withdrawal of UP resource from these area has, of course, been compensated by the injection of new money from TWDC. North Shields, for example, now benefits from the development corporation's work at Fish Quay, while Riverside and Chirton wards benefit from the Royal Quays development. However, there has been a clear qualitative shift in the types of development now being implemented by TWDC, compared with those funded under the Urban Programme. In the case of the Royal Quays development, for example, North Tyneside MBC has expressed concern about the proposals for retailing and their potential impacts on existing shopping provision at Wallsend and North Shields. Moreover, the council has also stated its concern about the development's emphasis on leisure, recreation and up-market private housing, which, it argues, underscore a shift away from attempts to regenerate the industrial base of the riverside through projects such as those funded by the UP at Point Pleasant. Indeed, this conflict over the direction of policy seems to have been accentuated still further by the DoE's restriction on UP spending within the Urban Development Area. For example, North Tyneside MBC has been prevented from using UP money to fund security improvements at Point Pleasant because it now falls within the UDA - even though TWDC itself supported the idea. In general, this inability to spend UP money within the UDA is seen as a major problem by local authority and development corporation alike, and one which militates against any continuity in terms of the types of initiative funded in a particular area. But while there has clearly been a shift in the orientation of projects targeted at the Riverside area as TWDC has taken over from the Urban Programme, some degree of continuity and co-operation has remained. In the case of Fish Quay, for example, North Tyneside MBC and TWDC jointly commissioned management consultants to investigate the opportunities for greater private-sector investment in the area. Unlike Royal Quays, the council generally has been happier with the direction of Fish Quays since Urban Programme funding for the area has ceased and TWDC have taken over.

With the arrival of TWDC, the focus for UP-funded attempts at industrial regeneration has switched to other areas, including the Tyne Tunnel Corridor, and Hadrian and Silverlink business parks, which have also been targeted for action under the borough's successful City Challenge bid. There has also been help for the Tyne Tunnel Industrial Estate, mainly in the form of security improvements, which are now seen as a major requirement by many of Tyne and Wear industrial estate-based businesses.

Although the share of the Urban Programme budget going to the Riverside area has declined in recent years, wards such as Wallsend and North Shields have continued to take a relatively large slice of available resources. In 1990/91, for example, Wallsend and North Shields received the largest and third largest share of the total UP budget. To a large extent this continued policy focus can be explained by funding for projects which seek to maintain the commercial health of both towns. Substantial UP resources have been invested in the towns in order to counter the threat of 'out of town' shopping development at Silverlink Retail Park, Royal Quays and North Tyneside Industrial Estate. The Urban Programme has funded a range of town centre schemes, including environmental improvements (landscaping, tree planting, street furniture), traffic management measures and grants for local businesses to improve building appearance.

Howdon, Longbenton and the Meadow Well (Chirton and Riverside wards) have been the principal beneficiaries of housing improvements funded under the HIP, Estate Action and Urban Programme budgets. The Urban Programme has funded Priority Project Teams to co-ordinate the housing management and renewal programmes at Longbenton, the Howdon/Willington/Holy Cross area and on the Meadow Well. Urban Programme money has most frequently been used for a range of small-scale environmental improvements and, increasingly, for security improvements aimed at creating 'defensible space' for residents. Urban Programme funding for such projects has normally been used in support of schemes funded from the HIP budget or, to a lesser extent, by Estate Action, housing associations and UDG/City Grant funds for private developers. At Kings Court in east North Shields, for example, HIP money was used to carry out the major part of the slicing of four story maisonettes to provide 'traditional' housing, but UP money was used to support demolition costs and fund environmental improvements on open space and gardens. Likewise, Urban

Programme money has been used as a prop for much larger injections of Estate Action money at Willington Square in Howdon (which received £330,075 from Estate Action between 1897/88 and 1988/89) and on the Meadow Well (£416,944 in 1988/89 and 1989/90). In this sense, the Urban Programme can be seen as having an important role in anchoring, and making viable, spending under other programme headings like HIP and Estate Action.

The co-ordination of these packages of funding for housing renewal and rehabilitation has been undertaken centrally by the former Urban Housing Renewal Unit (UHRU), and locally by the UP-funded Priority Project Teams (and their predecessors, the Intensive Housing Management Teams). Together, the regional DoE, North Tyneside MBC, the Priority Projects Teams and UHRU have been able to put together packages of money targeted at particular estates. This has also frequently involved partnership with voluntary and community organisations. In Longbenton, for example the Priority Project Team worked with NACRO (security improvements to housing), community businesses such as Keep North Tyneside Warm (for house insulation) and Longbenton Advice Centre (for housing benefit advice for residents).

The Urban Programme has also supported a large number of social and community projects in the borough, many related to social need in the areas of housing stress mentioned above. The UP has funded a welfare benefit take-up campaign in the borough, an idea later used in Newcastle's successful round one City Challenge bid for the West End of the city. Moreover, there have been several noteworthy local examples of developments of this type including a Community Rights Centre at Meadow Well, an information and advice centre at Wallsend and a CAB at North Shields. On the peripheral Longbenton estate alone, the UP had funded the Longbenton Community High School, which offers a creche, nursery, adult education facilities and elderly day centre; Benton Resource Centre, which helps voluntary and community groups; and Longbenton Advice Service, which offers a wide range of advisory services to residents of the estate.

These types of social project clearly are carefully targeted and linked, in many cases, to UP-supported housing improvements. However, the criticism remains that UP money is 'pepper potted' around too many small-scale initiatives. The Community Chest programme, for example, has offered small grants for leisure and recreation projects, play groups and the like, while the Project Support Fund (also UP supported) has offered 'rapid response' capital grants for MSC voluntary and community projects in the inner area. While both these initiatives may be criticised for spreading resource too thinly and in an untargeted way, the IAP documents do spell out a clear commitment to concentrating small-scale social projects within the inner area and in 'activity areas' and, later, in designated priority areas.

*South Tyneside*

According to the UPCS database, South Tyneside's Urban Programme budget of £36.96m over the period 1983/84 to 1990/91 was shared between nineteen of its twenty wards, eighteen of which fall within the 'inner area'. These range, at one end of the funding scale, from the Rekendyke ward, which covers much of the inner and riverside parts of South Shields, and which received almost £6m of UP resource, to Fellgate which received less than £10,000.

As in the case of North Tyneside, the location of the borough and its role within the Tyneside conurbation go some considerable way to explaining the shape and structure of South Tyneside's Urban Programme budget. South Tyneside devoted less than one third of its UP budget towards projects whose benefits were shared amongst most or all of the borough's wards. This figure is significantly lower than in the Newcastle/Gateshead partnership where around half of all expenditure went on borough wide projects. But whereas the partnership authorities have placed considerable emphasis on large-scale promotional and marketing initiatives, city centre leisure and tourist activities and sizeable industrial and commercial investment, much of South Tyneside's UP activity has taken the form of projects of an altogether smaller scale. Unlike Newcastle's city centre or the Metro Centre in Gateshead, for example, South Shield's town centre caters predominantly for more localised forms of retailing and commerce, which have attracted UP support at a much lower level. This is not to say, of course, that South Tyneside has avoided projects aimed at a conurbation-wide market - the recent 'Catherine Cookson' promotional initiatives clearly testifies to this - but that borough-wide projects reflect the smaller scale of the borough itself.

The UPCS database indicates that spending on borough-wide projects has comprised around one third of the entire UP budget over the period of study, a finding which is supported by the borough's own estimate that 31.5% of expenditure on new projects programmed for 1992/93-1994/5 is accounted for by borough-wide projects. But, unlike the other Tyne and Wear authorities, South Tyneside is unusual in that the proportion of spending allocated to borough-wide projects rose in 1990/91, despite the increasing emphasis in DoE Annual Programme Guidelines, and in other urban policy programmes, on the need for more precise spatial targeting. At the same time, however, this increase was small and tells us little about the shape of the borough's budget. South Tyneside's borough-wide total has remained relatively constant over the period of study, ranging from 35.96% of the total in 1986/87 to 29.79% in 1989/90. Moreover, as Figure C78 shows, larger amounts of UP cash have increasingly gone on 'targeted' projects, with year-on-year increases between 1987/88 and 1990/91.

*Figure C78*    **South Tyneside - shares of Urban Programme expenditure**

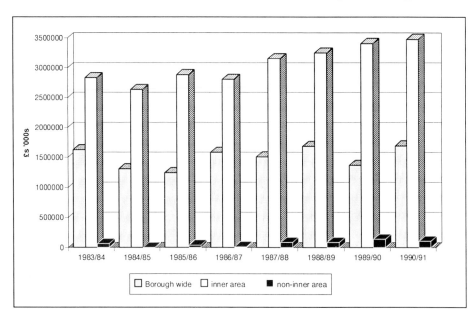

Of South Tyneside's total Urban Programme budget over the period of study, around two thirds (67.54%) went on targeted (that is, non-borough-wide) projects. Over the whole period, targeted expenditure ranged from 64.04% (1986/87) to 72.22% (1989/90). Clearly, the borough's Urban Programme budget has placed more emphasis on targeted projects than is the case for either of the partnership authorities. Equally, however, geographically-grounded projects of this sort have been shared amongst a larger number of the wards than in North Tyneside, where the borough's UP budget has been shared amongst only twelve of its twenty wards. In contrast, nineteen of South Tyneside's twenty wards have received some amount of Urban Programme resource, even if in the case of seven wards (West Park, Harton, Cleadon Park, Horsley Hill, Westoe, Westburn and Fellgate) this amounted to less than one hundredth of the total UP budget for the borough.

Rather strangely, the only ward in South Tyneside which received no Urban Programme funding - Biddick Hall - falls within the defined 'inner area'. UPCS records show no sign of spending in the ward, while IAP documents, which from 1986/87 onwards specify the ward or group of wards affected by proposed and current projects, list only one project which impacts on the ward, and even that is scheduled for 1992/93 onwards, outside the period of study. Conversely, Cleadon and East Boldon - the only ward in the borough not included within the 'inner area' - received over half a million pounds between 1983/84 and 1990/91, the tenth best-funded ward in the borough. The bulk of the funding for Cleadon and East Boldon went towards the Cleadon Lane Improvement Area, the first of the borough's Industrial Improvement Areas to be located away from the riverside area. Urban Programme and Derelict Land Grant budgets helped support site assembly, environmental improvements, site access and infrastructure work, and grant aid to companies, which, it was hoped, would generate employment growth and compensate for the large-scale job losses in the surrounding area following the closure of Boldon Colliery in summer 1982. Despite being outside the 'inner area', and despite the relatively low unemployment rate in the ward itself, it was hoped that the benefits of the Improvement Area would accrue principally to people within the 'inner area'.

The wide geographical extent of South Tyneside's 'inner area' is acknowledged and justified by the borough on the grounds that 'the particular areas of South Tyneside where deprivation is most intense are dispersed throughout the inner area'. Unlike North Tyneside, which contains areas of contrasting characteristics, South Tyneside has a more uniform social and economic geography. With the exception of Cleadon and East Boldon, unemployment levels have been high throughout the borough and frequently in excess of one in ten of the economically active population. This widespread distribution of economic, social and environmental problems throughout South Tyneside has led some councillors and senior officials to conclude that policy approaches emphasising spatial targeting too heavily are inappropriate for the borough. This feeling that economic and social problems need to be tackled over a large geographical area was evidenced by the borough's unsuccessful City Challenge bid for 1993/94-1997/98, which focused upon an area of some 2000 hectares covering the riverside area already targeted by TWDC, and much of Hebburn, Jarrow and inner South Shields. North Tyneside, by contrast, targeted an area of 1128 hectares in its successful bid, while Gateshead's proposed City Challenge area ran to only 174 hectares. At the same time, however, it should be noted that Sunderland's bid, which, like North Tyneside's, proved successful, covered an area larger than South Tyneside's (2850 hectares).

While some officials of the borough council view the economic landscape as inimical to the geographical targeting of policy, the annual Inner Area Programme documents do betray a clear commitment towards concentrating Urban Programme funding on a small number of places within the inner area where problems are particularly intense or opportunities particularly great. Indeed, South Tyneside's designation in 1978 of eight priority areas within the 'inner area' (and a further one in 1981) predates by some fourteen years the advice on target areas given in the UP Annual Programme Guidance notes. Although economic and social problems may be evident throughout the borough, these are particularly severe in a smaller number of places. In Rekendyke, All Saints, Beacon and Bents and Bede wards, for example, unemployment rates ran in excess of 15% in 1991, well above the average ward unemployment rate in the borough of 12.51%.

Despite the area's geography, and despite the views of some within the council, Urban Programme resources have been focused upon a relatively small number of wards. In fact, over two thirds (67.88%) of targeted Urban Programme monies went to just four wards over the period 1983/84-1990/91 (Figure C79). Moreover, three of these four wards - Rekendyke, Bede and Beacon and Bents - occupy three of top four positions in terms of average unemployment rates in the borough between 1986 and 1991. Almost three quarters (74.55%) of UP spending was concentrated in just five wards (the four mentioned above, plus Hebburn Quay); over nine tenths was concentrated in the nine best funded wards. Clearly, the focus of Urban Programme expenditure, in broad terms, has predominantly been on the declining area of largely traditional industry and older housing along the riverside and in the inner parts of Hebburn, Jarrow and South Shields; and on the area surrounding Boldon Colliery ward, particularly in the wake of the closure of the colliery itself in 1982.

*Figure C79*    **South Tyneside - % share of 'targeted' (ie non-borough wide) Urban Programme expenditure (1983/84-1990/91)**

|  | TOTAL | % |
|---|---|---|
| REKENDYKE* | 5817385 | 23.31 |
| BEDE* | 3754473 | 15.04 |
| BOLDON COLLIERY* | 3699697 | 14.82 |
| BEACON AND BENTS* | 3672259 | 14.71 |
| HEBBURN QUAY* | 2165215 | 8.67 |
| WHITELEAS* | 1062848 | 4.26 |
| MONKTON* | 889163 | 3.56 |
| HEBBURN SOUTH* | 784401 | 3.14 |
| TYNE DOCK* | 744892 | 2.98 |
| CLEADON AND EAST BOLDON | 534903 | 2.14 |
| ALL SAINTS* | 531799 | 2.13 |
| PRIMROSE* | 504712 | 2.02 |
| WEST PARK* | 180890 | 0.72 |
| HARTON* | 178123 | 0.71 |
| CLEADON PARK* | 164408 | 0.66 |
| HORSLEY HILL* | 151112 | 0.61 |
| WESTOE* | 65001 | 0.26 |
| WHITBURN* | 53351 | 0.21 |
| FELLGATE* | 6646 | 0.30 |
| **TOTAL** | **24961282** | **100.00** |

\* 'inner area' ward

In total, Boldon Colliery ward received around £37m of Urban Programme resource between 1983/84 and 1990/91, representing one tenth (10.01%) of all UP expenditure in the borough and 14.82% of all expenditure on targeted projects. Much of this has taken the form of support for Boldon Business Park and Hi-tech Village, marketed by the council as its flagship industrial development, suitable for large-scale prestige investors. The eastern part of the site already contains advance factory provision completed by English Estates and Washington Developments Ltd, together with 21 factory units provided by British Coal Enterprises. Part of the western portion of the site has been developed and marketed by South Tyneside MBC as a Hi-tech Village, providing

314

around a dozen units for hi-tech companies, with another ten units due to come on stream once phase II of the development is completed. Urban Programme support has taken the form of environmental, infrastructural and site access improvements, linking the site with the A19 and A1 trunk routes south. Funding has also been provided by Derelict Land Grant monies, which funded reclamation and preparation works at the colliery to the tune of around £250,000 between 1986/87 and 1989/90; by City Grant, which provided an extra £1,228,042 for the area in 1991/92; and, most significantly, by English Estates, to the tune of £3.12m between 1987/88 and 1990/91. The council has designated the site a 'Strategic Employment Area', although South Tyneside MBC and Tyne and Wear County Council had earlier sought (and been refused) Enterprise Zone status following the closure of Boldon Colliery. Despite this, the financial commitment from TWCC, South Tyneside MBC and, since the wind up of the county council, by English Estates has been significant. Indeed, around one third of South Tyneside's economic development budget for 1992/93 is being spent on Boldon Business Park.

The riverside areas of South Shields, Jarrow and Hebburn have also been the subject of significant Urban Programme expenditure, again with the aim of regenerating the area's industrial base of shipbuilding and marine engineering. Rekendyke ward has gained UP funding in the form of support for the Riverside Industrial Improvement Area (designated in 1978) which contains Rekendyke and Millbank industrial estates and covers much of the industrial area of inner South Shields. The Urban Programme has funded a range of infrastructure and site assembly works, access improvements and environmental projects on declining industrial sites such as the former Singer factory at Templeton and the former Coal Board mineral line running through the riverside area. English Estates has also been active in funding advance factory construction at the Garwood Street and Rekendyke industrial estates, while the conversion of vacant industrial property at Mill Dam to workshop and office space was supported with Urban Programme and ERDF money.

In recent years, some rather tentative attempts have been made to link the benefits of economic development and industrial regeneration in the riverside area with the resident population in nearby areas. For example, the Simonside Employment Initiative, funded under the Urban Programme and the DoE's Inner City Programme Development Fund, has attempted to ensure that any benefits from economic regeneration are linked to the needs of residents of deprived areas like the Lower Simonside and West Harton estates. Funding was secured for two full-time staff, with the aim of encouraging 'self help' initiatives in training and business development, by promoting training and employment opportunities for local people and by improving community facilities.

Over the last few years the focus of Urban Programme attention has moved away from the riverside industrial area. Since the arrival of Tyne and Wear Development Corporation, the DoE has prevented South Tyneside, in common with other local authorities, from spending UP money within the UDC area. The council estimates that around 23% of all Urban Programme expenditure in 1987/88 went towards projects located within the UDA, falling to 19% during the subsequent year. The upshot of this, as in North Tyneside, has been that the share of the Urban Programme budget taken by the riverside wards has declined, while that of Boldon Colliery - the other main area targeted for economic regeneration - has increased. In Rekendyke, for example, the share of total UP resource fell from 12.08% in 1987/88 and 16.63% the following year, to 7.72% in 1989/90 and 5.67% in 1990/91.

This inability to spend Urban Programme money in the UDC area is viewed as a particularly serious problem for South Tyneside for two reasons. First, the borough has a shortage of developable land and premises, and much of the potential industrial land supply is located in the riverside area within the UDC area. A second problem, according to the council, is posed by the fact that flagship developments of the type often favoured by TWDC are likely to be more viable in the central part of Tyneside at Newcastle, where private investment is more likely to be forthcoming. The result, according to the council, will be that 'South Tyneside may therefore benefit from few, if any, flagship schemes, and at the same time see major reductions in on-going programmes of smaller scale ... in the UDA'.

As well as economic and industrial regeneration projects - which account for the bulk of Urban Programme spending and are now the focus for TWDC activity in the borough - the riverside wards have also benefited from Urban Programme, HIP, Estate Action and UHRU Support for housing rehabilitation and redevelopment. Rekendyke ward, for example, has been the subject of Urban Programme supported Housing Action Areas at Wallas Road, Dacre Street and Dean Road. In accordance with Annual Programme Guidance notes, this has normally taken the form of funding for environmental and landscape works in support of major work funded through HIPs and, to a lesser extent, UHRU and Estate Action, or by housing associations and private developers. At the Laygate Flats and the Woodbine Estate, both in South Shields, Urban Programme funding went towards small-scale environmental works in support of the HIP-funded rehabilitation programmes and, in the case of Laygate, the introduction of secure door entry systems. In the Rekendyke area, for example, it was estimated that the Urban Programme contributed only 15% of the total cost of housing improvements in the area between 1979 and 1984, whereas HIP and housing association finance accounted for three quarters of the total cost.

Many of the Urban Programme funded housing projects have drawn support from a wide range of bodies and programme headings. For example, Urban Development Grant (UDG) funding of £174,589 was utilised in harness with UP funding to support the conversion of rundown commercial property to low cost housing for sale at Mill Dam, South Shields between 1985/86 and 1986/ 87. The development was undertaken in partnership with the Enterprise Five Housing Association and Northern Rock Housing Trust (a Newcastle-based company). Similarly, UDG support - amounting to £3,125,993 between 1987/ 88 and 1990/91 - was given to Bellway Urban Renewals (another company based in the North East) for a proposed 456-dwelling scheme to be called Hebburn Village on the site of a former shipyard at Hebburn. In general, however, applications for UDG/City Grant from private developers have been fewer than expected, something that the council attributes to a 'deep-seated reluctance to consider investment in the borough'.

As in the other Tyne and Wear authorities, the Urban Programme has helped fund a diverse range of social and community projects, often small in scale, localised in impact and targeted at particular client groups such as South Shields' Bangladeshi and Yemeni populations. These types of project are often criticised on the grounds that they are spread too finely over a wide area, based, in many cases, on ad hoc demands emanating from the network of disparate voluntary and community groups. In the case of South Tyneside, this is a criticism which has been levelled with particular force on the grounds that the borough's Area Advisory Committees (AACs) encourage the 'pepper potting' of social and community resources. The AACs were established with funding from the Urban Programmes Area Management Initiatives Scheme, and have small budgets to 'bid' for UP resources and to spend money themselves on a range of small-scale environmental and social schemes such as landscaping small sites, holiday schemes for children and small grants to community groups. At the same time, however, the AACs can also be viewed as an institutional framework to monitor the co-ordination and targeting of UP expenditure on social projects. In this sense, they can be seen as serving a similar function to the South Tyneside Industrial Strategy Committee, which comprises representatives of the local authority, central government departments, development agencies, quangos like TWDC and the private sector. The committee's strategy for 1990-95 is currently in place, and the annual Economic Development Plans and UP economic development projects must be formulated in accordance with the strategy's objectives. The Urban Programme's Grants and Loans to Industry pool, for example, is overseen by TEDCo (Tyneside Economic Development Company), South Tyneside's local enterprise agency, with applications for funding scrutinised by a panel comprising representatives from the borough council, South Tyneside Task Force and local business. TEDCo, like the AACs, aims to ensure that UP funding is scrutinised and monitored, and that resources are matched to needs and opportunities. Nevertheless, the criticism remains that support for social and community services in the borough has been untargeted, uncoordinated and unfocused, even if this can be explained to a limited extent by the widely dispersed nature of social need in the borough.

The Urban Programme has helped support numerous social and community services which have also drawn funds from mainstream council budgets or other programmes such as ESF or, indeed, the Traditional Urban Programme. Services of this type include nursery provision, child minders, the Nursery Transport scheme, elderly sheltered accommodation (at South Shields Hospital and Deans Hospital, for example) and environmental improvements in schools (for example, demolition and landscaping to provide additional play space at Boldon Colliery Primary School). Urban Programme support is often vital to ensure the viability of such projects, particularly where they impose recurring revenue demands on mainstream service budgets in addition to 'one-off' capital funding from the Urban Programme. Indeed, in some cases the Urban Programme has become important to the viability of such services as mainstream service budgets have progressively been squeezed by reductions in Rate Support Grant (as outlined in Section 3.2). The result has been that pressure has increased to use Inner Area Programme funds as a partial substitute for lost mainstream resources. This emphasises just how important the Urban Programme is to a local authority like South Tyneside, both for revenue and capital expenditure. In fact, South Tyneside was reliant on the Urban Programme for around half (50.8%) of all capital expenditure by the council in the first five years of the Urban Programme, rising to almost three quarters (74%) in 1983/84 and remaining at that level thereafter.

*Sunderland*

Sunderland's Urban Programme budget amounted to £41.75m over the period 1983/84-1990/91. Of the city's twenty-five wards, twenty-one received Urban Programme funds, ranging from the £12.58m spent in Central ward, to only £49,281 in St Michael's. Washington East and South wards, Hetton and Shiney Row received no Urban Programme funding over the study period.

Over the eight years covered by the UPCS database, the share of Urban Programme expenditure devoted to projects which benefited most or all of the city amounted to almost one third (31.68%) of the total, a calculation which is supported by the council's recent estimate that borough-wide spending for

1992/93 is likely to come to 33% of the Inner Area Programme. This is broadly similar to the borough-wide share of spend in the other programme authorities, North and South Tyneside, but significantly lower than the Newcastle/Gateshead Partnership, where around half of all UP spending went on non-targeted projects. That Sunderland should have devoted such a low proportion of its UP budget to borough-wide projects is, perhaps, rather surprising given the city's geographical position within Tyneside and Wearside. Whereas North and South Tyneside are very much tied into Newcastle and the central part of the Tyneside conurbation, Wearside is, in many ways, quite separate from Tyneside. Within Wearside, Sunderland is very much the dominant place, a fact which is recognised by the recent acquisition of city status. It might be expected that Sunderland would fulfill many of the central place functions which Newcastle performs for the Tyneside conurbation - an expectation which, initially at least, is not borne out by the UPCS figures.

There are two factors which may go some way to explaining these figures. First, although Sunderland does perform some of the same kinds of central place functions as Newcastle, the latter is very much the regional capital and serves a much wider area than even Tyneside or Wearside. Moreover the 'policy community' in Newcastle - the City Council, Tyne and Wear Development Corporation, The Newcastle Initiative and the like - have tried to reinforce this by presenting an image of the city as an attractive location for high status office employers, retailing and financial services, attempting to build upon the city's existing concentration of regional offices of major companies and public sector bodies. Sunderland, by contrast, has modelled itself more as a location for manufacturing industry - as evidenced by The Wearside Opportunity's 'Make it Wearside' campaign - and building on past success in attracting inward investment, most notably, of course, Nissan's move to Washington. A second reason for Sunderland's low borough-wide total centres on the way in which UPCS data records have been compiled. Central ward received nearly one third (30.13%) of all Urban Programme spending in the city over the eight-year period from 1983/84 to 1990/91. Furthermore, in the first four years of this period, Central ward actually received a greater share of spending than did borough-wide projects, reaching a peak of 43.07% of total spending in 1986/87. Conversely, borough-wide expenditure amounted to less than one sixth of all Urban Programme expenditure in 1983/84 and 1984/85 - by far the lowest totals of any of the five Tyne and Wear authorities. This can be explained, to a certain extent, by the concentration of the city's shopping facilities in this ward, with a series of Urban Programme funded projects to provide loans and grants to businesses in the Town Centre Commercial Improvement Areas, together with associated environmental improvements and pedestrianisation schemes. Projects of this type clearly benefit a wider area than just Central ward, but nonetheless have been allocated solely to Central ward in the UPCS database. But while this clearly will have artificially inflated the total spend in Central ward, much of the Urban Programme spending there has been on projects whose impacts are more limited in geographical terms. In 1984/85, for example, almost half of the total spend in Central ward was explained by just two projects: site preparation works for the Parrs Bank Industrial Improvement Area and access and environmental improvements for Webster's Ropery Workshops.

Expenditure on borough-wide projects in Sunderland has ranged from 15.10% in 1984/85, to 48.45% in 1988/89. To a limited extent, this high degree of variation can be explained by changes from year to year in the ways in which project expenditure is recorded in the UPCS database, as outlined above. This is certainly borne out by comparison with the other Tyne and Wear authorities, each of which have had rather more stable patterns of spending on borough-wide projects. At the same time, however, the pattern of spending on borough-wide projects does reflect some of the changing themes underpinning the Urban Programme. For example, the growth of borough-wide projects during 1988/89 reflected the growing emphasis on training initiatives (funding for the MARI computer training agency, for example) and small business development (UP support for Entrust in 1988/89). As in Newcastle/Gateshead and North Tyneside, 1989/90-1990/91 saw a fall in expenditure on borough-wide projects in the city. Again, this reflects a more general trend in the direction of the Urban Programme, this time the growing concern that economic development, training and small business initiatives of the type mentioned should be targeted towards particular areas of greatest social and economic need, or, in the case of tourism, retail or commercial related developments, towards areas of greatest potential for growth.

Over two thirds (68.31%) of all Urban Programme expenditure over the eight years examined went towards particular wards or groups of wards. Although this figure may be artificially inflated by the inclusion of some borough-wide projects in the total for Central ward - particularly in earlier years, as already noted - it is clear that Sunderland has devoted a higher proportion of its budget to targeted projects than is the case in either of the partnership authorities. At the same time, however, much of this can be explained by the high degree of targeting in 1983/84 and 1984/85, when targeted expenditure accounted for over four fifths of all expenditure, mainly as a result of the large expenditure totals in Central ward. Moreover, while Urban Programme spending in the 'inner areas' of Tyne and Wear has, in general terms, increased over the period of study, in Sunderland the 'inner area' has taken a progressively lower share of the total spend. Indeed by 1988/89-1990/91, the 'inner area' share of total urban programme spend had declined to around half (Figure C80).

Sunderland also differs from the general pattern amongst Tyne and Wear authorities in terms of the extent of Urban Programme funding for projects which fall outside the inner urban area. From 1985/86 to 1990/91, but with the exception of 1988/89, wards outside the 'inner area' received between 3.43% and 16.17% of the city's Urban Programme budget. In part, this is a reflection of the distribution of Sunderland's economic and social problems, which is very different from other parts of Tyne and Wear. In particular, Sunderland

*Figure C80*     **Sunderland - shares of Urban Programme expenditure**

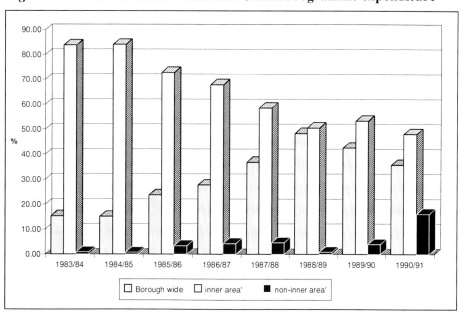

319

possess 'an unusual urban structure, with many of the adverse conditions being experienced on the periphery of the borough rather than being concentrated around the town centre'. This was recognised by the DoE in 1988 when it was agreed that 'inner area' status should be applied to the peripheral estates of Town End Farm and Thorney Close, both of which had previously been designated 'Special Priority Outer Areas' and had received some Urban Programme monies. But even though this led to the virtual doubling of the 'inner area', containing some 42% of the city's population, the Urban Programme has continued to fund projects which fall outside the 'inner area'. Indeed, non-'inner area' wards received a greater share of UP resource (16.17%) in 1990/91 than in any year previously (Figure C80). In total, spending in wards outside the 'inner area' amounted to 7% of all 'targeted' (i.e. non borough-wide) expenditure in the city - a significantly higher proportion than elsewhere in Tyne and Wear.

The result of spending outside the 'inner area' has been a somewhat irregular distribution of UP resource amongst Sunderland's wards. On one hand, the dominance of Central ward, which took a 44.10% share of targeted resource of the city, has led to a top heavy distribution of Urban Programme funds. The second best funded ward in the city - Thornholme - received less than one third of the Urban Programme money spent on projects in Central ward (Figure C81). On the other hand, a large number of wards - both inside and outside the 'inner area' - have received relatively small amounts of UP funding. Around one hundredth of the total UP spend was shared amongst four wards, two of them (Thorney Close and St Michael's) covered by the 'inner area', and two (Washington East and Ryhope) lying outside. The ten best funded wards received 88.64% of all targeted UP money in this city, the remainder being shared amongst eleven wards, all of which received less than one fiftieth of all targeted project monies. Two of this group of ten best funded wards - Houghton

*Figure C81*  **Sunderland - % share of total 'targeted' (ie non-borough wide) Urban Programme expenditure 1983/84 - 1990/91**

|  | TOTAL | % |
|---|---|---|
| CENTRAL* | 12,579,760 | 44.10 |
| THORNEHOLME* | 3,662,254 | 12.84 |
| SOUTHWICK * | 2,216,043 | 7.77 |
| COLLIERY* | 1,395,402 | 4.89 |
| ST PETERS* | 1,236,122 | 4.33 |
| HENDON* | 1,225,621 | 4.30 |
| SOUTH HYLTON* | 1,219,254 | 4.27 |
| HOUGHTON | 590,502 | 2.07 |
| FULWELL | 580,754 | 2.04 |
| TOWN END FARM* | 578,510 | 2.03 |
| CASTLETOWN* | 568,104 | 1.99 |
| SILKSWORTH* | 563,761 | 1.98 |
| EPPLETON | 563,502 | 1.98 |
| PALLION* | 549,410 | 1.93 |
| GRINDON* | 480,508 | 1.68 |
| ST.CHADS* | 108,197 | 0.38 |
| WASHINGTON N | 102,002 | 0.36 |
| THORNEY CLOSE* | 94,002 | 0.33 |
| WASHINGTON E | 93,002 | 0.33 |
| RYHOPE | 67,001 | 0.23 |
| ST MICHAEL'S* | 49,281 | 0.17 |
| **TOTAL** | **28,522,991** | **100.00** |

* 'inner area' ward

and Fulwell - lie outside the 'inner area', while seven of the eleven worst funded wards are covered by the designated 'inner area'.

Like North and South Tyneside, the focus of Sunderland's inner area programme has been on economic regeneration, with a geographical focus on the Wear Corridor. This area suffered the brunt of the long-term decline in manufacturing industry, culminating with the final demise of shipbuilding on the Wear with the closure of the VESL yard in the late 1980s. Moreover, of the relatively small amount of new employment created in the 1980s most was located in peripheral areas and, in particular, in Washington New Town. In the 'inner area', fewer than 400 jobs have been provided by the attraction of flagship employers such as Kigas, Leibherr and Ti-Well.

Urban Programme monies have been targeted at the Wear Corridor through a combination of promotion and advice for businesses, grants and loans to companies, site assembly and workspace provision. Much of this has been channelled through Industrial Improvement Areas at Panns Bank, Queen Alexandra Bridge, Bonnersfield and Monkwearmouth. The Queen Alexandra Bridge IIA, for example, has received Urban Programme and Derelict Land Grant support for the derelict former shipyard area at Ayres Quay on the south bank, providing low-cost workshop provision for small firms, including 'bad neighbour' uses at Wellington Lane. The Farringdon Row Site within the Queen Alexandra Bridge IIA has also received Urban Programme and DLG support for site reclamation and preparation, with UP money being used for advance nursery units for small business start-ups. The area has also seen Urban Programme funding for conversion of redundant premises, most notably the refurbishment of the Webster's Ropery building to provide craft workshop space and hi-tech offices.

In addition to site preparation and associated infrastructural and environmental works, the riverside industrial area has also benefited from Urban Programme loans and grants to companies. Sunderland MBC and the former County Council have used the 1976 Tyne and Wear Act and the Urban Programme to help companies with plant and machinery investment costs, rent and rate relief and costs incurred in relocation. This has often been linked with other programmes such as the European Social Fund, which supported the council's Industrial and Commercial Training Fund, a programme of grants to companies to encourage employment of more trainees. There have also been UP-funded advice and support services, particularly for small firms and new companies. The New Enterprise Advisory Unit, for example, is a CAB-run service which provides counselling and advice for potential small retail firms. Likewise, the Sunderland Common Ownership Enterprise Resource Centre, which received UP cash for a new base at Hendon, has the aim of encouraging the development of workers co-operatives.

The geographical focus of Urban Programme attention on the riverside area has faded somewhat with the advent of Tyne and Wear Development Corporation, which, as in North and South Tyneside, has taken over responsibility for much of the riverside corridor. The result has been the gradual emergence of new priorities for Urban Programme spending. This has involved the continued emphasis on environmental improvements in the town centre, with a third commercial improvement area covering the town centre's core designated in 1990 to complement the existing CIAs on the edge of the town centre at Villiers Street/High Street West and Silksworth Row/Mary Street, both of which were designated in 1983. The Urban Programme has helped fund major town centre environmental improvements, including the refurbishment of the Town Centre Park and the pedestrianisation of the High Street, together with a range of improvements funded through the CIAs. In recent years, many such improvements have been related to wider attempts to boost the city's image, with UP support for tree planting, sign posting, floodlighting, street furniture and the creation of local landmarks.

Linked to these attempts to develop the city's image through environmental improvements in the city centre have been the increasing policy inputs to the Roker/Seaburn coastal foreshore area to the north of the river mouth. Urban Programme money has been used over recent years to fund visitor attractions in this area, including the Sunderland Illuminations and the Wearside Festival. There has also been UP support for Seaburn Ocean Park, a mixed housing/ retail/leisure development marketed at incoming visitors.

Promotional and marketing activities of this sort have also been evident with the beginnings of a move away from 'traditional' forms of Urban Programme support for economic regeneration - site preparation, advance factory construction and loans and grants to companies - as UP efforts have increasingly gravitated towards the marketing of opportunities for incoming investors. Urban Programme monies have helped to set up The Wearside Opportunity, whose marketing of the city's merits is pitched at potential investors and incoming companies. Urban Programme money in Sunderland has increasingly gone towards the marketing of industrial development opportunities, such as site availability in the new Enterprise Zone and the availability of advance factory premises. At the same time, however, Urban Programme efforts have retained part of their focus upon traditional site assembly and servicing of industrial land, for example at the Enterprise Zone-funded Doxford International site.

In addition to the geographical focus on the Wear Corridor, the Urban Programme has also funded a range of social and housing-based projects spread throughout the city. This explains why a relatively large number of wards have received UP funds of varying amounts. Quite simply, social and economic problems are widely distributed throughout the city, and unlike some other parts of Tyne and Wear, Sunderland's outer estates display particularly impoverished conditions. In the early years of the programme, resources were concentrated on three areas of greatest need: East End/Hendon/ Bishopwearmouth, Ford and Pennywell and Southwick/Monkwearmouth. But in the mid-1980s, the feeling was that the targeting of these areas during earlier years meant that it would now be possible 'to direct more money towards the secondary areas of need'. As a result, a greater share of UP resource went to areas like Town End Farm and Downhill on the north western edge of the city. Town End Farm ward received over £100,000 of Urban Programme funds per annum during 1985/86, 1987/88 and 1988/89.

Areas like Town End Farm would have received a still greater share of Urban Programme resource were it not for the particular way in which Sunderland's Inner Area Programme has supported housing improvements. In general, the city's IAP has placed much less emphasis on housing renewal than is the case in other authorities, where, despite increasingly tight Annual Programme Guidance restrictions, UP support for housing renewal funded from HIP, Estate Action and UDG/City Grant budgets have been altogether more intense. Initiatives like the Avenues Agency in Bensham, Gateshead - a multi-agency housing improvement project using money from several budgets and including UP money - arguably have no real parallel in Sunderland. Urban Programme support for housing improvements has consisted mainly of relatively minor landscaping and environmental works, as in the rehabilitation of the difficult-to-let 'Squares' area of central Southwick, which received over £400,000 in Estate Action support between 1986/87 and 1989/90. Indeed, the Inner Area Programme for 1986/87 notes that the bulk of environmental improvements were funded from the city's HIP budget, rather than its UP budget.

Town End Farm has received considerable sums of public money for the improvement of the area's housing stock. However, most of this public funding has come from sources other than the Urban Programme, principally HIP and Estate Action, the latter alone providing the Downhill and Town End Farm areas with £1.3m between 1987/88 and 1989/90. There has also been Urban Development Grant funding of around £800,000 during the same period for the conversion of the area's 'S' blocks to traditional type dwellings, in conjunction with Wimpey and Two Castles Housing Association. In other cases, Urban Programme funding has gone towards housing management services rather than environmental improvements. In Pennywell (another peripheral estate), for example, the Urban Programme provided funding for seven staff as part of the area's Intensive Housing Management Service.

Sunderland's peripheral estates have also received Urban Programme support in the form of funding for a range of social and community services. Pennywell, for example, has received funding for a Community Centre managed by the local community association, while Town End Farm has had UP money for the Turning Point project, which offers advice on training, employment and enterprise to young unemployed people on the estate and some workspace facilities housed in a converted block of flats. In the early years of the Urban Programme, the majority (around 64% in 1979/80) of the budget went towards social projects, many of them revenue-funded and inherited from the Traditional Urban Programme. In recent times, however, expenditure on social projects has comprised around one quarter of total expenditure. Funding for many mainstream social services such as libraries and community centres has now been absorbed into the council's main programme. Indeed, with the tightening of Urban Programme rules over the years, most social and community projects have been funded through voluntary sector groups, thereby countering the criticism that UP spending of this sort is merely a substitute for funding which would normally come from the council's main budget.

Much of the funding for voluntary groups has been small in scale and scattered amongst a range of groups throughout the city. Initiatives such as the Community Seed Fund, which gives small grants for start-up costs for new voluntary groups, and the Community Chest, which hands out 'one-off' grants, by their very nature lack any clear geographical focus, but are vital nonetheless for the existence of many voluntary bodies.

While the Urban Programme in recent years has shifted much of its effort to the city centre and various promotional and image-based initiatives, and TWDC has taken over responsibility for the regeneration of the Wear Corridor area, the north west area of the city has emerged as a target area for action through City Challenge. Many of the new projects proposed in the city's City Challenge bid simply continue on from the range of housing improvements funded by Estate Action, HIPs and, to a lesser extent, the Urban Programme, but with increased emphasis on tenure diversification through a combination of 'right-to-buy' sales and transfers of council stock to housing associations and tenant co-ops. However, there are also two major flagship schemes proposed, the first of which is the Concord Centre, which will house a sports stadium and conference centre, plus associated retail and leisure facilities. The second is the proposed Glass City, a heritage centre featuring various visitor attractions and recreation facilities. Sunderland's City Challenge is also linked into some of the other publicly-funded initiatives targeted in the north west Sunderland area, notably the TWDC and English Estates development of Sunderland Enterprise Park on the north bank of the Wear and the Sunrise Business Park at Castletown, both of which have Enterprise Zone status.

# *Appendix D*  Local analysis: the three conurbations

## 1  INTRODUCTION

The quantitative interpretation of the impacts of policy looked at both the national and local scales. For the local scale, the three conurbations of Greater Manchester, Merseyside and Tyne and Wear were selected for more detailed examination. The national level analysis includes all the districts within these conurbations, but the evaluation was solely at the scale of districts. Although much urban policy is derived at a district scale, much of the allocation of resources and the implementation of policy is based at neighbourhood level, targeted mainly on sub-areas of districts where problems are most concentrated. It is necessary therefore to evaluate whether such areas have been receiving the major amounts of overall monies within districts and whether they are catching up with less disadvantaged areas within the districts. The first question is reported on in Appendix C - the reports on the three conurbations - where conclusions are drawn on the targeting of the designated 'inner areas' within districts. The second question is examined here.

### 1.1  Aims

The aims of this section of the report are:

- to analyse change in the outcome indicators within districts based on ward-level data;

- to establish whether the gaps between inner and outer area wards, measured on the outcome indicators, have narrowed or widened over the period;

- to analyse whether there is a relationship between amounts of resource inputs and changes in the outcome indicators; and

- to evaluate the impact of government monies at a number of scales.

### 1.2  Data

While the ward scale of analysis is most appropriate for evaluating the overall impacts of urban policy, it is one at which data on inputs and indicators are often inaccessible. The assembly of ward-level data has presented major difficulties. As described in the local accounts in Appendix C, input data have been gathered for the three conurbations and attributed to wards. The reliability and availability of the data varies between and within conurbations. As much attribution of expenditure to the ward level has been carried out as is possible. With all its limitations this process in itself provides a picture of policy inputs that has not been available before. Most of the districts have designated parts of their overall areas as 'inner areas' with the intention of giving priority to them in the resource allocation process. These designated areas vary over time. In some districts their boundaries do not coincide with current ward boundaries (no doubt as a consequence of ward boundary changes in the early 1980s). In some districts the implication of the designated 'inner areas' is less clear than in others. In some districts a large proportion of the overall area is designated, while in others the 'inner area' is a small fraction of the total. While much of the monies have been directed towards these 'inner areas', there are a number of anomalies and there is considerable variation of allocation within the set of 'inner areas'. This makes any straightforward analysis of the relationship between inputs and outcomes unlikely. The intention was to group the wards into sets with major amounts of inputs and sets with little or no inputs. The variation of inputs which we have discovered within both the set of 'inner areas' and the set of non-'inner areas' makes an analysis based on an assumption that the first set has been well resourced and the second set less well resourced untenable. The patterns are likely to be complex.

The outcome indicators available at ward level are few. This analysis is therefore based on job change, unemployment and long-term unemployment. At the ward level, job change has limitations which have been discussed earlier. The statistics are company-based and do not necessarily refer to the number of jobs actually held in the ward. They are only indicative of change of employment opportunities and economic health over time. The unemployment data are simple numbers. Unemployment is only available from 1983 while long-term unemployment is only available from 1984. They are not rates. The data are not available to calculate rates since there are no accurate age-related population estimates at ward scale. Although population estimates of the denominators could be made to provide rates, it is likely that the errors may be larger than the real changes in the rates. We have therefore decided to use the numbers alone in one part of the analysis and have examined the changing share of total unemployment and total long-term unemployment for wards within districts. This might still reflect the changing number of economically active over time, but there is no accurate way of measuring this since even the census results have a spatially variable undercount which makes even these figures questionable. In order to remove the size difference of wards (as much as to produce rates), the unemployment numbers have also been divided by the number of economically active in the ward according to the 1981 census (the reults of the 1991 census not having been available at the time of the analysis). These data only accurately represent rates in 1981 and do so less and less as the decade progresses. The other major problem with analysis at the ward scale is the changes in ward boundaries which have taken place during the 1980s. In some districts such changes have been minor. In others whole wards have disappeared. The unemployment data are only available for the 1981 wards throughout the period. This makes analysis of the changing shares of unemployment easy, but it does not permit a straightforward analysis of the relationship between unemployment change and inputs, because the input data are available only for present ward boundaries. Reallocations of input data have been made to permit some correlation between inputs and outcomes. The data for jobs are available for both sets of ward boundaries but, of course, are in themselves less interpretable than the unemployment data. We await the census change files for the most appropriate analysis of the net migration of 25-34 year-olds.

**1.3 Methods**

To a large extent, therefore, the availability of data has constrained the methods open to us. A number of approaches have been used. The 'gap' analysis is based on the changing share of total unemployment or jobs within districts. The two points of time used to compare the gaps are determined by data availability. As with the national level analysis, the points do not correspond to similar positions on the economic cycle. They are simply the best we have. The gaps are examined throughout the period as well as between the two end points.

The gap analysis has been carried out using different clusters of wards. One set is based on 1981 census data, distinguishing an inner area and a number of different peripheral areas within every district. The other is a two-fold classification based on designated 'inner areas' and non-'inner areas'. The first then is based on the characteristics of the wards according to a set of indicators from the 1981 census, while the second is based on the policy-oriented criterion of targeted wards.

The gap analysis examines the outcomes. It can be interpreted only as a general indication of the relationship between inputs and outcomes. This relationship is tested by the application of a set of multi-level models and standard multiple regression analysis. The multi-level model uses the wards as the first level, a grouping of wards as the second level and the districts as the third. Various groupings of wards were tried: the two described above; and one based entirely on the indicator variables. The logic of the census-based groupings is obvious. This is a set of areas based on wards grouped according to common characteristics. They may have been expected to respond in similar ways to inputs and may have been expected to receive similar amounts of inputs. The second grouping is based on intended targeting of inputs. The 'inner areas' may have been expected to have received most inputs and to have responded differently to non-'inner areas'. The third grouping is based on the outcome indicator and poses the question of whether certain outcomes arise as a response to particular levels or presence/absence of inputs.

The multi-level model allows inputs to be entered as explanatory variables at different levels and permits contextual variables to be introduced at different levels too. Multiple regression is only resorted to where the data fail to fit the model; where, in other words, the classes of wards have insufficient variation between classes compared to the variation within classes.

An analysis of shares and gaps was first carried out for unemployment and long-term unemployment based on the census groupings. The share analysis was first carried out at the conurbation level by district to set the context for the intra-district share analysis.

## 2.1 Greater Manchester

Within Greater Manchester, Manchester itself had an increasing share of unemployment over the period 1983-90. It rose from 24.36% in 1983 to 29.12% in 1990. It was fairly stable until 1986 and in subsequent years, a period of unemployment decline, its share rose rapidly. The share of long-term unemployment increases even more dramatically by 6.37% to 33.88%. Oldham is the only other district to increase its share over the period as a whole. Its share declined until 1986 but, like Manchester, rose during the period of unemployment decline. Obviously both are faced with increased long-term unemployment, the share of which increases steadily for both throughout the period 1984-90.

At the other end of the spectrum lie: Stockport, down 1.7% for unemployment and 2.1% for long-term unemployment; Bury, down 1.15% and 1.09% respectively; and Trafford, down 0.58% and 0.34%. Rochdale and Salford are down overall on unemployment, but after falling until 1988 have both risen again. In Salford this corresponds to a rapid recent increase in the share of long-term unemployment which put its 1990 share above its 1984 share. Rochdale's share of long-term unemployment went down, along with all the other districts except Manchester, Oldham and Salford. Tameside had a stable share of unemployment until 1987 and then it declined. Wigan's share varied until 1988 and then it fell.

At the beginning of the period, Manchester, Salford and Wigan had greater shares of long-term unemployment than ordinary unemployment. At the end, only Manchester and Salford stood out, both with proportionally more long term than at the start.

Within the context of the conurbation shares, we can see that all of the inner areas of districts, with the exception of Manchester's, had increased shares of unemployment from 1983 to 1990. The gap within districts had widened for nine districts. For Wigan, Trafford and Bolton this change was a very marked one. Manchester's gap may be explained by a loss of population or the poor state of the east and north areas which both gain in share.

**Shares of unemployment in the inner areas of Greater Manchester districts**

|            | 1983  | 1990  |           | 1983  | 1990  |
|------------|-------|-------|-----------|-------|-------|
| Bolton     | 58.84 | 63.02 | Salford   | 46.16 | 46.89 |
| Bury       | 37.97 | 41.59 | Stockport | 38.90 | 41.98 |
| Manchester | 37.37 | 36.99 | Tameside  | 49.14 | 49.99 |
| Oldham     | 56.81 | 57.35 | Trafford  | 54.48 | 59.35 |
| Rochdale   | 38.73 | 40.24 | Wigan     | 40.53 | 50.03 |

These changes still conceal much variation between wards within the inner areas. Only Bury has all its inner area wards increasing their share. In all the others, there are varying experiences.

The increasing share of inner areas is less clear for long-term unemployment. It is increasing for Bolton, Rochdale, Salford, Stockport and Trafford. The increase is substantial for Trafford (3.59%). The east and north of Manchester again have increasing shares. West Oldham, west Tameside and north Wigan have substantially increased shares. In all cases except Tameside, the inner areas have a higher share of long-term unemployment than ordinary unemployment.

**Summary of Greater Manchester**

Overall, Manchester has an increasing share of the conurbations unemployed but this is not concentrated more in the inner areas over time; while in all the other districts, unemployment and often long-term unemployment, too, is increasingly concentrated into the inner areas. While there is considerable variation within all the inner areas excepting Bury, the gap within most districts between the inner area as a whole and the rest is increasing.

## 2.2 Merseyside

As in Greater Manchester, the share of the main district, Liverpool, increases over the period from 40.63% to 43.60% for unemployment and 43.32% to 47.92 % for long-term unemployment. Again it should be noted that Liverpool's share of long-term unemployment is higher than its ordinary unemployment. Wirral is the only other area to increase its share slightly. Its share increased to 1986 and then came down, to levels just above their starting point. So its share was at its highest when unemployment was at its peak level. Unlike Liverpool its share of long-term unemployment is less than its ordinary unemployment. Knowsley is the only other district to have a larger share of long-term unemployment than ordinary unemployment. The gap between the two shares narrowed over the period from 0.73 to 0.35, whereas the gap for Liverpool widened from 2.69 to 4.32. There is therefore an increasing concentration of Merseyside's long-term unemployment in Liverpool.

Knowsley, St. Helens and Sefton all had declining shares of both kinds of unemployment. In Knowsley's case it declined until 1988 (1989 long term) and then rose. St. Helen's shares rose initially until 1985 and then dropped. Its share of long-term unemployment is down by 2.18%. Sefton increased until 1986, the peak year of unemployment, and then declined. In this it matches Wirral but unlike Wirral there is an overall decline in the share of both.

The changing share within districts is less clear-cut than in Greater Manchester. The inner areas' share in both St. Helens and Sefton has gone up considerably (2.06 and 3.15 respectively). In Wirral it has increased marginally. In Liverpool it is static. In Knowsley it has declined. The inner area of Knowsley, however, includes much of the district, with a share of over 70%. In Liverpool there are increases in both the north and the south. In St. Helens the north west increases and in Wirral the north east does.

**Shares of unemployment in the inner areas of Merseyside districts**

|  | 1983 | 1990 |
|---|---|---|
| Knowsley | 73.16 | 72.51 |
| Liverpool | 40.27 | 40.31 |
| St Helens | 54.07 | 56.13 |
| Sefton | 53.27 | 56.43 |
| Wirral | 49.07 | 49.74 |

For long-term unemployment the picture is slightly clearer. Sefton's inner area again shows a clear increase. All the others, except Knowsley, have a marginal increase in share or in Wirral's case, exactly the same share. In Wirral it is the north east again that has the largest increase in share.

Again there is considerable variation at the ward level within the inner areas with some having increasing and others decreasing shares. At the very local level, then, the picture is complex.

Summary of Merseyside

There is an increasing concentration of unemployment within Liverpool as a district but, as in Manchester, this is not increasingly concentrated in the core of the district. In most of the other districts, however, there is an increasing concentration or the same concentration in the inner areas. The exception is Knowsley where there has been declining concentration.

**2.3 Tyne and Wear**

Again as in the other conurbation the central district has an increasing share of both unemployment and long-term unemployment; Newcastle rises from 24.82% to 26.94% and 25.63% to 31.47% respectively. The increasing gap between the two levels at the start of the period and at the end can also be clearly seen. Sunderland's and South Tyneside's shares of unemployment marginally rise, but as with the other districts their shares of long-term unemployment decline. Only Newcastle has a rising share of long-term unemployment.

**Shares of unemployment in the inner areas of Tyne and Wear districts**

|  | 1983 | 1990 |
|---|---|---|
| Gateshead | 55.11 | 55.97 |
| Newcastle | 47.40 | 50.53 |
| N.Tyneside | 23.10 | 24.41 |
| S.Tyneside | 57.90 | 59.47 |
| Sunderland | 50.99 | 53.92 |

The story for overall unemployment and the inner areas is very clear. All of the inner areas increase their share over the period. In Newcastle and Sunderland there is a substantial increase of about 3.0%. In North and South Tyneside there is a rise of more than 1%. In Gateshead it is a more marginal increase. In all but Newcastle, where there has been a steady increase, the share declined to 1986 and then rose. Again at the peak level of unemployment there was some diminution in share as people in outer areas experienced unemployment at much higher levels than previously.

The picture for long-term unemployment is less clear. Newcastle's and Sunderland's inner area shares rose considerably; in the case of Sunderland only in 1990. In South Tyneside there was a marginal increase. In the other two there was a decrease.

Within the inner areas at the ward level, again the picture is complex with some wards increasing and others decreasing.

Summary of Tyne and Wear

There is an increasing concentration of unemployment in the district of Newcastle and, unlike the other two conurbations, for Tyne and Wear there is an increasing concentration in the inner area of its largest district. For overall unemployment the inner areas' shares have increased over the period. The picture is more complex for long-term unemployment.

Summary for the three conurbations

Unemployment has increasingly concentrated in the main district of all three conurbations. Within most districts the inner areas have increased their share of unemployment. In some cases their share declined slightly in 1986 (the peak level of unemployment) presumably as unemployment spread to areas where it was normally less common. In Manchester and Liverpool the inner areas did not have a rising share. This may be because of declining populations or possibly the impact of government schemes. It may also be that the areas prone to unemployment within these districts have become more numerous.

## 2.4 Jobs' analysis

The changing share of the total number of jobs was examined for the same grouping of wards. First the changing district share within the conurbation is given as context. Whereas Manchester is receiving an increasing share of the unemployed, it is losing its share of jobs, from 27.6% in 1984 to 26.3% in 1989. Rochdale, Salford and Tameside are also losing, while Bolton, Bury, Oldham, Stockport and Trafford were gaining. Apart from Manchester, no district, however, was a major gainer or loser of jobs. They seem less sensitive to change than unemployment.

Within the districts nearly all the inner areas lost their share of jobs. For Rochdale (5.27), Bolton (4.41), Wigan (3.99) and Trafford (3.73) the loss was substantial. Salford (2.31) and Manchester (1.35) also lost, while Oldham had a marginal gain, Stockport and Tameside remained the same and Bury had a marginal loss.

The analysis of shares of jobs within districts, therefore, supports the findings of the unemployment analysis. The gaps between the inner areas and the rest are widening for both sets of indicators.

Designated 'inner area' groupings

A similar analysis of changing shares was carried out using the designated areas, that is the grouping based on whether the wards are formally 'inner areas' or not. For each district this time there is a simple dichotomy between 'inner area' and non-'inner area', and the changing shares are examined for the two groups of wards.

The proportion of unemployment in the 'inner areas' varies considerably from district to district showing that in some districts there are many more wards included than in others. In Salford only 36.15% of unemployment is included within its 'inner areas', whereas for Rochdale over two thirds is included. For all the districts in Greater Manchester, except Salford, there is a rising share of unemployment between 1983 and 1990. In all cases the share rose in the last few years of the decade. This even applies to Salford. Bolton's 'inner area' share increases by over 5%, Rochdale's by nearly 4%, Wigan and Oldham by over 2% and Manchester's more marginally by 0.47%. This all suggests that the 'inner areas' are left at the end of a period of unemployment decline with a relatively larger share of the people who find it difficult to obtain or retain employment.    In Merseyside the changing shares are less dramatic. Wigan rises by over 4%. Sefton and St. Helens rise by less than 2% while Knowsley only increases marginally. Liverpool, on the other hand, clearly declines by over 4%.

These general increases suggest a number of possible explanations. It is possible that government monies have not been sufficiently targeted despite the designations of the areas. There is some evidence of this in the reports on the inputs to the conurbations. It is possible that monies have been targeted on these areas but it has not worked. It also possible that without the monies the gap would have increased even further. It is also possible that if two equivalent points in time on the economic cycle had been observed, then there would not have been any change in the extent of the gaps. The last explanation does not seem likely. The gaps have widened too much. However there is some small part of the explanation here. It has been observed in the residential survey that some 'inner areas', such as Dingle, have improved with relatively generous government monies whereas others, such as Granby, have not significantly improved even though they have received as much if not more. There is evidence then of 'success' and the continued need for resources. In still other areas, such as Ordsall, there seems to have been some success with considerable inputs. These successes can easily be offset by other stories in the aggregate grouping of wards.

Equally, the decline in Liverpool and to a lesser extent Salford may be due to the success of government programmes or to the decline in the number of economically active in these 'inner areas'. The census data may give a clue to this, but the undercount should be noted immediately.

# 3 IMPACTS

The relationship between outcome indicators and inputs formed the final element of the local analysis. Various types of multi-level models were applied to the changes in the indicators to see the extent to which change could be accounted for by government inputs. Job change per capita between 1984 and 1990 and unemployment change between 1983-86 and 1986-90 are the indicators.

The census-based groupings of wards proved to have too much internal variation and relatively too little variation between groups to fit the model; the groupings are therefore not a good classification for reflecting changes in the indicators. This is not surprising, given the results of the share analysis. There it was noted that, although the shares had increased for the inner areas as a whole, there was considerable variation at the ward level within the inner areas.

The wards were also grouped according to the changes on the indicators, paying no attention to spatial contiguity. Although such groupings fit the model and gave significant differences at both the ward and grouping levels, no explanatory variables were found to have a significant association with either level.

# 4  CONCLUSIONS

- Unemployment has increasingly been concentrated in the main districts (Liverpool, Manchester and Newcastle) of the three conurbations.

- The inner areas of most districts have increased their share of the district's unemployment.

- In Liverpool and Manchester the incidence of unemployment appears to have spread to areas outside the 'inner areas'.

- The great variability of experience of the wards within both census and policy-based groupings means that multi-level modelling cannot be applied. More importantly, it means that there are areas of 'success' and areas of 'failure' within 'inner areas' (as, indeed, is confirmed by the residents' survey).

- There is no simple direct relationship between levels of inputs and socio-economic outcomes.

# *Appendix E*    Residents' survey

## 1  INTRODUCTION

### 1.1  Aims

The aims of the residents' survey were:

- to analyse the views of some recipients of urban policy on its overall impacts;

- to focus on some aspects of policy that were impossible to measure by quantitative methods either because of the unavailability or unreliability of data - crime, appearance and overall attractiveness as a place to live;

- to focus in addition on the residents' views of employment opportunities, the other major objective of urban policy;

- to use a design that permitted comparison between areas with considerable and areas with few policy inputs, and between areas with different degrees of success in terms of outcomes;

- to focus on a particular subset of the population, non-white ethnic groups, whose responses to policy had not been examined elsewhere in the research.

### 1.2  Choice of sample areas

The survey was designed to use a set of clustered samples in different parts of the three conurbations. Clustered sampling was chosen rather than a random sample drawn from across the inner cities because it is important to obtain a set of views from within areas for which some estimate of overall inputs can be made. The clusters were not randomly chosen. Rather, they were selected as neighbouring pairs, so that a relative measure can be established of the views of people of their own area compared to a neighbouring one. By comparing the views of people from the two neighbouring areas, area loyalty or a grass-is-greener effect can be isolated and some idea of the relative overall outcomes can be arrived at. Since some estimate of the relative policy inputs to the areas is known, the impacts of policy can be evaluated in a general and indirect way. If high policy input areas are judged to have been more successful, causality cannot be assumed, but at least the association is in the right direction for a positive effect.

Six areas were chosen in Greater Manchester: two paired areas in Salford inner city; two paired in east Manchester; and two areas with concentrations of ethnic minority groups in south Manchester. Four areas were chosen in Tyne and Wear: two paired areas in central Newcastle; and two in Sunderland which compared an inner city area with a peripheral estate. Five areas were chosen in Merseyside: one pair in inner city Liverpool; one pair on the borders of Knowsley and Liverpool; and one area in Birkenhead that was comparable with inner-city Liverpool areas.

In each area a sample of 80 residents was selected. The sample was clustered. Every other house was selected so that the resulting sample could represent the view of a neighbourhood. Where there were rather different types of housing or tenure in the area, the selection of houses was designed to achieve a representative set of residents from within the small area. A larger sample of 120 residents was surveyed in the 'ethnic areas' so that the sample was large enough for comparisons of groups within the areas as well as between them.

## 1.3 Questionnaire design

The questionnaire (a copy of which is provided as an annexe to this Appendix) was divided into three parts. The first dealt with the factors which the residents felt were important dimensions in their concept of their 'quality of life'; and, in relation to these dimensions, how they viewed the past, present and future quality of life in their area and neighbouring area. The second examined three specific aspects of quality of life in the areas: appearance; safety from crime; and employment opportunities. The third part sought contextual information about the individual respondents.

The quality-of-life variables were adapted from Glasgow-based research so that some connection could be made to other surveys on quality of life as well as to focus respondents' minds on aspects of quality of life that are potentially important at the scale of inner city neighbourhoods. The aim was to assess the respondents' views of the area at the time of the interview, of change over the last three years and expected change over the next three. This enabled us to derive some idea of the trajectory of areas.

Attitudes to overall attractiveness, appearance, safety from crime and employment opportunities were each examined over time. If areas with considerable policy inputs showed greater change over the last three years and greater expected change than their neighbouring area, then this may be some sign of a successful impact.

The respondents were also asked about their neighbouring area and about change within it. This is a more difficult issue to probe, but it enables some relative measure between places, rather than just a view of one place over time. It also allows us to assess the degree to which residents' comparative view of their own area is biased favourably (a 'loyalty' effect), or unfavourably (a grass-is-greener effect).

Most questions used a standard Likert scale. In some cases, in order to measure the present situation, a Thurstone scale was employed. This enables us to obtain a score between 0 and 11 for a respondent on their view of the area at present. A number of statements had previously been tested to determine whether they reliably represented a particular position on the scale from 0 to 11 and allocated a value (the 50% point on a cumulative frequency graph of experts' opinions). Statements were discarded if experts did not agree sufficiently on their position. The selected statements were then presented to the respondent to reflect different positions along a scale measuring, say, the safety of the area from crime. The respondents were asked to tick those statements with which they agreed. The median of the scores of these statements were taken to represent the respondent's position on the scale. If the range of the statement scores is greater than 5 for a particular respondent, then a median score is not recorded and the respondent is not viewed as having a reliable position on the scale.

The questionnaire was discussed with and piloted by MORI before being administered. In the final version certain questions were presented in reverse and in inverted orders to check that the order of statements did not affect the results. Similarly some Likert scales were reversed to check that their order did not influence answers. In general the order of the scale or statement did not affect the answers. There is some difference for desirability of the area in that relatively fewer people ticked 'very desirable' when it was the last point of the scale, but there is no statistical difference based on the order of presentation in the numbers saying 'desirable' or 'undesirable' (i.e. grouping the 'fairly' and 'very' categories). There is, however, a difference for comments about change over the last three years, in both desirability and appearance. There is a bias towards 'worse' rather than 'better' if 'worse' comes first on the scale. This bias is not removed by amalgamating categories. More people say that desirability has declined for both sequences of order, but relatively more such responses were recorded if 'worse' appeared first on the scale. There is therefore a bias towards decline. In change in appearance, the order is important, because it changes the conclusion. If 'improves' was first in the scale, the number saying 'improved' is greater than those saying 'worsened', but the reverse is the case if 'worse' comes first. This question is therefore somewhat suspect and little weight is put on it in the analysis. For both of these questions, however, area and conurbation comparisons are possible because the order of the scales occurs equally across the areas. There is no bias at all for comments about the future. The order of the scale does not affect these results.

The order of the statements in the crime and employment scales had little affect on the results. There is some effect on the first statement in the crime scale, but none on the rest. Overall these seem quite reliable.

The results have been analysed in a straightforward descriptive fashion, by simple counts and cross-tabulations, with chi-square analysis being used to determine where significant differences occur. When differences are reported here, they are statistically significant ones. For ease of reading the chi-square values are not included in the text.

An area is suggested to have performed well if more people make positive comments about it and, to some extent, if these comments are more strongly felt. In most of the analysis the 'fairly' and 'very' categories have been combined so that the order in which the Likert scale was presented does not affect the results.

## 2 RESULTS FROM THE TOTAL SAMPLE

**2.1 Characteristics of the sample**

There were 1299 people in the sample, with 574 in the 6 areas of Greater Manchester, 402 in the 5 areas of Merseyside and 323 in the 4 areas of Tyne and Wear. This is slightly more than required to enable statistical comparisons to be made. The age profile below shows that there was a fair representation of age groups and no bias to the elderly:

| Age group | % |
|---|---|
| 18-24 | 14.6 |
| 25-34 | 26.2 |
| 35-44 | 16.9 |
| 45-54 | 12.0 |
| 55-64 | 12.6 |
| 65-74 | 11.7 |
| 75+ | 6.0 |

A number of indicators suggest that poorer people were well targeted by the survey. For example:

| | % |
|---|---|
| no car | 67.8 |
| no telephone | 42.5 |
| social class AB* | 1.9 |
| social class C1* | 11.8 |
| social class C2* | 13.0 |
| social class D* | 23.4 |
| social class E* | 49.7 |

\* head of household

The household composition of the total sample suggests that, again, a good cross-section of inner-city residents was included:

| | % |
|---|---|
| 2 parent with 1+ child(ren) | 21.9 |
| 1 parent with 1+ child(ren) | 18.6 |
| single <60 | 13.5 |
| 3+ adults | 12.3 |
| single 60+ | 11.6 |
| 2 adults with at least 1 60+ | 11.0 |
| 2 adults, both <60 | 10.5 |

The tenure composition partly reflects the high proportion rented from the local authority in inner cities and partly the choice of areas:

| | % |
|---|---|
| owned outright | 10.0 |
| buying on a mortgage | |
|    house previously owner occupied | 10.5 |
|    house previously council rented | 8.9 |
|    house previously HA rented | 2.0 |
| rented from council | 52.1 |
| rented from housing assoc. | 5.2 |
| rented from private landlord | 8.2 |

Employment status shows quite a high proportion of unemployed:

|  | % respondents |
|---|---|
| Full time working | 20.7 |
| Part time working | 8.2 |
| <8 hrs per week | 0.3 |
| housewife | 27.2 |
| retired | 16.4 |
| registered unemployed | 16.8 |
| "unemployed" not registered | 3.5 |
| student | 3.2 |
| other | 3.8 |

The ethnic mix of the sample is mainly white (86.1%) but there are other ethnic groups, particularly in the intentionally-selected 'ethnic' areas of Manchester.

|  | % |
|---|---|
| Black Caribbean | 3.1 |
| Black African | 0.8 |
| Black other | 1.2 |
| Indian | 0.9 |
| Pakistani | 4.8 |
| Bangladeshi | 0.5 |
| Chinese | 1.2 |
| other | 0.9 |

Since questions were asked elsewhere in the questionnaire about change over the last three years, it was important to ask the length of time that residents had been in the house and the area (although, even if they had not been in the area for three years, respondents still might have views on how the area had changed). 82% had lived in the area for over three years. 65% had lived there over 10 years. Merseyside was the most stable with 90% living there over 3 years while Greater Manchester was the least stable with only 75%. Not surprisingly, there were more people in Greater Manchester than in Merseyside who said that they did not know when asked about change over the last three years. The views on change then are based almost entirely on direct experience.

## 2.2 Quality of life

The frequency with which people rated variables as 'very important' to their quality of life in the area (with 'fairly important' within brackets) is shown below:

%

| | | |
|---|---|---|
| violent crime | 79.3 | (93.6) |
| quality of health care | 73.7 | (93.9) |
| cost of living | 71.9 | (93.7) |
| non-violent crime | 67.2 | (91.3) |
| quality of housing | 64.2 | (91.0) |
| quality of welfare services | 61.7 | (85.8) |
| what the area looks like | 61.3 | (91.5) |
| employment prospects | 59.2 | (79.2) |
| pollution | 58.2 | (86.2) |
| unemployment levels | 58.0 | (81.1) |
| quality of schools/colleges | 55.5 | (82.9) |
| quality of shops | 55.4 | (89.9) |
| house rents | 52.6 | (74.6) |
| public transport | 52.3 | (82.9) |
| availability of council housing | 49.1 | (73.8) |
| racial harmony | 48.4 | (73.5) |
| availability of job training | 44.0 | (70.7) |
| quality of leisure facilities | 37.7 | (73.8) |
| house prices | 34.7 | (59.3) |
| quality of sports facilities | 34.3 | (68.4) |

The order is not markedly different for the cumulative percentage of those responding either 'very' or 'fairly' important. Employment prospects ranks less highly, while public transport gets a higher value without moving up the ranking very much.

These results are quite consistent across the conurbations. For employment prospects there is only 0.6% difference between the 3 conurbations. Some variables show more than a 10% difference in frequency mentioned as very important, but in many cases the order of importance is little different. These are non-violent crime (61.2 in Merseyside, but 71.8 in Tyne and Wear), quality of housing (57.5 in Greater Manchester, but 71.5 in Tyne and Wear), availability of council housing (40.6 in Greater Manchester, but 59.1 in Tyne and Wear), house rents (48.3 in Merseyside, but 60.4 in Tyne and Wear), quality of welfare services (59.9 in Greater Manchester, but 72.4 in Merseyside), racial harmony (38.4 in Tyne and Wear, but 52.2 in Merseyside), and what the area looks like (55.1 in Greater Manchester, but 68.7 in Tyne in Wear). Some of these differences reflect the local contexts.

While the order of the Likert scale affects the number of times a factor is ticked in the 'very important' category, it does not affect the order of importance of the factors. The only effect of the order of presentation of the factors is that non-violent crimes gets ticked more often when it appears ahead of violent crime than when it occurs after it, and that public transport receives more support when it is slightly higher up the order. Apart from these two factors the order of presentation has no significant effect on the numbers responding to particular factors and no effect on the order of importance. The variables are examined in more detail later in the questionnaire - crime, appearance and employment opportunities - are all reasonably important to people.

It is useful to make some comparisons between these results and those from the Glasgow-based study on quality of life which examined views in a national opinion survey, and on which much of the content of our questions was based. There were some minor differences between the questions in the two surveys since certain variables were omitted or changed in our conurbation survey: climate, travel-to-work time and wage levels were omitted; scenic quality was amended to "what the area looks like" and various housing variables were altered; public transport was added to the conurbation survey. Despite these small differences in the content of the two questionnaire schedules, there is a considerable degree of similarity between the results of our conurbation study and those of the national survey. Violent crime is top in both. Health care, cost of living and non-violent crime also appear towards the top of both lists. The major difference is the position of pollution which is 9th for the conurbations but 4th for the national study. Presumably inner-city residents, generally more accustomed to experiencing higher pollution levels, are less sensitive to this issue. Employment prospects and unemployment levels are somewhat further down the national list, but that could reflect the timing of the two surveys; in neither study are employment-related issues particularly high in the order. Sports and leisure facilities come towards the bottom of both lists. Most of the other variables are slightly changed and not exactly comparable.

Overall, this level of agreement suggests that the conurbation survey is reliable. Some differences would be expected because of the geography of the two samples.

## 2.3 Desirability of neighbourhoods

It is instructive to outline the results from some of the other questions at the level of the whole sample. The desirability of their own area compared to the neighbouring area shows that there is a loyalty to their own area rather than a grass-is-greener-elsewhere effect. This is so both for the present desirability and for change over the last three years:

### Desirability

| | Present | | | Last three years | |
| | Own area | Neighbouring area | | Own area | Neighbouring area |
|---|---|---|---|---|---|
| *Positive* | | | *Positive* | | |
| very | 9.5 | 2.9 | much | 11.2 | 2.8 |
| fairly | 38.2 | 9.5 | a little | 15.7 | 7.9 |
| indifferent | 16.7 | 9.7 | same | 25.3 | 16.7 |
| *Negative* | | | *Negative* | | |
| fairly | 17.1 | 17.4 | a little | 18.2 | 9.3 |
| very | 16.7 | 33.4 | much | 23.1 | 14.5 |
| don't know | 27.0 | 48.0 | | | |

It is important to notice that, although there is a dominantly positive view of the own area at present, there is a dominantly negative view of change over the last three years. A larger proportion of people thought that things had got worse than had got better or indeed stayed the same. Although this is somewhat biased by the order of presentation of the Likert scale, the tendency towards things getting worse still holds.

The relative position of the inner cities was also viewed as worsening. The gap between their area and the suburbs was seen as widening by 60% of respondents and narrowing by only 9%. The view of the future was more optimistic with 36.4% forseeing improvement compared with 33.6% seeing things getting worse. However, of those answering the question, more than twice as many felt that the gap between their area and the outer suburbs will widen in the future or thought it would narrow.

The views on change in appearance over the last three years were influenced by the order of presentation and so are not reliable. So, although overall they show more people saying there has been an improvement than a decline, this does depend upon the order of presentation.

## 2.4 Crime

This dominance of decline is echoed for the change in safety from crime over the last three years. Again respondents' views of their own area were generally better than their views of their neighbouring area, but there were some people who saw things as relatively worse in their own area:

| | | **View of neighbouring area** | | | | |
| --- | --- | --- | --- | --- | --- | --- |
| | | safer | same | less safe | don't know | **Totals** |
| **View of own area** | safer | 17 | 42 | 26 | 79 | 164 |
| | same | 9 | 208 | 52 | 167 | 436 |
| | less safe | 15 | 60 | 278 | 223 | 576 |
| | **Totals** | 41 | 310 | 356 | 469 | 1176 |

**Safety from crime in their own area**

| | | **Next three years** | | | |
| --- | --- | --- | --- | --- | --- |
| | | safer | same | worse | **Totals** |
| **Previous three years** | safer | 89 | 47 | 18 | 154 |
| | same | 85 | 220 | 64 | 369 |
| | worse | 118 | 112 | 277 | 507 |
| | **Totals** | 292 | 379 | 359 | 1030 |

Of those who were able to make comparisons with the outer suburbs and thought that there was a gap between safety from crime in their own area and the outer suburbs, with the suburbs being safer (144), 61% thought the gap had widened over the last three years and would widen further in the next three. Again a pessimistic view was dominant.

There are some important differences associated with ethnic status. Although Blacks as a whole did not view crime as getting any worse than Whites do, Pakistanis had a much more pessimistic view with over 67% saying things had got worse compared to 49% in the whole sample of those answering the question. This difference in the view of crime is not shown in their relative views of change in the general desirability of their area, where there was little difference according to ethnic status. Pakistanis' views of changes in safety from crime over the next three years were equally pessimistic, with over 65% believing that it will get worse. This compares with only 34% of the whole sample.

## 2.5  Job opportunities

The generally pessimistic views of job opportunities and those particularly for young people are shown for the conurbations below in detail. Of those agreeing or disagreeing with the statement in the whole sample, 92.9% disagreed that there were plenty of jobs available while 92.4% believed that it was very difficult for young people to get jobs. 66% of people answering the question thought that over the last three years the job opportunities for people in their area had got worse. While this is not surprising given the recessionary conditions at the time of the interviews, 42% thought that they will get worse in the future while only 22% thought that they will improve. The dominantly pessimistic view is shown below:

**Job opportunities**

| | | **Next three years** | | | |
|---|---|---|---|---|---|
| | | will get better | same | will get worse | **Totals** |
| **Previous three years** | has got better | 39 | 16 | 5 | 60 |
| | same | 76 | 176 | 51 | 303 |
| | has got worse | 104 | 192 | 394 | 690 |
| | **Totals** | 219 | 384 | 450 | 1053 |

Of those expressing an opinion, 58% thought that it was very difficult for someone from their area to set up a business. Of those saying it was 'fairly difficult' or 'very difficult' (785), the following reasons were given:

| | % |
|---|---|
| lack of capital | 28.0 |
| no financial backing | 4.5 |
| crime rate | 10.0 |
| reputation of area | 10.0 |
| recession | 9.0 |
| no opportunities | 3.8 |
| no qualifications | 3.5 |
| no premises available | 2.8 |

Clearly, lack of capital/finance was most frequently mentioned, while the nature of the area was mentioned more than the recession.

Of those who thought that it was 'very' or 'fairly easy' for people from the area to set up a business (82), 18.3% mentioned that the government would help; thereby suggesting some degree of awareness of possible assistance. The question of capital/finance came up again, with 13% saying "if you have the money". Many gave reasons which suggested the importance of the individual or group. 20% said it depended on the person. 11% said they knew people who had, while 11% commented that Asians had managed to do so. 7.3% said that people from their area had as good a chance as those from anywhere else.

The view of change in employment opportunities over the last three years was, not surprisingly, predominantly negative with 66% saying that things had got worse. Notably, Blacks had an even more negative view, with nearly 82% thinking that opportunities had got worse. Their view of the future was also more pessimistic, with nearly 60% saying things will get worse, compared to 42% of the whole sample.

There is an interaction between people's views on overall desirability and appearance, safety from crime and job opportunities. Respondents who thought that the desirability of the area had gone up were more likely to say that its appearance had improved, its safety had improved and job opportunities had got better. Conversely, those who said that desirability had gone down were more likely to say that appearance, safety from crime and job opportunities had got worse. This is as expected. It confirms the reliability of the answers.

## 2.6 Subsets of the sample

Some comments are made here about subsets of the sample. It should be remembered that the local context may affect the composition of the sample, especially its ethnic composition, and that variations for the whole sample may reflect particular local situations rather than circumstances common to all the areas in the three conurbations.

### Gender

More women had an optimistic view of the situation than men (more agreed with the statements 'no trouble finding jobs' and 'plenty of jobs available'). Their greater reliance on local job opportunities was reflected by many more women thinking they would have to move area within the city to obtain better jobs.

### Age

The 18-24s were somewhat more optimistic about their own opportunities than those 35 and over, and even sometimes more than 25-34s. In particular, they were less frequently concerned about their address being a difficulty in getting interviews. In general men were less concerned about this than women. There is very little difference between ages on safety from crime.

### Class

The socio-economic class of the head of the household affected the responses in a predictable way, even though it was not necessarily the class of the respondent. Relatively fewer As Bs and C1s thought that one would have to move to another city or another part of the city to get a better job. Relatively fewer agreed that the only jobs available were low paid and insecure.

### Ethnicity

While it is more appropriate to look at the effect of ethnicity at the local scale, it is nevertheless worth noting that the responses of the Pakistanis on employment opportunities were similar to those of whites, but that for some statements relatively more of the Blacks (Caribbean, African and other), the Indians and the Bangladeshis were negative about opportunities; for example, on the statements 'no trouble in finding a job' and 'plenty of jobs available', only 3.8% agreed as against 7.8% of the rest. Pakistanis were much more likely than the other ethnic groups to think that safety from crime had decreased and to be pessimistic about crime in the future.

## 2.7 Summary of results for the whole sample

The predominant view of respondents was that things had got worse over the last three years within their own area on a number of dimensions. This absolute comparison is supported by a relative comparison. Most people thought that the gap with outer suburbs had widened over the last three years.

The view of the future was less bleak for the overall desirability of their area than it was for crime and job opportunities which most people thought would worsen. However even though more had an optimistic view of the future desirability of their area, more still thought that the gap with the outer suburbs would widen further.

There are significant differences related to ethnic status. Pakistanis had a poor view of safety from crime. They viewed the changes in the last three years much more pessimistically and saw the future as much bleaker than the sample as a whole. Blacks, on the other hand, had a bleaker past and future view of employment opportunities compared to the whole sample. Although no direct connection can be made, it would be reasonable to infer that Pakistanis are more vulnerable to crime and Blacks more vulnerable to poor employment prospects than the population as a whole.

Some results, particularly those on employment opportunities, are worth noting at the conurbation scale. It is important to remember that these results reflect views in particular areas of the conurbations and are not necessarily representative of the conurbations as a whole. They may be indicative of differences, but strictly they represent differences between the areas chosen within the three conurbations rather than differences between the conurbations in their entirety.

The responses to statements about the availability of job opportunities shows that respondents in the areas in Tyne and Wear were least optimistic about the present situation. The difference between Merseyside and Greater Manchester was less than expected with one being higher on one statement and the other higher on another:

|  | Gr.Man | Mersey | Tyne & Wear |
|---|---|---|---|
| only low paid jobs | 76.4 | 66.6 | 80.4 |
| only insecure jobs | 76.9 | 70.4 | 81.9 |
| very little chance of getting better jobs | 77.4 | 80.0 | 83.7 |
| to get better jobs need to move city | 58.3 | 66.9 | 77.4 |
| to get better job have to move within city | 58.6 | 45.4 | 65.0 |
| no trouble finding job (disagree) | 94.2 | 91.1 | 94.2 |
| plenty of jobs available (disagree) | 90.7 | 95.2 | 93.2 |

The greater occurrence of concern about employment opportunities in Tyne and Wear is repeated to some extent for opportunities specifically for young people. The relative position of Merseyside and Greater Manchester varies somewhat with the question:

|  | Young people | | |
|---|---|---|---|
|  | Gr.Man | Mersey | Tyne & Wear |
| very difficult to get jobs | 90.3 | 94.4 | 93.6 |
| can only get jobs requiring few skills | 71.7 | 66.3 | 67.4 |
| address makes it difficult to obtain interviews | 52.7 | 49.4 | 47.9 |
| only those with good qualifications find it easy to get jobs (disagree) | 57.4 | 61.5 | 62.8 |
| plenty of jobs (disagree) | 90.7 | 93.8 | 95.5 |

While the view of job opportunities seems worse in Tyne and Wear, the situation seems to have worsened more in Greater Manchester in the last three years. Of those answering the question, many fewer thought that the job situation had improved and many more thought it had got worse than in either Tyne and Wear or Merseyside. Over this period in Tyne and Wear there seem to be relatively more with optimistic or less pessimistic views than in Merseyside:

**Job opportunities in last three years: own area**

|  | Gr.Man | Mersey | Tyne & Wear |
|---|---|---|---|
| improve | 4.0 | 5.6 | 8.2 |
| same | 21.9 | 36.7 | 29.7 |
| a little worse | 27.8 | 17.0 | 25.8 |
| a lot worse | 46.1 | 40.6 | 36.2 |

On the other hand, there were fewer respondents who were optimistic about the future in Merseyside than the other two conurbations, while there were more pessimistic people in Greater Manchester.

**Job opportunities in the next three years**

|  | Gr.Man | Mersey | Tyne & Wear |
|---|---|---|---|
| improve | 23.8 | 14.5 | 30.1 |
| same | 30.4 | 44.3 | 36.6 |
| a little worse | 17.9 | 15.7 | 13.4 |
| a lot worse | 30.0 | 25.5 | 19.9 |

Summary of conurbation comparisons

The situation was seen to be bad by more people in Tyne and Wear than in Greater Manchester and Merseyside. Overall there are signs that things were thought to be getting worse in Greater Manchester by more people than in either Tyne and Wear or Merseyside. More people were pessimistic about the future in Greater Manchester than in the other conurbations but fewer were optimistic in Merseyside than in the other two.

# 4 RESULTS: COMPARISONS OF PAIRS OF AREAS

## 4.1 Ordsall and Pendleton in Salford

The interviews were carried out in the northern part of Ordsall in an area adjacent to the enterprise zone, a new Sainsbury's store and a privately-rehabilitated block of erstwhile council flats. The housing varies from low-rise council of varying quality, some of the better ones having been sold, to rehabilitated early-20th century housing which has either been sold by a housing association, run by a cooperative for the council or managed directly by the council. Pendleton is close to the town centre of Salford. It consists of a major council area with low- and high-rise accommodation and some old terraced housing which has been improved.

Ordsall has received considerable government assistance in comparison to Pendleton. If this has had a successful overall impact, then residents would be expected to respond more positively in Ordsall than in Pendleton. The results show that residents' views of their own area at present and over the last three years show that more people are positive and less negative about Ordsall than Pendleton:

### Views on own area

| | Present desirability | | | Change in last three years | |
|---|---|---|---|---|---|
| | Ordsall | Pendleton | | Ordsall | Pendleton |
| very desirable | 5.0 | 6.3 | much improvement | 21.3 | 5.3 |
| fairly desirable | 45.0 | 25.0 | some improvement | 30.7 | 19.7 |
| neither desirable nor undesirable | 8.8 | 17.5 | same | 10.7 | 9.2 |
| fairly undesirable | 22.5 | 28.8 | somewhat worse | 18.7 | 28.9 |
| very undesirable | 17.5 | 22.5 | much worse | 18.7 | 36.8 |

The better view of Ordsall than Pendleton is confirmed by future expectations. Not only did more of those in Ordsall have an optimistic view than those in Pendleton, but people in Pendleton had a more optimistic view of Ordsall's future than those in Ordsall had of Pendleton's. More significantly, given the observed area loyalty effect, more of those in Pendleton had an optimistic view of Ordsall's future than that of their own area:

### Views on future desirability

| | Own area | | Pendleton on Ordsall | Ordsall on Pendleton |
|---|---|---|---|---|
| | Ordsall | Pendleton | | |
| will improve | 56.7 | 32.0 | 39.3 | 33.3 |
| same | 13.4 | 20.0 | 27.8 | 33.3 |
| will worsen | 29.9 | 48.0 | 32.7 | 33.3 |

The overall view is confirmed strongly by the views on appearance. 83.1% of Ordsall's residents thought that its appearance had improved while only 33.3% of Pendleton's did. Indeed there were more (40%) in Pendleton that thought it had declined. Again there were more in Pendleton who thought that Ordsall had improved (44%) than had their own area.

There is very little difference between the areas on the safety-from-crime scale. Both areas were split between those who thought that their area was safe and those who thought that it was very unsafe. Both areas had over half of the residents who felt that things had got worse over the last three years, with Pendleton having a few more than Ordsall. Pendleton also had more people who have a pessimistic view of the future.

The comparison between the areas is not quite as straight-forward for job opportunities. Ordsall had more people with more favourable views both of the last three years and the next three years, but there were also more with negative views of the last three years and about the same for the future:

### Job opportunities

|  | Last three years | | Next three years | |
|---|---|---|---|---|
|  | Ordsall | Pendleton | Ordsall | Pendleton |
| a lot better | 0.0 | 0.0 | 2.9 | 1.3 |
| a little better | 10.0 | 3.8 | 26.5 | 20.5 |
| no change | 12.9 | 26.9 | 33.8 | 42.3 |
| a little worse | 32.9 | 32.1 | 13.2 | 16.7 |
| a lot worse | 44.3 | 37.2 | 23.5 | 19.2 |

Nearly all the signs are that Ordsall has improved more and declined less than Pendleton over the last three years. There appears to be a close association with greater government inputs.

## 4.2 Miles Platting and Beswick in Manchester

Miles Platting is part of Central Ward. It comprises mainly council housing some of which has received attention in the last few years. Beswick is a mixed area. Interviews were carried out on an old estate where most of the houses had been very recently replaced, a post-war estate of low-rise and maisonettes, and a road of old terraced housing. Miles Platting has received somewhat more inputs than Beswick.

Neither area was thought very desirable, but more in Miles Platting had a positive view. Many more in Miles Platting thought that it had improved over the last three years, but there were still some who saw things as having got worse. The majority view in Beswick was one of decline. The greatest difference between the areas was in their view of the future. Many more in Miles Platting were optimistic. It seems to be on an upward trajectory:

### Views on desirability of own area

|  | Miles Platting | | | Beswick | | |
|---|---|---|---|---|---|---|
|  | now | last three years | future three years | now | last three years | future three years |
| positive | 44.1 | 43.1 | 77.1 | 24.0 | 11.3 | 19.5 |
| same | 14.3 | 16.6 | 10.8 | 36.7 | 36.6 | 48.0 |
| negative | 41.6 | 40.3 | 12.1 | 39.3 | 52.1 | 32.5 |

There is little difference between the areas on their appearance over the last three years. Both had most respondents saying 'no change', and more of the rest thinking it had got worse than got better, but in neither case is the number saying getting worse significantly more than those saying it had improved.

Beswick was viewed as safer than Miles Platting. On the safety-from-crime scale, 63% saw it as safe, whereas only 39% saw Miles Platting as safe. 58.6% in Miles Platting compared to 46% in Beswick thought it had got worse in the last three. Yet 10% thought that Miles Platting had got safer while hardly anyone said that of Beswick. 44% compared to 38% thought that things would get worse. Again there were a few more in Miles Platting who were optimistic about the future. The differences on their view of past change and future expectations are not great.

There is also little difference in their views on job change. Large majorities thought that things had got worse. On the job-related statements, Miles Platting people were more positive about opportunities at present than those of Beswick. This is also the case for young people's job opportunities. However, more people in Miles Platting thought that their address made a difference for access to interviews, perhaps reflecting greater labelling of the area. In both areas it was felt to be difficult to start up a business.

Although the differences between the areas is not great, there was a somewhat better overall view of change in Miles Platting than Beswick. Both areas still have problems, but it seems that the recent inputs into Miles Platting might have helped to give its residents a somewhat better view of the future than is the case for Beswick.

## 4.3 Ardwick and Longsight in Manchester

These areas were selected because they each include a variety of ethnic groups. Ardwick is a mixed area nearer the city centre than Longsight. Both have some council and some private housing. Neither area has had much attention from government programmes. If anything, Ardwick has received somewhat more resources.

In the Ardwick sample there are 75 Whites, 24 Blacks, 9 Pakistanis and 12 others from ethnic minority groups. In Longsight there are only 42 Whites, 51 Pakistanis, 16 Blacks and 12 others from ethnic minority groups. The ethnic minority groups include Indians and Bangladeshis. These are not grouped with Pakistanis because their answers were not sufficiently similar. Caribbean and African Blacks have been grouped together along with other Blacks because their answers were similar.

There is little difference between perceptions of the general desirability of the areas. Slightly more people thought that Ardwick was desirable. There is however a difference in the view of change over the last three years with more people thinking that Ardwick had got worse.

There is some ethnic difference in Longsight. More Blacks had a favourable view of the area and change over the last three years. In Ardwick the Blacks again had a more favourable view, this time compared to the Pakistanis, more of whom viewed the area negatively. They also had a more dominant view that the area had grown worse over the last three years. These differences are reflected in more Blacks and Pakistanis finding Longsight desirable than Ardwick, the reverse of the Whites. The Blacks also saw change in the two areas rather differently. Relatively more saw Ardwick as having got worse than did the sample as a whole:

### Desirability of own area

|  | Longsight | | | Ardwick | | |
|---|---|---|---|---|---|---|
|  | All | Blacks | Pakistanis | All | Blacks | Pakistanis |
| desirable | 38.0 | 61.1 | 40.0 | 47.4 | 54.1 | 33.3 |
| neither | 23.0 | 22.2 | 32.0 | 17.0 | 12.5 | 22.2 |
| undesirable | 37.3 | 16.7 | 28.0 | 35.6 | 33.3 | 44.4 |

### Changes in last three years

|  | | | | | | |
|---|---|---|---|---|---|---|
| improved | 14.0 | 12.5 | 17.4 | 6.5 | 5.0 | 11.1 |
| same | 43.0 | 56.3 | 39.1 | 30.5 | 25.0 | 11.1 |
| worsened | 43.0 | 31.2 | 43.5 | 63.0 | 70.0 | 77.8 |

More people saw a poorer future for Longsight than Ardwick. This view was shared by people from both areas; respondents from Ardwick viewed Longsight less favourably than respondents from Longsight viewed the prospects for Ardwick. More Pakistanis in Ardwick had a poorer view of Longsight than the Whites and Blacks. More Whites in Longsight had a poorer view of Ardwick than did the Pakistanis.

Both in Ardwick and Longsight, more Pakistanis thought that crime had got worse than did Whites or Blacks. More people in general saw Longsight as having got worse than Ardwick. Whereas more saw a poorer future for Ardwick than Longsight. In Longsight it was the Pakistanis who had the most pessimistic view.

For changes in job opportunities in the last three years, more people thought that things had got worse in Ardwick than Longsight. It was especially the Blacks in Ardwick who expressed this opinion.

## 4.4 Granby and Dingle in Liverpool

Both areas comprise recently built housing in redevelopment areas. There have been more housing-related problems in Granby than in Dingle. Both have received considerable amounts of inputs. The 'experts' think that these have been more successful in Dingle.

The views of Granby and Dingle are very different. On a whole series of questions, more people saw Granby as undesirable and viewed it as having changed for the worse. Dingle, on the other hand, had more people seeing it in a positive light and thinking that it had improved over the last three years. More people were optimistic about Dingle's future than Granby's:

|  | Granby | | | Dingle | | |
|---|---|---|---|---|---|---|
|  | now | last three years | future three years | now | last three years | future three years |
| positive | 36.3 | 20.2 | 34.4 | 69.2 | 50.0 | 41.4 |
| same/neither | 13.7 | 25.3 | 26.6 | 7.6 | 14.1 | 24.3 |
| negative | 50.0 | 54.4 | 39.1 | 23.1 | 35.9 | 34.3 |

The views of the residents of their own area were supported by the views of their neighbours. Dingle residents had a poor view of Granby and recent changes there, while those of Granby who had an opinion of Dingle suggested that it had improved and more said that it was a desirable area. While most of those in Granby saw a widening gap with the outer suburbs, both in the past and for the future, there was more of a balance between those who, for the past, saw a widening gap or no change, and who, for the future, saw a widening or a narrowing gap.

The views on crime are again clearly different. Granby had some people whose views lay at the better end of the safety-from-crime scale, but conversely had more at the poor end, while Dingle had 60% at the very top. 34% thought that crime had got worse in Dingle while 39% thought so in Granby - not a major difference, but the extremess are very different.

More people in Granby thought that job opportunities had got worse and had poorer expectations of the future. There is, however, one major topic about which people in Dingle were very pessimistic. 76% thought that it was very difficult for people in Dingle to start up a business. Only 62% thought this in

Granby. So while there are other positive signs about Dingle, this is not the case for enterprise.

In summary, there are major differences between the two areas according to their views on both their own and their neighbouring areas. Dingle seems to have been something of a success story, with the exception of residents' perceptions of a decrease in safety from crime and of the difficulty of setting up businesses. While the residents' views confirm those of the experts, there are still problems to be tackled.

**4.5 Granby (Liverpool) and Egerton (Wirral)**

A comparison was also made between Granby on one side of the Mersey and Egerton, a ward in the Wirral to the south of Birkenhead. Egerton comprises inter-war housing; some private, some council. It has received very little government inputs, but is viewed by the 'experts' as having survived the difficulties of the 1980s relatively well. Egerton has improved relative to Granby on most aspects with the exception of employment opportunities. The predominant view of residents, however, was one of 'no change'. Two thirds of respondents thought that it was a desirable area to live in while 80% viewed Granby as undesirable. 72.6% thought that the area had not changed in desirability over the last three years (one of the most frequent views of stability in any area sampled), whereas over a third thought that Granby had worsened. Their view of the future was again dominated by views which suggested that it would stay the same. There was a slightly greater number of optimists than pessimists. Again, in respect to the appearance of the area, the view of 'no change' dominated.

On the safety-from-crime scale, most people thought positively about the area, although not as many views were at the top of the scale as were between middling scores of 3 and 6. Again it was viewed as not having changed greatly over the last three years.

Respondents in the area were, however, very pessimistic about job opportunities. Over half thought that they had got worse over the last three years and almost the same proportion was pessimistic about the future as was agnostic about it. Unlike Granby, Dingle and Cantril Farm - where there were at least some people who thought that there was no problem about getting a job after redundancy - there were none in Egerton. There was very little optimism about jobs at all.

In summary, there has been little investment in the area. It does not seem to have a view of decline, but it is not very optimistic about improvement either.

**4.6 Cantril Farm (Knowsley) and Clubmoor (Liverpool)**

Cantril Farm, a ward that includes Stockbridge Village, has received quite large amounts of government financial inputs compared to Clubmoor. Stockbridge has a variety of tenures of new and rehabilitated housing. It has been the subject of a major public-private initiative involving Knowsley Council and the private-sector firms of Barrett, Abbey and Barclays. Clubmoor has mainly council housing. It is not an 'inner area' and has received few inputs.

More people in Cantril Farm found their area desirable and thought that it had improved than did people in Clubmoor. More were also optimistic of the future. Very few were pessimistic. In contrast, a large proportion was pessimistic about the future in Clubmoor and by far the majority viewed it as having declined recently:

|  | Cantrill Farm | | | Clubmoor | | |
|  | now | last three years | future three years | now | last three years | future three years |
|---|---|---|---|---|---|---|
| positive | 78.2 | 75.0 | 48.7 | 49.4 | 7.8 | 22.4 |
| same | 16.0 | 18.8 | 46.0 | 11.4 | 34.2 | 30.2 |
| negative | 6.2 | 6.2 | 5.3 | 39.2 | 57.9 | 47.4 |

In Cantril Farm more thought that Clubmoor was undesirable and had got worse. While those in Clubmoor may not have thought highly of Cantril Farm, by far the majority thought that it had improved recently, in great contrast to the numbers thinking the same of their own area. In Cantril Farm, only a few people considered that their area had changed compared to the outer suburbs and, of those that did, as many thought that the gap had narrowed as considered that it had widened. Most thought that there would be little change relative to the outer suburbs in the future and of those that thought there would be, they were equally split between a narrowing and a widening. Again this is in contrast to Clubmoor where many more thought that the gap with the outer suburbs had widened. Although more thought that there will be little future change relative to the outer suburbs, of those that did most considered that the gap would widen.

In Cantril Farm, 82.3% thought that its appearance had improved while in Clubmoor 55.1% considered that their own area had got worse. Even 70% of those in Clubmoor thought that the appearance of Cantril Farm had improved.

About two thirds of those in Cantril Farm scored their area at the top of the safety-from-crime scale, whereas the majority in Clubmoor assessed their area as near the bottom. Less than 16% thought that it had got less safe in Cantril Farm, whereas 50% thought that within Clubmoor. While only 7% were pessimistic about crime in the future in Cantril Farm, 37% thought that it would get less safe in Clubmoor. Again more were optimistic in Cantril Farm.

Most respondents in both areas were negative about the possibility of setting up a business. While the majority in Cantril Farm considered that job opportunities had not changed, most people in Clubmoor viewed them as having got worse. There was not much difference in their views on the statements about job opportunities. The only significant difference is that more people in Cantril Farm than Clubmoor thought that there would be few problems in finding a job after redundancy.

In summary, there is a major difference between the two areas' views. Undoubtedly there is evidence to suggest that inputs into Cantril Farm, whether directly or indirectly, have had a positive impact on its residents.

## 4.7 Cruddas Park (West City) and Scotswood in Newcastle

The interviews were carried out in Cruddas Park, an area of council housing with high-rise blocks, three-storey blocks and recently-built terraces. Some of the high-rises have been used to house problem households. Scotswood is further from the city centre. The area surveyed was a 1930's-1950's cottage-style council estate. According to the 'experts', there are problems with the quality of the housing and the appearance of the estate. There are many economic and social problems.

Both areas have had considerable policy inputs over the years, but more recently West City - or parts of it - have received the greater attention.

As can be seen from the table, there were more residents with a better view of West City than there were ones with good views of Scotswood. While by far the majority saw Scotswood as having declined in the last three years, somewhat more saw West City as having improved as against declined. There was, however, a major reversal in their views of the future, with far more people in Scotswood being optimistic than in West City:

**Desirability of own area**

| | West City | | | Scotswood | | |
|---|---|---|---|---|---|---|
| | now | last three years | future three years | now | last three years | future three years |
| positive | 50.6 | 39.4 | 42.9 | 26.0 | 6.7 | 66.1 |
| same | 10.2 | 16.9 | 15.5 | 10.4 | 18.9 | 19.4 |
| negative | 39.2 | 33.8 | 41.6 | 63.6 | 74.3 | 14.5 |

The differences in views of the last three years are confirmed by the perceptions of changes in appearance. 48% in West City thought it had improved whereas 70% in Scotswood thought that their area had got worse. Those in Scotswood who were able to compare the overall change in their area with that of West City were clearly weighted to the worsening of their own area. Such a view completely outweighs the generally-observed loyalty factor that respondents showed to their own area. Whereas 72% of people in Scotswood thought that it had got less safe over the last three years, only 31% of those in West City thought this about their area. A third of West City thought that the situation had improved. Their views of the areas on the safety-from-crime scale also reflect a major difference; Scotswood was predominantly in the worse part of the scale, whereas West City had many more in the better part:

| | safe | | risky | | | |
|---|---|---|---|---|---|---|
| | 0-3 | >3-6 | >6-7.5 | >7.5-8.5 | >8.5-10 | >10 |
| Scotswood | 7 | 24 | 0 | 3 | 52 | 14 |
| West City | 32 | 29 | 6 | 0 | 29 | 3 |

Both areas expressed many pessimistic views about job opportunities, but again Scotswood people were more pessimistic about the last three years. No Scotswood respondent thought that things had improved, whereas 14% did in West City; and in West City only 43% thought that things had got worse while 78% did in Scotswood. In this case more were optimistic about the future in West City than Scotswood. Many more in Scotswood than West City thought that they would have to move to another area of the city to get better jobs and thought that they had very little chance of getting a better job. Finally it is significant that many more thought that young people's opportunities were affected by their address in Scotswood than in West City.

In summary, there are major differences between the areas on all of the aspects of the survey. Scotswood regards itself as worse than West City and this is confirmed in a number of questions. Scotswood has got worse over the last three years while West City shows many more signs of improvement. There is therefore indirect evidence of the success of recent policy inputs into West City. Overall the inputs over the longer period into West City seem to have been much more successful than those into Scotswood.

**4.8 Southwick and Town End Farm in Sunderland**

Southwick is very much a 'traditional' inner-city area, with a mix of 1930s-50s cottage-style council housing and some older terraced housing. The area relied heavily on the shipbuilding and marine engineering of the River Wear which have now gone. It has long been the focus of policy attention.

Town End Farm is a peripheral council estate located to the north west of Sunderland with South Tyneside to the north and the A19 to the west. It is in reasonable condition physically, but it has economic and social problems. It has only been included as an inner area since the mid-1980s. It has received considerable amounts of Estate Action and HIPS resources. There has also been some private rehabilitation using City Grant. The Nissan plant is nearby.

More respondents thought the areas were desirable than undesirable, but many more had a positive view of Town End Farm than Southwick. People in both areas regarded their neighbouring area as undesirable, but there were more people in Town End Farm who saw Southwick as undesirable than there were in Southwick who viewed Town End Farm as undesirable. Many more thought that the area had improved its desirability in the last three years in Town End Farm and fewer thought that it had got worse. The contrast between the two areas was even greater for future expectations with many more in the peripheral estate having an optimistic view. Those in Southwick had a more optimistic view of their neighbouring area than they did of their own:

Desirability of own area

|  | Southwick | | | | Town End | | |
|---|---|---|---|---|---|---|---|
|  | now | last three years | future three years |  | now | last three years | future three years |
| positive | 47.6 | 15.2 | 32.5 |  | 71.9 | 62.2 | 82.9 |
| same | 23.8 | 42.5 | 36.4 |  | 14.6 | 11.0 | 15.9 |
| negative | 28.8 | 44.3 | 31.2 |  | 13.4 | 26.8 | 1.2 |

These differences are confirmed in the responses on gaps with the outer suburbs and on change in appearance. More in Southwick thought that the gap would widen or stay the same whereas more in Town End Farm thought that it would narrow or stay the same. Both areas thought it had widened rather than narrowed over the last three years. Over three quarters thought that the appearance of Town End Farm had improved over the last three years and only 16% thought it had deteriorated. In Southwick only 14% thought it had improved while 36% thought it had got worse.

The two areas both had a positive view of safety from crime, with Southwick showing a greater number of people who thought that it was very safe. The dominant view in Southwick was that there had been little change over the last three years whereas the majority view in Town End Farm was of a worsening situation. However many more in Town End Farm had an optimistic view of the future safety of the area.

This greater optimism was also evident in views on future job opportunities. Although the general view of both areas was that opportunities had decreased recently, more in Town End Farm than Southwick saw the recent period positively. There were no differences between the areas on their view of the job opportunity statements, but there were some differences on views about job opportunities for young people. Fewer agreed that an address can hinder opportunities in Town End Farm and fewer thought that only low-skill jobs were available.

In general, Town End Farm seems to have had a greater boost from recent initiatives, whether public or private, than Southwick, where there is evidence of some decline despite policy inputs.

# 5 CONCLUSIONS

- Many inner-city residents show loyalty to their area. There is a base on which to build in all areas.

- Overall, there are more negative views than positive ones about change. This applies to overall desirability, crime and job opportunities. While this changing overall desirability is correlated with people's views on declining job opportunites, this should not be used to account for the overall view of decline. Their views on changing desirability are also strongly correlated with their views on changes in safety from crime and appearance. A simple improvement in the economy is unlikely in itself to reverse their views.

- Results from the areas and from the whole sample show that Blacks are more concerned than others about changing job opportunities and that Pakistanis are more concerned than others about changes in safety from crime.

- Although there is more optimism than pessimism about the future for overall desirability, this is not the case for safety from crime and job opportunities.

- On the basis of these areas only, there seem to be some differences between the conurbations on job opportunities. More people in Tyne and Wear think that the present situation is bad in various ways. But it is people in Greater Manchester who say more frequently that opportunities have declined. This links to the poor showing of Manchester on the quantitative analyses at national and local level.

- Nearly all of the area comparisons substantiate the experts' views on where policy has been more successful. Ordsall, Dingle, Cantril Farm and West City have all clearly done better over the last three years than their paired area. Ordsall and Cantril Farm have both had much more inputs than their pairs. In Dingle, similar policy inputs have worked better than in Granby. More recent initiatives in West City and Town End Farm seem to have had more of an impact than the longer period of initiatives in Scotswood and Southwick. There is also some evidence to suggest that the inputs into Miles Platting have been somewhat successful, though there is a growing problem about crime.

- The overall conclusion from the survey is that more residents are responding positively in areas where there have been more inputs, even when the predominant views within the pair of areas is one of decline. From the residents' viewpoints the policy inputs have been worthwhile.

Serial No...............
(5-8)
CARD 1                    9

URBAN POLICY

Name: Initials  Mr/Mrs/Miss  .................................

Address:  ...........................................................
...........................................................

Postcode  ...........................  Telephone  Yes ...................... 1
(10)
No ........................ 2        10
Tel No. (incl exch name)  ..........

Sample number.  ☐☐☐☐☐☐
(11)(12)(13)(14)(15)(16)                                    11/16

| Sex | (17) |
| --- | --- |
| Male | 1 |
| Female | 2 |

**Age  WRITE IN EXACT AGE**    (18)
| | |
| --- | --- |
| 18-24 | 1 |
| 25-34 | 2 |
| 35-44 | 3 |
| 45-54 | 4 |
| 55-64 | 5 |
| 65-74 | 6 |
| 75+ | 7 |

**Work status of respondent**    (19)
| | |
| --- | --- |
| Full time (30 hrs/wk+) | 1 |
| Part time (8-29 hrs/wk) | 2 |
| Working (under 8 hrs) | 3 |
| Housewife | 4 |
| Retired | 5 |
| Registered unemployed | 6 |
| Unemployed but not registered | 7 |
| Student | 8 |
| Other | 9 |

Occupation of Head of Household
Position/
rank/grade  ......................
Industry/type
of company  ......................
Qualifications/
degrees/apprenticeships  ..............
No of staff responsible for  ...........
PROBE FOR CWE/PENSION

**Class**    (20)
| | |
| --- | --- |
| AB | 1 |
| C1 | 2 |
| C2 | 3 |
| D | 4 |
| E | 5 |

Q   SHOWCARD S   And how would you
describe the composition of your
household?    (21)
| | |
| --- | --- |
| Single adult under 60 | 1 |
| Single adult 60+ | 2 |
| Two adults both under 60 yrs | 3 |
| Two adults at least one aged over 60 yrs | 4 |
| 3+ adults all over 16 | 5 |
| 1-parent family with child/ren, at least one under 16 | 6 |
| 2-parent family with child/ren at least one under 16 | 7 |
| Don't know | 9 |

Car in Household  CIRCLE NUMBER

0   1   2   3+                        22

**Tenure**
(23)
| | |
| --- | --- |
| Owned outright | 1 |
| Buying on mortgage: This house was | |
| Previously owner occupied | 2 |
| Previously rented from Council | 3 |
| Previously rented from HA | 4 |
| Rented from Council | 5 |
| Rented from Housing Association | 6 |
| Rented from private landlord | 7 |
| Other | 8 |        23

Q   How long have you lived in this area?
(24)
| | |
| --- | --- |
| 1 year or less | 1 |
| Over 1 up to 3 yrs | 2 |
| Over 3 up to 7 yrs | 3 |
| Over 7 up to 10 yrs | 4 |
| Over 10 yrs | 5 |
| Don't know | 6 |        24

Q   How long have you lived in this house/flat?
(25)
| | |
| --- | --- |
| 1 year or less | 1 |
| Over 1 up to 3 yrs | 2 |
| Over 3 up to 7 yrs | 3 |
| Over 7 up to 10 yrs | 4 |
| Over 10 yrs | 5 |
| Don't know | 6 |        25

Ethnic Origin
Q   SHOWCARD T  Can you tell me, from this card,
which ethnic group you belong to?
(26)
| | |
| --- | --- |
| White | 1 |
| Black-Caribbean | 2 |
| Black-African | 3 |
| Black-other | 4 |
| Indian | 5 |
| Pakistani | 6 |
| Bangladeshi | 7 |
| Chinese | 8 |
| Other ethnic group | 9 |
| Refused | 0 |        26

SHOWCARD PACK STARTS
(27)
| | |
| --- | --- |
| Showcard A | 1 |
| Showcard A1 | 2 |        27

Appendix E.16

START INTERVIEW HERE

NOTICE THAT SOME OF THE SHOWCARDS USED IN THIS SURVEY ARE REVERSED, SO THAT THE ITEMS ON THE SHOWCARDS MAY NOT BE IN THE SAME ORDER AS THEY APPEAR ON THE QUESTIONNAIRE. REMEMBER TO CODE SHOWCARD PACK TYPE ON FRONT PAGE.

Good morning/afternoon/evening, I'm from MORI, the market research and polling organisation. We are carrying out some research on peoples' attitudes to living in this and other areas of Greater Manchester/Merseyside/Tyne and Wear. The interview will take about 30 minutes.

Q1    SHOWCARD A I am going to read out a number of things that might affect the quality of life that people have. From this card, can you tell me how important to you each of the following is in affecting the quality of your life here in . . . (NAME OF AREA) ?
READ OUT. ALTERNATE ORDER. TICK START

| | | Very impor-tant | Fairly impor-tant | Neither impor-tant nor un-impor-tant | Fairly un-impor-tant | Very un-impor-tant | Don't know/no opinion | |
|---|---|---|---|---|---|---|---|---|
| a) | Quality of health care | 1 | 2 | 3 | 4 | 5 | 6 | 28 |
| b) | Pollution | 1 | 2 | 3 | 4 | 5 | 6 | 29 |
| c) | Cost of living | 1 | 2 | 3 | 4 | 5 | 6 | 30 |
| d) | Employment prospects | 1 | 2 | 3 | 4 | 5 | 6 | 31 |
| e) | Violent crime | 1 | 2 | 3 | 4 | 5 | 6 | 32 |
| f) | Non-violent crime | 1 | 2 | 3 | 4 | 5 | 6 | 33 |
| g) | Quality of housing | 1 | 2 | 3 | 4 | 5 | 6 | 34 |
| h) | Availability of Council housing | 1 | 2 | 3 | 4 | 5 | 6 | 35 |
| i) | House rents | 1 | 2 | 3 | 4 | 5 | 6 | 36 |
| j) | House prices | 1 | 2 | 3 | 4 | 5 | 6 | 37 |
| k) | Unemployment levels | 1 | 2 | 3 | 4 | 5 | 6 | 38 |
| l) | Public transport | 1 | 2 | 3 | 4 | 5 | 6 | 39 |
| m) | Quality of schools and colleges | 1 | 2 | 3 | 4 | 5 | 6 | 40 |
| n) | Quality of welfare services | 1 | 2 | 3 | 4 | 5 | 6 | 41 |
| o) | Racial harmony | 1 | 2 | 3 | 4 | 5 | 6 | 42 |
| p) | Quality of sports facilities | 1 | 2 | 3 | 4 | 5 | 6 | 43 |
| q) | What the area looks like | 1 | 2 | 3 | 4 | 5 | 6 | 44 |
| r) | Quality of shops | 1 | 2 | 3 | 4 | 5 | 6 | 45 |
| s) | Availability of job training | 1 | 2 | 3 | 4 | 5 | 6 | 46 |
| t) | Quality of leisure facilities | 1 | 2 | 3 | 4 | 5 | 6 | 47 |

X   Y

Q2    SHOWCARD B Thinking about the area in general, how desirable or undesirable do you find .... (NAME OF LOCAL AREA) as a place to live in these days?

Q3    SHOWCARD B AGAIN   And by comparison, I'd like you to think about . . . (NEIGH-BOURING AREA). How desirable or undesirable do you think . . . (YOUR NEIGHBOURING AREA) would be as a place to live?

| | Q2 Local area (48) | Q3 Neighbouring area (49) | |
|---|---|---|---|
| Very desirable | 1 | 1 | |
| Fairly desirable | 2 | 2 | |
| Neither desirable nor undesirable | 3 | 3 | |
| Fairly undesirable | 4 | 4 | |
| Very undesirable | 5 | 5 | |
| Don't know/no opinion | 6 | 6 | 47/48 |

Appendix E.17

Q4    SHOWCARD C  To what extent, if at all, do you think this area has changed in the last three years? (IF LIVED IN AREA LESS THAN 3 YEARS, ASK FOR THEIR IMPRESSION)

Q5    SHOWCARD C AGAIN  And to what extent, if at all, do you think (YOUR NEIGHBOURING AREA) has changed in the last three years?

|  | Q4 Local area (50) | Q5 Neighbouring area (51) |  |
|---|---|---|---|
| Improved a great deal | 1 | 1 | BOX |
| Improved a little | 2 | 2 | A |
| Stayed the same | 3 | 3 ←GO TO Q10 |  |
| Got a little worse | 4 | 4 | BOX |
| Got a great deal worse | 5 | 5 | B |
| Don't know/no opinion | 6 | 6 ←GO TO Q10 | 50/51 |

ASK IF IMPROVED (CODES 1 OR 2) OR GOT WORSE (CODES 4 OR 5) AT Q4.  OTHERS GO TO Q7

Q6    In what ways has the (LOCAL) area around here improved/got worse?
PROBE FOR DETAIL

. . . . . . . . . . . . . . . . . . . . . . . . . . . . . . . . . . . . . . . . .    52

. . . . . . . . . . . . . . . . . . . . . . . . . . . . . . . . . . . . . . . . .    53

. . . . . . . . . . . . . . . . . . . . . . . . . . . . . . . . . . . . . . . . .    54

ASK IF IMPROVED (CODES 1 OR 2) OR GOT WORSE (CODES 4 OR 5) AT Q5.  OTHERS GO TO Q8

Q7    And in what ways have things in . . . (YOUR NEIGHBOURING AREA) improved/got worse?
PROBE FOR DETAIL

. . . . . . . . . . . . . . . . . . . . . . . . . . . . . . . . . . . . . . . . .    55

. . . . . . . . . . . . . . . . . . . . . . . . . . . . . . . . . . . . . . . . .    56

. . . . . . . . . . . . . . . . . . . . . . . . . . . . . . . . . . . . . . . . .    57

ASK IF BOTH RESPONSES AT Q4/5 IN BOX A - *OTHERS GO TO Q9*

Q8    SHOWCARD D  You say that you think the quality of life in . . . (THIS AREA) and . . . (NEIGHBOURING AREA) has improved.  On balance, to what extent would you say this area has improved more or less than . . . (NEIGHBOURING AREA)?

|  | (58) |
|---|---|
| Improved a lot more | 1 |
| Improved a little more | 2 |
| About the same | 3 |
| Improved a little less | 4 |
| Improved a lot less | 5 |
| Don't know | 6 |

58

ASK IF BOTH RESPONSES AT Q4/5 IN BOX B - *OTHERS GO TO Q10*

Q9    SHOWCARD W  You say that you think the quality of life in . . . (THIS AREA) and . . . (NEIGHBOURING AREA) has got worse.  On balance, would you say this area has worsened more or less than . . . (NEIGHBOURING AREA)?

|  | (59) |
|---|---|
| Worsened a lot more | 1 |
| Worsened a little more | 2 |
| About the same | 3 |
| Worsened a little less | 4 |
| Worsened a lot less | 5 |
| Don't know | 6 |

59

Appendix E.18

ASK ALL

Q10 Generally speaking, do you consider the quality of life in the outer suburbs, such as (NAME OF SUBURB) to be better, worse or the same as the quality of life here in this area?

|  | (60) |  |  |
|---|---|---|---|
| Better | 1 | ASK | |
| Worse | 2 | Q11 | |
| The same | 3 | GO | |
| Don't know | 4 | TO Q12 | 60 |

ASK IF BETTER OR WORSE

Q11 SHOWCARD E  In the last three years, would you say the difference between the quality of life here and in the outer suburbs, such as  (NAME OF SUBRUB) has widened, narrowed or remained the same?

|  | (61) |  |
|---|---|---|
| Widened a lot | 1 | |
| Widened a little | 2 | |
| Remained the same | 3 | |
| Narrowed a little | 4 | |
| Narrowed a lot | 5 | |
| Don't know/no opinion | 6 | 61 |

ASK ALL

Q12 SHOWCARD F  Now, thinking about the future, what do you expect to happen to the quality of life in this (LOCAL) area in the next three years?

Q13 SHOWCARD F AGAIN  And what do you expect to happen to the quality of life in ... (NEIGHBOURING AREA) in the next three years?

|  | LOCAL Q12 (62) | NEIGHBOURING Q13 (63) |  |
|---|---|---|---|
| Improve a great deal | 1 | 1 | |
| Improve a little | 2 | 2 | |
| Stay the same | 3 | 3 | |
| Get a little worse | 4 | 4 | |
| Get a great deal worse | 5 | 5 | |
| Don't know/no opinion | 6 | 6 | 62/63 |

ASK IF IMPROVE OR GOT WORSE (CODES 1,2,4 OR 5) AT Q12.  OTHERS GO TO Q15

Q14 In what ways do you think the (LOCAL) area around here will improve/get worse? PROBE FOR DETAIL

|  |  |
|---|---|
| . . . . . . . . . . . . . . . . . . . . . . . . . . . . . . . . . . . . . . . . . . . . . . . . . . . . . . . | 64 |
| . . . . . . . . . . . . . . . . . . . . . . . . . . . . . . . . . . . . . . . . . . . . . . . . . . . . . . . | 65 |
| . . . . . . . . . . . . . . . . . . . . . . . . . . . . . . . . . . . . . . . . . . . . . . . . . . . . . . . | 66 |
| . . . . . . . . . . . . . . . . . . . . . . . . . . . . . . . . . . . . . . . . . . . . . . . . . . . . . . . | |

ASK ALL

Q15 Do you think the quality of life in ... (LOCAL AREA) will change compared to the outer suburbs such as ... (SUBURB) in the next three years?

|  | (67) |  |  |
|---|---|---|---|
| Yes, will change | 1 | ASK Q16 | |
| No, will not change | 2 | Go TO Q17 | |
| Don't know/no opinion | 3 | | 67 |

Appendix E.19

ASK IF YES AT Q15 - OTHERS GO TO Q17

Q16   SHOWCARD G  To what extent, if at all, would you say the difference between the quality of life here and in the outer suburbs, such as . . . (NAME OF SUBURB) will change in the next three years?

|  |  | (68) |
|---|---|---|
| Widen a lot | | 1 |
| Widen a little | | 2 |
| Remain the same | | 3 |
| Narrow a little | | 4 |
| Narrow a lot | | 5 |
| Don't know/no opinion | | 6 |

68

ASK ALL

Q17   Now I would like to ask you some questions about the general appearance of this area, that is, whether it is attractive to look at or not.  First of all, I'd like you to tell me whether you agree or disagree with the following statements about the appearance of this area? READ OUT.  ALTERNATE ORDER.  TICK START

|  |  | Agree | Disagree | No opinion |  |
|---|---|---|---|---|---|
| x ☐ | a) | This area is attractive to look at | 1 | 2 | 3 | 69 |
| | b) | They should knock down all the buildings in this area and start all over again | 1 | 2 | 3 | 70 |
| | c) | There is very little litter in this area | 1 | 2 | 3 | 71 |
| | d) | This area is generally unattractive to look at | 1 | 2 | 3 | 72 |
| | e) | There is far too much graffiti in this area | 1 | 2 | 3 | 73 |
| Y ☐ | f) | Only parts of this area are attractive to look at | 1 | 2 | 3 | 74 |

Q18   SHOWCARD C  To what extent, if at all, would you say the appearance of the (LOCAL) area around here has changed in the last three years?

Q19   SHOWCARD C  AGAIN  And to what extent, if at all, do you think the appearance of .... (NEIGHBOURING AREA)  has changed in the last three years?

|  | Q18 Local area (75) | Q19 Neighbouring area (76) |
|---|---|---|
| Improved a great deal | 1 | 1 |
| Improved a little | 2 | 2 |
| Stayed the same | 3 | 3 |
| Got a little worse | 4 | 4 |
| Got a great deal worse | 5 | 5 |
| Don't know/no opinion | 6 | 6 |

75/76

ASK IF IMPROVED/GOT WORSE (CODES 1,2,4 OR 5) AT Q18.  OTHERS GO TO Q21

Q20   In what ways has the appearance of the (LOCAL) area around here changed? PROBE FOR DETAIL

. . . . . . . . . . . . . . . . . . . . . . . . . . . . . . . . . . . . . . . . . . . . . . . . . . . . . . . . . . .

77

. . . . . . . . . . . . . . . . . . . . . . . . . . . . . . . . . . . . . . . . . . . . . . . . . . . . . . . . . . .

. . . . . . . . . . . . . . . . . . . . . . . . . . . . . . . . . . . . . . . . . . . . . . . . . . . . . . . . . . .

78

. . . . . . . . . . . . . . . . . . . . . . . . . . . . . . . . . . . . . . . . . . . . . . . . . . . . . . . . . . .

79

Appendix E.20

CARD ②    9

ASK IF IMPROVED/GOT WORSE (CODES 1,2,4 OR 5) AT Q19.  OTHERS GO TO Q22

Q21    And in what ways has the appearance of .... (NEIGHBOURING AREA) changed?
PROBE FOR DETAIL

. . . . . . . . . . . . . . . . . . . . . . . . . . . . . . . . . . . . . . . . . . . . . . . . . . . . . . . . . . .    10

. . . . . . . . . . . . . . . . . . . . . . . . . . . . . . . . . . . . . . . . . . . . . . . . . . . . . . . . . . .    11

. . . . . . . . . . . . . . . . . . . . . . . . . . . . . . . . . . . . . . . . . . . . . . . . . . . . . . . . . . .

. . . . . . . . . . . . . . . . . . . . . . . . . . . . . . . . . . . . . . . . . . . . . . . . . . . . . . . . . . .    12

ASK ALL

Q22    And now some questions about whether this area is safe to live in.  By safe I mean the amount of crime in the area.  Do you agree or disagree with the following statements about crime and how safe it is in this area?  READ OUT.  ALTERNATE ORDER.  TICK START

|   |   | Agree | Disagree | No opinion |   |
|---|---|---|---|---|---|
| X [ ] a) | It is safe to walk through the streets at night | 1 | 2 | 3 | 13 |
| b) | It is safe to walk through the streets during the day | 1 | 2 | 3 | 14 |
| c) | It is only safe to walk along certain routes at night | 1 | 2 | 3 | 15 |
| d) | People in this area feel unsafe in their homes at night | 1 | 2 | 3 | 16 |
| e) | It is only safe to walk along certain routes during the day | 1 | 2 | 3 | 17 |
| Y [ ] f) | This area is very safe to live in | 1 | 2 | 3 | 18 |

Q23    SHOWCARD H From this card, how safe from crime would you say this area is compared with . . . (NEIGHBOURING AREA)?

Q24    SHOWCARD H And how safe from crime would you say this area is compared with the outer suburbs such as . . .(SUBURB)?

|   | Q23 Neighbouring area (19) | Q24 Outer suburbs (20) |   |
|---|---|---|---|
| Much safer | 1 | 1 | |
| A little safer | 2 | 2 | |
| About the same | 3 | 3 | |
| A little less safe | 4 | 4 | |
| Much less safe | 5 | 5 | |
| Don't know/no opinion | 6 | 6 | 19/20 |

Q25    SHOWCARD I To what extent, if at all, would you say this area has changed in the level of crime in the last three years?

Q26    SHOWCARD I  And, in the last three years, to what extent would you say . . . (NEIGHBOURING AREA)  has changed?

|   | Q25 Local area (21) | Q26 Neighbouring area (22) |   |
|---|---|---|---|
| Much safer | 1 | 1 | |
| A little safer | 2 | 2 | |
| Stayed the same | 3 | 3 | |
| A little less safe | 4 | 4 | |
| Much less safe | 5 | 5 | |
| Don't know/no opinion | 6 | 6 | 21/22 |

Appendix E.21

ASK IF MORE OR LESS SAFE (CODES 1,2,4 OR 5) AT Q25. OTHERS GO TO Q28

Q27 In what ways has the area around here got more/less safe in terms of crime? PROBE FOR DETAIL

. . . . . . . . . . . . . . . . . . . . . . . . . . . . . . . . . . . . . . . . . . . . . . . . . . . .  23

. . . . . . . . . . . . . . . . . . . . . . . . . . . . . . . . . . . . . . . . . . . . . . . . . . . .  24

. . . . . . . . . . . . . . . . . . . . . . . . . . . . . . . . . . . . . . . . . . . . . . . . . . . .

. . . . . . . . . . . . . . . . . . . . . . . . . . . . . . . . . . . . . . . . . . . . . . . . . . . .  25

ASK ALL

Q28 Do you feel there is any difference in safety from crime here in this area compared with . . . (NEIGHBOURING AREA)?

                                                                          (26)
Yes, difference . . . . . . . . . . . . . . . . . . . . . . . . . . . . . . . . . . . . . . . . . . . 1
No, no difference . . . . . . . . . . . . . . . . . . . . . . . . . . . . . . . . . . . . . . . . . . 2
Don't know/no opinion . . . . . . . . . . . . . . . . . . . . . . . . . . . . . . . . . . . . . . 3        26

ASK IF YES AT Q28. OTHERS GO TO Q30

Q29 In what ways do you think safety from crime is different in this area compared with . . . (NEIGHBOURING AREA)? PROBE FOR DETAIL

. . . . . . . . . . . . . . . . . . . . . . . . . . . . . . . . . . . . . . . . . . . . . . . . .  27

. . . . . . . . . . . . . . . . . . . . . . . . . . . . . . . . . . . . . . . . . . . . . . . . .

. . . . . . . . . . . . . . . . . . . . . . . . . . . . . . . . . . . . . . . . . . . . . . . . .  28

ASK ALL . . . . . . . . . . . . . . . . . . . . . . . . . . . . . . . . . . . . . .  29

Q30 Generally speaking, do you think the safety from crime in this area is better, worse or the same as the safety from crime in . . .(NAME OF SUBURB)?

                                                      (30)
Better . . . . . . . . . . . . . . . . . . . . . . . . . . . . . . . . . . . . . . . . . 1 } ASK
Worse . . . . . . . . . . . . . . . . . . . . . . . . . . . . . . . . . . . . . . . . . 2 } Q31
The same . . . . . . . . . . . . . . . . . . . . . . . . . . . . . . . . . . . . . . . 3 } GO TO
Don't know . . . . . . . . . . . . . . . . . . . . . . . . . . . . . . . . . . . . . . 4 } Q32        30

ASK IF BETTER OR WORSE AT Q30-

Q31 SHOWCARD J In the last three years, would you say the difference between safety from crime here and in the outer suburbs, such as . . . (NAME OF SUBURB) has widened, narrowed or remained the same?

                                                          (31)
Widened a lot . . . . . . . . . . . . . . . . . . . . . . . . . . . . . . . . . . . . . . 1
Widened a little . . . . . . . . . . . . . . . . . . . . . . . . . . . . . . . . . . . . . 2
Remained the same . . . . . . . . . . . . . . . . . . . . . . . . . . . . . . . . . . . 3
Narrowed a little . . . . . . . . . . . . . . . . . . . . . . . . . . . . . . . . . . . . 4
Narrowed a lot . . . . . . . . . . . . . . . . . . . . . . . . . . . . . . . . . . . . . 5
Don't know/no opinion . . . . . . . . . . . . . . . . . . . . . . . . . . . . . . . . . 6        31

Q32  SHOWCARD H From this card, thinking about the next three years, do you expect this area to be more or less safe from crime?

Q33  And do you expect, in the next three years, . . . (NEIGHBOURING AREA) to become more or less safe from crime?

| | Q32 Local area (32) | Q33 Neighbouring area (33) |
|---|---|---|
| Much safer | 1 | 1 |
| A little safer | 2 | 2 |
| About the same | 3 | 3 |
| A little less safe | 4 | 4 |
| Much less safe | 5 | 5 |
| Don't know/no opinion | 6 | 6 | 32/33 |

Q34  In the next three years, do you think that there will be a change in safety from crime in this area, compared with the outer suburbs such as ..... (NAME OF SUBURB)?

| | (34) |
|---|---|
| Yes, will be a change | 1 ASK Q35 |
| No, will not be a change | 2 } GO TO Q36 |
| Don't know/no opinion | 3 } | 34 |

ASK IF YES AT Q34
Q35  SHOWCARD G In the next three years, would you say the difference between safety from crime here and in the outer suburbs, such as . . . (NAME OF SUBURB) will widen, narrow or remain the same?

| | (35) |
|---|---|
| Widen a lot | 1 |
| Widen a little | 2 |
| Remain the same | 3 |
| Narrow a little | 4 |
| Narrow a lot | 5 |
| Don't know/no opinion | 6 | 35 |

Now, I'd like to ask you a few questions about employment and training.

ASK ALL
Q36  I am now going to read out some statements about job opportunities in this area. I'd like you to tell me whether you agree or disagree with each statement? READ OUT. ALTERNATE ORDER. TICK START

| | | Agree | Disagree | No opinion | |
|---|---|---|---|---|---|
| X ☐ a) | If people from this area left their present jobs, or were made redundant, they would have no trouble finding another job | 1 | 2 | 3 | 36 |
| b) | In order to get a better job, people from this area would have to move house to another area of the city | 1 | 2 | 3 | 37 |
| c) | The only jobs that people from this area can get are low paid ones | 1 | 2 | 3 | 38 |
| d) | There is very little chance for people from this area to get better jobs | 1 | 2 | 3 | 39 |
| e) | There are plenty of jobs available for people from this area | 1 | 2 | 3 | 40 |
| f) | The only jobs that people from this area can get are insecure ones | 1 | 2 | 3 | 41 |
| Y ☐ g) | In order to get better jobs, people from this area would have to move to another city | 1 | 2 | 3 | 42 |

Appendix E.23

Q37 Now.some statements about young people and their chances of obtaining jobs and skills. I'd like you to tell me whether you agree or disagree with the following statements? READ OUT. ALTERNATE ORDER. TICK START

|  |  | Agree | Disagree | No opinion |  |
|---|---|---|---|---|---|
| X ☐ a) | There are plenty of job opportunities for young people from this area | 1 | 2 | 3 | 43 |
| b) | Young people from this area find it very difficult to get jobs | 1 | 2 | 3 | 44 |
| c) | Only young people from this area who have good qualifications find it easy to get jobs | 1 | 2 | 3 | 45 |
| d) | An address in this area makes it difficult for young people to obtain job interviews | 1 | 2 | 3 | 46 |
| Y ☐ e) | Young people from this area can only get jobs that require few skills | 1 | 2 | 3 | 47 |

Q38 SHOWCARD K From this card, can you tell me how easy or difficult you think it is for people in this area to set up their own business?

|  | (48) |  |
|---|---|---|
| Very easy | 1 |  |
| Fairly easy | 2 |  |
| Neither easy nor difficult | 3 |  |
| Fairly difficult | 4 |  |
| Very difficult | 5 |  |
| Don't know/no opinion | 6 | 48 |

ASK IF EASY OR DIFFICULT (CODES 1,2,4 OR 5) AT Q38

Q39 Why do you say it is easy/difficult for people in this area to set up their own business? PROBE FOR DETAIL

.................................................................. 49

.................................................................. 50

.................................................................. 51

..................................................................

ASK ALL

Q40 SHOWCARD L In the last three years, how much, if at all, do you think job opportunities for people in this area have changed?

|  | (52) |  |
|---|---|---|
| Got a lot better | 1 |  |
| Got a little better | 2 |  |
| Not changed | 3 |  |
| Got a little worse | 4 |  |
| Got a lot worse | 5 |  |
| Don't know/no opinion | 6 | 52 |

Q41 SHOWCARD M And thinking about the next three years, how do you expect job opportunities in this area to change, if at all?

|  | (53) |  |
|---|---|---|
| Get a lot better | 1 |  |
| Get a little better | 2 |  |
| No change | 3 |  |
| Get a little worse | 4 |  |
| Get a lot worse | 5 |  |
| Don't know/no opinion | 6 | 53 |

GO TO DEMOGRAPHICS

Appendix E.24

# Respondent Feedback

PLEASE COMPLETE THIS SECTION AT THE END OF THE INTERVIEW. <u>AFTER</u> THE DEMOGRAPHICS.

I would like to end the interview by asking you what you thought about the interview.

How interesting did you find the interview? Would you say . . .
READ OUT. ALTERNATE AND TICK START

|  |  | (54) |
|--|--|------|
| ☐ | . . . very interesting | 1 |
|  | . . . fairly interesting | 2 |
|  | . . . not very interesting | 3 |
| ☐ | . . . not at all interesting | 4 |
|  | Don't know | 5 |

And how long did you find the interview? Would you say . . .
READ OUT. ALTERNATE AND TICK START

|  |  | (55) |
|--|--|------|
| ☐ | . . . much too long | 1 |
|  | . . . a little too long | 2 |
|  | . . . about right | 3 |
| ☐ | . . . too short | 4 |
|  | Don't know | 5 |

Did you think the questions were difficult to understand or not? Would you say . . .
READ OUT. ALTERNATE AND TICK START

|  |  | (56) |
|--|--|------|
| ☐ | . . . very difficult | 1 |
|  | . . . fairly difficult | 2 |
|  | . . . not very difficult | 3 |
| ☐ | . . . not at all difficult | 4 |
|  | Don't know | 5 |

Finally, how interested would you be in participating in future surveys on similar subjects? Would you be . . .
READ OUT. ALTERNATE AND TICK START

|  |  | (57) |
|--|--|------|
| ☐ | . . . very interested | 1 |
|  | . . . fairly interested | 2 |
|  | . . . not very interested | 3 |
| ☐ | . . . not at all interested | 4 |
|  | Don't know | 5 |

LENGTH OF INTERVIEW

☐☐ minutes
(58) (59)

<u>Interviewer Declaration</u>
I declare that I have carried out this interview within the MRS Code of Conduct, and according to MORI's specification and with a person previously unknown to me.

Signed . . . . . . . . . . . . . . . . . . . . . . . . . . . . . . . . . . . . . . . . . . . . . . . . .

Interviewer Name . . . . . . . . . . . . . . . . . . . . . . . . . . . . . . . . . . . . . . . . . . .

Interviewer ☐☐☐☐   ☐

Appendix E.25

# Employer's survey

## 1 AIMS AND METHODOLOGY

Over the past five years a substantial number of public-private partnership initiatives have been developed to tackle economic and employment issues. Training and Enterprise Councils, various training initiatives and, most recently, City Challenge, have all represented government attempts to address the need to develop partnerships to assist in urban regeneration. The aim of the survey was to develop a qualitative analysis of employers' knowledge and views about such public-sector support.

Many of the programmes included in the evaluation do have statistically measurable economic outcomes; examples include employment change and business start-up rates. These are assessed elsewhere in the Report. The employers' survey aimed to explore the 'softer' aspects of the impact of policy on employment and economic issues. This Appendix concentrates on these more elusive concepts - on image generation and business confidence, for example - to tease out the links between these and government action and to assess the extent to which policy has been directly or indirectly beneficial to businesses.

A sample of 50 firms was drawn from within each of the three conurbations. The fact that the ideas of 'image' and 'confidence' do not lend themselves to an extensive sample meant that it was not necessary to construct a comprehensive population of firms to be surveyed. As a result it was decided that a final subset of twenty firms would provide adequate variation; six from Merseyside and seven each from Greater Manchester and Tyne and Wear.

The criteria for the initial selection of firms was based upon size, economic sector and whether or not the firm was known to have received any form of government aid. Firms were initially selected from two sub-groups: a 'policy-on' and a 'policy-off' group. Drawing on the data previously collected on government expenditure it was possible to classify a set of firms that had been the recipients of assistance from government programmes ('policy-on'); the second group was selected without any prior knowledge of their financial past. As this was a semi-random process, it was impossible to judge if these firms had or had not had any involvement with government policy ('policy off'). There was no guarantee that the 'policy-off' sub-group had not been in receipt of government funds, as there are no data bases which list firms that have operated totally independently. However, because of this uncertainty, the semi-random exercise was able to explore the penetration of government programmes into the wider business community as well as testing the degree to which firms were aware of policy initiatives.

So that the level of comparative analysis could be maintained, the programmes selected for the 'policy-on' sub-groups were kept constant for all three conurbations. The larger firms were predominantly selected if they had received some form of regional policy (Regional Development Grant/Regional Selective Assistance) or City Grant. The medium to small companies were chosen if they had benefited from being located in an Enterprise Zone or an Urban Development Corporation area, or if they had received Urban Programme funds.

The final firms in each conurbation were then selected on the basis of size and sector so as to include; large (over 250 employees) service sector companies, medium-sized (50 to 250 employees) companies (both manufacturing and service sector), and small-sized (below 50 employees) manufacturing companies.

In order to offset the classic survey problem of poor response rates, a total of sixteen firms were approached in each location from which the final sample was drawn. This helped to achieve the required quota. The schedule of issues discussed in the semi-structured interviews is provided in an annexe to this Appendix.

The analysis will initially outline the findings from the three areas, directly contrasting the different firm types and sizes, and in particular the 'policy-on' and 'policy-off' groups. Following this, the final section will draw together some of the most significant findings, highlighting a list of the central themes articulated by the various business communities.

# 2 MERSEYSIDE

## 2.1 Large companies

On Merseyside the views of the larger service-sector businesses were represented by a banking and a shipping organisation, the latter being the 'policy-off' establishment. Both are long-established companies, each employing well in excess of 1000 and both, since 1988, having reduced their workforce by approximately 1000. Both companies have several major establishments within the area, as well as having extensive national and international networks. Both interviewees had worked in Merseyside for over thirty years and were therefore well placed to give a long-term view of the relationship between the business community and government policy.

### Training and recruitment issues

The banking company estimated that labour costs had remained constant over the past five years, mainly as a result of a combination of reduced numbers and increased salaries. However, over the past five years the labour costs for the shipping establishment had decreased, based upon rapid increases in productivity, reductions in the labour force, the introduction of more 'flexible' work regimes and the development of new technology.

The shipping establishment had not altered its training programme over the last five years, and as a result its expenditure on training had remained the same. However, due to the increasing level of computer technology in the banking company, its technical staff had been extensively retrained. This, along with emphasis on promoting 'Total Quality Management' meant that expenditure on training had increased markedly over the last five years. The shipping company had no direct contact with the Merseyside TEC or CEWTEC, apart from some business training courses.

Both companies indicated that there had been virtually no recruitment problems within the Merseyside area over the last decade. They stated that this was indicative of the health of the local labour market, which offered a massive pool of under-utilised labour. Only in very specialised cases involving information technology had they encountered any difficulty in recruiting from the local area, but this type of personnel was in any case difficult to find nationally.

### Image and attractiveness

Both interviewees talked firstly of the general state of the local economy and its prospects for the future. The shipping company had dramatically improved its productivity and profit rates over the past five years, and this was identified as resulting primarily from a restructuring of the company. However, some other local factors were noted, such as comparatively low land prices, good transport links and the comparatively high quality of life, all of which were seen as essential to the company's well-being. As a result, confidence in the area had increased in comparison to all other locations and as a business site Merseyside was now seen as more attractive in comparison to other regions of the country than was the case before. In contrast, the banking company felt that, even though the political climate of the area was now much more stable, there were still problems with the area which hindered any improvement in business confidence. These problems were attributed largely to wider macro-economic concerns, but also to Merseyside's over-dependence for employment upon large companies, and to the problems faced by the financial services sector in the area. This last comment related directly to the over-capacity created by the boom of the late 1980s and the effects of technological developments, both of which resulted in the shedding of labour.

As a business location, the representative from the banking organisation believed Merseyside had become more attractive. Over the next five years this situation was likely to improve, he felt, due to the hoped-for upturn in the national economy, which Merseyside would, he believed, be prepared for through the work of The Mersey Partnership, Business Opportunities On Merseyside (BOOM) and City Challenge. If the levels of co-ordination and partnership could be maintained, he felt that the area would become more attractive as a business location. But at the same time he insisted that this could only be achieved if the processes were supported by the public sector, as transport and infrastructure were in need of vital investment.

Perceptions of policy

Both respondents deliberated long over Merseyside's supposed 'image problem' and the implications of this for businesses. Both concluded that, outside the area, the image of Merseyside's business community had not improved to any great extent and that, even though the general image of the area had improved slightly, it remained precarious due to the continued 'talking down' of the region in the national press. Within Merseyside itself, it was felt that the self-image of the area had improved because of the more stable political climate and the increasingly co-ordinated efforts of the various development agencies to boost the area's image. But this process, it was argued, had been hampered by the large number of organisations involved, and both interviewees believed that any future improvement in Merseyside's image was conditional upon the streamlining of these institutional networks.

Rather more surprising than the somewhat predictable views of Merseyside's image, however, was the common belief of both respondents that the image of Merseyside was either only 'fairly important' to their business or that it was 'neither important nor unimportant'. This was because the companies' business success was based upon the image and reputation of the company itself rather than the area. It was also implied that they had never knowingly lost any business because of the image of Merseyside and that they did not attach much importance to it. In any case, there was a strong sense that the area's image had been unfairly distorted in the past.

Both respondents were then prompted to establish the extent of central and local government influence on the area. In terms of general government economic policy, there was a strong feeling that the level of support offered to the area had been insufficient, reflected, for example, in a lack of action regarding the barrage and Speke airport developments. However, there was more support for the government's policy of decentralising services, with strong support for the relocation of the VAT registration office to Merseyside.

On specific sets of policy initiatives, both noted the positive work of Merseyside Development Corporation (MDC), despite certain reservations concerning its ability to attract private investment. In addition, the shipping organisation had had difficulties in dealing directly with the MDC, as the corporation had proved 'obstructive and economically misguided' when the two organisations had come into contact. City Challenge was also viewed positively, primarily because of the physical regeneration it would bring. But there was also scepticism as to whether this sort of action would create jobs in the long term, or provide any real and lasting economic stimulus to the local economy.

The shipping company, which was supposedly a 'policy-off' company, had in fact made extensive use of Derelict Land Grant and was presently involved in acquiring City Challenge and City Grant funds. Conversely, the banking company (a 'policy-on' company) had, according to the respondent, only utilised regional policy. This included Regional Development Grants, Regional Selective Assistance and the general benefits of being located in a Development/ Assisted Area.

In the case of the shipping organisation, the approximate total of public financial assistance was £10 million. Public support of this sort, it was argued, had helped make projects viable and ultimately had increased profit levels. The main complaint about these programmes was that the process for acquiring resources was too lengthy and complicated, a problem which, in some cases had meant the loss of associated private investments. Other problems identified included the inability of the DoE to be more flexible with unrecoverable expenditure (which ideally would be included in grants awarded), and the failure to agree upon and fix interest rates for loans. In addition, problems had arisen as a result of the clawback mechanism, which was seen as an unfair one-way mechanism biased in favour of the government department involved. It was suggested that if project costs overrun or there is a delay in the payments, then the level of grant should be increased to compensate for additional costs. The shipping organisation made a direct comparison between government programmes such as City Grant and the way in which EC funds (ERDF and ESF) are administered. The government programmes were criticised for not adopting more of the broad 'objective' approach of the EC; government programmes, he argued, have often been too specific, with unrealistic and sometimes unworkable guidelines.

The regional policy programmes utilised by the banking organisation amounted to approximately £5 million in all over a ten-year period. Other factors were identified as helping to explain the company's location on Merseyside, most notably the area's proximity to mail distribution outlets at Crewe. After the initial establishment of the company in Merseyside, additional funds (RSA) were used to expand their range of services and increase their workforce. Regional monies were also used to 'rationalise' the workforce, to increase the use of Information Technology, and to boost productivity rates. However, Regional assistance was criticised by the banking company interviewee on a number of grounds. First, he argued that regional policy was of limited significance in face of wider and stronger macro-economic pressures. Second, it was criticised for being overly mechanistic. There had been little or no flexibility in its application, he argued, with the result that regional funds had not always been used where they would be most effective. He also considered it questionable whether or not regional policy provided any real additionality since the funding process was highly laborious, causing time delays which undermined the operation of the rest of the business. As a result, a streamlining of the process was thought essential if the full benefits from the funds were ever to be achieved.

Asked to consider an extensive list of further government programmes, neither respondent knew of the Industrial Improvement Areas or Safer Cities programmes, although both recognised the remainder of the list. The bank respondent was openly critical that there were so many programmes of apparently broad similarity, which, he felt, lead to confusion between departments over programme remits and objectives. The shipping respondent reiterated this view, but did pinpoint Derelict Land Grant as one of the more successful and useful programmes. It was praised for being 'well set out', with the only criticism being that its end-use assessment strategy does not take into account the viability of future projects on the development site.

On assistance from bodies other than central government, only the shipping organisation had used other forms of public support and this had involved extensive use of ERDF over the past eight years (and planned to continue for the next five years). The total cost of the schemes undertaken was in excess of £300 million, with ERDF support running at between 75% and 50% depending on the project in question. Plans for the next five years included a programme of 37 schemes which needed similar levels of financial support, for which they already had the full support of the EC. The respondent expressed a strong view that these funds had proved to be the 'life-line' of the company, and that their highly functional approach should be replicated in central government programmes.

On their views on local government in Merseyside, neither company had utilised any direct form of support from local government and the only real contact had involved the shipping company's links with individual local authority officers through conflict over environmental legislation, working together to develop submissions for EC funds and collaboration over City Challenge. In all cases the interviewee had found the local authority in question 'neither supportive nor obstructive, just over-worked'. However, both respondents stated that local government had been a negative influence on the more general economic development of the area. Even though local government had made attempts to develop economic strategies and promote business, its hands had been tied through externally imposed financial constraints and the area's political instability. However, the banking respondent was reasonably optimistic for the future involvement of local government in business development, due mainly to the more professional approach of the various chief executives' departments in recent times, particularly through City Challenge.

Respondents' views of local authorities were also conditioned by their experience of business rates over the last five years. Both companies noted that their business rates had not altered over the past five years, but for different reasons. In the case of the shipping company the premises are concentrated around one site and the introduction of the Unified Business Rate (UBR) had not brought about the reductions promised. The banking company has premises on three separate sites; rates have increased in one of these, been reduced in a second and in the third location (where the interview took place) have remained the same.

Finally, on the ideal shape for future central and local government policy for businesses on Merseyside, both stressed the need for increased co-ordination between central government departments in order to provide more effective and flexible schemes: 'Money should not be offered in boxes', as one put it. The respondents also offered some personal views on the future direction of policy. The banking respondent believed that central government should provide more support for the transport infrastructure of the area and, in particular, for the railway system, which, he argued, should not be left to the private sector. The shipping respondent was critical of MDC's focus on leisure development. In addition, he also expressed concern over management of the airport and the need to come to some definite decision over its future shape and direction.

Comments on the future role for local government were altogether more vague, reflecting the general belief that local authorities possess only limited resources to intervene in the local economy. The main conclusion was that while local government in the area now has a better profile and improved image, the lack of resource at their disposal means they have to rely on co-operation with the private sector and government agencies.

| Links with local communities | Both companies stated that they were members of the Merseyside Chamber of Commerce. However, both interviewees believed that their membership was more a result of a sense of community responsibility to local organisations of this sort, rather than any real benefits of membership. Both companies claimed to be involved with the community in a number of ways, ranging from Compacts to providing guide dogs for the blind. Both companies believed involvement of this sort was necessitated by a general sense of 'corporate responsibility'. |
|---|---|

## 2.2 Medium-sized companies

Interviews were held with three medium-sized manufacturing establishments (a 'policy-on' clothing manufacturer and a 'policy-off' engineering company), and one medium-sized service-sector establishment (a 'policy-off' banking company). The engineering firm interviewed is based solely on Merseyside in one location; the clothing company is also based exclusively on Merseyside, but in two locations; and the banking company is part of a large multi-national company. All three companies have been present on Merseyside for over eighty years, but they have occupied their existing sites for different lengths of time: the engineers have been based on Liverpool waterfront for twenty five years; the banking establishment in the centre of Liverpool throughout the duration of their time on Merseyside; and the clothing company on one of the main arterial routes in north Liverpool for six years. Each interviee had worked on Merseyside for a minimum period of seven years. The banking and clothing respondents had held their present position for approximately two years, and the engineering representative had worked for the company for eighteen years.

Training and recruitment issues

All three companies noted an increase in labour costs as a proportion of total costs. In the cases of the banking and clothing companies, this resulted from a general increase in salaries above the rate of inflation. According to the engineering respondent, even though labour costs had increased due to the excessive labour demands of the late 1980s, this process had now stopped and in real terms salaries were now being cut.

Both the banking and engineering organisations had increased their expenditure on training, whilst the clothing company had maintained a consistent level of expenditure. The engineering firm had been attempting to develop and 'get more out of' their in-house staff, for example through career development schemes designed to generate 'loyalty' to the firm. The banking company had rapidly increased its technical training to compensate for the reduction in staff and it was also concentrating on 'risk management' courses in order to allow staff to cope with the looser lending criteria of the 1980s.

None of the businesses had experienced any problems with recruiting staff from the area. Three reasons were offered for this: first, all three companies had maintained similar, or even reduced, staffing levels; second, there had been a consistently abundant supply of the type of labour required from the local labour market; and third, any recruitment problems for key positions had been addressed by recruiting in different areas.

Image and attractiveness

The three respondents proffered a wide range of viewpoints on the extent of business confidence in Merseyside. The respondent for the 'policy-on' clothing company felt that while business confidence in Merseyside was similar to that in the rest of the North West, it was considerably lower than in the rest of the country. He identified the main problem as the poor attitude of the local authority to local businesses - a problem which he believed would not be resolved simply by pumping public funds into the area. The respondent for the 'policy-off' engineering company felt that business confidence in Merseyside was no different from elsewhere. He argued that business confidence levels in Merseyside were similar to those Manchester or Warrington. Moreover, the 'hype' concerning grand projects on Merseyside, particularly the barrage and airport development, was now accepted as overly optimistic. The 'policy-off' banking representative, however, was more optimistic about the developments of this sort in the area in recent years and felt these had had a positive knock-on effect for business confidence. He described the situation on Merseyside as having been 'rock bottom' several years ago, but felt it had now started to improve. The increased stability of the local authority, and the stronger links with the business community though initiatives like City Challenge, meant that confidence had increased in comparison to other parts of the country.

These opinions were repeated in terms of the attractiveness of Merseyside as a business location. The clothing company respondent stated that its attractiveness had remained at a similar level over the past five years in comparison with the rest of the country, but felt that its attractiveness had declined at the international level because other European cities were doing more to promote and encourage a healthy business environment and marketing 'quality of life' to potential investors. The engineering representative believed that places such as Chester, Warrington and Manchester had become more attractive locations, to the detriment of Merseyside. However, Merseyside had become more attractive relative to the south east, although this did not signify any absolute improvement in Merseyside's attractiveness to businesses. The banking respondent was once again optimistic about the development of the area and considered it had become more attractive compared to other places in the region. This, he argued, was because Merseyside had begun to sell itself and exploit its most saleable assets: heritage, culture, arts, leisure and 'life style'.

These viewpoints were maintained in the concluding responses to the multiple choice section of the questionnaire, which sought to uncover interviewees' thoughts about the future development of the area as a location for businesses. The clothing representative offered a pessimistic view of the area's future, citing the instability in local politics, the inability of the local authority to help business and the 'profligacy' of agencies such as MDC as continuing problems. This interviewee argued that high profile projects such as the regeneration of the dock have had few spill-over benefits for the business community; they have failed to build the sound economic wealth-generating basis required for real regeneration and image development. The engineering respondent felt that Merseyside will become less attractive as a business location, but the area's image will continue to improve. He based this view on the continuing competition from Manchester and its airport; the 'artificial' way in which central government has supported business with public funds; and the emphasis on job relocations (such as the VAT registration company) rather than creating new wealth and jobs. The banking representative continued in his optimistic vein, arguing that the area would continue to become much more attractive as a business location and its image would continue to improve in the future. These assumptions were based upon the expected success of the Merseyside Partnership and City Challenge, together with what he viewed as vital improvements already undertaken by MDC.

Interviewees also talked of the area's image, how this has affected the business community and how it might be improved in future. The clothing representative considered the image of Merseyside to be neither important nor unimportant to his business; the company's own image was of much greater importance. The engineering respondent considered the image to be 'fairly important', arguing that it may have affected the judgement of (potential) clients, especially when compared to the generally positive image of 'competitors' like Manchester and Chester. The banking respondent felt the image of Merseyside was 'very important' and would be tied inextricably to attempts to regenerate the area.

Perceptions of policy

The 'policy-on' company had received Regional Development Grant support in excess of £10,000, and a smaller sum under the Enterprise Initiative to employ a business consultant. In addition, they had received £65,000 of Urban Programme funds in 1981. The respondent had no knowledge of this latter subsidy, but was able to discuss RDG and Enterprise Initiative. His view was that the RDG award was very effective not only in sustaining the firm's expansion, but in accelerating it. This was because it enabled the company to reinvest capital and thereby expand into wider geographical and product markets. The Enterprise Initiative was identified as being less useful, largely because of the cumbersome process of applying for funding. Indeed, for both RDG and Enterprise Initiative, the largest draw-back to using the programmes was seen as 'excessive form-filling'.

Respondents also offered some support for the work of MDC and Liverpool City Challenge. The banking representative was attracted by the idea of spatial targeting under both City Challenge and the MDC. The respondent from the 'policy-on' clothing firm pointed towards what he saw as the positive work of MDC, particularly in funding environmental improvements, although he noted the continuing problem of the lack of private finance. He was also highly supportive of regional policy subsidies, arguing that direct financial assistance to firms has allowed them to reinvest, become more competitive and generate more business outside the area.

Neither of the 'policy-off' companies had received any direct financial assistance on Merseyside. For both companies, contact with government schemes had been limited to work with development agencies such as MDC or participation in the planning of Liverpool's City Challenge project. The two respondents felt these contacts had not only boosted their own businesses, but had also provided knock-on regeneration effects for the rest of the city.

Respondents were prompted with a series of further policy programmes in order to gauge their awareness of the support on offer to businesses. Leaving aside those programmes (outlined above) which had been used directly, responses in general were extremely vague. In response to the list of programmes, interviewees proved to be less aware than was the case for respondents from the large firms. The only programmes which were widely recognised were those which had been highly publicised, such as the Enterprise Initiative, English Estates, UDCs and Enterprise Zones. All thought they may have heard of the various training initiatives, but apart from the clothing representative, had had no experience of any of the schemes. The respondent from the clothing company noted his firm's involvement in the Job Interview Guarantee project, but stated that the low standard of applicant under this programme had prompted the company to pull out of the scheme. Both the banking and engineering representatives believed their establishments had benefited indirectly from government programmes in the area: the former because of their involvement with City Challenge and the general image improvement created by the MDC; and the latter, because they had won contracts to work with the UDC and English Estates. In addition, the engineering representative pointed to their success in tendering for local public services since deregulation, with the main draw-back being that 'some of the work is so competitive that it's done at a loss'. He added that as other private work progressively has become less available, they have been forced to take on such loss-making public services, which ultimately will result in a 'rationalisation' of the firm.

The 'policy-on' firm suggested that central government could help business on Merseyside in future years by cutting down on 'layers of bureaucracy' so that a larger proportion of government funds actually reach 'the coal face'. The banking representative identified national economic policies, arguing that central government had to stem the outflow of capital from Britain. The engineering representative thought central government should standardise its objectives for business development across all departments and agencies, and encourage more co-operation with local authorities 'on the ground'.

None of the organisations had ever used any support from local government and they were unaware of the precise nature of local authority assistance to businesses. Only the engineering respondent had a view as to whether the local authority was supportive or obstructive and he felt it was entirely dependent upon the individual officer with whom contact was made. The engineering respondent felt local government was severely overworked and that the responsibility for City Challenge would add to this burden. This was especially true, he argued, in cases where local authorities had prepared bids unsuccessfully; this work was wasted. Other comments on local government reflected those of the larger firms (outlined earlier) that local authorities could best advance business by becoming more co-operative with all the network of agencies involved in business support and development. At the same time, though, there was a feeling that this was as much a responsibility of central government as of local government.

|  | Of the three interviewees, all but the clothing company were members of the |
| --- | --- |
| Links with local communities | Chamber of Commerce. However, both member-firms were unsure about the effectiveness of the organisation, the engineering representative arguing that BOOM did a better job in articulating the interests of the business community. All had had some contact with the TEC, but this received only lukewarm support; the TEC either being felt to be a waste of resources, or at best having done no harm. None of the respondents knew any details of the TEC's functions. |

Interviewees listed their links with the community: the engineering company had run an exchange scheme with a local school and provided expert advice through career evenings organised by the Engineering Council; the banking company had appointed a community manager to deal with the bank's involvement in the local area, school visits, charity support or career advice; and the clothing company had very little contact with the local community, apart from making donations to charities.

Crime was not perceived as a major problem by any of the companies. Only the banking company had increased its expenditure on security, whilst the other two companies had not felt any increased threat to security from the surrounding communities. In fact, the increase in security expenditure by the bank had not taken the form of improved physical defences, but of a large investment in protection against computer fraud.

## 2.3 Small companies

The final firm surveyed on Merseyside was chosen because of its location within the Speke Enterprise Zone and was therefore considered a 'policy-on' company. It is a single-site company and has been established for six years in the same location. It specialises in the manufacture of protective clothing and since 1988 has doubled its workforce to six.

### Training and recruitment issues

Labour costs had not changed as a general proportion of turnover during the last five years. Costs had successfully been capped by accessing support under the Enterprise Allowance Scheme, which subsidised the wages of two employees for a year. There had been a slight increase in the proportion of turnover spent on training, because they had made use of Youth Training. This required payments to a training agent, but wages were low and had little impact on the company's budget. Poor off-the-job training was identified as a major problem with Youth Training. The interviewee also felt that the quality of YT trainees had been disappointingly low. Of the seventeen staff taken on under YTS, only two had been considered of sufficient quality to be given full-time jobs. The company had had indirect contact with the TEC via a training agent organising YTS, but the interviewee felt it was felt impossible to comment on the TEC from this limited position.

The firm had had some problems recruiting semi-skilled manual workers, but this was a problem of quality rather than quantity; finding workers was unlikely to be a problem in a labour market such as Merseyside's.

### Image and attractiveness

The interviewee's perception of business confidence on Merseyside was based solely on comparisons with other parts of the North West region. As a business location, he believed that Merseyside had become more attractive, firstly, because Wavertree Technology Park had been successful in attracting business to the area, and secondly, because the Freeport had helped generate business for the area as a whole and for his company. In general, the respondent believed the image of Merseyside had improved and was likely to improve further in future. This was premised upon the hope of more favourable publicity for the area, a real increase in business activity and high profile developments such as the Albert Dock. At the same time, however, he considered the area's image to be fairly unimportant in terms of its effect on the company's business.

### Perceptions of policy

The company was established with the aid of a Regional Development Grant of £8,000. Its early development and growth was also helped by the Enterprise Zone rate holiday period from 1986-91, an Enterprise Allowance wage subsidy of £80 per week wage, and the employment of seventeen YTS trainees. These subsidies, he believed, had accelerated the firm's growth beyond the rate which would otherwise have been achieved. He also echoed some of the more general criticisms voiced by other interviewees, in particular noting the excessive bureaucracy involved in applying for the support of government programmes.

The company had also had support from English Estates, but experience had been more mixed. The company's rent and rates bill had increased greatly over the past five years. Rent alone had doubled in 1989 as a result of a decision taken by English Estates to attract private property speculators into the area. In fact, this had resulted in a large proportion of existing tenants moving out. Conversely, the company had been much more satisfied with English Estates' role in meeting vitally important site security costs.

377

The respondent was not aware of any other programmes which could have benefited his company, but felt it would help if government programmes were more widely publicised. Apart from the programmes already mentioned, he could recognise Enterprise Initiative, Employment Training, Consultancy Training and 'Other Training Schemes'. However, the firm had not benefited from any of these programmes.

Several suggestions were made as to how central government could cater for small business needs in a more effective way. He stressed the need for better publicity of assistance on offer (perhaps a single 'one stop shop' source of advice); improvement to the general economic climate; and, specifically, improvement to the transport infrastructure of the area, which was especially poor in comparison to Manchester.

The company had not used any support from the local authority, but had explored the possibility of moving to another site with their help, especially since rates had increased so dramatically following the wind-up of the Enterprise Zone in 1992. The firm had found the local authority very helpful in this respect and had considered seeking local government support for any future relocation. However, the local authority had been less helpful in imposing a rates bill of £500 per annum. This, he believed, had been a major discouragement to further investment.

**Links with local communities**

The company is not a member of the Chamber of Commerce and has not developed any links with the local community.

# 3  GREATER MANCHESTER

## 3.1  Large companies

The two companies selected were distinctly different. The 'policy-off' retail company had been based in central Manchester for over 100 years, whilst the 'policy-on' hotel company had only recently been established, within the Central Manchester Development Corporation (CMDC) area. Both companies had increased their market share within the local area. The two companies had significantly increased their financial commitment to the area. The hotel company had invested in the tourist industry in other parts of Manchester, while the retail company had taken on additional space in its existing building. However, the retail company was frustrated with its central Manchester location, due to access restrictions, and was not certain whether it would remain in its present site, even though it will stay in Manchester. Rent and rates for the retail company had increased over the past five years, with the UBR making no difference to the amount of rates paid. The hotel company, with its parent company as landlord, had paid lower rent and rates.

### Training and recruitment issues

The retail company had reduced its workforce by 25% to 250, since 1988, while the hotel company had doubled its staff to 200 in the same period. Only the retail company had experienced difficulties with recruitment, in key management positions, R&D and marketing. However, it had become less of a problem as personnel were being attracted to the North, as the South East has suffered the worst of the recession.

The retail company had greatly increased its training, due to improved in-house courses, and because of a 'Total Quality Management' programme developed in conjunction with the TEC (who covered half the costs). The hotel company had also increased its in-house training, but not to the same extent. Its only contact with the TEC had been to arrange some informal work experience.

### Image and attractiveness

There was a difference of opinion on the image of Manchester. The retail company thought it had not changed, but would improve due to a decline in the South East, while the hotel company thought it had improved through urban regeneration, but would deteriorate because of the increasing crime levels. The importance they attached to the image of Manchester was related to their business. The retail company did not want to be associated with 'a sleepy northern city', and therefore thought that image was of more significance.

As a business location, the retail company felt that Manchester had not changed, but would become more attractive, especially if it were to be successful in its Olympic bid, but primarily because 'pride has come back to Manchester'. Conversely, the hotel company believed the area had become more attractive on a regional and national scale, particularly because of the urban regeneration programmes in and around the city. In future years, however, it was felt the Manchester would be less attractive because investment (both by business and by CMDC) had reached a peak and would now fall away, especially if the Olympic bid failed.

Both companies felt that business confidence in Manchester in comparison to the rest of the North West had increased, the retail company simply because Liverpool was the main competitor and 'anywhere's better than Liverpool', and the hotel company because redundancies in Manchester, especially amongst white-collar professionals, were much less severe than in other areas. However, in comparison to the rest of the nation and other countries, confidence had been hampered by the bad publicity focused on Moss Side and its crime problem. Both companies had increased their investment in security measures, which involved fences, barriers and patrolled car parks. This was a reaction both to increased thefts from vehicles, and in order to maintain a stable image.

Perceptions of policy

The retail company had no experience of any central government programme, apart from some help from DTI with Eastern European projects. However, they found the Department to be very bureaucratic and 'not keen to hand out actual grants'. The company had received much more satisfactory help from similar organisations in other countries, and it was felt that the UK government should take a similar attitude. The hotel company had received a grant of £2.5 million from the CMDC for new developments and felt that CMDC had improved the environment in the immediate locality. The hotel company felt that CMDC was very important in fostering change in Manchester and, together with the tourist boards and general government policy, had helped to create a business in leisure. The grant received meant the project could actually go ahead and it was felt the CMDC 'shared a similar vision with the company' as to how the area should be developed. They found the CMDC very helpful and there were no serious drawbacks to the assistance. Both companies only had knowledge of the UDC, the DTI initiative and Youth Training. Neither had received any other form of public assistance, but the retail company had (unsuccessfully) been looking to attract EC funds. Central government could help business in Manchester by: the DTI being far more helpful and less bureaucratic; widening the sphere of influence of the CMDC so that it helps firms not located within its boundaries; and helping to 'unlock' sources of funding. Finally, it was felt that, ultimately, business should not rely on central government at all and should be able to survive on its own.

Although neither company had received any direct assistance from local government, the retail company had several contacts in the local authorities of Salford and Manchester. Salford were supportive, and very anxious to develop good relations with the company. The authority was seen as being informative and helpful, especially with regard to planning applications. However, Manchester City Council did not see the company as 'high-profile', and were not so helpful. The hotel company thought that local government made no real contribution, and in certain ways was a hindrance, creating problems with licensing laws, for example. With regard to improving local government, the hotel company once again made the distinction between Salford and Manchester, and how Manchester should be less obstructive.

Links with local communities

Both companies were members of the Chamber of Commerce, and both considered it to be 'fairly useful', providing informative discussions on marketing and sales development. However, neither was prepared to state if the Chamber actually served the interests of the whole business community.

The retail company was the only one to have developed any links with the local community. These associations were quite extensive, but only within Salford, and included school visits, career advice and supporting charities.

## 3.2 Medium-sized companies

The four firms selected were: two manufacturers, comprising an engineering 'policy-on' company and a paint manufacturing 'policy-off' company; and two service-sector organisations, comprising a hotel 'policy-on' establishment and a security 'policy-off' service. The hotel was the only company operating solely within Manchester. The security service has another establishment in Liverpool, the engineering firm has its headquarters in Dorset and the paint producers have other operations in Wales and Ireland. The engineers and hotel establishment have only been in Manchester since 1989, the security service has been working in the area for 17 years, but only based on the same site for two years, and the paint manufacturers have been based in Manchester for 62 years and on the same site for 32 years.

All the companies had increased their share of the Manchester market, apart from the engineers, all of whose products are exported. The reasons for the increased sales in the area were seen to be due to a general increase in business and the general growth that has occurred in Manchester over the past five years. All had increased their financial commitment to Manchester, although the engineering company had greatly increased its commitment because it had moved a third of its business to the area from Dorset.

|                          |                                                                                                                                                                                                                                                                                                                                                                                                                           |
|--------------------------|---------------------------------------------------------------------------------------------------------------------------------------------------------------------------------------------------------------------------------------------------------------------------------------------------------------------------------------------------------------------------------------------------------------------------|
| Training and recruitment issues | All the companies had increased their staffing levels. In terms of labour costs, neither the hotel nor the paint producers had noted any increase over the past five years. However, the security firm had doubled its workforce which had caused an increase in labour costs, and the engineering company thought their increased costs were a result of wage rates catching up with those in the south of the country. |

Only the security firm had encountered problems in recruiting suitable staff, and this was due to 'low pay, shift work, long hours, plus a high level screening process', all of which result in unattractive employment, 'even during a recession'. The other firms had no recruitment problems, mostly due to high unemployment. This was especially true for the engineering company, which had taken on several ex-British Aerospace employees. The same pattern applied to the recruitment of young people.

The hotel and engineering companies had an increase in training costs, which in both cases was due to more in-house training, especially 'on-the-job' training for young people. The security and paint companies' training costs had greatly increased, because they have both established a training officer/consultant and have very intensive in-house training. In addition, the paint producers are involved in 'Investors in People'.

Only the paint firm had had any involvement with the TEC, as the chair of the company holds a position on the board of the TEC. However, it was felt that the TEC did not support firms who make an effort to conduct their own training, and that such activity should be rewarded in some way.

|                          |                                                                                                                                                                                                                                                                                                                                                                                                                   |
|--------------------------|-------------------------------------------------------------------------------------------------------------------------------------------------------------------------------------------------------------------------------------------------------------------------------------------------------------------------------------------------------------------------------------------------------------------|
| Image and attractiveness | Three of the companies believed the image of Manchester had improved and would improve in the future, based on the strong supply of attractive office space, the possibility of attracting the Olympics and the fact that many organisations, such as the British Council, have already relocated there. Only the hotel company thought the city's image was important to their business, in that a positive image can boost trade. The other companies thought the image of Manchester was 'fairly unimportant' to their business. |

In terms of attractiveness, the area was described as second to London, but considerably more attractive than Liverpool. The paint producers thought that any firm would choose Manchester for its location over Liverpool, but that Manchester may have suffered some loss of confidence in the last six months, but little by comparison to the rest of the country. The others, apart from the security firm, offered similar responses with regard to Manchester as a business location. They considered it has become more attractive in relation to the North West and the rest of the country. All the companies, except the engineering, believed Manchester would become more attractive on a regional and national scale. The paint producer based its optimism on the development of the airport, self confidence and the more stable labour conditions in the area in comparison to other places, especially Liverpool.

All the representatives responded that business confidence had increased on a regional and national basis. The security firm thought Manchester had remained 'the same' as a business location, because even though 'it had held its own during the recession', the increases in crime had had a definite effect on the area's image. All apart from the engineers increased their security operations in the last five years, which for the hotel meant investing in security guards and cameras. But for the paint producers it has meant a dramatic improvement in security systems, because the area was felt to have become a 'high-crime zone'.

Perceptions of policy

The 'policy-on' engineering firm was selected because it had received support from the Urban Programme, and the 'policy-on' hotel because it was located within the Central Manchester Development Corporation (CMDC) area. Both the engineering firm and the paint firm mentioned the influence of government policy on the changes described above. The engineering respondent believed that the firm's receipt of Urban Programme funds and Regional Selective Assistance had definitely helped their position within the area. The paint firm mentioned the Business Improvement Scheme (DTI), which they had used to pay for consultancy and for training middle managers. Only the two 'policy-on' firms noted that they had received financial assistance from central government. The engineering company confirmed they had received UP and RSA but could not give any details concerning amounts or effectiveness. The hotel acknowledged a grant of approximately £2 million from CMDC, without which the business would not have been viable. The government programmes recognised by the firms were limited solely to those they had come directly into contact with. The paint producers and the security firm knew of the Youth Training Scheme. The engineering company, meanwhile, was the only firm to have used other forms of public assistance, which were described as 'EC grants for job creation' and totalled several thousands of pounds.

None of the companies had had any financial assistance from local government, but the engineering firm had found Salford City Council very supportive and encouraging, offering advice and help when they located in the area. In fact, the choice of the area as a location was strongly based on the positive attitude of the council. The paint company had found Manchester City Council also to be very supportive and positive in offering advice and help. The other two companies had had no contact with any local authority.

Interviewees offered views on the shape which future government activity should take. The security firm thought that government at all levels was unimportant to the role of business in Manchester. The hotel, by contrast, thought the involvement with CMDC was very important, especially in terms of financial support offered. The paint company argued that central government should 'leave business alone' as far as possible and only reward good practice; there were too many schemes operating already, it was argued, and this had created a confusing picture. However, local government should be 'unashamedly partisan' and do as much as possible to help local business.

| | |
|---|---|
| Links with local communities | All of the firms bar the security company found the Chamber of Commerce very useful. For example, the Chamber has helped the engineering firm to develop its export market and the hotel company allows the Chamber to hold meetings on its premises. None of the companies had any definite contacts with the local community. The hotel company has an informal arrangement with the University of Manchester to accept student placements and the engineering firm is sometimes involved in supporting local charities on an ad hoc basis. The paint company was particularly critical of the Compact model of community involvement, which, it felt was 'immoral' because it involves promises of jobs that companies might not be able to fulfil. |

## 3.3 Small Companies

The small company was a 'policy-off' clothing manufacturer, which has been based in Manchester for 65 years, but only on the present site for 3 years. The firm's commitment to Manchester over the past five years had greatly increased, because they had rented new buildings within the area. The rents and rates for the company have greatly increased over the past five years and in the near future the rents were set to double. However, this was considered to be the price of the past success that Manchester had enjoyed.

| | |
|---|---|
| Training and recruitment issues | In 1988 the company had a workforce of 29 and it presently employs 22; the labour costs had increased proportionately. No new staff had been taken on for a considerable time and those who were there at present were highly experienced and needed no extra training. As a result, expenditure on staff development had remained constant. However, the firm had had some problems with recruiting skilled staff and young people. This had greatly increased over the past five years, but was a problem with the clothing industry in general, due to its poor image rather than any reflection of the local labour market's characteristics. The company had had no contact with the TEC. |
| Image and attractiveness | As a business location, the firm thought that the area had stayed 'the same' in comparison to the rest of the North West; Manchester was 'still an excellent location'. However, as opposed to the rest of the country, it had become less attractive. Being generally optimistic about Manchester, the firm considered that it would become more attractive on a regional and national scale over the next five years, although no reason was offered for this view. |
| | The company felt that business confidence in Manchester in comparison to the rest of the North West had 'greatly decreased', particularly as Altrincham and Wilmslow had become much more attractive. The respondent felt that people were not so keen to travel into Manchester to shop. In comparison to the rest of the nation, the firm thought that confidence had declined. |
| Perceptions of policy | What little influence central government had had on company, it was argued, had been detrimental. For example, the firm could had been unable to access grant money by staying in Manchester and the only help available was if they moved to Salford, it was stated. A DTI representative had informed the company that there was 'no money in the area available for them', but if they employed over 30 people it might be possible to get some form of assistance. This view of government policy support was doubtless influenced by the firm's recent locational experiences. CMDC had already forced the firm to relocate without compensation because, within the area, the UDC was turning warehouses into flats. Were Manchester to win its Olympic bid, the firm would be forced to move again since it is located on the site of the planned Olympic village. This could mean the closure of the company. |

Apart from the DTI 'advice' the firm had no other support from central and local government. They had tried to use City Grant to help their relocation, but were refused. The company had also heard of Enterprise Zones and the Urban Programme, and the company had taken on YTS trainees. Indirectly, the company felt that the CMDC had helped the development of business in the area, but that this was the only indirect influence government policies had had on the company. The company felt that CMDC could do more to help small businesses, rather than concentrating mainly on larger companies, as at present.

The company did not consider the local authority important, unless it were to move to Salford. Moreover, it appeared that, because there was no help forthcoming from Manchester City Council, the local authority did not wish to promote manufacturing in central Manchester.

Links with local communities

The organisation has had no contact with the Chamber of Commerce, and as yet has not developed any type of relationship with the local community.

# 4 TYNE AND WEAR

## 4.1 Large companies

The two large companies selected from Tyne and Wear were a national insurance firm and a national building society. The insurance company had been in the area for sixteen years, but had only recently moved to its present site. The building society had originated in the north east and had been on the same site for the last 25 years or so. Both companies have been recipients of policy support in a number of contrasting ways, both directly and indirectly. Both of the people interviewed had been with their respective companies for less than three years, although the building society representative had considerable knowledge of the region having worked there for the last 27 years.

### Training and recruitment issues

The workforces of both companies had increased significantly over the last five years, with employment with the insurance firm growing to a current figure of around 1500 and the building society to 720. The implications of this growth for labour costs were contrasting: the insurance company noted an increase in its labour costs over the last few years, due principally to this increase in staff numbers, while the building society, by contrast, recorded a decrease in labour costs as increasing automation helped boost productivity.

A second implication of workforce growth was that both companies had increased their expenditure on training over the last five years. Moreover, the growth in training expenditure had been reinforced by the introduction of automation and new technology, both of which frequently necessitated 'costly' forms of training provision. At the same time, however, neither firm had had any major external support for this increased commitment from agencies like the Training and Enterprise Councils (TECs) or Tyne and Wear Development Corporation (TWDC). Although the insurance firm had used the TEC to help employees gain business qualifications, he felt the TEC was not sufficiently 'pro-active', with the company constantly having to approach the TEC for help.

The insurance company has had no recruitment problems over the past five years, but the building society has had problems finding people with training in information technology, a problem which the interviewee felt reinforced the need for more expenditure on training. Moreover, this problem had increased over recent years and, he argued, has been compounded by competition from other firms for the small pool of trained labour. However, recruitment was less of a problem when it came to young people. As one of the interviewees noted, the lack of obvious employment opportunities for young people in the regional labour market means that there can be as many as 200 applicants for every post.

### Image and attractiveness

Both interviewees commented upon the image of Tyneside both within the region and conurbation and from outside north east. One interviewee noted that business confidence was increasing relative to the rest of the country, and, moreover, that this was now being reflected by his company's increased investment and growing workforce. This, he felt, was having important knock-on benefits for the image of the region, both in terms of the growing sense of pride within the region and in terms of the way in which the region is now perceived elsewhere. The building society representative also felt that business confidence over the past five years had increased in comparison to the North East and had greatly increased in comparison to the country as a whole. He felt that in this respect the work of the Tyne and Wear Development Corporation

(TWDC) had played a vital role for his company in presenting a positive image of Newcastle to other businesses and potential customers.

In contrast to the views in the other conurbations surveyed, both interviewees agreed that growing business confidence and the region's improving image were inextricably tied together, and that both had been underpinned by the region's 'policy network'. The insurance representative thought Tyneside had become more attractive on a regional and national scale as a business location, due principally to the publicly-funded developments of business parks and the financial incentives on offer to potential investors. The building society representative thought that, as a business location, Tyneside had become more attractive regionally, nationally and internationally, based upon the work of TWDC, the region's traditional strength in attracting inward investment and the general 'business friendliness' which characterised much of the Tyneside 'policy community'.

The insurance company respondent was bullish about prospects for the area's image to outside investors, and for existing companies, in future years. Equally, he was doubtful about the extent to which company location decisions were affected by 'image' concerns, other than at the margins. The building society respondent tempered this with a more cautious assessment and some uncertainty about the regional and national economic picture over the next five years. He considered that the prospects for regional economic growth had been hampered as a result of recent developments, notably problems with riots in the area, which, he argued, had done much to undermine previous improvements in the area's image. Increasing crime - and fear of crime - had also had more tangible effects in that many companies were now faced the added burden of extra costs on security measures. At the same time, he was confident that the region's image would improve once more in future years. This, he argued, was of vital importance since image is crucial in attracting new business. For his own company, a positive regional image conferred direct benefits in that it can directly affect their borrowing capacity and investment levels.

Perceptions of policy

Interviewees were prompted with a list of government programmes in order to gauge the business community's awareness of public support on offer, and the extent to which these had been used in the past. The insurance representative knew of the Enterprise Initiative, Employment Training, Youth Training, Investors in People and Job Interview Guarantee. The building society interviewee, having been involved in many government programmes, knew of the majority of programmes apart from Safer Cities, Business Growth Training, Employment Training, Consultancy Training and the Management Charter Initiative.

Even though the building society had not received any financial assistance for its own development, it had been involved with administering and financing several programme initiatives. Therefore, even as a representative of a 'policy-off' company, he was able to comment on a number of programmes which he felt had influenced changes in the area. He listed a number of policy instruments which he had experience and knowledge of. City Grant and Urban Development Grant, for example, had benefited South Tyneside and allowed housing investment at Mill Dam; the Urban Programme had been used for improvement grants for 'The Avenues' area of Bensham; and the company had also been involved with the TWDC in a range housing, hotel and security developments. He considered that all of these had benefited and improved the area by bringing down the cost of development and allowing projects to go ahead which would otherwise be unviable. The only improvement suggested was that TWDC could become more 'business-like' and speed up its 'over-bureaucratic' processes. At a more general level, though, he felt government policy had indirectly benefited the area by reducing national labour costs and discouraging trade unions. But at the same time these gains had been offset because macro-economic policy had caused problems by creating an unstable housing market and a general lack of business confidence.

Ironically, the 'policy-on' interviewee, representing a major insurance company, had less knowledge of the range of policy support for firms. He was aware, though, of some of the support on offer from TWDC. He felt that TWDC had been successful in allowing companies to centralise their staff on single sites and to gain new offices which may be an attraction to potential recruits. Similarly, he pointed towards TWDC's successes in improving the area's image and boosting business confidence (as outlined above). He also noted some of the drawbacks with TWDC. First, he felt that TWDC offered insufficient help with meeting costs for childcare and other facilities, such as shops in business park areas. He also pointed out that TWDC was seen by many employers on TWDC-managed business parks as calling too many meetings of employers. Improvements could arise, he argued, were TWDC to take responsibility for providing the full range of services required by the companies on its business parks.

The interviewees commented upon how they would like to see government policy evolve from a business perspective. The building society respondent felt the best way in which central government could help business in the area was by the most direct routes possible: lowering taxes on profits, giving higher allowances on capital investment, ensuring a higher quality of education and following a policy of 'non-intervention' with business. He felt that local government had a less important role, but could help by minimising business rates and speeding up planning applications. The insurance representative thought the most effective way in which both central and local government could help business in the area was by improving its image through publicising and marketing the benefits of working and living in Tyneside.

Links with local communities

Both companies claimed to have been actively involved with community relations: helping community trusts, promoting and sponsoring arts and sport, helping play groups, developing crime-prevention initiatives and supporting Housing Associations. Indeed, the building society considered itself to be so involved with community work that it has 'stronger links with the community than the church has'.

## 4.2 Medium-sized companies

The firms in this group comprised two 'policy-on' firms: a computer software company and an engineering firm; and a 'policy-off' distribution company. The 'policy-on' companies were chosen because of their location within the Enterprise Zone at Team Valley Trading Estate in Gateshead; both are relatively young, rapidly expanding and 'glamorous' companies. The engineering firm only operates from one site in Tyneside, whereas the other two firms have additional plants outside the North East. The two 'policy-on' firms have been based at their present location for four years and the distribution company has been at its present site since 1967. The two representatives from the 'policy-on' firms have worked on Tyneside for over twenty years, whilst the distribution representative has only been within the area for five years.

| Training and recruitment issues | All three companies had increased their workforce since 1988, the software company witnessing the largest growth by more than doubling its employees from 100 to 250, principally as a result of increased exports. The distribution and software companies noted an increase in their labour costs over the past five years due to their increasing labour force. |
| :--- | :--- |

Unlike the 'policy-off' company, the 'policy-on' companies both increased their proportional expenditure on training. The software company had paid for a range of training, which included developing personal skills and encouraging educational qualifications from 'A' levels to MBAs. The engineering firm has focused on 'Total Quality Management' with advice from the TEC. Both of the 'policy-on' companies have had some form of contact with the TEC, but this was not directly related to training. The TEC has tended to fill more of a consultancy role and the companies have found this both helpful and positive.

Only the 'policy-on' companies had experienced recruitment problems, very much reflecting their need for people with technical qualifications. The software company had found it difficult to find technical staff - a problem which apparently had been increasing. The engineering company had found it difficult to locate skilled manual operators and literate young people.

| Image and attractiveness | Both 'policy-on' firms felt that business confidence had remained at a similar level within the region, but had increased nationally and internationally. However, the 'policy-off' company thought there had been no change in the confidence of the area in comparison to any other location. |
| :--- | :--- |

All three companies felt that the area had become more attractive as a business location. This was largely due to the grants and incentives on offer, which was especially true of the Enterprise Zone. Indeed, it was this incentive which had encouraged the 'policy-on' firms to locate there. The distribution and engineering companies felt that in the future Tyneside would become more attractive, largely as a result of continuing environmental improvements, particularly along the riverside. They also noted the importance of the work of English Estates, which had successfully offered attractive purpose-built accommodation to potential investors. The software company was slightly less confident, although the interviewee did point towards the developing technological base and improving quality of life as positive signs for the area's future as an attractive location for businesses.

All the interviewees responded to the 'image' questions by saying that they felt the image of the area had improved, will improve in future and that it is reasonably important for their businesses. This improvement, they argued, has been created through developments such as the Metro Centre, the marketing of the area by bodies such as the regional CBI (through The Newcastle Initiative) and the inward investment of large companies such as Nissan. All of these developments have boosted business confidence, attracted skilled people and helped in the regeneration of the area, it was argued.

| Perceptions of policy | Both of the 'policy-on' companies were extremely positive about the Tyneside Enterprise Zone, indicating that their location within the EZ had been of definite benefit in business terms. The EZ was felt by the respondents to have been vital to their success and has enabled them to expand their companies. The only drawback was simply that EZ allowances have now ended, despite the strong feeling amongst respondents that capital allowances should have been continued. One interviewee felt the removal of the EZ benefits will have |
| :--- | :--- |

a 'devastating effect on [Team Valley]'. By contrast, views on the role of the DTI in the area were somewhat less unequivocal. The software company had received financial support in the form of RDG and felt that the DTI had been extremely helpful and were able to be of assistance in most aspects of business life. This help had included advice and financial support, but he felt there was a need to publicise these services more. The engineering company had a different view, stating that the information they had received from the DTI was 'useless', and that the services offered to help exports and promote the firm abroad was 'very poor'.

In addition to awareness of EZ benefits and DTI support, interviewees offered views on a range of further programmes. First, both 'policy-on' companies had used the various Youth Training schemes. These had, on the whole, provided potential full-time staff, but the feeling amongst interviewees was that YT-trained staff would often require further training if they were to be taken on in a permanent position. Second, all of the firms had come into contact with English Estates, but as yet the distribution firm had not used their services. The other two companies had found English Estates to be a reasonable landlord, but had little knowledge of the business support services on offer.

In general, the 'policy-on' firms were very aware of the majority of the programmes available and were able to recognise a wide range of schemes on the questionnaire list. The only programmes they were unaware of were: Safer Cities, Derelict Land Grant, the Management Charter Initiative and Job Interview Guarantee. By contrast, the 'policy-off' company, while aware of some of the more high-profile programmes such as City Grant, the Urban Programme, UDCs, Enterprise Initiative and English Estates, were unaware of the large range of training and job start initiatives. The software company was the only firm to indicate it had benefited indirectly from government action, which involved sales of their product to local government. The software company felt it had pursued all the grants that are available to it, but it was not entirely satisfied with the approach of central government, which, it felt, had tended to favour and target manufacturing companies.

In addition to help from central government, both of the 'policy-on' companies had received EC funds to support their businesses. The software company obtained a grant of £500,000, which allowed them to develop new office accommodation, while the engineering company had obtained an EC grant of £1.5 million, which was used to build new accommodation.
The software firm was the only company which had had contact with the local authority and had found them to be 'tremendous'. This, the interviewee argued, was because the business unit in Gateshead had been very active and had been able to promote and market the company in other locations. The company had also received direct financial assistance, help with marketing initiatives and direct promotion by the local authority. They were found to be very helpful and the only criticism was that their marketing initiatives could be more intensive. The distribution company had also found the local authority very supportive, though not directly in terms of business development. The main influence the local authority had was in granting swift planning permissions and in implementing environmental health legislation in a flexible way.

Interviewees went on to discuss their views of the ways in which future policy might best be shaped in order to support business. The distribution 'policy-off' firm felt there were no policies or programmes designed to support an established business such as theirs. This also applied to local government, which was considered helpful in a limited way but unimportant and lacking in real powers. The only way in which government was considered to be an influence on their company was through the Home Office, which sets the drug tariffs. The 'policy-on' companies felt that central government could do far more to promote a national business development programme, which would improve confidence during the recession. In addition, there was a continuing need for government to inform and prepare business for the European Single Market. Both firms believed that capital allowances should be maintained within the Enterprise Zone areas, particularly as the timing of their removal could be fatal to many companies.

Respondents also commented on their preferred shape for local government. The software company felt local government could do far more to improve links between the multitude of existing development agencies to make the 'resource environment' less confusing. It could also improve the contacts between young businesses and establishments which provide training and education, as there is a gap in the market for an agency to help stabilise established businesses, rather than generate new business. This might be a role which TECs could perform, according to one interviewee. The engineering company felt that the role of local government could also focus more on improving the general physical environment, which would have a knock-on effect for the quality of life and the image of the area. The distribution company and software firm had both increased their expenditure on security costs, and both felt that local government could have a part to play in helping with this.

Links with local communities

Only the 'policy-on' companies had developed links with the community. The software company had adopted a local school for career advice and placement schemes and the engineering company was a strong supporter of local charities.

## 4.3 Small companies

The two firms selected for this group were both small branch establishments of larger national companies. The 'policy-on' firm was a plastics manufacturer and the 'policy-off' company a producer of catering equipment. The plastics company was the younger of the two, having been in Tyneside for nine years and on its present site for just over a year. The catering company had been on Tyneside for 50 years and on its present site for 18 years. Both interviewees had been with the same company for approximately the same time (between 6 and 8 years) and both had worked on Tyneside for over 30 years.

Training and recruitment issues

The plastics company had increased its share of the Tyneside market over the last five years, due mainly to their expansion in the area. The result was that the number of employees had increased from 7 to 15. By contrast, the catering company had reduced its turnover in the area and, having shed staff, its labour-force had decreased from 29 to 24 since 1988. Not surprisingly, the contrasting fortunes of the two companies had meant that the plastics firm had spent a consistent amount on training over the past five years, whereas the catering company had been forced to cut-back and offer more 'in-house' training provision. Neither of the firms had encountered any problems with recruitment over the last five years, feeling that the local labour supply was adequate for their needs in terms of both quality and quantity. The 'policy-off' firm was the only one to have had any contact with the TEC, although this was because of their location in the City Challenge area rather than any real need for help with training requirements. Under the City Challenge scheme the TEC has co-ordinated a business-school link, which has developed career advice and placement schemes. The contact with the TEC was felt to be limited at the moment - partly because the company had reduced its commitment to training as a result of workforce cutbacks - but they were found to be reasonably helpful.

Image and attractiveness

The two interviewees had contrasting views on changes in confidence amongst the business community over the last five years. The 'policy-on' interviewee was more positive about business confidence during this period, arguing that it had increased, regionally, nationally and internationally. The catering company interviewee took the opposite view, arguing that it had decreased at each of these scales. However, the plastics company respondent felt the increase in confidence and the improvement of the area as a business location was only relative to the rest of the country, and the area had suffered internally over the past five years, with increases in deprivation and violent crime. This was reiterated by the catering representative, who felt that Tyneside, as a business location, had become less attractive within the North East. The plastics company representative was, however, less optimistic about the future of the area as a business location, feeling that it would remain at a similar level in comparison to other areas. But the catering respondent was more optimistic, arguing that it would become more attractive as a result of continuing area renewal programmes, including the City Challenge programme in Newcastle's West End.

There was also a difference of opinion concerning the image of the area. The plastics respondent believed it had improved greatly and would improve further still in future years. This was primarily based upon the decline of the 'cloth cap' image, which, he argued, had resulted from the introduction to the area of hi-tech companies such as Nissan at Washington. The catering respondent, in contrast, felt that the riots on Tyneside in 1991 and the general level of crime in the area had diminished its image over the past five years, but that this would improve in future years with the renewal and regeneration of the most problematic areas (he was particularly hopeful for City Challenge in this respect). Both representatives felt that the image was very important to the their business in that it impacted in a clear way upon sales.

Perceptions of policy

Both respondents felt that government policy had done little to improve the lot of local companies. While the establishment of business parks was welcomed to some extent, this was offset by a feeling that many business parks had been set up in isolated locations, and that even previously successful firms had been unable significantly to boost their businesses by relocating. Both interviewees believed that wider economic policy was the main cause of problems suffered by businesses, and that urban or regional policy had negligible impacts by comparison. Thus, the main points for government to address from a small business perspective were levels of personal and corporate taxation, interest rates, general economic stability and the creation of greater economic confidence amongst businesses and consumers alike. The key, it was argued, was to create a climate whereby businesses could reinvest a larger proportion of profits, rather than lose these through taxation. However, the current government approach to industry and taxation was likened to 'a cow that has to be milked indefinitely, to the ultimate detriment of the cow'.

The 'policy-on' plastics firm had received a Regional Selective Assistance grant of £70,000, which went towards £1 million worth of investment in new machinery, new factory space and extra staff. The company thought that, even though the DTI had been supportive, the grant offer was extremely 'meagre' and that, despite all the bureaucracy involved in applying for the grant, it had not made a vast amount of difference. This negative view was also repeated for English Estates, who were described as very 'anti-business' and a 'Rachman-type' landlord.

In addition to the views offered on the DTI and English Estates, the 'policy-on' interviewee was also prompted for views on a further series of government programmes. The respondent recognised the majority of those listed on the questionnaire, with the exception of City Grant, Safer Cities, Industrial Improvement Areas, the Management Charter Initiative and Investors in People. The advantages offered to companies in Enterprise Zones were felt to be extremely unfair since firms located nearby - such as the plastics firm - lost out in comparison. Inclusion in the EZ area, the interviewee argued, would have made a major difference in financial terms.

The 'policy-off' respondent recognised half of the schemes from the same list, but these did not include RSA/RDG or the Urban Programme. He tended to be more aware of the mainstream/high profile initiatives such as UDCs, EZs, Youth Training and the Enterprise Initiative.

Even though neither company had used any form of direct support from the local authorities, both had found them to be supportive and a good provider of general services. Gateshead was noted as being far more supportive than Newcastle in this respect, with the latter felt to be almost 'anti-business' in some respects. Gateshead MBC was felt to be more supportive and had provided good advice, along with certain limited exhibition facilities. However, local government's powers were felt by both respondents to be too limited, especially in relation to the importance of government macro-economic policy. The correct role for future local government activity was thought to be providing a better range of local services which would improve the general environment and help with security problems. There would also be benefit to local companies were local government to offer quicker processing of planning permissions.

The two companies had had contrasting experiences of the introduction of the Unified Business Rate. On one hand, the plastics company noted that the introduction of the UBR had successfully 'capped' rate increases (which had been a major problem) and that rates levels were now in decline. The catering company, by contrast, had suffered rate increases as a result of the introduction of UBR.

## Links with local communities

The 'policy-on' company, being located in the middle of an industrial estate, felt it had no connections with the local community, and the only contact the 'policy-off' firm had experienced were links with local traders and police. Both companies had recently been concerned by increasing problems of criminal damage and vandalism to property and as a result had greatly increased their expenditure on security.

# 5 GENERAL CONCLUSIONS

- Rents have tended to increase and part of this has been the result of the English Estates policy of trying to make areas economically viable for investment.

- Rates in general have increased and the introduction of the UBR has not been of particular benefit to most companies. There is a general demand for the introduction of 'rate holidays' in the areas suffering most from the recession, which includes keeping the EZs in operation.

- Sales within the local areas have tended to increase with firm contraction. This was especially the case with the larger firms and particularly within Merseyside. Regional Policy grants to medium-sized establishments have meant they were better able to exploit wider geographical markets by allowing reinvestment and expansion.

- Labour costs, being largely dependent on numbers employed, have in general decreased through the effects of recession.

- Firms have been trying to boost productivity by increasing training. However, this tends to be on an in-house basis in order to minimise cost. There is a tendency for only the larger firms to have had contact with the TEC. Most firms have used only the Youth Training schemes, because of a lack of awareness of other programmes. There is a need for the training programmes and organisations to become pro-active and to seek out clients.

- In general firms are more security conscious due to increasing levels of crime and violence. There is potential for the Home Office to develop a 'Safer Firms' programme through the local authorities.

- In general there appear to be very few recruitment problems in most of the locations. This is unsurprising in light of economic contraction and an over-supply of potential employees. Only in certain specialised technical and IT areas was there any indication of a labour shortage.

- In the main, the firms which had received some form of financial assistance were more likely to have increased their financial commitment to their respective area. Wider economic success was nevertheless an important determinant of local commitment.

- The comparative views of the areas were strongly dependent upon the performance of the individual firm and their profile within the area. The larger companies tended to be more bullish about their areas in comparison to other locations; and, since they were more likely to be involved in high profile government programmes, they were more supportive of government policy.

- For most respondents the image of the area was not seen as being very important to their business, especially - and not surprisingly - in areas where the image has perhaps not improved. However, there was a tendency to consider the image of an area more important if it was felt to have dramatically improved through, for example, the influence of UDCs.

- Local government was conspicuous by being largely disregarded. Few firms had contact with the local authority and few knew of any business support local government may offer. This is a promotional problem that could be rectified since most of the authorities do offer business services. The ones which were especially noted for supportive effort were Salford and Gateshead. Others such as Manchester and Newcastle were seen by some companies as being uninterested at best and almost anti-business at worst. In Liverpool the authority was seen as an irrelevance and its actions were of no consequence to the companies.

- There is a widespread ignorance of the details of government policy. Where policy is known, respondents did not mention it because it is considered largely ineffective. There is scope for the respective departments to be more pro-active by approaching business as an integral part of their service.

- The only programmes or initiatives that were widely recognised tended to be the high-profile one, most notably UDCs. These have created divided camps amongst the business communities, as have the EZs, with those inside the areas predictably giving a more favourable impression than those outside.

- It was noticeable that City Challenge is far more prominently recognised in the Merseyside area than in the other areas. It is seen as a vital step forward in co-ordination, whereas the respondents from Manchester and Tyneside did not refer to it as a key influence for change.

- Those who had used some form of government assistance were consistently unhappy about the bureaucracy involved and the over-strict guidelines that needed to be followed. In contrast, EC funding, based on broader guidelines, was widely praised; it was suggested that there should be open-day surgeries - as with ESF - to explain the procedures for acquiring funds before firms become involved in the time consuming bureaucracy.

- The isolated locations for business development were disliked.

- Even though most firms were members of their local Chamber of Commerce, they generally appear to be ineffective organisations which, while having the potential to offer considerable help, need to be more pro-active in their approach.

- There needs to be more flexibility in government programmes, so that, for example, if a firm is one employee short of a specified requirement this does not exclude them from any assistance. Also, programmes should be more open to recognising the needs of the service sector, especially since it is suffering at least as much as the manufacturing sector in the current recession.

- There is a general impression that government programmes have been more successful in Tyneside as opposed to Merseyside.

- By far the strongest message to come from all the firms is that government urban and regional programmes have a minute effect in comparison to wider economic policy. The majority thought that the efforts of UDCs (no matter how geographically limited), business support initiatives, direct financial assistance and training development had all helped to improve certain parts of the areas concerned. But this did not make any significant difference to the performance of business in the areas in the face of a depressed economy. Government would serve business and industry better by improving the national economy, through addressing problems with interest rates, business rates, company taxes, capital allowances and exchange mechanisms.

*Annexe to Appendix F*

## Schedule for business interviews

The interview is divided into three parts. **First** I would like to ask you some questions about your firm's activities and your own role. **Then** we would like <u>you</u> to complete some questions about your own view of how things have changed over the last five years. **Finally** I would like to ask you some questions about these changes.

— — — — — — — — — — — — — — — — — — — — — — — — — — — —

### SECTION 1

1. What are the main products/services of your company here?

2. Is this the only plant/office - in Greater Manchester Y / N
 - in the North West Y / N
 - in the UK  Y / N

3. How long has this plant/office been established

 - on this site ..........

 - in Manchester ..........

4a. How many people does it <u>now</u> employ (approx) ..........

 b. How many did it employ in 1988? ..........

5a. (if not already known) What is your role in the company?

 b. How long have you occupied this position in the company?
 ..........

 c. Have you played any other role in the company in the past?
 Y / N (If Y, specify) ..........

6. How long have you personally worked in Manchester? ..........

— — — — — — — — — — — — — — — — — — — — — — — — — — —

### SECTION 2

The following questions relate to various aspects of your business here in Manchester over the last five years. Could you record your response by ticking the most appropriate box.

7. In the last five years, as a proportion of your total costs here, have rents

| greatly increased | increased | not changed | decreased | greatly decreased | don't know |
|---|---|---|---|---|---|
| .......... | .......... | .......... | .......... | .......... | .......... |

<u>or</u>
have they varied over time without any trend) (please specify)
.............................

8. In the last five years, as a proportion of your total costs here, have rates/business rates

| greatly increased | increased | not changed | decreased | greatly decreased | don't know |
|---|---|---|---|---|---|
| .......... | .......... | .......... | .......... | .......... | .......... |

<u>or</u>
have they varied over time without any trend) (please specify)
................

9. In the last five years, has the proportion of your sales turnover that has come from the Greater Manchester market

| greatly increased | increased | not changed | decreased | greatly decreased | don't know |
|---|---|---|---|---|---|
| .......... | .......... | .......... | .......... | .......... | .......... |

<u>or</u>
has it varied over time without any trend) (please specify)
................

10. In the last five years, as a proportion of your total costs here, have labour costs

| greatly increased | increased | not changed | decreased | greatly decreased | don't know |
|---|---|---|---|---|---|
| .......... | .......... | .......... | .......... | .......... | .......... |

<u>or</u>
have they varied over time without any trend) (please specify) ................

11. In the last five years, has the proportion of your turnover spent on training

| greatly increased | increased | not changed | decreased | greatly decreased | don't know |
|---|---|---|---|---|---|
| .......... | .......... | .......... | .......... | .......... | .......... |

or
has it varied over time without any trend) (please specify) ................

10. In the last five years, has your expenditure on security

| greatly increased | increased | not changed | decreased | greatly decreased | don't know |
|---|---|---|---|---|---|
| ........... | ........... | ........... | ........... | ........... | ......... |

or
has it varied over time without any trend) (please specify)

13a. With regard to your workforce, in the last five years have you experienced any problems in recruiting suitable personnel when vacancies arose?

Yes ...    No ....

**If no**, go to Question 13b.

**If yes**, in what areas?
management ....    skilled manual ....    semi-skilled manual ....
clerical ....                other (please specify) ....

Over the last five years, has the problem

| greatly increased | increased | not changed | decreased | greatly decreased | don't know |
|---|---|---|---|---|---|
| ........... | ........... | ........... | ........... | ........... | ......... |

or
has it varied over time without any trend) (please specify) ................

13b. In the last five years, have you experienced problems in the recruitment of young people to your workforce?

Yes.....    No......

**If No**, go to Question 14

**If Yes**, have the problems
worsened greatly ..... worsened ..... stayed the same ....

14. In the last five years, has your financial commitment to investment in Manchester (e.g to purchase/lease buildings and plant or to refurbish)

| greatly increased | increased | not changed | decreased | greatly decreased | don't know |
|---|---|---|---|---|---|
| ........... | ........... | ........... | ........... | ........... | ......... |

or
has it varied over time without any trend) (please specify) ................

The final questions ask you to make comparisons between Manchester and other places:

15a. Over the last five years, do you feel that business confidence in Manchester, compared to other places in the North West, has

| greatly increased | increased | not changed | decreased | greatly decreased | don't know |
|---|---|---|---|---|---|
| .......... | .......... | .......... | .......... | .......... | ......... |

15b. Over the last five years, do you feel that business confidence in Manchester, compared to the nation as a whole, has

| greatly increased | increased | not changed | decreased | greatly decreased | don't know |
|---|---|---|---|---|---|
| .......... | .......... | .......... | .......... | .......... | ......... |

15c. Over the last five years, do you feel that business confidence in Manchester, compared to other countries, has

| greatly increased | increased | not changed | decreased | greatly decreased | don't know |
|---|---|---|---|---|---|
| .......... | .......... | .......... | .......... | .......... | ......... |

16a. As a business location, compared to other places in the North West, has Manchester over the last five years become

| much more attractive | more attractive | neither more nor less attractive | less attractive | much less attractive | don't know |
|---|---|---|---|---|---|
| ..... | ..... | ..... | ..... | ..... | ..... |

16b. As a business location, compared to the nation as a whole, has Manchester over the last five years become

| much more attractive | more attractive | neither more nor less attractive | less attractive | much less attractive | don't know |
|---|---|---|---|---|---|
| ..... | ..... | ..... | ..... | ..... | ..... |

16c. As a business location, compared to locations outside Britain, has Manchester over the last five years become

| much more attractive | more attractive | neither more nor less attractive | less attractive | much less attractive | don't know |
|---|---|---|---|---|---|
| ..... | ..... | ..... | ..... | ..... | ..... |

17a. In the next five years, as a location for business, compared to other places in the North West, do you expect Manchester to become

| much more attractive | more attractive | neither more nor less attractive | less attractive | much less attractive | don't know |
|---|---|---|---|---|---|
| ..... | ..... | ..... | ..... | ..... | ..... |

17b. In the next five years, as a location for business, compared to the nation as a whole, do you expect Manchester to become

| much more attractive | more attractive | neither more nor less attractive | less attractive | much less attractive | don't know |
|---|---|---|---|---|---|
| ..... | ..... | ..... | ..... | ..... | ..... |

17c. In the next five years, as a location for business, compared to locations outside Britain, do you expect Manchester to become

| much more attractive | more attractive | neither more nor less attractive | less attractive | much less attractive | don't know |
|---|---|---|---|---|---|
| ..... | ..... | ..... | ..... | ..... | .... |

18. As a business person, in the last five years do you think the image of Manchester has

| greatly improved | improved | not changed | deteriorated | greatly deteriorated | don't know |
|---|---|---|---|---|---|
| ........... | ........... | ........... | ........... | ........... | .......... |

19. As a business person, do you expect the image of Manchester in the next five years, to

| greatly improve | improve | not change | deteriorate | greatly deteriorate | don't know |
|---|---|---|---|---|---|
| ........... | ........... | ........... | ........... | ........... | .......... |

20. How important is the image of Manchester to your business
very fairly neither fairly very don't

| very important | fairly important | neither important nor unimportant | fairly unimportant | very unimportant | don't know |
|---|---|---|---|---|---|
| ........... | ........... | ........... | ........... | ........... | .......... |

Thank you. Please hand these sheets back to the interviewer.

— — — — — — — — — — — — — — — — — — — — — — — — — — — —

## SECTION 3

Thank you for answering those questions. I would finally like to ask you about some of the changes that you have noted.

Then ask open-ended questions to explore reasons behind the responses in Section 2. For example:

In your opinion, what are the reasons for the increased/decreased proportion of your sales in the Manchester region? (Interviewer to probe)

What is it that explains the fact that the image of Manchester over the last few years has improved/deteriorated compared to other places in the NW and more generally within the country? (Interviewer to probe)

**Record answers on separate sheet**

(After completing these questions about reasons, the interviewer then asks questions about policy.)

————————————————————————————————————

## SECTION 4

You have/have not mentioned government policy and activity as one of the reasons for these changes.

21. Are there any (further) ways in which <u>central</u> government policy or action have influenced these changes?

      regional policy (prompt and probe)
      inner city/urban policy (prompt and probe)
      general policy (prompt and probe)

22. Are there any (further) ways in which <u>local</u> government has influenced these changes?

Could I now ask for your views on the impact of particular programmes?

23. Has your plant/office here in Manchester had experience of any particular national government policy or programme?

               Yes... No....

**If No**, go to q.24

**If Yes**, Can you give me details of what this entailed?

      What sums of direct financial assistance were involved?

      What were the benefits (prompt, job creation, speeding up production processes, subsidising production)?

      What were the drawbacks (if any)?

      In what ways could it have been improved?

      Are there any other programmes? (repeat above set of questions).

24. Are there other particular government programmes of which you are aware which are available to firms but which you have not pursued?
(For each)

      How helpful do you think they are?

      In what ways could they be improved?

      Why did your firm not pursue them?

25. May I mention some other specific policies or programmes that have been available to firms in parts of the country and ask your views on them if you know about them (note only those not already mentioned and record reactions under each).

Enterprise Initiative.
English Estates.
City Grant.
Safer Cities
Urban Programme.
Industrial Improvement Areas.
Derelict Land Grant.
UDC.
EZ.
Regional Selective Assistance/Development Grant.
Business Growth Training
Enterprise Training
Consultancy Training
Youth Training
Other training schemes
Management Charter Initiative
National Training Awards
Investors in People
Job Interview Guarantee

26. Would you say that, whether your company has or has not benefited directly from such policies, you have experienced any <u>indirect</u> benefits from government policy and actions (prompt, through winning contracts, general improvements in the local business climate).

27. Have you taken up any support/programmes from <u>local</u> government?

**If Yes**, Can you give me details of what this entailed.

How helpful were they?

Were there any drawbacks to them?

In what ways could they be improved?

28. Are there other local government programmes of which you are aware but have not pursued (prompt, business advice, technical help, financial assistance, provision of premises).

How helpful are they?

Are there any drawbacks to them?

In what ways could they be improved?

Any reasons for not having pursued them?

29. In general, do you find the local authority supportive ...... obstructive ........

In what ways?

30. Have you been in receipt of any other forms of public support (e.g. European monies)? Y / N

**If Yes**, could you provide details of the schemes and the amounts of assistance?

31. Is your company a member of the Chamber of Commerce? Y / N

How helpful have you found the Chamber?

Are the collective interests of local business/industry articulated effectively (by the Chamber or by other bodies)? Y / N

32. Has your company had any involvement with the TEC (prompt, either formal connection or contact through the TEC clubs, networks, databases, gatherings)? Y / N

**If Yes**, Could you give details?

How helpful have you found the TEC?

33. May I ask you about the relationship of the plant/office with the local community in which you are located.

Are there any ways in which you have developed links with the community (e.g. Compact, Enterprise in HE)? Y / N

**If Yes**, Could you specify?

Finally, may I ask you two general questions covering what we have been discussing.

34. What do you think are the most effective ways in which <u>central</u> government can help business/industry in Manchester, either directly or indirectly (probe)?

35. What do you think are the most effective ways in which <u>local</u> government can help business/industry in Manchester, either directly or indirectly (probe)?

Thank you very much for your co-operation. Are there any points which you think we have not covered?

The following accounts draw on interviews with around one hundred key figures in the policy communities in Greater Manchester, Merseyside and Tyne and Wear. In broad terms, the aim of the discussions was to explore respondents' perceptions of the areas' problems, the ways in which policies have been implemented and the impacts of those policies on the conurbations over the last decade.

Interviews were conducted with a diverse range of people from public, private and voluntary sector backgrounds. Respondents included senior civil servants, local government officers, business people, local and national politicians and people from quangos and community organisations. This Appendix presents some of the major themes arising from these discussions. Each of the three accounts provides a brief resume of the views of respondents. The emphases differ across the three areas, although there are obviously recurring themes. These contrasts and similarities are explored in greater depth in the accounts of the three areas in Appendix C which also draws on some of the rich detail provided by our discussions with key figures.

## 1 GREATER MANCHESTER

The Manchester conurbation is the largest and most complex of the three areas. It is difficult to characterise the area as a whole since the conurbation neither operates nor sees itself in a unitary way. It has long been politically fragmented and its constituent parts are very different economically and socially. It was not surprising that the impression of balkanisation was one which kept recurring throughout the discussions.

Such fragmentation was seen at both a regional and local scale. Respondents from within some of the districts spoke of their areas still feeling part of Lancashire rather than the conurbation. At a regional level, the authorities in the North West have seemed incapable of developing a single strategic view and this has meant that the image that it presents is blurred. This has helped neither to attract inward investment into the region nor to develop strategic thinking. INWARD - potentially the most potent of the regional agencies - has failed to attract members from across all the authorities, especially the conurbations. The Chambers of Commerce are of very variable size and effectiveness, although discussions are now underway through the Manchester Chamber to explore a federation across the region.

At a local level, the real or perceived variation in local political flavour has created jostling between authorities and considerable suspicion of Manchester as the 'lead' body. Frequent contrasts were drawn between, on one hand, the pragmatism of Labour authorities like Salford or Wigan and of non-Labour authorities like Trafford or Stockport, as against the 'ideological purity' of Manchester. Against this, however, many respondents argued that in practice such contrasts were more apparent than real and that even the more 'ideological' authorities were in practice ready to work both with central government departments and with the private sector. Some part of the local fragmentation was seen as a reflection of the smallness of Manchester vis-a-vis the other authorities in the conurbation. Frequent comparisons were made with Birmingham which was seen as larger, more powerful and more visionary and therefore in a better position to exert leadership for the West Midlands as a whole.

The private sector was seen as playing very different roles in different parts of the area. Many of the peripheral authorities (like Tameside or Bury) emphasised the difficulties that they faced because they had few large employers within their areas and that partnerships were more difficult to establish in this context. To this extent, it was more difficult for them to respond to the imperative to collaborate with the private sector, one of the main thrusts of urban policy in the 1980s. Even in Manchester, senior figures from both the public and private sectors made the point that most companies had little commitment to the area since they were run from headquarters elsewhere and owed little allegiance to their local area. As one respondent put it, 'the Manchester context is a million miles from Boston where local firms are local'. The Co-operative Bank was seen as a striking exception and its role in the Eastlands project reflected that. A senior figure in the commercial sector commented that 'business is willing to contribute time, but not to dip its hands into its pockets'.

Yet, in discussing the potential strengths of Greater Manchester, most respondents included its business resilience as a factor: pharmaceuticals and foodstuffs were seen as a node of strength, as was the continuing importance of banking and insurance in the area. Other of its strengths were the airport and higher education complex; the City's potential for tourism and leisure and cultural activities; the large population within the catchment of the conurbation as a whole. Its weaknesses were the familiar ones: a continuing dependence on a 'traditional' industrial structure; squalor, crime and unrest; a large dependent' population; a lack of vision and the fragmentation of the various districts.

Networking was continually stressed. A strength of Manchester was that it was less introverted and 'provincial' than many conurbations. It has 'movers and shakers' who can get things done. A large number of people passed through the area, and those who were successful were not seen as outsiders. Networks, however, were seen as being diffuse. The various groups tended not to interlock, so that in the eyes of one respondent, 'the academics, the Jewish groups, the professionals, the fly-boys, the media, the business leaders each have their own circles'.

The respective roles of the public and private sectors were a recurring focus of discussion. In the eyes of one private sector respondent, the local authority was largely an irrelevance in getting things done in Manchester; it was too small, had too little resource and too little power. Any significant projects were 'private-sector led, central government-financed and local-authority approved'.

## 1.1 Constraints on implementation

There was considerable uncertainty about the aims of policy. A senior local authority politician characterised it pithily as being aimed at freeing the market, since local authorities were seen as sitting on land and were large employers who squeezed out private capital. He argued that the government's view was that urban areas would look after themselves if only local authorities didn't get in the way.

A senior local authority officer recalled the UP initially as a topping-up programme which involved the bending of mainstream resources, while another described the Partnerships as being 'supposed to reach the parts other programmes didn't reach'. Most local authority officers noted that urban policy has been directed at the physical manifestations of urban decline through physically directed policy instruments. These have been supplemented by a series of employment-type initiatives which founder one after another, seemingly at odds with the real problem.

In general, local authorities felt that urban policy had been designed to diffuse influence among many players, often consciously at the expense of local government. There is a feeling that urban policy has increasingly been about targeting, and this is a view shared by actors from all kinds of organisations, notably the housing associations and the development corporations. The cynical view that policy had simply been about managing decline more gently was only rarely heard.

Housing policy was seen as having little to do with renewal until Mr Heseltine's second spell at the DoE. Prior to this, most respondents saw housing policy throughout most of the decade as having been driven by the wish to increase home ownership. Even in recent years, however, there were doubts about the extent to which housing had been given an urban dimension. One respondent, for example, noted that since 1988 the focus had been on new-build rather than refurbishment and that this was not to the benefit of big cities.

Clearly, there is some ambiguity over problem-definition. Some part of this is a reflection of regional diversity across the country and the tendency for policy emphases to reflect a London-dominated perspective. This was illustrated, in the housing field, by comments from one of the government departments. In this view 'the South' (i.e. government ministers) sees the housing problem as one of homelessness, while those in 'the North' (i.e. the Regional Offices) see the problem as stemming from the fact that households have insufficient income to maintain and improve the stock. Failure to recognise the latter has meant that policy has merely accelerated the decline of housing stock in the North West.

One of the most frequently cited constraints on policy was the supposed incompatibility of aims between central and local government. The classic illustration of this is the reform of local government finance. The local authorities made two major complaints: first, they have lost great amounts of revenue support through rate/charge capping and what they see as the arbitrary calculation of Standard Spending Assessments, whose tendency to fluctuate wildly made for difficulties in forward planning. The second problem is the introduction of capital controls, the most frequently cited of which, unsurprisingly, was the restriction on the use of capital receipts from council house sales. One senior local authority politician, however, noted wryly that a side benfit of financial squeezes was that 'if you haven't got the money, then you have to think'.

Some of the private-sector respondents drew attention to the revenue/capital dilemma, but unsurprisingly it was amongst the local authorities that this was most widely articulated. Local authority officers argued that central government takes no account of the revenue consequences of the capital schemes which it approves and funds through urban policy. A Manchester officer pointed out that money spent on greening parts of East Manchester in the early 1980s had not had the full impact expected because there had been insufficient revenue resource to maintain these areas to the required standard. This is identified as a problem with grants like UP since, while anxious to attract resources, authorities were aware that the local authorities' 25% contribution counts as 'growth' for capping purposes. In the opinion of one local authority, the revenue/capital problem dilutes the final benefit to the public. 'UP acts as a pump-primer, but the limits on revenue mean that there is no-one to man the pump in the longer term.'

Another common complaint from local authorities concerned the familiar problem of the compartmentalised nature of the various grant regimes, and the different rules which accompany each. The up-side of this, however, was that many authorities and agencies have successfully 'stitched together' different types of grant on an area basis. This undoubtedly is one of the explanations for the favourable reception given to City Challenge, since one of its strongest attractions was seen as the encouragement it gives to strategic corporate action across a range of service sectors.

This question of inter-agency co-ordination was widely raised. It was seen as a problem both at central and local level. There is a widespread feeling that government departments work poorly together, with the Department of Transport in particular being singled out, and with frequent criticism of the apparent incompatibility of the aims of DoE and DTI. Different departments were argued to take starkly different views of what was or was not relevant to urban policy: DoE and DTI had disparate views on the relevance of airports policy to urban regeneration; there was varying enthusiasm for incorporating a conscious arts and culture dimension to urban policy. A civil servant noted the failure to integrate land-use policy and industrial strategy across departments but that this was needed to create the new industrial structure needed by the area.

Some respondents argued that it was only forms of regional devolution that would tackle the problem of the lack of departmental co-ordination. One respondent argued that the need was to persuade government to think regionally and that this would create 'national government rather than central government'.

The City Action Team was not widely credited with overcoming such departmental rivalries, being seen in its early years as concerned principally with how best to spend its own limited budget. There is a frustration with 'Treasury rules', which forbid the carrying over of funding from year to year. Some authorities have obtained 'rolling programmes' of Derelict Land Grant from the Regional Office by clubbing together, an example of this being Bolton/Bury/Salford. Although these do not strictly circumvent annualisation, they seem to be a tacit guarantee of continued funding, allowing councils to undertake longer-term projects with relative security. The authorities involved regard this as something of an achievement, a reward from the Regional Office for their ability to deliver in the past. But the same point about longer-term funding was directed at Housing Renewal Areas which, while generally seen as being successful, were criticised because their expected ten-year life-span was not matched by a similar medium-term financial commitment.

A further problem of co-ordination was seen as lying within the local authorities themselves. There is a view that the committee structure is no longer the best one for delivering policy on the ground, an experience reinforced in Salford by the Trinity and Ordsall projects. The benefits of a 'corporate approach' become clearer when one moves toward an area-based approach. Again City Challenge has stimulated further valuable experimentation with different structures of decision-making. The need for functional co-ordination is felt to be a lesson for central government, and indeed there are many who support the introduction of delegated budgets for regional offices.

## 1.2 Partnership and implementation

The concept of partnership has become so central to urban policy that it was difficult to find anyone who disagreed with its theoretical virtues. One politician, however, argued that so far as central/local partnership is involved, partnership in practice has been centre-led. Perhaps surprisingly, none of the discussants referred specifically to the Manchester/Salford Partnership itself. It is clear that in practice the two authorities operate in a quite discrete way. Nevertheless, at local level, there was a widespread view from local authorities that their relations with the regional DoE were supportive and good.

In terms of inter-authority co-ordination, there was no consensus on the role of AGMA and the demise of the GMC. A few mourned the passing of the GMC, but the general view was that its role had never been clear or effective. Most respondents emphasised the unpopularity of the upper tier with both the public and with some of the districts. We encountered no majority support for a return to metropolitan or regional government.

In terms of local authorities' relations with the private sector, many within the private sector itself pointed out that authorities varied widely in their approach and in their potential for developing good working relations with the private sector. Many mentioned the large projects undertaken by Salford in the 1980s, and contrasted this with Manchester's less pragmatic approach. With regard to housing, such inter-authority variation was especially marked. One respondent noted Bolton's pro-active co-operation with housing associations, and also praised Rochdale. By comparison, Oldham's efforts were described as 'unconvincing'.

Some of the most forthright comments on the respective roles of the public and private sectors drew on comparisons with Birmingham. The view was expressed that, not only did Manchester's local government operate in a less sophisticated way than Birmingham, but that while Birmingham represents more than 60% of the West Midlands, Manchester forms just 19% of its county and thus has neither the resources nor political strength to offer a firm lead. For example, the support of GMC had been very important for the Arts in the City, and without it some of the City's theatres might well never have come into being. Since abolition, however, there had been a revival of inter-district rivalry. That - and the small size and limited resources of the ten districts - had meant that the key player in making things happen in the Arts' world was now the private sector rather than the local authorities, according to one respondent.

The private sector has always played a critical role in the life of the City. It is, however, less cohesive than, say, in Tyne and Wear and, rather than forming a small interlocking network, it consists of a large number of only partly overlapping spheres. The role of the Chambers of Commerce within the region may provide a new mechanism through which greater local involvement and co-ordination might be achieved. The Business Leadership Team is felt to be less influential than it should be due to poor co-ordination, but its 24 members have a total turnover of £30b, and this represents a potentially formidable financial muscle.

## 1.3 Targeting and implementation

There were mixed views on the effectiveness of targeting. On one hand, most respondents identified the growing degree of spatial targeting as helpful since it introduced a degree of coherence to the policy context. It potentially began to recognise the interconnected nature of many of the problems associated with poverty, unemployment, low skills and infrastructural and environmental problems. There was, for example, widespread support for the decision to appoint a Minister for Manchester and Salford since potentially this helped to create a more integrated view of its problems. On the other hand, there was criticism of the inevitably patchy response to problems which were seen as widely scattered throughout the conurbation.

Targeting at a national level, through which the '57' UPAs were recognised, was resented by those authorities which had earlier qualified for Traditional UP resources but were subsequently not included in the 57. There remains unhappiness at some of the designations made. Many of the peripheral authorities made the point that their needs were ignored merely because their deprivation was more scattered - but no less real - than that in the central parts of the conurbation. One respondent argued that the selection of targeted areas was based on a concept of single-centred areas rather than multi-centred conurbations and that those on the periphery suffered in consequence. The authority thought to have been most unfairly excluded was Tameside, since it has a similar social profile to a place like Oldham, yet receives no UP. This is less true of Bury, another recipient of Traditional UP before 1987. In each case the authority feels that UP status brings benefits over and above the simple resources that follow allocation of grant; programme status gives influence and a degree of political muscle. There is a view that the decision to handle Channel Tunnel freight on a site in Trafford Park - rather than in the non-UP areas of Guide Bridge within Tameside - can be seen as an example of how urban policy has distorted the working of the market. Another example quoted from work done by Greater Manchester Research on the take-up of industrial floorspace, shows that take-up was 1-2% in Tameside compared to 20% in Oldham. Tameside's adjacent neighbours are: Stockport - a relatively wealthy council; Oldham, which does receive UP funding; and East Manchester which is currently the recipient of resources for its Eastlands initiative. The view was expressed that this puts an authority which is not UP funded and yet which lies within a conurbation large parts of which do receive targeted government resource, in the worst possible position: associated with deprivation and yet not benefiting from funding; handicapped by social profile, yet unable to compete on a level playing field even with similarly poor areas.

Within local authorities themselves, there is some ambivalence towards spatial targeting. Many of the local government officers acknowledge that 'pepper-potting' achieves limited and short-lived results. The advantage of concentrating resources in a small ring-fenced area is that, like Salford Quays, the results are highly visible and there may be spin-offs from a successful project acting as a magnet. This obviously applies to buildings which are overtly commercial such as Multiplex cinemas or other forms of entertainment. The point was also made that with many housing projects, there is a very high threshold to reach before they become self-sustaining and hence that targeting with sufficient resources and over a sufficiently long period is a necessary condition for turning around an area.

Outer boroughs with less of a natural inner area have experienced difficulties in solving their own particular problems. Wigan has twin centres, in Wigan and at Leigh. Tameside experiences similar drawbacks, and has been dogged by rivalries between the two towns of Stalybridge and Ashton. In Manchester, the concentration of resources into 470 acres of the City Centre could be seen as controversial, except that the UDC has continued many of the projects begun earlier by the City Council, the City having long been committed to the concept of the Regional Centre. Politicians and local authority officers were both alive to the problems of equity associated with concentrating resources and the implied acceptance of 'writing-off' areas not covered by targeted programmes.

## 1.4 Successes

UDCs

The resurgence of the City Centre since the late 1970s was seen as a key success. Part of this is attributed to the successful working of the Central Manchester Development Corporation which was widely applauded. Even though many of its schemes were inherited from the local authority, it was seen as having done things more quickly than the local authority would have managed and as having involved the right mix of key local actors. To offset such plaudits, one politician saw UDCs as being like local government in the 1960s; 'with more money than they know what to do with and needing to spend up to the limits. They are not creative; they spend whether it's sensible or not'. Yet even this view was tempered since he saw exposure to the market as having benefits in that 'politicians seem to behave better when there are real-live capitalists present'.

The experience of Trafford UDC was often used as a contrast to CMDC. It was widely felt that it had worked too slowly, had not been successful in negotiating the world of central government and had little vision of what it wanted to achieve. Against this, there was a recognition of the value of the recent change of emphasis to incorporate a training and community-related dimension to its work and that its problems have included the slow speed with which CPOs have been confirmed; 'the powers of UDCs are really no more draconian than those of local government'.

Partnerships

The co-operation of Salford City Council with Regalion at St. James's Park, with Wimpey at Canterbury Gardens, with Barratt's in Trinity, and with Norwest Holst in Pendleton, were seen to represent the positive side of 1980s' urban policy. Similar housing projects were widely praised in Rochdale. Economic initiatives such as Bolton Business Ventures have been seen as representing the new entrepreneurial face of local authorities. Various of the specific schemes had been used successfully to involve the private sector; Derelict Land Grant and City Grant being noted in particular. City Grant was seen in a generally favourable light, but was criticised for its slowness and its cumbersome bureaucracy especially where schemes involving inward investment were concerned since speed was usually of the essence in persuading overseas or out-of-region companies to invest.

Policy instruments which encouraged collaborative implementation across departments were generally welcomed. Reference has already been made to Housing Renewal Areas, which were widely praised as having offered incentives to co-ordinate action across a range of economic, social and environmental agendas. So too were Estate Action and Safer Cities. The latter was widely valued both for being closer to the grassroots and for the potential inter-agency co-ordination that it encouraged. Many of the problems, for example dealing with long-term offenders, necessitated co-operation across sectors; since co-ordination between the Home Office and the DoE was not seen as being very effective, the kinds of local co-ordination (or, more strictly, bilateral agreements) which could be achieved at a local level under Estate Action were seen as invaluable. Such praise was tempered. Many respondents recognised that the various agencies differed in the enthusiasm with which they responded to this potential; co-ordination required great effort and that 'if the community isn't convinced, you get nowhere'. Furthermore, inevitably, much of the success or failure of schemes depended critically on the coordinator as much as on the principle of the programme itself. Eventually, driven by the Treasury's need to spend money, some respondents saw the imperative of speed overtaking the slow long-term needs to address issues of crime; 'glitz takes over once the need to spend to budget has to be faced'. Nevertheless, the success of specific projects like the Kirkholt scheme was universally recognised.

The **City Challenge** principle was generally seen as being helpfully galvanising because of its organisational thrust and the implication of the new role that it appeared to assume for local authorities; it had brought local authorities closer to the private sector and to the regional DoE; and it had brought the DoE closer to other government departments. The area focus was welcomed. Contrary views emphasised the inappropriateness of the competitive principle - 'a farcical way of allocating money' - and that, while City Challenge promised to be good on the physical renewal side and raised the image of areas, the process would largely merely displace poor residents and their problems. Disparaging views also emphasised the implausibility of extending the scheme to more authorities: 'the mind boggles at the thought of 48 cities doing what Manchester had to do for Hulme and of the bureacracy of appearing to make rational decisions about winners and losers'.

## 1.5 Failures

Many of the failures, by their nature, are less tangible and visible. Local authorities claim that mainstream resources have all but dried up, as capital programmes have been pruned. This makes urban policy grants more significant than ever, and compels local authorities to play more tightly by central government's rules. As one Chief Executive commented, 'If there's a good deal on white bread, we buy it, even though we know brown bread's better for us'. In a sense, there is a feeling among local authorities that 'we are all pragmatists now'.

The Moss Side **Task Force** was widely criticised, at least in its early years, for not having better consulted the local community and for having taken at face value the belief that the self-elected members of its forum represented the wider views of the local community and were not involved partly to press for their own pet schemes. There was a strong sense of civil servants having been 'parachuted in' to a difficult and sensitive area. Even more focused criticism was directed at the Rochdale Task Force. It too was seen as having failed to get close to the grassroots and was characterised by one as having merely 'operated with a cheque book'. The Task Force and the CAT were both criticised for having underspent their budgets. The CAT was seen as providing some liaison but not enough since each director is not obliged to set out corporate plans and, because of departmental budgets, does not have freedom to fit in with other departments' plans.

**TECs** were also widely criticised. Many respondents had found them impenetrable and difficult to get on with. One saw it as a profound mistake to have combined the notions of training and enterprise. Others saw them as a step backwards since they created yet another agency concerned with enterprise when the need was to co-ordinate those which already existed. Yet another likened their policies to doughnuts, lacking a strategy in the middle. Another argued that, on training, they had failed to engage the skills of the voluntary sector.

Meanwhile, the issues of poverty and inequality remained largely hidden and rarely mentioned in many of our discussions. One local authority respondent noted the new jobs in financial services which have been created in the City, and pointed out that amidst the physical improvements, rents have risen as incomes have fallen, and that Manchester's homelessness problem has worsened.

While the city as a whole seems to be recovering its confidence, Manchester's poor are now more highly concentrated, and in a less favourable economic position than they were in 1978. Many of our respondents felt that there had indeed been a growing social polarisation during the 1980s and that most of the urban policy initiatives had done little to address this - indeed had in many ways exacerbated it. One respondent from the voluntary sector characterised urban policy as being a process of removing attractive old flagstones from his deprived neighbourhood and re-laying them in the glitzy Castlefield redevelopment for the benefit of tourists.

The voluntary sector was seen as having partly been sidelined over the period of the late 1980s. Housing associations, for example, were ill-equipped to take a wider role in tackling many of the problems since housing was often not the place to start; it should be poverty, structural unemployment and general deprivation. The assumption that the voluntary sector can take on extra tasks is doubtful in light of their financial difficulties. The two biggest bodies in Manchester, for example, had just had their budgets halved by the local authority. Despite their experience and their sensitivity to local communities, this made it unrealistic to look to the voluntary sector as a replacement for local authorities. On the other hand, one respondent from within the voluntary sector saw opportunities in the jostling of the multiple big bodies since this gives a chance for small bodies within the voluntary sector to jump in.

To some respondents, the problems of many poor estates was one of a crisis of debilitated people. 'To break the dependency culture you have to do more than send people off on irrelevant training courses - everyone is doing courses on french polishing'. The need was to give them financial security. 'No-one has ever come up with a training scheme the size of City Challenge'. The danger was that policy had initially built up expectations which had not been realised. This had led to local leaders who had originally taken leading roles in community programmes subsequently becoming disillusioned or withdrawing from them, especially once the impacts of financial cuts had bitten. Such bitterness was levelled as much at local as at central government: 'The gap of perception is larger between the City Centre and Alexandra Park than between London and Manchester'. Such views led to the opinion that there had been a 'policy of indifference visited on inner cities', a 'sense of having to grovel for what you know is fifth-rate'.

**Ethnic communities** were a particular dimension of such criticisms. The view of one respondent from the voluntary sector, for example, was that in practice ethnic groups had received little or no benefit from urban policy. Much of the resource from the UP, for example, was first exploited by local authority officers to tackle their pet schemes and only 'funny money' was left for ethnic and other community groups. Their problems were compounded by their difficulty in getting access to timely information and, even when they did, in not being well placed to understand its significance; 'It's not enough to have the information, you have to know what it means'. The many ethnic groups in Manchester had received little direct resource - small sums for reburbishment which helped Asian textile businesses, nothing for those in the catering trades, some training help for Afro-Caribbean groups. Section 11 Grants were generally seen as having been widely misused and misplaced. Respondents with knowledge of ethnic groups spoke warmly of the role of the Employment Service, whose knowledge of the needs of local people was drawn from their 'frontline' experience in job centres. This was in stark contrast to most civil servants.

The view of the salience of the largely-ignored ethnic dimension was heightened by the fact that many respondents drew attention to the changing expectations of the new generations of ethnic groups. The obvious example was amongst Asian groups whose older generations, at least in the non-Manchester districts, had largely taken a subservient and docile view of their place within the wider society. They were now increasingly characterised by younger members whose expectations were little different from their white counterparts and who created similar problems of lawlessness in many estates. Future prospects look difficult with a less placid more disillusioned generation. Even where traditional forms of organisation existed, respondents foresaw problems. Amongst West Indians, for example, the potential role of churches had been stressed, but the pentecostal churches were too pure - 'too concerned with faith and too little with social concern'.

## 1.6 Conclusion

The sense in Manchester was of an area which has shown signs of a dramatic improvement in much of its physical infrastructure in the last three years and in which over that same period there has been a significant turning-around of business confidence vis-a-vis other parts of the country. The evidence of new building, the sense of a new vision associated with the Olympic bid, developments in the City Centre and the Eastlands area and the promise that the longstanding problem of Hulme might be tackled through City Challenge; all these represented the bullish side of the evaluations of the changes of recent years. As one respondent commented, 'there has been the start of a new pride in the area; people no longer apologise for Manchester'. Against this, the continuing and deepening erosion of the position of the poor and of the areas outside the centre were seen to remain as a problem which was only scratched by urban policy. As one respondent put it: 'Away from bricks and mortar, social conditions haven't really changed. Ordsall, Cheetham Hill and Moss Side have even deteriorated. Gangs have arisen not from derelict areas but from new council property'.

# 2 MERSEYSIDE

There was considerable agreement on the region's strengths; the most commonly noted elements being its heritage, waterfront, cultural industries, tourism, leisure, higher education, low-cost labour pool and accessibility to desirable areas. But there was general agreement that these are as much potential as actual strengths. Local and central government discussants were broadly agreed in this respect. However, many interviewees argued that too much emphasis has been placed on these service areas at the expense of manufacturing. There is a need to broaden the strategy. In this respect, the other potential attributes of the area were more relevant: the Freeport, the concept of the east/west Landbridge, the Mersey Barrage and the airport.

The offsetting weaknesses on which there was equal agreement were; location, communications and, particularly, the poor environment. Frequently-quoted examples included: the fact that the motorway does not enter the city, unlike the Manchester case; railway stock and services are appalling in relation, for example, to the North East; the airport has no real competitive chance, given its peripheral location. But, within the region, Knowsley and St. Helens were recognised as having good domestic motorway links. There is a desperate need for improved communications to Europe in the 1990s. The general infrastructure was in some respects seen as being even worse than transport. The radial routes into the city reveal dereliction not addressed in the past decade. The physical dereliction of Toxteth is seen as being worse now than in the 1981 riots.

To these infrastructural problems, a range of economic weaknesses was also added: poor skill levels in the labour force; a weak private sector; the decline in the manufacturing base; the dominance of MNCs; a lack of an entrepreneurial small-firm tradition; the over-representation in the local economy of traditional, low-growth sectors. One senior civil servant also highlighted aspects of the local political context: the poor performance of the key local authority of Liverpool; the impact of the confrontational politics of the 1980s; the absence of effective partnership; the lack of public and private civic leadership; the poor internal and external image. Broader threats were also identified in terms of peripherality in a European context and the political instability of the core local authority.

## 2.1 Government strategy

The most damning general criticism of urban policy was made by a local authority interviewee who saw urban policy as being largely irrelevant and insignificant when set against such major decisions as those on the Channel tunnel, airports strategy, R&D and defence contracts; decisions on all of which were seen as favouring other regions. Others made the related and familiar point that the expansion of AfC resources was drowned by cuts in main programmes. In the words of one, the programme 'treats the symptoms not the disease.' RDG has been cut substantially during the decade. Even though it had problems, it nevertheless attracted business. Its wider spatial spread and larger resources were argued to be a better principle than that of AfC. This lack of resources was endorsed by the private sector and conservative business interests in Liverpool. Particular criticism was directed at the resource cuts in the housing field. One senior official in the field emphasised the contrast between Estates Action, HATs and City Challenge resources, on one hand, and cuts in HIP which are creating a future crisis in the city, on the other. A view from an official within the housing associations cited the regional bias of housing resources to the south because of concern with homelessness as opposed to living conditions. A respondent from the voluntary sector equally argued that

AfC been undermined by deterioration in RSG, capital receipt restrictions and especially cuts in social security levels.

There were also some doubts about how aware senior policy-makers were of the impact that AfC as a whole had made on the area. Many of the senior figures in the region were familiar with the main programmes that constitute AfC. But they were not very aware of the rest of the package. In other words, the raft of programmes is clearly not seen as an integrated approach to things urban. While the government might think it has a coherent strategy - not many share that view. This is not surprising, but it underlies more detailed comments made below. One local authority chief executive made the point that AfC was supposed to do what City Challenge is now doing; but this was mere rhetoric. It took Heseltine to return to get strategy implemented. Another local authority interviewee made the point that the EC has a far more integrated policy on economic and social urban issues than does the government which simply has programme initiatives.

Many criticisms were more specific to the area. Few of the discussants believed that the government has a strategy for the Merseyside region. In the words of another local authority chief executive, AfC does not link a clear vision of what the region's future economic and social role might be, to institutional mechanisms and to resources. The Urban Programme, specifically, is resource led. It does not specify what it is trying to achieve. It silts up main budgets. It has no exit strategy.

Another familiar theme was the highly fragmented nature of central government. Again, this is not surprising. But this was identified as the major weakness of government policy in the region by one senior civil servant: 'Urban problems are multi-dimensional - government departments are not.' He cited the CAT as a useful way of integrating departmental activity - that is, it avoids egregious blunders. But there was no mechanism to get a genuinely co-ordinated government approach in the region. Even the three primary economic departments - DoE, DTI, DE - do not share the same strategy. They cannot focus or target in a coherent way. His view, shared by others, was the need for a single regional office. A senior figure in the housing association movement reinforced this by noting the problems faced by differences in approach to voluntary projects. The DTI was singled out by many respondents for its failure to contribute to urban regeneration. One private sector interviewee pointed out that DTI had absolutely no understanding of the needs of corporate customers.

A related point came from a local authority chief executive who argued that central policy was shaped by individual government departments and secretaries of state with individual political agendas. They had no view of the spatial impact of their collective decisions upon the structure of local governance. For example, DES allows Polytechnics or Colleges of Education to incorporate without regard to the impact that this has upon the institutional structures at local level.

A wider very familiar point from the same chief executive was of the institutional fragmentation of local governance. Too many agencies impinged upon the area, but it was not clear that they had the capacity to help the area. This point was endorsed by the regional director of a quango. The proliferation of agencies all trying to help has increased internal communication problems and left too many fingers in the pie.

The same chief executive emphasised the devaluation of local democracy, and the centralisation of power. Local authorities are losing resources and competence. But this eventually prevents them playing the role that central government wishes them to. Local authorities are supposed to generate vision, create partnerships, network and enable; but the capacity to play all of these roles has been removed. This view was endorsed by a senior businessman and a Conservative party member.

City Challenge is however seen by many as a more strategic model; 'the best thing the government has come up with'. There are obvious reservations about it; its competitive nature and its top-slicing. But many senior figures argued that 'what it has got is what previous programmes have lacked'. City Challenge's alleged virtues are the following: it encourages negotiations not confrontation; it forces local authorities to seek partners (the chief executives of two of the local authorities were both surprised at the extent to which it had encouraged their authorities to actively seek partners); it gives community a role; it gives local authorities a role; it has wider goals than physical regeneration and includes social capital; it encourages inter-departmentalism in both central and local government; it makes local authorities link resources to mechanisms, programmes and strategic vision; it encourages a concern with quality rather than expenditure. As one senior civil servant pointed out, it provides a method for giving incentives and rewards to those local authorities who deliver - and sanctions for those who do not. All of such plaudits say something about the implicit and explicit criticisms of AfC since this was taken as the counterpoint to City Challenge.

At the same time, however, there were obvious concerns about City Challenge. Core funding is needed to match the initiative. There needs to be safety net for the losers. It must be matched by bending of main programmes. A wider point was that City Challenge is still demand led. It requires local authorities to find partners, which was not easy. Giving an area City Challenge status will not necessarily make it any more attractive to private sector partners in an area with weak demand. But it will get progressively harder as Marks 2, 3, and 4 tackle even more problematic areas or groups in the city. Will resources eventually run out? Will the continually disappointed give up? Will departments other than DoE offer support? Will main programmes be bent?

The principle of competition to improve quality is one that many endorsed. It clearly extends beyond the Challenge initiative. The chief executive of a major housing association, who obviously benefited from the shift in resources from local authorities to his sector, emphasised the importance of this point. Local authorities should be forced to compete with the best in the housing field. In his view, healthy competition, privatisation, league tables, performance indicators, grant tied to performance are the best ways of increasing the quality of services for tenants. But equally, and more surprisingly, the chief executive of a local authority, who suffered resource cuts, confirmed the value of the principle of competition. Reduced resources and compulsory competitive tendering have allowed him to do on quality control in his local authority what he could not have done without it. A senior officer in Liverpool also confirmed the value of CCT in confronting overmanning. He raised the interesting theme that 'governmental resources are more than money - influence is also important'. But government has not thought enough about ways of using its influence, as well as its resources, to achieve things.

Considerable support was evinced for the need for spatial targeting of resources - it is here where the successes have been. One discussant cited the waterfront and the city centre as achieving results because of this. This principle emerges also in housing. The most commonly cited example of housing success was Estates Action, in which two underlying principles were emphasised: it involved tenants; and it focused and concentrated resources. Task Forces were also supported for this reason; they have a real basis, a specific remit and concentrated resources.

The downside of spatial targeting is the predictable one. Those inside the boundaries do well; those outside do not. In Liverpool the clearest example is the black community which has been excluded from the boundaries of the MDC during the 1980s and from City Challenge in the 1990s. The point was also made by a director of housing that targeting is often used to mask resource cuts. The director of a quango observed that there was no ripple effect from targeted areas, which have remained isolated developments; 'the syndrome of an oasis in the desert'. Equally, spatial targeting can distort local priorities. Again, a housing director emphasised that resources for Estates Action solves the problems of modern council estates, but it has diverted attention and resources from housing of older vintage. Given that such housing constitutes 70% of the housing stock, any decline in investment in the sector is merely storing up a major housing crisis for the future.

## 2.2 Partnership

There was common agreement that weakly developed partnership is one of the problems of Merseyside. There are too many agencies. There is too much local authority rivalry. The partners are not very efficient. A constant theme was the poverty of services offered by the major partner, Liverpool. The private sector is weak - but does not commit even its limited resources. A senior civil servant admitted a weakness of his government's strategy in its failure to get stronger partnership sooner. A senior figure in the financial world argued that the crucial role for government is to provide incentives, through taxation, to get the private sector to play in partnership. The chief executive of one local authority made the point that partners find it difficult to collaborate because of different boundaries, different competences, a lack of interest by some agencies (most obviously the health service). The antagonism of central to local government has weakened partnership and reduced the capacity of the local authorities to be partners.

But equally there was common agreement that most institutions are attempting to address such weaknesses. Local authorities are attempting to collaborate; Liverpool is attempting rationalisation and improvement of services. A Mersey Partnership is slowly emerging. City Challenge is encouraging this process in Birkenhead, Liverpool and Knowsley.

An exception to the picture of doom and gloom is St. Helens. Here, strong partnership and reasonably successful diversification and regeneration has been achieved through the Ravenshead Renaissance. The reasons for such difference were seen as lying in the fact that St. Helens is on the periphery of Merseyside, is a Company town, and is smaller in scale than others of the Merseyside districts.

## 2.3 Failures

A range of general and specific failures of policy were noted. The principal failure was policy's reliance on a market-led strategy. This view was shared by local authority chief executives and senior figures in the private sector who equally argued that government must take a larger lead in the region. The private sector has disengaged and caused the problems; alone, it will not solve the problems. The director of an enterprise agency made the point that government policy is to create enterprise and small business development, but both have historically been weak on Merseyside. A senior figure in the finance sector offered this as his strongest criticism. In his view, the private sector is particularly weak on Merseyside - but it does not even punch the weight that it has got. There is a lack of civic commitment by the private sector. The government must provide them with more incentive to play a part. Specifically, one private-sector respondent wanted to see a virtual doubling of MDC's budget. It was £30m throughout the 1980s; it needs to be boosted to £50m.

Second, was the failure to sustain programmes not just initiate them. Interviewees commented on the succession of initiatives meeting political imperatives which are subsequently abandoned. 'The charitable view is that it is an iterative process; alternatively it can be seen as government by spasm.'

Third was the failure of regional policy in the region and its failure to support manufacturing. This constantly emerged as a primary failing. This was linked with a view of the failure of the DTI to commit resources to urban regeneration. One local government officer argued the need for DTI to be more proactive, the need for it to co-ordinate better the agencies supporting business.

Fourth, was the failure of central priorities to match local needs. Central policies often seek the immediate, the politically visible which local authorities have to pursue.

Fifth was short-termism in programmes. The annuality rule was specifically mentioned by some in local government as preventing strategic approaches to housing. The director of a leading enterprise agency equally saw uncertainty and annual funding as being the major constraints upon his activity.

Sixth was the degree of bureaucratic central controls. One senior local government officer argued that the private sector wants quicker decisions on UP than the central government allows local authorities to make. Others reiterated the point specifically, for example, with respect to DLG rules on Wavertree Technology Park Mark 2, and on controls by the Housing Corporation. All wanted greater freedom to use resources and were willing to be judged on performance.

The most frequently quoted specific failure was the Enterprise Zones. The regional director of one quango made the point that the EZ failed even in comparative terms - on Merseyside it was not marketed well enough, in contrast for example to Swansea.

Another area widely identified as not having succeeded was training. Training schemes do not lead to jobs. Too much training is of low quality. TECs are not adequate to their task, being overly constrained by the civil service culture. They were seen as having confused responsibility for the delivery of training; as having no connections with other regeneration policies.

**2.4 Successes**

Many of the successes on Merseyside are in the housing arena rather than in economic development. This may not be surprising, but is worth stating. Wirral pointed to its five Housing Renewal Areas which do not have extra resources but extra powers encourage a multi-agency approach. Wirral also noted that the juxtaposition of housing association activity with the Safer Cities initiative has maintained and increased property values in some of its schemes. The chief executive of a housing association understandably approved of government focus on housing associations and applauded the move to greater tenant participation. He identified housing co-ops as one of the major successes in the region and specifically cited the Beechwood housing estate which was formerly Ford estate. Here, regeneration started with housing, but progressed to wider activities through the involvement of MTF, the CAT, the local authorities, the Wirral Task Force, Enterprise Agency and the Department of Employment; all of whom began to work together and to do so alongside the local community.

There were familiar criticisms of MDC: it had not achieved enough development; it had not co-operated with adjacent local authorities; it had not done enough for local communities, especially black groups in Toxteth; it had placed too much emphasis on tourism and leisure at the expense of manufacturing. Nevertheless, most interviewees agreed that, comparatively, it has been one of the most successful institutions. It had achieved environmental improvement, flagship projects, high profiles and exploited the tourism and leisure potential of the area.

A number of specific projects were singled out for praise. Wavertree Technology Park, Freeport, Housing Action Areas, Housing Co-operatives, Ravenshead Renaissance (which one discussant claimed to be the model for City Challenge); all received praise, not least on the grounds that they were spatially confined and targeted.

Equally, some institutions received plaudits. The Merseyside Task Force, despite some sniping, is regarded as important. It gives access to central government; it helps to offset the economic and institutional dominance of Manchester.

Perhaps the most striking aspect of our discussions was that, despite the diversity of respondents' backgrounds, much common ground exists throughout the policy community. Indeed, consensus - and the idea of consensus - is one of the dominant features of the region. There is considerable agreement about both problems and solutions and this has helped create and maintain effective policy networks. Almost all interviewees came originally from outside the region yet now feel a strong loyalty and commitment to the North East. And, while recognising its problems, most felt confident that there are grounds for cautious optimism about the area's future.

Interviewees talked in wide-ranging terms of the area's key urban problems and how these might be addressed in terms of broad policy strategies. Respondents also offered views on the impacts of specific policy initiatives, and also the role of the private sector in formulating and implementing policy. The issue of policy targeting was also discussed, with particular reference to notions of 'people-based' and 'place-based' targeting and the specific issue of a regional development agency.

## 3.1 Defining urban problems

Among interviewees there was a widespread feeling that the region's key problem is one of structural change in the economy. While other problems were identified - notably the area's image, crime problems and cuts in public expenditure - these were often seen as secondary in importance to the more fundamental structural problems. Interviewees saw major structural economic changes and their attendant impacts as fundamental to the area's fortunes during the 1980s. They often referred to deindustrialisation and the loss of large-scale manufacturing plants. On Wearside, for example, the closure of the last remaining ship yards at the end of the 1980s was frequently identified as exemplifying the larger process of deindustrialisation. And although the loss of traditional industries has been a feature of the North East for many years, the massive losses during the recession of the early 1980s were seen as especially intense and traumatic.

The implications of these economic changes were noted: unemployment, physical dereliction, poverty, crime and urban unrest were often viewed essentially as flowing from structural change. One widely shared concern was the problem of increasing social polarisation, leaving some marginalised groups trapped in unemployment and poverty. This issue seems to be rising in importance on the local political agenda and has been given greater prominence since the Tyneside riots in September 1991. One civil servant interviewee thus spoke of the need to tackle 'local blackspots' of poverty, as well as dealing with the larger regional structural issues. Some also pointed towards 'cultural' barriers making it difficult for people to respond to changes in the economy, such as lack of enterprise, low educational attainment and insufficient skills. Undoubtedly, there was a widespread concern by many of the institutions to intervene to ameliorate these problems - while at the same time recognising their apparent intractability.

While there was something of a shared feeling that the basic problems remain, there was less agreement about the extent of progress towards resolving them. Some of the more optimistic interviewees pointed towards the growth of new economic activity, the 'pragmatic' adjustment to new economic realities, and an improving image of the region. The area was said to be holding up well in the current recession: unemployment is now 'more of a cyclical than a structural phenomenon', according to one interviewee.

By contrast, some respondents noted that little had changed over the last decade, with unemployment still high and the region once again experiencing recession. Some believed that policy had not addressed - and was not intended to address - structural problems. As one otherwise supportive local government official put it, government programmes like the Urban Programme have amounted to nothing more than 'sticking plaster....a tacit admission that we can't solve the problems of inner areas'. Despite a whole raft of urban initiatives, this respondent felt the region was no further on in terms of remedying the structural deficiencies of the economy.

Policy solutions proffered by interviewees were, in the main, based along the lines of current initiatives and their limitations were acknowledged. Many respondents seemed resigned to what they saw as the intractability of the area's problems. A senior official noted that one of the central aims of the UDC - namely to 'lever' £1b of private investment over a ten year period - was insignificant in comparison to the GDP of the area over a ten year period, which he estimated at £160b. The aims of urban policy, in the eyes of this interviewee, were essentially modest when placed beside the immense scale of the area's problems.

There was a shared sense of the area having undergone fundamental structural change and a belief that this is irreversible. Traditional industries have declined but some new economic activities have been established; many interviewees made particular reference to Nissan and also noted increased property investment. However, in many cases interviewees felt unsure whether these new activities are of sufficient scale and of the right type to resolve what were acknowledged as profound structural problems. But there was widespread recognition that, ultimately, there is little or no alternative to a reliance on market forces in shaping the local economy.

## 3.2 Defining policy solutions

Interviewees talked generally of how policy strategies might address urban problems. First, they discussed the philosophy of public sector intervention in urban areas and how best the role and scope of public intervention might be defined. Second, interviewees offered views on various broad strategies for economic regeneration, most notably inward investment and small business development.

### The role of the public sector in urban regeneration

While most interviewees argued that economic change is largely a result of market forces and that the private sector is central to wealth creation, there was a strong consensus on the relevance and value of public sector intervention. Local authorities, as well as central government, were identified as key 'players' in the policy community. Intervention - through regional policy, urban policy and local economic development initiatives - is a familiar feature of the local landscape, accepted by public and private sector alike. The area's traditional right wing Labourism finds much common ground here with the interventionist Conservatives in the business community.

The public sector's role in the economy is seen mainly as providing, or ensuring the provision of, conditions for economic development. In the case of such organisations as the UDC and English Estates, this means fostering the development of land and property, with the extent of intervention and subsidisation conditioned by the strength of the market. Likewise, the area's local authorities - all of which are active in economic development - offer small business advice services, use planning to zone land, and provide a wide range of infrastructure and services to support the economy. The public sector, with solid private sector encouragement, also works hard at promoting the area, selling a 'positive image' outside the region. Crucially, public sector activities of this sort go largely unchallenged by the business community. Indeed, the creation of a stable and less uncertain environment for business - through, for example, public sector planning and land ownership - is welcomed. As the chief executive of one government agency put it, public sector intervention can 'remove some of the uncertainties from the development process'.

Many interviewees did, however, allude to the constraints on public sector activities. Local authorities complained about spending cuts undermining their ability to solve or ameliorate the area's economic and social problems. Some respondents pointed towards the need for more stability in public sector finance over the long-term. One senior official noted the limitations of a property-led approach to regeneration in times of recession in the property market and felt there is a need to 'commit more resources, even during the bad times [and to]... spend through a recession'. The UDC, he argued, requires substantial funding in the long-term in order 'to regenerate something which has been eighty years in the dying'.

The public sector is constrained not only in terms of resources but also - and this was widely recognised - in relation to its abilities actually to solve economic problems since the economic development process itself is largely the province of the private sector. On the other hand, some interviewees noted the important economic role of the public sector as an employer and thus as an important source of incomes spent in the local economy. In addition, there was a general belief that the public sector has to be responsible for dealing with social problems and issues; the private sector is felt to be neither willing nor competent to address these concerns.

Regeneration strategies

Interviewees outlined a number of potential policy strategies which might contribute towards the area's regeneration. There was a clear recognition that no single strategy can succeed on its own. Many interviewees spoke of the need for a diverse range of strategies for economic regeneration, covering inward investment, small business support, self-employment, and encouraging both manufacturing and service industries.

There was a degree of nervousness about over-reliance on inward investment because of past experience of branch plant closures in the early 1980s. However, inward investment was seen as crucial to the region because a large relocation offers a major boost to job creation much more quickly than a longer-term strategy of promoting indigenous small business. Respondents hoped that more recent relocations to Tyne and Wear would be more permanent owing to the scale of their investment (notably Nissan) and lesser dependence on grants. Some of the newer inward investors - particularly the Japanese - were seen as providing useful models to others in the region and serving to encourage their local suppliers to adopt improved practices. Similarly, inward investment was viewed as having a central role in improving the region's 'image'.

The dangers of external control and the insecurities of the 'branch plant syndrome' were acknowledged, while at the same time most interviewees saw the arrival of Nissan as one of the most important and encouraging events of the 1980s. However, inward investment was regarded by some respondents as essentially a short-term strategy: necessary but limited. In the longer-term, the establishment of indigenous enterprise was felt to be crucial in creating a sustainable economy and fostering what one interviewee called 'provincial regeneration'. The general feeling amongst respondents appeared to be that self-employment and the small business sector had had to be built up from a low base, and this process is now being suitably encouraged through the now considerable support infrastructure for indigenous enterprise in Tyne and Wear which appears to have reached some maturity.

One interviewee supported the existing pattern of support for local enterprise, arguing that the area 'makes the best out of a bad system', with money coming in a 'fairly unstructured way' and 'welded together at the local level' to provide a useful support for small business development. Another was more critical, arguing that complex funding arrangements supporting enterprise initiatives create an 'unbelievable mess'. This, he argued, fostered an 'opportunistic' approach, whereby projects are tailored according to the often conflicting criteria laid down by the various funding regimes. The ideal solution, according to this interviewee, would be for small firm support to be co-ordinated by a single lead department. Similarly, there were calls for a rationalisation of enterprise agencies, although many respondents were unclear about how this could be achieved. Indeed, some interviewees saw it as a virtue: the variety of agencies adds 'flexibility', and 'competition between the diversity of bodies is good and stimulating'.

Like inward investment and indigenous enterprise, a balance between both manufacturing and service industries also has to be encouraged. As one local authority official said, 'there's still a need to diversify, both in manufacturing and services'. Many respondents argued that in a market economy, any choice between manufacturing and service industries inevitably would be artificial. However, one local politician summed-up the general feeling by admitting that he was unsure whether the area could restore its manufacturing base, but felt that the service sector, though expanding, could not be the solution since so much of it is characterised by low pay.

## 3.3 Implementing policy

Interviewees talked in broad terms of the successes and failures of policy and the ways in which the various policy initiatives have evolved over time. In addition, two specific issues of implementation were discussed: first, the extent and nature of public-private partnership and the role of the private sector in policy formulation and delivery; and second, the different conceptions of targeting in policy implementation.

### Constraints on policy implementation

The limited nature of public sector intervention in structural-economic issues was discussed by interviewees in relation to some of the specific policy initiatives of recent years. Several noted the downgrading of **regional policy** during the 1980s. Although most bemoaned the decline of regional policy expenditure, some admitted that traditional regional policy had its drawbacks. Automatic grants on investment, for example, were seen as inefficient and wasteful. Moreover, grants had distorted the relocation process so that, as one put it, some branch plants were set up in the area only to move away 'once the cash flow benefits of those grants had worked their way out of the system'. This respondent was pleased to see more genuine company relocations now that 'we don't offer the same degree of bribes'.

Because of its greater visibility and its spatially concentrated aspect, the **Enterprise Zone** seemed to be regarded with perhaps more enthusiasm. One interviewee pointed out that, contrary to the initial 'free market' rhetoric, the Enterprise Zone had constituted straightforward state subsidisation - particularly important at a time when local authorities were denied resources. Interviewees felt it had been effective in generating or drawing in development and were able to point to the new Vickers plant, Newcastle Business Park, the MetroCentre and the southern section of Team Valley - all located within the Zone and all cases of development attracted to it.

In general, the reaction to the **UDC** was favourable. It was viewed as a valuable source of much needed funding denied to local authorities. Although there had been some initial friction with some local authorities, the UDC was generally regarded as a useful policy vehicle, even if local authorities claim that, given adequate resources, they would have been able to do much the same job. Most interviewees saw the smooth relationship between UDC and exiting institutions in Tyne and Wear as very different from the situation in other parts of the country. Interviewees also noted the benefits of the UDC as a catalyst stimulating development, as an agency able to bring back into the market derelict land and, more strategically, as a way of re-focusing the conurbation on its rivers.

Views on the **Urban Programme** were more mixed; local authorities saw it as important not least because such a significant proportion of capital spending now comes from this source, but several interviewees thought its 'pepper pot' approach gave it a lack of focus and impact. Several were critical of its emphasis on capital, rather than revenue, expenditure, although many local authority respondents pinned the blame for this on wider central government restrictions on local spending. One civil servant concluded that the UP was 'now a bit stale' and certainly, because it has been operating so long, it is now regarded by some rather mundanely as just part of the system of finance. A much broader and critical perception of the UP was given by a local government officer who saw it as an admission that 'we can't solve the problems of inner city areas but that we can make life more bearable'.

One senior local government official commented that it was surprising that, even after ten years of fiscal retrenchment, the Urban Programme had remained pretty much intact. Yet even though the UP continues to support a variety of projects, he argued that the increasingly rigid guidelines mean the programme is more constrained than ever. These constraints, he argued, are all the more severe given the desire of his authority to use UP cash to substitute for cuts to mainstream budgets - ironically, something which the authority had been able to do in the early '80s.

Another official, from the same authority, noted the importance of formal and informal constraints on how authorities make use of the UP. The increasingly inflexible formal rules constrain where and what UP money can be used for. Moreover, these are compounded by the informal constraint posed by the limited ability of authorities to meet future recurring revenue commitments on UP funded projects. In other words, regardless of how well the UP itself is funded, local authorities are constrained by the wider restrictions on local government finance. This official felt this was already resulting in a tendency towards increased short-termism in the UP as one-off projects which incur little or no future revenue expenditure are favoured.

One of the impacts of cuts in local government finance has been the renewed significance of funding from the Urban Programme and City Challenge. A senior officer in one of the smaller authorities noted that the combination of 'residual' UP and City Challenge funding was likely to outmatch the main capital programme during the next financial year. By contrast, an official of a larger authority characterised City Challenge money as 'loose change', with little importance in relation to the scale of mainstream service budgets.

The **City Challenge** initiative was very much a live issue at the time of the interviews, when many respondents were directly involved in preparing bids. Newcastle had successfully bid for City Challenge in the first round, selecting an area in the city's West End, and all five Tyne and Wear authorities have submitted bids this year. While views of the initiative were mixed, the level of support from local government officials was strong, notwithstanding some reservations about the initiative's competitive dimension. Interviewees welcomed the restoration of a stronger role for local authorities previously denied them in the late 1980s. There was also support for the idea of a corporate approach, spatial targeting and a more direct involvement for local communities. However, some interviewees feared that local communities would not be allowed real power and influence and that mechanisms intended to ensure this were weak and underdeveloped. There was some cynicism, too, about the resources involved both because money is 'top sliced' from the UP and also because in some cases this funding has been accompanied (and often exceeded) by cuts in mainstream local authority expenditure.

Nevertheless, local authorities felt obliged to bid for these resources. Several interviewees from the local authorities viewed with distaste the competitive element, preferring allocation based on need; one made the point that competition also raises expectations in a situation where they are more likely than not to be dashed. Another interviewee also pondered the sustainability of a competition based on the quality of bids, feeling that sooner or later the pressure to award City Challenge on the basis of political criteria would prove irresistible.

A few respondents mentioned the need for greater inter-agency **co-ordination**. One civil servant, with wide ranging experience of several government departments, identified the establishment of the City Action Team as one of the key landmarks in the last decade. The general feeling appeared to be that there was (and is) insufficient inter-agency co-ordination, even though the system manages to muddle through quite effectively via existing informal networks.

One interviewee felt that inter-agency co-ordination would be improved considerably by delivering policy to precisely targeted areas, as with City Challenge. A senior local authority planner argued that the money provided by City Challenge was not important in terms of its actual impact on the areas targeted, but in terms of encouraging local authorities to take a more 'corporate' approach by 'dangling big bucks' in front of them. This, he argued, would encourage good practice for future policy. Indeed, the City Challenge approach, he argued, should be extended still further by creating formal bodies designed to target specific areas, and with 'not just a City Challenge bid, but a corporate plan'.

Partnership in policy implementation

Like 'co-ordination', the notion of 'partnership' was accorded virtual consensual support, albeit often in a vague and ill-defined way. Most interviewees felt that public-private partnership in the region is based on a strong, well-developed consensus shared by both the public and private sectors alike. Some mentioned that this consensus was not always present in the past, and was born mainly of the area's problems during the '80s. The attraction of the Nissan plant was often pin-pointed as the key project which brought together a diversity of interests and convincingly demonstrated the value of working together. Equally important in fostering this sense of 'collective togetherness' in the region was the formation of the Northern Development Company - a promotional agency established 'naturally' from within the region, which was successful in drawing together local and central government, business and the trade unions.

Some interviewees commented that the regional consensus relies heavily on a series of intimate, well-developed networks revolving around personal contacts. In turn, this was said to rely upon the geographical cohesiveness of the North East, its single 'capital city' (unlike the North West) and its stable political environment ('less scoring of political points'). There was a sense, too, in which the area settled on a form of political realism or pragmatism in the mid-1980s, especially after the 1987 election, acknowledging even more than before the wisdom of working co-operatively with government and the private sector.

This regional consensus was also attributed to the fact that a limited number of players crop up across a whole series of networks. This coherence is manifest in the density and effectiveness of networks within the policy community. In Tyne and Wear (and within the North East generally) the various institutional 'players' regularly meet; personalities, not structures, it appears, determine and explain how things work. Thus, institutions and personalities come together - often on an ad hoc basis - to respond, for example, to a potential inward investor or to 'stitch together' funding for an initiative. The network of key people driving the system in Tyne and Wear seemed to interviewees to comprise quite a small group. They seek consensus and there are few points of friction between these different players. Through multiple membership of institutions policy makers in the region appear able effectively to 'broker' deals between them.

A particularly striking point to emerge from the interviewees was the extent to which private sector figures appear comfortable with what could be construed essentially as a public sector led consensus. This faith in public-sector - and, in particular, local-authority - solutions appears to contrast with the situation in Manchester, where local authorities are seen more as bit players, secondary in importance to the private sector and central government. Local authorities, according to one Manchester interviewee, are important only insofar as they approve of, and co-operate with, private sector and/or central government led initiatives. Conversely, many in the private sector in the North East identified a more central - and sometimes pivotal - role for local government. This is especially true in terms of social policy and service delivery, which many in the private sector saw exclusively as the responsibility of the public sector. The upshot of all this is that even supposedly business-oriented initiatives such as the Business Leadership Teams have, ironically, become dominated by public sector ideas.

Linked to this public-sector dominance is the narrow range of private sector partners. Private sector involvement is quite limited despite the strenuous efforts to draw in businesses through the creation of various quangos, enterprise agencies and Business Leadership Teams. According to most interviewees, private sector involvement in public policy is confined mainly to a relatively small number of companies, often represented by a few active senior businessmen. Several large multi-national companies have little or no involvement in public policy, in terms either of policy formulation or delivery - perhaps reflecting a general lack of 'civic consciousness' on the part of companies, as one voluntary sector interviewee put it. Moreover, even where private sector business people have become involved, some interviewees were critical of their limited contribution. A number of respondents pointed out that the input of 'active' firms is often limited in scope: and that business interest is not matched by business resources. By contrast, a few companies are very active, with senior managers on the boards of numerous quangos and initiatives. Some interviewees felt that the different responses of companies could be attributed to the degree of enthusiasm of individuals, although others pointed towards the more rigid corporate structure of some of the 'inactive' MNCs. Whatever the explanations, a common view was that too few businesses are involved in policy, even though existing involvement is effective.

A similar concern was expressed about voluntary sector participation. Whereas the general view appeared to be that private-public and central-local relationships have been fairly strong and steady, especially since the mid-'80s, links with the voluntary sector are perceived as working less smoothly. One interviewee commented that the high level, tight knit networks were good at delivering the 'big deals', but were less good at delivering projects and help to the local community level. One voluntary sector figure felt the position of the various voluntary and community groups would be exacerbated still further with what she saw as the likely demise of the UP and its gradual replacement by City Challenge. This respondent thought that the much criticised 'pepper-pot' spread of UP money was a valuable - and highly flexible - source of 'seed corn' funding for a whole range of voluntary organisations which otherwise might not exist.

In general, then, respondents were impressed by how smoothly the informal networks of key players operates. There was, however, the broader criticism that while the region possesses an 'extraordinary good officer class at chief executive level', there is a general lack of visionary leadership. The lack of powerful political leadership, it was argued, has left the area operating efficiently, if mundanely, in policy terms, but lacking any clear vision for the future.

## 3.4 Targeting in policy implementation
### Places and people

The bulk of interviewees felt that the focus of policy has been predominantly to target particular places. However the selection of places changes in response to shifting priorities, as exemplified by the recent designation of greenfield industrial sites in the draft UDP for Newcastle. Conversely, there appeared to be a fairly widespread acceptance (although some interviewees were more enthusiastic) that 'letting the market decide' inevitably entailed a focus on greenfield locations.

One respondent argued that the geographical focus of policy is now rotating more amongst areas. With the growth of 'corporate' approaches targeting precisely defined areas - as in City Challenge - he felt that a greater number of small areas were likely to be targeted, each for a short period of time.

Many interviewees pointed towards a shift from place-based to people-based targeting - or at least a coupling of the two. According to one TEC official, this shift is evidenced by Action for Cities' 4 'E's - employment, enterprise, environment and, significantly, employability. Some interviewees argued that recent events (the riots at Meadow Well being the most obvious example) had hardened the increasing realisation that regeneration must be linked positively to people, in contrast to the conventional policy-makers' view that regeneration by itself automatically benefits people. One interviewee argued that the increasing focus on employability and training is a belated reflection of the growth of service and office based employment, which, even at the lowest grades, require basic literacy and numeracy skills which were of less importance in manufacturing industry.

While much public policy is focused on places, increasing concern about marginalised groups has been leading to a new emphasis on 'outreach' initiatives to deliver public policy to particular groups and communities, notably on deprived estates. Several interviewees had become sensitised to the difficult issues involved. One spoke of the need to initiate programmes to 'help people with no prospect of finding work', and identified the need for 'missionary' work to bring services like Jobcentres to people on the estates; another talked of the need to rebuild the individual's confidence, likening the search for ways out of long-term unemployment to 'retirement in reverse'. There seems to be agreement that both spatial targeting and a 'people-based' approach are highly relevant.

Some interviewees agreed that there is also the potential for conflict between places which have been targeted. Sunderland's strategy of attracting inward investment and marketing the city as the 'Advanced Manufacturing Centre of the North' could come into conflict with the designation of greenfield industrial sites in Newcastle's draft UDP. Equally, though, Sunderland's emphasis on inward investment and manufacturing was seen by some interviewees as complementing Newcastle's dominance in financial and commercial services. One prominent businessman argued that from a regional perspective, any such 'conflict' would be better interpreted as offering 'choice' to potential inward investors.

One respondent felt that conflict between places could also prove problematic at borough level as the various interest groups within each district make demands for funding. This has been a classic problem under the Urban Programme and it was felt by a senior civil servant that this problem could also undermine City Challenge. This was thought to be a particular danger in South Tyneside, where the City Challenge bid covers a wide area of the district. This is partly as a response to the wide distribution of high levels of unemployment throughout the borough, but also arguably a reflection of the competing demands made by the six Area Advisory Committees, which comprise local councillors, and which can each bid for UP cash.

**3.5 Regional intervention**

One way of resolving some of these geographical conflicts would be through some form of regional development agency. A number of interviewees argued that the defunct county council was reasonably successful in fulfilling this role, and in presenting a powerful single case for resources from central government. At the same time, however, it has been argued that the county council was an inappropriate vehicle for resolving any conflicts between two distinct parts of the conurbation - Tyne & Wear exists as nothing more than a postcode, as one interviewee put it.

This ambiguity over the need for a regional perspective on regeneration was mirrored through some respondents' support for existing regional bodies. The NDC, it was argued, already takes a regional view of inward investment, while English Estates likewise co-ordinates a regional property and land portfolio. Contrary to the usual argument that the regional dimension of policy has been neglected over the past decade or so, one interviewee noted that there is already a well-developed infrastructure of often inter-locking regional bodies of this type. They range though government departments' regional offices to regional quangos and ad hoc regional bodies like NDC.

Interviewees identified the status of Newcastle as a major impediment to the establishment of any formal regional agency. Some felt that the city possesses neither the financial nor political strength to dominate the wider region and emerge clearly as the 'unchallenged regional capital'. This situation was contrasted with the dominance of Birmingham in the West Midlands and the supposed strength of Manchester in the North West. What this illustrates is that while there appeared to be a consensus that some form of regional-level intervention is desirable, it is altogether less clear precisely what 'regional' should mean. Although it was generally agreed that regional co-ordination already works pretty well, there was some disagreement about whether this could be made to work better still. On one hand, there was the view that formal multi-purpose regional institutions - at whatever spatial scale - would undermine the existing informal network of organisations. Some argued that without a real devolution of budgets to the region - which many viewed as unlikely - regional institutions would constitute little more than a 'talking shop'. There was also considerable uncertainty about the precise spatial focus of any such agency; should the focus be region-wide (North or North East) or sub-regional (Tyne & Wear)?

Conversely, some interviewees took the view that existing regional institutions already constitute something of an embryonic regional agency which could easily evolve into something more formal. The general feeling, however, seemed to be that existing institutions such as the CAT and NDC already fulfilled the need for a limited degree of co-ordination. As one civil servant put it, existing institutions already 'work to the same game plan'.

Taking more of a middle way was the chief executive of a government agency, who advocated a regional plan which could ensure that the various existing regional bodies pull in the same direction, but without leading towards the cumbersome bureaucracy of a regional development agency. By contrast, another senior official of a government agency argued that the formulation of any such 'holistic' regional plan would prove impracticable because there could never be any firm agreement amongst local authorities over the plan's content. The result would be that any plan 'would never catch up with the market'.

Interestingly, many interviewees felt that regional intervention, whether within the existing framework or through a new development agency, would be undermined by any accountability to a regional assembly. Some interviewees, however, did suggest that the existing Northern Regional Councils Association might evolve into just such an assembly, unlikely though this may seem following the General Election.

One of the reasons for the demand for increased regional powers is the feeling that the North East is at a disadvantage in competing with the former Scottish Development Agency (now Scottish Enterprise) and the Welsh Development Agency. The latter, for example, was seen as having more effective powers in attracting inward investment because it offers a 'one stop shop' - in contrast to the plethora of agencies in the North East. Some interviewees felt that further devolved powers for Scotland would leave the North East in an ever weaker position, particularly in the context of competing regions within Europe.

# 4 FUTURE NEEDS

A summary of views on the needs for the future would include the following:

- There is not a great deal of optimism about the future of inner areas.

- There is need for a more strategic approach to the areas at national and local level.

- There is a need for regional agencies: at its weakest, this view supports the need for an integrated regional office of government or for some form of federation of the multiplicity of existing agencies; at its strongest it argues the need for regional development agencies.

- There is need for a better fit between urban and regional industrial policy; such a development was seen as more likely given the recent move of Mr Heseltine to DTI.

- There is a need for a more integrated approach to training, economic development and physical regeneration.

- There is a need for a more coherent private-sector contribution to regeneration: this would include tax incentives for the sector to play a more active part and stronger chambers of commerce on the German model.

- There is a need to face European threats and opportunities more systematically.

- There is a need for longer-term planning and longer-term funding.

- There is a need for more flexibility on central grant regimes.

- There is a need for further substantial flagship projects.

- There is a need for a greater focus on the losers - the marginal social groups and the excluded areas - and this calls for a better linkage between regeneration and the excluded.

- There is a need to build on the promise inherent in the City Challenge principles which offer valuable new ways of developing and implementing renewal if commitment to the programme and resources is maintained.

- There is a need for greater local input to national strategies to avoid distortion of local policy priorities.

- There is a need for greater flexibility in the national regulation of resource deployment locally.

- There is a need for better monitoring of the collective impact of national programmes upon local authorities and region.

- There is a need to increase local capacity to sustain government initiatives.

- There is a need to recognise the revenue implications of capital programmes.

*Appendix H*     Summary of recommendations from the feasibility study

Phase I of the project investigated the feasibility of developing methods of evaluating the impact of the overall urban policy of central government. It was from this work that the research design of the evaluation was developed. Most, but not all, of the recommended approaches were incorporated into the final study. The programme of work of the Feasibility Study was divided into a series of inter-related blocks of work (Figure H1) which addressed the following six main questions:

*Figure H1*   **Design of feasibility study**

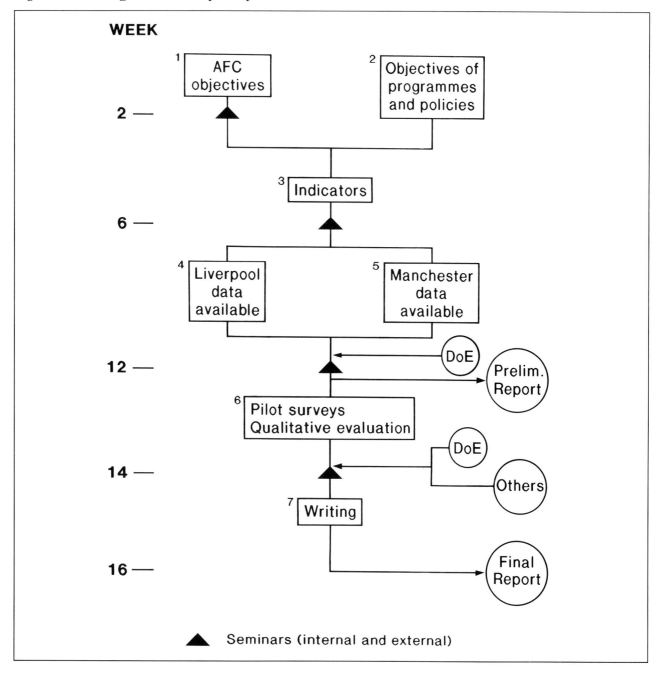

431

# 1 HOW CAN ONE SPECIFY THE PRINCIPAL AIMS UNDERLYING THE GOVERNMENT'S APPROACH TO URBAN POLICY?

To explore this, a national audit was used, holding a series of interviews with senior officers in central government departments to determine the formal objectives used by departments for elements of urban policy and to explore what kinds of impact assessment are used by those departments and what are the perceived shortcomings and lessons which might be learned from such assessment. These interviews covered 30 of the 33 programmes listed in Action for Cities. Four issues emerged from these discussions:

## 1.1 How well AfC represents 'urban policy'

AfC was initially put together through joint departmental discussions about their policy contributions to inner-city revival. The precise contribution of programmes is inevitably somewhat arbitrary. The AfC package included; national programmes which by default were delivered to inner cities, specific targeted inner city programmes, and selective area programmes which were substantially geared toward inner cities. That the same programmes should not continue to constitute the overall inner city package is unsurprising: in an experiment-dominated policy area, it is inevitable that some programmes should lapse whilst new ones appear. This makes future-orientated impact research problematic. The potential difficulties are exacerbated however by the lack of any obvious rationale behind the inclusion of some programmes within AfC and the exclusion of others. The current make-up of AfC suggests, for example, that the DES's main contribution to the inner cities is through City Technology Colleges whilst ignoring both the massively more substantial impact of the new educational reforms and the efforts made by the department to bend its main programmes toward inner cities. Likewise it is difficult to appreciate the logic of including the DTp's TSG programme within the UPAs whilst excluding all of the HIP expenditure (except for the targeted Estate Action resources), particularly when improvements in housing quality are stressed more directly than transport issues in AfC objectives. It is difficult to design impact analysis measures for a set of policy objectives which lack any neat identity with the programmes serving them, and when the programmes themselves lack any internal logic and are peculiarly subject to change or termination.

## 1.2 The varying definition of the 'inner city'

Put simply, there is no commonality across AfC programmes on the definition of the inner city or the degree to which policy instruments target inner city areas. Departmental definitions of the inner city tend on the whole to utilise the 57 Urban Programme-designated local authority areas; in other words, the entire administrative boundary of the designated local authorities rather than the smaller inner area laid down in regulations which, in some but not all cases, serves to channel the use of Urban Programme expenditures. Adoption of the larger, rather than the constricted, area definition of the inner city means, for example, that a relatively affluent area such as Dulwich would fall under the inner city definition simply because it lies within the London Borough of Southwark which merits UP-designation because of the problems suffered in Peckham and Bermondsey.

The relation of AfC programmes to the 57 UPAs also varies enormously. A small number operate only in the 57 (although some which were promoted heavily as inner city programmes fall outside in some cases - UDCs and CTCs being cases in point). Others operate in the 57 because they are national programmes and may or may not make special efforts to ensure that the programmes are tailored to an inner city context, however understood. Further programmes tend to benefit inner cities partially and co-incidentally because they treat particular types of problems or target groups that are found in inner cities - an example would be the Race Relations Employment Advisory Service. Others lag much further behind in recognising the 'inner city' as a spatial unit or an interconnected set of conditions. The use of the 57 UP cities as a proxy for inner cities is mainly limited to accountancy procedures: programme expenditures in the 57 (often estimated rather than known) are 'claimed' as inner city-related even though they may not cover all of the issues generally felt to be important within inner cities.

## 1.3 How the objectives of policy are defined and delivered on the ground

Two issues arose in considering how objectives are determined: first, the adequacy of objectives attached to programmes at the national level for operational purposes and for deriving specific indicators of performance; and second, the need to balance this with flexibility in local programme formulation and delivery. Clearly, central departmental officials have, in recent years, become much more involved in the detail of local programme delivery as both overseers and direct implementors. The structural logic of government remains dominated by the notion that a central policy framework is translated into consistent but sensitive local action by local agencies. Hence there remains a need for good understanding of programme purposes between national and local levels if there is to be a good flow of information between the two on what the programmes are achieving. AfC programmes have acquired their national objectives in many different ways. Some adopt relevant passages from the legislation directly; others arrive at post-hoc rationalisations of previous practice. At worst, objectives are absent until consultancy studies or reviews are put in place and they have to be imputed for any sensible judgement to be made.    Overall, there is a variance between:

- the existence, quality and feasibility of operationalising national objectives;

- the degree to which lower-level, more operational objectives are required of implementing agencies; and

- the seriousness with which the objectives of ii) are used and linked to particular programme outputs.

All three points have implications for the information base available for impact studies.

## 1.4 The extent to which departments evaluate their success in meeting policy objectives

There is a huge variation in the range and quality of data routinely kept by or readily available to central departments on AfC programmes, reflecting the adequacy of objective-setting, different management systems, and a range of department-delivery agency relationships. Whilst accepting that much of the data necessarily refer to programme management - that is, to the use of agreed levels of resource for more or less specified purposes - such variance in monitoring systems has significance for wider impact assessment. At the 'good practice' end of the monitoring continuum, would be a stable programme which had clearly specified national objectives, a range of lower-level operational objectives to which particular indicators of performance would be attached, a pattern of close working relationships between departmental sponsor and programme deliverers, and a computerised monitoring system which, at the lowest feasible level of generality - usually the project, could identify the following: programme inputs (staff and finance); direct outputs across the whole range of the programme; and some estimate of indirect outputs, that is to say positive and negative spin-off effects. Outputs would be disaggregable to the lowest geographical unit - address or grid reference - and across all categories: of intermediate or final beneficiary type of firm, by size and sector; of individuals, by gender, ethnic group, level of disability, age, etc. At the other end of the spectrum would be a programme in which all of the above were absent.

In practice, of course, the two ends of the continuum do not exist, but most positions in between do. To the extent that there is a trend, it is that more recent programmes take output measures and monitoring procedures more seriously and have had better systems in place from the beginning. Other programmes have developed them as a result of internal or external reviews, whilst some still have a long way to go. One promising development is for the preparation, at the beginning of a programme's life, of base-line studies, generated through existing data sources and special surveys. This, for example, was partly true of the later UDCs and has been true of City Challenge. When combined with good operational objectives, a set of performance indicators and a commitment to review at regular intervals, such a tool can provide a critical basis for impact assessment and will remove the need for expensive and time-consuming retrospective research.

Variations across programmes which make the aggregation of programme-specific data sources difficult include: different start dates for particular data-sets - particularly the date on which computerisation took place (if at all); different frequencies of data-collection; and, most importantly, different levels of disaggregation. Whilst some programmes can in principle get down to ward if not even address or grid reference level, others find it difficult to manipulate their data sets to give an accurate picture at a geographical level lower than the region. A final obvious point is that data systems, however sophisticated in design, are never any better than their respondents and there exists a whole host of reasons as to why the latter are sometimes less than fulsome in their responses.

Even those programme managers/monitorers who presided over a monitoring system which approximated to our 'good practice' model were firm in their conviction that departments were not capable of carrying out impact studies. This was for reasons of limited skill, time and resources, or objectivity. Opinions varied as to the role of implementing agencies in impact assessment. Some departmental managers felt that they could serve their programming and resource-attracting purposes better by providing more critical evidence than was included on standard monitoring forms. Others were wary of the possible lack of impartiality. A general consensus was apparent for the use of external agencies (usually consultants, but sometimes 'disinterested' wings of government) for impact assessment purposes, although the degree of support to be provided for such a process through departmental monitoring procedures varied both in theory and in practice.

## 2 WHAT INDICATORS MIGHT BE MOST APPROPRIATE IN ASSESSING THE ACHIEVEMENT OF POLICY INPUTS?

**2.1 Policy objectives**

Our scrutiny of the published aims of urban policy, together with the results of the National audit, produced an extensive list of over 100 avowed objectives. Our consideration of the overlaps between them led us subsequently to refine them into ten lower-level stated objectives of government policy which, in turn, were collapsed into a shorter summary list of two high-level objectives. The lower-level comprised:

- Enterprise development;

- Sites for economic development;

- Skills development;

- Motivation to work;

- Inter-agency co-ordination;

- Access to employment and services;

- Housing development;

- Built environment;

- Social fabric; and

- Safety and security.

The higher-level objectives were in turn constructed from an examination of the ten lower-level objectives to produce two generalised objectives:

- the creation of employment opportunities; and

- the creation of cities which are more attractive places in which to live.

Given the overlaps between the lower-level objectives, it is inevitable that any impact assessment will be forced to use combinations of objectives rather than specifically test on the basis of one-to-one relationships between individual objectives and individual indicators.

**2.2 Indicators**

Despite the difficulties of assessment, four factors helped to guide our approach to the selection of indicators:

i) most of the policy objectives have a focus on an essentially spatial view of the working of urban policy. This suggests the appropriateness of using a geographical approach to our analysis (using aggregative spatial data rather than data for categories of individuals);

ii) the central requirement of impact evaluation is to identify measures of outcome rather than input or output. It is more important to know what substantive changes have occurred to employment or to the attractiveness of cities, than to know how much has been spent on environmental improvement or how many new houses have been built;

iii) any evaluation will need to focus on measures which are readily available at both the spatial scales and the temporal frequencies which might make evaluation practicable, even though this will force us to adopt imperfect and crude measures. There is therefore an inevitable compromise between what might be ideal and what is available; and

iv) it is inevitable that one will have to use general indicators rather than ones which claim to be highly specific to one or another objective. This is a result of the high degree of overlap between the aims of different policy instruments which means that any element of social and economic change will be affected by the inputs from a variety of policy instruments.

These points led us to consider a large range of potential evaluative measures and from them to select five indicators. Many others which we considered were rejected principally for one of three reasons: they were measures of input or output rather than of outcomes; their relationship to the objectives of policy were too ambiguous; or data were not available at appropriate scales or at the necessary sequential time intervals. The five indicators are far from perfect; nor would we claim that they provide a comprehensive overview of the impacts of policy. Nevertheless, in conjunction with the 'contextual' variables which are suggested as part of the quantitative interpretation of policy impact, they do offer valuable indicators of subsets of the ten stated policy objectives. The first three fall within the first higher-level objective; the remaining two within the second higher-level objective:

- Changes in unemployment and long-term unemployment 1983-90, which addresses policy objectives 1, 2, 4 and 6;

- Net job changes 1981-87, which addresses policy objectives 1, 2, 3, 4 and 6;

- Percentage change in the number of small businesses 1981-90, which addresses policy objectives 1, 2, 4 and 5;

- House price changes 1983-90, which addresses policy objectives 2, 6, 7, 8, 9 and 10; and

- Net change in the number/proportion of 25-34 year-olds 1981-91, which addresses policy objectives 1,7,8,9 and 10.

# 3 HOW AVAILABLE AND ACCESSIBLE ARE THE DATA NEEDED TO MEASURE SUCH INDICATORS?

The availability of data to measure changes was studied through two local audits. These involved a series of interviews and discussions held with local agencies in Liverpool and Manchester, covering national and local government bodies, non-government or quasi-government organisations, and private-sector agencies. The aim was to explore the nature of local data holdings and to investigate the degree to which evaluation is undertaken by agencies at a local level and the problems which prevent such assessment. Here, we highlight some of the difficulties which emerged from our investigation.

## 3.1 The lack of local evaluation

Despite the fact that Liverpool has probably seen more urban policy experimentation over the last two decades than any other urban area and that Manchester has been a recipient of most of the urban policy instruments, there is a marked absence of evaluation work carried out locally, especially relating to the collective impact of different policies and programmes. The audit exercise revealed that this can be explained by a variety of reasons:

- methodological difficulties. The problems of evaluation identified from our reading of previous work have been confirmed by numerous agencies as making assessment difficult especially given the lack of resources with which they are usually faced.

- organisational priorities. The emphasis of many agencies upon achievement tends to result in narrow monitoring of programme outputs rather than outcomes which deal with gross rather than net effects. Many local arms of government carry out relatively little data analysis themselves but rather pass information to their respective headquarters for collation and review. Certain governmental organisations do not even possess a designated information officer. Impact assessment seems to lie at some distance from policy formulation and, at least at the local level, does not always seem to be integral to the policy process. There was evidence to suggest that additional local involvement of agencies in devising the exact form monitoring takes may well improve programme delivery especially if they possess appropriately qualified staff and the necessary resources.

- narrowness of remit. Many organisations have quite narrow objectives and are therefore not obliged to take into account wider effects or distributional and dispacement issues (e.g. English Estates, Development Corporations). The narrowness of objectives is compounded by Treasury rules which encourage assessment of specific programmes and the achievement of specifically defined financial guidelines; even where the agencies themselves may be alive to the importance of the wider implications of specific programmes. Occasionally, in the case of initiatives that are both a catalyst and demonstration vehicle (eg. Business Growth Training), some attempt is made at gauging wider effects such as the economic performance of the firms involved and the knock on effects (e.g. promotion of good practice etc.) on other firms. This, however, is unusual.

- volume of operational performance data. Many agencies are sufficiently pre-occupied with completing comprehensive monitoring forms from Whitehall reflecting financial performance and the need for general accountability for public use of money. Some organisations did suggest that procedures could be simplified. Monitoring systems seem to be better at justifying money spent rather than revealing the broader impact of policies; again this emphasises some of the limitations produced by Treasury rules.

- lack of baseline information. With a few exceptions, (eg. Estate Action, the Development Corporations) most initiatives cannot accurately be evaluated because of a lack of information on the pre-policy situation. Furthermore, the additionality of many initiatives is difficult to establish because non-policy locations have not been monitored (e.g. Estate Action, Compacts).

- tenuous links between programme deliverers and AfC. Data are rarely collected by individual agencies with broader goals in mind e.g. AfC aims. Apart from the reasons already specified, agencies often remarked that they had not had much involvement in the formulation of the AfC package and felt it lay at some distance from their immediate operational concerns. However, in practice the presence of the CATs, MTF and local Task Forces has encouraged an increasing amount of joint action between agencies which seems to achieve a number of AfC's aims quite effectively. A prime Liverpool example is the involvement of the CAT and the Granby Task Force in stimulating joint projects between housing associations, the Training Agency, local authorities and community groups which combine housing and environmental programmes and the provision of training opportunities for local residents in Speke and Granby.

- frequency of policy change. Costly evaluation exercises have often been viewed as unjustifiable within a highly unstable policy environment. Reasons include frequent policy experimentation by central government and vicissitudes in local political control and consequently policy making.

- emphasis upon strategic information. Certain agencies have commissioned research in order to guide their forward planning rather than explicitly evaluate previous initiatives. Whilst some studies have produced useful data (e.g. Merseyside Enterprise Board commissioned reports on the local clothing and food industries etc.) this prospective approach can lead to rather uneven data coverage.

- lack of longitudinal data. Especially with training programmes, the central requirement of evaluation is for longitudinal data to 'track' the development and subsequent careers of the beneficiaries of programmes. The absence of such data - and the cost of collecting appropriate information - makes it difficult for relevant agencies to contemplate genuine evaluation of outcomes.

- lack of independent local watchdogs. As most agencies are understandably pre-occupied with their own internal performance, an independent organisation charged with taking an overview of the collective local impact of government policy might be the only means of establishing broad outcomes rather than measuring individual outputs. No such organisation exists. The local authority partially fulfils this role, but could not claim full impartiality and its intelligence functions suffer from fragmentation and being under-resourced. The major Liverpool data processing agency in this sphere, Merseyside Information Service, specialises in survey design and data analysis; the Manchester equivalent, Greater Manchester Research and Information Policy Unit, specialises in comparable data analysis. The client organisations of both agencies are relied upon to supply hard data and to draw policy implications from their survey work. With the demise of the two metropolitan councils there is no organisation well placed to look at the joint impact of various expenditure programmmes at a regional level - a task formerly carried out quite effectively by the regional planning boards in the 1960s and 1970s.

## 3.2 Data problems

With one or two exceptions (e.g. Small Firms Service) there was a marked absence of information on recipients' views of government initiatives and programmes. Related to this, most agencies demonstrate an understandable preference for quantifiable, hard information rather than softer, qualitative data which may be equally important, if more difficult to specify and use as a basis for drawing conclusions.

Much monitoring is client based. This can have important consequences for programme monitoring. In some cases, spatial analysis of impact does not receive the same priority. In others, follow-up information on firms and individuals no longer in receipt of varying forms of assistance is lacking, raising questions about the permanency of benefits and the value for money of many initiatives in the longer term. On the other hand, such monitoring can be difficult, costly and extensive particularly where programmes emphasise maximisation of throughput (e.g. major government training programmes).

Historical data relating to individual programmes are uneven and at best partially computerised. Longitudinal data which relates to policy areas are generally less comprehensive and less frequently updated (e.g. ACE, Census of Distribution, DOE floorspace statistics). However, much data are now presented in a more useful form due to computerisation (e.g. JUVOS) and the volume and quality of information on some policy topics is set to improve in future (e.g. local housing conditions).

Data held by government departments are often not available on the same spatial basis. Administrative boundaries vary and only some government agencies specifically relate their policies to the Urban Programme areas. Often it is not possible to compare the impact of programmes on specific areas because postcoding of information is not standard practice.

Information produced by individual organisations is often affected by their policy procedures and the broader context (e.g. the use and take-up of training facilities are affected by government Social Security legislation and forthcoming changes in training organisations' access policies associated with TECs and changes in funding regimes).

Agency interdependency also affects the collection and availability of data. Although many agencies assembled their own data there is inevitably considerable interchange of data. Certain organisations (e.g. Task Forces) are heavily reliant upon other government agencies and produce little data themselves. Government departments also draw heavily upon information collected by local government and other local organisations because in a number of spheres (e.g. housing, tourism) government information is not good below a regional level. At present there are no special mechanisms for ensuring that quality data exchange occurs. An obvious implication for the future is that it should be imperative that central and local government and other agencies act in partnership and that the importance of each agency's role is recognised by appropriate allocation of resources.

Analysis of local data resources by topic revealed marked variation in the quality and amount of data. For instance, housing information is relatively good and improving, whilst information on the local skills base and skill shortages and the stock of varying kinds of land and premises is relatively poor. Data on business confidence and investment, which has traditionally been poor, is improving and will continue to do so (Merseyside Business Survey, Merseyside Economic Bulletin, Merseyside Image Campaign monitoring, MDC, CMDC and TDC commissioned surveys, GMRIPU Bulletins and Occasional Papers, Manchester Chamber of Commerce quarterly business surveys, TEC monitoring proposals, proposed monitoring of City Grant equivalent by English Estates).

# 4 HOW MIGHT ASSESSMENT BEST BE INCORPORATED FORMALLY INTO FUTURE POLICY?

The national and local audits suggested some of the difficulties of evaluating policy which arise from the nature of policy formulation and from the nature of existing data. Our subsequent exploration of ways of developing retrospective evaluation recognised some of the very considerable difficulties of looking back at what has or has not been achieved by urban policy. It is not simply that data are not always available to measure impacts, but that the aims of policy are frequently ambiguous and that evaluation itself is an exercise fraught with great conceptual problems. The importance of assessing the effects of policy has increasingly been recognised by government. One aspect of this is doubtless the argument about value for money; another must be concern about the direction in which policy is or is not steering urban areas. If evaluation is now more centrally on the agenda, government is presented with an opportunity for a fresh start which might make it easier to develop more robust approaches to the assessment of future impacts.

Our starting point would be that, if assessment is important (as we think it is and as we assume the Department thinks it to be) then future policy ought consciously to incorporate evaluation and assessment. This could be translated into a recommendation that, on the model of Environmental Impact Assessment, future policy and future programmes should formally be required to embody statements about their intended aims and anticipated effects and that this should accompany a parallel move to ensure the identification and provision of information through which monitoring can be effected. It should be a requirement of future major programmes with a spatial dimension to their remit; that they formulate their objectives clearly and identify the outcomes at which they are aimed, that they incorporate baseline data on the existing state of relevant areas (and possibly of control areas too), that they maintain records of the incidence of financial inputs on a spatially disaggregated basis and that they make provision for regular monitoring of changes over time. Such practice (which would clearly involve additional costs) would help to ensure that future evaluation of outcomes would be more securely based and would present fewer difficulties than are currently faced in making retrospective evaluation.

There are also specific issues connected with the collection and flow of data. It would be important that the interdependence of agencies is recognised and reflected in the development of mechanisms to encourage the exchange of quality data. It is therefore imperative that central and local government and other agencies act in partnership and that the importance of each agency's role is recognised by appropriate allocation of resources. Some fields in which there are good-quality data available could benefit from the establishment of national data-collection guidelines so that data could be produced in a form which permitted both intra- and inter-urban analysis. Ongoing evaluation of such a wide ranging programme as AfC may eventually require a national information strategy to which a number of governmental and non-governmental agencies could work. The local audit revealed countless examples of surveys being undertaken which, in a slightly revised form, would have provided the base line for a series of government programmes. In resource terms, joint working makes sense. Indeed, given the interdependence of so many areas of policy, there must be strong arguments for the development of regionally-based corporate strategies.

We considered a variety of approaches to quantitative modelling. In particular, we explored the feasibility of adapting the new technique of multi-level modelling to investigate the relationships between urban policy inputs and socio-economic change in cities. This involved importing and modifying the relevant software from the London Institute of Education and developing a conceptual framework for using the technique in the innovative context of assessing urban policy (rather than educational performance, for which the technique was devised).

In assessing the relationship between the inputs and the outcomes of policy, the most obvious statistical technique is the use of multiple regression analysis since this assesses the relationship between dependent and independent variables. As a technique, regression analysis has the advantage of being well understood and widely used. It suffers, however, from a, by now, well known range of technical limitations; including the problems associated with the inter-dependence of spatial data. Consequently, we explored the potential of using multi-level modelling. We were attracted to this technique not because it offered a seductive and shiny new tool, but because it appeared to address at least some of the problems of making retrospective impact evaluations using imperfect data of the sort which we have outlined. The technique was developed in the educational field where robust quantitative data have long been collected on the performance of different groups which 'nest' into each other; individuals, school classes and whole schools. This 'nesting' makes it possible to use explanatory variables at a variety of 'levels' or scales. Multi-level modelling approaches the analysis of data through 'nesting' finer spatial scales within coarser scales (e.g. wards nested within local authority areas) and thereby can explore the way in which relationships between variables can differ from one scale to another.

Much of our exploration of the technique involved us in trying to translate its approach into the very different context of a more diffuse set of objectives and a less tractable set of 'levels'. The requirements of an evaluation model are:

- to incorporate areas which have received varying amounts of policy input so that differential change in a chosen outcome indicator can partly be 'accounted for' by differences in input;

- to disentangle the effects of policy from those of other processes;

- to take account of the prior conditions or prior states of areas at the start of the period during which the relevant policy has been operating;

- to take account of the effects of other government policies that are not ostensibly inner-area focused;

- to handle relatively large quantities of data, either for a large number of areas within a few cities or for a large number of cities;

- and, perhaps most importantly, to take account of the hierarchical nature of spatial data and the likelihood of intra-group relationships through the nesting of small areas within larger spatial units.

This final point is of importance. Evaluation demands a model which produces conservative estimates of the degree of statistical 'explanation' of the relationship between inputs and outcomes. This is critical in a situation in which policy is likely to explain only a small part of the overall variance amongst the data. Conservative estimates of the effect of variables, including policy, will produce a much more powerful argument for the impact of policy where it is found to exist.

Multi-level modelling appeared to meet all of these requirements. It can be used to interpret the relationship between a set of inputs (which can include the prior states of areas) and a set of outcomes over a period of time and to do this at a number of spatial scales or levels. Its particular attraction is that it takes some account of the inter-dependence of spatial data by allowing the data to be grouped and nested, currently at three levels. This nesting has a number of distinct advantages. It would permit the variation in any indicator to be decomposed into that due to differences between wards, sub-areas such as inner-city/non-inner-city areas, and whole districts. It also means that the effects of policy inputs can be incorporated at a variety of scales (for example, the variation in outcomes at a ward level could be accounted for by variations in the inputs at the larger scale of sub-areas). Furthermore, explanatory variables included at higher levels may be treated as aggregates of variables that are available for lower scales, thereby producing contextual variables for the area as a whole (e.g. net job change and net migration change could be used at the local authority scale as contextual variables). Prior states can be included at all scales. Finally, the analysis of residuals can allow the regrouping of wards so that a better demarcation of inner areas may be made for particular cities.

For the purposes of using the technique to assess urban policy the three levels appropriate for a ward-scale analysis would be the ward, groupings of wards which comprise inner-city and non-inner-city areas, and whole local authority districts. For a district-scale analysis, the three appropriate levels would be local authorities, conurbations and regions. The data used in the model can be thought of in three categories: inputs, prior states and outcomes. Input variables could either be continuous data (such as amounts of resource channelled to various of the urban priority areas) or dichotomous data (such as whether an area has or has not received support under the Safer Cities programme or whether an area has or has not had a UDC). The input variables would also include, in addition to government urban policy, the inputs of other programmes (for example, local authority activity) in order to take into account the wider context in which urban policy needs to be assessed. Prior state variables would include descriptors of the occupational composition of an area, levels of unemployment, etc. Outcome variables would be the changes in the five indicators discussed above.

Sequences of runs of the model could be used to address the following questions:

- what amount of variation in outcomes is explained at the three levels by government policy?;

- what is the direction of the relationship between the indicator variables and government policy inputs?; and

- what is the amount of change in the indicator produced by a given input of government policy at the three levels?

It may also be used to test whether the relationships between an indicator and policy differ for different sub-areas, conurbations or regions. Any such differences would suggest that similar policy inputs have had different effects in different areas, which may point to the role played by the form of implementation of policy. It may also be used to test for the effects of interaction between, for example, the effects of policy and prior states.

Such uses of the model suggest some of the potential flexibility of multi-level modelling. Its use would be applied in two distinct analyses: at a ward level for two (or a very few) cities; and at a local authority district level for a large number of cities sampled (both from the 57 urban priority areas and from non-policy areas) so as to enable comparisons between places which have experienced different amounts of policy input and different socio-economic contexts. Clearly, the application of the model must depend on whether or not the data prove to be spatially structured in such a way that, for the different levels, the within-group variance is less than the between-group variance. In the event of this not being the case, formal statistical exploration of the relationships between inputs and outcomes would be forced to rely on regression techniques.

There are clear limitations to any formal quantitative assessment of policy outcomes. Any sensitive interpretation of the results of such modelling demands an informed and broader awareness of the economic, social and political context of the areas whose performance is being assessed. There are few substitutes for intimate knowledge of areas 'on the ground' if one is to avoid drawing hasty and ill-judged conclusions based only on aggregate data. It is for that reason that we suggested complementing the 'extensive' modelling exercise with a more qualitative and 'intensive' assessment based on discussions with 'experts' who might be expected to have an informed view of what policy inputs have been made, what effects have been achieved and what constraints have been faced by cities or parts of cities over the ten-year period. Were such qualitative assessment also to be seen through the eyes of researchers who were themselves familiar with the development of urban policy and with the contexts of the particular cities to be studied, considerable confidence could be placed on the resulting interplay between quantitative and qualitative assessment of the ten-year period.

# 6  WHAT APPROACHES COULD BE USED TO ASSESS THE SHORTER PERIOD OF THE LAST FEW YEARS?

Our approach to assessing changes in the more recent period focused on qualitative surveys since questionnaire respondents could be expected to have an informed view of recent change. Since one would be dealing with a sufficiently short time span, it was considered feasible to rely on the perceptions and impressions of those directly involved in urban policy. We can therefore more confidently turn to looking at qualitative data drawn from interviews with a range of 'actors' in inner-area localities.

As part of our work, we developed a set of three types of interview schedules on which we conducted some initial piloting. This piloting aimed to test the robustness and interpretability of the attitude scales which are part of the interviews. The sampling design aimed to enable comparisons to be made between a variety of types of cities, sub-areas and sub-groups.

Three types of interviews were considered appropriate.

## 6.1  Residents' interviews

This set of interviews was designed to probe the views of recipients of some aspects of urban policy and aimed to test objectives 2,3,4,6,7,8,9 and 10. The questions covered residents' views on the safety and attractiveness of areas and on employment opportunities and involved comparisons over time (the previous and the future three years) and across various areas (for example, comparing their own and other named areas). The design of the questionnaire involved the selection of four wards in Liverpool and four in Manchester, with wards selected either because of their residual status as shown by the multi-level model or because of known differences in policy inputs into them. In each city, one pair of wards would be in an area with relatively high concentrations of ethnic minority groups. In each ward an optimum sample size would be 50 respondents, although a number as low as 30 would be feasible if a clustered sample design were used. Comparison could be made between the scores and profiles of wards with greater and lesser amounts of policy input so as, crudely, to measure the impacts of policy. In addition to such quantitative analysis, impacts may be interpreted qualitatively through respondents' responses to questions about the reasons for past or anticipated changes in areas. The latter would rely on careful probing and recording of comments using the now-extensive range of established qualitative techniques.

## 6.2  Business interviews

This set of interviews would be targeted at people making decisions about investment and dis-investment in the inner city (decisions which may or may not be affected by government policy) and therefore primarily addresses objectives 1,2,3,4 and 5. Questions covered perceived changes in the investment context of the locality, its labour market context and in levels of business confidence. Comparisons would be invited over time and across different areas. Separate questions covered the perceived reasons for changes and the role that policy has played. The sample design would help to throw light on differences between areas since four sets of samples would be selected: two in the inner areas of Liverpool and Manchester; one in an economically buoyant area such as Stockport near Manchester; and a fourth in Warrington, a new town outside Liverpool. A matched-pairs sample from each conurbation would be used with the sample based on SIC category and taking account of firm size, ownership and date of establishment. The aim would be to select 33 respondents from each area. Such a design would allow comparison between areas but within commercial/industrial sectors and would therefore produce comparisons both across two conurbations and across inner and outer areas within each.

**6.3 Experts' interviews**

This set of interviews was designed to obtain a direct evaluation of the impact of policy from those who are themselves involved in the delivery or management of policy. It would concentrate on the last three years, but where respondents have sufficient knowledge about the ten-year period the interviews would also be used to supplement the findings of the modelling exercise. Its aims would be: to establish views about the amount of inputs going to different areas within the cities; to determine the impacts in terms of outputs and outcomes; to discover spillover and shadow effects; to probe views on the nature and causes of countervailing processes which work against the achievement of policy objectives; and to discover any unintended effects of policy. 'Experts' would be drawn from a list including: senior government officials in regional offices of central government departments; local authority officers in departments such as economic development and housing; senior officers in chambers of commerce; senior officials in bodies such as TECs and UDCs. Interviews would be semi-structured, incorporating both the ranking of areas and open-ended discussion.

Printed in the United Kingdom for HMSO
Dd297789 5/94 C8 G531 10170